Sweden

Benedict Walker,
Craig McLachlan, Becky Ohlsen

May 2018

PLAN YOUR TRIP

KUNGLIGA SLOTTET P43, STOCKHOLM

RAMONESPELT/GETTY IMAGES ©

DALA HORSE P127

ALLANW/SHUTTERSTOCK ©

ON THE ROAD

Contents

SKANSEN P50, STOCKHOLM

SPECIAL FEATURES

Welcome to Sweden

Frozen wastelands, cosy cottages, virgin forest, rocky islands, reindeer herders and Viking lore – Sweden has all that plus impeccable style and to-die-for dining.

Landscape

Truth be told, the best thing about Sweden is its natural beauty. To really appreciate this country's charms, you have to leave the city behind. Whether that means sailing across an archipelago to visit a lonely island or trekking along a kingly trail through the northern wilderness just depends on your preferences – why not try both? Hiking, camping, cycling, skiing, skating, boating, fishing and foraging for mushrooms and berries are all major Swedish pastimes, and it's easy to get in on the action from just about anywhere in the country.

Swedish Style

In some ways, visiting Sweden feels like walking right into a fashion or home-decor magazine. There are no boring outfits on the streets of Stockholm, and the care with which houses, cottages, cafes and public spaces are decorated and kept up throughout the country is truly inspiring. But Swedish style is never too showy; form and function are tightly linked in this society known for valuing moderation, practicality, order, simple lines and clever designs. Whether you decide to shop for your own versions or just enjoy the scenery, it's hard not to fall for the cool aesthetics of this place.

The Sami

The northern part of Sweden is home to the indigenous Sami people, whose traditionally nomadic lifestyle is built around reindeer herding. Sami culture, including handicrafts, homes and villages, methods of transport and style of cooking, is one of the many things a visitor can become immersed in while spending time in Lappland: spend a night or two in a Sami reindeer camp or take a dogsledding tour. If you're on a more limited schedule, have a meal in a Sami restaurant or pick up some handmade Sami woodwork or leather goods to take home as a souvenir.

Vikings & History

Ancient rune stones poke up out of the grass in parks all over Sweden; huge stone-ship settings and unobtrusive burial mounds are almost as common. Walled medieval cities and seaside fortresses are regular stops on the travellers' circuit. Viking ruins and the stories surrounding them are very much a part of the modern Swedish landscape, and it's easy to feel as if you're walking through history when you wander around the country. In fact, you are. As a bonus, several Swedish museums do an excellent job of distilling and explaining that history in fascinating ways.

By Becky Ohlsen, Writer

There's something so wholesome and healthy about Sweden. People here really know how to take advantage of their gorgeous country, from its scenic beauty to its edible bounty. My earliest trips here were to visit my grandparents, and no day would be complete without a long walk on the forested trails around their apartment. Dinner was usually local fish and produce gathered from one of Stockholm's market halls – and for dessert, Swedish strawberries from a Hötorget vendor. To this day, being in Sweden means appreciating the outdoors, be it hiking, foraging or just happily wandering.

For more about our writers, see p352

Above: Bohuslän Coast (p151)

Sweden

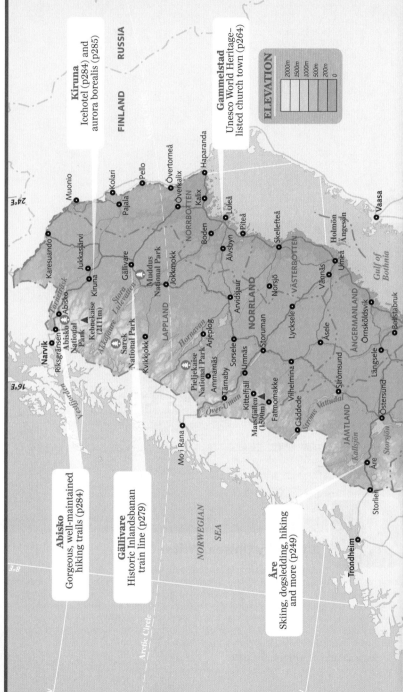

Abisko
Gorgeous, well-maintained hiking trails (p284)

Gällivare
Historic Inlandsbanan train line (p279)

Åre
Skiing, dogsledding, hiking and more (p249)

Kiruna (p284) and aurora borealis (p285)

Gammelstad
Unesco World Heritage-listed church town (p264)

ELEVATION

2000m
1500m
1000m
500m
200m
0

FINLAND   RUSSIA

Muonio
Karesuando
Kolari
Jukkasjärvi
Pajala
Pello
Övertorneå
Överkalix
Kiruna
Gällivare
Haparanda
Kalix
Boden   Luleå
Muddus National Park
Jokkmokk   Piteå
Älvsbyn
Kvikkjokk   Skellefteå
NORRBOTTEN
Sarek National Park
Kebnekaise (2111m)
Abisko National Park
Abisko
Riksgränsen
Narvik
LAPPLAND
Hornavan
Arvidsjaur
Norsjö
Holmön
Ångesön
Vaasa
Gulf of Bothnia
Umeå
Vännäs
VÄSTERBOTTEN
Lycksele
Pieljekaise National Park
Ammarnäs
Arjeplog
Sorsele
Tärnaby   Umnäs
Storuman
Åsele
NORRLAND
Moi Rana
Marsfjället (1590m)
Kittelfjäll
Fatmomakke
Vilhelmina
Gäddede
Strömsund
Örnsköldsvik
ÅNGERMANLAND
Långsele
Bollstabruk
JÄMTLAND
Åre
Östersund
Storsjön
Kallsjön
NORWEGIAN SEA
Storlien
Trondheim
Arctic Circle

Tärendö
Stora Luleälven
Akkajaure
Över-Uman
Ströms Vattudal

200 km
100 miles

N

24°E
20°E
16°E

68°N
64°N

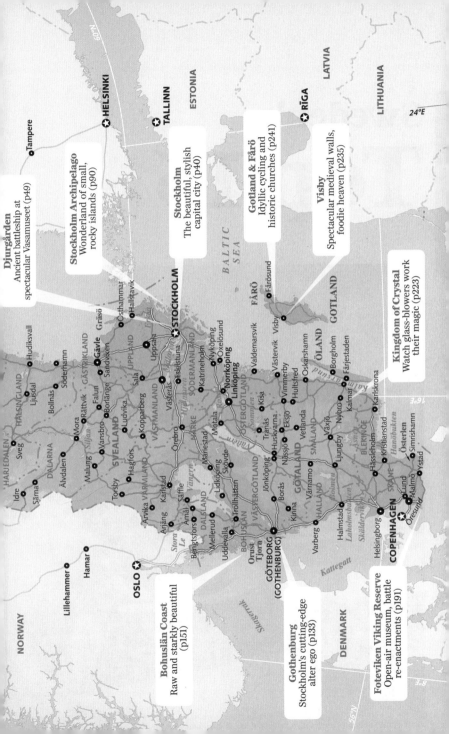

Djurgården
Ancient battleship at
spectacular Vasamuseet (p49)

Stockholm Archipelago
Wonderland of small,
rocky islands (p90)

Stockholm
The beautiful, stylish
capital city (p40)

Gotland & Fårö
Idyllic cycling and
historic churches (p241)

Visby
Spectacular medieval walls,
foodie heaven (p235)

Kingdom of Crystal
Watch glass-blowers work
their magic (p223)

Bohuslän Coast
Raw and starkly beautiful
(p151)

Gothenburg
Stockholm's cutting-edge
alter ego (p133)

Foteviken Viking Reserve
Open-air museum, battle
re-enactments (p191)

NORWAY

FINLAND

ESTONIA

LATVIA

LITHUANIA

DENMARK

*BALTIC
SEA*

HELSINKI

TALLINN

RĪGA

OSLO

STOCKHOLM

COPENHAGEN
(GOTHENBURG)
GÖTEBORG

Tampere

Hamar

Lillehammer

Hudiksvall

Ljusdal

Söderhamn

Bollnäs

Sveg

Idre

Särna

Älvdalen

Mora

Orsa

Rättvik

Falun

Borlänge

Ludvika

Kopparberg

Sala

Sandviken

Gävle

Uppsala

Östhammar

Hallstavik

Gräsö

Eskilstuna

Västerås

Örebro

Katrineholm

Nyköping

Oxelösund

Norrköping

Linköping

Motala

Mariestad

Skövde

Lidköping

Trollhättan

Vänersborg

Karlstad

Säffle

Årjäng

Arvika

Torsby

Hagfors

Malung

Vansbro

Åmål

Bengtsfors

Mellerud

Uddevalla

Orust

Tjörn

Kinna

Borås

Jönköping

Tranås

Nässjö

Huskvarna

Eksjö

Vetlanda

Vimmerby

Kisa

Hultsfred

Västervik

Valdemarsvik

Oskarshamn

Borgholm

Färjestaden

Kalmar

Nybro

Växjö

Ljungby

Värnamo

Gislaved

Halmstad

Varberg

Laholm

Båstad

Ängelholm

Helsingborg

Landskrona

Lund

Malmö

Ystad

Simrishamn

Österlen

Kristianstad

Hässleholm

Karlskrona

Karlshamn

Ronneby

Visby

Färösund

FÅRÖ

GOTLAND

ÖLAND

SKÅNE

BLEKINGE

SMÅLAND

HALLAND

VÄSTERGÖTLAND

ÖSTERGÖTLAND

GÖTALAND

BOHUSLÄN

DALSLAND

VÄRMLAND

SVEALAND

DALARNA

HÄRJEDALEN

HÄLSINGLAND

GÄSTRIKLAND

UPPLAND

VÄSTMANLAND

SÖDERMANLAND

NÄRKE

Vänern

Vättern

Siljan

Mälaren

Hjälmaren

Hanöbukten

Kattegat

Skagerrak

Öresund

60°N

24°E

16°E

8°E

56°N

Sweden's
Top 15

1

Ambitious Menus, Stockholm

1 Traditionally, basic Swedish cuisine is a humble, healthy enterprise based on fish, potatoes and preserved meat. But in recent years the country's top chefs have pushed the boundaries, so that alongside classic everyday dishes such as fried herring or meatballs, or even more exotic northern fare like Arctic char or reindeer with wild berries, you'll find innovative, experimental dishes that are fiercely global in influence and ambition. There's also a new emphasis on vegetarian cuisine (p74). Dining out can be an adventure and an experience.

Bohuslän Coast

2 Caught between sky and sea, the coast of Bohuslän is raw and starkly beautiful, its skerries thick with birds and its villages brightly painted specks among the rocks. Choose from myriad quaint seaside boltholes. Film star Ingrid Bergman loved pretty Fjällbacka (p155), the bargain-hunting Norwegians flock to Strömstad and every sailor knows Tjörn is the place to be in August for the round-island regatta. For a real taste of Swedish summer, spread your beach blanket on a smooth rock and tuck into a bag of peel-and-eat shrimp.

Below right: Fjallbacka (p155)

ASTRAKAN IMAGES/GETTY IMAGES ©

ROLF57/GETTY IMAGES ©

Norrland Hiking, Abisko

3 Sweden has some absolutely gorgeous hiking trails, most of which are well maintained and supplied with conveniently located mountain huts along the way. The season is relatively short, but it's worth a bit of extra planning to get out into the wilderness: its natural landscape is one of Sweden's best assets. A good place to start your venture is the Norrland village of Abisko (p284), at the top of the Kungsleden long-distance trail – it's a hiker headquarters and easily reached by train.

Top: Kungsleden trail (p284)

Vasamuseet

4 Stockholm's unique Vasamuseet (p49) is a purpose-built preservation and display case for an ancient sunken battleship. The ship was the pride of the Swedish Crown when it set out in August 1628, but pride quickly turned to embarrassment when the top-heavy ship tipped and sank to the bottom of Saltsjön, where it would await rescue for 300 years. The museum explains – in fascinating multimedia – how it was found, retrieved and restored, why it sank in the first place, and what it all means to the Swedish people.

Gothenburg

5 The humble sibling to Stockholm's confident polish, Gothenburg (p133) is a city of slick museums, raw industrial landscapes, pleasant parks, can-do designers and cutting-edge food. Try delectable shrimp at one of the city's five Michelin-rated restaurants. There's the thrill-packed chaos of Sweden's largest theme park, the quiet of the many museums, and window-shopping in the Haga and Linné districts. For a unique way of getting there, jump on a boat and wander the 190km of the Göta Canal.

Northern Delights, Kiruna

6 The twin phenomena that have made the north of Sweden so famous – one natural, one artificial – are both found beyond the Arctic Circle. No other natural spectacle compares to the aurora borealis: the shape-shifting lights that dance across the night sky during the Arctic winter (October to March). The Icehotel, humble igloo turned ice palace just outside Kiruna (p280), takes its inspiration from the changeable nature of the northern lights – once re-created each winter, it is now a year-round phenomenon.

KARAMBOL/GETTY IMAGES ©

Medieval Visby

7 It's hard to overstate the beauty of the Hanseatic port town of Visby (p235), in itself justification for making the ferry trip to Gotland. Inside its thick medieval walls are twisting cobblestone streets, fairy-tale cottages draped in flowers and gorgeous ruins atop hills with stunning Baltic views. The walls themselves, with 40-plus towers and the spectacular church ruins within, are a travel photographer's dream, and the perimeter makes an ideal scenic stroll. The city is also a food-lover's heaven, packed with top-notch restaurants accustomed to impressing discriminating diners.

Vikings Village – Foteviken

8 There are still real, live Vikings, and you can visit them at one of Sweden's most absorbing attractions. An evocative 'living' reconstruction of a late–Viking Age village, Foteviken Viking Reserve (p191) was built on the coast near the site of the Battle of Foteviken (1134) and contains some 22 reed-roofed houses. You can tour all of these, check out the great meeting hall, see a war catapult and buy Viking-made handicrafts. It's all admirably legit, too – the reserve's residents hold to old traditions, laws and religions.

Stockholm

9 The nation's capital calls itself 'beauty on water', and it certainly doesn't disappoint in the looks department. Stockholm's many glittering waterways reflect slanted northern light onto spice-hued buildings, and the crooked cobblestone streets of Gamla Stan are magic to wander. Stockholm (p40) also has top-notch museums, first-class dining and all the shopping anyone could ask for. Its clean and efficient public transport, and multilingual locals, make it a cinch to navigate, and at the end of the day you can collapse in a cushy designer hotel. Top far right: Nordiska Museet (p51)

Winter Sports, Åre

10 Winter sports in Lappland are a major draw. To go cross-country skiing, just grab a pair of skis and step outside; for downhill sports, be it alpine, heli-skiing or snowboarding, Åre (p249) is your best bet. And those are far from your only options. Few pastimes are as enjoyable as rushing across the Arctic wasteland pulled by a team of dogs, the sled crunching through crisp snow – but if you prefer something with a motor, you can test your driving (and racing) skills on the frozen lakes instead.

MKALLSTROM/GETTY IMAGES ©

10

MICHAEL715/SHUTTERSTOCK ©

Inlandsbanan to Gällivare

11 Take a journey through Norrland along this historic train line (p280; summer only), which passes small mining towns, deep green forests, herds of reindeer and, if you're lucky, the occasional elk (moose). Built during the 1930s and rendered obsolete by 1992, the line has more than enough charm and historical appeal to make up for its lack of speed – you'll have plenty of time to contemplate the landscape, in other words. It's a beautiful, odd-ball means of transport, best suited to those for whom adventure trumps efficiency.

Gotland & Fårö

12 Merchants in the 12th and 13th centuries dotted the beautiful island of Gotland (p234) with fabulous churches. Today, Gotland's lovely ruins, remote beaches, idyllic bike- and horse-riding paths, peculiar rock formations, excellent restaurants and rousing summer nightlife attract visitors from all over the world. The event of the season is Medieval Week, which brings Visby's old town alive with costumes, re-enactments and markets. Film buffs and nature lovers will want to head north to visit Ingmar Bergman's stomping ground of Fårö (p241). Top right: Gotland (p234)

Gammelstad

13 There is an abundance of Unesco World Heritage–recognised treasures in Sweden. A fine example is Gammelstad church town (p264) near Luleå. The largest church town in the country, it was the medieval centre of northern Sweden; visiting feels a bit like time travel. The village's stone Nederluleå Church (built in 1492) has a reredos worthy of a cathedral and choir stalls for a whole consistory, and there are 424 wooden houses where rural pioneers stayed overnight on their weekend pilgrimages.

Stockholm Archipelago

14 Scattered between the city and the open Baltic Sea, this archipelago (p90) is a mesmerising wonderland of small rocky isles, some no more than seagull launch pads, others studded with deep forests and fields of wildflowers. Most are within easy striking distance, a few hours from the city, with regular ferry services in summer and several organised tours designed for island-hopping. Hostels, campgrounds and more upmarket slumber options make an overnight stay a good option, as does the growing number of excellent restaurants.

Kingdom of Crystal

15 In the Glasriket (p223; Kingdom of Crystal) a rich mix of skill and brawn combine to produce stunning works of art. Watch glass-blowers spin bubbles of molten crystal into fantastic creatures, bowls, vases and sculptures. Choose something for the mantelpiece or try glass-blowing yourself at the centres in Kosta and Orrefors. For background on the 500-year-old industry there's Smålands Museum in Vaxjo, and for the ultimate finish enjoy a cocktail at Kjell Engman's cobalt-blue bar at the Kosta Boda Art Hotel.

14

15

Need to Know

For more information, see Survival Guide (p321)

Currency
Krona (kr)

Language
Swedish (official), Finnish, Sami dialects, English

Visas
Americans don't need a visa to enter Sweden; some nationalities will need a Schengen visa, good for 90 days.

Money
ATMs widely available. Credit cards accepted in most hotels and restaurants.

Mobile Phones
In many cases you can buy a local SIM card to use in your own mobile phone (check with your provider). Barring that, it may be worthwhile buying a cheap mobile phone you can load with prepaid minutes.

Time
Central European Time (GMT/UTC plus one hour)

When to Go

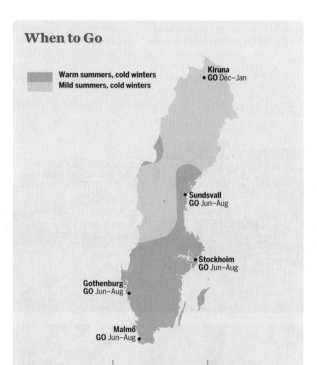

Warm summers, cold winters
Mild summers, cold winters

Kiruna
● GO Dec–Jan

● Sundsvall
GO Jun–Aug

● Stockholm
GO Jun–Aug

Gothenburg
GO Jun–Aug ●

Malmö
GO Jun–Aug ●

High Season
(mid-Jun–Aug)

➡ Season starts at midsummer; expect warm weather. Most sights and accommodation will be open.

➡ Some restaurants and shops close in July or August as Swedes take their own holidays.

Shoulder
(Sep–Oct)

➡ Weather is still good, even if no one's around to enjoy it.

➡ Many tourist spots are closed, but you'll have the rest all to yourself.

➡ Hotel rates return to normal but drop at weekends.

Low Season
(Nov–May)

➡ Best season for winter-sports adventures, the northern lights and holiday markets.

➡ Book accommodation and winter activities in advance.

➡ Many campgrounds and hostels close for the winter.

Useful Websites

Visit Sweden (www.visitsweden.com) Official tourism website.

Swedish Institute (www.si.se/English) Scholarly info on Swedish culture.

The Local (www.thelocal.se) News from Sweden in English.

Lonely Planet (www.lonelyplanet.com/sweden) Destination information, hotel bookings, traveller forum and more.

Important Numbers

Country code	⌨46
International access code	⌨00
International directory assistance	⌨118 119
Directory assistance within Sweden	⌨118 118
Emergency	⌨112

Exchange Rates

Australia	$1	6.36kr
Canada	$1	6.46kr
Europe	€1	9.50kr
Japan	¥100	7.31kr
New Zealand	$1	5.72kr
UK	£1	10.39kr
US	$1	7.96kr

For current exchange rates see www.xe.com.

Daily Costs

Budget: Less than 1000kr

➡ Dorm bed or campsite: 250–450kr

➡ Fast-food meal (kebab, quiche, sandwich): 65–85kr

➡ 24-hour bus and metro ticket: 120kr

➡ Admission to museum: 100kr

Midrange: 1000–2000kr

➡ Double room in midrange hotel: 1000–1600kr

➡ Happy-hour beer: 55–75kr

➡ Meal at a midrange restaurant: 100–295kr

➡ 72-hour bus and metro ticket: 240kr

Top End: More than 2000kr

➡ Double room in top-end hotel: 1600–2600kr

➡ Dinner with drinks at a nice restaurant: 350–600kr

➡ Taxi from airport: 520kr

Opening Hours

Except where indicated, we list hours for high season (mid-June to August). Expect more limited hours the rest of the year.

Banks 9.30am to 3pm Monday to Friday; some city branches open to 5pm or 6pm.

Bars & Pubs 11am or noon to 1am or 2am.

Government Offices 9am to 5pm Monday to Friday.

Restaurants 11am to 2pm and 5pm to 10pm, often closed on Sunday and/or Monday; high-end restaurants often closed for a week or two in July or August.

Shops 9am to 6pm Monday to Friday, to 1pm Saturday.

Arriving in Sweden

Stockholm-Arlanda Airport The Arlanda Express train runs from the airport to Stockholm central station (adult/child one way 280/150kr, 20 minutes, every 10 to 15 minutes). Airport buses (Flygbussarna) also run to the centre (adult/child one way 99/89kr, 45 minutes, every 10 minutes).

Gothenburg Landvetter Airport Flygbussarna run from the airport to the city centre (adult/child one way 95/79kr, 30 minutes, every 15 minutes).

Sturup Airport (Malmö) Flygbussarna run from the airport to the city centre (adult/child one way 105/85kr, 40 to 50 minutes, every 10 to 15 minutes). Öresund trains operated by Skånetrafiken (www.skanetrafiken.se) run every 20 minutes from 6am to midnight (and once per hour thereafter) between Copenhagen and Malmö (one way from 99kr, 45 minutes) via the bridge. The trains usually stop at Copenhagen airport.

Getting Around

Transport in Sweden is reliable and easy to navigate. Roads are generally in good repair, and buses and trains are comfortable, with plenty of services on board and in stations. There's a good trip planner at https://reseplanerare.resrobot.se.

Car Expensive but great if you want to explore smaller roads and remote places; especially ideal for camping and outdoor activities.

Bus More thorough coverage than the train network, and often equally quick and cheap (if not more so).

Train Affordable and extensive; speed depends on whether the route is local, regional or express.

For much more on **getting around**, see p329

If You Like...

Alpine Adventures

Norrland in winter is home to all manner of exciting cold-weather activities.

Åre A fabulous ski resort in a chic little town. (p249)

Riksgränsen Primarily for expert skiers, this resort nestles right up against the Norwegian border. (p286)

Tärnaby A fun town at the edge of a gorgeous lake, with a growing ski resort that's more laid-back than its neighbour at Hemavan. (p273)

Båtsuoj Sami Camp If you've never had a chance to meet a reindeer before... (p272)

Jokkmokk Winter Market Apart from great shopping and street theatre, this huge market also features reindeer races. (p278)

Abisko At this well-equipped national park you can go hiking, snowmobiling, dogsledding, or just kick back and gaze at the northern lights. (p284)

Boat Trips

Don't forget, this is the land of 100,000 lakes (maybe even a few more). Go ahead and get your feet wet.

Stockholm Archipelago Sailing around the archipelago is what Stockholmers wish they had time to do on holiday. (p91)

Göta Canal Float between locks and lakes on a tour of this peaceful canal. (p218)

Bohuslän ferries Hop from ferry to ferry in the Bohuslän archipelago. (p151)

Luleå Archipelago The northern archipelago is well worth exploration. (p266)

Tiveden National Park Hire a canoe and explore the wilderness. (p118)

Under the Bridges of Stockholm Strömma Kanalbolaget offers a number of good tours of Stockholm's waterways, including this two-hour canal tour. (p64)

Cycling

Most towns in Sweden have a place where visitors are able to rent or borrow a bicycle to ride around. Plus, not only is cycling a far greener mode of transportation, it forces you to slow down the pace and really take in your surroundings.

Gotland Wide bike paths and sea views make for lovely island cycling. (p235)

Öland Cycle between farmers markets and nature reserves on this peaceful island. (p230)

Göta Canal Cycle alongside the locks en route to Vättern. (p218)

Örebro Everyone in this college town rides a bicycle. (p112)

Stockholm Car traffic can be hectic, but the shared-bike program and bike paths make Stockholm a cycle-friendly city. (p60)

Åre The mountain-bike park here delivers an amped-up cycling experience. (p249)

Fine Dining

Given the number of superstar chefs in the media, the focus on organic, sustainable ingredients and a devotion to great atmosphere, it's no surprise Sweden has some fantastic places to fill up.

Matbaren Celebrated chef Mathias Dahlgren's double-Michelin-starred restaurant fits right in at the Grand Hôtel. (p75)

Finnhamns Café & Krog Great restaurant on a remote, pastoral archipelago island. (p94)

Sånninggården A foodie beacon serving game in classic Lappland style. (p273)

Länsmansgården A historic building and a picturesque place for a fine, traditionally Swedish lunch. (p117)

Hiking

Sweden is an awesome place to hike around, with its springy, well-kept trails and excellent network of huts and campgrounds.

Kungsleden The King's Trail, a popular, accessible northern route. (p286)

Höga Kusten Leden Awesome views from high coastal cliffs. (p257)

Sarek National Park Challenging terrain for expert hikers. (p290)

Skåneleden Lush path along Sweden's southern coast. (p184)

Arctic Trail An 800km joint development of Sweden, Norway and Finland, entirely above the Arctic Circle. (p28)

Kebnekaise Sweden's tallest peak is a highlight of hiking in Norrland. (p283)

European long-distance paths E1 and E6 run from Varberg to Grövelsjön (1200km) and from Malmö to Norrtälje (1400km). (p166)

Finnskogleden A 240km-long route along the border between Norway and the Värmland region in Sweden. (p120)

Sami Culture

The Sami, Sweden's indigenous population, have a rich, often embattled culture that fascinates visitors and locals alike. There are many opportunities to learn more, be it a visit to an absorbing museum or an overnight (or longer) stay in a traditional Sami reindeer camp.

Ájtte Museum A stellar museum presenting the history and current status of the Sami people in Sweden. (p277)

Top: Kayaking in Abisko National Park (p284)

Bottom: Sami man with reindeer, Lappland (p268)

Båtsuoj Sami Camp Stay overnight with traditional reindeer herders at this forest camp. (p272)

Arjeplog Silvermuseet This museum in a former nomad school has a stunning collection of Sami silver objects. (p276)

Nutti Sámi Siida Take a reindeer-sled excursion with this ecotourism expert. (p285)

Shopping

Shopping in Sweden is easy to do – almost too easy. Look for glass and crystal, authentic handicrafts marked with the *slöjd* (handicraft) sticker, fine linens, chic designer clothing and funky gadgets IKEA doesn't have yet.

Stockholm's shopping streets The pedestrian thoroughfares of Biblioteksgatan, Drottninggatan and Västerlånggatan are retail heaven. (p83)

NK Nordiska Kompaniet is a Stockholm city landmark – great for stocking up on souvenirs and gourmet groceries. (p83)

Formargruppen Cooperative designer shop and gallery in Malmö. (p180)

Sami Duodji Gallery and shop with authentic Sami handicrafts. (p277)

Small Villages

The country is dotted with tiny masterpieces: red cottages, cobblestone town squares or windswept fishing huts clinging to the coastline.

Eksjö One of Sweden's best-preserved wooden towns. (p217)

Vadstena A rewarding end for pilgrims visiting St Birgitta. (p212)

Skanör An idyllic summer beach town. (p191)

Höga Kusten The tiny fishing villages here are to die for. (p256)

Tällberg A lovely collection of red-painted wooden buildings set along a twisty scenic road. (p123)

Nora Not only gorgeous but also a premier source of ice cream. (p112)

Sigtuna Within easy reach of Stockholm and Uppsala, this adorable village boasts numerous church ruins. (p94)

Vaxholm A photogenic harbour and a famous fortress entice flocks of visitors to this archipelago town. (p91)

Swedish Design

Gorge yourself on the sleek and spartan, the rounded corner, the clever tool, the vividly printed fabric and the inventive glasswork that define Swedish design – from established artists now part of the canon to new talents making a name for themselves.

Nordiska Museet Huge building filled with objects illustrating the evolution of Swedish design, arranged by theme for various changing exhibitions. (p51)

Svenskt Tenn Home of Josef Frank's signature fabrics and other iconic pieces. (p83)

DesignTorget Great selection of clever gadgets and decor from up-and-coming designers. (p84)

Velour Chic jeans, knits and jumpsuits from a savvy Gothenburg designer. (p147)

Kosta outlets Stock up on gorgeous glass in the heart of the Glasriket (Crystal Kingdom). (p224)

Month by Month

January

This is the peak of winter, with freezing temperatures and snow in most regions. Winter-sports activities draw the crowds.

☆ Göteborg International Film Festival

Sweden's 'second city' hosts this annual festival, which draws some 200,000 visitors each year, with short films, documentaries and features, plus seminars and parties. (p140)

Kiruna Snow Festival

Based on a snow-sculpting competition, this annual Snöfestivalen draws artists from all over to carve elaborate shapes out of the snow. It also features reindeer-sled racing, with Sami traditions emphasised. (p281)

February

It's still peak winter weather, with snow sports the main draw.

Jokkmokk Winter Market

A large gathering of Sami people from across Scandinavia, this festival includes a market, meetings, craft shows, performances and more. (p278)

Vasaloppet

This huge ski race between Sälen and Mora, started in 1922, commemorates Gustav Vasa's history-making flight on skis in 1521; it has grown into a week-long ski fest. (p126)

March

The winter season begins to wind down in the southern half of the country, though winter sports are still going strong in Norrland.

◉ Liljevalchs Spring Salon

The Djurgården gallery's annual springtime launch of the new year in art brings to the fore up-and-coming artists as well as new work from established names. The gallery (www.liljevalchs.se) was under restoration at the time of research, so check online to find the current location of the salon.

April

The weather's still cold, but the days are longer and brighter.

Walpurgis Night

This public holiday, a pagan holdover to celebrate the arrival of spring, involves lighting bonfires, singing songs and forming parades; parties are biggest in the student towns, such as Uppsala.

May

Spring tourism starts to pick up as the days get longer and warmer; summer-only hostels and campgrounds start to open for the season.

May Day

Traditionally a workers' marching day in industrial

towns and cities, it's observed with labour-movement events, brass bands and marches.

June

Midway through June is the official beginning of summer. The weather is perfect, hotel rates are low and travelling is effortless.

Midsummer

Arguably the most important Swedish holiday, Midsummer's Eve traditionally falls on the Friday between 19 and 25 June; revellers head to the countryside to raise the maypole, sing, dance, drink and eat pickled herring. Midsummer Day is primarily spent recovering from the long night.

Smaka På Stockholm

Taste samples from some of Stockholm's top kitchens in manageable quantities, and watch cooking duels at this week-long food fest in Kungsträdgården. (p65)

Sweden Rock Festival

This large three-day rock festival is held in Sölvesborg (www.swedenrock. com) and features huge metal and hard-rock acts like Ministry, Aerosmith and Ozzy Osbourne.

Swedish National Day

Known merely as Swedish Flag Day until 1983, the public holiday (6 June) commemorates the crowning in 1523 of King Gustav Vasa

and Sweden's independence from the Danish-led Kalmar Union.

Öjeby Church Market

This market near Piteå (www.pitea.se) attracts some 20,000 visitors each year.

July

July is peak summer-tourism season: the weather is fine and everyone is cheerful. Many Swedes (especially in larger cities) go on holiday, though, and lots of shops and restaurants are closed for vacation.

Classic Car Week

Rättvik hosts this gathering of motorheads and the objects of their devotion; there are monster-truck battles, drive-in movies, laid-back cruising and lots of chrome. (p125)

Musik vid Siljan

A midsummer music festival, it takes place in the towns around Lake Siljan, and includes chamber, jazz and folk music; tourist offices for Mora, Leksand and Rättvik will have up-to-date schedules. (p126)

Piteå Dansar

One of Sweden's biggest street festivals, the PDOL (www.pdol.se) draws some 120,000 visitors for music, dance, crafts, food and a carnival.

Stockholm Pride

This massive, exuberant annual parade and festival is dedicated to creating an

atmosphere of freedom and support for gay, lesbian, bisexual and transgender people. (p326)

August

The weather is as nice as in July, but many Swedes (especially Stockholmers) have gone out of town on their own holidays, and some restaurants are still closed for vacation.

Kräftskivor (Crayfish Parties)

Swedes celebrate the end of summer by wearing bibs and party hats while eating lots of crayfish and drinking *snaps* (usually aquavit). In the north, parallel parties take place but with *surströmming* (strong-smelling fermented Baltic herring).

Visby Medieval Week

Find yourself an actual knight in shining armour at this immensely popular event (www.medeltids veckan.se), which puts Gotland's medieval city to great use with a market, games, costumes and a banquet. Be sure to reserve your accommodation and transportation to the island in advance.

September

Days begin to grow shorter and cooler, and many seasonal tourist facilities (campgrounds, some hostels, outdoor cafes) close for the season, but the weather can still be gorgeous.

✸ Göteborg International Book Fair

Scandinavia's biggest book fair (www.goteborg-book fair.com), this event brings together authors, readers, publishers, agents, teachers, librarians and the media.

☆ Lidingöloppet

Enshrined in the *Guinness World Records* as the world's largest terrain race, this annual event takes place on Lidingö, just northeast of Stockholm.

☆ Tjejmilen

Sweden's biggest sporting event for women (www.tjejmilen.se) features 30,000 runners of all ages in a race that begins at Gärdet in Stockholm.

✸ Öland's Harvest Festival

This celebration of the local harvest (www.skordefest.nu) takes place each autumn in Borgholm, Öland.

October

Though the travel infrastructure can feel largely abandoned, autumn is a lovely time of year in Sweden, and you'll essentially have the place to yourself.

☆ Hem & Villa

This is the country's largest interior decor and design fair, with furniture trends, textiles, lighting schemes, and arts and crafts. The event (www.hemochvilla.se), held in Stockholm and Gothenburg, includes displays, lectures and great shopping.

☆ Stockholm Jazz Festival

Held in clubs all over town, this internationally known jazz fest brings big names like Van Morrison and Mary J Blige; evening jam sessions at famed Stockholm jazz club Fasching are a highlight. (p65)

☆ Stockholm Open

A huge event among the international tennis crowd, this tournament draws its share of top-100 players. (p65)

☆ Umeå International Jazz Festival

International jazz musicians have filled Umeå's stages for this event (www.umeajazzfestival.se) for 50 years running.

☆ Uppsala Short Film Festival

For the past 33 years, this film festival (www.shortfilmfestival.com) has screened more than 300 short films a year at four cinemas in central Uppsala.

November

Grey winter is here, but the holiday season has yet to begin. A good time for movies, markets and museums!

✸ St Martin's Day

In Sweden, the 10th of November is St Martin's Eve, and, regardless of how the tradition originally began, these days the holiday is all about the goose. That means that, ideally, you'll see the traditional dinner of roasted goose on your plate.

🔒 Gamla Stan Christmas Market

Usually opening in mid-November, this adorable Stockholm market (www.stortorgetsjulmarknad.com) in Gamla Stan's main square (Stortorget) can lift the spirits on a cold winter night. Shop for handicrafts and delicacies, or just wander with a mug of cocoa and a saffron bun.

☆ Stockholm International Film Festival

Screenings of new international and independent films, director talks and discussion panels draw cinephiles to this important festival; tickets go quickly, so book early. (p65)

December

The month in which Sweden cheerfully rages against the dying of the light, aided by hot spiced wine and seasonal treats.

✸ Luciadagen (St Lucia Day)

On 13 December, wearing a crown of lit candles, 'Lucia' leads a white-clad choir in traditional singing in a celebration that seems to merge the folk tradition of the longest night and the story of St Lucia of Syracuse. Look for free performances in churches.

✸ Julafton (Christmas Eve)

The night of the smörgåsbord and the arrival of *jultomten* (the Christmas gnome), carrying a sack of gifts, this is the biggest celebration at Christmas time.

Itineraries

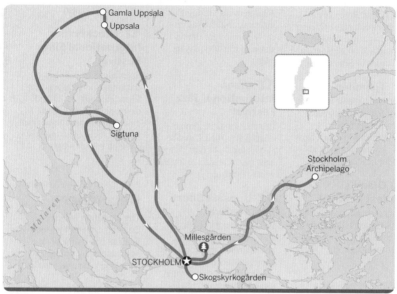

Stockholm & Its Surrounds

This itinerary brings you the highlights of the area around the capital, including ruins from early Swedish history and a few suburban delights.

Start in **Stockholm**, where mandatory attractions include the Kungliga Slottet (Royal Palace), Gamla Stan (the lovely Old Town) and Skansen (a family-friendly open-air museum that's basically Sweden in miniature). Kick off with a short boat tour of the city's waterways. You can do all of those in a couple of days, which leaves an evening for enjoying some nightlife in Södermalm – try the clubs and bars in the SoFo district. On day three, visit a museum or two.

The next day, check out the cathedral and palace at **Uppsala** and delve into early Swedish history via the burial mounds and museum at **Gamla Uppsala**. On the way back, explore **Sigtuna**, with its old-fashioned buildings, adorable cafes and atmospheric church ruins. The following day, visit the sculpture museum at **Millesgården**, or make a pilgrimage to Greta Garbo's memorial at Unesco-recognised cemetery **Skogskyrkogården**. Finally, take a leisurely boat ride out into the **Stockholm archipelago**, hopping off to explore one of the islands or even staying overnight if time allows.

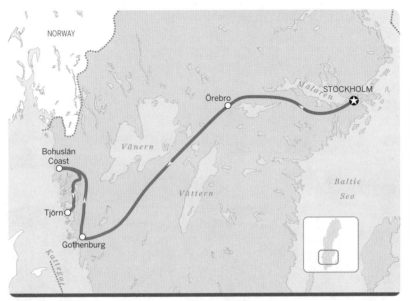

 Stockholm & Gothenburg

You can see a good stretch of Sweden in the space of two weeks. This itinerary makes its way through the heart of the country, taking in lush landscapes as well as the relics of industry.

To get a sense of the things that make the place so quintessentially Swedish, we suggest spending the first week of your trip exploring the sights in and around stylish capital **Stockholm**. Then, make your way west toward Gothenburg, Sweden's so-called second city, a worthy destination in its own right. Take your time getting there – you'll want to stop along the way to visit the lively college town of **Örebro**, tour its moat-protected castle and wander through the nearby Stadsparken, one of Sweden's most beautiful city parks.

Continue heading southwest, between the huge inland lakes Vänern and Vättern, and into **Gothenburg**. This engaging city is easily worth a few days of exploration: visit its theme park and museums, notably the nostalgiafest that is Mölndals Museum, but don't neglect to do some Michelin-star dining and trend-focused shopping, perhaps in the attractive and well-preserved Haga district, Gothenburg's oldest suburb. Take the whole clan along for the rides at the huge amusement park that is Liseberg, one of Sweden's most visited tourist attractions. Pick up some picnic supplies at Feskekörka, a fish market shaped like a church, or settle in for some locally sourced, gourmet burgers at Restaurang 2112. And don't miss the cool, retrofitted art space at Röda Sten, a gritty power-station-turned-gallery that exhibits some of the edgiest artwork around and has a range of evening events to boot.

Spend the rest of week two exploring the craggy coastline and rickety fishing villages of the **Bohuslän Coast**. Check out the Bronze Age rock carvings on the Tanum plain, then have a go at making sense of them with the help of the Vitlycke Museum. Cross the bridge from Stenungsund (on the Swedish mainland) to the island of **Tjörn**, a favourite of landscape artists and sailors alike. Wander the tiny villages admiring sailboats, have a summer barbecue on the deck of a youth hostel or make a meal of smoked fish from Åstols Rökeri.

ERNST HAAS/GETTY IMAGES ©

Top: Läckö Slott
(p162), Lidköping

Bottom: Bronze Age
rock carvings, Tanum
(p152)

2 WEEKS Stockholm to Kiruna

The journey from Stockholm to the northernmost city in Sweden actually merits the term 'epic'. You'll cross vast stretches that seem to be populated by nothing but reindeer. You'll also see the fertile, forested breadbasket of the country.

From **Stockholm** head toward the lovely **Lake Siljan** region, home to carved wooden Dala horses, red-painted huts and hobbitlike villages. Spend a day or two hopping between **Mora**, **Rättvik** and **Leksand**.

Continue north, tacking east towards the **Höga Kusten** region for glorious scenery and cliffside hiking. From there, it's an easy journey up to the urban centres of Norrland: **Umeå** and **Luleå**. From Luleå, jag inland to **Arvidsjaur** for a dogsledding or snowmobile tour, and then on to **Jokkmokk**, whose Sami museum, Ájtte, mustn't be missed.

Continue to **Kiruna** to explore some wild landscapes. Hike in the accessible but untamed **Abisko National Park**, a short train ride from Kiruna. From Kiruna, zip over to **Jukkasjärvi** to see the Icehotel and visit a Sami reindeer camp. Completists might opt to visit **Karesuando**, the northernmost village in Sweden.

3 WEEKS Stockholm to Malmö

You can cover a lot of the southern part of Sweden in three weeks, including two of the most dynamic urban centres in Scandinavia – Malmö and Gothenburg – as well as some gorgeous coastline and fishing villages.

Start your journey in **Stockholm**. The wonderful capital city will hold your attention for as many days as you can devote to it. When it's time to move on, head toward dynamic **Gothenburg** and its surrounding coastline, whose charms include pretty fishing villages and spectacular, otherworldly light. Make your way along the coast, jagging north to enjoy the eye candy in upscale **Marstrand**, then edging south to dodge mopeds in beachy **Brännö**.

Stop in at **Varberg** and see the preserved body of Bocksten Man displayed in its medieval fortress. Continue south to **Lund**, Sweden's second-oldest town, with a striking cathedral and the great cafe culture that goes along with a large student population. Just south of here is **Malmö**, a diverse and lively city that sometimes feels more a part of neighbouring Denmark – no surprise, really, as Copenhagen is only a bridge away.

Plan Your Trip

Outdoor Activities

Sweden is ideal for outdoor activities: it has thousands of square kilometres of forest with hiking and cycling tracks, vast numbers of lakes connected by mighty rivers, and a range of alpine mountains. And its concentrated population means you're likely to have the wildest places all to yourself.

Best Outdoors

Winter Sports

Abisko National Park Short-trip and full-day dogsledding; weekend multi-activity stays; snowmobile track along first section of the Kungsleden. (p284)

Kiruna Dogsledding under the northern lights, day and night snowmobiling and three-day wilderness excursions. (p280)

Arvidsjaur Over 600km of snowmobile tracks. (p275)

Hiking

Kungsleden Sweden's best-known and most accessible long-distance trail. (p286)

Sarek National Park Over 2000 sq km of rugged hiking terrain. (p290)

Padjelanteleden Easier hiking amid gorgeous wilderness. (p290)

Cycling

Örebro Central Sweden's urban centre seems built with bikes in mind. (p112)

Skåne Pastoral scenery, flat terrain and plenty of well-serviced cycling trails. (p170)

Gotland An enchanting island with extensive cycling trails, comfortable hostels and stunning scenery. (p234)

Hiking

Swedes love their hiking, and there are many thousands of kilometres of marked trails that make most of the country a trekker's dream.

European long-distance footpaths E1 and E6 run from Varberg to Grövelsjön (1200km) and from Malmö to Norrtälje (1400km) respectively. But the **Kungsleden**, in Lappland, is the best-known and most user-friendly trail in Sweden. **Finnskogleden** is a 240km-long route along the border between Norway and the Värmland region in Sweden. The **Arctic Trail** (800km) is a joint development of Sweden, Norway and Finland and is entirely above the Arctic Circle; it begins near Kautokeino in Norway and ends in Abisko, Sweden. The 139km **Padjelantaleden** is a generally easy route, with long sections of duckboards and bridged rivers. The mountainous part of western Jämtland is also one of Sweden's most popular hiking areas.

Mountain trails in Sweden are marked with cairns, wooden signposts or paint on rocks and trees. Marked trails have bridges across all but the smallest streams, and wet or fragile areas are crossed on duckboards. Overnight huts and lodges along these trails are maintained by Svenska Turistföreningen (p323).

RESPONSIBLE HIKING

Rubbish

Carry out all your rubbish, and make an effort to carry out rubbish left by others. Never bury your rubbish. Sanitary napkins, tampons, condoms and toilet paper should be carried out despite the inconvenience, as they burn and decompose poorly.

Human-Waste Disposal

Contamination of water sources by human faeces can lead to the transmission of all sorts of nasties. Where there is a toilet, please use it. Where there is no toilet, bury your waste. Dig a small hole 15cm deep and at least 100m from any watercourse. Cover the waste with soil and a rock. In snow, dig down to the soil.

Washing

Don't use detergents or toothpaste in or near watercourses, even if they are biodegradable. For personal washing, use biodegradable soap and a water container (or even a lightweight, portable basin) at least 50m away from the watercourse. Wash cooking utensils at a similar distance using a scourer, sand or snow instead of detergent.

Fires & Low-Impact Cooking

Don't depend on open fires for cooking or warmth. The cutting of wood for fires in popular trekking areas can cause rapid deforestation. Cook on a light-weight kerosene, alcohol or Shellite (white gas) stove and avoid those powered by disposable butane gas canisters.

Equipment

Hikers should be well equipped and prepared for snow in the mountains, even in summer. Prolonged bad weather in the northwest isn't uncommon – Sarek and Sylarna are the most notorious areas. In summer you'll need good boots, waterproof jacket and trousers, several layers of warm clothing (including spare dry clothes), warm hat, sun hat, mosquito repellent (a mosquito head-net is also highly advisable), water bottle, maps, compass and sleeping bag. Basic supplies are often available at huts, and most lodges serve meals (but check first, especially outside high season). If you're going off the main routes you should, obviously, take full camping equipment.

The best hiking time is between late June and mid-September, when trails are mostly snow free. After early August the mosquitoes have gone.

Mountaineering & Rock Climbing

Mountaineers head for Sylarna, Helagsfjället, Sarek National Park and the Kebnekaise region.

The complete traverse of Sylarna involves rock climbing up to grade 3. The ridge traverse of Sarektjåhkkå (2089m) in Sarek, the second-highest mountain in Sweden, is about grade 4. There are lots of other glacier and rock routes in Sarek. The Kebnekaise area has many fine climbing routes (grades 2 to 6), including the north wall of Kaskasapakte (2043m), and the steep ridges of Knivkammen (1878m) and Vaktposten (1852m).

For qualified guides, contact **Svenska Bergsguideorganisation** (Swedish Mountain Guide Association; www.sbo.nu). The website is in Swedish, but under *medlemmar* there's a list of guides and their contact details.

Rock climbers can practise on the cliffs around Stockholm and Gothenburg – there are 34 climbing areas with 1000 routes around Gothenburg, and some 200 cliffs around the capital. For further information, try the helpful **Svenska Klätterförbundet** (Swedish Climbing Federation; ☎08-618 82 70; www.klatterforbundet.se).

Cycling

Sweden is perfect for cycling, particularly in Skåne and Gotland. It's an excellent way to look for prehistoric sites, rune stones and quiet spots for free camping. The cycling season is from May to September in the south, and July and August in the north.

You can cycle on all roads except motorways (marked by a green sign with two lanes and a bridge on it) and roads for motor vehicles only (green sign with a car symbol). Highways often have a hard shoulder, which keeps cyclists well clear of motor vehicles. Secondary roads are mostly quiet and safe by European standards, and many roads have dedicated cycle lanes.

You can take a bicycle on some regional trains and buses. Long-distance buses usually don't accept bicycles; Sveriges Järnväg (SJ) allows them only if they're foldable and can be carried as hand luggage. Bikes are transported free on some ferries.

You can hire bicycles from campgrounds, hostels, bike workshops and sports shops; the cost is usually around 150kr a day or 500kr a week.

Some country areas, towns and cities have special cycle routes – contact local tourist offices for information and maps. Kustlinjen (591km) runs from Öregrund (Uppland) southwards along the Baltic coast to Västervik, and Skånespåret (800km) is a fine network of cycle routes. The well-signposted 2600km-long Sverigeleden extends from Helsingborg in the south to Karesuando in the north, and links points of interest with suitable roads (mostly with an asphalt surface) and bicycle paths.

Brochures and maps are available from **Svenska Cykelsällskapet** (Swedish Cycling Association; ☎08-751 62 04; www.svenska-cykelsallskapet.se).

Mountain Biking

One of the most thrilling summer and fall activities is downhill mountain biking. The sport takes over ski resorts after the snow melts; fully armoured, riders carry their sturdy little bikes up the hill on chairlifts, then barrel down along rough mountain trails at exhilarating speeds. Åre Bike Park (p249) is the mother lode, with 35km of slopes, 17 trails and a potential vertical drop of almost 900m. Multiday packages are available.

Boating & Sailing

Boating and sailing are hugely popular in Sweden. The 7000km-long coastline, with its 60,000 islands, is a sailor's paradise, but look out for the few restricted military areas off the east coast. (They're quite obvious, and marked on maps.)

Inland, lakes and canals offer pleasant sailing in spring and summer. The main canals are the Göta Canal, the Kinda Canal and the Dalsland Canal. Various companies offer short canal cruises; contact local tourist offices for details.

Those with private boats will have to pay lock fees and guest harbour fees (around 150kr per night, although some small places are free). A useful guide is the free, annual *Gästhamnsguiden*, which is published in Swedish by **Svenska Kryssarklubben** (Swedish Cruising Club; ☎08-448 28 80; www.sxk.se). It contains comprehensive details of 500 guest harbours throughout the country and is available from tourist offices.

Canoeing & Kayaking

With its countless lakes and rivers, not to mention the long coastlines, Sweden is a real paradise for canoeists and kayakers. The national canoeing body is **Svenska Kanotförbundet** (www.kanot.com). It provides general advice and lists approved canoe centres that hire out canoes (per day/week from around 350/1600kr).

Fishing

There are national and local restrictions on fishing in many of Sweden's inland waters, especially for salmon, trout and eel.

Top: Abisko (p284)

Bottom: Dogsledding
team, Lappland (p268)

THE RIGHT OF PUBLIC ACCESS

Allemansrätten, the right of public access to the countryside, is not a legal right but a common-law privilege. It includes national parks and nature reserves, although special rules may apply. Full details in English can be found on the website www.allemansratten.se.

You're allowed to walk, ski, boat or swim on private land as long as you stay at least 70m from houses and keep out of gardens, fenced areas and cultivated land. You can pick berries and mushrooms, provided they're not protected species. Generally you should move on after one or two nights' camping.

Don't leave rubbish or take live wood, bark, leaves, bushes or nuts. Fires fuelled with fallen wood are allowed where safe, but not on bare rocks (which can crack from the heat). Use a bucket of water to douse a campfire even if you think that it's completely out. Cars and motorcycles may not be driven across open land or on private roads; look out for the sign *ej motorfordon* (no motor vehicles). Dogs must be kept on leads between 1 March and 20 August. Close all farm gates and don't disturb farm animals or reindeer. Off-limits areas where birds are nesting are marked with a yellow or red-and-yellow sign containing the words *fågelskydd – tillträde förbjudet*.

If you have a car or bicycle, look for free camping sites around unsealed forest tracks leading from secondary country roads. Make sure your spot is at least 50m from the track and not visible from any house, building or sealed road. Bring drinking water and food, and don't pollute any water sources with soap or food waste.

Above all, remember the mantra: 'Do not disturb, do not destroy'.

Before dropping a line, check with local tourist offices or councils.

Local permits (*fiskekort*) can be bought from tourist offices, sports stores or camping shops and typically cost 50kr to 200kr per day, depending on season and location.

Summer is the best fishing time with bait or flies for most species, but trout and pike fishing in southern Sweden is better in spring or autumn and salmon fishing is best in late summer. Ice fishing is popular in winter.

An excellent web resource for fishing in Sweden is www.cinclusc.com/spfguide, or contact **Sportfiskarna** (Angling Association; ☏08-704 44 80; www.sportfiskarna.se).

Skiing

Large ski resorts cater mainly to downhill (alpine and telemark) skiing and snowboarding, but there's also scope for cross-country (Nordic) touring.

SkiStar (www.skistar.com) runs the ski resorts at Sälen, Vemdalen and Åre, among others. Check the website before travelling for early-bird deals on lodging and tickets.

For cross-country skiing, the northwest usually has plenty of snow from December to April. The Kungsleden and other long-distance hiking tracks provide great skiing. You can also ski along parts of the Vasaloppet ski-race track in Dalarna (the town of Mora is a good starting point). Most towns have illuminated skiing tracks.

Take the usual precautions: don't leave marked routes without emergency food, a good map, local advice and proper equipment including a bivouac bag. Temperatures of -30°C or lower (including wind-chill factor) are possible, so check the daily forecasts. Police and tourist offices have information on local warnings. In alpine ski resorts, where there's a risk of avalanche (*lavin*), susceptible areas are marked by yellow multilingual signs and buried-skier symbols. Make sure your travel insurance covers skiing.

Swimming

No Swedish summer is complete without a dip in the water, be it a lake, canal or sea. There are sandy beaches along the southwest coast, rocky launch pads in Bohuslän, and a combination of the two on the islands of the various archipelagos. Sweden's many lakes frequently have little public docks ideal for diving. In Stockholm there are several public beaches, but you can also swim from the terrace in front of Stadshuset (City Hall). Roped-off kid-friendly swimming areas are common and well marked across the country; many other spots are unofficial but easy to find if you just follow the crowds.

Skating

When the Baltic Sea freezes (once or twice every 10 years), fantastic tours of Stockholm's archipelago are possible. The skating season usually lasts from December to March. Less ambitiously, there's skating all winter on many city parks and ponds, including Kungsträdgården in Stockholm, with skate-rental booths nearby.

Dogsledding

Sweden's Sami have readily adopted dogsledding as a means of winter transport, following in the footsteps of the indigenous people of Siberia, and excursions are available in most northern towns. Apart from being the most ecofriendly means of exploring the Arctic regions, it's also one of the most enjoyable ways of getting around, allowing you to bond with your own husky team and to slow down and appreciate the surrounding wilds as the mood takes you. Most operators offer anything from a two-hour taster to fairly demanding multiday expeditions, staying overnight in rustic forest cabins or Sami winter tents.

Snowmobile Safaris

While some may argue that snowmobiles are noisy and not terribly ecofriendly, they are the Arctic equivalent of an all-terrain vehicle and essential for travel within isolated areas, not mention for rounding up reindeer. Travelling by snowmobile allows you to access difficult terrain and cover more ground than by dog- or reindeer sled. Snowmobile safaris (including night rides to see the northern lights) are offered by operators in all major northern towns. It's cheaper to ride as a passenger behind an experienced driver, though snowmobiles are available for hire to those with a valid driving licence (get a snowmobile permit from the nearest tourist office). Trails are marked with red crosses on poles.

Golf

Sweden has about 500 golf courses, open to everyone, and many hotel chains offer golf packages. Björkliden, near Abisko, is a golf course 240km above the Arctic Circle, and at the Green Line golf course at Haparanda, playing a round means crossing the Swedish–Finnish border four times. Green fees range from 550kr to 1450kr per day, depending on the season and the kind of course (prices are higher near metro areas); for more information, contact **Svenska Golfförbundet** (http://sgf.golf.se).

Birdwatching

There are many keen ornithologists in Sweden, and there are birdwatchers' towers and nature reserves everywhere. For further information, contact **Sveriges Ornitologiska Förening** (www.birdlife.se).

Horse Riding

Sweden's multitude of tracks, trails, forests, shorelines and mountains make for some fantastically varied riding. Everything from short hacks to full-on treks are on offer (two hours/half day/full day start around 400/650/950kr) on Swedish or Icelandic horses. Trips can be arranged through local tourist offices.

Plan Your Trip
Travel with Children

Sweden is a fantastically fun and easy place to travel with children, from infants up to teens. Most sights and activities are designed with kids in mind, with free or reduced admission for under-18s and plenty of hands-on exhibits. Dining, accommodation and transport providers are also well accustomed to handling families.

Best Regions for Kids

Stockholm & Around
Museums, a petting zoo and an amusement park make the capital city a delight for kids.

Uppsala & Central Sweden
A great water park, zoo, family-friendly ski slopes and tons of camping.

Gothenburg & the Southwest
The country's biggest amusement park, plus great museums and public parks.

Malmö & the South
One of Sweden's best open-air museums, plus a rad skatepark.

The Southeast & Gotland
Take the family on an easy, round-island bicycle trip on Gotland, or visit Astrid Lindgrens Värld in Vimmerby.

Östersund & the Bothnian Coast
A legendary sea monster, a great zoo, an open-air museum and several kid-friendly hostels.

Lappland & the Far North
Hit the ski slopes or take the kids on a dogsledding adventure in winter, or a good long hike in summer.

Sweden for Kids

If you've got kids, you're guaranteed an easy ride in Sweden. As a general tip, get the kids involved in your travel plans – if they've helped to work out where you're going, chances are they'll still be interested when you arrive! Remember, don't try to cram too much in. Lonely Planet's *Travel with Children* is a useful source of information.

Swedes treat children very well, and domestic tourism is largely organised around children's interests. Many museums have a kids' section with toys, hands-on displays and activities, and there are numerous public parks for kids, plus theme parks, water parks and so on. Most attractions allow free admission for young children – up to about seven years of age – and in many cases up to about 18. Tours and hostel beds are usually half-price for kids. Family tickets are often available.

High chairs and cots (cribs) are standard in most restaurants and hotels. Restaurant menus usually feature at least a couple of children's meals at a reasonable price. (These are generally along the lines of Swedish meatballs or pancakes with lingonberries and cream – a fairly easy sell even for fussy eaters.) Swedish supermarkets offer a wide choice of baby food, infant formulas, soy and cow's milk, disposable nappies (diapers) etc. There are nappy-changing facilities in most toilets (men's and women's), and breastfeeding in public is not an issue.

Children's Highlights

Theme Parks

Liseberg (p137) Sweden's most popular tourist attraction, for good reason.

Gröna Lund Tivoli (p46) Fun rides and concerts in the heart of Stockholm, with awesome views of the capital from the more gravity-defying rides.

Junibacken (p51) Pretend you're Pippi Longstocking at this book-based theme park.

Open-Air Museums

Skansen (p50) A miniature Sweden.

Himmelsberga (p233) A farm village with quaint cottages.

Kulturen (p183) A vast museum with buildings from all points in history.

Fredriksdals museer och trädgårdar (p186) An old manor house, a farm, lovely gardens and a French baroque theatre.

Vallby Friluftsmuseum (p108) A farmyard and several craft workshops.

Jamtli (p246) The north's answer to Skansen.

Murberget (p256) A traditional shop, smithy, church and school, in typical Norrland style.

Museums

Tekniska Museet (p47) Thrill tiny nerds with science and gadgetry.

Naturhistoriska Museet (p139) The forest comes to life in this diorama-filled museum.

Medeltidsmuseet (p45) Go back in time and underneath Stockholm for the gripping story of the city's foundations.

Värmlands Museum (p115) Everything there is to know about the region, plus great contemporary art.

Ájtte Museum (p277) Sami culture gets the attention it deserves, with beautiful multimedia presentations.

Rainy-Day Activities

Kulturhuset (p54) Crafts in Stockholm.

Science Fiction Bookshop (p85) In Stockholm's Gamla Stan.

Cinemas Catch a Hollywood blockbuster.

Planning

When to Go

Parents will find that travel in the summer tourist season (mid-June to August) is easier than outside those times, simply because more visitor facilities, sights and activities are up and running. Be sure to book ahead.

If your family is interested in outdoor activities, winter is also a great time to visit; several ski hills (including the world-class Åre) have family-friendly facilities, bunny slopes, ski schools, day care and so on.

Accommodation

Campgrounds have excellent facilities and are overrun with ecstatic, energetic children. They get very busy in summer, so book tent sites or cabins well in advance.

Hotels and other accommodation options often have 'family rooms' that sleep up to two adults and two children for about the price of a regular double. Cots for young children are available in most hotels and hostels, usually either free of charge or for a nominal fee.

Hotel staff are accustomed to serving families and should be able to help you with anything you need, from heating bottles to finding a babysitter for a parents' night out.

Transport

Car-rental companies will hire out children's safety seats at a nominal cost, but it's essential that you book them in advance. Long-distance ferries and trains may have play areas for children.

Ask about free rides on public transport for young children; this is offered at certain times of day in many cities (for instance, kids under 12 ride free at weekends in Stockholm). Buses are nicely set up for strollers/prams, and most of the time you'll be swarmed by locals trying to help you get the stroller on and off the bus.

Regions at a Glance

Stockholm & Around

Food
Museums
Shopping

World-Class Cuisine

Stockholm is a world-class foodie destination, with multiple Michelin stars to its name and a number of celebrity chefs known for transcending expectations with their bold takes on locally sourced, traditionally rooted dishes. You can eat as well here as in most any European capital.

Multimedia Museums

There's no chance you'll be bored in a Stockholm museum – this city does them right. Stockholm's museums present the best of the country's art and historical treasures in an inviting atmosphere. Exhibition rooms are as well planned and well lit as the rest of the city's stylish spaces.

Ready, Set, Shop

From tucked-away thrift stores to big-name retail boutiques, fine linens and handicrafts to cleverly designed kitchen gadgets, nearly every type of shopper will find plenty to pick through here.

p40

Uppsala & Central Sweden

History
Industry
Museums

Historical Relics

Uppsala is a treat for history buffs: from pre-Viking grave mounds to a hillside castle whose pink walls concealed decades of royal intrigue, plus the odd rune stone or ship setting, and a stash of museum treasures from art and artefacts to ancient manuscripts.

Industrial Artefacts

Central Sweden is the country's industrial workhorse, plying the rich landscape for iron, copper and silver. Many of these places have been transformed into quaint and atmospheric historical sites well worth a visit.

Regional Museums

Great museums are spread throughout the region, from Örebro's regional art museum to the ambitious Värmland Museum in Karlstad to the homes of beloved Swedish artists Carl Larsson and Anders Zorn and author Selma Lagerlöf.

p97

Gothenburg & the Southwest

Coastline
Food
Culture

Southwest Shore

From kitesurfing in Halland to island-hopping in Bohuslän, there are unlimited options for ocean-lovers in the southwest. Spend the night on one of the coast's remote skerries or join the crowds to watch summertime round-island regattas.

Fresh Seafood

Local chefs boast that seafood arrives first in Gothenburg and second in Stockholm, so if you want to experience truly fresh prawns, oysters, lobster or cod, look no further. Select your own dockside, or indulge in top-tier restaurants.

Urban Edge

Gothenburg's industrial roots make its artists practical – less talk, more action – and there's a gritty refinement to design, music and art across the region. Distinctive venues abound: repurposed power stations, basement boutiques and castle lawns.

p131

Malmö & the South

Variety
Nature
Mystery

A Bit of Everything

A thorough experience of southern Sweden may include sailing on a restored Viking ship, taking in avant garde architecture, climbing fortress steps and finishing up with a 5am falafel after a night out in Malmö. The best option is to try it all.

Outdoor Activities

Whether it's with apple picking, gorgeous beaches or some nice coastal hikes, southern Sweden is perfect for taking advantage of the great outdoors. More offbeat options include seal safaris, scuba diving and pony trekking.

Secrets of the South

Ancient and present-day mysteries thrive in southern Sweden. Come face to face with (hopefully fictional) crime scenes in Kurt Wallander's Ystad or puzzle over Bronze Age relics at Kivik and Ales Stenar.

p168

The Southeast & Gotland

Outdoor Activities
World Heritage
History

Ports, Roads & Trails

The southeast is paradise for the outdoorsy person, with grand ports for sailors, rocky beaches for sunworshippers, quiet lakeside roads for cyclists and miles of glorious woodland trails.

National Treasures

A wander through Visby's cobblestone streets, past fairy-tale cottages and haunting church ruins, and the gasp-inducing view of sky, sea and rock at Öland's southernmost point will make it clear why both have earned Unesco distinction.

Canals, Castles & Churches

Steeped in tales of industry and migration, boasting the engineering triumph of the Göta Canal and with some seriously impressive castles, the southeast has plenty of history to share. Not to mention Gotland's stunning churches and the pilgrim's route to St Birgitta's abbey.

p206

Jämtland & the Bothnian Coast

Wildlife
Activities
Islands

Mammals & Monsters

Quite apart from the musk oxen, elk and reindeer that you may meet in the wild (or pet at Järvzoo), the waters of Lake Storsjön hide the most elusive creature of all – Östersund's answer to the Loch Ness Monster.

Year-Round Adventure

Åre is adventure central, where you can try your hand at hillcarting, heli-skiing, zorbing and mountain biking. The mountains west of Östersund and the Bothnian Coast offer varied terrain for some superb hiking in summer and skiing in winter.

Jagged Coast

The waters of the Gulf of Bothnia are dotted with myriad forested islands. While some allow you to play out your Robinson Crusoe fantasies, others introduce you to traditional fishing culture and that devil of a delicacy, *surströmming* (fermented herring).

p244

Lappland & the Far North

Wildlife
Hiking
Sami Culture

Elusive Creatures

There are few places in the world where it's easier to see reindeer, elk and foxes. If you're lucky, you may even spot a brown bear, lynx or wolverine, though they are nocturnal and shy.

Top Trails

The Kungsleden is the most celebrated hiking trail, although Padjelanta and Stora Sjöfjallet offer trails that are no less picturesque. The ascent of Kebnekaise provides exceptional views, while Sarek National Park will challenge even the most experienced of hikers.

Sami Way of Life

Explore the past and present of the indigenous people of Scandinavian Europe: admire Sami silver jewellery through the ages at Áttje Museum, stay with Sami reindeer herders at Båtsuoj Sami Camp and visit the Jokkmokk Winter Market.

p268

On the
Road

Stockholm & Around

🌙 08 / POP 932,000

Best Places to Eat

➜ Kryp In (p71)

➜ Rosendals Trädgårdskafe (p73)

➜ Hermans Trädgårdscafé (p76)

➜ Grands Verandan (p74)

➜ Woodstockholm (p77)

Best Places to Stay

➜ Rival Hotel (p68)

➜ Vandrarhem af Chapman & Skeppsholmen (p66)

➜ Långholmen Hotell & Vandrarhem (p68)

➜ Hobo Hotel (p67)

➜ Grand Hôtel Stockholm (p67)

Why Go?

Stockholm's good looks and fashion sense could almost be intimidating. But this city is an accessible beauty, as easy to explore as it is to love. Though spread across 14 islands, connected by 57 bridges, it is compact and walkable. Each neighbourhood has a distinct character, yet they're so close together you can easily spend time in several areas. In each, you'll find trend-setting design, inventive cuisine, unbeatable museums, great shopping, pretty parks and loads of atmosphere. The old town, Gamla Stan, is one of Europe's most arresting historic hubs, all storybook buildings, imposing palaces and razor-thin cobblestone streets. Just a few metres from this time capsule, the modern city centre shines like the pages of a magazine. Downtown is a catwalk, showroom and test kitchen. Everything here is the very latest thing. And it's surrounded by pristine forests and a vast archipelago. What's not to love?

When to Go
Stockholm

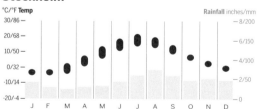

Mid-Jun–mid-Aug Stockholm's long days, uncannily pretty light and mild weather are dreamy.

Dec–Feb The city is a frosted cake, with holiday markets and mugs of *glögg* around every corner.

Sep & Oct Cooler weather, minimal crowds and beautiful autumn colours.

Stockholm & Around Highlights

❶ **Vasamuseet** (p49) Studying a shipwreck and Swedish history.

❷ **Gamla Stan** (p65) Wandering around the atmospheric old town.

❸ **Skansen** (p50) Visiting Sweden in miniature at this open-air museum.

❹ **Nordiska Museet** (p51) Exploring Swedish culture, art and daily life.

❺ **Moderna Museet** (p51) Admiring cutting-edge international artwork.

❻ **Biblioteksgatan** (p83) Shopping at big name boutiques.

❼ **Södermalm** (p80) Bar-hopping with lively locals and wayfarers.

❽ **Utö** (p92) Taking a boat to sample the Stockholm archipelago.

History

Rising land drove Stockholm's early destiny, forcing the centre of Swedish Viking political power to move from northern lake Mälaren to the lake's outlet for better trade routes. The town charter dates from 1250. Stockholm's official founder, Birger Jarl, commissioned the original royal castle, Tre Kronor, in 1252.

The Black Death of 1350 wiped out around a third of Sweden's population; then Danish Queen Margrethe Valdemarsdotter added insult to injury by besieging the city from 1391 to 1395, amalgamating the crowns of Sweden, Norway and Denmark under the unpopular Union of Kalmar in 1397. Stockholm was a key piece in control of the lands covered by the Kalmar Union, and from 1397 to the early 1500s it was constantly embattled as various Danish and Swedish factions struggled for power.

In what became known as the Stockholm Bloodbath of 1520, Danish King Christian II tricked, trapped and beheaded 82 rebellious Swedes on Stortorget in Gamla Stan. One of the victims had a son, Gustav Ericsson Vasa, who led a successful resistance to Danish rule and became Sweden's first king on 6 June 1523, now Sweden's national day.

Gustav Vasa's sons continued their father's nation-building, transforming Stockholm into a major military hub during the Thirty Years War. By the end of the 16th century, Stockholm's population was 9000, and the city had spread from the original old town onto Norrmalm and Södermalm. Stockholm was officially proclaimed the capital of Sweden in 1634.

By 1650 the city boasted a thriving artistic and intellectual culture and a grand new look, courtesy of father-and-son architects the Tessins, who built Drottningholms Slott and several other iconic Stockholm buildings.

The following decades weren't so kind to the capital. A devastating famine brought starving hordes to the city in 1696, and the beloved Tre Kronor went up in flames the following year. Russian military victories shrunk the Swedish empire, and a plague engulfed the city in 1711.

A now-fragile Stockholm traded state-building for character-building. Botanist Carl von Linné (1707–78) developed the template for the classification of plants and animals, Anders Celsius (1701–44) came up with the centigrade temperature scale and royal palace Kungliga Slottet rose from the ashes of

Tre Kronor. Swedish science, architecture and arts blossomed during the reign of Francophile King Gustav III (1771–92), but the theatre buff's tyrannical tendencies saw him assassinated by parliament member Jacob Johan Anckarström at a masked ball in the Opera House in 1792. The murder formed the basis of Giuseppe Verdi's opera *A Masked Ball*.

When Sweden's northern and southern train lines were connected via Stockholm's Centralstationen and Riddarholmen in 1871, an industrial boom kicked in. The city's population reached 245,000 in 1890 (an increase of 77,000 in ten years), and new districts like Östermalm expanded the city limits.

Stockholm hosted the 1912 summer Olympics, but the resulting elation quickly dissipated when Sweden refused to uphold a blockade against Germany during WWI. Britain attacked the country's supply lines, causing starving Stockholmers to riot in Gustav Adolfs Torg. During WWII Sweden's official neutrality made it a hot spot for Jewish, Scandinavian and Baltic refugees, the first of many successive waves of migrants.

The city's postwar economic boom saw the advent of Eastern Bloc–style suburban expansion. Along with growth and modernisation came increased violence, notably the still-unsolved murder of Prime Minister Olof Palme on Sveavägen in 1986, and the stabbing death of foreign minister Anna Lindh at the NK department store in 2003.

◉ Sights

Stockholm can seem a baffling city to navigate at first, strewn over 14 islands. Although the city centre and other neighbourhoods are easily walkable, the excellent transport system, comprising trams, buses and metro, is the best way to cover the city's more far-flung sights. Most people start their visit at Gamla Stan, a medieval tangle of narrow alleyways and colourful buildings which, although touristy, is extremely picturesque and home to several truly splendid sights.

Note that very few museums in Stockholm are open before 10am – often not until 11am. Plan to *ta det lugnt* ('take it easy').

◌ Gamla Stan

The old town is Stockholm's historic and geographic heart. Here, cobblestone streets wriggle past Renaissance churches, baroque palaces and medieval squares. Spice-coloured buildings sag like wizened old men, and

STOCKHOLM IN...

Two Days

Beat the crowds to the labyrinthine streets of **Gamla Stan**, the city's historic old town. Watch St George wrestle the dragon inside **Storkyrkan** (p46), the old-town cathedral, and join a tour of the royal palace, **Kungliga Slottet**. Then trek to **Södermalm** for dizzying views from the Söder Heights. See what's on at the photography gallery **Fotografiska** (p56) – you can grab a bite here, too. If the weather's nice, party on the terrace at **Mosebacke Etablissement** (p82) or the bars in **Medborgarplatsen**. Spend the next day exploring the outdoor museum **Skansen** (p50), before a seafood dinner at **Sturehof** (p73).

Four Days

On day three take a guided boat tour of Stockholm's waterways. Visit the impressive **Vasamuseet** (p49), then stroll up to **Hötorgshallen** (p74) for a big bowl of fish soup and speciality-food browsing. Next day, head to **Millesgården** (p59) for sculptures in a dreamy setting, then spend the afternoon doing what Stockholmers do best: shopping. Start with pedestrianised **Biblioteksgatan** off Stureplan, then transition to **Drottninggatan** for souvenirs.

One Week

A week gives you time to visit the royal palace of **Drottningholm** (p88), then take a boat to an island on the archipelago for a quiet, pastoral overnight stay.

narrow lanes harbour everything from dusty toy shops to candlelit cafes.

Västerlånggatan is the area's nerve centre, a bustling thoroughfare lined with galleries, eateries and souvenir shops. Step off the main drag and into the tinier alleyways for a surprisingly quiet chance to explore.

★**Kungliga Slottet** PALACE
(Royal Palace; Map p44; ☑08-402 61 30; www.theroyalpalace.se; Slottsbacken; adult/child 160/80kr, combo ticket incl Riddarholmen adult/child 180/90kr; ☺9am-5pm Jul & Aug, 10am-5pm May-Jun & Sep, 10am-4pm Tue-Sun Oct-Apr; ☐43, 46, 55, 59 Slottsbacken, ☒Gamla Stan) Kungliga Slottet was built on the ruins of Tre Kronor castle, which burned down in 1697. The north wing survived and was incorporated into the new building. Designed by court architect Nicodemus Tessin the Younger, it took 57 years to complete. Highlights include the decadent Karl XI Gallery, inspired by Versailles' Hall of Mirrors and Queen Kristina's silver throne in the Hall of State.

With 608 rooms, this is the world's largest royal castle still used for its original purpose. The first royal family moved here in 1754. The palace is not a museum but rather a working government building; though it contains fine examples of baroque and rococo furnishings and interiors, each room also bears the fingerprints of the many generations who have lived there. There are regular 45-minute guided tours (20kr per person) held in several languages which are well worth taking; check the website for the timetable.

Admission to the palace also includes the **Museum Tre Kronor**, devoted to Stockholm's original castle; the **Royal Treasury**; and **Gustav III's Antikmuseum** (the museum of antiquities). Tickets are good for seven days.

In the basement Museum Tre Kronor, you can see the foundations of 13th-century defensive walls and items rescued from the medieval castle during the 1697 fire. The museum also describes how the fire started (a fire watcher was off flirting with a kitchen maid, it seems) and explains rather vividly the meaning of 'run the gauntlet' (which in 1697 was how the court punished watchmen for flirting with kitchen maids while fire destroyed the castle).

The Royal Treasury contains ceremonial crowns, sceptres and other regalia of the Swedish monarchy, including a 16th-century sword that belonged to Gustav Vasa. Gustav III's Antikmuseum (closed mid-September to mid-May) displays Italian sculptures collected by King Gustav III in the 1780s.

It's worth timing your visit to see the **Changing of the Guard**, which takes place in the outer courtyard at 12.15pm Monday to Saturday and 1.15pm Sunday and public holidays

Gamla Stan

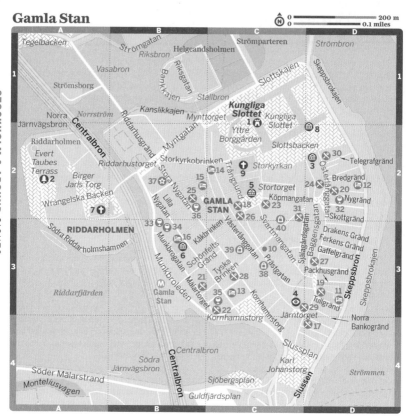

from May to August, and 12.15pm Wednesday and Saturday and 1.15pm Sunday and public holidays from September to May.

The apartments are occasionally closed for royal business; closures are noted on the website.

Riksdagshuset
NOTABLE BUILDING

(Swedish Parliament; Map p48; ☑020-34 80 00; www.riksdagen.se; Riksgatan 3; ⊙1hr tours in English noon, 1pm, 2pm & 3pm Mon–Fri mid-Jun–mid-Aug, 1.30pm Sat & Sun Oct–mid-Jun; ☐3, 59, Riddarhustorget, ☐Gamla Stan, T-Centralen) FREE Technically situated on Helgeandsholmen, the little island in the middle of Norrström, rather than on Gamla Stan, the Swedish Parliament building is an unexpected pleasure to visit. The building consists of two parts: the older front section (facing downstream) dates from the early 20th century, but the other more-modern part contains the current debating chamber. Tours offer a compelling glimpse into

the Swedish system of consensus-building government.

Nobelmuseet
MUSEUM

(Map p44; ☑08-54 43 18 00; www.nobelmuseet.se; Stortorget; adult/child 120kr/free; ⊙9am-8pm Jun-Aug, shorter hours rest of year; ☐53, ☐Gamla Stan) Nobelmuseet presents the history of the Nobel Prizes and their recipients, with a focus on the intellectual and cultural aspects of invention. It's a slick space with fascinating displays, including short films on the theme of creativity, interviews with laureates like Ernest Hemingway and Martin Luther King, and cafe chairs signed by the visiting prize recipients (flip them over to see!).

Royal Armoury
MUSEUM

(Livrustkammaren; Map p44; ☑08-402 30 30; www.livrustkammaren.se; Slottsbacken 3; ⊙10am-5pm, to 6pm Jul-Aug; ☐43, 46, 55, 59 Slottsbacken, ☐Gamla Stan) FREE The Royal Armoury

Gamla Stan

is housed in the cellar vaults of the palace but has separate hours. It's a family attic of sorts, crammed with engrossing memorabilia spanning more than 500 years of royal childhoods, coronations, weddings and murders. Meet Gustav II Adolf's stuffed battle steed, Streiff; see the costume Gustav III wore to the masquerade ball on the night he was shot in 1792; or let the kids try on a suit of armour in the playroom.

Evert Taubes Terrass PARK
(Map p44; Riddarholmen; ⊙ 24hr; ㉔ Gamla Stan) **FREE** Evert Taubes Terrass is a tranquil and relaxed spot and one of the best viewpoints in Stockholm, at eye level with lake Mälaren on the quiet island of Riddarholmen, with open sightlines across the water to Stockholm City Hall, Münchenbryggeriet and Södermalm's coastline. Sunset is the time to come. Taube, the park's namesake, was a beloved composer and troubadour who grew up on the Gothenburg archipelago; he's immortalised in the joyful statue at the corner of the park.

Riddarholmskyrkan CHURCH
(Riddarholmen Church; Map p44; ☎ 08-402 61 30; www.kungahuset.se; Riddarholmen; adult/child

50/25kr; ⊙ 10am-5pm mid-May–mid-Sep; ㉔ 3, 53 Riddarhustorget, ㉔ Gamla Stan) The strikingly beautiful Riddarholmskyrkan, on the equally pretty and under-visited islet of Riddarholmen, was built by Franciscan monks in the late 13th century. It has been the royal necropolis since the burial of Magnus Ladulås in 1290, and is home to the armorial glory of the Seraphim knightly order. There's a guided tour in English at noon (included with admission) and occasional concerts. Holiday closures are frequent; check the website for updates. Admission fee is by credit card only.

Medeltidsmuseet MUSEUM
(Medieval Museum; Map p48; www.medeltids museet.stockholm.se; Strömparterren; ⊙ noon-5pm Tue-Sun, to 8pm Wed; ㉔ 62, 65, Gustav Adolfs torg) **FREE** Tucked beneath the bridge that links Gamla Stan and Norrmalm, this child-friendly museum was established when construction workers preparing to build a car park here in the late 1970s unearthed foundations from the 1530s. The ancient walls were preserved as found, and a museum was built around them. The circular plan leads visitors through faithful reconstructions of typical homes, markets

and workshops from medieval Stockholm. Tickets are valid for one year.

Storkyrkan
CHURCH

(Great Church; Map p44; www.stockholms domkyrkoforsamling.se; Trångsund 1; adult/child 60kr/free; ⊙9am-4pm, to 6pm Jun-Aug; ☒Gamla Stan) The one-time venue for royal weddings and coronations, Storkyrkan is both Stockholm's oldest building (consecrated in 1306) and its cathedral. Behind a baroque facade, the Gothic-baroque interior includes extravagant royal-box pews designed by Nicodemus Tessin the Younger, as well as German Berndt Notke's dramatic sculpture *St George and the Dragon*, commissioned by Sten Sture the Elder to commemorate his victory over the Danes in 1471. Keep an eye out for posters and handbills advertising music performances here.

Kungliga Myntkabinettet
MUSEUM

(Royal Coin Cabinet; Map p44; ☑08-51 95 53 04; www.myntkabinettet.se; Slottsbacken 6; ⊙11am-5pm; ☒Gamla Stan) **FREE** Across the plaza from the Royal Palace, Kungliga Myntkabinettet – the National Museum of Economy – gleams with a priceless collection of currency spanning 2600 years. Treasures include Viking silver and the world's oldest coin (from 625 BC), largest coin (a Swedish copper plate weighing 19.7kg) and first banknote (issued in Sweden in 1661).

Postmuseum
MUSEUM

(Map p44; ☑010-436 44 39; www.postmuseum. se; Lilla Nygatan 6; adult/child 80kr/free; ⊙11am-4pm Tue-Sun, to 7pm Wed Sep-Apr; ☒Gamla Stan) Examining almost four centuries of Swedish postal history, the Postmuseum is not as mind-numbing as it might sound. It's actually rather evocative, featuring old mail carriages, kitsch postcards and a cute children's post office for budding postal workers. There's also a great cafe and a philatelic library with 51,000 books on stamps and postal history.

Mårten Trotzigs Gränd
AREA

(Map p44; ☒Gamla Stan) This tiny alley in Gamla Stan is Stockholm's narrowest street and a popular spot for a photo op.

Gröna Lund Tivoli
AMUSEMENT PARK

(Map p52; www.gronalund.com; Lilla Allmänna Gränd 9; entrance 115kr, unlimited ride pass 330kr; ⊙10am-11pm Jun-Aug, shorter hours rest of year;

STOCKHOLM FOR CHILDREN

Stockholm is well set up for travelling with children. There are baby-changing tables in almost every public bathroom, and even top-end restaurants have high chairs and children's menus. Likewise, hotel and hostel staff are accustomed to catering to families, while public transportation is generally easy to navigate.

In terms of entertainment, many of Stockholm's best attractions are targeted specifically at children and families. And even if they aren't particularly geared towards children, most of the city's museums have family playrooms available. Nobelmuseet (p44), for instance, has a 'Children's Club' (Barnens Nobelklubb) where kids aged between seven and 10 can share ideas and be creative. Other museums have rooms set aside for kid-friendly hands-on learning activities, such as painting, clay modelling or costume making.

Junibacken (p51) Draws young readers into Swedish author Astrid Lindgren's fantastic world, home to Pippi Longstocking and her friends.

Naturhistoriska Riksmuseet (p48) Offers a child's-eye view of the natural world, with an entire section for hands-on science experiments.

Medeltidsmuseet (p45) Provides multimedia displays that transport visitors back in time to the city's earliest days.

Postmuseum Includes a miniature post office for children who want to see how it all works.

Gröna Lund Tivoli Offers carnival-ride entertainment for slightly older kids and teens.

Tekniska Museet Interactive science exhibits will entertain inquisitive brains for hours.

Skansen (p50) Essentially a younger child's paradise, with dozens of mini-exhibits to explore, snacks everywhere, a petting zoo, singalongs and guides in old-timey costumes.

⊞ ; 🚌 44, 🚢 Djurgårdsfärjan, 🚋 7) Crowded Gröna Lund Tivoli has some 30 rides, ranging from the tame (a German circus carousel) to the terrifying (the Free Fall, where you drop from a height of 80m in six seconds after glimpsing a lovely, if brief, view over Stockholm). There are countless places to eat and drink in the park, but whether you'll keep anything down is another matter entirely. The Åkband day pass gives unlimited rides, or individual rides range from 25kr to 75kr.

Big-name concerts are often staged here in summer (admission free after 6pm if you're going to a concert). Gröna Lund is a stop on the Slussen–Djurgården ferry.

⊙ Östermalm & Ladugårdsgärdet

Östermalm is indisputably Stockholm's party district, where the beautiful, rich and famous come to play. It's also home to some of the city's best places to eat, drink and shop. But it isn't strictly about hedonism: this is also where you'll find two excellent history museums.

Just to the east is Ladugårdsgärdet, a wide-open, park-like area that once served as a military training ground. These days the smooth fields are popular for strolls, football matches and hot-air-balloon rides. The area boasts three fine museums and one of Stockholm's loftiest views.

⭐ **Historiska Museet**   MUSEUM
(☑ 08-51 95 56 20; www.historiska.se; Narvavägen 13-17; ⊙10am-5pm Jun-Aug, 11am-5pm Tue-Sun, to 8pm Wed Sep-May; 🚌 44,56, 🚢 Djurgårdsbron, 🚋 Karlaplan, Östermalmstorg) **FREE** The national historical collection awaits at this enthralling museum. From Iron Age skates and a Viking boat to medieval textiles and Renaissance triptychs, it spans over 10,000 years of Swedish culture and history. There's an exhibit about the medieval Battle of Gotland (1361), an excellent multimedia display on the Vikings, a room of breathtaking altarpieces from the Middle Ages, a vast textile collection and a section on prehistoric culture.

Ekoparken   PARK
(Royal National City Park; www.ekoparken.org; ⊙24hr; 🚻; 🚌 69) 🖉 **FREE** The vast Ekoparken, or Royal National City Park, is the world's first national urban park. Established in 1995, it incorporates 26 sq km, stretching all over Stockholm and into the suburbs

of Solna and Lidingö. The park is home to rare plant and insect species, some of which live nowhere else in Sweden. Several tourist attractions reside inside the park area (it incorporates Djurgården, Ladugårdsgärdet and the University area), so you'll probably end up wandering through it without even trying.

Etnografiska Museet   MUSEUM
(Museum of Ethnography; Map p52; ☑ 010-456 12 99; www.etnografiska.se; Djurgårdsbrunnsvägen 34; ⊙11am-5pm Tue-Sun, to 8pm Wed; 🚌 69 Museiparken) **FREE** The Museum of Ethnography stages evocative displays on various aspects of non-European cultures, including dynamic temporary exhibitions and frequent live performances. Recent examples include a display about the cultural treasures of Afghanistan, a look at gender norms in different cultures, and 'real-life' voodoo. If there's a dance or musical performance scheduled, don't miss it. The cafe is a treat, with great music, imported sweets and beverages, and authentic global dishes.

Tekniska Museet   MUSEUM
(Museum of Science & Technology; Map p52; ☑ 08-450 56 00; www.tekniskamuseet.se; Museivägen 7; adult/child 150/100kr, free 5-8pm Wed; ⊙10am-5pm Thu-Tue, to 8pm Wed; 🚻; 🚌 69 Museiparken) Tekniska is a sprawling wonderland of interactive science and technology exhibits. The Teknorama is a vast room of kinetic experiments and stations designed to do things like test your balance, flexibility and strength. In one corner is a dark and genuinely scary mining exhibit. There's also a model railroad, a survey of inventions by women, and a climate-change game.

Armémuseum   MUSEUM
(Artillery Museum; ☑ 08-51 95 63 00; www.armemuseum.se; Riddargatan 13; ⊙10am-7pm Jun-Aug, 11am-8pm Tue, to 5pm Wed-Sun Sep-May; 🚋 Östermalmstorg) **FREE** Delve into the darker side of human nature at Armémuseum, where three levels of engrossing exhibitions explore the horrors of war through art, weaponry and life-size reconstructions of charging horsemen, forlorn barracks and starving civilians. You can even hop on a replica sawhorse for a taste of medieval torture.

Swedish Museum of Performing Arts   MUSEUM
(Scenkonstmuseet; Map p48; ☑ 08-51 95 54 90; www.scenkonstmuseet.se; Sibyllegatan 2; adult/

Central Stockholm

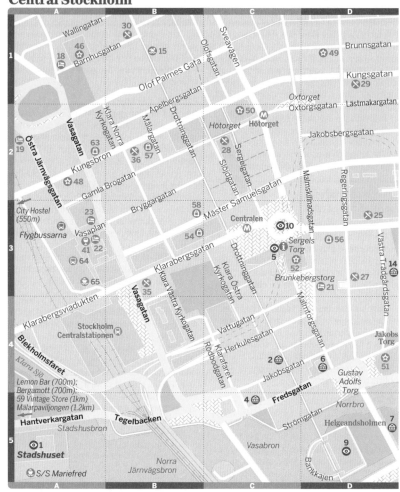

child 120kr/free; ⏱ 11am-5pm Jul & Aug, closed Mon Sep-Jun; 🚇 Östermalmstorg) Spanning over 400 years of history, the Swedish Museum of Performing Arts has a rich collection of set designs, original costumes and musical instruments detailing the visual arts. Housed in the old Crown Bakery originating from the 17th century and adjacent to the national theatre, this a must for anyone aiming to indulge their creative side.

Hedvig Eleonora's Church CHURCH
(Hedvig Eleonora Kyrka; ☎ 08-54 56 75 70; www. hedvigeleonora.se; Storgatan 2; ⏱ 11am-6pm; 🚇 Östermalmstorg) FREE A perfect example

of Swedish baroque architecture from the late-17th to early-18th centuries, Hedvig Eleonora church is an often-bypassed landmark in Stockholm. Centrally located in the Östermalm district overlooking the Östermalmstorg markets, it's great for a quick a visit to break up a day of shopping.

Naturhistoriska Riksmuseet MUSEUM
(Swedish Museum of Natural History; ☎ 08-51 95 40 00; www.nrm.se; Frescativägen 40; ⏱ 10am-6pm Tue-Sun, open select Mon; 🅿 ♿; 🚇 Universitetet) FREE A fantastic place to bring kids, the Natural History Museum has seen a lot of changes since Carl von Linné founded it

IMAX and 3D theatre with themes ranging from mummies and dinosaurs to the deep sea and prehistoric sea monsters. Films are screened on the hour (check the latest schedules online), and reservations by phone are recommended. No admittance for children under five.

Kaknästornet   VIEWPOINT
(www.kaknastornet.se; Mörka Kroken 28-30; adult/child 70/25kr; ⊙10am-6pm Sun-Thu, to 9pm Fri & Sat; ⊒69 Kaknästornet) A handy landmark for navigating this part of town, the 155m-tall Kaknästornet is the automatic operations centre for radio and TV broadcasting in Sweden. Opened in 1967, it's among the tallest buildings in Scandinavia. There's a small visitor centre (mainly a gift shop) on the ground floor and an elevator up to the observation deck, restaurant and cafe near the top, from where there are stellar views of the city and archipelago.

◎ Djurgården & Skeppsholmen

The parklike island of Djurgården is a museum-goer's dream. Not only are many of Stockholm's top museums gathered here but the setting is sublime: gardens, greenery, a lazy river, cycle paths, picnic places, and all of it just one footbridge away from the centre of town.

The small island of Skeppsholmen is home to a couple of major museums. To get here, take the footbridge from the city centre or hop on the Djurgården ferry from Slussen.

★Vasamuseet   MUSEUM
(Map p52; www.vasamuseet.se; Galärvarvsvägen 14; adult/child 130kr/free; ⊙8.30am-6pm Jun-Aug, 10am-5pm Sep-May; ℙ; ⊒44, ⊠Djurgårdsfärjan, ⊒7) A good-humoured glorification of some dodgy calculations, Vasamuseet is the custom-built home of the massive warship *Vasa*; 69m long and 48.8m tall, it was the pride of the Swedish crown when it set off on its maiden voyage on 10 August 1628. Within minutes, the top-heavy vessel tipped and sank to the bottom of Saltsjön, along with many of the people on board.

Tour guides explain the extraordinary and controversial 300-year story of its death and resurrection, which saw the ship painstakingly raised in 1961 and reassembled like a giant 14,000-piece jigsaw. Almost all of what you see today is original.

On the entrance level is a model of the ship at scale 1:10 and a cinema screening a

in 1739. These days, everything is interactive: you can crawl inside a human ear, sit through a forest fire or step into a chamber that mimics a swarm of mosquitoes. Of course, there are still countless displays of fossils, rock specimens, and whole forests' worth of taxidermied wildlife, marine life and the hardy fauna of the polar regions.

Cosmonova   PLANETARIUM, CINEMA
(✆08-51 95 51 30; www.nrm.se; Frescativägen 40, at the Naturhistoriska Riksmuseet; adult/child 110/50kr; ⊙10am-6pm Tue-Sun; ℙ⊞; ⊒Universitetet) Adjoining Naturhistoriska Riksmuseet is Cosmonova, a combined planetarium,

Central Stockholm

25-minute film covering topics not included in the exhibitions. There are four other
levels of exhibits covering artefacts salvaged
from the *Vasa,* life on board, naval warfare,
and 17th-century sailing and navigation,
plus sculptures and temporary exhibitions.
The bottom-floor exhibition is particularly
fascinating, using modern forensic science
to re-create the faces and life stories of several of the ill-fated passengers.

The bookshop is worth a browse and there's
a restaurant for a well-earned pit stop.

Guided tours are in English every 30 minutes in summer, less frequently the rest of
the year.

★ **Skansen**   MUSEUM
(Map p52; www.skansen.se; Djurgårdsvägen; adult/
child 180/60kr; ☉10am-6pm, extended hours in
summer; [P]; ☒69, ☒Djurgårdsfärjan, ☒7) The
world's first open-air museum, Skansen
was founded in 1891 by Artur Hazelius to
provide an insight into how Swedes once
lived. You could easily spend a day here

and not see it all. Around 150 traditional houses and other exhibits dot the hilltop – it's meant to be 'Sweden in miniature', complete with villages, nature, commerce and industry. Note that prices and opening hours vary seasonally; check the website before you go.

★**Moderna Museet**   MUSEUM
(Map p52; 📞08-52 02 35 00; www.moderna museet.se; Exercisplan 4; ⏱10am-8pm Tue & Fri, to 6pm Wed-Thu, 11am-6pm Sat & Sun; 🅿; 🚌65, 🚢Djurgårdsfärjan) FREE Moderna Museet is Stockholm's modern-art maverick, its permanent collection ranging from paintings and sculptures to photography, video art and installations. Highlights include works by Pablo Picasso, Salvador Dalí, Andy Warhol, Damien Hirst and Robert Rauschenberg, plus several key figures in the Scandinavian and Russian art worlds and beyond. There are important pieces by Francis Bacon, Marcel Duchamp and Matisse, as well as their contemporaries, both household names and otherwise.

Glassblowers' Workshop   WORKSHOP
(Map p52; www.stockholms-glasbruk.se; Skansen; ⏱10.30am-5pm Jul-Aug, shorter hours rest of year) The Glassblowers' hut, built in 1936, is one of the top attractions within Skansen. It's also possible to book your own glassblowing session – reserve online well in advance.

Skansen Zoo   ZOO
(Map p52; www.skansen.se) Inside Skansen is this excellent zoo, with native Nordic animals, farm animals and a kid-friendly petting zoo.

Junibacken   AMUSEMENT PARK
(Map p52; www.junibacken.se; Djurgården; adult/child 159/139kr; ⏱10am-6pm Jul-Aug, to 5pm rest of year; 👶; 🚌44, 69, 🚢Djurgårdsfärjan, 🚋7) Junibacken whimsically recreates the fantasy scenes of Astrid Lindgren's books for children. Catch the flying Story Train over Stockholm, shrink to the size of a sugar cube and end up at Villekulla cottage, where kids can shout, squeal and dress up like Pippi Longstocking. The bookshop is a treasure trove of children's books, as well as a great place to pick up anything from cheeky Karlsson dolls to cute little art cards with storybook themes.

Aquaria Vattenmuseum   MUSEUM
(Map p52; 📞08-660 90 89; www.aquaria.se; Falkenbergsgatan 2; adult/child 120/80kr; ⏱10am-

6pm Jun-Aug, 10am-4.30pm Tue-Sun rest of year; 👶; 🚌44, 69, 🚢Djurgårdsfärjan, 🚋7) This conservation-themed aquarium, complete with seahorses, sharks, piranhas and clownfish, takes you through various environmental zones – from tropical jungle and coral reef to sewer systems – with an emphasis on ecology and the fragility of the marine environment. If that sounds a bit of a drag, it's not – there's enough to do and see to keep the family entertained. Time your visit to coincide with a feeding, daily at 11am, 1.30pm and 2.30pm.

Thielska Galleriet   GALLERY
(📞08-662 58 84; www.thielska-galleriet.se; Sjötullsbacken 8; adult/child 130kr/free; ⏱noon-5pm Tue-Sun, to 8pm Thu; 🚌69) Thielska Galleriet, at the far eastern end of Djurgården, is a must for Nordic art fans, with a savvy collection of late-19th- and early-20th-century works from Scandinavian greats like Carl Larsson, Anders Zorn, Ernst Josephson and Bruno Liljefors, plus a series of Edvard Munch's etchings of vampiric women and several paintings from a bridge you'll recognise from *The Scream*. (Ernest Thiel, a banker and translator, was one of Munch's patrons.)

Nordiska Museet   MUSEUM
(Map p52; 📞08-51 95 47 70; www.nordiska museet.se; Djurgårdsvägen 6-16; adult/child 120kr/free; ⏱10am-5pm Sep-May, 9am-5pm rest of year, to 8pm Wed; 🚌44, 69, 🚢Djurgårdsfärjan, 🚋7) The epic Nordiska Museet is Sweden's biggest cultural-history museum and one of its largest indoor spaces. The building itself (from 1907) is an eclectic, Renaissance-style castle designed by Isak Gustav Clason, who also drew up Östermalms Saluhall (p72); you'll notice a resemblance. Inside is a sprawling collection of all things Swedish, from sacred Sami objects to clothing and table settings. The museum boasts the world's largest collection of paintings by August Strindberg, and a number of his personal possessions.

Prins Eugens Waldemarsudde   MUSEUM
(Map p52; 📞08-54 58 37 07; www.walde marsudde.com; Prins Eugens väg 6; adult/child 150kr/free; ⏱11am-5pm Tue-Sun, to 8pm Thu, gardens 8am-9pm; 🚋7) Prins Eugens Waldemarsudde, at the southern tip of Djurgården, is a soul-perking combo of water views and art. The palace once belonged to the painter prince (1865–1947), who favoured art over typical royal pleasures. In addition to Eugen's own work, it holds his impressive collection of Nordic paintings and sculptures,

Skeppsholmen & Djurgården

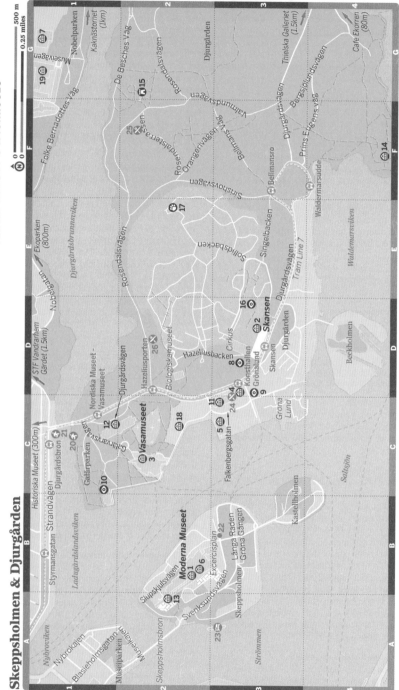

500 m
0.25 miles

Nobelparken

Kaknästornet
(1km)

Djurgården

De Besches Väg

Rosendalsvägen

Valmundsvägen

15

Museivägen

19

7

Folke Bernadottes Väg

Djurgårdsbrunnsviken

Ekoparken
(800m)

Nobelgatan

25

Rosendalsterrassen

Orangerivägen

Bellmans Väg

Sinnebovägen

Thielska Galleriet
(1.5km)

Djurgårdsvägen

Bergsjölundsvägen

Prins Eugens väg

Café Ekorren
(80m)

14

Bellmansro

Waldermarsudde

Waldemarsviken

17

Rosendalsvägen

Solliddsbacken

Singelbacken

Djurgårdsvägen

Tram Line 7

16

Skansen

2

Skansen

Djurgården

Beckholmen

STF Vandrarhem
Gärdet (1.5km)

Djurgårdsvägen

Nordiska Museet •
Vasamuseet

Hazeliusporten

26

Biologiskamuseet

Hazeliusbacken

Cirkus

8

Konsthallen

Grönalund

9

Skansen

Djurgården

Grona Lund

Salsjön

Historiska Museet (300m)

Djurgårdsbron

21

20

Djurgårdsvägen

12

Gåtärvarvsvägen

Vasamuseet

3

18

11

24 4

5

Falkenbergsgatan

Kastellholmen

10

Gåtärparken

Galärparken

Styrmansgatan

Strandvägen

Ladugårdslandsviken

Moderna Museet

Slupskjulsvägen

1

6

Exercisplan

22

Långa Raden

Grona Gången

Skeppsholmen

Svenksundsvägen

13

Nybroviken

Nybrokajen

Museikajen

Museiparken

Blasieholmsgatan

Skeppsholmsbron

23

Strömmen

Skeppsholmen & Djurgården

including works by Anders Zorn and Carl Larsson. The museum stages top-notch temporary exhibitions several times a year, usually highlighting the careers of important Scandinavian artists.

The buildings and galleries, connected by tunnels, are surrounded by gardens (free to wander) and an old windmill from the 1780s.

Spritmuseum   MUSEUM
(Museum of Spirits; Map p52; ☑08-12 13 13 00; www.spritmuseum.se; Djurgårdsvägen 38; adult/child 120kr/free; ⊙10am-5pm Mon, to 7pm Tue-Sat, noon-5pm Sun; ☒44, 69, ☲Djurgårdsfärjan, ☲7) The surprisingly entertaining Museum of Spirits is dedicated to Sweden's complicated relationship with alcohol, as mediated over the years by the state-run monopoly System Bolaget. The slick space, in two 18th-century naval buildings, covers the history, manufacture and consumption of all kinds of booze, plus holiday traditions, drinking songs, food pairings and so on. Best of all, you can combine your visit with a tasting kit (250kr), including various flavours of liquor to be sampled at specified points.

ABBA: The Museum   MUSEUM
(Map p52; ☑08-12 13 28 60; www.abbathemuseum.com; Djurgårdsvägen 68; adult/child 250/95kr; ⊙9am-7pm Mon-Fri Jun-Aug, shorter hours rest of year; ☒67, ☲Djurgårdsfärjan, Emelie, ☲7) A sensory-overload experience that might appeal only to devoted ABBA fans, this long-awaited and wildly hyped cathedral to the demigods of Swedish pop is almost aggressively entertaining. It's packed to the gills with memorabilia and interactivity – every square

inch has something new to look at, be it a glittering guitar, a vintage photo of Benny, Björn, Frida or Agnetha, a classic music video, an outlandish costume or a tour van from the band members' early days.

Rosendals Slott   CASTLE
(Map p52; ☑08-402 61 30; www.kungahuset.se; Rosendalsvägen 49; adult/child 100/50kr; ⊙hourly tours noon-3pm Tue-Sun Jun-Aug; ☒44, 69, ☲7) On the northern side of Djurgården, Rosendals Slott was built as a palace for Karl XIV Johan in the 1820s. One of Sweden's finest examples of the Empire style, it sparkles with sumptuous royal furnishings. Admission is by guided tour only. While you're out this way don't miss the wonderful Rosendals Trädgårdskafe (p73) – an organic cafe set among gardens and greenhouses.

Skansen Akvariet   AQUARIUM
(Map p52; ☑08-442 80 39; www.skansen.se; adult/child 100/60kr; ⊙10am-4pm or 5pm, closing times vary by season; ☲7) The Skansen Aquarium is worth a wander, its residents including piranhas, lemurs and pygmy marmosets (the smallest monkeys in the world). Intrepid visitors are allowed into the cages of some of the animals.

Östasiatiska Museet   MUSEUM
(Museum of Far Eastern Antiquities; Map p52; www.ostasiatiska.se; Tyghusplan; ⊙11am-5pm Wed-Sun, to 8pm Tue; ☒65) FREE This long, narrow building displays Asian decorative arts, including one of the world's finest collections of Chinese stoneware and porcelain from the Song, Ming and Qing dynasties. The museum also houses the largest and oldest

Asian library in Scandinavia, from which several notable specimens are displayed. The often refreshing temporary exhibitions cover a wide range of themes, with past shows including a look at Japanese anime characters and Chinese video art.

ArkDes · MUSEUM
(Map p52; ☑08-58 72 70 00; www.arkdes.se; Exercisplan 4; special exhibits adult/child 120kr/ free; ⏰10am-8pm Tue & Wed & Thu, 11am-6pm Sat & Sun; ☒65, ⏏Djurgårdsfärjan) 【FREE】 Adjoining Moderna Museet (p51) and housed in a converted navy drill hall, the architecture and design centre has a permanent exhibition spanning 1000 years of Swedish architecture and an archive of 2.5 million documents, photographs, plans, drawings and models. Temporary exhibitions also cover international names and work. The museum organises occasional themed architectural tours of Stockholm; check the website or ask at the information desk.

◎ Kungsholmen

Until recently something of an underappreciated gem, especially among visitors, Kungsholmen has really come into its own. This is a laid-back, mostly residential neighbourhood with great places to eat, kid-friendly parks and an amazingly long stretch of tree-lined waterside walking. Plus it's home to one of Stockholm's most important buildings, architecturally and practically, in Stadshuset (City Hall).

★Stadshuset · · · · · · · · · · · NOTABLE BUILDING
(City Hall; Map p48; www.stockholm.se/stads huset; Hantverkargatan 1; adult/child 100/50kr, tower 50kr/free; ⏰9am-3.30pm, admission by tour only; ☒3, 62 Stadshuset, ☒Rådhuset) The mighty Stadshuset dominates Stockholm's architecture. Topping off its square tower is a golden spire and the symbol of Swedish power: the three royal crowns. Entry is by guided tour only; tours in English take place every 30 minutes from 9am until 3.30pm in summer, less frequently the rest of the year. The **tower** is open for visits every 40 minutes from 9.15am to 4pm or 5pm from May to September; it offers stellar views and a great thigh workout.

Punctured by two courtyards, the building's interior includes the glittering, mosaic-lined **Gyllene salen** (Golden Hall), Prins Eugen's own fresco recreation of the lake

view from the gallery and the very hall used for the annual Nobel Prize banquet. Part of the tour involves walking down the same stairs you'd use if you'd won the big prize.

Rålambshovsparken · · · · · · · · · · · · · · · · PARK
(☒Fridhemsplan) In the warmer months, Rålambshovsparken is one of the city's favourite playgrounds, packed with picnicking Swedes fresh from a dip in the lake. Take a swim, hire a canoe or just get physical at the free alfresco aerobics sessions – there's nearly always a nightly exercise class of some kind through the summer.

◎ Norrmalm

The modern heart of the city, Norrmalm is where most visits to Stockholm begin: it's home to the main train and bus stations, Centralstationen and Cityterminalen respectively. It's also where you'll find the highest concentration of schmancy retail boutiques, glamorous bars and restaurants, hotels from functional to fabulous, and noteworthy cultural institutions.

Wetterling Gallery · · · · · · · · · · · · · · · GALLERY
(Map p48; ☑08-10 10 09; www.wetterlinggallery. com; Kungsträdgården 3; ⏰11am-5pm Wed-Fri, 1-4pm Sat; ☒Kungsträdgården) This cool gallery space at the edge of Kungsträdgården always has something interesting going on – usually a boundary-pushing contemporary painter, but there's also often photography or multimedia work, from big names (eg Frank Stella) to soon-to-be-big names.

Nationalmuseum · · · · · · · · · · · · · · · · MUSEUM
(National Art Museum; Map p48; www.national museum.se; Södra Blasieholmshamnen; ☒65) Sweden's largest art museum is home to the nation's collection of painting, sculpture, drawings, decorative arts and graphics from the Middle Ages to the present.

At the time of research it was undergoing a major renovation to expand public spaces, and add climate control and natural light, with the works due to be completed in early 2018. Highlights from the collection are temporarily on display at Stadsteatern inside Kulturhuset.

Kulturhuset · · · · · · · · · · · · · · · ARTS CENTRE
(Map p48; ☑tickets noon-5pm 08-50 62 02 00; www.kulturhusetstadsteatern.se; Sergels Torg; ⏰11am-5pm, some sections closed Mon; ♿; ☒52, 56, 59, 69, 91 Sergels Torg, ☒7 Sergels Torg, ☒T-Centralen) This architecturally divisive

building, opened in 1974, is an arts hub, with a couple of galleries and workshops, a cinema, three restaurants, and libraries containing international periodicals, newspapers, books and an unusually good selection of graphic novels in many languages. It's home to Stadsteatern (the City Theatre), with performances in various-sized venues (mostly in Swedish). Stockholm's main visitor centre (p86) is also here, on the lower level.

Medelhavsmuseet   MUSEUM
(Museum of Mediterranean Antiquities; Map p48; ☑ 010-456 12 98; www.medelhavsmuseet.se; Fredsgatan 2; ☺ noon-8pm Tue-Fri, to 5pm Sat & Sun; ⊠ Centralen, Kungsträdgården) **FREE** Housed in an elegant Italianate building, Medelhavsmuseet lures history buffs with its Egyptian, Greek, Cypriot, Roman and Etruscan treasures. A large portion of the main hall is devoted to the Swedish expedition to Cyprus in 1927, which unearthed masses of well-preserved artefacts that are attractively displayed here. Don't miss the gleaming gold room, home to a 4th-century BC olive wreath made of gold. And in the basement: mummies! The attached Bagdad Cafe (open 11.30am to 1.30pm) has great food and atmosphere.

Hallwylska Museet   MUSEUM
(Hallwyl Collection; Map p48; ☑ 08-402 30 99; www.hallwylskamuseet.se; Hamngatan 4; tours 40kr; ☺ 10am-7pm Tue-Sun Jul-Aug, to 4pm rest of year; ⊠ Östermalmstorg) **FREE** A private palace completed in 1898, Hallwylska Museet was once home to compulsive hoarder Wilhelmina von Hallwyl, who collected items as diverse as kitchen utensils, Chinese pottery, 17th-century paintings, silverware, sculpture and her children's teeth. In 1920 she and her husband donated the mansion and its contents to the state. Guided tours in English take place at 12.30pm Tuesday to Sunday, June to August (weekends only the rest of the year). The museum is not wheelchair accessible.

St Jakobs Kyrka   CHURCH
(Map p48; www.svenskakyrkan.se/stockholms domkyrkoforsamling/st-jacobs-kyrka; St Jakobs Torg, Kungsträdgården; ☺ 11am-5pm, to 6pm Thu, Fri & Sun; ⊠ Kungsträdgården) **FREE** St Jakobs kyrka is one of Stockholm's most notable and oldest – though often overlooked – churches, away from the central islands of the old town and Riddarholmen. Just across the water from the Royal Palace, it's been standing on the same spot since the 16th century. Its uniquely red complexion and

a number of facelifts make it perhaps the most eclectic church in the city.

It's also an excellent place to hear music. Check the schedule for upcoming special events.

Stora Synagogan   SYNAGOGUE
(Map p48; ☑ 0708-21 18 97; http://jfst.se/ stockholms-stora-synagoga; Wahrendorffsgatan 3b; tours 150kr; ☺ tours 11am & noon Mon-Thu, 11am Fri; ⊠ Östermalmstorg) Designed by Fredrik Scholander and completed in 1870, this unique building knows no counterpart in Stockholm. It's the centre of Sweden's Jewish community and its first permanent home. Open to visitors by guided tour (in English) on weekdays.

Konstakademien   MUSEUM
(Royal Academy of Fine Arts; Map p48; ☑ 08-23 29 25; www.konstakademien.se; Fredsgatan 12; ☺ 11am-5pm Tue-Fri, noon-4pm Sat & Sun; ⊠ Centralen) **FREE** The Royal Academy of Fine Arts has a beautiful gallery space and puts on several exhibitions a year, well worth investigating if you're interested in Swedish art.

Sergels Torg   SQUARE
(Map p48) Stockholm's living room, this circular square (which was undergoing major repairs on our last visit, but was still accessible to foot traffic) is a little on the grungy side, and you'll want to keep close tabs on your wallet, but it's a key transit hub as well as a great place to catch the pulse of the city. Something's always going on here, be it an impromptu classical music performance or a hundreds-strong political demonstration.

Dansmuseet   MUSEUM
(Map p48; ☑ 08-441 76 51; www.dansmuseet.se; Drottninggatan 17; adult/child 120kr/free; ☺ 11am-5pm Tue-Fri, noon-4pm Sat & Sun; ⊠ T-Centralen) Located on a heavily trafficked pedestrian shopping street and boasting a chic cafe (mains 165kr to 225kr), Dansmuseet (or the Rolf de Maré Dance Museum, after its founder) focuses on the intersections between dance, art and theatre. Collection highlights include traditional dance masks from Africa, India and Tibet, avant-garde costumes from the Russian ballet, Chinese and Japanese theatre puppets and one of the finest collections of early-20th-century Ballets Russes costumes.

☺ Södermalm

Slightly unvarnished and bohemian, Stockholm's southern island, Södermalm, or Söder, is where you'll find the coolest secondhand shops, art galleries, bars and espresso labs. The hills at the island's northern edge provide stunning views across Gamla Stan and the rest of the central city. A couple of museum heavyweights round out the to-do list, before taking in some of the city's most diverse nightlife.

★**Fotografiska** GALLERY

(Map p56; www.fotografiska.eu; Stadsgårdshamnen 22; adult/child 135kr/free; ⊙9am-11pm Sun-Wed, to 1am Thu-Sat; ﬕSlussen) Fotografiska is a stylish photography museum and a must for shutterbugs. Its constantly changing exhibitions are huge, interestingly chosen and well presented; examples have included a Robert Mapplethorpe retrospective, portraits by indie filmmaker Gus Van Sant and an enormous collection of black-and-white photos by Sebastião Salgado. The attached cafe-bar draws a crowd on summer evenings, with DJs, good cocktails and outdoor seating. Follow signs from the Slussen tunnelbana stop to reach the museum.

Tantolunden PARK

(Zinkens Väg; ﬕ Zinkensdamm, Hornstull) Located in southwest Södermalm, adjacent to trendy Hornstull, Tantolunden is one of Stockholm's most extensive and varied parks. Its combination of allotments, open expanses, outdoor gym, play area and waterside walks make it a great getaway from the city centre. Although the park becomes a focal point of the city in the summer, with crowds flocking to swim and picnic, locals wind down with relaxing walks here throughout the year.

Leksaksmuseet MUSEUM

(Toy Museum; ☎08-641 61 00; www.leksaks museet.se; Tegelviksgatan 22; adult/child 50/25kr; ⊙10am-5pm Mon-Fri, 11am-4pm Sat & Sun; ﬔ; ☒2, 66 Spårvägsmuseet) Sharing an entrance with Spårvägsmuseet, the Toy Museum is packed with everything you probably ever wanted as a child (and may still be hankering for as an adult). If anybody in your family just happens to be crazy about model

Southern Stockholm

trains, model aeroplanes, toy soldiers, toy robots, Barbie dolls or stuffed animals, don't miss it.

Spårvägsmuseet   MUSEUM
(Transport Museum; ☑ 08-686 17 60; www.sparvags museet.sl.se; Tegelviksgatan 22; adult/child 50/25kr; ⊙ 10am-5pm Mon-Fri, 11am-4pm Sat & Sun; ⊠ 2, 66 Spårvägsmuseet) In a former bus depot near the Viking Line terminal, Stockholm's charmingly old-school transport museum is an atmospheric spot to spend a rainy afternoon. An impressive collection of around 40 vehicles includes several very pretty antique horse-drawn carriages, vintage trams and buses, and a retro tunnelbana carriage (complete with original advertisements). Kids can play tunnelbana driver (there's video from the driver's seat). Displays about the construction of the tunnelbana system starting in 1933 are pretty mind-blowing.

The museum shares a space and entrance with the toy-filled Leksaksmuseet (one admission covers both).

Stockholms Stadsmuseum   MUSEUM
(City Museum; Map p56; www.stadsmuseum. stockholm.se; Ryssgården, Slussen; ⊠ Slussen) The evocative exhibits here cover Stockholm's development from fortified port

to modern metropolis via plague, fire and good old-fashioned scandal. It's housed in a late-17th-century palace designed by Nicodemus Tessin the Elder. Temporary exhibitions are fresh and eclectic, focused on the city's ever-changing shape and spirit. Admission gets you a card good for one year here and at Medeltidsmuseet (p45).

Note that the museum was closed for renovations on our last visit; it was due to reopen in late 2018.

Münchenbryggeriet   HISTORIC BUILDING
(☑ 08-658 20 00; www.m-b.se/en; Torkel Knutssonsgatan 2; ⊠ Mariatorget) Münchenbryggeriet is a dominant feature of Södermalm's coastline – anyone gliding by in a boat or taking in the view is bound to wonder what it is. The name means 'Munich brewing company' – this was once the royal brewery. Since 1971, when brewing operations moved to the suburbs, Münchenbryggeriet has been an event venue and conference centre. The building is a unique landmark, a relic of Stockholm's industrial past.

◉ Vasastan

This relaxed, residential neighbourhood has some of the best places to eat in Stockholm, along with several great hotels and a couple

Southern Stockholm

Northern Stockholm

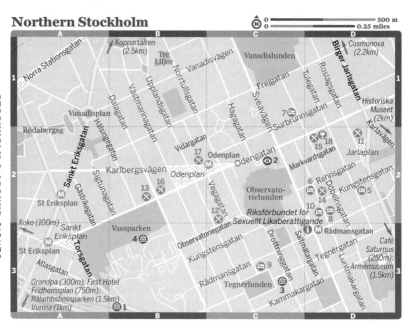

Northern Stockholm

of slick art galleries in impressive buildings. It's also home to one of the greatest examples of Scandinavian architecture, Stadsbiblioteket. Wander around, take a nap in a park and join the laid-back locals in just hanging out.

Stadsbiblioteket　　　　　　　LIBRARY
(Map p58; ☏ 08-50 83 10 60; Sveavägen 73; ⊙10am-7pm Mon-Fri, noon-4pm Sat; ☐ Odenplan) FREE The main city library is north of the centre. Designed by architect Erik Gunnar Asplund and sporting a curvaceous, technicolor reading room, it's the finest example of Stockholm's 1920s neoclassicist style.

Bonniers Konsthall　　　　　　GALLERY
(Map p58; ☏ 08-736 42 48; www.bonnierskonsthall.se; Torsgatan 19; ⊙noon-5pm Thu-Sun, to 8pm Wed; ☐ St Eriksplan) FREE This ambitious gallery keeps culture fiends busy with a fresh dose of international contemporary art, as well as a reading room, a fab cafe and a busy schedule of art seminars and artists-in-conversation sessions. The massive, transparent flatiron building was designed by Johan Celsing. There are discussions about the exhibitions in English at 1pm, 3pm, 5pm and 7pm Wednesdays, and 1pm and 4pm Thursday to Sunday. Curators lead free guided tours on Sunday at 2pm.

Sven-Harrys Konstmuseum MUSEUM
(Map p58; ☑08-51 16 00 60; www.sven-harrys. se; Eastmansvägen 10-12; adult/child 100kr/free; ⊙11am-7pm Wed-Fri, to 5pm Sat & Sun; ⓡ Odenplan) This ultramodern building houses an art gallery with interesting temporary exhibitions (recently a collection of August Strindberg's paintings, borrowed from Strindbergsmuseet), as well as a recreation of the former Lidingö home of owner and art collector Sven-Harry Karlsson. Access to the home is by guided tour (150kr, 45 minutes, currently in Swedish only). There's also an award-winning restaurant with terrace seating facing the park.

Strindbergsmuseet MUSEUM
(Map p58; ☑08-411 53 54; www.strindbergs museet.se; Drottninggatan 85; adult/child 75/50kr; ⓡ Rådmansgatan) The small but evocative Strindbergsmuseet in the Blue Tower is the well-preserved apartment where writer and painter August Strindberg (1849–1912) spent his final four years. Visitors can peep into his closet, scan his study and library (containing some 3000 volumes), do a round of the dining room and take in the often absorbing temporary exhibits.

The museum was closed for renovations on our last visit, but is expected to reopen in early 2018.

◉ Further Afield

★ **Millesgården** MUSEUM
(☑08-446 75 90; www.millesgarden.se; Herserudsvägen 32; adult/child 150kr/free; ⊙11am-5pm, closed Mon Oct-Apr; ⓡ Ropsten, then bus 201, 202, 204, 206, 207) Beautiful Millesgården was the home and studio of sculptor Carl Milles, whose delicate water sprites and other whimsical sculptures dot the city landscape. The grounds include a crisp modern gallery for changing exhibitions of contemporary art, Milles' elaborately Pompeiian house and an exquisite outdoor sculpture garden where items from ancient Greece, Rome, medieval times and the Renaissance intermingle with Milles' own creations. There's also a museum shop and a cafe.

Skogskyrkogården CEMETERY
(☑08-50 83 17 30; www.skogskyrkogarden.se; Söckenvagen; ⊙24hr, visitor centre 11am-4pm mid-May–Sep, Sat & Sun only Oct; Ⓟ; ⓡ Skogskyrkogården) FREE One of Stockholm's more unusual attractions, Skogskyrkogården (the Woodland Cemetery) is a beautiful graveyard

set in soothing pine woodland. Designed by Gunnar Asplund and Sigurd Lewerentz, it's on the Unesco World Heritage List and famed for its functionalist buildings. Famous residents include Stockholm screen goddess Greta Garbo. A visitor guide is available on the website in several languages. Guided tours (100kr) in English are available at 10.30am Sunday, from June to September.

Ulriksdals Slott CASTLE
(☑08-402 61 30; www.kungahuset.se; Slottsallén, Ulriksdal, Solna; adult/child 120/80kr; ⊙noon-4pm Tue-Sun Jun-Aug; ⓡ Bergshamra, then bus 503) The 17th-century royal pad Ulriksdals Slott was home to King Gustaf VI Adolf and his family until 1973. Several of their exquisite apartments, including the Carl Malmsten–designed drawing room from 1923, are open to the public by guided tour (in Swedish). The **stables** house Queen Kristina's magnificent 17th-century coronation carriage, while the **Orangery** contains Swedish sculpture and Mediterranean flora.

Fjärilshuset-Haga Ocean MUSEUM
(Butterfly House; ☑08-730 39 81; www.fjarilshuset. se; Hagaparken; adult/child 165/80kr; ⊙10am-5pm; Ⓟ; ⓡ515, Haga Norra) The steamy Fjärilshuset ('butterfly house') is a great choice for a cold-weather visit. It recreates a tropical environment, complete with free-flying birds and butterflies, and some very friendly fish, plus a large shark aquarium. Temporary exhibits range from wildlife photography to animatronic rain-forest creatures.

Take the tunnelbana to T-Odenplan to catch the bus.

Koppartälten MUSEUM
(Copper Tent; ☑08-27 42 52; www.koppartalten.se; Hagaparken; ⊙10am-5pm Jun-Aug; ⓡ515, Haga Norra) FREE The exotic Koppartälten looks a bit like part of the circus that got left behind. It consists of three magical copper tents created by set designer Louis-Jean Desprez in 1787. Originally a stable and barracks for Gustav III's personal guard, the central tent now houses the Haga Parkmuseum while the eastern tent boasts a slick cafe (11am-4pm) designed by Torbjörn Olsson.

Bergianska Trädgården GARDENS
(☑08-612 09 59; www.bergianska.se; Gustafsborgsvägen 4; adult/child växthus (conservatory) 80kr/free, Victoriahuset 25kr/free; ⊙växthus and Victoriahuset 11am-4pm Mon-Fri, to 5pm Sat & Sun; Ⓟ; ⓡ50) ✐ This expansive botanical garden, bordering the university on one

side and Brunnsviken lake on the other, is a wonderful oasis. Stroll the grounds learning about rare types of Swedish flora, then relax with lunch or *fika* (coffee and cake) at the cafe in the Orangeriet (mains 105kr to 140kr). Be sure to take a gander at Victoriahuset, an elegant greenhouse from 1900 built to display the giant water lily it's named for.

Activities

One thing visitors will notice about Stockholm, particularly during the summer months, is how fit and active the majority of locals are. Outdoor activity is a well-integrated part of the city's healthy lifestyle, and there are numerous ways in which a visitor can get in on the action.

Tolv
AMUSEMENT PARK

(☑020-10 40 00; www.tolvstockholm.se/en; Arenavägen 69; activities priced individually; ☻11am-11pm Sun-Tue, to midnight Wed & Thu, to 1am Fri & Sat; ㉓Globen, Gullmarsplan) Eat, drink, play, dance, sleep! Tolv is a giant entertainment complex, named after its 12,000-sq-metre floorspace. Located underneath the Tele2 Arena, it has a range of restaurants and bars, as well as activities: bowling, curling, miniature golf, karaoke, ping pong, even a ceramics studio. (What says 'party' like making ceramics?) Good place to bring a large group.

After you've indulged your inner child, you can head over to one of the two in-house nightclubs then sleep it off at Tolv's own capsule-inspired hotel.

Cycling

Stockholm is a very bicycle-friendly city. Cycling is best in the parks and away from the busy central streets and arterial roads, but even busy streets usually have dedicated cycle lanes. There's also a separate network of paved walking and cycling paths that reaches most parts of the city; these paths can be quite beautiful, taking you through green fields and peaceful forested areas. Tourist offices carry maps of cycle routes. Borrow a set of wheels from City Bikes (p87).

Sjöcaféet
CYCLING

(Map p52; ☑08-660 57 57; www.sjocafeet.se; Djurgårdsvägen 2; per hour/day bicycles 80/275kr, canoes 150/400kr, kayaks 125/400kr; ☻9am-9pm Apr-Sep; ㉓7) Rent bicycles from the small wooden hut below this restaurant, cafe and tourist-info centre beside Djurgårdsbron; it also offers canoes and kayaks for hire.

Sailing & Boating

Water surrounds and permeates the city, and it's hard not to want to get out there if you're walking around on a warm, sunny day. Fortunately, getting out there is easy to do. The city canals are mostly gentle and easily navigable, even for novices; if you're unsure, discuss your level of experience with staff before you rent equipment. Some places also offer guides.

Fjäderholmarna
BOATING

(Feather Islands; ☑08-21 55 00; www.fjaderholms linjen.se; Nybroplan, Berth 13; adult/child round-trip 145/70kr; ☻hourly 10.30am-10.30pm May–early Sep) A trip to the Feather Islands takes about 25 minutes from Stockholm, and is a fantastic way to get a taste of the archipelago in a very short time. You can swim and sunbathe, visit traditional workshops including smiths and glassblowers, admire old boats, visit a brewery and stuff yourself on smoked fish. Recommended!

The ferry leaves from Nybroplan; check signboards at the dock for updated departure times.

Strandbryggan
BOATING

(Map p52; ☑070-564 93 58, 08-660 37 14; www. strandbryggan.se; Strandvägskajen 27, Strandvägen; per hour from 2000kr; ☻10am-dusk Apr-Sep; ㉓7) Across the water from Sjöcaféet, floating restaurant-bar Strandbryggan offers yachts for charter for up to 12 passengers. Prices start at around 2000kr per hour (minimum 2½ hours), and you can add catering from the restaurant.

Göta Canal
CRUISE

(☑031-80 63 15; www.gotacanal.se/en; 5 days per person 19,860kr; ☻mid-May–mid-Aug) Float along the Göta Canal from Stockholm to Gothenburg (and back, if you like), stopping for off-boat excursions and guided tours along the way. The full journey takes six days, five nights, including all meals and excursions. Shorter segments are available; check timetables online.

Swimming

Swimming is permitted just about anywhere people can scramble their way to the water. Popular spots include the rocks around Riddarfjärden and the leafy island of Långholmen, the latter also sporting a popular gay beach.

Centralbadet
SWIMMING

(Map p48; ☑08-54 52 13 00; www.central badet.se; Drottninggatan 88; weekday/weekend

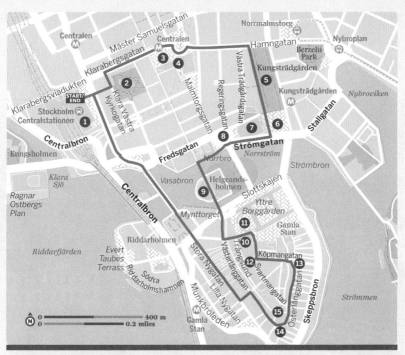

City Walk
Central Stockholm

START CENTRALSTATIONEN
END CENTRALSTATIONEN
LENGTH 3KM; TWO HOURS

Starting at ❶ **Centralstationen**, cross Vasagatan and enter side street Klara Vattugränd. Turn left onto Klara Västra Kyrkogatan, past the church ❷ **Klara Kyrka**. Follow Klarabergsgatan to ❸ **Sergels Torg** (p55), home to frenzied commuters, casual shoppers and the odd demonstration. Pop into arts hub ❹ **Kulturhuset** (p54), with its exhibitions, theatres, cafes and creative spaces.

Continue a short way along Hamngatan before turning right into the grand ❺ **Kungsträdgården**. Originally the kitchen garden for the Royal Palace, this park is now a popular spot for sun soaking in the warmer months and ice skating in the colder ones.

At ❻ **Karl XII's Torg** there's a statue of the warmongering King Karl XII. On your right is ❼ **Operan**, the Royal Opera House (opened in 1896), and across the road you'll see the narrow strait Norrström, the freshwater outflow from lake Mälaren. Continue along the waterfront, past

❽ **Gustav Adolfs Torg**, then turn left and cross the bridge known as Riksbron. Continue across the islet ❾ **Helgeandsholmen**, between the two parts of Sweden's parliament building, Riksdagshuset. Cross Stallbron to arrive on Stadsholmen, Stockholm's medieval core.

Cross Mynttorget, follow Västerlånggatan for a block, then turn left (east) into Storkyrkobrinken to reach the city's oldest building, ❿ **Storkyrkan** (p46). Facing the cathedral across the cobblestone square is ⓫ **Kungliga Slottet** (p43). Källargränd leads southward to ⓬ **Stortorget**, the cobblestone square where the Stockholm Bloodbath took place in 1520.

Head east along Köpmangatan to small square ⓭ **Köpmantorget** and the statue of St George and the Dragon. Turn right into Österlånggatan and follow it until you reach ⓮ **Järntorget**, where metals were bought and sold in days long past. From there, keep right and turn into Västerlånggatan, looking out for ⓯ **Mårten Trotzigs Gränd** (p46; Stockholm's narrowest lane) by No 81.

Turn left (northwest) into Stora Nygatan before crossing over Vasabron to head back to Centralstationen.

MIKAEL DAMKIER/SHUTTERSTOCK ©

. Stockholm
tockholm is an accessible beauty, as
asy to explore as it is to love.

. Swedish cuisine
tockholm's dining scene (p70) has
enty to offer, from the traditional to the
novative.

. Kungliga Slottet (p43)
tockholm's Royal Palace is the world's
rgest royal castle still used for its
riginal purpose.

. Skansen (p50)
he world's first open-air museum is
esigned to be 'Sweden in miniature',
omplete with villages, nature,
ommerce and industry.

MICHEL SETBOUN/GETTY IMAGES ©

250/350kr; ⊙8am-7.30pm Mon-Fri, to 5.30pm Sun) Worth exploring for its art-nouveau building and gardenlike atmosphere alone, Centralbadet is almost literally a relaxing oasis in the middle of the busy city. Entry includes pool, sauna and gym access. Treatments available for an additional fee include massage, facials and body wraps; these are best booked two weeks ahead. You can also hire towels (35kr) and robes (50kr).

Eriksdalsbadet   SWIMMING
(☑08-50 84 02 58; www.eriksdalsbadet.se; Hammarby Slussväg 8; indoor pool adult/child 90/40kr, outdoor pool 70/20kr; ⊙6am-8pm Mon-Thu, to 7pm Fri, 8am-6pm Sat, 8am-7pm Sun May-Aug, shorter hours rest of year; ⊞; ⊠Skanstull) At the southern edge of Södermalm is this sprawling complex, with both indoor and outdoor pools (and all the trimmings). A popular place to bring kids in the summertime.

Sturebadet   SPA
(Map p48; ☑08-54 50 15 00; www.sturebadet.se; Sturegallerian 36, Stureplan; day pass from 595kr; ⊙6.30am-10pm Mon-Fri, 8.30am-8.30pm Sat & Sun; ⊠Östermalmstorg) Old Norse meets Ottoman chic at Stockholm's poshest pool, gym and spa, once the haunt of Greta Garbo and still a favourite with the rich and famously frazzled. While day passes are readily available, treatments should be booked two weeks in advance. Over-18s only.

Rock Climbing
Climbers will find around 150 cliffs within 40 minutes' drive of the city, plus a large indoor climbing centre in Nacka.

Klätterverket   CLIMBING
(☑08 641 10 48; www.klatterverket.se; Marcusplatsen 17, Nacka; adult/child 120/80kr; ⊙10am-10pm Mon-Fri, 10am-8pm Sat & Sun; ⊠Sickla) One of Sweden's largest indoor climbing centres, with around 1000 sq metres of artificial climbing. It rents shoes (35kr) and harnesses (25kr). Next to the J-train Sickla stop.

☞ Tours

Taking a tour can be an efficient way of getting a handle on Stockholm's highlights. For a unique perspective, try seeing the city from the water or from up in the air.

Millennium Tour   WALKING
(www.stadsmuseum.stockholm.se; per person 130kr; ⊙11.30am Sat year-round, 6pm Thu Jul-Sep) Fans of Stieg Larsson's madly popular crime novels (*The Girl with the Dragon Tattoo*)

will enjoy this walking tour (in English) pointing out key locations from the books and films. While the Stadsmuseum is closed for renovations, buy tickets online or at the Medeltidsmuseet (p45). Tour meeting points are printed on the tickets.

The museum runs several other guided walking tours; check online.

Strömma Kanalbolaget   BOATING
(Map p52; ☑08-12 00 40 00; www.stromma. se; Svensksundsvägen 17; 200-400kr) This ubiquitous company offers tours large and small, from a 50-minute 'royal canal tour' around Djurgården (200kr) to a 50-minute ABBA tour, which visits places where the *ABBA* movie was shot and drops you off at the ABBA museum (p53; 315kr). There are also hop-on, hop-off tours by bus (from 300kr), boat (180kr) or both (400kr).

Recommended: 'Under the Bridges of Stockholm' (250kr), a two-hour canal tour running daily 10am to 7pm mid-April to October. Book ahead if possible, as this tour sometimes sells out.

Svenska Turistföreningen   TOURS
(STF | Swedish Touring Association; ☑08-463 21 00; www.svenskaturistforeningen.se) Events and tours are generally affordable, ecologically minded and fun, and mostly based on outdoor activities (eg kayaking and hiking). Equipment rental is often available. Prices are usually lower for STF members.

Far & Flyg   BALLOONING
(☑070-340 41 07; www.farochflyg.se; 10-person group 25,000kr; ⊙late May–mid-Sep) Float over Stockholm in a hot-air balloon for up to an hour and see the city from a rare vantage point. Note that only groups can book trips, so bring your friends, and reserve well ahead.

Stockholm Ghost Walk   WALKING
(Map p44; ☑07-61 46 66 00; www.stockholm ghostwalk.com; Tyska Brinken 13; adult/child 200/100kr, cash only; ⊙7pm; ⊠Gamla Stan) This 90-minute walking tour features tales of murder, mayhem, hauntings and executions, narrated with gusto by multilingual costumed guides. The walk starts at Järntorget in Gamla Stan. Dinner packages available (from 575kr per person). Check online for tour availability on particular days.

★☆ Festivals & Events

Stockholm Marathon   SPORTS
(www.stockholmmarathon.se; ⊙late May or early Jun) About 21,000 runners participate in this annual marathon.

Smaka På Stockholm
FOOD & DRINK

(A Taste of Stockholm; www.smakapastockholm. se; ⊙early Jun) **FREE** A five-day celebration of the Stockholm area's food scene. The program includes gourmet food stalls (including representatives from several archipelago restaurants), cooking demonstrations and entertainment on Kungsträdgården. It's free to get in, and food offerings tend to be good value.

Stockholm Pride
LGBT

(www.stockholmpride.org/en; ⊙late Jul or early Aug) Stockholm goes pink with a week of parties and cultural events, including a pride parade.

Stockholms Kulturfestival
CULTURAL

(www.kulturfestivalen.stockholm.se; ⊙mid-Aug) **FREE** This festival is one big party week, with everything from sidewalk opera to street theatre and dancing in and around Sergels Torg. Free admission.

Lidingöloppet
SPORTS

(☑08-765 26 15; www.lidingoloppet.se; ⊙late Sep) The world's largest cross-country foot race, with an estimated 60,000 participants, is held in Lidingö, on Stockholm's outskirts.

Stockholm Jazz Festival
MUSIC

(www.stockholmjazz.com; ticket price varies by venue; ⊙Oct) One of Europe's premier jazz festivals, headquartered at Fasching (p82).

Stockholm Open
SPORTS

(www.ifstockholmopen.se; ⊙Oct) Over a week of international tennis and courtside celebrity spotting.

Stockholm International Film Festival
FILM

(www.stockholmfilmfestival.se; tickets 170kr; ⊙Nov) A major celebration of local and international cinema whose guest speakers include top actors and directors. The ticket office is in Kulturhuset.

🛏 Sleeping

Expect high-quality accommodation in Stockholm, although it can be expensive. Major hotel chains are invariably cheaper booked online and in advance; rates are also much cheaper in summer and at weekends.

Stockholm's Svenska Turistföreningen (STF) hostels are affiliated with Hostelling International (HI); a membership card yields a 50kr discount. Many have options for single, double and family rooms.

REGIONAL TOURS

From Stockholm it's easy to arrange various half-day or day tours, whether your interests run toward ancient history, royal palaces or seaside picnics. For something more ambitious, book a multiday journey along the **Göta Canal** (p60) from coast to coast.

Just 25 minutes away by boat, the **Fjäderholmarna** (p60) make for an easy escape from the city and are a favourite swimming spot for locals.

Other options include an atmospheric all-day trip from Stockholm to the Unesco World Heritage site of **Birka** (p96) on the island of Björkö; and a romantic jaunt to **Drottningholm** (p88) via turn-of-the-century steam ship.

🛏 Gamla Stan

Ideal for romantics, though pricier than other parts of the city, Stockholm's medieval nexus has several atmospheric hotels that put you in easy reach of other neighbourhoods.

2kronor Hostel Old Town
HOSTEL €

(Map p44; ☑08-22 92 30; www.2kronor.se; Skeppsbron 40; dm from 195kr, s/d from 495/590kr; ⊙reception 3-6pm; ➐@🖀; 🚇Gamla Stan, Slussen) This small, quiet, family-run hostel has a fantastic location and a friendly vibe. Rooms are on the basement level, slightly cavelike but pretty and well kept (and there are windows). Shared bathrooms are down the hall. Breakfast isn't available, but there's a guest kitchen and dining area by the reception upstairs. Dorms (six- and eight-bed rooms with bunks) are mixed.

Victory Hotel
HOTEL €€

(Map p44; ☑08-50 64 00 00; www.thecollectors hotels.se/en/victory-hotel/; Lilla Nygatan 5; r from 1120kr; ➐✸@🖀; 🚇Gamla Stan) Nautical antiques, art and model ships define the wonderfully quirky Victory. Most rooms are fairly small (though perfectly comfy), while the museum-like suites (from 2300kr) are larger. There are also four apartments available for long-term rentals (three nights or more).

Lord Nelson Hotel
HOTEL €€

(Map p44; ☑08-50 64 01 20; www.lordnelson hotel.se; Västerlånggatan 22; r from 1500kr; ➐🖀; 🚇Gamla Stan) Yo-ho-ho, me scurvy barnacles!

It's a tight squeeze, but this pink-painted, glass-fronted building feels like a creaky old ship loaded with character. At just 5m wide, the 17th-century building is Sweden's narrowest hotel. Its nautical theme extends to brass and mahogany furnishings, antique sea-captain trappings and a model ship in each of the small rooms.

Lady Hamilton Hotel HOTEL €€€
(Map p44; ☑ 08-50 64 01 00; www.lady hamiltonhotel.se; Storkyrkobrinken 5; s/d from 1600/1950kr; ⊜ 🛜; 🚇 Gamla Stan) Expect old-style luxury (with modern touches where it counts, such as in the bathrooms). The building dates back to the 1470s, and is packed with antiques and portraits of Lady Hamilton herself. If you're not a fan of church bells, request a room away from Storkyrkobrinken.

Hotel Scandic Gamla Stan HOTEL €€€
(Map p44; ☑ 08-723 72 50; www.scandichotels. com; Lilla Nygatan 25; r from 1750kr; ⊜✳@🛜; 🚇 Gamla Stan) The former Rica chain has been absorbed by Scandic, and this is one of the most atmospheric hotels in its vast collection. Each of the smallish 52 rooms is individually decorated in classic Swedish style – think powder-blue wallpaper and vintage chandeliers. The 17th-century building has up-to-the-minute modern amenities, and the location is perfect for soaking up Gamla Stan's history.

First Hotel Reisen HOTEL €€€
(Map p44; ☑ 08-22 32 60; www.firsthotels.com; Skeppsbron 12; r from 1668kr; ⊜🛜; 🚇 Gamla Stan) Stockholm's oldest hotel once hummed with sailors. These days the impressive waterfront building draws in passers-by with a slinky restaurant-bar. Some rooms have exposed brick walls, others are light and open in classic Scandi style; several have French doors with sea views. There's also a gym in the 16th-century vault-ceilinged basement, as well as a candlelit plunge pool and spa.

Östermalm & Ladugårdsgärdet

Ostentatious Östermalm melds A-league boutiques, restaurants and nightclubs with some outstanding museums. There's a good range of accommodation options, too, from friendly hostels to top-of-the-line design hotels.

STF Vandrarhem Gärdet HOSTEL €€
(☑ 08-463 22 90; www.swedishtourist association.com; Sandhamnsgatan 59; s/d from 845/895kr, breakfast 85kr; 🅿⊜@🛜; 🚇1 Östhammarsgatan, 🚇 Gärdet) Surrounded by forested trails and open fields in quiet Gärdet, this efficient hostel works more like a no-frills hotel. Rooms are tiny but well planned, and all have their own bathroom and TV. Towels, sheets and cleaning are included in the prices of some rooms. There's a good guest kitchen.

Djurgården & Skeppsholmen

★**Vandrarhem af Chapman & Skeppsholmen** HOSTEL €€
(Map p52; ☑ 08-463 22 66; www.stfchapman.com; Flaggmansvägen 8; dm/s/d from 325/595/940kr; ⊜@🛜; 🚇65 Skeppsholmen) The *af Chapman* is a storied vessel that has done plenty of travelling of its own. It's anchored in a superb location, swaying gently off Skeppsholmen. Bunks are in dorms below deck. Apart from showers and toilets, all facilities are on dry land in the Skeppsholmen hostel, including a good kitchen, a laid-back common room and a TV lounge.

Kungsholmen

This fun part of town is home to one of the city's nicest hostels, a great base from which to explore its fantastic neighbourhood restaurants.

City Hostel HOSTEL €
(☑ 08-41 00 38 30; www.cityhostel.se; Fleminggatan 19; dm 240-300kr, s/d/tr from 495/680/960kr; ⊜@🛜; 🚇1, 50, 61, 69, 🚇 Rådhuset) A modern and quiet budget option, this tidy, functional hostel in the friendly Kungsholmen neighbourhood is close to the city centre but away from most of the hustle and bustle, handy to the train station as well as Stadshuset and the old town. There's a good guest kitchen, free coffee and tea, wi-fi, and laundry. Sheets included in the price.

First Hotel Fridhemsplan HOTEL €€
(☑ 08-653 88 00; www.fridhemsplan.se; St Eriksgatan 20; r from 1250kr; @🛜; 🚇 Fridhemsplan) This modern hotel near the Fridhemsplan tunnelbana stop has pleasant, if somewhat bland, rooms, featuring expansive bathrooms with rain showers. Some rooms have windows with city views and there are also suites with either a spa bath or sauna (2650kr). There's a cool lounge in the lobby to hang out in, and a better-than-average breakfast buffet.

☷ Norrmalm

★City Backpackers
HOSTEL €

(Map p48; ☑08-20 69 20; www.citybackpackers. org; Upplandsgatan 2a; dm 300-360kr, s/d/tr from 550/690/920kr, breakfast 65kr; ☺@☎; ⓡT-Centralen) The closest hostel to Centralstationen has clean rooms, friendly staff, free bike hire and excellent facilities, including sauna, laundry and kitchen (with a free stash of pasta). En suite private rooms are also available. Bonus for female guests: there are four- and eight-bed female-only dorms if you prefer, and you can borrow a hairdryer from reception.

★Hobo Hotel
BOUTIQUE HOTEL €€

(Map p48; ☑08-57 88 27 00; https://hobo.se; Brunkebergstorg 4; r without/with windows from 1000/1250kr, breakfast 120kr; ☺; ⓡT-Centralen) This new 200-room boutique hotel has a great location in the city centre, plus a mega-hip style that feels both cool and comfortable. The cheapest rooms are small and windowless, but well designed, with full bath and comfy beds. Details like comic books on the bedside table and borrowable umbrellas add to the fun vibe.

There's a gym and a laundry in the basement and a fun bar/cafe with outdoor seating.

Hotel 'C' Stockholm
HOTEL €€

(Map p48; ☑08-50 56 30 00; www.nordicchotel. com; Vasaplan 4; s/d from 795/850kr; ☺✳@☎; ⓡT-Centralen) A fantastic deal if you time it right and book ahead (especially in summer when prices drop), this sister hotel to the Nordic Light has small but well-designed rooms, great service and an enormous breakfast buffet. The cheapest rooms are windowless and tiny but comfortable, with evocative Swedish wallpaper. One of the two hotel bars is the famous Icebar (p80).

The Arlanda Express (p87) is just steps from the lobby, and you can buy tickets at the front desk.

Nordic Light Hotel
HOTEL €€

(Map p48; ☑08-50 56 30 00; www.nordiclight hotel.com; Vasaplan 7; r from 1400kr; ☺✳@☎; ⓡT-Centralen) Extremely convenient to Centralstationen, the Nordic Light is a minimalist Scandi design hotel, with modern, well-equipped rooms. The signature 'mood rooms' ditch conventional artwork for custom-designed light exhibits, which guests can adjust to suit their mood. Additional perks include mini gym, sauna and chic lobby bar, plus a restaurant with fancy cocktails and DJs most nights.

★Grand Hôtel Stockholm
HOTEL €€€

(Map p48; ☑08-679 35 00; www.grand hotel.se; Södra Blasieholmshamnen 8; s/d from 2340/3300kr; Ⓟ☺✳@☎; ⓠ2, 43, 55, 62, 65, 76 Karl XII's Torg, ⛴Strömkajen, ⓡKungsträdgården, T-Centralen) This is where the literati, glitterati and nobility call it a night. A waterfront landmark, with several exclusive restaurants and a see-and-be-seen piano bar, it remains Stockholm's most sumptuous lodgings. Room styles span royal Gustavian to contemporary chic.

Clarion Hotel Sign
HOTEL €€€

(Map p48; ☑08-676 98 10; www.clarion sign.com; Östra Järnvägsgatan 35; s/d from 1600/1800kr; Ⓟ☺✳@☎; ⓡT-Centralen) Stockholm's largest hotel is also among its most stylish. Behind the striking granite-and-glass facade, trendsetters lounge on Arne Jacobsen egg chairs, dine at chef Marcus Samuelsson's American Table Brasserie, and recharge at the rooftop spa, complete with 35°C plunge pool. The high-concept rooms showcase design objects from across Scandinavia, with each floor dedicated to a particular Nordic nation's designers.

Berns Hotel
HOTEL €€€

(Map p48; ☑08-56 63 22 00; www.berns.se; Näckströmsgatan 8; s/d from 2280/2470kr; Ⓟ☺@☎; ⓠ7 Kungsträdgården, ⓡKungsträdgården) The rooms at Berns come equipped with entertainment systems and styles ranging from 19th-century classical to contemporary sleek. Some are more impressive than others (the balcony rooms get our vote); room 431 was once a dressing room used by Marlene Dietrich and Ella Fitzgerald. The cheapest rooms don't include breakfast, but it can be added for 195kr.

Crystal Plaza Hotel
HOTEL €€€

(☑08-406 88 00; www.crystalplazahotel.se; Birger Jarlsgatan 35; s/d from 1200/1880kr; ☺@☎; ⓡÖstermalmstorg) Housed in an 1895 building with an eight-storey tower and neo-classical columns, this friendly hotel offers wonderfully cosy rooms (albeit smallish, especially the economy class), decorated in homey Swedish traditional style. There's also a sauna, a gym and a tiny lobby bar.

☷ Södermalm

This district is only a 15-minute walk or quick subway ride from Viking Line boats and Centralstationen; it's also the most happening section of Stockholm and is your best bet for interesting budget or midrange accommodation.

★ Långholmen Hotell & Vandrarhem
HOSTEL, HOTEL **€**

(🗷 08-720 85 00; www.langholmen.com; Långholmsmuren 20, Långholmen; dm from 290kr, cell with bath s/d from 650/810kr, hotel r from 1095kr; P 🖭 @ 🛜; 🖵4, 40, 77, 94 Högalidsgatan, 🚇Hornstull, 🖵54 Bergsunds strand) Guests at this hotel-hostel, in a former prison on Långholmen island, sleep on bunks in a cell, with either shared or private baths (it's much nicer than that sounds; there's a playful vibe throughout). There's laundry service, a good guest kitchen, excellent breakfast, a restaurant serving meals all day June to August, and a popular Långholmen bathing spot a towel flick away.

Hotel-standard rooms are also in cells but spruced up with textured wall coverings and mod fixtures; some of the budget doubles are in bunks, so be sure to clarify the room configuration you want. The hostel contains a prison museum; guests visit free (open 11am-4pm, nonguest adult/child 25/10kr). Bicycles are available to rent from reception, and cycling/jogging trails line the surrounding area.

Zinkensdamm Hotell & Vandrarhem
HOTEL, HOSTEL **€**

(🗷 08-616 81 00; www.zinkensdamm.com; Zinkens Väg 20; dm from 270kr, s/d from 490/850kr; P 🖭 @ 🛜; 🚇Zinkensdamm) 🏊 In a cheery yellow building next to the adorable Tantolunden park, the Zinkensdamm STF is fun, attractive and well equipped – complete with a sleek guest kitchen and personal lockers in each room – and caters for families with kids as well as pub-going backpackers. It can be crowded and noisy, but that's the trade-off for an upbeat vibe.

Mosebacke Hostel
HOSTEL **€**

(Map p56; 🗷 08-641 64 60; www.mosebackehostel.se; Högbergsgatan 26; s/d from 625/720kr; 🕑reception 8am-11pm; 🖭 @ 🛜; 🚇Slussen) This hostel in the Söder Heights is a decent crash-pad with a great location. Common areas have a modern design, with a slick, IKEA-catalogue kitchen for guests. You can choose shared-bath or en suite rooms. Be warned that soundproofing between rooms is not great; bring earplugs. Breakfast is included in the price.

Clarion Hotel
HOTEL **€€**

(🗷 08-462 10 00; www.clarionstockholm.com; Ringvägen 98; budget/standard r from 1190/1290kr;

P 🖭 ❄ @ 🛜; 🚇Skanstull) This design hotel feels like a modern-art museum, its wide ramp leading into the foyer dotted with stylish furniture and modelled on the Tate Modern. Standard rooms are compact but uncluttered and ultramodern, with 'deluxe' options and suites available for those wanting more space. There are several bars and restaurants, and it's in a great location for exploring Södermalm.

Den Röda Båten – Mälaren/Ran
HOSTEL **€€**

(Söder Malärstrand; Map p56; 🗷 08-644 43 85; www.theredboat.com; Kajplats 10; dm from 395kr, hostel s/d from 550/900kr, hotel r from 1350kr; 🖭 @ 🛜; 🚇Slussen, Gamla Stan) The 'Red Boat' is a hotel and hostel on two vessels, *Mälaren* and *Ran*. The hostel section is the cosiest of Stockholm's floating accommodations: lots of dark wood, nautical memorabilia and friendly staff. Linens are included in the price. Hotel-standard rooms are bigger, with blond wood, maritime paintings and breakfast; sea-view rooms are worth the extra 200kr or so.

Hilton Stockholm Slussen
HOTEL **€€**

(Map p56; 🗷 08-51 73 53 00; www.hilton.com; Guldgränd 8; r from 1300kr; P 🖭 ❄ @ 🛜; 🚇Slussen) Perched between the chaotic Slussen interchange and Södermalm's underground highway, Stockholm's unmissable Hilton sports modern, comfortable (if a bit small) rooms with swirly marble bathrooms and everything you'd expect in a top-notch business hotel. Several rooms have stunning city views. There's a nice terrace bar, and the lobby is well suited to meeting friends before a night exploring Söder.

Hotel Anno 1647
HISTORIC HOTEL **€€**

(Map p56; 🗷 08-442 16 80; www.anno1647.se; Mariagränd 3; s/d economy from 925/970kr, standard from 1500/1700kr; P 🖭 @ 🛜; 🚇Slussen) Just off Götgatan, with many rooms overlooking the colourful roofs of Gamla Stan across the water, this historic hotel in two beautiful buildings has labyrinthine hallways, gorgeous wooden floors and spiral staircases, and affable staff. The economy rooms have shared showers and (tiny) bathrooms in the hall. Standard rooms have antique rococo wallpaper, all modern amenities and the occasional chandelier.

★ Rival Hotel
HOTEL **€€€**

(Map p56; 🗷 08-54 57 89 00; www.rival.se; Mariatorget 3; s/d from 2395/2695kr; 🖭 ❄ @ 🛜; 🚇Mariatorget) Owned by ABBA's Benny

Andersson and overlooking leafy Mariatorget, this ravishing design hotel is a chic retro gem, complete with vintage 1940s movie theatre and art-deco cocktail bar. The super-comfy rooms feature posters from great Swedish films and a teddy bear to make you feel at home. All rooms have luxurious, well-equipped bathrooms.

Vasastan

Hostel Bed & Breakfast   HOSTEL €
(Map p58; ✐08-15 28 38; www.hostelbed andbreakfast.com; Rehnsgatan 21; dm 320kr, s/d 550/780kr; ⊗reception 9am-8pm; ➔@🖾; ⛎Rådmansgatan) Located only a few steps from T-Rådmansgatan tunnelbana station, in an up-and-coming neighbourhood full of great restaurants and pretty parks, this pleasant, informal basement hostel has modern (shared) bathrooms, floral wallpaper, TVs in the rooms, a tidy guest kitchen, hang-out-friendly common area, and a laundry for guests (50kr). Breakfast is included in the prices; sheets can be rented (50kr).

Birger Jarl Hotel   HOTEL €€
(Map p58; ✐08-674 18 00; www.birgerjarl. se; Tulegatan 8; cabin r from 1190kr; s/d from 1200/1400kr; P➔✳@🖾; ⛎43 Tegnérgatan, ⛎Rådmansgatan) One of Stockholm's original design hotels, the Birger Jarl has a wide variety of room choices. Cabin rooms are tiny and windowless; local fashion designers customised one wall in each. Standard rooms are all done up in modern Swedish style, and the superior rooms are interior-design showpieces, some of them by big-name Swedish designers – they're well worth the price upgrade.

Rex Hotel   HOTEL €€
(Map p58; ✐08-16 00 40; www.rexhotel.se; Luntmakargatan 73; s/d from 1390/1690kr; ➔✳@🖾; ⛎Rådmansgatan) While a little less luxe than its sibling Hotel Hellsten across the street, Rex has small but stylish rooms with flat-screen TVs, rich colour schemes and Greek-stone bathrooms. Ultra-budget rooms on a lower level are recommended only if you don't plan to spend much time there – they are *very* tiny and windowless. Breakfast is in the lovely, exposed-brick atrium.

Hotel Tegnérlunden   HOTEL €€€
(Map p58; ✐08-54 54 55 50; www.hoteltegner lunden.se; Tegnérlunden 8, Norrmalm; s/d from 2090/2280kr; P✳🖾; ⛎69, ⛎T-Centralen) This chic small hotel enjoys a choice location,

overlooking the leafy Tegnérlunden park and near the vibrant Drottningatan pedestrian shopping street. Rooms are tight on space but are an excellent example of efficient Swedish design with swivel bedside lamps, decent work desks, comfy armchairs, full length mirrors and slick black-and-white decor. The 6th-floor breakfast room offers sweeping panoramic views.

Hotel Hansson   HOTEL €€€
(Map p58; ✐08-15 04 20; www.hotelhansson.se; Surbrunnsgatan 38; classic s/d from 1285/1885kr; P ➔@🖾; ⛎Rådmansgatan) This friendly, family-run boutique hotel is in a quiet but vibrant part of town and is loaded with atmosphere. The standard rooms are basic and spacious, with all the trimmings; a step up are the design rooms, with intense wallpaper, sumptuous fabrics and chandeliers. There's a beautiful lounge area and a fabulous breakfast buffet.

Hotel Hellsten   HOTEL €€€
(Map p58; ✐08-661 86 00; www.hellsten.se; Luntmakargatan 68; r from 2000kr; ➔✳@🖾; ⛎Rådmansgatan) Hotel Hellsten is owned by anthropologist Per Hellsten, whose touch is evident in the common areas, which are furnished and decorated with objects from his travels and life, including Congan tribal masks and his grandmother's chandelier. Standard rooms are comfortable and individually styled; the cheapest rooms are on the small side.

Further Afield

Bredängs Vandrarhem & Camping   HOSTEL, CAMPGROUND €
(✐08-97 62 00; www.bredangvandrarhem.se; Stora Sällskapetsväg 51; sites 295-315kr, dm 240kr, s/d 440/600kr; ⊗campsites early Apr–early Oct; P➔@🖾; ⛎Bredäng) This lakeside option is 10km southwest of central Stockholm, with good public-transport connections. It's a well-equipped campground, with a hostel and 4-person cabins (990kr). There's free wi-fi, free parking, mini golf, multiple guest kitchens and laundry facilities. It's about a 700m walk from the Bredäng tunnelbana station; if you're driving, it's well signposted from the E4/E20 motorway.

Hotel J   HOTEL €€€
(✐08-601 30 00; www.hotelj.com; Ellensviksvägen 1, Nacka Strand; r from 1440-2350kr; P➔@🖾; ⛎Nacka Strand, ⛎Slussen, then bus 404, 443) This upscale hotel with a breezy, blue-and-white Hamptons vibe is a popular weekend

getaway for Stockholmers. Initially a summer house built in 1912, it's named after the boats used in the America's Cup. The scent of nonchalant wealth wafts unmistakably through the air here. Rooms are decorated with comfortable furniture and fine linens; several have balconies.

✕ Eating

Stockholm is a city of food obsessions. The relatively small city has more than half a dozen Michelin-starred restaurants, with new and exciting places opening constantly, serving everything from vegie-minded superfoods to fast-food fads like the indefatigable burger. It's not unusual for people to plan their visits here around restaurant menus.

Gamla Stan

Chokladkoppen CAFE €
(Map p44; www.chokladkoppen.se; Stortorget 18; cakes & coffees from 35kr, mains 85-125kr; ⊙ 9am-11pm Jun-Aug, shorter hours rest of year; 🛜; 🚇 Gamla Stan) Arguably Stockholm's best-loved cafe, hole-in-the-wall Chokladkoppen sits slap bang on the old town's enchanting main square. It's an atmospheric spot with a sprawling terrace and pocket-sized interior with low-beamed ceilings, custard-coloured walls and edgy artwork. The menu includes savoury treats like broccoli-and-blue-cheese pie and scrumptious cakes.

Gamla Stans Fisk SEAFOOD, DELI €
(Map p44; ✆ 08-10 25 85; www.gamlastansfisk.se; Mälartorget 21; deli mains 85-100kr; ⊙ 10am-6pm Tue-Fri, to 3pm Sat; 🚇 Gamla Stan) 🖉 Located close to the tunnelbana station, Gamla Stans Fisk has been in business since 1907. The shop focuses on providing premium quality and ethically sourced seafood, while the delicatessen serves the best of Swedish meats and cheeses. Perfect opportunity to cook up your own seafood or to grab some lunch.

Cafe Järntorget ICE CREAM €
(Map p44; Västerlånggatan 81; ice cream 1/2/3 scoops 40/50/60kr; ⊙ 8am-6pm Mon-Fri, 10am-6pm Sat & Sun, open late in summer; 🚇 Gamla Stan) Just off Järntorget, this busy ice-cream shop reliably offers such quintessentially Swedish flavours as lemon licorice (*lakrits*), forest berries (*skogsbär*) and the ambrosia that is saffron-and-honey ice cream.

Grillska Husets Konditori BAKERY, CAFE €
(Map p44; ✆ 08-68 42 33 64; www.stadsmissionen.se/vad-vi-gor/grillska-huset; Stortorget

3; mains 90-125kr, lunch special 125kr; ⊙ 10am-8pm Mon, to 9pm Tue-Sat, 11am-8pm Sun; 🚇 Gamla Stan) The cafe and bakery run by Stockholms Stadsmission, a chain of secondhand charity shops, is an excellent spot for a sweet treat or a traditional shrimp sandwich, especially when warm weather allows for seating at the outdoor tables in Gamla Stan's main square. There's a bakery shop attached, selling goodies and rustic breads to take away.

Sundbergs Konditori CAFE €
(Map p44; ✆ 08-10 67 35; Järntorget 83; mains 85-129kr; ⊙ 9am-8pm; 🚇 Gamla Stan) Dating from 1785, this is Stockholm's oldest bakery-cafe, complete with chintzy chandeliers, a subdued parlour atmosphere and a copper samovar full of self-serve coffee. Mix and match with gleaming pastries and a soothing selection of bagels, ciabattas and quiches. Outdoor seating is primo for people watching in summer.

★ Hermitage VEGETARIAN €€
(Map p44; www.hermitage.gastrogate.com; Stora Nygatan 11; buffet weekday/weekend 130/140kr; ⊙ 11am-8pm Mon-Fri, noon-8pm Sat & Sun, to 9pm Jun-Aug; 🖉; 🚇 Gamla Stan) Herbivores love Hermitage for its simple, tasty vegetarian buffet, easily one of the best bargains in Gamla Stan. Salad, homemade bread, tea and coffee are included in the price. Pro tip: don't miss the drawers of hot food hiding under the main buffet tabletop. Vegan fare is also available, including cakes.

Under Kastanjen SWEDISH €€
(Map p44; ✆ 08-21 50 04; www.underkastanjen.se; Kindstugatan 1; mains 182-289kr, dagens lunch 105kr; ⊙ 8am-11pm Mon-Fri, 9am-11pm Sat, 9am-9pm Sun; 🛜; 🚇 Gamla Stan) This has to be just about the most picturesque corner of Gamla Stan, with tables set on a cobbled square under a beautiful chestnut tree surrounded by ochre and yellow storybook houses. Enjoy classic Swedish dishes like homemade meatballs with mashed potato. The downstairs wine bar has a veritable Spanish-bodega feel with its whitewashed brick arches and moody lighting.

It also offers a good range of gluten-free dishes and cakes.

Cafe Nova CAFE €€
(Map p44; ✆ 08-411 49 53; Järntorget 82; mains 105-149kr; ⊙ 8.30am-10pm Mon-Sat, from 9.30am Sun Jun-Sep, shorter hours rest of year; 🛜; 🚇 Gamla Stan) Enjoying a prime people-watching position on a picturesque square, this cafe is good for such standards as salads, pastas

and a particularly delicious goulash with crème fraiche. The cakes raise the bar a notch, in particular the blueberry-and-apple crumble pie. They also serve excellent ice cream, smoothies and cappuccino.

Hairy Pig Deli   DELI €€

(Håriga Grisen; Map p44; ☑073-800 26 23; www.hairypigdeli.se; Österlånggatan 9; sausage 85kr, mains 135-280kr; ☺5-9pm Tue-Fri, noon-10pm Sat; ⌂Gamla Stan) Follow your nose to this cute little corner deli, where the personable owners make all their own sausages and serve beer brewed by a family friend. Try the sausage of the day or a home-smoked pulled-pork sandwich, paired with a couple of tapas – olives, roasted potatoes, shrimp, various salamis. They've also opened a tapas restaurant nearby.

★Kryp In   SWEDISH €€€

(Map p44; ☑08-20 88 41; www.restaurangkrypin.nu; Prästgatan 17; lunch mains 135-168kr, dinner mains 198-290kr; ☺5-11pm Mon-Fri, noon-4pm & 5-11pm Sat & Sun; ☎; ⌂Gamla Stan) Small but perfectly formed, this spot wows diners with creative takes on traditional Swedish dishes. Expect the likes of salmon carpaccio, Kalix roe, reindeer roast or gorgeous, spirit-warming saffron aioli shellfish stew. The service is seamless and the atmosphere classy without being stuffy. The three-course set menu (455kr) is superb. Book ahead.

Fem Små Hus   SWEDISH €€€

(Map p44; ☑08-10 87 75; www.femsmahus.se; Nygränd 10; mains 205-410kr; ☺11.30am-11pm Mon-Tue, to midnight Wed-Fri, 1pm-midnight Sat, 1-11pm Sun; ⌂Gamla Stan) Fem Små Hus offers the perfect combination of authentic historical setting with traditional cuisine, just a short walk from the Royal Palace in the heart of the old town. The menu features Swedish classics with a French touch – think reindeer fillets with port wine sauce, seared Arctic char, Swedish farm chicken confit – served in 17th-century vaulted cellars.

Den Gyldene Freden   SWEDISH €€€

(Map p44; ☑08-24 97 60; www.gyldenefreden.se; Österlånggatan 51; mains 200-380kr; ☺11am-2pm Mon-Fri, 5.30-9pm Mon-Sat; ⌂Gamla Stan) Open since 1722, this venerable barrel-vaulted restaurant is run by the Swedish Academy, where (rumour has it) its members meet to decide the winners of the Nobel Prize. Personally, we think it should go to the chefs, whose sublime offerings include civilised *husmanskost* (home-style) dishes like roast lamb with chanterelles, cabbage and country cheese, or old-school Swedish meatballs.

Tradition   SWEDISH €€€

(Map p44; ☑08-20 35 25; www.restaurangtradition.se/en; Österlånggatan 1; dinner mains 195-275kr, lunch mains 120-140kr; ☺11.30am-11pm Mon-Fri, 4-11pm Sat, to 9pm Sun; ⌂Gamla Stan) Located in the heart of Gamla Stan only a short distance from the Royal Palace, Tradition brings a touch of class to traditional Swedish favourites like shrimp salad, *falukorv* (sausage), gravadlax (cured salmon) or baked cod in a buttery sauce. The restaurant is set in fresh and airy surroundings, and the inner courtyard is perfect during long summer nights.

Magnus Ladulås   SWEDISH €€€

(Map p44; ☑08-21 19 57; http://magnusladulas.se; Österlånggatan 26; mains 195-289kr; ☺11am-10pm Mon-Thu, to 11pm Fri, 1-11pm Sat, to 8pm Sun; ⌂Gamla Stan) Named after King Magnus III, Restaurang Magnus Ladulås is housed on the site of a 16th-century eatery. Tables hug sloped ceilings in this authentic and intimate setting where the menu is built around Swedish classics – think meatballs with potatoes and lingonberries, seafood stew, or pike-perch with roe and lobster sauce.

Flying Elk   PUB FOOD €€€

(Map p44; ☑08-20 85 83; www.theflyingelk.se/en; Mälartorget 15; mains 225-395kr; ☺6pm-midnight Sun-Tue, 6pm-1am Wed & Thu, 5pm-1am Fri & Sat; ⌂Gamla Stan) Not just your average pub – Michelin-starred chef Björn Frantzén has added a touch of Swedish style and class to the traditional pub experience, serving up hearty Nordic dishes like oven-baked Arctic char alongside fancied-up pub standards like fish and chips and burgers. There's also a good selection of craft ales. Check it out at the weekends when there's music and dancing.

Sjätte Tunnan   SWEDISH €€€

(Map p44; ☑08-440 09 19; www.sjattetunnan.se; Stora Nygatan 41-43; mains 230-295kr; ☺5pm-1am Sun-Thu, to 3am Fri & Sat; ⌂Gamla Stan) Situated in a medieval cellar in the heart of the old town, Sjätte Tunnan offers a glimpse into a forgotten world. Venture deep into the bowels of old Stockholm to discover hearty fare based on original recipes, such as wild hog meatballs or tender, baked deer steak, washed down with mead brewed in-house. Waiting staff, fully clad in medieval garb, complete the setting.

✖ Östermalm & Ladugårdsgärdet

Östermalms Saluhall   MARKET
(www.saluhallen.com; Östermalmstorg; ⊕9.30am-7pm Mon-Fri, to 5pm Sat; ⍟Östermalmstorg) **FREE** Östermalms Saluhall is a gourmet food hall that inhabits a delightful many-spired brick building. It's a sophisticated take on the traditional market, with fresh produce, fish counters, baked goods, butcher shops and tea vendors and some top places to grab a meal. For best results, arrive hungry and curious.

Closed for refurbishment when we last visited, the market was temporarily located in a sleek space right next door. It was due to reopen in mid-2018.

Café Saturnus   CAFE €
(☑08-611 77 00; Eriksbergsgatan 6; sweet rolls 50kr, salads & sandwiches 68-138kr; ⊕8am-8pm Mon-Fri, 9am-7pm Sat & Sun; 🚇2 Eriksbergsgatan) For velvety caffè latte, Gallic-inspired baguettes and perfect pastries, saunter into this casually chic bakery-cafe. Sporting a stunning mosaic floor, stripy wallpaper and a few outdoor tables, it's a fabulous spot to flick through the paper while tackling what has to be Stockholm's most enormous sweet roll (cinnamon or cardamom, take your pick).

Sturekatten   CAFE €
(Map p48; ☑08-611 16 12; www.sturekatten.se; Riddargatan 4; pastries from 35kr; ⊕9am-7pm Mon-Fri, 9am-6pm Sat, 10am-6pm Sun; ⍟Östermalmstorg) Looking like a life-size doll's house, this vintage cafe is a fetching blend of antique chairs, oil paintings, ladies who lunch and servers in black-and-white garb. Slip into a salon chair, pour some tea and nibble on a piece of apple pie or a *kanelbulle* (cinnamon bun).

Phil's Burger   BURGERS €
(☑08-40 88 40 60; www.philsburger.se; Birger Jarlsgatan 34; burgers 69-155kr; ⊕11am-10pm Sun-Tue, to 11pm Wed & Thu, to midnight Fri & Sat; ⍟Östermalmstorg) Burgers made from scratch in-house, served on bread baked in Phil's own bakery, are the name of the game here. It's a simple menu, with only a handful of choices (plus a couple of vegetarian options and a bunch of sides – get the sweet-potato fries!), but everything is well-executed, the atmosphere is classy and service is quick and smooth.

Sibyllans Kaffe & Tehandel   CAFE €
(☑08-662 06 63; Sibyllegatan 35; ⊕10am-6pm Mon-Fri, to 4pm Sat; ⍟Östermalmstorg) Stockholmers are obsessed with their coffee, but what if you're craving a nice cuppa? Looking venerable with its sombre wooden interior and rows of giant tea tins, this tea and coffee peddler has been filling pots and plungers since WWI. Try the house blend of mixed green teas or go Latin with a Bialetti cafeteria and a block of Colombian-bean chocolate.

Sabai-Soong   THAI €€
(☑08-663 12 77; www.sabai.se; Linnégatan 39B; ⊕11am-2pm Mon-Fri, 5-10pm daily; ⍟Östermalmstorg) Super-kitsch Sabai-Soong is keeping it real despite the snooty address. A hit with families and fashionistas alike, its tropical-trash day-glo interior is the perfect place to chow down on simple and faithful versions of *tod man pla* and fiery green curry.

★Ekstedt   SWEDISH €€€
(Map p48; ☑08-611 12 10; http://ekstedt.nu/en; Humlegårdsgatan 17; 4/6 courses 890/1090kr; ⊕from 6pm till late Tue-Thu, from 5pm Fri, from 4pm Sat; ⍟Östermalmstorg) Dining here is as much an experience as a meal. Chef Niklas Ekstedt's education in French and Italian cooking informs his approach to traditional Scandinavian cuisine – but only slightly. Choose from a four- or six-course set menu built around reindeer and pike-perch. Everything is cooked in a wood-fired oven, over a fire pit or smoked in a chimney.

The Michelin-starred restaurant is frequently named among the best in the world; reservations are essential.

Gastrologik   SWEDISH €€€
(☑08-662 30 60; www.gastrologik.se; Artillerigatan 14; tasting menu 1595kr; ⊕6-11.30pm Tue-Fri, 5-11.30pm Sat; ⍟Östermalmstorg) Gastrologik is at the forefront of dynamic and modern Scandinavian cooking. Diners choose from a set three- or six-course menu, which changes frequently, as the chefs work closely with suppliers to deliver the freshest and most readily available produce with a nod to sustainability and tradition. Reservations are essential.

Lisa Elmqvist   SEAFOOD €€€
(☑08-55 34 04 10; www.lisaelmqvist.se; Östermalmstorg, Östermalms Saluhall; mains from 215kr; ⊕11am-11pm Mon-Sat; ⍟Östermalmstorg) Seafood fans, look no further. This Stockholm legend is never short of a satisfied lunchtime crowd. The menu changes daily, so let the waiters order for you; classics include

shrimp sandwiches and a gravadlax plate. There's also an excellent selection of wine.

On our last visit, the restaurant was located inside the temporary Östermalms Saluhall; its usual home, the historic market across the road, is due to reopen in 2018.

Sturehof SEAFOOD €€€
(Map p48; ☑ 08-440 57 30; www.sturehof.com; Stureplan 2; mains 185-495kr; ⊙ 11am-2am; ⓡ Östermalmstorg) Superb for late-night sipping and supping, this convivial brasserie sparkles with gracious staff, celebrity regulars and fabulous seafood-centric dishes (the bouillabaisse is brilliant). Both the front and back bars are a hit with the eye-candy brigade and perfect for a postmeal flirt.

Djurgården & Skeppsholmen

★ **Rosendals Trädgårdskafe** CAFE €€
(Map p52; ☑ 08-54 58 12 70; www.rosendals tradgard.se; Rosendalsterrassen 12; mains 99-145kr; ⊙ 11am-5pm Mon-Fri, to 6pm Sat & Sun May-Sep, closed Mon Feb-Apr & Oct-Dec; ⓟ ☑; ⓡ 44, 69, 76 Djurgårdsbron, ⓡ 7) 🌱 Set among the greenhouses of a pretty botanical garden, Rosendals is an idyllic spot for heavenly pastries and coffee or a meal and a glass of organic wine. Lunch includes a brief menu of soups, sandwiches (such as ground-lamb burger with chanterelles) and gorgeous salads. Much of the produce is biodynamic and grown on site.

Cafe Ekorren SWEDISH €€
(www.cafeekorren.se; Biskopsvägen 5; mains 185-225kr; ⊙ 10am-8pm May-Sep; ⓡ 47, 69) This summer cafe, in a little yellow hut near the Biskopsudden marina in Djurgården, has outdoor tables set on decks beside the water. It makes a lovely rest break on a long walk through the park island – refuel with a coffee or an ice cream.

Blå Porten Café CAFE €€
(Map p52; ☑ 08-663 87 59; www.blaporten.com; Djurgårdsvägen 64; ☑; ⓡ 47 Liljevalc Gröna Lund, ⓡ 7 Liljevalc Gröna Lund) This lovely cafe with a courtyard garden is located in the shadow of **Liljevalchs Konsthall** (Map p52; ☑ 08-50 83 13 30; www.liljevalchs.se; Djurgårdsvägen 60; ⓡ 44, 69, ⓡ Djurgårdsfärjan, ⓡ 7) – and, at the time of our last visit, was more or less demolished to enable repairs to the art gallery. It's scheduled to reopen in summer 2018.

Wärdshuset Ulla Winbladh SWEDISH €€€
(Map p52; ☑ 08-53 48 97 01; www.ulla winbladh.se; Rosendalsvägen 8; mains 175-425kr;

⊙ 11.30am-10pm Mon, 11.30am-11pm Tue-Fri, 12.30-11pm Sat, 12.30-10pm Sun; ⓡ Djurgårdsfärjan, ⓡ 7) Named after one of Carl Michael Bellman's lovers, this villa was built as a steam bakery for the Stockholm World's Fair (1897) and now serves fine food in intimate rooms and a blissful garden setting. Sup on skilfully prepared upscale versions of traditional Scandi favourites, mostly built around fish and potatoes – try the herring plate with homemade crispbread.

Book ahead in summer.

Kungsholmen

Mälarpaviljongen SWEDISH, AMERICAN €€
(☑ 08-650 87 01; www.malarpaviljongen.se; Norr Mälarstrand 63; mains 185-225kr; ⊙ 11am-1am; ⓡ Rådhuset) 🌱 When the sun's out, few places beat this alfresco waterside spot for some Nordic dolce vita. Its glassed-in gazebo, vast floating terraces and surrounding herb gardens are only upstaged by the lovely and supremely welcoming service. Both food and cocktails are beautified versions of the classics: meatballs, fried herring, gravadlax and the like. Opening times vary with the weather.

Bergamott FUSION €€€
(☑ 08-650 30 34; www.restaurangbergamott.se; Hantverkargatan 35; mains 195-325kr; ⊙ 5.30pm-midnight Tue-Sat; ⓡ Rådhuset) The very cool French chefs in this kitchen don't simply whip up to-die-for French-Italian dishes, they'll probably deliver them to your table, talk you through the produce and guide you through the wine list. It's never short of a convivial crowd, so it's best to book, especially when jazz musicians drop in for a soulful evening jam. Menu changes daily.

Norrmalm

Holy Greens VEGETARIAN €
(Map p48; ☑ 08-22 62 22; www.regeringsgatan. holygreens.se; Regeringsgatan 28; mains 85-105kr; ⊙ 8am-7pm Mon-Fri, 11am-5pm Sat & Sun; ☑; ⓡ T-Centralen) This crisp, friendly cafe serves huge, healthful bowls of greens, grains and superfoods at good prices – try the Laxokado, with baked salmon, black rice, avocado, pickled vegies, sunflower seeds and greens, or the falafel bowl with a creamy lemon sauce, baby tomatoes and snap peas. Everything is also available gluten-free. Add a shot of grapefruit-beet juice (20kr) for extra virtue.

La Neta MEXICAN €
(Map p48; www.laneta.se; Barnhusgatan 2; tacos & quesadillas 22-52kr; ⊙ 11am-9pm Mon-Fri,

noon-9pm Sat, noon-4pm Sun; ⓡHötorget) Competition for the title of 'Stockholm's Best Taqueria' is not fierce, but La Neta wins hands down. Fast-food pseudo-Mexican eateries are all over town, but this is the real deal, with homemade corn tortillas, nuanced flavours and zero frills in the dining area (unless you count the bowls of delicious salsa). It's great value for money.

The kitchen is bigger than the dining area, and there's a perpetual line halfway around the block from the minute the place opens. Cheap beer and soft drinks are available, and the daily specials are worth trying.

Vetekatten
CAFE €

(Map p48; www.vetekatten.se; Kungsgatan 55; lunch mains 88-128kr; ⓧ7.30am-8pm Mon-Fri, 9.30am-7pm Sat & Sun; ⓡHötorget) A cardamom-scented labyrinth of cosy nooks, antique furnishings and oil paintings, Vetekatten is not so much a cafe as an institution. Wish back the old days over filling sandwiches, heavenly scrolls and warming cups of tea. (The cosiest nooks are in the back rooms.)

Hötorgshallen
FOOD HALL €

(Map p48; Hötorget; prices vary; ⓧ10am-6pm Mon-Thu, to 6.30pm Fri, to 6pm Sat; ⓡHötorget) Located below Filmstaden cinema, Hötorgshallen is Stockholm at its multicultural best, with stalls selling everything from fresh Nordic seafood to fluffy hummus and fragrant teas. Ready-to-eat options include Lebanese spinach parcels, kebabs and vegetarian burgers. For the ultimate feed, squeeze into galley-themed dining nook **Kajsas Fiskrestaurang** for a huge bowl of soulful *fisksoppa* (fish stew) with aioli (110kr).

While you're here, don't neglect to buy some produce from the vendors in the square outside – they're entertainers as much as they are retailers, and it's a fun way to get a good deal on some nice locally grown fruit and vegies.

Wiener Caféet
CAFE €€

(Map p48; ☎08-68 42 38 50; www.wienercafeet.com; Biblioteksgatan 6-8; mains 185-269kr, sandwiches 85-95kr, afternoon tea 329kr; ⓧ7am-9pm Mon-Fri, 9.30am-9pm Sat, 9.30am-7pm Sun; ⓢ; ⓠ291, ⓡÖstermalmstorg) Step into the lavish art-deco interior here and you are transported to the grand cafes of Vienna and Paris. Pastry chef Per Bäckström has ensured that this is the place to come in town for tea (2pm to 5pm). And not just a cuppa, but a lavish Ritz Hotel-style experience including scones and cream, choux puffs and assorted cakes.

Breakfasts are similarly mouthwateringly lavish and varied; light lunches are also served.

K25
FOOD HALL €€

(Map p48; ☎08-21 29 29; www.k25.nu/en; Kungsgatan 25; mains incl drink 100-200kr; ⓧ10am-10pm Mon-Fri, 11am-10pm Sat; ⓡHötorget) K25 is a sleek food court that provides a fast and affordable option for breakfast, lunch or dinner in the upmarket area of Norrmalm. With various counters offering gourmet burgers, Chinese dumplings, Mexican burritos and more, it's handy for a break while shopping, sightseeing or before you head out for the night.

Eco Baren
CAFE €€

(Map p48; ☎08-24 10 81; www.centralbadet.se; Drottninggatan 88, Centralbadet; mains 165-198kr; ⓧ9am-7.30pm Mon-Sat, to 5.30pm Sun; ⓢⓙ; ⓡT-Centralen) ⓿ Step away from the bustle of Drottninggatan's fine shops and into this green oasis with its lily pond, mature trees, birdsong and pervading air of tranquillity. Located within the historic Centralbadet spa, this excellent small restaurant and cafe fittingly specialises in healthy colourful dishes made solely with organic ingredients, including raw food salads, soups and vegan burgers.

★ Rutabaga
VEGETARIAN €€€

(Map p48; ☎08-679 35 84; www.mdghs.se; Södra Blasieholmshamnen 6, Grand Hôtel Stockholm; dishes 125-295kr; ⓧ5pm-midnight Mon-Sat; ⓙ; ⓡKungsträdgården) At Rutabaga, celebrity chef Mathias Dahlgren pushes vegetarian cuisine into the realm of art: the menu features vividly colourful salads and other unusual combinations (an egg-truffle-white-bean dish, a mango and mozzarella salad) which, as always, Dahlgren presents impeccably on the plate. Most dishes are meant for sharing (if you can bear to give any up). Closes in July.

★ Grands Verandan
SWEDISH €€€

(Map p48; ☎08-679 35 86; www.grandhotel.se; Södra Blasieholmshamnen 6, Grand Hôtel Stockholm; smörgåsbord 545kr, mains 205-365kr; ⓧ7-10.30am & 11.30am-11pm; ⓡKungsträdgården) Head here, inside the Grand Hôtel, for the famous smörgåsbord – especially during the Christmas holidays, when it becomes even more elaborate (reservations recommended). Arrive early for a window seat and tuck into both hot and cold Swedish staples, including gravadlax with almond potatoes, herring, meatballs and lingonberry jam. It's like a belt-busting crash course in classic Nordic flavours.

The Market
SWEDISH €€€

(Map p48; ☑08-51 73 42 00; www.scandic hotels.com; Klarabergsgatan 41; mains 185-265kr; ⊙7am-noon daily, 6-11pm Mon-Sat; ⓶T-Centralen) Handy for the station, this restaurant inside the Scandic Continental hotel has an expansive buffet breakfast and a menu focused on sustainable, locally sourced, seasonal ingredients. The atmosphere is rustic chic with wooden shelves, racks of wine and arty lamps; squeeze in at the bar, a cosy table for two or at the communal tables.

Matbaren
INTERNATIONAL €€€

(Map p48; ☑08-679 35 84; www.mdghs.se; Södra Blasieholmenshamnen 6, Grand Hôtel Stockholm; mains 145-385kr; ⊙noon-2pm Mon-Fri & 6pm-midnight Mon-Sat; ⓶Kungsträdgården) One of celebrity chef Mathias Dahlgren's restaurants at the Grand Hôtel (the other is Rutabaga; p74), the bistro-style Matbaren ('Food Bar') boasts a Michelin star and an inventive menu of seasonal ingredients. The food is elaborately gorgeous – matjes herring arranged like a still-life, 'Scandinavian sashimi', architectural desserts almost too pretty to eat – but the place never really feels overly formal.

Reservations are crucial. Note that it's closed for several weeks in summer (usually July to early August).

Vassa Eggen
SWEDISH €€€

(☑08-21 61 69; www.vassaeggen.com; Birger Jarlsgatan 29; mains 225-450kr; ⊙11.30am-2pm Mon-Fri, 5.30-10pm Mon, to midnight Tue-Thu, to 2am Fri & Sat; ⓶Östermalmstorg) Featuring a domed dining room sitting beyond a glassed birch forest, this stylish dining pad is named after Somerset Maugham's novel *The Razor's Edge*. With sharply executed dishes like oxtail tortellini with mascarpone cheese and a long and luscious wine list, it all makes perfect sense. Book ahead.

Operakällaren
FRENCH, SWEDISH €€€

(Map p48; ☑08-676 58 00; www.operakallaren.se; Karl XII's Torg 10, Opera House; tasting menus 1050-5950kr; ⊙6pm-1am Tue-Sat, closed mid-Jul–mid-Aug; ⓶Kungsträdgården) Inside Stockholm's show-off opera house, the century-old Operakällaren is a major gastronomic event. Decadent chandeliers, golden mirrors and exquisitely carved ceilings set the scene for French-meets-fusion adventures like seared scallops with caramel, cauliflower purée, *pata negra* ham and brown-butter emulsion. Book at least two weeks ahead.

Bakfickan
SWEDISH €€€

(Map p48; ☑08-676 58 00; www.operakallaren. se; Opera House, Karl XII's Torg; mains 195-375kr; ⊙11.30am-10pm Mon-Thu, to 11pm Fri, noon-11pm Sat, noon-5pm Sun; ⓶Kungsträdgården) The small, casual 'hip pocket' of Operakällaren, this comfy restaurant is crammed with opera photographs and deco lampshades. Dexterous old-school waiters serve upscale comforting Swedish *husmanskost* (matjes herring, cured salmon, Isterband sausage, Swedish meatballs) and the counter seats make it a perfect spot for solo dining. Late at night, rumour has it, this is where the opera singers hang out.

Bobergs Matsal
SWEDISH €€€

(Map p48; ☑08-762 81 61; www.bobergsmatsal. se; Yxsmedsgränd 12, Nordiska Kompaniet; mains 215-420kr; ⊙11am-3pm Mon-Fri, noon-5pm Sat; Ⓟ🛜; ⓶T-Centralen) In this restaurant on the top floor of the swanky Nordiska Kompaniet department store, celebrated local chef Björn Frantzén offers a menu of contemporary art-on-a-plate interpretations of traditional Swedish recipes (shrimp salad, cognac-spiced blood pudding, cured salmon), all beautifully assembled. The dining room is fabulous and a culturally protected site, with 100-year-old carved birch wood panelling and twinkling chandeliers.

✖ Södermalm

Kafé 44
VEGAN €

(Map p56; ☑08-644 53 12; www.kafe44.org; Tjärhovsgatan 44; mains 60-80kr, coffee 10kr; ⊙noon-6pm Tue-Fri, 11am-4pm Sat & Sun; 🍴; 🚌93 Tjärhovsplan) The heart and soul of Stockholm's punk scene back in the 1980s is now a vegan cafe that doubles as an anarchist-leaning community centre. Everything served is vegan (the burgers are made of aubergine), but you can request milk or cheese if you want. Live music regularly; check schedules online.

Söderhallarna
FOOD HALL €

(Map p56; Medborgarplatsen 3; ⊙10am-7pm Mon-Fri, to 4pm Sat, shorter hours Jul & Aug; 🍴; ⓶Medborgarplatsen) This food hall on Medborgarplatsen contains a cinema as well as shops selling everything from cheese and smallgoods to decent vegetarian grub. There are several cafes and a burger joint; we like fish restaurant **Melanders** (11am-3pm Mon-Fri, mains 145-280kr).

String
CAFE €

(Map p56; ☑08-714 85 14; www.facebook.com/cafestring; Nytorgsgatan 38; sandwiches 65-95kr, breakfast buffet 90kr; ☺9am-10pm Mon-Thu, to 7pm Fri-Sun; ⓡMedborgarplatsen) This retro-funky SoFo cafe does a bargain weekend brunch buffet (9am to 1pm Saturday and Sunday). Load your plate with everything from cereals, yoghurt and fresh fruit to pancakes, toast and amazing homemade hummus. Its daily lunch specials (lasagne, quiche) are good value, too.

Nystekt Strömming   SWEDISH €
(Map p56; Södermalmstorg; mains 40-75kr; ☺11am-9pm; ⓡSlussen) For a quick snack of freshly fried herring, seek out this humble cart outside the tunnelbana station at Slussen. Large or small combo plates come with big slabs of the fish and a selection of sides and condiments, from mashed potato and red onion to salads and crispbread; more-portable wraps and the delicious herring burger go for 55kr.

★Hermans Trädgårdscafé   VEGETARIAN €€
(Map p56; ☑08-643 94 80; www.hermans.se; Fjällgatan 23B; buffet 195kr, desserts from 35kr; ☺11am-9pm; ☑; ☐2, 3, 53, 71, 76 Tjärhovsplan, ⓡSlussen) ✎ This justifiably popular vege-tarian buffet is one of the nicest places to dine in Stockholm, with a glassed-in porch and outdoor seating on a terrace overlook-ing the city's glittering skyline. Fill up on inventive, flavourful vegie and vegan crea-tions served from a cosy, vaulted room – you might need to muscle your way in, but it's worth the effort.

The desserts (sold separately) are mostly vegan, gluten-free, or both, and they look amazing, though it's a challenge to save room. If you have a valid student ID, you may be able to get a two-for-one deal on the buffet. Worth asking!

Blå Dörren   SWEDISH €€
(Map p56; ☑08-743 07 43; www.bla-dorren.se; Sö-dermalmstorg 6; mains 148-258kr; ☺10.30am-11pm Mon, to midnight Tue-Thu, to 1am Fri, 1pm-1am Sat, 1-11pm Sun; ⓡSlussen) A stone's throw from Gamla Stan and facing Stockholm City Muse-um, Blå Dörren (The Blue Door) honours its historic surroundings with a variety of tradi-tional Swedish dishes. You can't go wrong with the pan-fried herring or elk meatballs, both ac-companied with fresh lingonberries.

Mahalo   VEGAN €€
(Hälsocafet; ☑08-42 05 65 44; www.halsocafet. se; Hornsgatan 61; mains 85-139kr; ☺9am-7pm Mon & Tue, 9am-8pm Wed-Fri, 10am-8pm Sat, 10am-7pm Sun; ☎☑❋; ⓡMariatorget, Zinkensdamm) ✎ You'll start to feel healthier just walking

into this vegan cafe (formerly Hälsocafet), humming with plants and vivid colours. The focus is on huge, filling, eco-friendly su-perfood bowls, like the Buddha bowl (spicy tofu, greens, glass noodles, avocado) or the homemade-falafel and hummus bowl. Cof-fee is included. There are also vegan sweets, wraps, breakfast bowls, smoothies, and tur-meric or matcha lattes.

Meatballs   SWEDISH €€
(Map p56; ☑08-466 60 99; www.meatballs.se; Nytorgsgatan 30; mains 179-195kr; ☺11am-10pm Mon-Thu, to midnight Fri & Sat, limited hours Jul & Aug; ☎; ⓡMedborgarplatsen) The name says it all. This restaurant serves serious meatballs, including moose, deer, wild boar and lamb, served with creamed potatoes and pickled vegetables, washed down with a pint of Sleepy Bulldog craft beer. It's a novel twist on a traditional Swedish dining experience, accentuated by the rustic decor and delight-ful waiting staff.

Chutney   VEGETARIAN €€
(Map p56; ☑08-640 30 10; www.chutney.se; Kata-rina Bangata 19; daily special weekday/weekend 105/135kr; ☺11am-10pm Mon-Fri, noon-10pm Sat, noon-9pm Sun; ☑; ⓡMedborgarplatsen) Sitting among a string of three inviting cafes along this block, Chutney is one of Stockholm's many well-established vegetarian restau-rants, offering excellent value and great atmosphere. The daily lunch special is usu-ally a deliciously spiced, Asian- or Indian-influenced mountain of vegies over rice, and includes salad, bread and coffee.

Plant   VEGAN €€
(☑08-21 51 52; www.theplant.se; Götgatan 132, Rin-gens Shopping Centre; mains 105-115kr; ☺11am-9pm Mon-Thu, to 10pm Fri & Sat, to 8pm Sun; ☑; ⓡS-kanstull) ✎ This simple but ambitious vegan kitchen, part of the sleek, chef-showcasing food court Teatern inside the Ringen Shop-ping Centre, creates flavour-packed meals us-ing only plant-based foods. Its calling card is Piston Peas, crispy-baked slices of yellow peas that taste totally decadent despite being good for you. There are also vegan burgers, hum-mus and desserts. Indulge guilt-free!

Van der Nootska Palace   CAFE €€
(Map p56; ☑08-644 99 60; www.vandernootska. se; St Paulsgatan 21; mains from 105kr; ☺11am-2pm Mon-Fri; ⓡSlussen, Mariatorget) Van der Nootska Palace was built in the 17th century and has been a private residence, a foreign embassy and even a tobacco factory. These days it's a

wedding and conference venue with a lunch restaurant serving hearty salads and soups, so why not indulge in the aristocratic experience? Lunch is served in the original courtyard during the warmer months.

Östgöta Källaren
SWEDISH €€

(Map p56; ☑ 08-643 22 40; Östgötagatan 41; mains 168-235kr; ⊙5pm-1am Sun-Fri, 3pm-1am Sat; ⊜Medborgarplatsen) The regulars at this soulful pub-restaurant range from multipierced rockers to blue-rinse grandmas, all smitten with the dimly lit romantic atmosphere, amiable vibe and hearty Swedish, Eastern European and French-Mediterranean grub. Try the saffron shellfish casserole.

The restaurant shares an entrance with the underworldy Vampire Lounge (p81).

Koh Phangan
THAI €€

(Map p56; ☑ 08-642 50 40; www.kohphangan. se; Skånegatan 57; mains 175-250kr; ⊙4pm-1am Mon-Fri, noon-1am Sat & Sun; ⊜Medborgarplatsen) Best at night, this outrageously kitsch Thai restaurant has to be seen to be believed. Tuck into your *kao pat gai* (chicken fried rice) in a real *tuk-tuk* to the accompanying racket of crickets and tropical thunder, or kick back with beers in a bamboo hut. DJs occasionally hit the decks and it's best to book ahead.

Crêperie Fyra Knop
CAFE €€

(Map p56; ☑ 08-640 77 27; Svartensgatan 4; crêpes 82-126kr; ⊙5-11pm Mon-Fri, noon-11pm Sat & Sun; ⊜Slussen) Head here for perfect crêpes in an intimate setting, plus a hint of shanty-town chic – think reggae tunes and old tin billboards for Stella Artois. A good place for a quiet tête-à-tête before you hit the clubs down the street.

Folkets Kebab
FAST FOOD €€

(☑ 08-669 91 66; Hornsgatan 92; buffet 119kr, kebabs from 50kr; ⊙10am-2am; ⊜Zinkensdamm) For a late-night after-bar soaker-upper, it's hard to beat the buffet at Folkets Kebab. The kebabs on the regular menu are also good value. Don't expect culinary genius, but you certainly won't leave hungry or feeling like you overpaid.

★ Woodstockholm
SWEDISH €€€

(Map p56; ☑ 08-36 93 99; www.woodstockholm.com; Mosebacketorg 9; mains 265-285kr; ⊙11.30am-2pm Mon, 11.30am-2pm & 5-11pm Tue-Sat; 🐾🖋; ⊜Slussen) 🖋 This hip dining spot incorporates a wine bar and furniture store showcasing chairs and tables by local designers. The menu

changes weekly and is themed, somewhat wackily: think Salvador Dalí or Aphrodisiac, the latter including scallops with oyster mushrooms and sweetbreads with yellow beets and horseradish cream. This is fast becoming one of the city's classic foodie destinations. Reservations essential.

Overlooking the delightful Södermalm park, diners have the choice of communal tables or bar seats (the latter reserved for drop ins). Sustainability is taken seriously with small local producers used as far as possible and there are always vegetarian options.

Eriks Gondolen
SWEDISH €€€

(Map p56; ☑ 08-641 70 90; www.eriks.se; Stadsgården 6; mains 215-335kr; ⊙5-11pm Mon, to 1am Tue-Sat, bar from 4pm Mon-Thu & 3pm Fri & Sat; ⊜Slussen) Perched above Slussen atop the antique lift Katarinahissen, this place is known for top-notch Swedish food, refined service, perfect cocktails and endless views. There's a formal dining room (reservations recommended), or you can keep it casual in the bar area. In summer there's seating outdoors – not ideal for the acrophobic.

Pelikan
SWEDISH €€€

(Map p56; ☑ 08-55 60 90 90; www.pelikan.se; Blekingegatan 40; mains 188-335kr; ⊙5pm-midnight or 1am; ⊜Skanstull) Lofty ceilings, wood panelling and no-nonsense waiters in waistcoats set the scene for classic *husmanskost* (home cooking) at this century-old beer hall – think roasted reindeer, Västerbotten cheese pie and Arctic char. The herring options are particularly good (try the 'SOS' starter, an assortment of pickled herring, 135kr to 195kr) and there's usually a vegetarian special. There's a hefty list of aquavit, too.

✕ Vasastan

Konditori Ritorno
CAFE €

(Map p58; ☑ 08-32 01 06; Odengatan 80-82; sandwiches from 50kr; ⊙7am-10pm Mon-Thu, to 8pm Fri, 8am-6pm Sat, 10am-6pm Sun; ⊜Odenplan) The cosy backroom at this unpresumptuous cafe looks like the lobby of an old movie house fallen on hard times. A hit with writers, students and pensioners, its worn leather couches and miniature jukeboxes at every table make it a perfect pit stop for old-school shrimp sandwiches and heavenly *semla* buns.

Tennstopet
PUB FOOD €€

(Map p58; ☑ 08-32 25 18; www.tennstopet.se; Dalagatan 50; dagens lunch 129kr; ⊙11.30am-1am Mon-Fri,

1pm-1am Sat & Sun; 🚇Odenplan) Had there been a Swedish version of *Cheers,* it would've been filmed here. Oil paintings, gilded mirrors and winter candlelight set the scene for a loveable cast of wizened regulars, corner-seat scribes and melancholy dames. Watch the show with a soothing *öl* (beer) and a serve of soulful *husmanskost.* Try the traditional herring platter for two (196kr).

Caffé Nero   CAFE €€
(Map p58; www.nerostockholm.se; Roslagsgatan 4; lunch mains 110-145kr, dinner mains 145-175kr; ⊙7am-4pm Mon-Fri, 9am-5pm Sat & Sun; 🚇Odenplan, Rådmansgatan) Packed with local hipsters during the busy lunch hour, this stylish but casual neighbourhood cafe serves substantial Italian meals (fish, pasta, salads) at good prices, plus sublime coffee and pastries. Next door is a more formal bar-restaurant, Buco Nero, with DJs most nights.

Flippin' Burgers   BURGERS €€
(Map p58; ✆08-30 62 40; http://flippinburgers.se/en; Observatoriegatan 8; burger 95-130kr, fries 35kr; ⊙4-10pm Mon-Thu, 11am-10pm Fri, noon-10pm Sat & Sun; 🚇Odenplan) 🍴 Part of Stockholm's current obsession with burgers, FB has a brief menu (just a few types of burger, fries and shakes) and a perpetual line out the front door. But things move quickly; squeeze into the bar for a Sam Adams beer while you wait. Burgers are simple and delicious, relying on high-quality ingredients (sustainably raised beef, ground in-house daily).

The restaurant also has a food truck, Sliders, that roams the city; check its whereabouts online.

Lao Wai   VEGETARIAN €€€
(Map p58; ✆08-673 78 00; www.laowai.se; Luntmakargatan 74; dagens lunch 110kr, dinner mains 220-240kr; ⊙11am-2pm Mon-Fri, 5.30-9pm Mon-Sat; ✐; 🚇Rådmansgatan) 🍴 Tiny, herbivorous Lao Wai does great things to tofu and veg, hence the faithful regulars. Everything here is gluten-free and vegan. A different Asian-fusion lunch special is served each weekday; the dinner menu is more expansive, offering virtuous treats like Sichuan-style smoked tofu with shiitake, chillies, garlic shoots, snow peas and black beans.

Tranan   SWEDISH €€€
(Map p58; ✆08-52 72 81 00; www.tranan.se; Karlbergsvägen 14; mains 160-395kr; ⊙11.30am-11pm Mon-Fri, noon-11pm Sat & Sun, 5-11pm daily Jul & Aug; 🚇Odenplan) Locals pack this former beer hall, now a comfy but classy neighbourhood bistro with a seafood-heavy menu and chequered tablecloths. The food combines Swedish *husmanskost* (home cooking) with savvy Gallic touches; don't miss the fried herring. In summer, choose an outdoor table and watch the human dramas across Odenplan. On the weekends, DJs and live bands perform in the basement bar.

Storstad   FRENCH, SWEDISH €€€
(Map p58; www.storstad.se; Odengatan 41; plates 125-325kr; ⊙4pm-1am Mon-Wed, to 3am Fri & Sat; 🚇Odenplan) This attractive bistro near Odenplan, which shares a corner (and owners) with **Olssons bar** (Map p58; ✆08-673 38 00; ⊙9pm-3am Wed-Sat), serves Scandi classics like *toast skagen* or Swedish meatballs alongside traditional French favourites like *moules frites* and tarte Tatin. It transforms into a lively cocktail bar later in the evening.

🍸 Drinking & Nightlife

Stockholm is a stylish place to drink, whether you're after cocktails or coffee. The coolest, most casual drinking holes are on Södermalm, the bohemian island in the southern part of town. For glamour, head to Östermalm's late-night clubs. Even hotel bars draw an ultrachic cocktail crowd.

Note that many places charge a mandatory coat-check fee (30 to 50kr) outside of summer.

🍺 Gamla Stan

Wirströms   PUB
(Map p44; ✆08-21 28 74; www.wirstromspub.se; Stora Nygatan 13; beer 60-80kr; ⊙noon-midnight Sun & Mon, to 1am Tue-Thu & Sat, 11am-1am Fri; 🚇Gamla Stan) A friendly, atmospheric Irish pub (despite the name), Wirströms is a lively, sports-friendly bar upstairs and a cavernous series of seemingly endless tunnels and dark little alcoves underground. There's regular live music with an emphasis on the blues, and a popular quiz night.

The owners have recently opened the Shebeen, a beer bar sharing an entrance with the original pub and serving dozens of varieties of Swedish craft beer.

Monks Wine Room   WINE BAR
(Map p44; ✆08-23 12 14; www.monkscafe.se; Lilla Nygatan 2; ⊙5pm-midnight Tue-Thu, 4pm-midnight Fri & Sat; 🚇Gamla Stan) Set in atmospheric 17th-century surroundings in the heart of the old town, Monks Wine Room has a well-stocked cellar with hundreds of bottles to choose from. Stop by for a quick glass of wine

to recharge the batteries or take some time to sample a cheese and wine pairing.

Monks Porter House PUB

(Map p44; 08-23 12 12; www.monkscafe.se; Munkbron 11; 6pm-1am Tue-Sat; Gamla Stan) This cavernous brewpub has an epic beer list, including 56 taps, many of which are made here or at the Monks microbrewery in Vasastan. Everything we tried was delicious, especially the Monks Orange Ale – your best bet is to ask the bartender for a recommendation (or a taste). Check online for beer-tasting events.

Le Rouge BAR

(Map p44; 08-50 52 44 30; www.lerouge.se; Brunnsgränd 2-4; 5pm-1am; Gamla Stan) Fin-de-siècle Paris is the inspiration for this decadent lounge in Gamla Stan, a melange of rich red velvet, tasselled lampshades, inspired cocktails and French bistro grub. DJs hit the decks Thursday to Saturday.

Torget BAR

(Map p44; 08-20 55 60; www.torgetbaren.com; Mälartorget 13; 5pm-1am; Gamla Stan) For camp and Campari, it's hard to beat this sparkling gay bar – think rotating chandeliers, mock-baroque touches and different themed evenings, from live burlesque to handbag-swinging *schlager*. The crowd is a good source of info on upcoming underground parties, so grab yourself a champers and chat away.

Östermalm & Ladugårdsgärdet

Spy Bar CLUB

(Map p48; Birger Jarlsgatan 20; cover from 160kr; 10pm-5am Wed-Sat; Östermalmstorg) Though it's no longer the super-hip star of the scene it once was, the Spy Bar (aka 'the Puke'; *spy* means vomit in Swedish) is still a landmark and fun to check out if you're making the Östermalm rounds. It covers three levels in a turn-of-the-century flat (spot the tile stoves).

Sturecompagniet CLUB

(Map p48; 08-54 50 76 00; www.sture compagniet.se; Stureplan 4; 10pm-3am Thu-Sat; Östermalmstorg) Swedish soap stars, flowing champagne and look-at-me attitude set a decadent scene at this glitzy, mirrored and becurtained hallway. Dress to impress and flaunt your wares to commercial house. Big-name guest DJs come through frequently.

Lilla Baren at Riche BAR

(Map p48; 08-54 50 35 60; Birger Jarlsgatan 4; 5pm-2am Tue-Sat; Östermalm) A darling of Östermalm's hip parade, this pretty, glassed-in bar mixes smooth bar staff, skilled DJs and a packed crowd of fashion-literate media types; head in by 9pm to score a seat.

Kungsholmen

Lemon Bar BAR

(08-650 17 78; www.lemonbar.se; Scheelegatan 8; 5pm-1am Tue, to 3am Wed-Sat; Rådhuset) A favourite among locals for its laid-back vibe, the Lemon Bar epitomises the kind of comfy neighbourhood joint you can drop into on the spur of the moment and count on finding a friendly crowd and good music, mostly Swedish pop hits that may or may not result in dancing.

Norrmalm

★Berns Salonger BAR

(Map p48; 08-56 63 22 00; www.berns.se; Berzelii Park; club 11pm-4am Thu-Sat, occasionally Wed & Sun, bar from 5pm daily; Kungsträdgården) A Stockholm institution since 1862, this glitzy entertainment palace remains one of the city's hottest party spots. While the gorgeous ballroom hosts some brilliant live-music gigs, the best of Berns' bars is in the intimate basement, packed with cool creative types, top-notch DJs and projected art-house images. Check the website for a schedule of events; some require advance ticket purchase.

★Café Opera CLUB

(Map p48; 08-676 58 07; www.cafeopera.se; Karl XII's Torg; cover from 160kr; 10pm-3am Wed-Sun; Kungsträdsgården) Rock stars need a suitably excessive place to schmooze, booze and groove, one with glittering chandeliers, ceiling frescoes and a jet-set vibe. This bar-club combo fits the bill, but it's also welcoming enough to make regular folk *feel* like rock stars. If you only have time to hit one primo club during your visit, this is a good choice.

★East BAR

(Map p48; 08-611 49 59; http://east.se; Stureplan 13; dinner mains 247-385kr; 11.30am-3am Mon-Sat, 5pm-3am Sun; Östermalmstorg) East is a bar, restaurant and club rolled into one. Great cocktails make it a bartender hangout. Dishes have a predominantly modern Asian twist (locals recommend the sushi),

STOCKHOLM & AROUND DRINKING & NIGHTLIFE

carrying influences from Vietnam, Korea and Japan. Set right in the heart of Öster-malm on Stureplan, it's a good place for fuel-ling up before or during a club night.

Solidaritet CLUB
(Map p48; 08-678 10 50; www.solidaritet.eu; Lästmakargatan 3; 11pm-5am Wed-Sat; Öster-malmstorg) Solidaritet plays host to both Swedish and internationally renowned DJs with an emphasis on electronic music. The interior decor, designed by leading Swedish architects, is sleek and stylish. The club is set just off Stureplan, the centre of Stockholm's club and party scene.

Bianchi Cafe & Cycles CAFE
(Map p48; 08-611 21 00; www.bianchicafe cycles.com; Norrlandsgatan 16; 11am-10pm Mon-Sat; Östermalmstorg) This cycle-centric Ital-ian spot is ideal for an espresso and a pastry.

Icebar BAR
(Map p48; 08-50 56 35 20; www.icebar stockholm.se; Vasaplan 4, Nordic 'C' Hotel; entry incl drink 170-210kr; 4.30pm-midnight Sun-Thu, 3.45pm-1am Fri & Sat, from 11.15am May–mid-Sep; T-Centralen) It's touristy. Downright gim-micky! And you're utterly intrigued, admit it: a bar built entirely out of ice, where you drink from glasses carved of ice on tables made of ice. The admission price gets you warm booties, mittens, a parka and one drink. Refill drinks cost 95kr; entry is cheap-er if you book online.

Södermalm

Kvarnen BAR
(Map p56; 08-643 03 80; www.kvarnen.com; Tjärhovsgatan 4; 11am-1am Mon & Tue, to 3am Wed-Fri, noon-3am Sat, noon-1am Sun; Medbor-garplatsen) An old-school Hammarby football fan hang-out, Kvarnen is one of the best bars in Söder. The gorgeous beer hall dates from 1907 and seeps tradition; if you're not the clubbing type, get here early for a nice pint and a meal (mains from 210kr). As the night progresses, the nightclub vibe takes over. Queues are fairly constant but justifiable.

Akkurat BAR
(Map p56; 08-644 00 15; www.akkurat.se; Hornsgatan 18; 3pm-midnight Mon, to 1am Tue-Sat, 6pm-1am Sun; Slussen) Valhalla for beer fiends, Akkurat boasts a huge selection of Belgian ales as well as a good range of Swedish-made microbrews and hard ciders. It's one of only two places in Sweden to be recognised by a Cask Marque for its real ale. Extras include a vast wall of whisky and live music several nights a week.

Himlen COCKTAIL BAR
(Map p56; 08-660 60 68; www.restaurang himlen.se; Götgatan 78, Skrapan, 26th fl; 4pm-midnight Mon, to 1am Tue-Thu, to 3am Fri & Sat; ; Medborgarplatsen) Cruise up the elevator to this elegant cocktail bar on the dizzying heights of the 26th floor; this is easily the the

LGBT STOCKHOLM

Stockholm is a dazzling spot for queer travellers. Sweden's legendary open-mindedness makes homophobic attitudes rare, and party-goers of all persuasions are welcome in any bar or club. As a result, Stockholm doesn't really have a gay district, although you'll find most of the queer-centric venues in Södermalm and Gamla Stan.

The national organisation for gay and lesbian rights is **Riksförbundet för Sexuellt Likaberättigande** (RFSL; Map p58; 08-50 16 29 00; www.rfsl.se; Sveavägen 59; 10am-3pm or 4pm Mon-Fri, closed most of Jul & Aug; Rådmansgatan), with an attached bookshop, restaurant and nightclub.

For club listings and events, pick up a free copy of street-press magazine *QX*, found at many clubs, shops and cafes around town. Its website (www.qx.se) is more frequently updated and has listings in English. *QX* also produces a free, handy *Gay Stockholm Map*, available at the tourist office.

Good bars and clubs include the following:

Lady Patricia This is a perennial Sunday-night favourite – two crowded dance floors, drag shows and a *schlager*-loving crowd. It's all aboard a docked old royal yacht (now open five nights a week, on Söder Mälarstrand).

Side Track This establishment has a low-key, publike ambience.

Torget (p79) In Gamla Stan, this is Stockholm's premier gay bar-restaurant, with mock-baroque touches and a civilised salon vibe.

tallest building in Södermalm. After you have finished ogling the view, indulge in a fabulous cocktail, accompanied by oysters (175kr for six). There's also more-formal dining in the 25th-floor restaurant (closed July and August).

Lady Patricia BAR
(Map p56; ☑08-743 05 70; www.patricia.st; Söder Mälarstrand, Kajplats 19; ⊙5pm-midnight Wed & Thu, to 5am Fri-Sun; ᵼSlussen) Half-price seafood, nonstop dance music and decks packed with sexy Swedes and drag queens make this former royal yacht a gay Sunday-night ritual (though you can now visit five nights a week). Head to the upper dance floor (past the pirates in the riggings) where lager-happy punters sing along to Swedish Eurovision entries with a bemusing lack of irony.

Debaser Strand BAR
(☑08-658 63 50; www.debaser.se; Hornstulls Strand 4; ⊙restaurant 5-11pm Tue-Thu, to 1am Fri & Sat, 11am-4pm Sun, bar Fri & Sat 4pm-3am; ᵼHornstull) Located in trendy Hornstull, Debaser is a Mexican restaurant, bar, nightclub and live-music venue all rolled into one big night out – it's a key draw to this area. The Brooklyn Bar is a comfy, unpretentious hang-out, with worn-in sofas and outdoor tables, and a good place to catch live music or DJ sets.

Den Gröne Jägaren BAR
(Map p56; ☑08-640 96 00; www.grone-jagaren. com; Götgatan 64; ⊙11am-1am; ᵼMedborgarplatsen) An institution since the 17th century. Legend has it that military officer Jacob Johan Anckarström had his last meal at Den Gröne Jägaren (The Green Hunter) before assassinating King Gustav III. The modern-day establishment is a favourite local hang-out, especially for karaoke and Hammarby football matches.

Rival BAR
(Map p56; ☑08-54 57 89 24; www.rival.se; Mariatorget 3; ⊙5pm-midnight Thu-Sat; ᵼMariatorget) You'll find this sleek art-deco number, complete with circular bar, inside designer hotel the Rival (p68; co-owned by ABBA's Benny Andersson). While not Söder's top choice for atmospheric toasting, its architectural prowess merits a quick trip.

Snotty's BAR
(Map p56; Skånegatan 90; ⊙4pm-1am; ᵼMedborgarplatsen) This mellow hang-out is friendly and free of attitude, and one of the most comfortable and unpretentious places to drink in Stockholm. It has a vaguely retro vibe, a

smooth wooden bar and record covers all over the walls.

Vampire Lounge BAR
(Map p56; ☑08-643 22 40; www.vampirelounge. se; Östgötagatan 41; ⊙5pm-1am Fri, 7pm-1am Sat; ᵼMedborgarplatsen) The name says it all: this dark basement bar is bloodsucker-themed all the way through. There are perspex 'windows' in the walls showing buried caches of anti-vamp supplies such as holy water, crosses and garlic – just in case. The cocktail menu ranges from a strawberry daiquiri to a frothy frangelico-and-egg-white concoction. The lounge shares an entrance with Östgöta Källaren (p77) restaurant.

Marie Laveau BAR
(Map p56; www.marielaveau.se; Hornsgatan 66; ⊙5-11pm Mon & Tue, to 3am Wed-Sat; ᵼMariatorget) In an old sausage factory, this kicking Söder playpen draws a boho-chic crowd. The designer-grunge bar (think chequered floor and subway-style tiled columns) serves killer cocktails and good sandwiches during the day, while the sweaty basement hosts club nights at the weekend.

Side Track BAR
(Map p56; ☑08-641 16 88; www.sidetrack.nu; Wollmar Yxkullsgatan 7; ⊙6pm-1am Wed-Sat; ᵼMariatorget) Claiming the title of Stockholm's oldest gay bar, this establishment has a low-key, publike ambience and decent bar food (fish and chips, curry, quesadillas). Check online for a schedule of theme nights and events.

Nada BAR
(Map p56; ☑08-644 70 20; Åsögatan 140; ⊙5pm-1am Mon-Sat; ᵼMedborgarplatsen) With its soft orange glow, mini chandelier and decadent black-toned back bar, this cosy spot pulls Söder's 20- and 30-something party people. Nightly, DJs play everything from alternative pop to '80s retro, while behind the bar mixologists sling elaborate summery cocktails.

Bara Enkelt BAR
(Map p56; ☑08-669 58 55; www.baras.se; Skånegatan 59; ⊙4pm-1am Mon-Fri, 3pm-1am Sat & Sun; ᵼMedborgarplatsen) Decked out in colourful furniture and delightfully busy decor, Bara Enkelt (formerly Bara Vi) is a popular hang-out for trendy 30-somethings who like their drinks list long and smooth.

🍷 Further Afield

Nya Carnegie Bryggeriet BEER
(New Carnegie Brewery; ☑08-51 06 50 82; www. nyacarnegiebryggeriet.se/en; Ljusslingan 15-17,

Hammarby Sjöstad; ⊙4pm-midnight Tue-Sat; ⬛Emelie to Hammarby Sjöstad) A shiny new brewery in a shiny new part of the city, Nya Carnegie is a collaborative effort between Swedish brewmasters and New York City's Brooklyn Brewery. The building is a cool, industrial-chic behemoth right by the ferry dock in Hammarby Sjöstad, Stockholm's newest neighbourhood. Tastings are 350kr; check online for times, as well as special releases and events.

The boat *Emelie* (one-way 60kr) ferries passengers here from Nybrokajen hourly (7.50am-9.50pm Mon-Fri, from 9.50am Sat & Sun).

Slakthuset CLUB
(www.slakthuset.nu; Slakthusgatan 6; prices vary; ⊙10am-3am Fri & Sat; ⬛Globen) Consistently hosting groundbreaking DJs from Sweden and beyond, Slakthuset (The Slaughter House) is the centre of Sweden's dance and techno scene. During the warmer months, Stockholm's hippest partygoers flock to its open rooftop terrace for a daytime drink before heading downstairs as the sun slowly begins to fade. Check the website for upcoming events and tickets well in advance.

☆ Entertainment

Stockholm has a good variety of entertainment, from spectator sports to live music, theatre and opera. The city also hosts a number of festivals that are worth planning a trip around.

For an up-to-date events calendar, see www.visitstockholm.com. Another good source, if you can navigate a little Swedish, is the Friday 'På Stan' section of *Dagens Nyheter* newspaper (www.dn.se/pa-stan).

Operan OPERA
(Map p48; ☑08-791 44 00; www.operan.se; Gustav Adolfs Torg, Operahuset; tickets 240-1070kr; ⬛Kungsträdgården) The Royal Opera is the place to go for thunderous tenors, sparkling sopranos and classical ballet. It has some bargain tickets in seats with poor views, and occasional lunchtime concerts for 275kr (including light lunch).

Mosebacke Etablissement LIVE MUSIC
(Map p56; http://sodrateatern.com; Mosebacketorg 3; ⊙6pm-late; ⬛Slussen) Eclectic theatre and club nights aside, this historic culture palace hosts a mixed line-up of live music. Tunes span anything from home-grown pop to Antipodean rock. The outdoor terrace (featured in the opening scene of August Strindberg's

novel *The Red Room*) combines dazzling city views with a thumping summertime bar. It adjoins Södra Teatern and a couple of other bars.

Södra Teatern THEATRE, LIVE MUSIC
(Map p56; ☑08-53 19 94 90; www.sodrateatern.com; Mosebacketorg 1; ⊙8am-4pm Mon & Tue, to 11pm Wed & Thu, to 2am Fri, 11.30am-2am Sat, noon-4pm Sun; ⬛Slussen) Accessible from Mosebacketorg and adjoining Mosebacke Etablissement, up the winding streets of old Södermalm, Södra Teatern is the original multifunctional event space, with its assortment of bars, stages and a restaurant. Whether you're relaxing in the beer garden or simply soaking up the ornate decor, this is a great place to dine and dance, or mingle with locals. Check the website for upcoming events.

Fasching JAZZ
(Map p48; ☑08-53 48 29 60; www.fasching.se; Kungsgatan 63; ⊙6pm-1am Mon-Thu, to 4am Fri & Sat, 5pm-1am Sun; ⬛T-Centralen) Music club Fasching is the pick of Stockholm's jazz clubs, with live music most nights. DJs often take over with Afrobeat, Latin, neo-soul or R&B on Friday night and retro-soul, disco and rare grooves on Saturday.

Stampen JAZZ
(Map p44; ☑08-20 57 93; www.stampen.se; Stora Nygatan 5; cover free-200kr; ⊙5pm-1am Tue-Fri & Sun, 2pm-1am Sat; ⬛Gamla Stan) Stampen is one of Stockholm's music-club stalwarts, swinging to live jazz and blues six nights a week. The free blues jam (currently on Sundays) pulls everyone from local noodlers to the odd music legend.

Zinkensdamms Idrottsplats SPECTATOR SPORT
(www.svenskbandy.se/stockholm; Ringvägen 16; tickets around 130kr; ⬛Zinkensdamm) Watching a bandy match is great fun. A precursor to ice hockey but with more players (11 to a side) and less fighting, the sport has grown massively popular since the rise of the Hammarby team in the late '90s. The season lasts from November to March; you can buy tickets at the gate.

Folkoperan THEATRE
(Map p56; ☑08-616 07 50; www.folkoperan.se; Hornsgatan 72; tickets 145-455kr; ⬛Zinkensdamm) Folkoperan gives opera a thoroughly modern overhaul with its intimate, cutting-edge and sometimes controversial productions. The under-26s enjoy half-price

tickets. The attached restaurant-bar draws a loyal crowd on its own.

Dramaten
THEATRE

(Kungliga Dramatiska Teatern; Map p48; ☑08-667 06 80; www.dramaten.se; Nybroplan; tickets 150-450kr; ⊠Kungsträdgården) The Royal Theatre stages a range of plays in a sublime art-nouveau environment. You can also take a guided tour in English at 4pm most days (adult/child 30/60kr), bookable online. Half-price tickets may be available an hour before showtime, for those willing to gamble.

Dansens Hus
DANCE

(Map p48; ☑08-50 89 90 90; www.dansenshus.se; Barnhusgatan 12-14; tickets around 300kr, under 20yr half-price; ⊠T-Centralen) This place is an absolute must for contemporary-dance fans. Guest artists have included everyone from British choreographer Akram Khan to Canadian innovator Daniel Léveillé.

Konserthuset
CLASSICAL MUSIC

(Map p48; ☑08-50 66 77 88; www.konserthuset.se; Hötorget; tickets 85-325kr; ⊠Hötorget) Head to this pretty blue building for classical concerts and other musical marvels, including the Royal Philharmonic Orchestra. The bronze sculpture of nymphs frolicking out front (*Orpheus Well*) is by Carl Milles.

Stockholms Stadsteatern
THEATRE

(Map p48; ☑08-50 62 02 00; www.stadsteatern.stockholm.se; Kulturhuset, Sergels Torg; tickets 200-350kr; ⊠T-Centralen) Regular performances are staged at this theatre inside Kulturhuset, as well as guest appearances by foreign theatre companies. It's also the temporary home to some of the collections from the National Gallery, which is closed for renovations.

Glenn Miller Café
JAZZ, BLUES

(Map p48; ☑08-10 03 22; Brunnsgatan 21A; ⊙5pm-1am Mon-Thu, to 2am Fri & Sat; ⊠Hötorget) Simply loaded with character, this jazz-and-blues bar draws a faithful, fun-loving crowd. It also serves excellent, affordable French-style classics like mussels with white wine sauce. Live music Wednesday to Saturday.

Globen
LIVE MUSIC

(☑077-131 00 00; www.globen.se; Arenavägen; SkyView adult/child 150/100kr; ⊙SkyView 10am-6pm Mon-Fri, to 4pm Sat & Sun, to 8pm daily Jul-mid-Aug; ⊠Globen) This huge white spherical building (it looks like a giant golf ball) just south of Södermalm hosts regular big-name pop and rock concerts, as well as sporting events and trade fairs. Even if nothing's going on inside, you can take a ride up and over the building inside SkyView, a mini-globe whose glass walls offer great views across town.

🛍 Shopping

Stockholm is a seasoned shopper's paradise. For big-name Swedish and international retail outlets, hit the pedestrianised Biblioteksgatan from Östermalm to Norrmalmstorg, as well as the smaller streets that branch off it.

For slightly funkier and artier stores and galleries, head to Södermalm. And for souvenirs and postcards, check out picturesque Gamla Stan.

★Svenskt Tenn
ARTS, HOMEWARES

(Map p48; ☑08-670 16 00; www.svenskttenn.se; Nybrogatan 15; ⊙10am-6pm Mon-Fri, 10am-4pm Sat; ⊠Kungsträdgården) As much a museum of design as an actual shop, this iconic store is home to the signature fabrics and furniture of Josef Frank and his contemporaries. Browsing here is a great way to get a quick handle on what people mean by 'classic Swedish design' – and it's owned by a foundation that contributes heavily to arts funding.

★NK
DEPARTMENT STORE

(Map p48; ☑08-762 80 00; www.nk.se; Hamngatan 12-18; ⊙10am-8pm Mon-Fri, 10am-6pm Sat, 11am-5pm Sun; ⊠T-Centralen) An ultraclassy department store founded in 1902, NK (Nordiska Kompaniet) is a city landmark – you can see its rotating neon sign from most parts of Stockholm. You'll find top-name brands and several nice cafes, and the basement levels are great for stocking up on souvenirs and gourmet groceries. Around Christmas, check out its inventive window displays.

Åhléns
DEPARTMENT STORE

(Map p48; ☑08-676 60 00; Klarabergsgatan 50; ⊙10am-9pm Mon-Fri, 10am-7pm Sat, 11am-7pm Sun; ⊠T-Centralen) For your all-in-one retail therapy, scour department-store giant Åhléns. It's especially good for housewares, bedding and Swedish-made items to bring home as gifts.

E Torndahl
DESIGN

(Map p44; www.etorndahl.se; Västerlånggatan 63; ⊙10am-8pm; ⊠Gamla Stan) This spacious design shop, operated by the women of the Torndahl family since 1864, is a calm and civilised oasis on busy Västerlånggatan, offering jewellery, textiles and clever Scandinavian household objects.

DesignTorget DESIGN
(Map p56; www.designtorget.se; Götgatan 31; 10am-7pm Mon-Fri, 10am-6pm Sat, 11am-5.30pm Sun; Slussen) If you love good design but don't own a Gold Amex, head to this chain, which sells the work of emerging designers alongside established denizens. There are several other locations, including one right next to the main tourist information office in Sergels Torg.

Studio Lena M GIFTS & SOUVENIRS
(Map p44; www.studiolenam.wordpress.com; Kindstugan 14; 10am-6pm, to 5pm Sat; Gamla Stan) This tiny, dimly lit shop is chock full of adorable prints and products featuring the distinctive graphic design work of Lena M. It's a great place to find a unique – and uniquely Swedish – gift to bring home, or even just a cute postcard.

Marimekko CLOTHING, HOMEWARES
(Map p48; 08-440 32 75; www.marimekko.com; Norrmalmstorg 4; 10am-7pm Mon-Fri, to 5pm Sat; Östermalmstorg) Marimekko's bright, bold, retro patterns are the stuff of legend. And like its Swedish equivalent, the Finnish textile company has plastered almost everything with its iconic prints, from towels, cups and coasters to notebooks, bags, napkins and clothes.

Kartbutiken MAPS
(Map p48; 08-20 23 03; www.kartbutiken.se; Mäster Samuelsgatan 54; 10am-6pm Mon-Fri, 10am-4pm Sat, noon-4pm Sun; T-Centralen) This huge, helpful store has all kinds of maps and guidebooks for Scandinavia and elsewhere, from urban centres to remote hiking areas, plus a variety of gifts and gadgets. You can also ask staff about geocaching and various other map-based pursuits.

Rönnells Antikvariat BOOKS
(08-54 50 15 60; www.ronnells.se; Birger Jarlsgatan 32; 10am-6pm Mon-Fri, noon-4pm Sat; Östermalmstorg) From vintage Astrid Lindgren books to dusty 19th-century travel guides, the 100,000-strong collection of books here, many in English, make this one of the meatiest secondhand bookshops in town. Forage through the sales rack for a new dog-eared friend.

Iris Hantverk DESIGN
(Map p48; 08-21 47 26; Kungsgatan 55; 10am-8pm Mon-Fri, to 3pm Sat; T-Centralen, Hötorget) This shop has impeccably made woodwork, linens, textiles, candlesticks, handmade soaps, glassware and crafting books.

Chokladfabriken CHOCOLATE
(Map p56; www.chokladfabriken.com; Renstiernas Gata 12; 10am-6.30pm Mon-Fri, 10am-5pm Sat; Medborgarplatsen, Slussen) For an edible souvenir, head to this chocolate shop, where seasonal Nordic ingredients are used to make heavenly treats. In addition to chocolate boxes and hot-cocoa mix in gift boxes, there's a cafe for an on-the-spot fix, occasional tastings, and a stash of speciality ingredients and utensils for home baking.

WESC FASHION & ACCESSORIES
(Map p48; 08-21 25 15; www.wesc.com; Kungsgatan 66; 11am-6pm Mon-Fri, 10am-4pm Sat; Hötorget) This street-smart label got started by dressing up underground artists and muses. It has since become one of Swedish fashion's big guns, opening up stores from Seoul to Beverly Hills. The look is indie-meets-skater cool.

BLK DNM FASHION & ACCESSORIES
(Map p48; 08-678 83 00; www.blkdnm.com; Mäster Samuelsgatan 1; Östermalmstorg) Here you'll find skinny jeans, painfully hip leather jackets and other clothing worthy of strutting around Stockholm, by designer Johan Lindeberg.

Acne FASHION & ACCESSORIES
(Map p48; 08-611 64 11; www.acnestudios.com; Norrmalmstorg 2; 10am-7pm Mon-Fri, to 5pm Sat, noon-4pm Sun; Östermalmstorg) This is the flagship store for Stockholm's hottest label. Acne's threads, shoes and accessories for guys and girls cram the pages of American fashion magazines. The cult item here is the jeans, though we say good luck stopping there.

59 Vintage Store VINTAGE
(08-652 37 27; www.59vintagestore.se; Hantverkargatan 59; 11am to 6pm Mon-Fri, 11am-4pm Sat; Rådhuset) This rack-packed nirvana of retro threads will have you playing dress-up for hours. Both girls and boys can expect high-quality gear from the 1950s to the 1970s, including glam, midcentury ballgowns, platform boots, Brit-pop blazers, *Dr Zhivago* faux-fur hats and the odd sequinned sombrero.

Judits VINTAGE
(08-84 45 10; www.judits.se; Hornsgatan 75; 11am-6.30pm Mon-Fri, to 4.30pm Sat Sep-May, 11am-6pm Mon-Fri, to 4pm Sat Jun-Aug; Zinkensdamm) A highly curated and well-loved secondhand clothing store, Judits carries premier brands and organises them beauti-

SWEDISH DESIGN

Now that Ingvar Kamprad's unmistakably huge blue-and-yellow IKEA stores have sprouted up all over the world, Swedish design may have lost some of its exotic appeal. But that just means more people can know the sleek, utilitarian joy of invisible drawers, paper chandeliers and round squares.

Most of the clever designs IKEA brings to the masses originated among Stockholm's inventive designers, and you can see these artefacts in their undiluted form all over the city in museums, shops, and a few shops so exclusive they may as well be museums.

Functional elegance defines Swedish design, although in recent decades a refreshing tendency towards the whimsical has lightened the mood. For a good collection of design objects arranged chronologically and by theme, head to **Nordiska Museet** (p51). You can also find examples of both historic and contemporary design at upmarket shops like **Svenskt Tenn** (p83), home to floral fabric prints by design legend Josef Frank, and **Nordiska Galleriet** (Map p48; ☑08-442 83 60; www.nordiskagalleriet.se; Nybrogatan 11; ⊙10am-6pm Mon-Fri, to 5pm Sat; ☒Östermalmstorg), with its dizzying array of neat things to look at.

For something a little more accessible, Södermalm's main drag, Götgatan, is home to democratically priced **DesignTorget** (with several other locations around town).

fully, creating the effect of a clothing museum. It's a fun place to browse even if your budget doesn't quite stretch far enough for a vintage Acne jacket.

Grandpa ACCESSORIES, CLOTHING
(☑08-643 60 81; www.grandpa.se; Fridhemsgatan 43; ⊙11am-7pm Mon-Fri, to 5pm Sat, noon-4pm Sun; ☒Fridhemsplan) With a design inspired by the hotels of the French Riviera during the '70s, Grandpa's second Stockholm location is crammed with atmosphere, as well as artfully chosen vintage and faux-vintage clothing, cool and quirky accessories and whatnots, random hairdryers, suitcases and old radios, plus a cool little cafe serving good espresso.

Lisa Larsson Second Hand VINTAGE
(Map p56; ☑08-643 61 53; Bondegatan 48; ⊙1-6pm Tue-Fri, 11am-3pm Sat; ☒Medborgarplatsen) A local fave among Södermalm's stylish thrift shops, this small space is packed with treasures dating from the '30s to the '70s. Look for leather jackets, handbags, shoes and vintage dresses.

Naturkompaniet SPORTS & OUTDOORS
(Map p48; www.naturkompaniet.se; Kungsgatan 4; ⊙10am-6.30pm Mon-Fri, 10am-5pm Sat, noon-4pm Sun; ☒Östermalmstorg) Find everything you might need for an excursion into the Swedish wilderness here, from backpacks and sleeping bags to woolly socks, headlamps, cooking stoves and compasses. There are several other locations across the city.

English Bookshop BOOKS
(Map p56; ☑08-790 55 10; Södermannagatan 22; ⊙10am-6.30pm Mon-Fri, to 5pm Sat, noon-3pm

Sun; ☒Medgorbarplatsen) Excellent bookshop with secondhand and new titles, storytelling for kids, regular book signings (including Nell Zink of *The Wallcreeper* fame), writing workshops and plenty of seating space for perusing the pages.

Science Fiction Bookshop BOOKS
(Map p44; www.sfbok.se; Västerlånggatan 48; ⊙10am-7pm Mon-Fri, to 5pm Sat, noon-5pm Sun; ☒Gamla Stan) In some ways this seems an unlikely location for a science fiction–fantasy comic bookshop, but in other ways it makes perfect sense. Regardless, this is the place to come for comics and graphic novels both mainstream and obscure (in English and Swedish), as well as books, games, toys and posters. Friendly staff will help you hunt down treasures.

Papercut BOOKS
(☑08-13 35 74; www.papercutshop.se; Krukmakargatan 24; ⊙11am-6.30pm Mon-Fri, 11am-5pm Sat, noon-4pm Sun, closed Sun Jul; ☒Zinkensdamm) This artfully curated shop sells books, magazines and DVDs with a high-end pop-culture focus. Pick up a new Field Notes journal and a decadent film journal or a gorgeous volume devoted to one of the many elements of style.

Mall of Scandinavia MALL
(☑08-40 00 80 00; www.mallofscandinavia.se/en; Stjärntorget 2; ⊙shops 10am to 9pm, restaurants to 10pm; ☐67, 103, 176, 177, 502, 505, 508, 509, 515, ☒Solna) Opened in November 2015, this modern, spacious mall houses 224 stores and features some of the best-known Swedish and

international brands including Björn Borg, Naturkompaniet and J. Lindeberg. Mall of Scandinavia also has an IMAX cinema and a number of restaurants catering to a wide variety of tastes.

Gallerian MALL
(Map p48; 08-53 33 73 00; Hamngatan 37; ⊙10am-8pm Mon-Fri, to 6pm Sat, 11am to 6pm Sun; ⦿T-Centralen) Stockholm's first shopping mall, Gallerian is right in the middle of the city's shopping districts. It hosts some of Sweden's best-known brands as well as international favourites. A great opportunity to update your wardrobe with some Swedish style or a central point to take a break.

ⓘ Information

EMERGENCY

Sweden's country code	📞46
24-hour medical advice	📞08-32 01 00
AutoAssistans (roadside assistance)	📞020-53 65 36
Emergency	📞112

INTERNET ACCESS

Nearly all hostels and most hotels have a computer with internet access for guests, and most offer wi-fi in rooms (though some hotels charge a fee). There is also wi-fi in Centralstationen, and most coffee shops offer free wi-fi to customers.

MEDIA

Dagens Nyheter (www.dn.se) Daily paper with a great culture section and a weekend event listing ('På Stan'). The website (in Swedish) is a good place to look for bar and restaurant news.

Nöjesguiden (www.nojesguiden.se) Entertainment and pop-culture news and event listings.

Svenska Dagbladet (www.svd.se) Daily news, in Swedish.

MEDICAL SERVICES

Apoteket CW Scheele (www.apoteket.se; Klarabergsgatan 64; ⦿T-Centralen) A 24-hour pharmacy located close to T-Centralen.

CityAkuten (📞010-601 00 00; www.city akuten.se; Apelbergsgatan 48; ⊙8am-5pm) Emergency health and dental care.

Södersjukhuset (📞08-616 10 00; www.sodersjukhuset.se; Ringvägen 52; ⦿Skanstull) The most central hospital.

MONEY

ATMs are plentiful, but many businesses in Stockholm are now cash-free and accept payment by credit or debit card only.

POST

You can buy stamps and send letters at most newsagents and supermarkets – keep an eye out for the Swedish postal symbol (yellow on a blue background). There's a convenient outlet next to the Hemköp supermarket in the basement of central department store **Åhléns.** (p83)

TELEPHONE

Smartphones are ubiquitous in Stockholm; coin-operated public telephones are virtually nonexistent. To call abroad from Sweden, dial zero and the country code. Within Sweden, dial the full area code including zero.

In many cases you can buy a local SIM card to use in your own mobile phone (check with your provider). Barring that, it may be worthwhile to buy a cheap mobile phone you can load with prepaid minutes and use as needed. The main providers are Tre, Telia, Comviq and Telenor. You can buy SIM cards from Pressbyrå locations, including at Arlanda Airport.

TOURIST INFORMATION

Stockholm Visitors Center (Map p48; 📞08-50 82 85 08; www.visitstockholm.com; Kulturhuset, Sergels Torg 3; ⊙9am-7pm Mon-Fri, 9am-4pm Sat, 10am-4pm Sun May–mid-Sep, shorter hours rest of year; ☎; ⦿T-Centralen) The main visitors centre occupies a space inside Kulturhuset on Sergels Torg.

ⓘ Getting There & Away

AIR

Stockholm Arlanda Airport (ARN; 📞10-109 10 00; www.swedavia.se/arlanda) Stockholm's main airport, 45km north of the city centre, is reached from central Stockholm by bus, local train and express train. Terminals two and five are for international flights; three and four are domestic; there is no terminal one.

Left Luggage Stockholm Arlanda Airport has self-service lockers for luggage storage (small/large locker for 24 hours 70/90kr), payable with a credit card. There's also a baggage counter.

Bromma Airport (BMA; 📞010-109 40 00; www.swedavia.se/bromma; Ulvsundavägen; ⦿Brommaplan) Located 8km west of the city centre, Bromma is handy for domestic flights but services only a handful of airlines, primarily British Airways, Brussels Airlines and Finnair.

Stockholm Skavsta Airport (Nyköping; NYO; 📞0155-28 04 00; www.skavsta.se/en; General Schybergs Plan 22, Nyköping; ⦿Flygbussarna) Small airport 100km southwest of Stockholm, near Nyköping, served by low-cost carriers Ryanair and WizzAir.

BOAT

The main ferry lines with routes from Stockholm are **Silja Line** (Map p48; 📞08-22 21 40; www.

tallinksilja.com; Silja & Tallink Customer Service Office, Cityterminalen; ⊙9am-6pm Mon-Fri, to 3pm Sat) and **Viking Line** (p331), which operate a regular ferry line to both Turku and Helsinki in Finland. **Tallink** (p331) ferries head to Tallinn (Estonia) and Riga (Latvia).

BUS

Most long-distance buses arrive at and depart from **Cityterminalen** (Map p48; www.city terminalen.com; ⊙7am-6pm), which is connected to Centralstationen. The main counter sells tickets for several bus companies, including **Flygbuss** (airport coaches), **Swebus** (Map p48; www.swebus.se) and **Ybuss** (Map p48; www. ybuss.se). You can also buy tickets from Pressbyrå shops and ticket machines. Destinations include:

Gothenburg from 419kr, six hours, eight daily
Halmstad from 569kr, 12 hours, two daily
Jönköping from 269kr, five hours, six daily
Malmö from 549kr, 8½ hours, two to four times daily
Nyköping from 89kr, two hours, eight daily
Uppsala 79kr, one hour, six daily

CAR & MOTORCYCLE

The E4 motorway passes through the city, just west of the centre, on its way from Helsingborg to Haparanda. The E20 motorway from Stockholm to Gothenburg via Örebro follows the E4 as far as Södertälje. The E18 from Kapellskär to Oslo runs from east to west and passes just north of central Stockholm.

Car hire companies have offices at Arlanda airport, near Centralstationen and elsewhere in town.

TRAIN

Stockholm is the hub for national train services run by **Sveriges Järnväg** (SJ; ☑ 0771-75 75 75; www. sj.se), with a network of services that covers all the major towns and cities, as well as services to the rest of Scandinavia. Destinations include:

Gällivare from 795kr, 15 hours, one daily
Gothenburg from 422kr, three to five hours, hourly
Jönköping from 696kr, 3½ hours, one daily
Kiruna from 795kr, 17 hours, one daily
Lund from 632kr, 4½ hours, four daily
Malmö from 632kr, five hours, frequent
Oslo from 1000kr, five hours, four daily
Uppsala from 95kr, 35 to 55 minutes, frequent

Centralstationen's lower level has left luggage lockers (small/large locker for 24 hours 70/90kr).

ⓘ Getting Around

TO/FROM ARLANDA AIRPORT

Arlanda Express (www.arlandaexpress.com; Centralstationen; one-way adult/child 280/150kr,

2 adults one-way in summer 350kr; ⊠ Centralen) Trains between the airport and Centralstationen run every 10 to 15 minutes 5am to 12.30am (less frequently after 9pm), taking 20 minutes.

Flygbussarna (Map p48; www.flygbussarna. se; Cityterminalen; ⊠ Centralen) Buses to/from Cityterminalen leave from stop 11 in Terminal 5 every 10 to 15 minutes (adult/child one-way 119/99kr, 40 minutes). Tickets can be purchased online, at Cityterminalen or at the Flygbuss self-service machine in Terminal 5.

Airport Cab (☑ 08-25 25 25; www.airportcab. se), **Sverige Taxi** (p88), **Taxi Stockholm** (p88) Reliable taxi services.

TO/FROM BROMMA AIRPORT

Flygbussarna Runs to/from Cityterminalen every 20 to 30 minutes (adult/child 85/69kr, 20 minutes).

TO/FROM SKAVSTA AIRPORT

Flygbussarna Runs to/from Cityterminalen every 30 minutes (adult/child 159/135kr, one hour 20 minutes).

BICYCLE

Bicycles can be carried free on SL local trains as foldable 'hand luggage' only. They're not allowed in Centralstationen or on the tunnelbana (metro), although you'll occasionally see some daring souls.

Stockholm City Bikes (www.citybikes.se; 3-day/season card 165/300kr) has self-service bicycle-hire stands across the city. Bikes can be borrowed for three-hour stretches and returned at any City Bikes stand. Purchase a bike card online or from the tourist office. Rechargeable season cards are valid April to October.

BOAT

Djurgårdsfärjan city ferry services connect Gröna Lund Tivoli on Djurgården with Nybroplan (summer only) and Slussen (year round) as frequently as every 10 minutes in summer; SL transport passes and tickets apply.

CAR & MOTORCYCLE

Driving in central Stockholm is not recommended. Skinny one-way streets, congested bridges and limited parking all present problems; note that Djurgårdsvägen is closed near Skansen at night, on summer weekends and some holidays. Don't attempt driving through the narrow streets of Gamla Stan.

Parking is a hassle, but there are *P-hus* (parking stations) throughout the city; they charge up to 100kr per hour, though the fixed evening rate is usually lower.

PUBLIC TRANSPORT

Storstockholms Lokaltrafik (SL; ☑ 08-600 10 00; www.sl.se; Centralstationen; ⊙SL Center Sergels Torg 7am-6.30pm Mon-Fri,

10am-5pm Sat & Sun, inside Centralstationen 6.30am-11.45pm Mon-Sat, from 7am Sun) runs the tunnelbana (metro), local trains and buses within Stockholm county. You can buy tickets and passes at SL counters, ticket machines at tunnelbana stations and Pressbyrå kiosks. Refillable SL travel cards (20kr) can be loaded with single-trip or unlimited-travel credit. Fines are steep (1500kr) for travelling without a valid ticket.

➡ The city's **Tunnelbana** underground rail system is efficient and extensive.

➡ Local **buses** thoroughly cover the city and surrounds.

➡ **Tram** lines serve Djurgården from Norrmalm.

➡ In summer, **ferries** are the best way to get to Djurgården, and they serve the archipelago year-round.

➡ The same tickets are valid on the tunnelbana, local trains and buses within Stockholm County, and some local ferry routes.

➡ Single tickets are available, but if you're travelling more than once or twice it's better to get a refillable Access card.

➡ Keep tickets with you throughout your journey.

➡ A single ticket costs 30-60kr and is valid for 75 minutes; it covers return trips and transfers between bus and metro.

➡ A 24hr/72hr/7-day pass costs 120/240/315kr for an adult, and 80/160/210kr for a child. Add another 20kr for a refillable Access card.

TAXI

Taxis are readily available but fees are unregulated – be sure to check for a meter or arrange the fare first. Use one of the established, reputable firms, such as **Taxi Stockholm** (☑ 15 00 00; www.taxistockholm.se) or **Sverige Taxi** (☑ 020-20 20 20; www.sverigetaxi.se). The ridesharing company **Uber** (www.uber.com) also covers Stockholm.

AROUND STOCKHOLM

With royal palaces, vintage villages and Viking traces, the greater Stockholm county is certainly worth a venture or three. Conveniently, SL travel passes allow unlimited travel on all buses and local trains in the area. Free timetables are available from the SL office in Centralstationen, most tunnelbana stations and the SL website.

Just to the east of Stockholm, the magical islands of the Stockholm archipelago have inspired the likes of writer August Strindberg and artist Anders Zorn. Ferry services aren't expensive and there's a travel pass available if you fancy a spot of island-hopping.

Drottningholm

The royal residence and parks of Drottningholm on Lovön are justifiably popular attractions and easy to visit from Stockholm city centre.

◉ Sights

★ **Drottningholm Slott**   PALACE
(☑ 08-402 62 80; www.kungahuset.se; Ekerö; adult/child 130/65kr, combined ticket incl Kina Slott 190/90kr; ⊙ 10am-4.30pm May-Sep, 11am-3.30pm Oct & Apr, noon-3.30pm Sat & Sun rest of year (closed mid-Dec–Jan); 🅿; ⛴ Stadshuskajen (summer only), 🚇 Brommaplan, then bus 301-323 Drottningholm) Home to the royal family for part of the year, Drottningholm's Renaissance-inspired main palace was designed by architectural great Nicodemus Tessin the Elder and begun in 1662, about the same time as Versailles. You can roam around the palace on your own, but it's well worth taking a one-hour guided tour (30kr; in English at 10am, noon, 2pm and 4pm June to August, noon and 2pm other months). Guides are entertaining, and provide insight into the cultural milieu that influenced some of the decorations.

The Lower North Corps de Garde was originally a guard room, but it's now replete with gilt-leather wall hangings, which used to feature in many palace rooms during the 17th century. The Karl X Gustav Gallery, in baroque style, depicts this monarch's militaristic exploits, though the ceiling shows classical battle scenes. The highly ornamented State Bedchamber of Hedvig Eleonora is Sweden's most expensive baroque interior, decorated with paintings that feature the childhood of Karl XI. The painted ceiling shows Karl X and his queen, Hedvig Eleonora.

Although the bulk of Lovisa Ulrika's collection of 2000 books has been moved to the Royal Library in Stockholm for safekeeping, her library here is still a bright and impressive room, complete with most of its original 18th-century fittings.

The palace's elaborate staircase, with statues and trompe l'oeil embellishments at every turn, was the work of both Nicodemus Tessin the Elder and the Younger. The geometric gardens, angled to impress, are well worth exploring.

Kina Slott   CASTLE
(Chinese Pavilion; adult/child 100/50kr, combined ticket incl royal palace 190/90kr; ⊙ 11am-4.30pm

Drottningholm

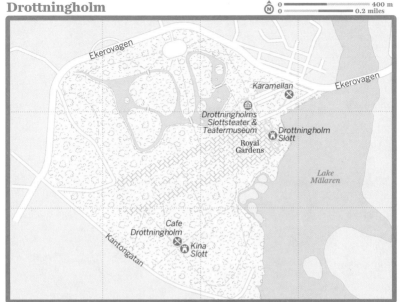

May-Sep) At the far end of the royal gardens is Kina Slott, a lavishly decorated Chinese pavilion built by King Adolf Fredrik as a birthday surprise for Queen Lovisa Ulrika in 1753. Restored between 1989 and 1996, it boasts one of the finest rococo chinoiserie interiors in Europe. The admission price includes guided tours, which run at 11am, 1pm and 3pm daily from June to August (fewer in May and September). There's a cafe on the premises serving good waffles.

Drottningholms Slottsteater & Teatermuseum
MUSEUM

(Court Theatre & Museum; www.dtm.se; entry by tour adult/child 100/70kr; ⊙tours hourly noon-3.30pm Fri-Sun Oct & Apr, noon-3.30pm Sat & Sun Nov & Mar, 11am-4.30pm May-Aug, 11am-3.30pm Sep) Slottsteater was completed in 1766 on the instructions of Queen Lovisa Ulrika. Remarkably untouched from the time of Gustav III's death (1792) until 1922, it's now the oldest theatre in the world still in its original state. The fascinating guided tour takes you into other rooms in the building, where highlights include hand-painted 18th-century wallpaper and an Italianate room (*salon de déjeuner*) with fake three-dimensional wall effects and a ceiling that looks like the sky.

🍴 Eating

Cafe Drottningholm
SWEDISH €

(🗷08-759 03 96; Kantongatan; waffles 65kr; ⊙9am-4.30pm May-Sep) Next to Kina Slott, this cute cafe in a low-ceilinged old stone building serves coffee and good waffles with jam; outdoor tables are available.

Karamellan
SWEDISH €€

(Drottningholms Slottskafé; 🗷08-759 00 35; www.drottningholm.org; Drottningholm; mains 89-215kr; ⊙9.30am-5pm May-Sep, 11am-4pm Sat & Sun rest of year) Within the palace grounds, this cafe-restaurant serves coffee and pastries as well as full meals, with both indoor and outdoor seating for plenty of atmosphere.

ℹ️ Getting There & Away

Bicycle If you have time, you can cycle out to the palace along a well-marked path (roughly 13km).

Tunnelbana To Brommaplan, then change to any bus numbered between 301 and 323 (SL passes are valid).

Boat For a more scenic and leisurely approach, Strömma Kanalbolaget (p64) will take you to the palace by boat (two hours; round trip 210kr). Departs frequently from Stadshusbron (Stockholm) daily between May and mid-September, with less frequent departures in September and October.

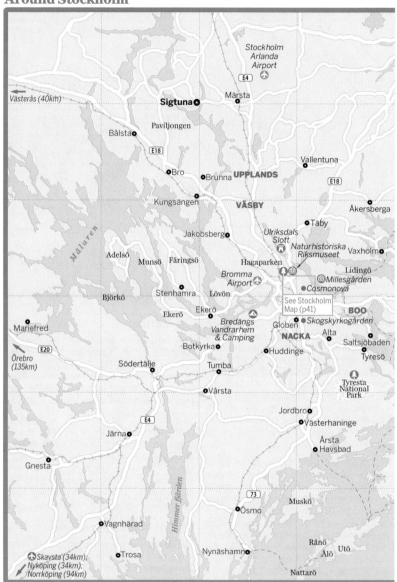

Stockholm Archipelago

Mention the archipelago to Stockholmers and prepare for gushing adulation – well-deserved, too. Buffering the city from the open Baltic Sea, it's a mesmerising wonder-land of rocky isles carpeted with deep forests and fields of wildflowers, dotted with yachts and picturesque red wooden cottages.

Exactly how many islands there are is debatable, with the count ranging from 14,000 to 100,000 (the general consensus is 24,000).

worth staying overnight and exploring if you have the time.

Most have good boat connections. Check timings in advance – although there are worse places in the world to get stranded!

ℹ️ Getting There & Around

Waxholmsbolaget (Map p48; ☎ 08-600 10 00; www.waxholmsbolaget.com/visitor; Strömkajen; ⊗ 7am-2pm Mon, 8am-2pm Tue-Thu, 7.30am-4.30pm Fri, 8am-noon Sat, 8.30am-noon Sun; ⊠ Kungsträdgården) in Stockholm runs most archipelago ferries plus tours on antique steamboats (adult 47-140kr, child 35-92kr, 5-/30-day pass 445/790kr). Timetables are available online or from offices on Strömkajen and at Vaxholm harbour. Also runs ferries to and from Djurgården in summer. Buy tickets onboard and hand them over when you disembark.

Strömma Kanalbolaget operates boats to and from various islands in the archipelago, as well as themed tours, including the full-day **Thousand Island Cruise** (Map p48; ☎ 08-12 00 40 00; www.stromma.se/en/stockholm/excursions; Nybrokajen; per person 1235-1450kr; ⊗ 9.30am Tue-Sun Jul–mid-Aug).

Vaxholm

There are plenty of reasons to come to Vaxholm, the most obvious being that this is the closest archipelago island to Stockholm and thus provides a charming taster to this extraordinarily diverse array of pine-clad islands and islets. Vaxholm is more than just a gateway, however. With cobbled sloping streets flanked by well-preserved wooden houses painted in candy-coloured pastels, plus a slew of excellent restaurants and idiosyncratic family-owned shops, it holds its own as a charming place to visit.

Vaxholm dates from 1647; to glean a sense of its history head to Norrhamn, just north of the town hall and home to the oldest buildings.

👁 Sights

Hembygdsgård   MUSEUM
(☎ 08-54 13 19 80; Trädgårdsgatan 19; ⊗ 11am-5pm May–mid-Sep) 🆓 The Hembygdsgård preserves the finest old houses in Norrhamn. The fiskarebostad is an excellent example of a late-19th-century fisherman's house, complete with typical Swedish fireplace. The award-winning cafe here is open daily from mid-May to mid-September (mains 145kr to 175kr).

Whatever the number, it's an unmissable area, unique in the world and much closer to the city than many visitors imagine (Vaxholm is less than an hour away), with regular ferry services and various tours. You can see most of the islands on day trips, but it's

Vaxholm Fortress Museum
HISTORIC SITE, MUSEUM

(☑ 08-54 17 18 90; www.vaxholmsfastning.se; Vaxholm Kastellet; adult/child 80kr/free; ☺ noon-4pm May-Jun, 11am-5pm Jul & Aug, noon-5pm Sep) King Gustav Vasa ordered the construction of Vaxholm Fortress in 1544 to protect the Swedish capital and mainland. It repelled an attack by the Danes in 1612 and the Russians in 1719, among others. It was a prison from the mid-18th century until 1842. Occupying an islet just east of town, it's now home to a museum and a B&B. The ferry to the island leaves Vaxholm harbour every 20 minutes from 11am to 5pm and costs 50kr return.

🛏 Sleeping & Eating

Vaxholm/Bogesunds Slottsvandrarhem
HOSTEL €

(☑ 08-54 17 50 60; www.bogesundsslottsvandrarhem.se; Bogesunds Gård; s 430-525kr, d per person 280-375kr, B&B from 475kr; P @ 🛜; 🚌 681 Bogesunds Gård) Behind Bogesunds Castle 5.5km southwest of Vaxholm town, this pleasant STF hostel has a pretty, farmlike setting. There's a nice guest kitchen, but you'll need to get groceries in Vaxholm. Bus service to the hostel is infrequent even in summer; buses depart Vaxholm's Söderhamnsplan at 11am, 2.12pm, 5.20pm and 6.40pm Monday to Friday, and 11.40am, 2.40pm and 5.40pm on weekends.

Waxholms Hotell
HISTORIC HOTEL €€€

(☑ 08-54 43 07 00; www.waxholmshotell.se; Hamngatan 2; r from 2300kr; P 🛜) This mid-20th-century hotel has a grand facade that overlooks the harbour; try to snag a room with a balcony to appreciate the breathtaking views. Rooms are simple and spotless, with parquet floors, maritime-themed artwork and pale fabrics. The breakfast buffet should set you up well for the morning with a fine array of hot and cold choices. There's no lift.

Bistro Magasinet
SWEDISH €€

(☑ 08-54 13 25 00; www.magasinetwaxholm.se; Fiskaregatan 1; mains 145-175kr; ☺ 11am-10pm; 🛜 🍴) 🖉 The produce here is mainly organic and the menu has plenty of vegetarian options. Our local informant swears by the excellent seafood soup with crayfish on the side, but the salmon and goat's cheese pie is equally divine. There are also tasty colourful salads topped with fresh seasonal fruit. Head to the second floor for unparalleled views of the fortress.

Waxholms Hotell
SWEDISH €€

(☑ 08-54 13 01 50; www.waxholmshotell.se; Hamngatan 2; buffet 395kr, mains 169-305kr; ☺ noon-10.30pm Mon-Sat, to 9pm Sun) In a historic building located opposite the harbour, grand Waxholms offers fine dining and unbelievable views. Grab a pint in the vaguely British woodsman-esque lobby bar or head upstairs to the formal dining room. In summer, stop for lunch on the popular outdoor terrace at Kabyssen bar-cafe – the fish dishes are highly recommended (Baltic herring is a speciality).

Utö

Star of the archipelago's southern section, tiny Utö was once an active mining community. Today, the history and architecture live on, but the island also offers plenty of up-to-the-minute activities.

The mostly flat island, lush with fairy-tale forests, is particularly suited to low-impact cycling and walking – there's a delightful 3.5km nature trail with information on the local fauna and flora along the way. The island is also popular for sailing, fishing or simply flopping on a tranquil sandy beach. Like much of the archipelago, Utö is on the migratory path for a variety of seabirds, as well as the snow goose and the more unusual Arctic puffin, so it is a popular destination with birdwatchers.

For the best views, head to the Dutch-style windmill on Kvarnbacken hill, 10 minutes' walk from the harbour.

👁 Sights & Activities

Iron Mine
MINE

(Utö Gruvbryggan, Haninge; ☺ 24hr) The most unusual of Utö's sights is the remains of Sweden's oldest iron mine, which opened in 1150 and closed in 1879. The three pits are now flooded – the deepest is Nyköpingsgruvan (215m). They're an atmospheric and impressive sight. The tiny mining museum (in a wooden cottage opposite the Värdshus hotel) keeps variable hours (roughly 11am to 3pm in summer); check locally.

Stora Sand
BEACH

The best sandy beach is Stora Sand on the south coast; it's a gorgeous 40-minute bike ride from the Värdshus hotel. Routes to the beach are occasionally closed due to military training exercises; ask at the tourist office or Värdshus front desk for updates.

🛏 Sleeping & Eating

Utö Värdshus
HOTEL, HOSTEL, CABINS €€

(☑08-50 42 03 00; www.utovardshus.se; Gruvbryggan; r hostel/hotel from 690/1600kr) This is the only hotel on the island, with good facilities and a sterling gourmet restaurant (closed January; mains from 200kr). It also runs the very pretty **STF hostel**, with comfy bunks in smallish rooms overlooking the picturesque harbour. Note there's no lift, and rooms on four floors. Hostellers can purchase the hotel's elaborate breakfast buffet for 150kr.

Utö Bageri
BAKERY €€

(Gruvbryggan; breakfast 85-145kr, lunch from 150kr, sandwiches 45-95kr; ⊙8am-5pm) This adorable bakery in a cottage by the harbour serves one of the best cups of coffee in Sweden, as well as champion baked goods; don't pass up the cardamom *bulle* (bun), delicious and filling sandwiches (perfect if you're on the go), fruit smoothies and hot meals. Show up before 9am or so to beat the crowds.

Nya Dannekrogen
EUROPEAN €€

(☑08-50 15 70 79; www.nyadannekrogen.se; Bygatan 1; mains 180-295kr, pizzas from 135kr; ⊙May-Sep) Near the Gruvbryggan harbour, this lively restaurant looks formal but has a young, casual vibe, with grub ranging from hearty fish stew to quinoa salad. The fried herring (180kr) with lingonberries and mashed potatoes is recommended; weirdly, pizza seems to be the most popular thing on the menu.

Arholma

Situated in the northern part of the Stockholm archipelago, Arholma barely survived a Russian invasion in 1719, when everything was burnt to the ground and all the villagers fled. Today it is one of the prettiest islands in the archipelago, with some fine historic houses and farms reflecting the traditional architecture of the region; many are summer homes for mainland Swedes.

The entire island is a nature reserve, well-geared towards activities, with hiking trails, cycle paths, kayaking routes and even a zip line; the latter has a stunning forest setting. Added to this are fine sandy beaches and tranquil rocky bathing spots.

On a more cultural note, the landmark lighthouse is home to a fine art gallery, while the church is also a venue for art, showcasing the work of local artist Harald Lindberg. Arholma is also the departure point for sailors heading for Åland and mainland Finland.

◉ Sights

Batteri Arholma
HISTORIC SITE

(www.roslagen.se; Riddarviksvägen 40, Arholma Nord; adult/child 145/75kr; ⊙tours at 10.30am, 11.45am, 1.30pm & 2.45pm late Jun–mid-Aug) Fans of military history can tour this formerly top-secret Cold War–era base, complete with cannons aimed at sea and underground living space for 340 men. There is information in English, but if you book ahead you can usually arrange an English tour. The views are amazing, whether you opt to delve further or not.

🛏 Sleeping & Eating

★ STF Arholma/ Bull-August Gård
HOSTEL €

(☑0176-560 50; https://bullaugust.com; Arholma Södra Byväg 8; d from 650kr, breakfast 80kr; P🛜) This comfortable hostel on beautiful grounds is a treat. Rooms are in a refurbished old homestead about 1km from the harbour, some in the main house and some in rustic wooden side buildings. The guest kitchen is huge and modern, and there's a TV room, laundry, bicycle rental, a sunny grassy courtyard and a good breakfast.

Arholma Nord Archipelago Lodge
HOSTEL €€

(☑0176-560 40; www.arholmanord.se; Riddarviken; s/d/q from 596/995/1090kr; ⊙year-round; P🛜) This hotel-hostel complex offers a variety of accommodation, most in simple bunk rooms but also a few really nice cabins. Price includes breakfast and bedding. There's a sauna, outdoor grill, bicycle and kayak rentals (from 150/350kr), small restaurant and beach access. Tours to Arholma's Cold War defence battery are booked here. It's about 1.2km from the harbour, well signposted.

Arholma Dansbana
SWEDISH €€€

(☑073-521 55 01; www.arholmadansbana.se; Norra Bryggan 7; mains 165-265kr; ⊙11am-9pm mid-Jun–mid-Aug) The only dining option near the harbour, this hilltop restaurant offers amazing views from its glassed-in dining room as well as a few outdoor tables. Seating is arranged around a dance floor (hence the name), which can get lively on summer weekend nights. The menu is brief but well executed; try the seafood stew or the *röding* (Arctic char).

Finnhamn

This 900m-long island, northeast of Stockholm, combines lush woods and meadows with sheltered coves, rocky cliffs and visiting eagle owls. It's a popular summertime spot, but there are enough quiet corners to indulge your inner hermit.

There's a sauna (100kr per person per hour) near the beach that can be booked through the hostel. You can rent kayaks, canoes and SUPs at a kiosk at Paradisviken, in the middle of the island (per day rowboats 300kr, kayaks 500kr, SUPs 950kr). Walking trails cover most of the island, taking in awesome panoramic views at various points.

🛏 Sleeping & Eating

STF Vandrarhem Utsikten HOSTEL €
(☑ 08-54 24 62 12; www.finnhamn.se; 2-/3-/4-bed r 820/1050/1250kr, 2-/4-bed cabins 820/890kr, breakfast 100kr; ☉ year-round; @ 🛜) This hostel in a large wooden villa has a killer view, tiny rooms and cheerful staff who go above and beyond. It's an old building, which means no lift and no soundproofing; if crowded it can get noisy. But it's fun and lively and an excellent base for exploring the island. Advance booking is essential.

The hostel is about 1km along a rough dirt track, well signposted from the harbour. If you have a ton of luggage, you can ask one of the ATV drivers at the ferry dock to haul it up. It also has 'sea cabins' just outside the hostel. Campsites nearby cost 120kr per night (limited space). Breakfast is available at the hostel, but there's also a good guest kitchen.

★ Finnhamns Café & Krog SWEDISH €€
(☑ 08-54 24 62 12; www.finnhamn.se; Ingmarsö; lunch mains 145-165kr, dinner mains 165-285kr; ☉ 11.30am-9pm Fri & Sat, to 4.30pm Sun May & Sep) 🌿 The kitchen and service at Finnhamns Krog, steps away from the ferry dock, are top notch: classy yet comfortable, and capable of transforming seafood into gold. Try the pickled-herring platter ('SOS'), or the daily lunch special (choose among meat, fish or vegetarian – you can't go wrong with fish). Sustainable ingredients are a priority. Reservations are recommended for dinner.

There's also a rooftop bar here in summer, with live music on some weekend nights and a good selection of Swedish beers.

Siaröfortet

The tiny island of Kyrkogårdsön, in the important sea lane just north of Ljusterö (40km due northeast of Stockholm), is one of the archipelago's most fascinating islands, and easy to visit on a day trip.

The ferry stop, Siaröfortet, is named for a fortress built here in 1916, when, after the outbreak of WWI, military authorities decided that the Vaxholm fortress just didn't cut it. The fortress and its museum are the main draw, but the island is also one of several in the archipelago that was used as a cemetery (*kyrkogård*) for victims of cholera, and the graveyard site can still be visited.

There's also great swimming, canoes for rent, boules and a sauna (adult/child 95/60kr, book at the hostel). It's a popular stop for parents; kids can basically be turned loose on arrival, although the signs warning of barbed wire and other scraps of military history aren't kidding around.

Kapellskär

Kapellskär is so tiny it can't really even be described as a village – there's little to it except for a campsite, a hostel and a large ferry terminal. The coastline, however, is spectacular, dotted with small fishing villages, and the surrounding countryside is delightfully pastoral. Most people come here for ferry connections to Finland and Estonia.

There's also a small memorial for the 852 passengers killed in the Estonia ferry disaster of September 1994; it's up the hill across the main road from the ferry terminal.

Viking Line's direct bus from Stockholm Cityterminalen to meet the ferries costs 65kr, but if you have an SL pass take bus 676 from Tekniska Högskolan tunnelbana station to Norrtälje and change to bus 631, which runs every two hours or so weekdays (three times Saturday and once Sunday).

Sigtuna

Just 40km northwest of Stockholm, Sigtuna is one of the cutest, most historically relevant villages in the area. Founded around AD 980, it's the oldest surviving town in Sweden, and the main drag, Storagatan, is very likely Sweden's oldest main street.

Around the year 1000, Olof Skötkonung ordered the minting of Sweden's first coins in the town, and ancient church ruins and rune stones are scattered everywhere.

👁 Sights

Mariakyrkan CHURCH
(Uppsalavägen; ☉ 9am-5pm) During medieval times, Sigtuna boasted seven stone-built churches, though most have since crumbled.

TYRESTA NATIONAL PARK

Some of the best hiking and wilderness scenery can be found in the 4900-hectare **Tyresta National Park** (National Parks Naturum; ☑ 08-745 33 94; www.tyresta.se; Tyresta by; guided hikes adult/child 40kr/free; ☉ visitor centre 9am-4pm Tue-Fri, 10am-5pm Sat & Sun; ⓟ; 🚍 834, 807, 809, 🚍 Haninge centrum), only 20km southeast of Stockholm. Established in 1993, the park is noted for its two-billion-year-old rocks and virgin forest, which includes 300-year-old pine trees. It's a beautiful area, with rocky outcrops, small lakes, marshes and a wide variety of bird life. Don't miss **Naturum**, an exhibition centre where you can learn about all 29 of Sweden's national parks through exhibitions and slide shows.

The centre itself is built in the shape of Sweden, complete with all 41 corners! There are even 'lakes' on the floor, indicated by different stones. Ask for the national park leaflet in English and the *Tyresta Nationalpark och Naturreservat* leaflet in Swedish, which includes an excellent topographical map at 1:25,000 scale. From the visitor centre there are various trails into the park; 45-minute guided hikes discussing the park's history and nature leave from the visitor centre at 10am daily June to August. Sörmlandsleden track cuts across 6km of the park on its way to central Stockholm.

The easiest way to reach the park is by car: exit south onto route 73 (signposted Nynäshamn). After about 15km exit right to Haninge, then turn left at the first T-junction. At the roundabout, take the first exit to Brandbergen and follow the signs.

By public transport, take the *pendeltåg* (commuter train) to Haninge centrum on the Nynäshamn line, then change to bus 834. You can also take bus 807 or 809 from Gullmarsplan tunnelbana station. Some buses run all the way to the park, while others stop at Svartbäcken (2km west of Tyresta village).

Mariakyrkan is the oldest brick building in the area – it was a Dominican monastery church from around 1250 but became the parish church in 1529 after the monastery was demolished by Gustav Vasa. Pop in for restored medieval paintings and free weekly concerts in summer.

Rosersbergs Slott　　　　　CASTLE
(☑ 08-59 03 50 39; www.kungahuset.se; adult/child 100/50kr; ☉ tours hourly 11am-4pm Jun-Aug, Sat & Sun only May & Sep; 🚍 J-Slottsvägen, Rosersberg) Rosersbergs Slott is on lake Mälaren about 9km southeast of Sigtuna. Built in the 1630s, it was used as a royal residence from 1762 to 1860; the interior boasts exquisite furnishings from the Empire period (1790–1820) and is noted for its textiles. Highlights include the lavishly draped State Bedchamber and Queen Hedvig Elisabeth Charlotta's conversation room. The palace cafe serves delicious light meals and cakes in regal surrounds.

Sigtuna Museum　　　　　MUSEUM
(☑ 08-59 12 66 70; www.sigtunamuseum.se; Storagatan 55; adult 50kr May-Sep, free Oct-Apr; ☉ noon-4pm daily Jun-Aug, Tue-Sun rest of year) This museum looks after several attractions in the town and has a small exhibition area. The main display covers Sigtuna's history; temporary displays are drawn from the permanent collection, which includes 150,000 archaeological objects from the Middle Ages, household items, photos and documents from the area's early days, and artwork by significant regional painters.

Sigtuna Rådhus　　　　　HISTORIC BUILDING
(Town Hall; ☑ 08-59 12 66 70; www.sigtunamuseum.se; ☉ noon-4pm Tue-Sun) **FREE** The smallest town hall in Scandinavia, Sigtuna *rådhus* dates from 1744 and was designed by the mayor himself. It's on the town square opposite the tourist office. There's a small local-history display just inside the entrance.

🛏 Sleeping & Eating

Sigtunastiftelsens Gästhem　　　HOTEL **€€**
(☑ 08-59 25 89 00; www.sigtunastiftelsen.se; Manfred Björkquists allé 2-4; s/d from 800/1100kr; ⓟ ☺ 🛜) This attractive, imposing place is run by a Christian foundation. It might look something like a cross between a cloister and a medieval fortress, but its unique hotel rooms – each named for a historical figure and decorated accordingly – are much cosier than you'd think. As is usual, rates go up outside peak summer season.

Stora Brännbo　　　　　HOTEL **€€**
(☑ 08-59 25 75 00; www.storabrannbo.se; Stora Brännbovägen 2-6; s/d from 800/1100kr; ⓟ ☺ @ 🛜; 🚍 570) Just north of central Sigtuna, this large hotel and conference centre

WORTH A TRIP

A VIKING VISIT IN BIRKA

The Viking trading centre of **Birka** (www. birkavikingastaden.se/en; Björkö; adult/child 395/198kr; ☉ May-Sep; 🚢 Stromma), founded around AD 760, is now a Unesco World Heritage site. Exhibits at the **Birka Museum** (🖅 08-56 05 15 40; www.birkavikinga staden.se/en; Björkö; adult/child 100/50kr; ☉ hours vary, check schedule online) include finds from the excavations, copies of the most magnificent objects, and an interesting model of the village in Viking times. Most visitors arrive by ferry with Strömma Kanalbolaget (p64); ferry tickets include museum admission.

offers small, contemporary rooms in neutral hues with TVs and fluffy bathrobes. There's a sauna, Jacuzzi and well-equipped gym for guests, and the bountiful breakfast includes waffles and freshly squeezed orange juice.

Tant Brun Kaffestuga　　　　CAFE €
(🖅 08-59 25 09 34; Laurentii gränd; coffees & cakes from 35kr; ☉ 10am-5pm Mon-Fri, to 6pm Sat & Sun) In a small alley off Storagatan, this delightful 17th-century cafe is set around a pretty courtyard. It's well worth seeking out for its home-baked bread and pastries (the apple pie is divine); just watch your head as you walk in, as the roof beams sag precariously (did we mention it's adorable?).

❶ Getting There & Away

Travel connections from Stockholm are easy. Take a train to Märsta, from where there are frequent buses (570 or 575, SL pass is valid) to Sigtuna.

Mariefred

Tiny lakeside Mariefred is a pretty village that pulls in the crowds with its grand castle, **Gripsholm Slott** (🖅 0159-101 94; www.kungahuset.se; adult/child 130/65kr; ☉ 10am-4pm mid-May–Sep, noon-3pm Sat & Sun Oct-Nov; 🚢 S/S Mariefred from Stadshuset, 🚆 towards Eskilstuna, station Läggesta). About 70km from Stockholm, the castle – with its round towers, spires, drawbridge and creaky wooden halls – was built in the 1370s and had passed into royal hands by the early 15th century. In 1526 Gustav Vasa took over and ordered the demolition of the adjacent monastery. A new castle with walls up to 5m thick was built using materials from the monastery; extensions continued for years. The

oldest 'untouched' room is Karl IX's bedchamber, from the 1570s.

❶ Getting There & Away

Mariefred isn't on the main railway line – the nearest station is Läggesta, 4km to the west, with trains from Stockholm every two hours in summer. A **museum railway** (🖅 0159-210 06; www.oslj.nu; one-way/return from 60/80kr; ☉ 10am-5pm Jun-Aug, Sat & Sun only May & Sep) from Läggesta to Mariefred runs roughly every hour during the day in peak summer; go online to check the schedule. Bus 303 runs hourly from Läggesta to Mariefred.

The steamship **S/S Mariefred** (Map p48; 🖅 08-669 88 50; www.mariefred.info; one-way/return 210/300kr; ☉ 10am Tue-Sun Jul–mid-Aug, 10am Sat & Sun mid-Aug–mid-Sep) departs daily from Stadshuset in Stockholm for Mariefred.

Sandhamn

One of the easiest archipelago destinations to reach from Stockholm (it's only about an hour away), Sandhamn, on the island of Sandön, is a popular summer day's excursion and an excellent place to get a taste of island life. Activity is centred around the Seglarhotel and its restaurant, and on the sandy beaches scattered around.

🍴 Sleeping & Eating

Seglarhotellet　　　　　　HOTEL €€€
(🖅 08-57 45 04 00; www.sandhamn.com/boende; Sandhamn; r from 2700kr; 🛜🆒) Luxury digs with all the modern touches you'd expect in a beach resort hotel, plus a gym and spa, several saunas and views over the harbour.

Seglarrestaurangen　　　　SWEDISH €€€
(🖅 08-57 45 04 21; www.sandhamn.com; mains 220-365kr; ☉ 11.30am-3pm & 5.30-11pm) Inside Seglarhotellet, this top restaurant serves high-end Swedish food, from exceptional seared Lofoten cod to coffee-roasted venison. The lunch seafood buffet (195kr) is a big draw, and in August people flock here for crayfish parties.

❶ Getting There & Away

Take bus 433/434 from Slussen (in Stockholm) to Stavsnäs; from here, **Waxholmsbolaget** (p91) ferries depart frequently.

Cinderella boats (🖅 08-12 00 40 45) depart from Kajplats 14 on Strandvägen in Stockholm at 9.30am and 12.45pm daily and 6pm Sat and Sun.

Strömma canal tours depart from Nybroplan in Stockholm at 9.45am daily late July to August for a day trip (370kr round-trip). Buy tickets on board.

Uppsala & Central Sweden

Best Places to Eat

➡ Frank (p109)

➡ Güntherska (p102)

➡ Jay Fu's (p102)

➡ Tällbergsgårdens Hotell (p124)

➡ A-mano (p114)

Best Places to Stay

➡ Steam Hotel (p108)

➡ Green Hotel (p123)

➡ Grand Hotell Hörnan (p101)

➡ Clarion Collection Hotel Borgen (p114)

➡ Gruvgården B&B (p110)

Why Go?

Central Sweden is the perfect distillation of all the things that make Sweden so Swedish, plopped not *exactly* in the nation's geographical centre, but in the middle of its population belt, making access to a diverse range of sights and experiences a cinch. You'll see plenty of old Volvos, Dalahäst (carved wooden horses), saunas, sunsets over lakes and candles in the windows out here. It's a paradise of forests, mountains and meadows and oh so much water,and is within easy reach of Stockholm and Gothenburg.

The Lake Siljan area, with its idyllic villages of Falu Red cottages, represents the country's historic heartland. Beyond Falun, the landscape becomes wilder and more rugged – a tease of Lappland and the far north.

The region is anchored to the south by the cities of Örebro, Uppsala and Västerås. All are lively cultural centres boasting well-preserved architecture, a wealth of museums and plenty of scope for wining, dining and shopping.

When to Go
Uppsala

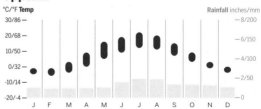

| **Mid-Jun–Aug** The weather's fine, accommodation prices are low and attractions are open. | **Sep & Oct** Many sights are closed, but the weather's fair and autumn leaves mean gorgeous scenery. | **Dec–Feb** Winter means bundling up, but central Sweden during the Christmas holidays is lovely. |

Uppsala & Central Sweden Highlights

1. **Museum Gustavianum** (p99) Pondering the weird and wonderful in Uppsala's fabulous old museum.

2. **Carl Larsson-gården** (p119) Getting inspiration for living in Sweden's favourite heritage home, outside Falun.

3. **Dalhalla** (p125) Enjoying outdoor opera in this amphitheatre outside Rättvik.

4. **Sala Silvergruva** (p109) Exploring the caverns of this defunct silver mine in Sala.

5. **Örebro Slottet** (p112) Getting medieval at this fort.

6. **Nils Olsson Hemslöjd** (p127) Watching iconic Dala horses being made in Nüsnas.

7. **MS Gustaf Wasa** (p122) Cruising the crystal waters of Lake Siljan.

8. **Nora Glass** (p112) Slurping on ice cream as you wander the streets of Nora.

9. **Orsa Rovdjurspark** (p128) Marvelling at majestic predators in this animal-friendly zoo outside Orsa.

10. **Engelsberg Bruk** (p110) Wandering among the heritage buildings of Ängelsberg's old iron works.

Uppsala

📞 018 / POP 214,559

The historical and spiritual heart of the country, Uppsala is one of Sweden's oldest yet most dynamic cities; the latter thanks in part to a student population nudging 40,000. Peaceful by day and lively by night, the resulting youthful buzz manifests most strikingly in the sheer number of laid-back boho-vibe cafes and bars – as well as all those bicycles on the streets. The city's charm also lies in its sheer picturesque value, with the meandering river Fyris flowing through the centre, flanked by pathways and still more cafes. History buffs have plenty to soak up here, with Gamla (Old) Uppsala just up the road. This fascinating archaeological site was once a flourishing 6th-century religious centre where human sacrifices were made, as well as an ancient burial ground.

The city makes an easy day trip from Stockholm, though it's worth lingering overnight to wander the deserted streets and soak up the atmosphere.

⦿ Sights

Aside from Gamla Uppsala, which is a short distance outside of town, Uppsala's sights are located centrally and many focus on the university, which is Sweden's oldest, and one of the oldest and most esteemed in the world.

The city is eminently walkable and rarely is anything more than a 15-minute walk away. Uppsala dates back to the 3rd century; among its more ancient sights are the fascinating rune stones to be seen around town. Other noteworthy sights include both the castle and the Domkyrka (cathedral).

★ Gamla Uppsala   ARCHAEOLOGICAL SITE

(www.arkeologigamlauppsala.se; ⊙24hr; **P**; 🚌2) **FREE** One of Sweden's largest and most important burial sites, Gamla Uppsala (4km north of Uppsala) contains 300 mounds from the 6th to 12th centuries. The earliest are also the three most impressive. Legend has it they contain the pre-Viking kings Aun, Egil and Adils, who appear in *Beowulf* and Icelandic historian Snorre Sturlason's *Ynglingsaga*. More recent evidence suggests the occupant of Östhögen (East Mound) was a woman, probably a female regent in her 20s or 30s.

★ Domkyrka   CHURCH

(Cathedral; 📞018-430 35 00; www.uppsala domkyrka.se; Domkyrkoplan; ⊙8am-6pm, tours in English 11am & 2pm Mon-Sat, 4pm Sun Jul & Aug)

FREE The Gothic Domkyrka dominates the city and is Scandinavia's largest church, with towers soaring an inspiring 119 m. The interior is imposing, with the French Gothic ambulatory flanked by small chapels. Tombs here include those of St Erik, Gustav Vasa and the scientist Carl von Linné. Regular tours in English are conducted in July and August and at other times by appointment.

★ Museum Gustavianum   MUSEUM

(📞018-471 75 71; www.gustavianum.uu.se; Akademigatan 3; adult/child 50/40kr; ⊙10am-4pm Tue-Sun Jun-Aug, from 11am rest of year) A wonder cabinet of wonder cabinets, the Museum Gustavianum rewards appreciation of the weird and well organised. The shelves in the pleasantly musty building hold case after case of obsolete tools and preserved oddities: stuffed birds, astrolabes, alligator mummies, exotic stones and dried sea creatures. A highlight is the fascinating 17th-century **Augsburg Art Cabinet** and its thousand ingenious trinkets. Not to be missed is Olof Rudbeck's vertiginous **anatomical theatre**, where executed criminals were dissected. Admission includes a tour in English at 1pm Saturday and Sunday.

Tropical Greenhouse   GARDENS

(📞018-471 28 38; www.botan.uu.se; Villavägen 6-8; 50kr; ⊙7am-9pm) In contrast to the stunning baroque design of the Linnaean Gardens of Uppsala (p101), where it is located, the greenhouse exhibits tropical species from around the world. Tours of the gardens in English (50kr) begin here, on Saturdays and Sundays at 2pm from June to August, and on the first Sunday of the month for the rest of the year. The tour cost includes admission into the greenhouse.

Gamla Uppsala Museum   MUSEUM

(📞018-23 93 01; www.raa.se/in-english; Disavägen; adult/child 80kr/free; ⊙10am-4pm Apr-late Jun & mid-Aug–Sep, 11am-5pm late Jun–mid-Aug, noon-4pm Mon, Wed, Sat & Sun Oct-Mar; **P**) Gamla Uppsala Museum contains finds from the cremation mounds, a poignant mix of charred and melted beads, bones and buckles. More-intact pieces come from various **boat graves** in and around the site. The museum is arranged as a timeline – useful for recreating the history of the area.

Uppsala Slott   CASTLE

(📞018-727 24 82; www.uppsalaslott.com; Slottet; admission by guided tour only, adult/child 90/15kr; ⊙tours in English 1pm & 3pm Tue-Sun late Jun-Sep)

Uppsala

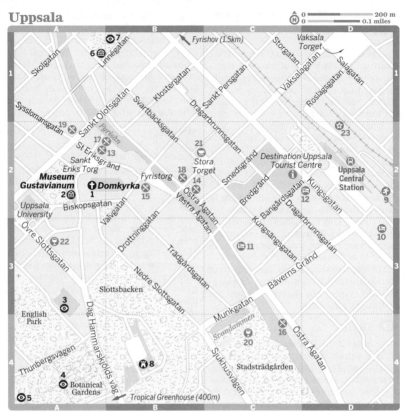

Uppsala

Uppsala Slott was built by Gustav Vasa in the 1550s. It contains the state hall where kings were enthroned and Queen Kristina abdicated. It was also the scene of a brutal murder in 1567, when King Erik XIV and his guards killed Nils Sture and his two sons,

Erik and Svante, after accusing them of high treason. The castle burned down in 1702 but was rebuilt and took on its present form in 1757. Contact Destination Uppsala Tourist Centre (p103) for tour bookings.

Carolina Rediviva bibliotek   LIBRARY
(☑018-471 39 00; www.ub.uu.se; Dag Hammarskjölds väg 1; ☺exhibition hall 9am-8pm Mon-Fri, 10am-5pm Sat) `FREE` Rare-book and map fiends should go directly to Carolina Rediviva, the university library. In a small, dark gallery, glass cases hold precious maps and manuscripts, including illuminated Ethiopian texts and the first book ever printed in Sweden. The star is the surviving half of the *Codex Argentus* (AD 520), aka the Silver Bible, written in gold and silver ink on purple vellum; aside from being pretty, it's linguistically important as the most complete existing document written in the Gothic language.

Linnémuseet   MUSEUM
(☑018-13 65 40; www.linnaeus.se; Svartbäcksgatan 27; adult/child 80kr/free; ☺11am-5pm Tue-Sun May-Sep) No matter how many times the brochures refer to the 'sexual system' of classification, the excitement to be had at Linnémuseet is primarily intellectual; still, botanists and vegetarians will enjoy a visit to the pioneering scientist's home and workshop, where he lived with his wife and five kids (1743–78). Visits to the adjoining Linnéträdgården (☑018-471 25 76; adult/child 60kr/free, admission with Linnémuseet ticket free; ☺shop & exhibit 11am-5pm Tue-Sun May-Sep, park 11am-8pm Tue-Sun May-Sep), a reconstruction of Sweden's oldest botanical garden, is included in the admission fee.

Linnaean Gardens of Uppsala   GARDENS
(☑018-471 28 38; www.botan.uu.se; Villavägen 6-8; ☺7am-9pm) `FREE` The Botanical Gardens, below the castle hill, show off more than 10,000 species and are pleasant to wander through. Attractions include the 200-year-old Linnaeum Orangery (☺9am-3pm Tue-Fri) `FREE` and the Tropical Greenhouse (p99) from where guided tours in English (50kr) begin. Tours are held on Saturdays and Sundays at 2pm from June to August, and on the first Sunday of the month for the rest of the year.

Disagården   MUSEUM
(☑018-16 91 80; www.upplandsmuseet.se/besok-oss/disgarden/; Ärnavägen; admission free, guided tours 30kr; ☺10am-5pm Jun-Aug, tours 1pm) `FREE` Follow signs from the grave mounds at Gamla Uppsala (p99) to reach Disagården, a 19th-century farming village turned open-air museum consisting of 26 timber buildings and a platform stage that serves as the focal point for Uppsala's Midsummer celebrations.

🏃 Activities

Lennakatten   RAIL
(☑018-13 05 00; www.lennakatten.se; Stationsgatan 11, track 10; day ticket adult/child 230/120kr; ☺9am-5pm Wed-Thu, Sat & Sun) Trainspotters, big kids and youngsters alike all get a thrill from riding this narrow-gauge steam train for 33km into the Uppland countryside. The train departs from the Uppsala Östra museum station, in Bergsbrunnaparken, toward the east side of Uppsala Central Station. Be sure to check online for timetable changes.

Fyrishov   WATER PARK
(☑018-727 49 50; www.fyrishov.se; Idrottsgatan 2; adult/child 100/80kr; ☺park 9am-9.30pm, pool from 6.15am; 🚻; ☒1, 13, 42, 111) Families with water-loving children should head for Fyrishov, one of Sweden's largest water parks. It features the full complement of slides, Jacuzzis, waterfalls and wave machines.

🛏 Sleeping

Hotel & Vandrarhem Central Station   HOSTEL €
(☑018-444 20 10; www.hotellcentralstation.se/en/; Bangårdsgatan 13; dm/s/d from 250/450/550kr; @🖥) The location of this hotel-cum-hostel is excellent, across from the train and bus station and close to the tourist office. The hostel rooms and dorms are tiny but spotless; the lack of windows may be a consideration for some, although there is adequate ventilation. The shared bathrooms are spacious and clean.

★Grand Hotell Hörnan   HOTEL €€
(☑018-13 93 80; www.grandhotellhornan.com/en/; Bangårdsgatan 1; d from 1495kr; 🅿🖥) This 1907 grand riverfront dame, re-invented in 2013, succeeds in blending that golden age of architecture with the amenities of today. You feel like you're staying in an old hotel, without that fusty furniture feeling, false airs and graces or failing to balance old and new. The Hörnan is smart, affordable and honours the tradition of which it is part.

★Sunnersta Herrgård   HOSTEL €€
(☑018-32 42 20; www.sunnerstaherrgard.se; Sunnerstavägen 24; dm 280kr, s/d from 715/850kr;

P @ 🛜; 🖵20) In a historic manor house about 6km south of the city centre, this hostel has a park-like setting at the water's edge and a good restaurant on site. You can rent bikes (per day/week 50/200kr) or borrow a boat. Hotel-standard rooms include breakfast and share a bathroom with one other room; hostel guests can add breakfast for 95kr.

Elite Hotel Academia HOTEL €€
(📲 018-780 99 00; www.elite.se/en/hotels/uppsala/hotel-academia/; Suttungs gränd 6; d from 1490kr; P ✳ 🛜) New in 2017, the Elite Academia has gotten off to a grand start, mostly by getting the service side of running a big, central hotel right. Rooms are as fresh and high-tech as you'd expect for a present-day build, while the design theme is understated, if not a little bland, and pricing is on the high-side. Still, it's a great choice.

🍴 Eating

Ofvandahls CAFE €
(📲 018-13 42 04; www.ofvandahls.se; Sysslomansgatan 3-5; cakes & light meals 35-90kr; ⊘ 8am-6pm Mon-Fri, 9am-5pm Sat, 11am-5pm Sun) An Uppsala institution, this classy but sweet *konditori* (bakery-cafe) dates back to the 19th century and is a cut above your average coffee-and-bun shop. It's been endorsed by no less a personage than the king, and radiates old-world charm with antique furniture and fittings. Try the star turn – homemade blueberry cake.

Feskarn Saluhallen MARKET €
(📲 018-10 44 45; www.feskarn.nu/saluhallen/; Vattugränd; items from 30kr; ⊘ 10am-6pm Mon-Thu, to 7pm Fri, to 4pm Sat; P) Stock up on meat, fish, cheese and fancy chocolate at this indoor market. Or you can hit one of the restaurant corners for a bite; a couple stay open late for dinner, with pleasant terrace bars available in summer.

★ Jay Fu's FUSION €€
(📲 018-15 01 51; www.jayfu.se; Sankt Eriks Torg 8; mains 145-295kr; ⊘ 5pm-late Mon-Sat; 🛜) Fusion doesn't always work, but while some of the combinations here sound mildly indigestible – like mac and cheese with grilled lobster, truffles and bok choy – they are actually well planned and beautifully presented. While steaks and the mixed grill take centre stage, lighter bites like corn fried crab cakes and salmon sashimi also receive rave reviews from diners.

★ Güntherska SWEDISH €€
(📲 018-13 07 57; www.guntherska.se; Östra Agatan 31; mains 145-220kr; ⊘ 9am-7pm Mon, Tue & Sat, to 9pm Wed-Fri, 10am-7pm Sun; 🛜) An 1870 grande dame of a cafe which enjoys an exemplary position with terraced seating across from the river, and a very elegant interior with regency-style wallpaper and chandeliers. The menu includes treats like hummus salad, and the sweet treats are in a league of their own, particularly the sticky buns. They also produce their own muesli, which is available for purchase.

Hamnpaviljongen SWEDISH €€
(📲 018-69 66 53; www.hamnpaviljongen.com; Hamnplan 5; mains 189-299kr, lunch menu 100kr; ⊘ 11am-2pm & 3-9pm Mon-Fri, from noon Sat & Sun; P 🛜) This restaurant may look pricey, but the reality is that it serves one of the best value lunchtime menus in town. However, when the sun goes down the prices go up for the evening's á la carte menu, which is of exactly the same quality. Head for the spacious glassed-in terrace for views across the water to the leafy park beyond.

Magnussons Krog SWEDISH €€
(📲 018-14 00 18; www.magnussonskrog.se; Drottninggatan 1; dagens lunch 109kr, mains 175-225kr; ⊘ 11am-midnight) Try any of the specials on the chalkboard at this sleek corner hangout. Late-night bar snacks (109kr to 129kr) help soak up delicious cocktails, which you can enjoy at outdoor tables on a busy riverside corner in fair weather. Great for people watching.

Hambergs Fisk SEAFOOD €€€
(📲 018-71 00 50; www.hambergs.se; Fyristorg 8; mains 155-305kr; ⊘ 11.30am-10pm Tue-Sat) Let the aromas of dill and the faint though not off-putting smell of fresh fish entice you into this excellent riverfront seafood restaurant. Shellfish platters (435kr per person) are mouthwatering and great value. Self-caterers should check out the market counter behind the dining room.

🍸 Drinking & Nightlife

★ Flustret CLUB
(📲 018-10 04 44; www.flustret.se; Flustergränd 5; ⊘ 10pm-3am Wed-Sat) Occupying a big 'ole mansion by the river, Flustret is Uppsala's most enduring nightclub/party venue, though it sounds a lot hotter than it actually is. Still, if you're a night owl and you're in

town, you're going to need to check it out for yourself.

⭐ **Kafferummet Storken**   CAFE
(☑018-15 05 22; Stora Torget 3; ⊙9.30am-10pm; 📶♿) Don't be deceived by the nondescript entrance tucked into the corner of Stora Torget. Climb the stairs and you are transported to a cool cafe hang comprising a series of eclectically furnished rooms filled with nostalgia, groaning bookshelves and an overall ambience of old-style comfort. There's also an outside terrace overlooking the rooftops.

Williams Pub   PUB
(☑018-14 09 20; www.williamspub.se; Åsgränd 5; ⊙4pm-midnight Mon-Thu, to 3am Fri & Sat) This is a cosy student/after-work pub near Domkyrka (p99) with a mellow vibe, a good selection of tap beers and a simple bar menu – what more could you ask for?

☆ Entertainment

Katalin and All That Jazz   LIVE MUSIC
(☑018-14 06 80; www.katalin.com; Godsmagasinet, Östra Station; ⊙from 2pm Mon-Thu, from 1pm Fri & Sat) Katalin, in a former warehouse behind the train station, hosts regular live jazz and blues, with occasional rock and pop bands. There's a good restaurant too, and in summer the sun-splashed back patio is jammed with great-looking people acting like they're not checking each other out.

ℹ Information

Destination Uppsala Tourist Centre (☑018-727 48 00; www.destinationuppsala.se; Kungsgatan 59; ⊙10am-6pm Mon-Fri, to 3pm Sat, plus 11am-3pm Sun Jul & Aug) Can offer helpful advice, maps and brochures covering the region and beyond.

ℹ Getting There & Away

Uppsala is 71km north of Stockholm on the E4 motorway.

Upplands Lokaltrafik (☑0771-14 14 14; www.ul.se) bus 801 shuttles between Uppsala and Arlanda Airport (91kr, 40 minutes).

SJ Rail (☑0771–75 75 75; www.sj.se) operates regular services to/from Stockholm (from 105kr, 40 minutes) and less frequent services to/from Gävle (from 116kr, 1¼ hours), Östersund (from 566kr, five hours) and Mora (from 407kr, 3¼ hours).

ℹ Getting Around

Upplands Lokaltrafik (p103) runs public transport within the city and county.

All local buses depart from the bus terminal at Uppsala Centralstation, with most stopping at Stora Torget. You can buy tickets at the UL office inside the station, via the website or by downloading the UL app to your smartphone. A single bus ticket costs 35kr but a variety of more economical options are available, depending on how much bus travel you are planning on doing. Check out the excellent English language homepage for details on how to save yourself money if you plan on sticking around.

For car rental, try **Sixt Biluthyrning** (☑018-430 01 01; www.sixt.se; Stationsgatan 1; ⊙7am-5pm Mon-Fri, 10am-2pm Sat) and **OKQ8** (☑018-29 04 96; www.okq8.se; Årstagatan 5-7).

Nyköping
☑0155 / POP 54,924

Nyköping (pronounced 'knee-sher-ping') was once the setting for one of Swedish royalty's greatest feuds, when in 1317 King Birger Magnusson invited his brothers to a royal feast, then subsequently imprisoned them. Drama ensued.

These days, the mid-sized city is a pretty, mellow place with far less subterfuge, although it was home to the reconnaissance division of the Swedish Air Force for many years: the museum in their honour is one of the town's main attractions. Otherwise, a big day out here doesn't usually get much more exciting than taking a pleasant riverside stroll or having a picnic by the harbour.

Although visitors to the city limits number in their tens of thousands each year, most people won't even know they've passed through – Stockholm's alternative international airport, Skavsta, popular with low-cost carriers, is located here.

⊙ Sights & Activities

On a fine day it's a nice idea to take a walk along the river or explore the Sörmlands archipelago, which extends more than 50km north of Nyköping, by canoe or boat. Enquire at Nyköpings Turistbyrå (p104) for suggested itineraries.

F11 Museum   MUSEUM
(☑0155-21 18 98; www.f11museum.se; Flygspanarvägen 3; 30kr; ⊙9am-noon Tue, 11am-4pm Sun; 🅿) You don't have to be a planespotter to enjoy this excellent little volunteer-run museum which gives an insight into the F11 aircraft and pilots who flew reconnaissance missions from the former base at Skavsta between 1965 and 1979. You can even take a

half-hour flight in a simulator (200kr; book in advance).

Nyköpingshus   CASTLE
(Vallgatan) FREE The ruined castle Nyköpingshus hosted some violent times in the Swedish monarchy. The bickering among King Birger and his two brothers, Erik and Valdemar, peaked in 1317 when Birger invited them to a 'peace banquet'. When they arrived, he hurled them into the dungeon and threw the keys in the river, letting them starve to death. It didn't do Birger much good, as he was driven to exile in Denmark the following year. You can wander around the ruins any time.

Sörmlands Museum   MUSEUM
(✆ 0155-24 57 20; www.sormlandsmuseum.se; Östra Trädgårdsgatan 2; ⊙ 11am-5pm Jun-Aug, 10am-4pm Sun only Sep-May) FREE Inside the grounds of Nyköpingshus, Sörmlands Museum includes Kungstornet (King's Tower), a whitewashed four-storey castle tower; Gamla Residenset, the old governor's residence; and the neighbouring Konsthallen, with interesting art exhibitions and a collection of 19th-century boathouses. Free guided tours of Kungstornet take place in English at 2pm Tuesday, Thursday, Saturday and Sunday in summer.

Sörmlandsleden   HIKING
(✆ 0155-355 64; www.sormlandsleden.se) The 1000km-long Sörmlandsleden walking trail passes through town on its way around the county: check the website for details.

🛏 Sleeping & Eating

Nyköpings Vandrarhem   HOSTEL €
(✆ 070-679 56 08; www.nykopingsvandrarhem.se; Brunnsgatan 4; dm/s/d 210/400/530kr; P) So close to the castle that you'd feel threatened if there were a siege, this independent hostel is homely and casual. The kitchen is great, there are picnic tables in the yard, and the folks in charge are accommodating and helpful. The riverside location is hard to beat.

Clarion Hotel Kompaniet   HOTEL €€
(✆ 0155-28 80 20; www.nordicchoicehotels.com/hotels/sweden/nykoping/clarion-collection-hotel-kompaniet/; Folkungavägen 1; r from 1080kr; P @ ☎) This enormous structure near the harbour features stylish modern rooms – not huge, but intelligently arranged, and many with nice views – in a building that was once home to a furniture factory. Prices vary seasonally, but all include breakfast and a dinner buffet (or a sandwich for those who arrive late).

Hellmanska Garden Cafe   CAFE €
(✆ 0155-21 05 25; Västra Trädgårdsgatan 24; mains 85-145kr; ⊙ 8am-6pm Mon-Fri, 9am-5pm Sat, 11am-4pm Sun) A charming cafe with a boutique shop attached, 'Hellmans' is a nice spot for lunch, with soups, salads, lasagne and focaccia, complimented by decent coffee and excellent cakes to enjoy in the summer courtyard.

★ Skafferiet   BISTRO €€€
(✆ 0155-26 99 50; www.mickesskafferi.se; Västra Storgatan 29; mains 195-280kr; ⊙ 11am-1.30pm & 6-11pm Mon-Fri, noon-2pm & 6-11pm Sat) Nyköping's more upmarket diners head to classy Skafferiet for its simple though beautifully presented locavore cuisine like grilled lamb, *moules-frites* and flank steak, served in arty farty surrounds. Après-dinner, folks tend to stick around for drinks at the bar.

ℹ Information

Nyköpings Turistbyrå (✆ 0155-24 82 00; www.nykopingsguiden.se; ⊙ 8am-6pm Mon-Fri, 10am-4pm Sat & Sun) Has plenty of brochures and rents bikes (75/250kr per day/week).

ℹ Getting There & Around

Nyköping is 110km southwest of Stockholm on the E4 motorway.

Nyköping's **Skavsta Airport** (✆ 0155-28 04 00; www.skavsta-air.se), 8km northwest of town, has flights to/from the UK and continental Europe with a variery of low-cost carriers.

Flygbussarna (✆ 0771-51 52 52; www.flygbussarna.se/en/; ⊙ customer service 8am-11pm) operates airport shuttle buses to meet most flights to/from Stockholm (139kr, 80 minutes). Local bus 515 runs regularly between Nyköping and Skavsta (42kr, 20 minutes); alternatively, catching a taxi with **Taxi Nyköping Oxelösund** (✆ 0155-21 75 00; www.taxinyox.se/eng) into Nyköping will set you back about 230kr.

SJ Rail (p103) trains run every hour or two to Norrköping (95kr, 40 minutes) and Stockholm (164kr, one hour).

Eskilstuna
✆ 016 / POP 67,359

Most visitors come to Eskilstuna for the vivid Viking Age rock carvings found just north of town and its family-centric city zoo, known for its collection of exotic and Nordic animals. There's also a pretty riverside old town, opportunities for walking, biking and swimming, and even a castle or two in the surrounding districts.

If visiting from abroad, don't be surprised if locals ask you, 'Why Eskilstuna, of all places?' as for them, their hometown might seem not unlike any other small Swedish city, with its well-ordered suburbs that won't strike you as particularly out of the ordinary. Although the question is valid, how you answer it might remind them of the significance of what lies on their very doorstep.

◉ Sights & Activities

★ Stora Sundby Slott   CASTLE
(Stora Sundby Castle; ☑016-620 01; www.stora sundby.com; Stora Sundby Gård, Stora Sundby; ☺by appointment; Ⓟ) **FREE** Occupying tranquil lands on the shores of Lake Hjälmaren, this outstanding castle was built in the 16th century in the Renaissance style and later transformed over 16 years (to 1848) into the turreted neo-Gothic fortress that's today home to the Klingspor family. The family has owned and occupied the estate since 1888. You're free to respectfully wander the castle's beautiful grounds and admire its fairy-tale form. Better still, contact the castle in advance to arrange a guided tour of its palatial rooms.

The castle is located just over 30km southwest of Eskilstuna – you'll need your own wheels to get here.

Sigurdsristningen   ARCHAEOLOGICAL SITE
(Sundbyholm Ramsund 1; ☺24hr; Ⓟ; ☒225) **FREE** The vivid, 3m-long Viking Age rock carving Sigurdsristningen illustrates the story of Sigurd the Dragon Slayer, a hero whose adventures are described in *Beowulf* and the Icelandic sagas. The story inspired Wagner's *Ring Cycle,* and *The Hobbit* and *The Lord of the Rings* also borrow from it. A walking path along the river starts from the parking lot. The carving is situated near Sundbyholms Slott (p106) and Mälaren lake, 12km northeast of Eskilstuna.

Rademachersmedjorna   AREA
(Rademacher Forges; ☑016-710 13 71; Rademach ergatan 42-51) **FREE** The Rademacher Forges uphold the 17th-century traditions of Eskilstuna's iron-working past in a series of pretty, well-preserved historic buildings that together form a kind of open-air museum. Visitors can observe workshops where the iron-, silver- and gold-smithing traditions continue. You can wander the cobblestone streets any time

of day, but the various forges, shops and cafes generally observe standard business hours (10am to 4pm Monday to Friday) with extended hours in summer (10am to 6pm Saturday and Sunday May to September).

Parken Zoo   ZOO
(☑016-10 01 01; www.parkenzoo.se; Flackstavägen 13b; adult/child from 300/230kr; ☺10am-6pm Jul–mid-Aug, shorter hours May, Jun & Sep, amusement park from noon, pool 10am-7pm Jun-Aug; Ⓟⓕ; ☒1) Parken Zoo, 1.5km west of the town centre, is one of central Sweden's most popular family attractions. The 80-plus animal species represented include monkeys, komodo dragons, lions and lemurs, as well as a large collection of animals native to the Nordic regions. Entry passes include admission to an amusement-park-style playground best suited to pre-teens and a small water park with three pools.

Admission fees and opening hours vary with the season: check the website for details.

Eskilstuna Konstmuseum   MUSEUM
(Eskilstuna Art Museum; ☑016-710 13 69; www. eskilstuna.nu/gora/sevardheter/eskilstuna-konst museum; Portgatan 2; ☺11am-4pm Tue-Fri, noon-4pm Sat & Sun; Ⓟ) **FREE** Of this ambitious art gallery's permanent collection of over 1000 works from the 17th century to today, around 120 pieces are displayed at any given time. Complimented by various visiting exhibitions, the museum has an emphasis on 20th-century Swedish art and occupies an attractive heritage site, formerly the Bolinder Munktell factory. There's a chic cafe on site.

★ Munktellbadet   BATHHOUSE
(Munktell Baths; ☑016-10 01 30; www.munktell badet.se; Holger Lindmarks seat 4; entry from 75kr; ☺10am-5pm; ⓕ) Sweden's newest family-centric public bathing facility opened in 2016 and boasts a variety of indoor pools, a climbing wall, a rushing river, a kids' pool with obstacles and even a 2.5m-deep lagoon replete with shoals of fish. Saunas, steam rooms, lounging areas and dining options complete the impressive package. Opening hours for the facility and individual pools vary seasonally: be sure to check the website for current opening times and pricing.

🛏 Sleeping & Eating

Comfort Hotel Eskilstuna   HOTEL €
(☑016-17 78 00; www.nordicchoicehotels.com/ hotels/sweden/eskilstuna/comfort-hotel-eskilstuna/;

Hamngatan 9; d from 805kr; P ≋) The light-filled, airy rooms of this central, riverside hotel are fresh and funky, featuring bold photographic wallpapers, plucky sofas, occasional tables and comfortable bedding. If you're familiar with the brand outside Scandinavia, synonymous with generic, low-cost motels, you'll need to throw that perception away: this hotel exemplifies the boutique style and professional service to which the Nordic Choice brand aspires.

Sundbyholms Slott Hotell   CASTLE €€
(🖉 016-42 84 00; www.sundbyholms-slott.se; Sundbyholm 8; d/ste from 1348/2220kr) The comfortable accommodation spread out over a number of buildings on the grounds of Sundbyholms castle (12km north of Eskilstuna) are the next best thing to sleeping in the castle itself. The property boasts a variety of room types, with cheaper hotel-style rooms furnished with a more modern touch and a number of classical suites.

A popular conference and wedding venue, the riverside estate has a variety of dining options, outdoor hot tubs and walking trails, and is a pleasant stroll from the impressive Sigurdsristningen (p105) rock carvings.

Jernberghska   SWEDISH €€
(🖉 016-14 65 05; www.jernberghska.se; Rademachergatan 48; mains 180-290kr; ⊙ 11.30am-2pm Mon, 11.30am-2pm & 5-11pm Tue-Fri, noon-11pm Sat) This charming restaurant that is housed in an 18th-century former smithy in the Rademachersmedjorna (p105) area oozes atmosphere of the rustic, romantic kind. From Tuesday to Friday you can enjoy a two-course set menu for 249kr, or otherwise dine a-la-carte from a modern Swedish menu, or just pop in for a beer, wine and cider accompanied by excellent tapas-style bar snacks.

Restaurang Tingsgården   SWEDISH €€
(🖉 016-51 66 20; Rådhustorget 2; dagens lunch 94kr, 2-course meal 240kr, mains 139-260kr; ⊙ 11am-11pm Mon-Fri, noon-11pm Sat, noon-10pm Sun) This intimate restaurant, inside a wonderful wooden 18th-century house in the old town, is a treat. Its menu is heavy on meat and fish, from lamb and steak to mountain trout. In summer, you can sit out on a large deck overlooking the twinkling river.

ℹ Information

You'll find most services around Fristadstorget and the pedestrianised part of Kungsgatan.
Eskilstuna Tourist Center (🖉 016-710 70 00; www.eskilstuna.nu; Fristadstorget 1; ⊙ 10am-

6pm Mon-Fri, 10am-2pm Sat & Sun, closed Sun winter) Dispenses helpful information.
Eskilstuna Station360 (🖉 0771-22 40 00; Resecentrum, Järnvägsplan, Centralstation; ⊙ 6am-5pm Mon-Fri, 7.30am-2pm Sat, 9.30am-4pm Sun) Head here for information on public transport in the region and beyond.

ℹ Getting There & Away

By road, Eskilstuna is 80km south of Västerås on the E18 and E20 motorways, and 113km west of Stockholm on the E20.
Swebus Express (🖉 0200-21 82 18; www.swebusexpress.se) operates one early morning service between Eskilstuna and Stockholm (from 79kr, one hour) while Karlstad-based BT Buss (www.bergslagstaget.se) also operates one service per day to Stockholm (209kr, 1½ hours) and Karlstad (269kr, 2¾ hours). Local buses 701 and 801 go to Nyköping (105kr, 1½ hours).

Most local and long distance bus services begin, terminate or stop at Resecentrum (Centralstation).

SJ Rail (p103) operates regular services to Örebro (125kr, one hour), Västerås (85kr, 30 minutes) and Stockholm (154kr, 1¼ hours).

Västerås

🖉 021 / POP 147,420

With its cobbled streets, higgledy-piggledy houses and flourishing flower gardens, Västerås' old town is an utter delight. But Sweden's sixth-largest city is a place of two halves: head just a few blocks southeast and you'll find modern shopping centres, industrial overloads and sprawling suburbs that bear no resemblance to the teeny lanes and crafts shops you've left behind. Indeed, if you're approaching the city from this direction, don't let initial appearances dismay – looking a little deeper will reveal some of Sweden's top museums, restaurants and attractions dotted throughout the city and in the surrounding countryside.

Västerås is also a handy base for exploring Mälaren lake and important pagan sites nearby and is the site of Sweden's newest (and zaniest) indoor water park and some of Sweden's most unusual places to lay your head.

All in all, quite the surprising package, really. Three cheers for the underdog!

◉ Sights & Activities

★**Karlsgatan 2**   MUSEUM
(🖉 021-16 13 00; www.karlsgatan2.se; Karlsgatan 2; ⊙ 10am-7pm Tue, Wed & Fri, to 8pm Thu, noon-4pm Sat & Sun; P) **FREE** Comprising the former

Västerås

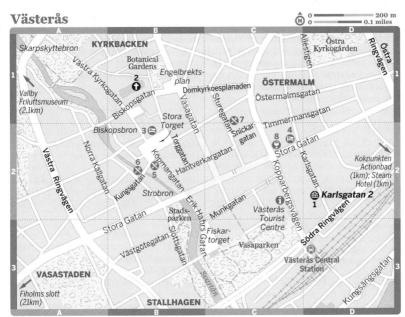

Västmanland Länsmuseum (county museum) and Västerås Konstmuseum (art gallery) in a re-imagined industrial block near Centralstation, Karlsgatan 2 packs a punch. The county museum is presented in a huge and elaborate space that introduces the region's history (and prehistory) in a kid-friendly, remarkably high-production-value fashion. In the opposite wing is the art gallery, with a permanent collection of regional highlights (Bror Hjorth, Aguelí) and ambitious, insightfully presented temporary displays.

★ **Anundshög**   ARCHAEOLOGICAL SITE
(📞 021-39 15 53; Anundshög 5; 🅿; 🚌12 Bjurhovda) **FREE** Västerås is surrounded by pre-Christian sites. The most interesting and extensive is Anundshög, the biggest *tumulus* (burial ground) in Sweden, 9km northeast of the city. You can get the bus 12 to Bjurhovda, from where it's a 2km walk east. The site has a full complement of prehistoric curiosities, such as mounds, stoneship settings and a large 11th-century rune stone. The two main ship settings date from around the 1st century.

Västerås domkyrka   CHURCH
(Västerås Cathedral; 📞 021-81 46 00; www.svenskakyrkan.se/vasteras; Västra Kyrkogatan 6;

Västerås

⊙9am-5pm) **FREE** The fine brick-built Domkyrka was begun in the 12th century, although most of what you see today is late-14th-century work. It contains carved floor slabs, six altarpieces and the marble sarcophagus of King Erik XIV, Gustav Vasa's son and successor, who died in 1577 after eating pea soup laced with arsenic. Ask about going into the **tower**; times vary, but it's generally open at 2pm Monday and Thursday and 10.30am Saturday (30kr).

Fiholms Slott
CASTLE

(🖉016-39 50 64; www.fiholm.se; Fiholms Säteri 3; 🅿) FREE This Dutch-French Renaissance-styled castle was completed around 1630. Private tours (price on application) can be booked for small groups, but otherwise, you'll have to settle for wandering around the beautifully manicured estate, where there's a small cafe and gift store.

Vallby Friluftsmuseum
MUSEUM

(🖉021-39 80 70; www.vallbyfriluftsmuseum.se; Skerikesvägen 2; ⊗10am-5pm; 🅿; 🚌10, 12) FREE Vallby Friluftsmuseum, off Vallbyleden near the E18 interchange, 2km northwest of the city, is home to an extensive open-air collection of traditional huts and cottages. Among the 40-odd buildings, there's an interesting farmyard populated by adorable Jämtland goats, bunnies and draft horses, a cute cafe with outdoor seating, and craft workshops for old-school carpentry and glassmaking.

★ Kokpunkten Actionbad
WATER PARK

(🖉021-448 55 00; www.kokpunkten.se; Kraftverksgatan 11; adult/child 160/120kr; ⊗11am-9pm Mon-Fri, 8.30am-8pm Sat & Sun; 🚼) While cities around the world are tearing down their post-industrial infrastructure, Västerås is reinventing its, like this wacky and wonderful indoor water park, complete with complex visuals and and special effects, housed in a former power station. It shares the same concrete bones as the Steam Hotel: why not package it all together?

🛏 Sleeping

Västerås Mälarcamping
CAMPGROUND €

(🖉021-14 02 79; www.nordiccamping.se/vara-anlaggningar/vaesteraas-maelarcamping/; Johannisbergsvägen; sites/cabins from 200/475kr; 🅿@🛜; 🚌25) The closest campground is this place 5km southwest of the city near Mälaren lake. It has up-to-date facilities including wi-fi and a pretty awesome miniature-golf course.

★ Steam Hotel
BOUTIQUE HOTEL €€

(🖉021-475 99 00; www.steamhotel.se/en/; Ångkraftsvägen 14; d from 1050kr; 🅿❋🛜🏊) What's not to love, love, love about this new-in-2017 boutique hotel housed in a towering, rock-solid former power station? You could be forgiven for thinking you're in downtown Manhattan when you step into the fabulous lobby or open the door to your sumptuously furnished guestroom. Thoroughly on-the-pulse, this imaginative property is a tribute to a legacy of Swedish design genius.

The hotel is owned and managed by a small Swedish consortium whose years in the business reflect in their attention to the guest experience. There are also restaurants, a killer day spa and...an indoor water park – Kokpunkten Actionbad. One to remember.

Hotel Plaza
HOTEL €€

(🖉021-10 10 10; www.plazavasteras.se; Karlsgatan 9a; d from 1095kr; 🅿❋@🛜) Bang in the centre of Västerås' modern sector, this 25-storey skyscraper was built for gravity-defying lounge lizards: its cocktail bar surveys the city from the 24th floor. Some rooms have views over lake Mälaren, and there's a spa with masseurs, sauna and gym, and a restaurant churning out upscale Swedish favourites. It's a Best Western Plus property.

Elite Stadshotellet
HOTEL €€

(🖉021-10 28 00; www.elite.se/en/hotels/vasteras/stadshotellet/; Stora Torget; s/d from 1050/1400kr; 🅿❋@🛜) Many of the rooms at the Elite, in a lovely art-nouveau building, have prime views over the main square – request one if you like people watching. The decor is tasteful (pale walls, leafy bedspreads and mahogany timber), the staff are obliging and there's a popular English-style pub attached. Parking is 90kr.

Utter Inn
HOTEL €€€

(Otter Inn; Lake Mälaren; s/d from 1250/2500kr) This small, red floating cabin situated in the middle of Mälaren lake is accessible only by boat. The bedroom is downstairs – 3m below the surface – and is complete with glass viewing panels to watch the marine life outside. There's room for two people, and a canoe is provided. Contact Västerås Tourist Centre for bookings and directions.

🍴 Eating & Drinking

Kalle på Spangen
CAFE €

(🖉021-12 91 29; www.kallepaspangen.se; Kungsgatan 2; set lunch 95kr; ⊗10am-10pm Mon-Sat, 11am-10pm Sun) This great cafe, right by the river in the old part of town, inhabits several cosy, creaky-floored rooms filled with mismatched furniture and gilt-edged grandfather clocks. Lunch specials, such as the lasagne, are hefty and include salad, beverage, bread and coffee. There's nice riverside outdoor seating in summer.

Spicy Hot
ASIAN €€

(🖉021-18 17 40; www.spicyhot.se; Sturegatan 20a; mains 75-185kr; ⊗11am-10pm Mon-Sat, noon-9pm Sun; 🖉) A favourite among local students, this Thai/Asian joint serves a wide variety of dishes as spicy as you like it. Portion sizes are large, meaning great value for hungry, budgeting diners. Vegetarians are happily catered for. Spicy hot is such a hit that it now has a number of branches in central Sweden.

★ Frank
BISTRO €€€

(☑ 021-13 65 00; www.frankbistro.se; Stora Torget 3; 4-course menu 595kr, wine pairings 375kr; ☺ 5pm-midnight Tue-Sat; ☑) A glance at Frank's place on the web will give you a sense of what to expect at this edgy bistro which is turning heads from Västerås to Stockholm. Here, you dine by Frank's rules: choose from meat, fish or vegetarian mains and sit back and wait to see what four courses and paired wines (optional) Frank comes back with. Bookings essential.

Sky Bar
ROOFTOP BAR

(☑ 021-10 10 10; www.plazavasteras.se/skybar; Kopparbergsvägen 10; ☺ 5pm-midnight) This almost-rooftop bar up on the 24th floor of Hotel Plaza offers killer cocktails and great views out over Västerås, Mälaren lake and the Västmanland countryside.

ⓘ Information

Västerås Tourist Centre (☑ 021-39 01 00; www.visitvasteras.se/en/; Kopparbergsvägen 10; ☺ 10am-6pm Mon-Fri, to 3pm Sat) Staff are particularly friendly and helpful and can load you up with pamphlets galore.

ⓘ Getting There & Away

Västerås is almost midway between Stockholm (108km to the east) and Örebo (95km west) on the E18 motorway.

The city is well serviced by road, rail and air. All local and long-distance buses and trains depart from Västerås Centralstation – the bus terminal is adjacent to the train station.

SJ Rail (p103) operates regular services between Västerås and Sala (65kr, 30 minutes), Stockholm (95kr, one hour), Örebro (105kr, one hour), Uppsala (116kr, 1½ hours) and Eskilstuna (84kr, 50 minutes).

Swebus Express (p106) offers less frequent coach services to a dwindling number of destinations including Stockholm and Örebro, but in most cases, it's cheaper and faster to get the train.

Västerås Airport (☑ 021-80 56 00; www.vasterasairport.se) is 6km east of the city centre. Budget carrier Ryanair flies here daily from the UK, and other budget airlines host a variety of destinations, including Crete and Turkey.

For taxis, try **Taxi Västerås** (☑ 021-18 50 00; www.taxivasteras.se).

Sala
☑ 0224 / POP 22,353

The source of Sala's park-like charm is distinctly unfrivolous. The local silver mine made Sweden rich in the 16th and 17th centuries, and its creation changed the face of the town: those small rivers, ponds and canals that weave so prettily through and around the neighbourhoods were actually built to power the mines.

Aside from the mine, which is itself enough of a reason to come to town, Sala, as pretty as it is, *isn't* big enough nor bold enough keep your attention for too long and probably has no plans to do so.

⊙ Sights

★ Sala Silvergruva
MINE, MUSEUM

(☑ 0224-67 72 60; www.salasilvergruva.se; Drottning Christinas-vägan; tours 1hr adult/child 195/95kr, 2hr 295/145kr; ☺ 10am-5pm May-Sep, 11am-4pm Oct-Apr) Even if you're reluctant to take the plunge, there's plenty to see and do above ground at this vast mine complex 2km south of the town centre. Underground, a staggering 20km of caverns and shafts contain galleries, artefacts and the world's deepest hotel suite! Tours go 60m or 150m deep into the mines, every half-hour from 11am to 3pm. Note: you'll need to walk down and up about 300 steps and it's freezing down there, so descent isn't for everyone.

Väsby Kungsgård
MUSEUM

(☑ 0224-106 37; www.vasbykungsgard.se; Museigatan 2; ☺ 1-4pm Mon-Fri; P) **FREE** In the main park in town is Väsby Kungsgård, a 16th-century royal farm where, according to a love letter from 1613, Gustav II Adolf met his mistress, Ebba Bruhe. Excitement for the traveller is confined to the beautifully preserved interiors, idyllic courtyard and 17th-century weapons collection.

Norrmanska Gården
AREA

(Gillegatan) **FREE** These pretty wooden houses arranged around a central courtyard, collectively known as Norrmanska Gården, were built in 1736. The pretty area is now home to a handful of boutiques and a funky cafe, Mat & Prat (p110).

Aguélimuseet
MUSEUM

(☑ 0224-138 20; www.aguelimuseet.se; Vasagatan 17; ☺ 11am-4pm Wed-Sun) **FREE** Aguélimuseet exhibits the largest display of oils and watercolours by local artist Ivan Aguéli (1869–1917)

WORTH A TRIP

ÅNGELSBERG

Looking more like a collection of gingerbread houses than an industrial relic, **Engelsberg Bruk** (☎0223-444 64; www.engelsberg.se; Ångelsbergsvägen 4) FREE, a Unesco World Heritage site in the tiny village of Ångelsberg, was one of the most important early-industrial iron-works in Europe. During the 17th and 18th centuries, its rare timber-clad **blast furnace** and **forge** (still in working order) were state-of-the-art technology, and a whole town sprang up around them. Today you can wander the perfectly preserved estate, made up of a mansion and park, workers' homes and industrial buildings. **Guided tours** (adult/child 65kr/free) run daily at 11am, 1.30pm and 3.30pm from June to August, and less frequently in May and September; call for details or pop into the tourist information hut near the parking area.

Nya Servering (☎0223-300 18; www.nyaserveringen.com; Palettvägen 2, Ångelsberg; mains 140-250kr; ⊗11.30am-2pm Mon-Fri, noon-5pm Sat & Sun) is not far from Ångelsberg train station, next to the tourist information hut, and serves fast food, coffee and simple sandwiches. There's a good view from here across to the island Barrön on Åmänningen lake, where the world's oldest surviving **oil refinery** is located – it was opened in 1875 and closed in 1902. You can take a ferry out to visit it in combination with Engelsberg Bruk (110kr; departures at 11am, 1.30pm and 3.30pm in summer, check www.oljeon.se or www.fagersta.se/turism for updated schedules).

Ångelsberg is around 60km northwest of Västerås, from where regional trains run every hour or two (from 89kr, 45 minutes); from Ångelsberg train station it's a 1.5km walk north to the Engelsberg Bruk site. If you have your own wheels, it's a gorgeous drive from pretty much any direction.

in Sweden, as well as work by some of his contemporaries. Aguéli was a pioneering Swedish modernist whose motto was 'One can never be too precise, too simple or too deep'. In summer there are also temporary exhibitions, usually of experimental young Scandinavian artists. The building is next door to the town library.

🛏 Sleeping & Eating

★ Gruvgården B&B   B&B €
(☎024-67 72 60; www.salasilvermine.com; Drottning Christinas-vägan 16; s/d from 595/890kr) Stay in a former 1920s miner's quarters in this character-filled, rustic B&B on the grounds of Sala Silvergruva (p109). A variety of room types are available, but shower and toilet facilities are shared. Rooms are furnished in period style with antiques and comfy, home-style linens and soft, natural fabrics and fibres.

If you really want to do something different, you can stay in the world's deepest hotel suite, 155m below ground, in the silver mine itself: no windows, no external light, but luxury furnishings, a CB-radio link to an on-call staff member above ground, and a toilet outside your door... all for the reasonable (?) price of 4495kr.

STF Sala/Sofielund   HOSTEL €
(☎0224-127 30; www.sofielundsala.se; Sofielund, Mellandammen; dm from 230kr, s/d from

290/580kr; P🐾) This haven of tranquillity is in the woods near the Mellandammen pond, 2km southwest of the town centre. It's a pet-friendly complex with camping, mini-golf and a cafe (open June to August). You can take bus 569 from Sala station to Nya vattentornet, then walk about 800m to the hostel. Reservations are necessary September to mid-May.

Cafe Stadsparken   CAFE €
(☎070-854 71 89; Ekebygatan 4; light meals 55-105kr; ⊗9am-5pm Mon-Fri, from 10am Sat & Sun) This bright little cafe in the town park serves sandwiches, snacks, light lunches and makes a mean cup o' Joe.

Mat & Prat   CAFE €€
(☎0224-174 73; www.matoprat.nu; Brunnsgatan 26; dagens lunch 80kr, mains 109-230kr; ⊗11am-2pm Mon & Tue, 11am-10pm Wed & Thu, noon-1am Fri & Sat) This restaurant, inside the rustic 18th-century wooden courtyard of Norr-manska Gården, has a great outdoor patio and includes a cute pub. On the menu you'll find everything from burgers and pasta to shrimp salad. It's a popular evening spot, too, with a decent happy-hour menu.

❶ Information

If **Sala Turistbyrå** (☎0224-552 02; www.sala. se/turism; Stora Torget; ⊗8am-5pm Mon-Fri year-round, plus 10am-2pm Sat May-Sep) isn't open when you're in town, you might be able to get brochures and local info from **Sala stads-bibliotek** (Sala City Library; ☑ 0224-555 01; Norra Esplanaden 5; ☉ 9.30am-7pm Mon-Thu, 9.30am-6pm Fri, 11am-3pm Sat), where there is also internet access.

ℹ Getting There & Away

Sala is 39km north of Västerås and 63km west of Uppsala.

SJ Rail (p103) operates regular local train services to Västerås (65kr, 30 minutes) and Uppsala (105kr, 35 minutes) and less frequent services to Stockholm (125kr, 1½ hours).

Ask about bike hire at the tourist office.

Nora

☑ 0587 / POP 10,665

One of Sweden's most seductive old wooden towns, Nora sits snugly on the shores of a little lake, clearly confident in its ability to charm the pants off anyone. Slow your pace and take the time to succumb to its captivating features, such as quaint cobbled streets, old-world steam trains, mellow boat rides and decadent ice cream.

◉ Sights & Activities

Kvarteret Bryggeriet   GALLERY
(☑ 072-742 65 65; www.norart.se; Prästgatan 27-42; ☉ 11am-5pm Jun-Aug) `FREE` At the end of Prästgatan is a collection of buildings that once housed a brewery and now contains several art galleries and studios. A collective of locals puts on a knockout gallery show in the main building each summer, including work by established and rising Swedish artists. The building itself is a work of art, restored just enough to be functional without losing any of its charm. Check online or ask at the main gallery for openings and evening events.

Göthlinska Gården   HISTORIC BUILDING
(☑ 0587-811 20; Kungsgatan 4; tours adult/child 80kr/free; ☉ 1pm Tue & Wed Jul & Aug, Sat May, Jun & Sep) This manor house just off the main square was built in 1739 and is now a museum featuring furniture, decor and accoutrements from the 17th century onward. Entrance is by guided tour only: contact Nora Turistbyrå (p112) for bookings.

★ Nora Bergslags Veteran Railway   RAIL
(☑ 0587-103 04; www.nbvj.se; Järnvägsgatan 1; to Järle 140kr, to Pershyttan 120kr; ☉ Tue-Thu, Sat & Sun Jun-Aug) From the train station down by the tourist office, a vintage train takes you 10km southeast to Järle (three times daily) or 2.5km southwest to the excellent old mining village at Pershyttan on an old steam train (once daily). The return trip is by bus (included in ticket price). Get tickets at the tourist office.

★ Alntorps Ö   CRUISE
(☑ 070-216 65 24; adult/child 20/10kr; ☉ 10am-6pm Jun-Aug; ⊕) Though it's technically a youngsters' activity, you don't need to be a child to appreciate the entertaining boat trips to Alntorps island. Boats depart roughly every half-hour from the jetty near STF Nora Tåghem. A walk around the island takes about an hour, and there are swimming spots, mini-golf and a cafe. Get tickets at Nora Turistbyrå (p112).

Camping and cabins (from 1000kr) can be booked through the tourist office (but if you plan to stay, bring supplies!).

⊨ Sleeping & Eating

Nora Camping   CAMPGROUND €
(☑ 0587-123 61; www.noracamping.se; Kungsgatan; sites from 235-310kr, cabins 395-995kr; ☉ May-Sep; 🅿🛜) This small campground is by the lake 1.5km north of Nora and can be reached by a lakeshore walking path from the train station. Although RVs are permitted, there are noticeably fewer here; it has a much more grassroots camping vibe, with basic amenities, a place for swimming and beach volleyball. Guests can hire boats and canoes (50/300kr per hour/day).

STF Nora Tåghem   HOSTEL €
(☑ 0587-146 76; www.noratåghem.se; Järnvägsområdet; s/d 350/450kr; ☉ May–mid-Sep; 🅿🛜) Outdoing its home town in the cuteness department, this hostel lets you sleep in the tiny but adorable antique bunks of 1930s railway carriages. All compartments have great views over the lake, and there's a cafe that does breakfast, plus sandwiches and snacks in summer. You can even jump right in the lake behind the carriages!

★ Nora Stadshotell   HOTEL €€
(☑ 0587-31 14 35; www.norastadshotell.se; Rådstugugatan 21; s/d from 790/1190kr; 🅿🛜) You can't miss this elegant building, planted smack on the main square, with 36 simple, white-furnitured rooms – some of them in a more modern annexe. There's a good-value lunch buffet (85kr) at the restaurant, which can

be eaten on the airy summer terrace, along with à la carte evening mains from 129kr and a comfortable pub.

★ **Strandstugan** CAFE €

(☑ 0587-137 22; www.noraglass.se/strandstugan; Storgatan 1; mains 40-66kr, sandwiches 50-75kr; ⊙ 10.30am-4.30pm May-Sep) Down by the lake is this delightful wooden cottage, set in a flower-filled garden, where you can get coffee, sandwiches, quiches, desserts and other home-baked goodies, as well as Nora Glass ice-cream creations. If it's available, try the local speciality, *Bergslags paj*, a quiche made with venison, chanterelles and juniper berries.

★ **Nora Glass** ICE CREAM €

(☑ 0587-123 32; Storgatan 11; ice cream 32-74kr; ⊙ 10.30am-6.30pm May-Aug) Nora is renowned for its incredible ice cream, made here for more than 80 years. You never know what flavours will be available – three or four different ones are churned out freshly each day – but you do know that they're worth queuing for. If hazelnut is among the day's selections, don't pass it up: seriously.

❶ Information

Nora Turistbyrå (☑ 0587-811 20; www.visit nora.se; Stationshuset; ⊙ 10am-6pm Mon-Sat, 10.30am-4pm Sun, shorter hours winter) Staff can provide you with a goodie bag of brochures to assist with your explorations of the town and beyond.

❶ Getting There & Away

Nora is 34km north of Örebro and 86km west of Västerås, as the crow flies (it's between 117km and 124km by road, depending on route).

Länstrafiken Örebro (☑ 0771-55 30 00; www. lanstrafiken.se/Orebro; ⊙ 8am-8pm) operates regular buses to Örebro (64kr, 40 minutes) and other regional destinations.

Ask at **Nora Turistbyrå** (p112) about bike rental.

Örebro

☑ 019 / POP 146,631

A substantial, culturally rich city, Örebro buzzes around its central feature: the huge and romantic castle surrounded by a moat filled with water lilies. The city originally sprang up as a product of the textile industry, but it continues to gain steam as a university town, since Uppsala University started offering some courses here in 1960. In 1999, the then Örebro University College became Sweden's 12th university, and though, by national standards, Örebro's pedagogical status hardly rates a mention, the presence of students on bikes, in cafes and in parks, is more evident with each passing year.

Örebro's proximity to Stockholm, which is fast outgrowing its borders, makes it an appealing city for young families, while the equally short distance to Vänern lake lends the city a relaxed, on-holidays kind of vibe: nursing a beer in a terrace cafe and shopping unhurriedly along cobbled streets are favoured local pastimes.

⊙ Sights

Örebro Konsthall (OBKHL) GALLERY

(Örebro Art Gallery; ☑ 019-21 49 00; Olaigatan 17b; ⊙ 11am-5pm) Örebro's excellent art gallery is responsible for the fact that there are over 200 public art pieces scattered about the city and is integral in the organisation of the Örebro Open Art festival (p114). With a diverse permanent collection of primarily contemporary art and frequent visiting exhibitions, there's always something going on.

Stadsparken PARK

(☑ 019-21 10 00; Stadsparken; ℗ 🚼) Stadsparken is an idyllic and kid-friendly park once voted Sweden's most beautiful. It stretches alongside Svartån (the Black River) and merges into the Wadköping museum village.

★ **Wadköping** MUSEUM

(☑ 019-21 10 00; www.orebro.se/wadkoping; Bertil Waldéns-gata 1; ⊙ 11am-5pm daily May-Aug, 11am-4pm Tue-Sun Sep-Apr; 🚼) **FREE** The Wadköping museum village contains craft workshops, a bakery and period buildings – including Kungsstugan (the King's Lodgings, a medieval house with 16th-century ceiling paintings) and Cajsa Warg's house (home of an 18th-century celebrity chef). You can wander the village at any time; there are guided tours (20kr) at 1pm and 3pm June to August.

Örebro Slottet CASTLE

(☑ 019-21 21 21; www.orebroslott.se; Kansligatan 1; tours adult/child 60/30kr; ⊙ tours noon & 2pm daily May-Sep, 1pm Sat & Sun rest of year, history exhibition 10am-5pm daily May-Aug) Örebro's hulking and magnificent castle is unmissable in town and now serves as the county governor's headquarters. It was originally built in the late 13th century, but most of what you see today is from 300 years later. The outside is far more dramatic than the interior. To explore you'll need to take a tour.

Örebro

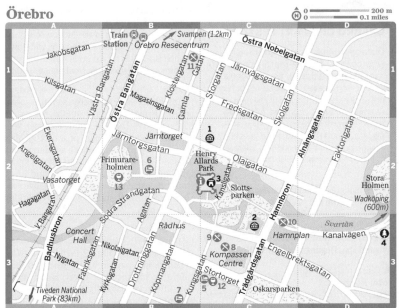

Örebro läns museum   MUSEUM

(Örebro County Museum; ☑019-602 87 00; www.
olm.se; Engelbrektsgatan 3; ☺9am-6pm Tue & Thu,
noon-9pm Wed, noon-4pm Fri-Sun) **FREE** The Länsmuseum has strong and topical temporary
exhibits – for example, a collection of protest
posters from the '60s, or a consideration of the
era's clothing and home furnishings as cultural indicators. It has a permanent collection
of artwork grouped by theme, and historical
displays about the region (mostly in Swedish).
The grounds are dotted with sculptures or outdoor art installations.

Svampen   TOWER

(☑019-611 37 35; www.svampen.nu; Dalbygatan
4; ☺11am-6pm Sun-Tue, to 9pm Wed-Sat; ▣11)
FREE The first of Sweden's modern 'mush-
room' water towers, Svampen was built in
1958 and now functions as a lookout tower.
There are good views of lake Hjälmaren at
the top, as well as a cafe (daily specials 98kr).

🛏 Sleeping

★ **STF Tivedstorp Vandrarhem**   HOSTEL €

(☑0584-47 20 90; www.tivedstorp.se/english/;
Tivedstorp; dm/s/d from 200/370/500kr, sites
100kr; ☺Apr-Oct; ℙ) This STF complex has
hostel accommodation in cute red grass-
roofed cabins, plus an activity centre and a

Örebro

tiny cafe (open noon to 7pm June to August,
and noon to 4pm Sunday March to May and
September to October). It's about 3km north
of the Tiveden National Park visitor centre;
you'll need your own transport to get here.

Clarion Hotel Örebro   HOTEL €€

(☑019-670 67 00; www.nordicchoicehotels.com/
hotels/sweden/orebro/clarion-hotel-orebro/; Kungsgatan 14; d from 1530kr; ℙ☺✳☎) This modern

DON'T MISS

ÖREBRO OPEN ART FESTIVAL

Örebro's biennial **Örebro Open Art** (www.openart.se; ⏲ Jun-Sep) is as good a reason to visit the city as any, when a diverse and sizeable collection of public art works are erected about town for all to enjoy. Different countries are usually asked to participate. In 2017, for example, Japan and Brazil were the guests, creating a dynamic fusion of disparate cultures on an overtly Swedish stage.

hotel is in a great spot along a shopping street just a block from the main square. It has comfortable rooms with all the amenities, done up in chic Swedish fabrics and fixtures. There's a popular and attractive lobby lounge area, a gym and spa. Parking is available (175kr).

★Clarion Collection Hotel Borgen HERITAGE HOTEL €€€
(☎019-20 50 00; www.nordicchoicehotels.com/hotels/sweden/orebro/clarion-collection-hotel-borgen/; Klostergatan 1; d from 1680kr) You can't miss this fabulous, central hotel by the Svartån river which looks like an extension of Örebro Slottet (p112). Occupying a building completed in 1891 that was once a bank, then a newspaper office, this otherwise thoroughly modern establishment boasts spacious, light flooded rooms with high ceilings, furnished in a contemporary style. The included afternoon tea, dinner and breakfast make for excellent value.

Behrn Hotell HOTEL €€€
(☎019-12 00 95; www.behrnhotell.se; Stortorget 12; s/d from 1395/1875kr; P ❄ @ 📶) Well positioned on the main square, the Behrn goes the extra mile with individually decorated rooms – ranging from strictly business to farmhouse or edgy modern Scandinavian. Do it right and get a room with a balcony or a suite with old wooden beams, chandeliers and a Jacuzzi. There's also a spa, and a restaurant serving dinner Tuesday to Friday.

Eating

★Hälls Konditori CAFE €
(☎019-611 07 66; www.hallsconditori.se; Engelbrektsgatan 12; pastries 20-45kr, lunch specials 84-98kr, brunch 85kr; ⏲7.30am-6pm Mon-Fri, 10am-4pm Sat; 👪) This bakery-cafe is a classic old-style *konditori* and a favourite hang-out for locals. Go for *fika* (coffee and cake) or more substantial salads, quiche and sandwiches. If the weather's nice, sit out back in the hidden courtyard area – part of Stallbacken, the tiny Old Town square. Brunch is served on Fridays from 8am to 11am and on weekends from 9am to noon.

Harrys PUB FOOD €€
(☎019-10 89 89; www.harrys.se/restauranger/orebro/; Hamnplan; beer from 60kr, pub snacks 65kr, mains 149-239kr; ⏲5pm-1am or 2am, from 2pm Sat) Though it's part of a sort of blah chain, this particular branch of Harrys has a good location in a cool old brick factory building by the river. It's popular and has a comprehensive menu of pub meals, live music on a Thursday, and a nightclub on Friday and Saturday.

Örebro Ölcafé GASTROPUB €€
(☎019-12 70 70; www.orebro-olcafe.se; Järnvägsgatan 8; mains 100-149kr; ⏲11am-10pm Tue-Thu, to 1am Fri, 4pm-1am Sat) More gastropub than cafe, this hipster joint does great burgers and killer fries, has daily home-style specials and hosts themed meal nights. With local craft beers on tap and a cosy vibe, it's a top spot for a classy but casual meal and a few ales.

★A-mano ITALIAN €€€
(☎019-32 33 70; www.a-mano.se; Kungsgatan 1; mains 178-298kr, set menus 365-735kr; ⏲6pm-midnight Mon-Sat) Escalated Italian fare, the likes of pistachio-crusted fillet of pesto-roasted lamb, from Gotland, served with fragrant gorgonzola gnocchi and baby red onions, and excellent value menus are the order of the day in this classy downtown restaurant off Stallbacken. It's best to dress to impress and is much more enjoyable if you're not dining alone.

Drinking & Nightlife

Örebro has some excellent nightlife for a city of its size and one very special club. Although Örebro isn't exactly party central, it's definitely a place where you'll have fun exploring the selection of bars and pubs.

★Villa Strömpis CLUB
(☎072-339 94 00; www.villastrompis.se; Strömparterren; ⏲9pm-2am Wed, Fri & Sat) This luxe manor house on its own island in the river is Örebro's coolest nightclub hang. Rumour has it the place even has its own secret society. Dress to impress, boys and girls, and keep it classy.

★Satin BAR
(☎019-10 89 89; www.satin.nu; Stortorget 14; ⏱3pm-2am) Part bar, part restaurant, part nightspot, this excellent multipurpose venue is a sure bet whether you're looking for casual dining, drinks with friends or a night on the tiles.

Information

The office of **Visit Örebro** (☎019-21 21 21; www.orebrotown.se; ⏱10am-5pm summer, noon-4pm Sat & Sun rest of year) is in the southwest tower of **Örebro Slottet** (p112), on the first floor.

Getting There & Away

Örebro is 202km west of Stockholm on the E18 motorway.

It is a popular hub for long-distance buses which leave from the **Örebro Resecentrum** (Östra Bangatan) adjoining the train station.

Swebus Express (p106) has direct connections to Norrköping (from 149kr, two hours), Karlstad (from 99kr, 1¾ hours) and Oslo (Norway; from 289kr, five hours), Västerås (from 69kr, 1¼ hours) and Stockholm (from 169kr, 2¾ hours).

SJ Rail (p103) operates direct trains to/from Stockholm (195kr, two hours) every hour with some via Västerås (95kr, one hour); and frequently to and from Gothenburg (145kr, three hours) and Borlänge (235kr, two hours), where you can change for Falun and Mora.

Karlstad

☎054 / POP 90,198

A pleasant and compact riverside town creeping down to the shores of Vänern lake, Värmland's largest city, Karlstad, makes itself useful as a base for travellers pursuing outdoor activities in the region.

The city has a handful of noteworthy sights and its large student population means it has a decent restaurant and bar scene for its size.

Sights

★Värmlands Museum MUSEUM
(☎054-14 31 00; www.varmlandsmuseum.se; Vastra Torgattan; adult/child 80kr/free; ⏱10am-6pm Mon-Fri, to 8pm Wed, 11am-4pm Sat & Sun) The award-winning and imaginative Värmlands Museum occupies two buildings on Sandgrundsudden (reclaimed land now converted into a pleasant park) near the library. Its multimedia displays cover local history and culture from the Stone Age to current times, including music, the river, forests and textiles. Some components of the museum are open-air, activity-based displays about local industry and working life, including a log-driving museum and a mineral mine, just outside of town; pick up brochures at the museum or tourist office.

Mariebergsskogen PARK
(☎054-29 69 90; www.mariebergsskogen.se; Treffenbergsvägen 20; ⏱7am-10pm; P) FREE For green spaces and picnic spots, seek out Mariebergsskogen, a combined leisure park, open-air museum and animal park in the southwestern part of town (about 1km from the centre). Also here is Naturum Värmland, with a cafe and shop, perched over Vänern lake.

Sleeping & Eating

CarlstadCity Hostel HOSTEL €
(☎054-21 65 60; www.carlstadcity.se; Järnvägsgatan 8; s/d hostel from 450/560kr, hotel from 540/610kr;) This very central hostel near the station, with hotel-standard rooms also available, has bunks in simple, basic whitewashed rooms with shared bathrooms. There's a guest kitchen and a good breakfast buffet available (60kr for hostellers). Hotel rooms have TVs and private bathrooms.

Skutberget Camping CAMPGROUND €
(☎054-53 51 20; www.firstcamp.se/skutberget-karlstad; Skutbergsvägen 315; sites from 150kr, cabins from 390kr; P; 18) This big, friendly lakeside campsite, 7km west of town off the E18 motorway, is part of a large sports and recreation area, with beach volleyball, a driving range, mini-golf, exercise tracks and a mountain-bike course. There are also sandy and rocky beaches nearby.

★Clarion Hotel Bilan HOTEL €€
(☎054-10 03 00; www.nordicchoicehotels.com/hotels/sweden/karlstad/clarion-collection-hotel-bilan/; Karlbergsgatan 3; r from 1580kr; P) The town's old jail cells have been converted into large, bright and cleverly decorated rooms with exposed-wood ceiling beams and funky shapes. You'll also find the **Old Town Prison Museum** (⏱10am-5pm) FREE in the basement, letting you in on the building's history. There's a guest sauna and complimentary afternoon tea, as well as a free evening meal and breakfast.

Kebab House FAST FOOD €€
(☎054-15 08 15; www.kebabhouse.kvartersmenyn.se; Västra Torggatan 9; pizza 85-112kr, kebabs

OFF THE BEATEN TRACK

HOTELL & CAMPING STORLUNGEN

If you really want to get away from it all, the pretty **Hotell & Camping Storlungen** (☑ 070-374 20 06; www. storlungen.se; Lungsund; sites 200kr, d from 995kr; P ☎) campground in the middle of nowhere, some 63km from Karlstad, is just the spot. Simple rooms (no TV) occupy the former schoolhouse building, or choose from a bunch of lovely waterfront campsites. Ask the friendly hosts about the private sauna on an island in the lake.

64-89kr, mains 99-249kr; ☺ noon-10pm) Don't be fooled by the name – the Kebab House is a cut above your average fast-food place and serves good-value pizza, kebabs and salads as well as steaks and fish. Check out its fancy striped wallpaper and chandeliers if you don't believe us. In summer, stake out one of the popular outdoor tables along the busy pedestrianised street.

❶ Information

Karlstads Turistbyrå (☑ 054-540 24 70; www. visitkarlstad.se; Västra Torggatan 26; ☺ 9am-7pm Mon-Fri, 10am-6pm Sat, 10am-3pm Sun) Centrally located in the same building as the public library.

❶ Getting There & Around

Karlstad is 109km west of Örebro on the E19 motorway and is a major transport hub for western central Sweden.

Swebus Express (p106) has daily services to Falun (from 299kr, three hours), Gothenburg (from 219kr, two to three hours), and Oslo (from 199kr, six hours). Services depart from **Karlstad Busstationen** (Drottninggatan 43).

SJ Rail (p103) runs frequent trains to Sunne (110kr, one hour), Stockholm (460kr, 2½ hours), Gothenburg (228kr, 2½ hours) and Oslo (Norway; 207kr, 2¾ hours).

Regional buses are operated by **Värmlandstrafik** (☑ 020-22 55 80). Bus 200 travels to Sunne (110kr, 1¼ hours) and Torsby (155kr, two hours).

Free bikes are available from **Solacykeln** (☑ 054-540 52 12; www.visitvarmland.se/en/do/sola-bike-30260; Västra Torggatan 26; ☺ 7.30am-5.30pm Jun-Sep). All you need is a valid ID.

Sunne

☑ 0565 / POP 4931

Sunne, a sprawly town with a happy sounding name hugs the waterway which connects so-called Övre Fryken (northern lake) and Mellan-Fryken (middle lake). Its famed for having one of southern Sweden's best-known ski areas, but southern Sweden isn't exactly renowned for its towering masstifs or thigh-deep cover... If you're a powder hound, don't get too excited.

In summer, it's a blissfully quiet spot with a handful of cultural attractions to keep most visitors busy for a day, but the town generally won't be on the radar for most international roamers as it's a little out of the way from, well, everything, really.

For those interested in Swedish literature, Sunne has a proud literary heritage, as the hometown of famed Swedish authors Selma Lagerlöf and Göran Tunström. Lagerlöf's birthplace is the town's star attraction (after the ski hill) while Tunström is buried near the east gable of Sunne Church.

◉ Sights & Activities

Selma Lagerlöfs Mårbacka MUSEUM
(☑ 0565-310 27; www.marbacka.com; Mårbacka 42, Östra Ämtervik; adult/child 40kr/free; ☺ 10am-4pm daily Jun-Aug, 11am-3pm Sat & Sun May & Sep, 11am-2pm Sat Oct-Dec & Feb-Apr, closed Jan; P) The area's main draw is this house at Mårbacka, 9km from Sunne, where Swedish novelist Selma Lagerlöf (1858–1940) was born. She was the first woman to receive the Nobel Prize for Literature, and many of her tales are based in the local area. Seeing the interior requires a guided tour (125kr, 45 minutes), which leaves on the hour from 11am to 3pm – a tour in English is given daily in summer at 2pm.

★ Rottneros Park PARK
(☑ 0565-602 95; www.rottnerospark.se; Rottneros; adult/child 120/40kr; ☺ 10am-4pm May, Jun & Sep, to 6pm Jul & Aug; P ♿; ☐ 200) Known as 'Ekeby' in Selma Lagerlöf's *Gösta Berling's Saga,* Rottneros Park, 6km south of Sunne, soothes travel-weary adults with flower gardens, a tropical greenhouse and an arboretum. There's lots for kids, including the rope-swinging delights of Sweden's largest climbing forest. The attached warehouse has temporary exhibitions. Rottneros has its own train station.

Stiftelsen Sundsbergs Gård　MUSEUM
(☑0565-103 63; Ekebyvägen; adult/child 50kr/
free; ☺noon-4pm Wed-Sun late Jun–mid-Aug)
Sundsbergs Gård, behind the Hotel Selma
Lagerlöf, was featured in *Gösta Berling's
Saga* and now contains a forestry museum,
a furniture and textiles collection, an art exhibition, a cafe and a manor house.

Ski Sunne　SNOW SPORTS
(☑0565-602 80; www.skisunne.se; Hån 67, Rottneros; day pass adult/child 320/260kr) Ski
Sunne, the town's ski resort, has nine different descents, a snowboarding area and
a cross-country skiing stadium, and night
skiing in some areas, plus all the usual ski-
area facilities (lodge, bar-restaurant, shop,
equipment rentals). In summer, the resort
becomes a mountain-bike park.

🛏 Sleeping & Eating

There are a few year-round accommodation
options to choose from, including a campground, youth hostel and quaint country inn.

Sunne Logi B&B　HOSTEL €
(☑0565-107 88; www.sunnevandrarhem.se; Hem-
bygdsvägen 7; dm 200kr, s/d from 300/440kr,
breakfast 60kr; ℗) This well-equipped hostel-
cum-B&B has beds in sunny wooden cabins.
There's a futuristic kitchen, an antique dining room and outside tables and chairs for
alfresco meals. Bikes can be rented.

**★Ulvsby herrgård
Länsmansgården**　INN €€
(☑0565-140 10; www.countrysidehotels.se/hotell/
ulvsby-herrgard-lansmansgarden; Ulvsby herrgård;
s/d from 895/1195kr; ℗☺🛜) This historic
'sheriff's house' features in Lagerlöf's *Gösta Berling's Saga*. It's a picturesque place
for a fine lunch or restful evening in one
of the romantic bedrooms, named after the
book's characters. The highly rated restaurant specialises in Swedish cuisine from the
Värmland region, using locally sourced pike,
salmon, beef, reindeer and lamb and fresh
seasonal ingredients.

Check the website for occasional hotel
packages with steeply discounted room
rates. The mansion is 4km north of Sunne
centre, by Rte 45 (toward Torsby).

Saffran & Vitlök　CAFE €
(☑0565-120 09; www.saffranvitlok.se; Storgatan
39; salads from 85kr; ☺11am-6pm Mon-Fri, to 3pm
Sat; ☑) Having expanded and moved into
the big, white library building on the main
square, this cafe serves giant bowls of hefty

salads to take away or dine in on (there's
indoor or courtyard seating), plus excellent
coffee, sandwiches, pastries and hot dishes.
It lives up to the name (*vitlök* is garlic), so
just follow your nose and you'll find it.

❶ Information

Sunne InfoPoint (☑0565-167 70; www.
sagolikasunne.se/sv; Storgatan 39; ☺9am-
6pm Mon-Thu, to 8pm Fri, plus 10am-3pm
Sat & Sun summer) Your port of call for local
information, maps and brochures.

❶ Getting There & Away

Sunne is 67km north of Karlstad on the E45
motorway.

Värmlandstrafik bus 200 and local **SJ Rail**
(p103) trains travel from Sunne to Karlstad
(112kr).

The fare is the same but trains run more
frequently and are quicker: 50 minutes versus
1½ hours.

Buses and trains also run to Torsby (73kr). The
bus takes an hour while the train takes about 40
minutes.

Torsby
☑0560 / POP 4503

Sleepy Torsby, deep in the forests of Värmland,
is only 38km from Norway. The area's history
and sights are linked to emigrants from Finland, who settled in western parts of Sweden
in the mid-16th century and built their own
distinctive farms and villages in the forests.
These homesteads, many of which have been
well preserved, are the main attraction for
visitors to the area, which also has some neat,
niche museums.

Public transport isn't great and sites
are far apart, so it's easier and more fun
to explore the town if you have your own
transport.

◎ Sights

★Torsby Finnskogscentrum　MUSEUM
(Torsby Finn Forest Centre; ☑0560-162 93; www.
varmlandsmuseum.se; Lekvattnet 84; adult/child
40kr/free; ☺11am-5pm mid-Jun–mid-Aug;　℗)
The ingeniously designed Forest Centre,
opened in June 2014 near Lekvattnet as
part of Värmlands County Museum, covers the 17th-century Finnish settlement of
the area, with displays on smokehouses,
hunting, music, witchcraft and the settlers'
trademark 'slash and burn' style of cultivat-
ing grain. (They planted rye in the ashes of

TIVEDEN NATIONAL PARK

Reopened in 2017 after extensive reconstruction works on its infrastructure and facilities, the landscapes of **Tiveden National Park** (☑ 0584-47 40 83; www.nationalparks ofsweden.se; ⊙ visitor centre 10am-4pm May-Sep, 11am-4pm Sat & Sun Apr & Oct) **FREE** were carved by glaciers tens of thousands of years ago. Reputedly the domain of trolls and the former stomping ground of highwaymen, the park, some 84km southwest of Örebro, is noted for its ancient virgin forests which are rare in southern Sweden. With plenty of dramatic bare bedrock, extensive boulder fields and a scattering of lakes, it makes for wonderful tramps through the wilderness.

Several self-guided walks, including the 6km Trollkyrka ('troll church') trail, start from the visitor centre in the southeastern part of the park, 5km north of Rd 49 (turn-off at Bocksjö) where you can pick up brochures and maps. Themed guided tours (150kr) are available Wednesday to Sunday from mid-June to August.

The area is also good for cycling (the Sverigeleden trail passes nearby), canoeing, fishing, cross-country skiing and horse riding. Ask at the visitor centre or speak to the friendly folks at Visit Örebro (p115) before you set out.

You can camp overnight in the park or stay in adorable little red huts at the STF Tivedstorp Vandrarhem (p113), but you'll need your own wheels to get here: there's no public transport, but that just keeps things pristine.

If you're a lover of the great outdoors, the park is well worth a look-see. For more info, check out www.tiveden.se/en.

burnt trees.) There's also a research library and a cafe. The centre is on the E16 road, 22km from Torsby, across from a small convenience shop.

Hembygdsgården Kollsberg   MUSEUM

(☑ 0560-718 61; www.hembygdsgarden.kollsberg. se; Levgrensvägen 36; adult/child 20kr/free, guided tours 40kr; ⊙ noon-5pm Jun-Aug; P) Hembygdsgården Kollsberg, down beside Fryken lake, is a dinky homestead museum with several old houses, including a Finnish cabin. A cafe serves coffee and waffles (40kr) and the traditional Finnish settlers' dish *motti och fläsk* (oat porridge with pork; 80kr).

Fordonsmuseum   MUSEUM

(☑ 0560-712 10; www.torsby-fordonsmuseum.se; Gräsmarksvägen 8; adult/child 40kr/free; ⊙ 10am-5.30pm Mon-Fri Jun-Aug, plus noon-5pm Sat & Sun May & Sep; P) At the edge of Torsby's town centre, the Fordonsmuseum will appeal to motorheads with its collection of rare and vintage cars, motorcycles and fire engines.

🏃 Activities

There are a number of summer activities and tours in the area, including fishing, canoeing, white-water rafting, rock climbing, mountain biking, and beaver and elk safaris. Contact the tourist office for information.

You can also catch boat trips on the *Freya af Fryken* from Torsby.

Torsby Skidtunnel   SKIING

(☑ 0560-270 00; www.skitunnel.se; Vasserudsvägen 11; adult/child rental packet 220/150kr, 1hr pass 180/120kr; ⊙ 10am-7pm Mon-Fri, to 5pm Sat & Sun) Looking like something you might use to smash atoms, Sweden's first ski tunnel (1.3km) offers controlled conditions and a gentle incline, making it a great workout or equipment-testing track. It also contains the world's only indoor biathlon shooting range.

Hovfjället   SKIING

(☑ 0560-313 00; www.hovfjallet.se; Överbyn 63; day pass adult/child 310/250kr, alpine ski hire per day from 255/210kr; ⊙ Dec-Apr) For skiing outdoors, check out Hovfjället, 20km north of Torsby. There are several ski lifts and a variety of runs. The resort also offers dog sledding on weekends, plus other activities such as snowshoeing, mountain-biking and wolf-viewing trips.

🍴 Sleeping & Eating

Vägsjöfors Herrgård   B&B €

(☑ 0560-313 30; www.vagsjoforsherrgard.com; Vägsjöfors 3; sites 200kr, dm 210kr, r without/with bathroom from 380/480kr; P 🛜) This large manor house is 20km north of Torsby, by a stunning lake. Rooms are individually and tastefully decorated, and there are hostel beds in little cabins and campsites on the grounds as well. Hostel breakfast is 65kr extra. There's also a guest kitchen. Family-size groups can rent a self-catering apartment (1200kr, sleeps up to six).

Hotell Örnen   HOTEL €€
(☑0560-146 64; www.hotellornen.se; Östmarksvägen 4; s/d from 895/1095kr; P⊖🛜) Cosy Örnen is a pretty lemon-coloured place set behind a white picket fence in the town centre. Cheerful, homey Swedish-style rooms practically vibrate with wholesomeness and folky charm.

Wienerkonditoriet   CAFE €
(☑0560-101 39; www.nyawienerkonditoriet.com; Järnvägsgatan 6; pastries from 20kr; ⊙8am-6pm Mon-Fri, 9am-4pm Sat, 11am-4pm Sun) This homey cafe on the main drag serving hot coffee and home-baked cakes and pastries feels like an auntie's living room, complete with family portraits on the walls.

ℹ️ Information
Torsby Turistbyrå (☑0560-160 50; www.visit torsby.se; Kyrkogatan 5; ⊙10am-4pm Mon-Fri) Near the main square.

ℹ️ Getting There & Away
Torsby is 37km north of Sunne on the E45 motorway.

Värmlandstrafik (p116) bus 212 runs from Torsby to Sunne (73kr, one hour).

It's quicker and the same price to catch a more frequent **SJ Rail** (p103) train from Torsby to Sunne (73kr, 40 minutes). Trains also run to Karlstad (155kr, two hours).

Torsby even has its own little **airport** (☑0560-717 24; www.torsbyflygplats.se), with flights to Stockholm Arlanda from 595kr.

Falun

☑ 023 / POP 57,685

An unlikely combination of industrial and adorable, Falun is home to one of Sweden's oldest and most important copper mines, now retired from service and a protected World Heritage site. As a consequence, the town was for hundreds of years the primary source of the ruddy red tint that renders Swedish country houses so uniformly cute.

Falun is the main city of Dalarnas *län* (Dalarna county), a region known for its year-round outdoor activities from lowlands hiking to biking, swimming and sailing, and in the colder months, cross-country and downhill skiing and even ski-jumping. It is positioned between lakes Runn and Siljan (50km north), and there's a selection of

worthwhile sights within striking distance of the city, including one of Sweden's best-loved historic home museums in the village of Sundborn.

⊙ Sights & Activities
The Unesco World Heritage listing encompasses a much larger area than just the centrally located Falu Gruva and includes sections of the historic old town.

★ Falu Gruva   MINE
(☑023-78 20 30; www.falugruva.se; Gruvplatsen 1; tours adult/child 220/90kr, above-ground only 90/50kr; ⊙tours hourly 10am-5pm Jun-Aug, less frequent rest of year; P; 🚌53, 708 Timmervägen) Falun's *kopparbergs gruva* was the world's most important copper mine by the 17th century. Called 'Sweden's treasure chest', it drove the small country's international aspirations, funded wars and helped paint all those summer cottages that distinctive red. You can opt to take a one-hour underground tour of the mines or simply explore above ground where you'll find the interesting and informative **Mine Museum** (adult/child 80/40kr; ⊙10am-5:30pm daily Jul & Aug, 10am-5:30pm Mon-Fri & noon-4pm Sat & Sun May, Jun & Sep) and some heritage outbuildings, cafes and boutiques.

★ Carl Larsson-gården   HISTORIC BUILDING
(☑023-600 53; www.clg.se; Carl Larssonsvägen 12, Sundborn; adult/child/family 180/60/550kr; ⊙tours 10am-5pm daily May-Sep, 11am Mon-Fri & 1pm Sat & Sun Jan-Apr; 🚻; 🚌64) Don't miss Sweden's 'most famous home', located 13km northeast of Falun in the picturesque village of Sundborn. After their deaths, the early-20th-century residence of artist Carl Larsson and his wife Karin was preserved in its entirety by their children, but it's no gloomy memorial: 'Lilla Hyttnäs' is itself a work of art, full of brightness, humour and love. Admission is by hour-long guided tour: call in advance to book English-language tours or grab an English handbook and follow the Swedes.

Lugnets Skidmuseum   MUSEUM
(☑023-864 00; www.lugnetsskidmuseum.se; Slaggatan 4; funicular adult/child 50/30kr, museum adult/child 50/30kr; ⊙10am-6pm; P) For something completely different, ride the funicular and elevator to this thoroughly original panoramic museum atop the iconic ski-jump tower looming over Falun from Lugnet (p120), 3km east of town. On offer

here are excellent views, the chance to learn about the history of the towers and the niche sport of professional ski-jumping, a ride on the ski-jump simulator (for those who like things a little more hands on) or a more subdued game of boules on the lawn outside.

Dalarnas Museum MUSEUM
([Z] 023-666 55 00; www.dalarnasmuseum.se; Stigaregatan 2-4; ⊙10am-5pm Tue-Fri, noon-5pm Sat-Mon, to 9pm Wed summer; [P][♠]) FREE Dalarnas Museum is a super introduction to Swedish folk art, music and costumes. It's kid-friendly, too, with the opposite of the usual 'Do not touch' signs (these say 'Be curious! Please touch!'). Selma Lagerlöf's study is preserved here, and there are ever-changing art and craft exhibitions, including a great regional collection of textiles. Don't miss the graphic-arts hall, with a display on the history of Swedish sketching and engraving techniques, or the gallery of traditional costumes from all parts of Dalarna.

Lugnet HEALTH & FITNESS
([Z] 023-835 00; www.lugnet.se; Slaggatan 4; ⊙reception 8am-7pm Mon-Fri, 9am-6pm Sat & Sun) If you're sporty and love the great outdoors, the Lugnet area, home to the massive Olympic ski jump you see as you drive into town, should be on your radar, whatever the season. In summer, cross-country, downhill ski-

ing and ski-jumping give way to mountain biking, hiking and swimming in Lugnet's excellent pool facilities; or take the funicular and elevator up to Lugnets Skidmuseum (p119). Hours and admission fees vary by facility: check the website for details.

🛏 Sleeping

Lugnets Camping & Stugby CAMPGROUND €
([Z] 023-654 00; www.lugnetscamping.se; Lugnetvägen 14; sites 270kr, 2-bed huts from 480kr, cabins from 795kr; [P][≈]; [🚌]705, 713) A variety of basic cottage-style lodging compliments the many campsites available in this long, thin campground 3km northeast of town in the Lugnet skiing and sports area. There's plenty to keep active adults occupied and crazy golf, boules and the nearby outdoor pool will keep the kids happy too.

Falu Fängelse Vandrarhem HOSTEL €
([Z] 023-79 55 75; www.falufangelse.se; Villavägen 17; dm/s/f 295/395/775kr; ⊙reception 8am-6pm; [@][🔊][🐾]) This hostel really feels like what it is – a former prison. Dorm beds are in cells, with heavy iron doors, thick walls, concrete floors and steel lockers for closets. The shower and toilet facilities are somewhat limited, so it's worth asking if a room with a bathroom is available.

THE GREAT OUTDOORS

Getting out into nature is one of the most rewarding things to do in this part of Sweden. And it's easy. Outdoors enthusiasts have a number of options within easy reach, for all types of weather.

Skiers are spoiled for choice, as sleepy little Sälen transforms itself in winter into a major destination for skiers of all abilities. There's also good skiing at the smaller, slightly more remote Grönklitt and at the bustling, snowboard-friendly Sunne. At Hovfjället (p118), you can opt for downhill or cross-country skiing, or choose something more unusual, like snowshoeing, dog-sledding or wolf-watching.

Torsby and its surrounds are also a good base for warm-weather activities like hiking and cycling. Finnskogleden is a well-marked 240km trekking path that roughly follows the Norwegian border. Dalarna has Siljansleden, a 300km network of walking and cycling paths surrounding the scenic Lake Siljan. And near Sälen it's easy to hop onto the southern section of Kungsleden, the popular walking trail through Norrland. Walking trails are also plentiful in and around Tiveden National Park (p118), which is a good place to enquire about fishing as well.

For a good summary of fishing in this part of Sweden, visit www.sportfiskeguide.se; the website has information on where to go, what's required, where to stay, and how to find a guide, in Swedish and English. Fishing generally requires you to purchase a Fiskekort, which must be bought locally where you intend to fish. Anglers will find some great fishing in and around Grövelsjön, along with excellent skiing, hiking, rock climbing, river paddling and most other outdoor activities. The village is inside a nature reserve.

★Clarion Collection
Hotel Bergmastaren   HOTEL €€
(☑ 023-70 17 00; www.nordicchoicehotels.se; Berg-skolegränd 7; d from 1280kr; [P][🛜]) This thor-oughly renovated modern hotel keeps the classics in mind. Antique styled furnishings, compact chandeliers, old-world wallpapers and wood-panelled walls shift your focus from the HDTV and high-speed wi-fi to the snuggly bed where it just feels right to read a book. A complimentary light dinner served between 6pm and 9pm and a decent breakfast spread round out this noteworthy downtown offering.

Scandic Hotel Lugnet Falun   HOTEL €€
(☑ 023-669 22 00; www.scandichotels.se/hotell/sverige/falun/scandic-lugnet-falun; Svärdsjöga-tan 51; d from 1160kr; [P][♿][@][🛜][🏊]) This large, modern building stands out a mile with its ski-jump design. It has something of a col-lege-dorm feel and heaps of facilities, includ-ing a restaurant, a bar and even a bowling hall in the basement. Steep summer and weekend discounts make it a smoking deal. The hotel is about 2km east of the centre, off the E16, close to Lugnet.

✖ Eating & Drinking
Sandbergs Skafferi   CAFE €
(☑ 023-176 70; www.sandbergsskafferi.se; Åsgatan 18; baguettes from 65kr, mains from 89kr; ⊙11am-6pm Mon-Fri, 10am-6pm Sat, 10am-3pm Sun) This cute little shop selling gifts and speciality foods is also a deli, with everything from cof-fee and pastries to delicious baguette sand-wiches and hot meals like quiche or lasagne. It's on a pedestrianised shopping street, with a handful of tables both inside and out.

★Kopparhattan   CAFE €€
(☑ 023-191 69; www.kopparhattan.se; Stigaregatan 2; lunch buffet 95kr, mains 149-259kr; ⊙11am-3pm Mon-Tue, to 10pm Wed-Sat, noon-5pm Sun; [☑]) An excellent choice is this funky, arty cafe-restaurant in the Dalarnas Museum com-plex. Choose from sandwiches, soup or a good buffet including vegetarian-friendly choices for lunch; and light vegie, fish and meat evening mains. There's an outside ter-race overlooking the river, and live music on Friday nights in summer. Oh, and burgers... really good burgers (from 85kr)... day and night.

Banken Bar & Brasserie   SWEDISH €€€
(☑ 023-71 19 11; www.bankenfalun.se; Åsgatan 41; mains 165-295kr, set menus 400-575kr; ⊙11.30am-11pm Mon-Thu, to midnight Fri, 1pm-midnight Sat) Based in a former bank, classy Banken has a splendid interior (thoroughly restyled in 2017) and matching service. The menu fea-tures decadent preparations of Swedish tra-ditional meals, like reindeer carpaccio with truffles, or saffron-scented roast salmon; im-pressive weekday set lunches are good value.

Engleska Puben   PUB
(☑ 023-292 61; www.engelskapuben.se; Bergslags-gränd 1; ⊙4pm-2am Tue-Fri, 6pm-2am Sat & Sun) This little, locally owned and operated pub with its regular punters really feels like a proper British hole-in-the-wall. With de-cor that could be straight from any British country pub, Brit beers on tap and fish and chips on the menu, there's no need to cross the Channel when you're craving old Blighty.

❶ Information
Falu Turistbyrå (Falu Tourist Office; ☑ 023-830 50; www.visitsodradalarna.se; Trotzgatan 10-12; ⊙10am-6pm Mon-Fri, to 4pm Sat) The friendly staff have maps and brochures which place Falun in its historical context and pinpoint the neighbourhoods, smelteries, slag heaps and mine estates protected under the World Heritage designation.

❶ Getting There & Away
By road, Falun is 223km northwest of Stockholm via the E18 motorway and Rte 70, and 91km west of Gävle on the E16.

Swebus Express (p106) operates operates daily buses on the Gothenburg–Karlstad–Falun route.

Regional transport is run by **Dalatrafik** (☑ 0771-95 95 95; www.dalatrafik.se), which covers all corners of Dalarnas *län*. Tickets cost 30kr for trips within a zone, and 15kr extra for each new zone. A 30-day *länskort* (county pass) costs 1390kr and allows you to travel through-out the county; cards in smaller increments are also available.

Regional bus 132 goes hourly to Rättvik (70kr, one hour) and Mora (96kr, 1½ hours).

SJ Rail (p103) operates at least hourly servic-es between Falun and Gävle (164kr, 1¼ hours), but if you're coming from Stockholm or Mora, you'll need to change at Borlänge.

Lake Siljan
It's difficult to imagine that 377 million years ago the area around picturesque Lake Siljan bore the brunt of Europe's greatest meteor impact, when a giant lump of space rock hit

with the force of 500 million atomic bombs, obliterating all life and creating a 75km ring-shaped crater.

Today, the area is a picture of tranquillity just a few hours' drive from Stockholm and is close to the hearts of many Swedes for whom it's a favoured summer destination.

The 354-sq-km lake and its surrounding countryside combine sparkling waters with lush green landscapes, outdoor activities galore, a rich tradition of folk arts and some of Sweden's prettiest villages. If outdoor pursuits aren't your thing, you'll be able to see Swedish folk art Dala horses being hand painted in Nusnäs, learn about the life of one of the nation's best-loved artists in Mora, or just relax and enjoy life in lovely Tällberg.

❶ Getting There & Away

Leksand is 260km northwest of Stockholm via Rte 70, which continues its journey around Lake Siljan's eastern shore for another 57km to Mora. Regional roads kiss the many inlets of the lake's less-touristed western shore. Renting your own vehicle will afford you the freedom to explore the more beautiful nooks and crannies of the lake outside its major towns.

Local **Dalatrafik** (p121) buses service Mora, Rättvik, Leksand and Orsa, with additional services to Falun and outlying communities.

SJ Rail (p103) operates daily Intercity services between Stockholm and Mora, stopping first at Leksand, Tällberg and Rättvik.

Leksand

📞 0247 / POP 15,507

For most of the year, the town of Leksand, the southernmost on the shores of Lake Siljan, is quiet. But for one weekend in summer (always from the Friday between 19 and 25 June) around 20,000 spectators flood the town for one of Sweden's most popular Midsummer Festivals where you can join in the festivities amid much singing and costumed dancing around maypoles.

Leksand is the southern gateway to Lake Siljan and a logical first port of call as you begin your explorations of the area. The town has strong trade ties with Japan and, in honour of its sister city, Tobetsu, there's a pleasant Japanese garden that's free to enjoy any time of year.

◎ Sights & Activities

★ **Munthe's Hildasholm**   HISTORIC BUILDING
(📞 0247-100 62; www.hildasholm.org; Klockaregatan 5; adult/child 140/60kr, garden only 40kr;

⊙ 10am-5pm Jun-early Sep, 11am-5pm Sat & Sun early Sep-Oct; ℗) Built by Axel Munthe (1857–1949), who served as the Swedish royal physician and wrote the best-selling memoir *The Story of San Michele*, this sumptuously decorated National Romantic–style mansion is set in beautiful gardens with views over Lake Siljan. Built for Munthe's second wife, an English aristocrat, in 1910–11, the mansion was rarely visited by Munthe as he spent most of his time attending to Queen Viktoria on the island of Capri. Admission is by guided tour only.

Tours (in Swedish) run every hour, with a guided tour in English at 2pm.

Japanska Parken   GARDENS
(Hjortnäsvägen; ℗) In recognition of the town's sister-city-hood with Tobetsu, Japan, you'll find this lovely (and authentic) Japanese garden by the shores of Lake Siljan. It's a wonderful, quiet place to sit and contemplate.

Naturum Dalarna   NATURE RESERVE
(📞 010-22 50 329; www.naturumdalarna.se; Buffils Annas vägen 36, Siljansnäs; ⊙ 10am-4pm May-Sep; ℗ ♿; 🚌 84 Siljansnäs) 🌿 **FREE** This visitor centre and nature park, 16km northwest of Leksand, has information about the meteor that hit several million years ago and local flora and fauna, with a slightly moth-eaten collection of 50 stuffed animals. There are activities for toddlers, nature walks and films; kids can even paint their own wooden horse. Two-hour guided tours of the park in English are available (book in advance). The highlight is the 22m-high viewing platform offering stunning 360-degree views around the lake.

M/S Gustaf Wasa   BOATING
(📞 070-542 10 25; www.wasanet.nu; Strandvägen 31; 125-175kr, incl meal 325-425kr; ⊙ Jun-Aug) A great way to enjoy Lake Siljan is by boat: in summer, M/S *Gustaf Wasa* runs a complex range of lunch, dinner and sightseeing cruises from the towns of Leksand, Mora and Rättvik. Updated schedules are posted online, in English. Tickets can only be booked by phone or in person.

🍴 Sleeping & Eating

STF Vandrarhem Leksand   HOSTEL €
(📞 0247-152 50; www.vandrarhemleksand.se; Källberget Parkgattu 6; dm member/non-member 200/250kr; ⊙ summer only; ℗ ♿ 📶) It's a little out of the way (2km south of town), but this is a lovely wee hostel and Dalarna's oldest,

with ultracute wooden huts built around a flowery courtyard. Bikes are available for rent (70kr per day). Breakfast is available, and there's a guest kitchen and laundry (40kr). Reserve early, as it's popular with groups.

Hotell Leksand HOTEL €€

(📞0247-145 70; www.hotelleksand.com; Leksandsvägen 7; s/d from 1095/1495kr; 🅿😊@🛜) Leksand's most dependable lodging is conveniently situated in the heart of town, with bright, spick and span single and double rooms and cheerful staff. There's even a video tour on the website so you'll have a fair idea of what to expect.

⭐**Siljans Konditori** BAKERY €

(📞0247-150 70; www.leksandresort.se/siljanskonditori/; Sparbanksgatan 5; sandwiches 45-85kr, dagens lunch 98kr, ice cream from 30kr; ⏱8.30am-7pm Mon-Fri, 9am-5pm Sat, 10am-5pm Sun) This large and inviting bakery-cafe serves hearty filled sandwiches on its own freshly baked bread, perfect for that lakeside picnic. If you're in the mood to dine in, daily set lunches offer good value. And you can finish off your meal with the tantalising ice cream you've been eyeing-off the whole time.

GC Bar & Lounge CAFE €€

(📞0247-132 60; www.gardscafe.se; Norsgatan 19; dagens lunch 98kr, sandwiches from 70kr; ⏱9am-9pm; 🍴) A cute old wooden house with front patio and back garden seating, this busy but friendly cafe serves tempting coffee and pastries as well as enormous, filling pasta salads and hot meals. The help-yourself *dagens* (daily) lunch buffet with salad bar is a great deal; you can also order just the salad bar for 88kr.

ⓘ Information

Siljan Turism Leksand Tourist Center

(📞0248-79 72 00; info@siljan.se; Norsgatan 28; ⏱9am-6pm Mon-Fri, 10am-4pm Sat & Sun) Has information on Dalarna county and Lake Siljan, and can assist with planning your explorations of the lake.

ⓘ Getting There & Away

Leksand is 260km northwest of Stockholm along Rte 70.

Dalatrafik (p121) buses and **SJ Rail** (p103) local trains run frequently between Leksand and the rest of the Lake Siljan region, including Mora (one hour, 105kr), Rättvik (from 65kr, 20 minutes) and Tällberg (from 55kr, 20 minutes).

Tällberg

📞0248 / POP 606

The reason to venture off the beaten track to visit Tällberg is not because there's any one thing to see or do here, but because it's downright adorable.

The perfect place to enjoy classy Swedish country life, Tällberg is a sprawling village of precious gingerbread houses and luxury private cottages (mostly painted Falu Red) sprinkled over rolling hillsides which tumble gently downward to a warren of sleepy, hidden coves and forested nooks on the shores of sparkling Lake Siljan.

Sound romantic? It is...and that's the other reason plenty of folks come here: for a weekend away with someone special, or to tie the knot. If you decide to make the trip, you're well advised to treat yourself to a night of blissfully quiet indulgence in one of the village's impressive lodgings, be it flying solo with the company of a good book, or on the arm of someone lovely.

🛏 Sleeping & Eating

Despite having only 600 or so permanent residents, the village is host to a number of upmarket hotels. Come here if you're looking to pamper yourself with peace and quiet or seeking a romantic country escape. If you're travelling on a budget, you might be better off visiting for the afternoon and spending the night in Rättvik or Leksand.

Dining options consist of a cafe or two and the several restaurants belonging to the village's boutique hotels. Tällberg has both romance and style going on in spades, so don't expect to front up solo for a stodgy takeaway or dine indoors in your scrubby fishing gear: epic fail.

Tällbergs Camping CAMPGROUND €

(📞0247-513 10; www.tällbergscamping.se; Sjögattu 38; powered sites 220-290kr, cabins 450-600kr; 🅿🛜) Tällberg's waterfront campground is just that, free from many of the amenities that have turned scores of Sweden's campgrounds into miniature 'family adventure parks'. RVs and caravans are still welcomed, but you'll find a more subdued crowd who appreciate the peace and quiet of camping and caravanning with simplicity.

⭐**Green Hotel** BOUTIQUE HOTEL €€

(📞0247-500 00; www.greenhotel.se/en/; Ovabacksgattu 17; d/ste from 1100/3200kr; 🅿🅿) 🍴 Originally built as a private residence in 1917

UPPSALA & CENTRAL SWEDEN LAKE SILJAN

and converted into a hotel 30 years later, Tällberg's quintessentially 'country Swedish' Green Hotel is something special. Privately owned and operated, the hotel feels like part of a more exclusive brand, from its exceptionally decorated guestrooms (many with gorgeous views) and decadent suites, to its attentive, personalised service. It's one to remember.

Opt for at least a 'Classic' room if you can – you won't regret paying extra for the balcony and wonderful views over Lake Siljan.

Hotell Siljanstrand   HOTEL €€

(☑0247-25 44 44; www.hotellsiljanstrand.se; Sjögattu 36; d 700-950kr; 🅿🛜) It doesn't get much more rustic than Hotell Siljanstrand, the closest hotel in Tällberg to the water, comprising a main lodge and a series of cute-as-a-button log cabins arranged around a sloping lawn. Woodsy rooms are less fluffy than neighbouring options, but if it's Swedish country life or old-fashioned romance you seek, you're on a winner.

★ Tällbergsgårdens Hotell   SWEDISH €€€

(☑0247-508 50; www.tallbergsgarden.se; Holgattu 1; mains 95-480kr, afternoon tea 165kr; ☺bar noon-10pm, kitchen 6-9pm; 🅿🛜🍴) Celebrating its 100th birthday in 2018, this luxe hotel restaurant offers locavore haute-Swedish dining of an evening, decadent Saturday afternoon teas and the opportunity to just pop in and enjoy the magnificent views and a glass of wine on the deck or to cosy up by the fire with coffee and a book or someone special in the rustic drawing room.

ℹ Getting There & Away

Tällberg is 13km north of Leksand and about the same distance southeast of Rättvik.

Dalatrafik (p121) bus 274 (55kr) runs between Leksand and Tällberg two to six times a day.

Tällberg is also a stop on the local **SJ Rail** (p103) line that travels around Lake Siljan, but the train station is inconveniently located about 2km east of the village proper.

Rättvik

☑0248 / POP 10,856

Rättvik is a totally unpretentious town on the shores of Lake Siljan in an area that sometimes borders on the precious. Nonetheless, it's a very pretty place, stretching up a hillside and gently hugging the shoreline. There are things to do year-round, for kids and adults alike, whether you like skiing,

cycling, hiking or just lolling around in the town's numerous parks and beaches.

A full program of special events in summer includes a folklore festival in late July, Classic Car Week in late July or early August, and a season of world-class opera from a unique and unforgettable outdoor venue.

⊙ Sights & Activities

Långbryggan   PIER

Scandinavia's longest wooden pier, the impressive 628m Långbryggan, runs out into the lake from just behind the train station.

Rättviks gammelgård   MUSEUM

(☑0248-514 45; www.hembygd.se/rattvik/rattviks-gammelgard/; ☺11am-5pm mid-Jun–mid-Aug) 🆓 You can get your open-air-museum fix at Rättviks gammelgård, 500m north of the *kyrka* – it's a collection of buildings that were moved here during the 1920s from villages around Rättvik parish (the oldest is from the 1300s). There's a good collection of furniture painted in the local style, and a unique '*ullkorgen*' (wool bin) from the 1200s. The grounds are always open for exploring, but the cafe and building interiors are summer-only.

Vidablick Utsiktstorn   TOWER

(☑0248-36 41 60; www.vidablickhantverk.se; Vidablicksvägen 50; adult/child 35/15kr; ☺10am-6pm Jun-Aug; 🅿) An enterprising 17-year-old built Vidablick Utsiktstorn, a viewing tower about 5km southeast of town, from where there are great panoramas of the lake. On your way up the tower, check out the miniature reconstruction of the village as it was at the turn of the century, made by a local carpenter in the 1930s. There's also a charming cafe and gift store selling handmade wares.

Rättviks Kulturhus   CULTURAL CENTRE

(☑0248-701 95; Storgatan 2; ☺11am-7pm Mon-Thu, to 4pm Fri, to 2pm Sat, 1-4pm Sun; 🅿) 🆓 This local museum complex houses the Rättviks *bibliotek* (library), art exhibitions and a display describing the Siljan meteor impact. The helpful staff go above and beyond to answer any questions you might have about the area.

Sommarrodel   ADVENTURE SPORTS

(☑073-671 00 10; http://sommar.rattviksbacken.se/sommarrodel-dalarna; Rättviksbacken Slalomvägen 36; 1/3 rides 60/165kr; ☺noon-7pm Jun-Aug, closed when raining) The 725m-long Sommarrodel, a sort of snowless bobsled chute, is lots of fun. You hurtle down a hill at speeds of up to 60km/h, which feels very fast so close to the ground. There's also paintball if you need more.

Rättviksbacken SKIING
(☑0736-71 00 10; www.rattviksbacken.se; Rättviksbacken Slalomvägen; day pass adult/child 260/200kr; ⓘ) Rättvik's easy-as-pie ski slopes and snowpark, just 1.5km from the centre of town, are great for kids and beginners. In summer the facility is home to the popular Sommarrodel bobsled.

🎊 Festivals & Events

⭐ **Classic Car Week** PARADE
(www.classiccarweek.com; ⊙end Jul/early Aug) Culminating in one lazy parade carousing down Rättvik's lakefront promenade, Classic Car Week is a must for motor buffs and attracts rev heads from Europe and around the world with their beautifully restored hot rods, saloons, limos and convertibles of all makes, shapes and sizes for a week of workshops, events and general showing-off.

🛏 Sleeping & Eating

Rättviksgårdens vandrarhem HOSTEL €
(☑0248-561 09; Enåbadsvägen 1; s/d from 530/760kr; ⊙reception 8-10am & 5-6pm; ℗@🛜) Towards the edge of town is this comfortable hostel with cosy rooms in three wooden buildings clustered around a grassy courtyard. It's a quiet place with good facilities, including a nice kitchen with a large dining/TV room in the main building, and picnic tables on the lawn for alfresco meals. Reception is at the Enåbadet campground office.

Siljansbadets Camping CAMPGROUND €
(☑0248-561 18; www.siljansbadet.se; Långbryggevägen 4; sites 295kr, cabins from 650kr; ℗) Between the station and Lake Siljan, this shady, woodsy campground has a plethora of powered sites, a bunch of simple camping cabins and a range of facilities, including a laundry, kids campground, showers, kiosk and even its own Blue Flag beach. It's popular with families and the RV crowd.

Jöns-Andersgården B&B B&B €€
(☑0248-130 15; http://bokasiljan.visitdalarna. se; Bygatan 4; r 495-995kr; ⊙mid-Apr–mid-Oct; ℗☺🛜) Beds here are in traditional wooden houses dating from the 15th century, high on a hill with superb views. Rooms are all in tip-top shape with modern interiors, and one suite has its own sauna. If you don't

DON'T MISS

OPERA UNDER THE STARS

Dalhalla (☑0455-61 97 00; www.dalhalla. se; Sätra Dalhallavägen 201; ticket prices vary), an old limestone quarry 9km north of Rättvik, is used as an open-air theatre and concert venue in summer; the acoustics are incredible and the setting is stunning. Check online for schedule and ticket information (prices vary depending on the act). From July to October, on non-concert days you can tour the theatre at 11am, 1pm and 2.30pm (125kr).

have transport, the owners will pick you up from the train station by arrangement. Breakfast is included in the price.

If you're staying here, it's well worth dining at the eponymous, on-site Restaurang Jöns-Andersgården.

Dala Wärdshus HOTEL €€
(☑0248-302 50; www.dalawardshus.se/hotell-rattvik-vid-siljan-dalarna/hantverksbyn-hotell/; Hantverksbyn 4; s/d from 675/1195kr, breakfast 90kr; ℗🛜) You might just fall in love with this rustic joint offering budget accommodation in basic, grass-roofed (real grass, not thatched) huts, some with lake views. The attached restaurant (open May to August; *dagens* lunch 89kr, coffee and cakes from 35kr) has a great view from its outdoor tables, and occasional live music. Wi-fi is patchy outside common areas.

Fricks Konditori CAFE €
(☑0248-136 36; www.frickskonditori.se; HSBgatan 1a; sandwiches from 45kr; ⊙8am-7pm Mon-Fri, 11am-6pm Sat & Sun) An old-fashioned bakery-cafe with a casual, neighbourhood vibe, Fricks offers good-value sandwiches, quiches and salads. That said, you really should save some room for its range of decadent, freshly baked cakes and pastries, which is where the place really shines.

Restaurang Jöns-Andersgården SWEDISH €€€
(☑0248-130 15; Bygatan 4; mains 185-265kr; ⊙5-10pm late May-Aug) If you can stir your stumps and make it up the hill, you'll find this rather sweet restaurant tucked at the top, attached to Jöns-Andersgården B&B. Dishes such as lemony chicken with gremolata potatoes, shellfish cannelloni, or herb-and-parmesan roasted lamb over gnocchi bring a taste of Italy to this very Swedish establishment.

❶ Information

Siljan Turism Rättvik Tourist Center
(☎ 0248-79 72 00; Riksvägen 40; ◔ 9am-6pm Mon-Fri, 10am-4pm Sat & Sun) Located at the train station; has info for the entire Siljan region.

❶ Getting There & Away

Rättvik is 20km north of Leksand and 39km southeast of Mora along Rte 70.

Dalatrafik (p121) bus 132 runs regularly between Falun, Rättvik and Mora. Buses depart from outside the train station.

SJ Rail (p103) operates up to three services per day from Stockholm which stop at Rättvik (492kr, 3¼ hours). Otherwise you have to change at Borlänge. Local trains from Leksand stop at Rättvik then continue on to Mora (85, 25 minutes).

Mora

☎ 0250 / POP 10,896

Mora is spliced with Sweden's historic soul. Legend has it that in 1520 Gustav Vasa arrived here in a last-ditch attempt to start a rebellion against the Danish regime. The people of Mora weren't interested and Gustav was forced to put on his skis and flee for the border. After he left, the town reconsidered and two yeomen, Engelbrekt and Lars, volunteered to follow Gustav's tracks, finally overtaking him in Sälen and changing Swedish history.

Today the world's biggest cross-country ski race commemorates that epic chase and its finish-line is in Mora. Participants number more than one and a half times the town's year-round population. Summer sees holidaymakers from Stockholm and beyond come for sunny antics on Lake Siljan, while year-round, lovers of Swedish folk art and lore visit the nearby village of Nusnäs for the chance to observe local artisans carving and painting the nation's beloved Dalahästar (Dala horses).

⊙ Sights & Activities

★ Zorngården   HISTORIC BUILDING
(☎ 0250-59 23 10; www.zorn.se/en/visit-us/ zorn-house/; Vasagatan 36; adult/child 100/40kr; ◔ 10am-4pm Jun-Aug, noon-4pm Tue-Fri Sep-May; ⓟ) The Zorn family house, Zorngården, is an excellent example of a wealthy artist's residence and reflects Anders Zorn's National Romantic aspirations (check out the Viking-influenced hall and entryway). Access to the house is by guided tour (in Swedish) on the hour and half-hour. Guided tours in English are conducted over the summer season at 11.15am and 2.15pm and must be booked in advance. Combination tickets including the adjacent Zornmuseet are 160kr (no child discount).

Vasaloppsmuseet   MUSEUM
(☎ 0250-392 00; www.vasaloppet.se; Vasagatan 30; adult/child 50/25kr; ◔ 10am-5pm May-Sep; ⓟ) Even if you have no interest in skiing, you may be pleasantly surprised by the excellent Vasaloppsmuseet, which really communicates the passion behind the world's largest cross-country skiing event. There's some fantastic crackly black-and-white film of the first race, a display about nine-times winner and hardy old boy Nils 'Mora-Nisse' Karlsson, and an exhibit of prizes. Outside the museum is the race finish line, a favourite place for holiday *snaps* (distilled alcoholic beverage).

Zornmuseet   MUSEUM
(☎ 0250-59 23 10; www.zorn.se/en/visit-us/ zorn-museum/; Vasagatan 36; adult/child 70kr/ free; ◔ 9am-5pm Jun-Aug, noon-4pm Sep-May; ⓟ) Zornmuseet displays many of the best-loved portraits and characteristic nudes of Mora painter Anders Zorn (1860–1920), one of Sweden's most renowned artists. His naturalistic depictions of Swedish life and landscapes are shown here, as is the Zorn family silver collection. A combined ticket including admission to the adjacent Zorngården costs 160kr (no discount for kids).

Vasaloppsleden   HIKING
(www.vasaloppet.se/en/about-us/the-vasaloppet-arena/) This 90km multi-use trail hugs the course taken in the Vasaloppet cross-country ski event, ending in Mora. Of course, the trail can be walked in reverse and there's plenty of food and lodging stops along the way. Check the website for full details and a downloadable map.

✷ Festivals & Events

Vasaloppet   SPORTS
(www.vasaloppet.se/en/; ◔ Mar) Each year, around 15,000 people take part in this 90km cross-country ski event which finishes in Mora. It's held on the first Sunday in March.

Musik vid Siljan   MUSIC
(www.musikvidsiljan.se; ◔ early Jul) Held in various venues around Mora and other lakeside

towns, Lake Siljan's biggest summer music festival draws crowds in their thousands.

🛏 Sleeping & Eating

Mora has a handful of lodging options, but if you've come to the region looking to appreciate the natural and rustic beauty of Lake Siljian, you'll find more appealing (and more expensive) digs in Tällberg, 50km south.

STF Hostel Mora Målkullan HOSTEL €

(📞0250-381 96; www.svenskaturistforeningen.se/anlaggningar/stf-mora-malkullan-vandrarhem/; Björnramsgatan 2; dm from 420kr; breakfast 50kr; P🖥🛜) This humble hostel occupies a handful of buildings around the Vasaloppsmuseet. There's a guest kitchen and rooms are simple but comfy, with mostly four- to six-bunk rooms. Breakfast is 50kr (book the night before). Free wi-fi and sauna are available.

Mora Parken CAMPGROUND €

(📞0250-276 00; www.moraparken.se; Parkvägen; sites 230kr, 2-/4-bed cabins from 305/350kr, hotel s/d 995/1245kr; P🛜🏊) This well-decked-out campground and hotel is in a great waterside spot, about 400m northwest of the main square. There's a beach, laundry, kitchen, minigolf, bicycle rentals and more. A hodgepodge of camping cabins are well equipped and full of rustic charm. The Vasaloppet track and Siljansleden trail pass through the grounds, and you can hire canoes to splash about on the pond.

Hotel rooms (all ground floor in the main building) have wooden floors and a sleek, modern look.

Mora Hotell & Spa HOTEL €€

(📞0250-59 26 50; www.morahotell.se; Strandgatan 12; r from 1295kr; P🖥❄🛜) There's been a hotel here since 1830, although its current incarnation is far from antique. Full of personality, modern rooms combine clean lines, wooden floors and earthy tones with bright folk-art accents. Head to the spa to relax and enjoy steam rooms, Jacuzzis, massage and body treatments.

Mora Kaffestuga CAFE €

(📞0250-100 82; Kyrkogatan 8; lunch specials from 85kr; ⏰9am-7pm Mon-Fri, to 5pm Sat, 10am-4pm Sun; 🖥) For a quick lunch – such as basic salads, quiches and sandwiches – or a coffee-and-pastry break, head to this popular, stylish little coffee shop. It has a grassy garden out back.

★Korsnasgarden EUROPEAN €€

(📞046-250 102 84; www.korsnasgarden.se; Moragatan 9; mains 195-385kr; ⏰11am-8pm Mon-Sat, shorter hours in winter) This delightful restaurant cafe serves a small selection of hot and cold meals and a plethora of freshly made sandwiches within Mora's most delightful dining environs – a smartly renovated historic house and garden. It's kid friendly too (but there's enough space that the place doesn't feel flooded with children).

THE DALA HORSE

What do Bill Clinton, Elvis Presley and Bob Hope have in common? They've all received a Swedish Dalahäst as a gift. These iconic, carved wooden horses, painted in bright colours and decorated with folk-art flowers, represent to many people the essence of Sweden.

The first written reference to a Dalahäst comes from the 17th century, when the bishop of Västerås denounced such horrors as 'decks of cards, dice, flutes, dolls, wooden horses, lovers' ballads, impudent paintings,' but it's quite likely they were being carved much earlier. Sitting by the fireside and whittling wood was a common pastime, and the horse was a natural subject – a workmate, friend and symbol of strength. The painted form that is so common today appeared at the World Exhibition in New York in 1939 and has been a favourite souvenir for travellers to Sweden ever since.

The best-known Dala horses come from Nusnäs, about 10km southeast of Mora. The two biggest workshops are Nils Olsson Hemslöjd (📞0250-372 00; www.nilsolsson.se; Edåkersvägen 17; ⏰8am-6pm Mon-Fri, 10am-4pm Sat) and Grannas A Olssons Hemslöjd (📞0250-372 50; www.grannas.com; Edåkersvägen 24; ⏰9am-6pm Mon-Fri, to 4pm Sat & Sun), where you can watch the carving and painting, then buy up big at the souvenir outlets. Wooden horse sizes stretch from 3cm to 50cm high (with prices from around 250kr to 5000kr).

To get to Nusnäs, take bus 324 to 'Nusnäs gamla affären' stop (40kr, 20 minutes).

❶ Information

Siljan Turism Mora Tourist Center (☑ 0248-79 72 00; Köpmannagatan 3a; ◷ 9am-6pm Mon-Fri, 10am-4pm Sat & Sun) The friendly folk can deck you out with maps of Siljansleden, an excellent network of walking and cycling paths extending for more than 300km around Lake Siljan, from among their wealth of local information.

❶ Getting There & Away

Mora is 39km northwest of Rättvik on Rte 70 and 17km southeast of Orsa on the E45.

All **Dalatrafik** (p121) buses depart from the main bus stop at Moragatan 23. Bus 132 runs to Rättvik and Falun and bus 141 runs to Orsa.

Mora is the Lake Siljan terminus for **SJ Rail** (p103) trains and the southern terminus of the Inlandsbanan (Inland Railway) which runs north to Gällivare (mid-June through mid-August). Mora train station is about 1km east of town. There's also a more central station called Morastrand but not all trains stop there: be sure to check timetables before setting out.

Mora has direct rail links year-round to Stockholm (545kr, 3¾ hours) and seasonally to Östersund (from 595kr, 6¼ hours) via the Inlandsbanan. Outside its operating season, you'll need to catch bus 45 (278kr, 5¼ hours).

Orsa

☑ 0250 / POP 5308

Orsa, 16km north of Mora, is a quiet town with a musical heart. It's located on the shores of Orsasjön which flows into Lake Siljan. The many postcard-perfect private cottages in the area make it a popular spot for local holidaymakers in the warmer months.

Orsa's main claims to fame are its eponymous lake, love of festivals, a thriving folk music scene and its location as a stopping point *en route* to Europe's largest predator park and the Orsa Grönklitt area. The latter is a popular, though isolated, winter ski area and in the green season, somewhat of a hotspot for hiking and adventure sports enthusiasts.

If you love the great outdoors and you're in the vicinity, you'll want to stop by, but if you're not fit and fabulous, or you simply prefer museums to mountain-biking or pints to pistes, there's not a great deal for you here.

◉ Sights & Activities

★ **Orsa Rovdjurspark**   ZOO
(☑ 0250-462 00; www.orsarovdjurspark.se; Björnparksvägen; adult/child 270/170kr, family 790kr;

◷ 10am-5pm; ℙ 🚻; 🚌 342) Fat-bottomed roly-poly bear cubs are the star attraction at the largest predator park in Europe, some 16km north of Orsa. Even if there are no cubs around during your visit, there's plenty to see: polar bears, Kodiak bears, leopards, Amur tigers, lynx, wolves, red foxes and wolverines. The park and the various possible activities here continue to expand, and now include cycling tours, themed hikes and more.

Orsa Grönklitt   SKIING
(☑ 0250-462 00; www.orsagronklitt.se; day pass adult/child 355/285kr; ◷ guest centre 9am-6pm; 🚻) With 23 slopes and 100 km of cross-country runs, this popular ski-ground and summer recreation area located 16km north of town is one of Orsa's star attractions, though with a peak altitude of just under 600m, hardened powder hounds might be somewhat disappointed. The area offers accommodation, activities and a variety of dining options year-round. It's also home to the Orsa Rovdjurspark zoo. Check the website for full details of the range of activities on offer.

🛏 Sleeping

★ **Orsa Camping**   CAMPGROUND €
(☑ 0250-462 00; www.orsacamping.se; Bowlingvägen 1; sites from 190kr, cabins from 795kr; ℙ 🛜 🏊) This enormous campground/caravan park is beautifully situated on the shores of Orsasjön. It's particularly suitable for families, with several playgrounds, a water slide, canoe hire, crazy golf and a beach to keep the kids happy. A range of campsites, camping cabins and rustic cottages are available. See the website for the full gamut of what's on offer.

STF Orsa Vandrarhem   HOSTEL €
(☑ 0250-421 70; www.orsavandrarhem.se; Gillevägen 3; dm/s/d from 120/330/480kr, breakfast 80kr; ℙ 🛏 🛜) This friendly hostel with a variety of small dorms and private rooms is located in the hills above Orsa with a view over Orsasjön. There's a kitchen for guests, as well as breakfast available for purchase. Linen hire is 100kr and exit cleaning will set you back a further 200kr. The hostel is near several hiking and cycling paths.

❶ Information

Orsa turistbyrå (☑ 0250-55 25 50; www.destinationorsa.se; Dalagatan 1; ◷ 9am-6pm Mon-Fri, 10am-4pm Sat & Sun)

ℹ Getting There & Away

Orsa is 16km north of Mora on the E45.

Dalatrafik (p121) bus 141 travels between Orsa and Mora (55kr, 20 minutes).

Sälen

📞 0280 / POP 652

A tiny spot in the wilds of Dalarna, the village of Sälen undergoes a stunning transformation from sleepy summertime fishing village into one of Sweden's largest conglomerations of ski resorts in the winter: its two selves are almost completely unrecognisable from each other.

In addition to its seven ski areas, the region offers a range of outdoor activities, including canoeing, horse riding and even wildlife safaris, but unless you're an avid fisherman or die-hard lover of hiking, mountain biking or adventure sports, most folks will only want to make the trek to visit when Sälen is wearing its snowsuit and skis.

🏃 Activities

Sälenfjällen's **ski areas**, replete with chalets, pubs and nightclubs, are spread out along a 20km stretch of road which cuts through the steep-flanked mountains west of the village. There are over 100 lifts and pistes of all degrees, monopolised by the giant resort group, SkiStar, where snow is guaranteed from 15 November to mid-April. About 45km north of Sälen, cheaper and quieter skiing is available at Näsfjället.

★**SkiStar Sälen**   SKIING
(📞 0771-84 00 00; www.skistar.com/en/Salen/; Sälfjällsgården; 3-day pass adult/child 1140/910kr; ▥) One of northern Europe's largest ski areas, SkiStar Sälen consists of four ski areas spread out over about 20km – Lindvallen, Högfjället, Tandådalen and Hundfjälle – which in total comprise a staggering 100 or so runs across all levels of difficulty, serviced by 87 lifts and 13 conveyors. Indeed, there's so much to cover here and such a range of activities that the resort has its own travel agency to help you decipher what's best for you.

Lindvallen   ADVENTURE SPORTS
(📞 0771-84 00 00; www.skistar.com/en/Salen/About-Salen/Summer/Biking-in-Salen/; Fäbodvägen 10c; ▥) In summer, the ski hills convert to mountain-bike parks; the ski area at Lindvallen has a whole summer season built

around the sport. Rent helmets and gear at the lift. The bike park is open Thursday to Sunday from mid-June to August.

Näsfjället   SKIING
(📞 0280-204 90; www.nasfjallet.se; Sörsjön; day pass adult/child 350/300kr; ▥) A quieter alternative to the SkiStar resorts, Näsfjället, some 47km north of Sälen near the Norwegian border, has 10km of groomed trails from a peak elevation of 890m with at least half of its runs ideal for beginners and families.

🛏 Sleeping & Eating

Summer offers very little by way of accommodation, aside from private cottage and chalet rentals through online booking portals. In winter, you're best advised to contact your travel agent, the Sälens Turistbyrå or SkiStar Sälen for packages.

Kläppen   HOTEL €
(📞 0280-962 00; www.klappen.se; Sjungarvägen, Transtrand; condos summer/winter from 695/1400kr; P🛰) Some of the area's most luxurious resorts become very affordable in summer; condos at Kläppen, 20km south of Sälen, for instance, are a smoking deal in July and August, when the price of an average hostel room fetches you a fully equipped apartment with kitchenette, patio, Jacuzzi and pool access. The resort can also book guided canoe tours and other activities.

Sälens Vandrarhem   HOSTEL €
(📞 0280-820 40; www.salensvandrarhem.se; Gräsheden 3; dm/s/d from 200/350/490kr, breakfast 70kr; P🛰) This rustic hostel 27km north of Sälen is a fantastic hideaway. It's based in a peaceful nature reserve at Gräsheden (near Näsfjället), with some great walks nearby – and the southern section of the Kungsleden trail passes 2km from the hostel. Order breakfast in advance.

Sälens Bageri & Konditori   CAFE €
(📞 0280-207 88; www.bullans.se; Sälenvägen; coffee 30kr, light meals 89-99kr; ⊙7am-5pm Mon-Fri, 8am-3pm Sat; P🖉) This surprisingly chic cafe is located inside the SälenGallerian shopping centre and serves up pizzas (89kr to 115kr), light lunches and a simple daily breakfast (59kr) from 7am to 10am.

ℹ Information

Sälens Turistbyrå (📞0280-187 00; www.salen.se; Centrumhuset; ⊙9am-6pm Mon-Fri, to 3pm Sat & Sun) Located inside the Centrumhuset shopping centre; your one stop shop for bookings and information. You can also get maps and advice on local hiking and biking trails here.

ℹ Getting There & Away

Sälen occupies a lonesome tract of pristine countryside 85km km west of Mora and 99km south of Idre.

Dalatrafik (p121) bus 133 runs from Mora Friedhemsplan to Sälen (105kr, 1¾ hours) once daily in the ski season (otherwise you have to change buses at Lima). In winter, jump on the ski bus (free with a ski pass), which tours around the ski area.

Idre

☑ 0253 / POP 794

Although part of the Swedish heartland, Idre and its surrounding wilderness feel utterly remote. Despite the region's rugged beauty, visitor numbers to this part of the county, whose wild landscapes look little like the rest of Dalarna, are relatively low. In summer, Idre's isolation keeps the crowds who cluster around Lake Siljan at bay – which, of course, is part of its charm.

In winter, sleepy Idre transforms ever so slightly into a popular ski area for those in the know. Wide open spaces and fewer crowds mean plenty of choice for downhill and cross-country aficionados who don't mind the five- to six-hour journey from Oslo or Stockholm.

Idre's closest neighbour, Grövelsjön, lies 38km northwest, close to the Norwegian border on the edge of the wild 664-sq-km Långfjällets Nature Reserve, noted for its lichen-covered heaths, moraine heaps and ancient forests. Reindeer from Sweden's southernmost Sami community wander throughout the area.

Idre Fjäll Ski Resort (☑ 0253-410 00; www.idrefjall.se/english.html; day lift passes adult/child from 400/300kr; ⊙ Nov-Apr), 9km east of Idre, is unique in that it offers skiing in every compass direction, with three chairlifts, 29 ski-tows and 40 downhill runs – including nine black runs to compliment its majority of family-friendly basic to intermediate

pistes and almost 60km of cross-country tracks.

🛏 Sleeping & Eating

Sörälvens Fiskecamping CAMPGROUND €
(☑ 0253-201 17; www.soralven-camping.com; Västanå 519; sites/cabins 210/550kr; ℗) Sörälvens Fiske Camping has rather shadeless camping areas but good, basic cabins. Popular with the fishing crowd (*fisk* means fish) the campground is 2.5km out of Idre in the direction of Grövelsjön.

★ **STF Fjällstation Grövelsjön** HOSTEL €
(☑ 0253-59 68 80; www.svenskaturistforeningen.se/grovelsjon; Grövelsjövägen 495, Grövelsjön; 2-/4-bed r from 695/1295kr; ⊙ mid-Jan–mid-Apr & mid-Jun–end Sep; ℗) The excellent STF Fjällstation Grövelsjön mountain lodge in Grövelsjön has a wide array of facilities, including kitchen, spa, shop and outdoor-gear hire. The restaurant serves breakfast, lunch and dinner; enquire about half-board and full-board arrangements.

Byvägen 30 SWEDISH €€
(☑ 0253-204 11; www.byvagen30.se/dagens-lunch/; Byvägen 30; buffet lunch 125kr; ⊙ noon-8pm; ℗ 🖋) Stop by for a good value buffet lunch at this compact lodge in the heart of town. The menu changes weekly, with a different spread on every day, so in the unlikely event that you're staying in town for a while, you won't get bored of the food! You can always just pop in for a coffee and excellent home-made cake.

ℹ Information

Idre Turistbyrå (☑ 0253-200 00; Framgårdsvägen 1; ⊙ 10am-5pm Mon-Fri) The tourist office has friendly staff and brochures and offers hiking advice and internet access.

ℹ Getting There & Away

Idre is 151km north of Mora on Rte 70, which continues north for another 39km to Grövelsjön,

Dalatrafik (p121) bus 104 travels once daily on a route between Mora, Idre and Grövelsjön. The journey from Mora to Idre (116kr) takes 2¼ hours; from Idre to Grövelsjön (45kr) takes 45 minutes.

Gothenburg & the Southwest

Best Places to Eat

➡ Thörnströms Kök (p144)

➡ Brygghuset (p154)

➡ Albert Hotell (p161)

➡ Magasinet Härön (p151)

➡ Restaurang Sjöboden (p163)

Best Places to Stay

➡ Stora Hotellet Bryggan (p156)

➡ Salt & Sill (p155)

➡ IQ Suites (p142)

➡ Utpost Hållö (p154)

➡ Tofta Gård (p152)

Why Go?

Sweden's southwest is diversity personified. Heading the cast is Sweden's 'second city' of Gothenburg and its kicking bars, cafes, museums and theme-park thrills. The islands of Gothenburg's southern archipelago are stunning and romantic, and surprisingly easy to reach.

South of Gothenburg, the coast around Halmstad is home to sandy Blue Flag beaches and Sweden's top surfing, windsurfing and kitesurfing. The attractions of inland Västergötland are low-key and eclectic, from Trollhättan's post-industrial museums and mighty locks to Lidköping's fairy-tale Läckö Slott.

North of Gothenburg, the Bohuslän coastline shatters into myriad granite islands with craggy cliffs and adorable red-and-white fishing villages. Yachts weave their way among uninhabited islets and skerries, while the area's mysterious Bronze Age rock carvings testify to the rich spiritual life of the region's early inhabitants. Further north, Dalsland, with its network of canals, locks and narrow lakes amid thick, dark forest, beckons boating and kayaking enthusiasts.

When to Go

Gothenburg

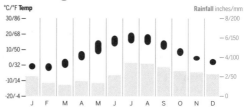

Jul & Aug Sailboat-loving Swedes beeline to Bohuslän. Gothenburg festivals run back to back.

May & Sep Ideal time for avoiding summer crowds and indulging in fine dining.

Dec & Jan Inland lakes and canals freeze over. Perfect skating and ice-fishing conditions.

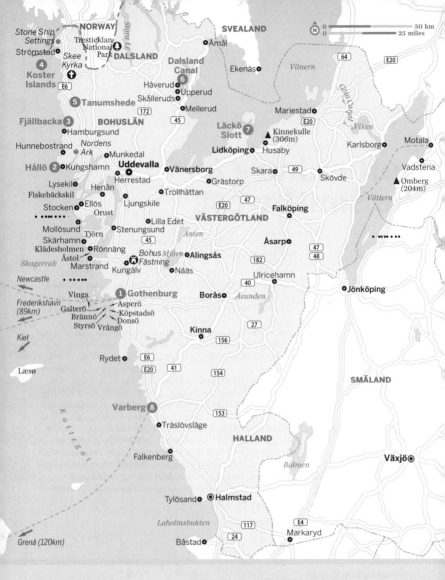

Gothenburg & Southwest Sweden Highlights

① Gothenburg (p133) Plummeting down scary roller coasters, taking in counterculture art and being surprised by advances in Swedish cuisine.

② Hållö (p154) Feasting on shrimp and archipelago views on this tiny island, located a short ferry trip from Smögen.

③ Fjällbacka (p155) Being charmed by Ingrid Bergman's favourite summer haunt.

④ Koster Islands (p156) Pedalling your way around these dazzling islands.

⑤ Tanumshede (p152) Decoding mysterious Bronze Age rock artwork at this Unesco World Heritage site.

⑥ Dalsland Canal (p158) Piloting a boat or paddling a kayak and watching boats navigate the Håverud aqueduct.

⑦ Läckö Slott (p162) Listening to opera staged on the broad lawns of this castle.

⑧ Varberg (p166) Surfing at Apelviken and sunning your bare behind on a rocky beach.

GOTHENBURG

📶 031 / POP 580,000

Gregarious, chilled-out Gothenburg (Göteborg) has considerable appeal for tourists and locals alike. Neoclassical architecture lines its tram-rattled streets, locals sun themselves beside canals, and there's always an interesting cultural or social event going on. Gothenburg is a very walkable city. From Centralstationen in the north, shop-lined Östra Hamngatan leads southeast across one of Gothenburg's 17th-century canals, through verdant Kungsparken (King's Park) to the city's boutique and upscale bar-lined 'Avenyn' (Kungsportsavenyn) boulevard.

The waterfront abounds with all things nautical, from ships, aquariums and sea-related museums to the freshest fish. To the west, the Vasastan, Haga and Linné districts buzz with creativity and an appreciation for well-preserved history.

History

Gamla Älvsborg fortress, standing guard over the river 3km downstream of the centre, is Gothenburg's oldest significant structure and was a key strategic point in the 17th-century territorial wars. The Swedes founded Gothenburg in 1621 to be free of the extortionate taxation rates imposed on Swedish ships by the Danes.

Fearful of Danish attack, the Swedes employed Dutch experts to construct a defensive canal system in the centre. The workers lived in what is now the revitalised Haga area: around a fifth of the original buildings are still standing. Most of Gothenburg's oldest wooden buildings went up in smoke long ago – the city was devastated by no fewer than nine major fires between 1669 and 1804.

Once Sweden had annexed Skåne in 1658, Gothenburg expanded as a trading centre. Boom time came in the 18th century, when merchants such as the Swedish East India Company made huge amounts of wealth from trade with the Far East, their profits responsible for numerous grand houses that are still standing.

Gothenburg was sustained largely by the shipbuilding industry until it went belly up in the 1980s. These days, the lifeblood of Scandinavia's busiest port is heavy industry (Volvo manufacturing in particular) and commerce.

◉ Sights

Most of the city's sights are located within walking distance of the centre and, after Liseberg, museums are Gothenburg's strongest asset: admission to most is covered by the Göteborg City Card (p140). All the museums have good cafes attached and several have specialist shops.

★ **Konstmuseum**   GALLERY
(www.konstmuseum.goteborg.se;   Götaplatsen; adult/child 40kr/free; ⊙ 11am-6pm Tue & Thu, to 8pm Wed, to 5pm Fri-Sun; 🚻; 🚊 4 Berzeliigatan) Home to Gothenburg's premier art collection, Konstmuseet displays works by the French Impressionists, Rubens, Van Gogh, Rembrandt and Picasso; Scandinavian masters such as Bruno Liljefors, Edvard Munch, Anders Zorn and Carl Larsson have pride of place in the **Fürstenburg Galleries**.

Other highlights include a superb sculpture hall, the **Hasselblad Center** with its annual *New Nordic Photography* exhibition, and temporary displays of next-gen Nordic art.

The unveiling of the bronze Poseidon fountain out front scandalised Gothenburg's strait-laced citizens, who insisted on drastic penile-reduction surgery.

The museum covers six floors of fabulous art dating from the Renaissance to the present day, so plan your visit accordingly and allow a sufficient amount of time.

★ **Universeum**   MUSEUM
(www.universeum.se; Södra Vägen 50; adult/child 250/195kr; ⊙ 10am-6pm, to 8pm Jul & Aug; 🅿 🚻; 🚊 2 Korsvägen) In what is arguably the best museum for kids in Sweden, you find yourself in the midst of a humid rainforest, complete with trickling water, tropical birds and butterflies flitting through the greenery and tiny marmosets. On a level above, roaring dinosaurs maul each other, while next door, denizens of the deep float through the shark tunnel and venomous beauties lie coiled in the serpent tanks. In the 'technology inspired by nature' section, stick your children to the Velcro wall.

If that's not enough, go button crazy with the fantastically fun, hands-on science exhibitions, where themes range from nanotechnology and space travel to mixing music.

★ **Röda Sten Konsthall**   GALLERY
(www.rodastenkonsthall.se; Röda Sten 1; adult/child 40kr/free; ⊙ noon-5pm Tue, Thu & Fri, to 8pm Wed, to

GOTHENBURG & THE SOUTHWEST GOTHENBURG

Gothenburg (Göteborg)

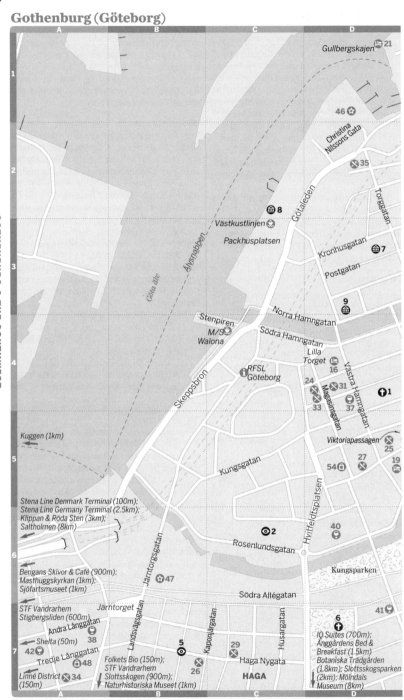

Gullbergskajen 🖼 21

46 ☆

Christina Nilssons Gata

✕ 35

Torggatan

🏛 8

Götaleden

Västkustlinjen ☺

Packhusplatsen

Kronhusgatan

🏛 7

Postgatan

9 🏛

Norra Hamngatan

Stenpiren
M/S
Walona

Södra Hamngatan

Lilla
Torget

16 🖼

Skeppsbron

RFSL
Göteborg

Västra Hamngatan

Magasinsgatan

24 ✕
✕ 31

33 ✕

37

❶1

Kuggen (1km)

Viktoriapassagen ✕ 25

27 ✕

19 🖼

54 🔒

Kungsgatan

Hvitfeldtsplatsen

Stena Line Denmark Terminal (100m);
Stena Line Germany Terminal (2.5km);
Klippan & Röda Sten (3km);
Saltholmen (8km)

⊙2

40

Rosenlundsgatan

Kungsparken

Bengans Skivor & Café (900m);
Masthuggskyrkan (1km);
Sjöfartsmuseet (1km)

☆ 47

Järntorgsgatan

Södra Allégatan

STF Vandrarhem
Stigbergsliden (600m)

Järntorget

6
❶

41

IQ Suites (700m);
Änggårdens Bed &
Breakfast (1.5km)
Botaniska Trädgården
(1.8km); Slottsskogsparken
(2km); Mölndals
Museum (8km)

STF Vandrarhem
Stigbergsliden (600m)

Andra Långgatan

38

Shelta (50m)

Landsvägsgatan

Kaponjärgatan

29 ✕

Husargatan

42

5 ⊙

Tredje Långgatan

🔒 48

Folkets Bio (150m);
STF Vandrarhem
Slottsskogen (900m);
Naturhistoriska Museet (1km)

✕ 26

Haga Nygata

HAGA

Linné District ✕ 34
(150m)

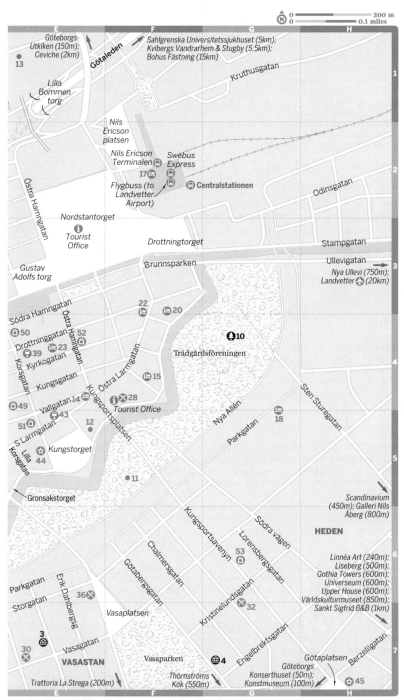

N 0 ————————————— 200 m
   0 ————————————— 0.1 miles

Göteborgs-
Utkiken (150m);
Ceviche (2km)

13

Götaleden

Sahlgrenska Universitetssjukhuset (5km);
Kvibergs Vandrarhem & Stugby (5.5km);
Bohus Fästning (15km)

Kruthusgatan

Lilla
Bommen
torg

Nils
Ericson
platsen

Nils Ericson
Terminalen

Swebus
Express

17

Flygbuss (to
Landvetter
Airport)

Centralstationen

Odinsgatan

Nordstantorget

Tourist
Office

Drottningtorget

Stampgatan

Ullevigatan
Nya Ullevi (750m);
Landvetter (20km)

Gustav
Adolfs torg

Brunnsparken

Södra Hamngatan

50

Östra Hamngatan

Drottninggatan

52

39   23

Kyrkogatan

Korsgatan

Kungsgatan

Vallgatan 14

49

51

43

S Larmgatan

Lilla
Korsgatan

44

Kungsportsplatsen

Kungstorget

12

11

22

20

10

Trädgårdsföreningen

15

28

Tourist Office

Nya Allén

Parkgatan

Sten Sturegatan

18

Gronsakstorget

Scandinavium
(450m); Galleri Nils
Åberg (800m)

HEDEN

Kungsportsavenyn

Chalmersgatan

Göteborgsgatan

Södra vägen

Lorensbergsgatan

53

Linnéa Art (240m);
Liseberg (500m);
Gothia Towers (600m);
Universeum (600m);
Upper House (600m);
Världskulturmuseet (850m);
Sankt Sigfrid B&B (1km)

Parkgatan

Storgatan

Erik Dahlbergsg

36

Vasaplatsen

Kristinelundsgatan

Engelbrektsgatan

32

Berzelligatan

3

30

VASASTAN

Vasagatan

Vasaparken

4

Thörnströms
Kök (550m)

Trattoria La Strega (200m)

Götaplatsen
Göteborgs
Konserthuset (50m);
Konstmuseum (100m)

45

Gothenburg (Göteborg)

6pm Sat & Sun; ☐ 3 Vagnhallen Majorna) Occupying a defunct power station beside the giant Älvsborgsbron, Röda Sten's four floors are home to such temporary exhibitions as edgy Swedish photography and cross-dressing rap videos by Danish-Filipino artist Lillibeth Cuenca Rasmussen that challenge sexuality stereotypes in Afghan society. The indie-style cafe hosts weekly live music and club nights, and offbeat one-offs like punk bike races, boxing matches and stand-up comedy. To get here, walk towards the Klippan precinct, continue under Älvsborgsbron and look for the brown-brick building.

Beside Röda Sten, check out the work-in-progress *Draken,* a 41m-long sculpture which visitors are welcome to decorate with graffiti; bring your own paint.

Mölndals Stadsmuseum MUSEUM
(☑ 031-431 34; www.museum.molndal.se; Kvarnbygatan 12; ☉ noon-4pm Tue-Sun; Ⓟ ♿; ☐ 752, 756, ☐ Mölndal) FREE Located in an old police station, this museum is like a vast warehouse, with a 10,000-strong collection of local nostalgia ranging from a 17th-century clog to kitchen kitsch and a re-created 1930s worker's cottage. With a focus on memories and feelings, it's an evocative place where you can plunge into racks of vintage clothes, pull out hidden treasures and learn the individual items' secrets on the digital catalogue.

One particular highlight is the eclectic collection of chairs, including beautifully crafted pieces from the nearby village of Lindome, one of Sweden's most historic furniture-making areas. The temporary exhibitions are clever (a circus exhibit will skip from art to brain research and finish up with a bit of history) and the in-house cafe boasts summertime seating right by the rapids. The museum also hires out a brilliant, hand-held computer guide (in Swedish), which leads you through Kvarnbyn's industrial landscape using a lively mix of historical anecdotes, animation and soundscapes.

From Gothenburg, catch a Kungsbackabound train to Mölndal station, then bus 752 or 756.

Liseberg   AMUSEMENT PARK
(www.liseberg.se; Södra Vägen; 1-day pass 455kr; ⊙11am-11pm Jun–mid-Aug, hours vary rest of year; 🅿 ♿; 🚋2 Korsvägen) The attractions of Liseberg, Scandinavia's largest amusement park, are many and varied. Adrenalin blasts include the venerable wooden roller coaster Balder; its 'explosive' colleague Kanonen, where you're blasted from 0km/h to 75km/h in under two seconds; AtmosFear, Europe's tallest (116m) free-fall tower; and the park's biggest new attraction, Loke, a fast-paced spinning 'wheel' that soars 42 m into the air. Softer options include carousels, fairy-tale castles, an outdoor dance floor, adventure playgrounds, and shows and concerts.

Entry to the park grounds is reasonable (100kr) which is ideal for those who just want to enjoy the charming landscaped grounds studded with impressive sculptures, but note that you pay for individual rides using coupons or an armband. Opening hours are varied – check the website.

When it comes to refuelling in between rides, Lisberg is also the first theme park in the world to offer a very high-quality, delicious, exclusively vegetarian buffet lunch (adult/child 165/65kr) at the Green Room (noon-10pm).

Haga District   AREA
(www.hagashopping.se; 🚋25 Hagakyrkan, 🚋2 Handelshögskolan) The Haga district is Gothenburg's oldest suburb, dating back to 1648. A hardcore hippie hang-out in the 1960s and '70s, its cobbled streets and vintage buildings now host a cool blend of cafes, trendy shops and boutiques. During some summer weekends and at Christmas, store owners set up stalls along Haga Nygata, turning the neighbourhood into one big market. Check out the charming three-storey timber houses, built as housing for workers in the 19th century.

Linné District   AREA
(www.facebook.com/AndraLangdagen/; 🚋1, 3, 5, 6, 9, 10) The Linné district holds fast to its grungy roots, especially along the Långgatan streets. Here, hip cafes, junk shops and street-smart boutiques mix with seedy sex shops and eclectic locals. It's home to the

CONTEMPORARY ART & ARCHITECTURE.

Gothenburg has imagination and creativity to spare. Independent galleries brim with up-and-coming talent, and architectural flights of fancy have sprung up like mushrooms after the rain. Take a peek at Kuggen (p138) for a taste of what 'green' engineering can mean. And even if you wanted to, you couldn't miss Göteborgs-Utkiken (p140), aka 'The Lipstick'. To dive into the art scene, visit Galleri Thomassen (p138), Galleri Ferm (p138) and Galleri Nils Åberg (p138).

kicking **Andra Långdagen block party**, a wild, one-day street bash organised by the street's traders and fans. Held annually between April and June (check Facebook for dates), it's a thumping concoction of DJ sets, film screenings, barbecues, clothes swaps and backyard B-boy battles.

Klippan Precinct   HISTORIC SITE
(🚋3, 9 Vagnhallen Majorna) Once a bustle of industry (with glassworks, foundries, breweries and salting houses) the Klippan precinct has been revamped into a rather fetching heritage centre. It includes 18th-century sailors' cottages, the remains of Gamla Älvsborg fort (ransomed from the Danes in 1619), a brewery opened by the Scot David Carnegie (now a hotel) and St Birgittas kapell. Klippan is just off Oscarsleden, about 400m east of Älvsborgsbron.

Trädgårdsföreningen   PARK
(www.tradgardsforeningen.se; Nya Allén; ⊙7am-8pm; 🚋3, 4, 5, 7, 10 Kungsportsplatsen) Laid out in 1842, the lush Trädgårdsföreningen is a large protected area off Nya Allén. Full of flowers and tiny cafes, it's popular for lunchtime escapes and is home to Europe's largest **rosarium**, with around 2500 varieties. The gracious 19th-century **Palmhuset** (open 10am to 8pm) is a bite-size version of the Crystal Palace in London, with five differently heated halls: look out for the impressive camellia collection and the 2m-wide tropical lily pads.

Nya Älvsborgs Fästning   CASTLE
(Elfsborgs Fortress; 📞031-10 10 15; www.vastkustlinjen.se; guided tours incl boat trip & lunch/dinner 275/495kr; ⊙lunch tours Thu-Sun mid-May–Jun & late Aug–mid-Sep, dinner Fri-Sun Jul-Aug;

Västkustlinjen) At the mouth of the Göta älv, squat red Elfsborgs Fortress was built in the 17th century to keep out the marauding Danes and saw action again in the early 18th century during the Great Nordic War. Tours take in the church built for Karl XII's troops, dungeons that discouraged escape by swimming, and the original tower. Boats leave at 10am and noon for the lunch tour, 5pm and 7pm for the dinner tour, from Maritiman behind Gothenburg Opera House.

Världskulturmuseet   MUSEUM
(Museum of World Culture; www.varldskultur museet.se; Södra Vägen 54; ⊙ 11am-5pm Tue-Sun; ▣ 4, 5, 6, 7, 8 Korsvägen) FREE In a striking building by London-based architects Cécile Brisac and Edgar Gonzalez, the Världskulturmuseet sees ethnography, art and global politics collide in immersive multimedia exhibitions. Recent ones have included a study of significant textile patterns in various cultures, enchantingly displayed with multicolored lights; and a collection of photos from various historic expeditions.

Kuggen   ARCHITECTURE
(Lindholmsplatsen; ▣ 55) Across the river and next to the Science Park is the city's most exciting new building – the epitome of green engineering. Kuggen, or 'Cogwheel', resembles a bright red Colosseum, only with triangular windows that make maximum use of daylight and a host of eco-credentials that include adaptive ventilation and interactive heating and cooling systems. Take the Älvsn ferry from the Rosalund stop along Skeppsbron to Lindholmspiren.

Maritiman   MUSEUM
(www.maritiman.se; Packhusplatsen 12; adult/5-15yr 125/70kr; ⊙ 10am-6pm Jun-Aug, shorter hrs rest of year; ▣; ▣ 5, 10 Lilla Bommen) Near the opera house, the world's largest floating ship museum is made up of 20 historical crafts, including fishing boats, a light vessel and a firefighter, all linked by walkways. Shin down into the 69m-long submarine *Nordkaparen* for a glimpse into underwater warfare. Inside the labyrinthine 121m-long destroyer *Småland*, in service from 1952 to 1979, hunched figures listen to crackling radio messages, and the bunks look just-slept-in – you half expect to meet uniformed sailors in the dim, twisting passages.

Volvo Museum   MUSEUM
(www.volvomuseum.com; Arendal Skans; adult/child 100/50kr; ⊙ 10am-5pm Mon-Fri, 11am-4pm Sat & Sun) Pay homage to one of Sweden's enduring icons at the Volvo Museum, which contains everything from the company's debut vehicle to its most experimental designs – including the first jet engine used by the Swedish Air Force.

The museum is about 8km west of the city centre at Arendal. Fittingly, it's tricky to get to without a car. Take tram 5 or 10 to Eketrägatan, then bus 32 to Arendal Skans.

Galleri Ferm   GALLERY
(www.galleriferm.se; Karl Gustavsgatan 13; ⊙ 11am-6pm Mon-Thu, to 5pm Fri, noon-3pm Sat & Sun; ▣ 1, 2, 3, 7, 10 Viktoriagatan) Constant surprises, mainly from Scandinavian artists such as Per Cederbank, Emil Olsson and Yrjö Edelmann, plus works by internationally renowned contemporary artists.

Galleri Nils Åberg   GALLERY
(www.gallerinilsaberg.se; Åvägen 24; ⊙ noon-6pm Wed-Fri, 11am-4pm Sat & Sun; ▣ 1, 2, 3, 7, 10 Vasaplatsen) This gallery shows works by fresh, young Scandinavian artists alongside established contemporary pieces by the likes of Picasso and Joan Miró.

Galleri Thomassen   GALLERY
(www.gallerithomassen.se; Götabergsgatan 32; ⊙ noon-6pm Tue-Thu, to 4pm Fri-Sun; by appointment only mid-Jul-Aug; ▣ 1, 2, 3, 7, 10 Vasaplatsen) Showcases up-and-coming talent in its Lilla Galleriet and contemporary art from all over Scandinavia as well as Berlin.

Feskekörka   MARKET
(www.feskekörka.se; Rosenlundsgatan; ⊙ 10am-6pm Tue-Fri, to 3pm Sat; ▣ 1, 3, 5, 6, 7, 9 Hagakyrkan) This peculiar fish market is shaped like a church. You may see the odd bride and groom posing with the shellfish; they're not lost – it's just that the market is also consecrated as a place of worship/matrimony.

Kronhuset   HISTORIC BUILDING
(Postgatan 6-8; ⊙ open for events; ▣ 6, 13 Nordstan) The city's oldest secular building, Kronhuset is a former arsenal built in Dutch style between 1642 and 1654. It was here that Karl X held the disastrous *riksdag* (parliament) in 1660 – he died while it was in session. Kronhusbodarna, across the courtyard from Kronhuset, houses workshops making and selling pottery, silverware, glass and textiles, as well as **Göteborgs Choklad & Karamellfabrik** (open 11am to 5pm): its chocolate balls are enough to lead the purest of angels into sugar-filled temptation.

BOHUS FÄSTNING

Survivor of no fewer than 14 sieges, **Bohus Fästning** (Bohus Fortress; ☎ 0303-23 92 03; www.bohusfastning.com; Fästningsholmen, Kungälv; adult/child 100/60kr; ⊙10am-6pm daily mid-May–mid-Aug, 10am-4pm daily mid-Aug–mid-Sep, 11am-4pm Sat & Sun mid-Sep–Oct & mid-Mar–mid-May; ▣ Grön Express) is a hulking ruin on an island in the Nordre älv, near Kungälv. Founded in 1308 by the Norwegian king to protect Norway's southern border, the fortress was inherited by Sweden at the Peace of Roskilde in 1658. Its substantial remains include a remarkable round tower, Fars Hatt, where unfortunates were once imprisoned for witchcraft and heresy; you can peer into the lightless dungeons, and climb the battlements for a lofty view.

Tourist information for the area is available at the fortress. To get here, take the Västtrafik Grön Express bus from Gothenburg to Kungälv (30 minutes, every 10 to 15 minutes); get off at the Eriksdal stop and walk the remaining 500m.

Sjöfartsmuseet
MUSEUM

(www.sjofartsmuseum.goteborg.se; Karl Johansgatan 1-3; adult/child 40kr/free; ⊙10am-5pm Tue-Sun, to 8pm Wed; ▣; ▣3, 9, 11 Stigbergstorget) Sjöfartsmuseet focuses on the city's maritime history through an entertaining collection of maps, model ships, recreated sailors' quarters, and period objects. Most compelling is the large darkened hall where you're surrounded by soaring figureheads – some regal, some pensive, some vicious. You may spot some scrimshaw and a tiny weaving loom in a bottle among the nautical booty.

The attached aquarium wriggles with goofy North Sea flatfish, lobsters and upside-down jellyfish, and you can find Nemo in the tropical fish tank.

Outside, the Sjömanstornet (Mariner's Tower), topped by a statue of a grieving woman, commemorates Swedish sailors killed in WWI.

Naturhistoriska Museet
MUSEUM

(Natural History Museum; www.gnm.se; Museivägen 10; adult/under 25yr 40kr/free; ⊙11am-5pm Tue-Sun, to 8pm Thu; ▣; ▣1, 2, 6 Linnéplatsen) The Natural History Museum is home to an incredible range of taxidermied wildlife, from the horned and hooved denizens of the savannah to all the big cats, the extinct Stellers sea cow, all manner of birds and pickled creatures of the deep. Its tour de force is the world's only stuffed blue whale (which visitors were allowed inside until an amorous couple was caught *in flagrante*, but Santa Claus still holds court here in the lead-up to Christmas).

Stadsmuseum
MUSEUM

(City Museum; www.stadsmuseum.goteborg. se; Norra Hamngatan 12; adult/child 40kr/free; ⊙10am-5pm Thu-Sun, to 8pm Wed; ▣; ▣1, 3, 4, 5, 6, 9 Brunnsparken) At Stadsmuseum, you can admire the remains of the *Äskekärrkeppet*,

Sweden's only original Viking vessel, alongside silver treasure hoards, weaponry and jewellery from the same period in the atmospheric semigloom. Walk through the history of the city from its conception to the 18th century, spiced up with period wares, including an impressive booty of East Indian porcelain, and play 'Guess the Object!'. Temporary art and photography exhibitions are also worth a peek.

Hagakyrkan
CHURCH

(Haga Kyrkoplan; Haga Kyrkogata; ⊙11am-3pm Mon-Thu, to 1pm Sat; ▣2, 7, 10 Handelshögskolan) The beautiful 19th-century Hagakyrkan, built in 1859, is well worth peeking inside. The park behind the church is home to a simple yet moving **monument** to Swedish hero Raoul Wallenberg. A Nordic Schindler of sorts, Wallenberg is credited with saving the lives of around 15,000 Hungarian Jews during WWII. Wallenberg himself was arrested by the Russian government in 1945 as an alleged spy and executed sometime after.

Domkyrkan
CHURCH

(Gustavi Cathedral; ☎ 031-731 61 30; Västra Hamngatan; ⊙8am-6pm Mon-Fri, 10am-6.30pm Sat & Sun; ▣1, 2, 5, 6, 9 Domkyrkan) FREE The elegant Domkyrkan was consecrated in 1815, the two previous cathedrals on this site having both been destroyed by town fires. Although many of the cathedral's contents are relatively modern, seasoned features include an 18th-century clock and reredos.

Masthuggskyrkan
CHURCH

(☎ 031-731 92 50; Storebackegatan; ⊙9am-6pm daily Jun-Aug, varies rest of year; ▣1, 3, 5, 6, 9 Stigbergstorget) One of Gothenburg's most distinctive buildings, this is a welcome landmark for sailors and is a smashing viewpoint over the

GOTHENBURG DISCOUNT CARDS

The brilliant **Göteborg City Card** (www.goteborg.com/citycard; 24-/48-/72hr card adult 395/545/695kr, child 265/365/455kr) is particularly worthwhile if you're into intensive sightseeing: it gives you free access to most museums and Liseberg amusement park, discounted and free city tours, unlimited travel on public transport and free parking in the city with the most dedicated traffic wardens. The card is available at tourist offices, hotels, Pressbyrån newsstands and online.

The **Göteborgspaketet** (http://butik.goteborg.com/en/package; adult from 635kr) is an accommodation-and-entertainment package offered at various hotels, with prices starting at 635kr per person per night in a double room. It includes the Göteborg City Card for the number of nights you stay; book online in advance.

western half of the city. Completed in 1914, its interior resembles an upturned boat.

Slottsskogsparken   PARK
(⊙24hr; ⬚1, 2, 6, 7, 10 Linnéplatsen) **FREE** Slottsskogsparken is an enormous park featuring dozens of walking trails and kid magnets **Barnens Zoo** and **Djurgårdarna**, an animal park with farm animals, elk, deer and other furry and feathered Swedish creatures.

Botaniska Trädgården   GARDENS
(📷010-473 77 77; www.gotbot.se; Carl Skottsbergsgatan 22A; by donation 20kr; ⊙9am-sunset; ⬚1, 2, 6, 7, 10 Linnéplatsen) Sweden's largest botanical garden breathes easy with around 16,000 plant species. Look for outdoor sculptures, and check online for special events and activities.

Göteborgs-Utkiken   ARCHITECTURE
(Lilla Bommen torg 1; adult/child 40/20kr; ⊙11am-4pm; ⬚6, 13 Nordstan) The red-and-white 'skyscraper' Göteborgs-Utkiken, nicknamed 'The Lipstick' for obvious reasons, has killer views of the harbour from the top.

🏃 Tours

Hop On Hop Off   BUS TOUR, BOAT TOUR
(www.stromma.se; from 297kr) Strömma runs the Hop On Hop Off bus-boat combo. A 24-hour ticket gives you access to the double-decker bus routes that take you past the city's main attractions, while the boats whisk you along the canals. You can also opt for separate bus and boat passes (189kr each). Catch the bus outside Stora Teatern just off Kungsportsavenyn.

Paddan City Boat Tour   BOATING
(www.stromma.se; tours from 175kr; ⊙Apr-Oct) Strömma runs 50-minute city tours on its Paddan boats from Kungsportsplatsen, right across from the tourist office. They're an information-packed way to get your bearings and

are free with the Göteborg City Card. Longer tours into the archipelago and various canals are also available.

Strömma Cruises   BOATING
(www.stromma.se; per person from 280kr) Along with several other tours, Strömma runs archipelago cruises of varying duration. Most leave from just southeast of Götaälvbron, but departure points vary.

🌟 Festivals & Events

Göteborg International Film Festival   FILM
(www.giff.se) One of Scandinavia's major film festivals, with flicks spanning all continents and genres. It's usually held in late January.

Kvarnbydagen   ART
(Kvarnbyn Day; www.kvarnbydagen.se) On a Saturday in April or early May, Kvarnbydagen sees local artists and designers open their studios to the public.

Metaltown   MUSIC
(www.metaltown.se) Metaltown is one of Sweden's biggest metal festivals. Held in June, it attracts the likes of Slipknot, Korn, Napalm Death and Motörhead, as well as a large number of attendees featuring heavy black eyeliner and spike-adorned clothing.

Clandestino Festival   MUSIC
(www.clandestinofestival.org) A hip-shaking line-up of world music, held in June.

Way Out West   MUSIC
(www.wayoutwest.se) In early August, Way Out West is a mighty three-day music festival pulling in big guns like the Pixies, Ryan Adams, Major Lazer, Regina Spektor, Band of Horses and the Shins.

Kulturnatt   ART, DANCE
(http://kulturnatta.goteborg.se/) In September or October, Kulturnatt is a starlit spectacle

of open studios and art installations, as well as dance and music performances and activities for adults and children.

🛏 Sleeping

Gothenburg has a solid range of accommodation in all categories. The majority of hotels offer decent discounts at weekends and during the summer. Check www.goteborg.com for deals. Most hostels are clustered southwest of the centre; all are open year-round.

Sankt Sigfrid B&B   B&B €
(📞 0735-51 52 80; www.sanktas.se; Sankt Sigfrids Plan 7; s/d from 480/730kr; 🅿🛜; 🚌5 Sankt Sigfrids Plan) Particularly handy for hitting Liseberg or Avenyn nightlife, this welcoming guesthouse in a quiet area offers all the perks of staying practically in the city centre, minus the city-centre prices. The rooms are snug, guests have access to a small kitchen, and the host couldn't be more attentive.

STF Vandrarhem Slottsskogen   HOSTEL €
(📞 031-42 65 20; www.sov.nu; Vegagatan 21; hostel dm/s/d from 195/395/540kr, hotel s/d 550/790kr, breakfast 75kr; 🅿@🛜; 🚌1, 2, 6 Olivedalsgatan) Like a good university dormitory, big, friendly Slottsskogen is a cracking place for meeting people. The facilities are top-notch, with comfortable beds, individual reading lights, lockable storage under the beds, a dressing table in the women's dorm and a good ratio of guests per bathroom. Proximity to the nightlife area is a bonus and the buffet breakfast is brilliant.

Kvibergs Vandrarhem & Stugby   HOSTEL €
(📞 031-43 50 55; www.vandrarhem.com; Kvibergsvägen 5; s/d from 490/585kr, cottage from 1100kr, breakfast 70kr; 🅿@🛜; 🚌6, 7, 11 Kviberg) This sterling hostel, a few kilometres northeast of the city centre, attracts families and travellers looking for a quiet spot with its extensive amenities that include a sauna and a pleasant outdoor area good for barbecuing. Hotel rooms throw in breakfast and bed linen and have their own bathrooms; dorm rooms don't. Cabins are particularly good value for groups.

STF Vandrarhem Stigbergsliden   HOSTEL €
(📞 031-24 16 20; www.hostel-gothenburg.com; Stigbergsliden 10; dm/s/d 390/500/675kr; ⊘reception 4-6pm; 🅿🛜🎒; 🚌3, 9, 11 Stigbergstorget) Rooms at Stigbergsliden have a certain monastic simplicity to them, in keeping with the hostel's history as a 19th-century seaman's institute. Staff are especially help-

ful, and besides the usual stuff (big kitchen, laundry, TV room) there is a pleasant sheltered garden. On the downside, the showers don't lock.

Linné Vandrarhem   HOSTEL €
(📞 031-12 10 60; www.linnehostel.com; Vegagatan 22; dm/s/d from 300/500/700kr; @🛜; 🚌1, 6, 7, 10 Prinsgatan) The helpful staff really brighten up this central, homey hostel. Make sure you have your door code if arriving after office hours and avoid the windowless 'economy' rooms (read: ovens) in summer.

★ STF Göteborg City   HOSTEL €€
(📞 031-756 98 00; www.svenskaturistforeningen. se; Drottninggatan 63-65; hostel r from 995kr, hotel s/d from 1400/1500kr, breakfast 85kr; @🛜; 🚌1 Brunnsparken) This large super-central hostel is all industrial chic in the cafe/dining area and lounge and plush comfort on each of its individually themed floors. All rooms are private, with en-suite bathroom, plush carpeting and comfortable bed-bunks, and – rarity of rarities! – your bed linen and towels are provided for you.

Hotel Allen   HOTEL €€
(📞 031-11 01 50; www.hotelallen.se; Parkgatam 10; s/d from 695/795kr; @🛜; 🚌3 Valand) Located parallel to the green oasis that is Trädgårdsföreningen, this small modern hotel has some inviting perks – like free waffles for guests until 9pm, complimentary hot drinks and cake, and even a shoe polisher (a machine that is!). Rooms are spacious with parquet floors, chic black-and-white fabrics and bathrooms with tubs, as well as showers.

First Hotel G   HOTEL €€
(📞 031-63 72 00; www.firsthotels.se; Nils Ericsonsplatsen 4; r from 1035kr; 🅿✳🛜; 🚌1, 2, 3, 4, 9 Centralstationen) In a you-couldn't-be-more-central location on top of the train station, this high-tech business hotel is completely soundproof, and its spacious rooms boast laminated wooden floors and thoroughly comfortable beds. Extensive breakfast is thrown in, and there's an in-house spa for pre- or post-journey relaxation. Substantial discounts online.

Vanilla Hotel   BOUTIQUE HOTEL €€
(📞 031-711 62 20; www.vaniljhotel.se; Kyrkogatan 38; s/d 1295/1445kr; 🅿🛜; 🚌1, 3, 5, 6, 9 Domkyrkan) This petite slumber spot has the cosy, welcoming feeling of a Swedish home. The compact rooms are pleasantly light and decorated in sparing Scandinavian style, with

wooden floors and furniture, crisp sheets and immaculate bathrooms, but they get rather hot in summer. Ask for a garden-view room, as the street gets noisy from early morning. Weekend rates drop sharply.

Hotell Barken Viking
HOTEL €€

(☑ 031-63 58 00; www.barkenviking.com; Lilla Bommens torg 10; r from 1395/1495kr; 🕾; 🚋 5, 10 Lilla Bommen) If staying aboard a schooner floats your boat, try the *Barken Viking*, an elegant four-masted sailing ship converted into a stylish hotel. The wood-panelled rooms are cosy (read: small), with Hamptons-style linen, and designed for those who travel light. You won't run into any seamen, however, as there's no access to the upper deck.

Änggårdens Bed & Breakfast
B&B €€

(☑ 070-554 47 60, 031-41 97 06; Änggårdsplatsen 1; s/d from 700/900kr; 🕾; 🚋 1, 2, 6, 8, 10 Botaniska Trädgården) Across the street from the Slottsskogen city park and surrounded by greenery, this appealing yellow-stone house welcomes you with its homey atmosphere; four compact, cosy rooms (the largest double has its own bathroom); and a chill-out garden area.

★ Dorsia Hotel
BOUTIQUE HOTEL €€€

(☑ 031-790 10 00; www.dorsia.se; Trädgårdsgatan 6; s/d from 1950/2950kr; P ❋ @ 🕾; 🚋 3 Kungsportsplatsen) If heaven had a bordello, it would resemble this lavish, flamboyant establishment that combines old-world decadence with cutting-edge design. Rooms delight with their heavy velvet curtains, purple-and-crimson colour scheme and opulent beds; thick carpet in the corridors muffles your footsteps; and the fine art adorning the walls comes from the owner's own collection.

★ Upper House
BOUTIQUE HOTEL €€€

(☑ 031-708 82 00; www.upperhouse.se; Mässans Gata 24; r from 2290kr; P ❋ 🕾 ≋; 🚋 2, 4, 5, 6, 7 Korsvägen) One of the highest hotels in Sweden, sumptuous Upper House takes up the top four floors of one of the Gothia Towers. The decor is cool Scandinavian chic, the beds are the ultimate in slumbering comfort, and the superlative spa comes with a hammam and a 19th-floor outdoor pool encased in glass, with killer views of the city.

Avalon
HOTEL €€€

(☑ 031-751 02 00; www.avalonhotel.se; Kungstorget 9; r from 1770kr; @ 🕾 ≋; 🚋 3, 4, 5, 7, 10 Kungsportsplatsen) Rooms at the design-conscious Avalon are packed with eye-popping Nordic

design, bright colours, curvaceous furniture and flat-screen TVs. Some rooms feature a mini-spa or their own gym equipment, and there's also a small rooftop pool. The over-the-top '90s bar excels at classic cocktails and is a favorite local hang-out on summer evenings.

Hotel Flora
BOUTIQUE HOTEL €€€

(☑ 031-13 86 16; www.hotelflora.se; Grönsakstorget 2; s/d from 1675/1760kr; @ 🕾; 🚋 1 Grönsakstorget) Fabulous Flora's slick, individually themed rooms flaunt black, white and spot colour interiors, designer chairs, flat-screen TVs and sparkling bathrooms, though lack of storage facilities may dismay those with extensive sartorial needs. The top-floor rooms have air-con, several rooms offer river views, and rooms overlooking the chic split-level courtyard are for night owls rather than early birds.

Gothia Towers
HOTEL €€€

(☑ 031-750 88 10; www.gothiatowers.com; Mässans Gata 24; r from 1790kr; P @ 🕾 ≋; 🚋 2, 4, 5, 6, 7 Korsvägen) The 23-storey Gothia Towers looms right above Liseberg. Its rooms ooze Nordic cool: all sharp angles and clean lines. Suites are available on two floors. 'Gothia Limited' budget rooms are also available, and guests have access to the luxurious spa at sister hotel Upper House. More bird's-eye views await at Sky bar and restaurant Heaven 23.

IQ Suites
APARTMENT €€€

(☑ 031-760 80 40; www.iqsuites.com; Besvärsgatan 3; s/d 1800/2000kr; P 🕾; 🚋 2 Brunnsgatan) Short of scanning your retinas upon entry, these luxurious, industrial-chic apartments are as high-tech as they come and are within walking distance of the city's main attractions. The fully equipped Miele kitchens are a boon for self-caterers, while the smaller of the two apartments comes with its own personal sauna and Jacuzzi, for the ultimate in pampering.

Elite Plaza Hotel
HOTEL €€€

(☑ 0771-78 87 89; www.elite.se; Västra Hamngatan 3; s/d from 1700/1900kr; P @ 🕾; 🚋 1, 3, 5, 6, 9 Domkyrkan) With stucco ceilings and lovely mosaic floors, the Elite Plaza is a grand, old-world establishment with all the modern trimmings. Most rooms are spacious and breakfast is ample (though chaotic when the hotel is full). The proximity to some of the city's best restaurants and bars is a boon, but the latter is also a bane if you're a light sleeper.

Hotel Royal
HOTEL €€€

(031-700 11 70; www.hotelroyal.nu; Drottninggatan 67; s/d from 1945/2395kr; @ ; 1, 2, 5, 6, 9 Domkyrkan) Gothenburg's oldest hotel (1852) has aged enviably. The grand entrance has been retained, complete with its flowery, art-nouveau painted ceiling and sweeping staircase, and the elegant, individually styled rooms make necessary 21st-century concessions such as flat-screen TVs and renovated bathrooms. There's also homemade cake for guests, and an excellent breakfast. Check the website for special offers.

⚔ Eating

Gothenburg's chefs are at the cutting edge of Sweden's Slow Food movement, and the city boasts top-notch restaurants. Happily, there are also more casual options for trying old-fashioned *husmanskost* (home cooking) and a good range of vegan and vegetarian options. Cool cafes, cheap ethnic gems and foodie favourites abound in Vasastan, Haga and Linné districts.

Da Matteo
CAFE €

(www.damatteo.se; Vallgatan 5; sandwiches & salads 65-95kr; 7.30am-6pm Mon-Fri, 8am-6pm Sat, 10am-5pm Sun; 1, 3, 5, 6, 9 Domkyrkan) The perfect downtown lunch pit stop and a magnet for coffee lovers, this cafe serves wickedly fine espresso, mini *sfogliatelle* (Neapolitan pastries), sandwiches, pizza and great salads. There's a sun-soaked courtyard and a second branch on Viktoriapassagen.

Saluhall Briggen
MARKET €

(www.saluhallbriggen.se; Nordhemsgatan 28; 9am-6pm Mon-Fri, to 3pm Sat; 1 Prinsgatan) This covered market will have you drooling over its bounty of fresh bread, cheeses, quiches, seafood and ethnic treats. It's particularly handy for the hostel district.

Green Food
VEGAN €

(Drottninggatan 59; mains from 85kr; noon-5pm Mon-Fri, to 7pm Sat; ; 1 Brunnsparken) This is one of several restaurants in the city that focuses on offering a vegetarian or vegan menu. Geared for the budget conscious, Green Food is Asian-inspired with dumplings, ramen and a green food plate with vegetarian sushi, avocado and salad. Grains like quinoa make a change from white rice. The interior is barebones, with some outdoor tables.

Beijing8
DIM SUM €

(www.beijing8.se; Magasinsgatan 3; meals from 96kr; 11am-9pm Mon-Fri, noon-10pm Sat; 1,

3, 5, 6, 9 Domkyrkan) Take six imaginatively filled types of dumpling (duck and ginger, pork and shiitake, courgette and aubergine, chicken and peanut...), cook 'em four different ways, add a few vegie sides, four types of sauce, a couple of desserts and a few types of tea and you have a winning formula.

Gourmet Korv
HOT DOGS €

(www.gourmetkorv.se; Södra Larmgatan; dogs 30-40kr, meals 67-95kr; 10am-6pm Mon-Fri, to 4pm Sat, to 3pm Sun; 2, 5, 6, 11 Grönsakstorget) A sausagefest to sate the hungriest of the carnivorously inclined. Choose from the likes of currywurst, bierwurst and the immensely satisfying, cheese-squirting käsekrainer and have it in a bun or with a full spread of salad and mash.

En Deli i Haga
DELI €

(Haga Nygata 15; combo plate weekday/weekend 105/135kr; 8am-7pm Mon-Fri, 10am-5pm Sat & Sun; ; 1, 3, 5, 6, 9 Järntorget) En Deli dishes out great Mediterranean-style salads and meze, as well as good soup and sandwiches. Can't decide? Try some of everything, with the deli plate. An extra perk is the locally brewed beer and organic wine to accompany your meal.

Hemköp
SUPERMARKET €

(www.hemkop.se; Östra Hamngatan; 8am-9pm Mon-Fri, 10am-6pm Sat & Sun; 5 Nordstan) Major supermarket in the Nordstan shopping complex.

Feskekörka
MARKET €

(www.feskekörka.se; Rosenlundsgatan; salads from 75kr; 9am-5pm Tue-Thu, to 6pm Fri, 10am-3pm Sat; 3, 5, 9, 11 Hagakyrkan) A market devoted to all things that come from the sea, the 'Fish Church' is heaven for those who appreciate slabs of gravadlax, heaped shrimp sandwiches and seafood-heavy salads. The outdoor picnic tables are the ideal place to munch on them.

★ Moon Thai Kitchen
THAI €€

(www.moonthai.se; Kristinelundsgatan 9; mains 139-189kr; 11am-11pm Mon-Fri, noon-11pm Sat & Sun; 4, 5, 7, 10 Göteborg Valand) The owners have opted to run with it a few miles, hence the kaleidoscopic whirl of tuktuks, flowers and bamboo everything. Luckily, the dishes are authentic, the whimsical menu features such favourites as *som tum* (spicy papaya salad) and the fiery prawn red curry will make you weep with pleasure and gratitude.

Restaurant 2112
BURGERS €€

(📋 031-787 58 12; Magasinsgatan; burgers 189; ⊘ 4pm-1am, from 2pm Sat; 🚇 1, 3, 5, 6, 9 Domkyrkan) Appealing to refined rockers and metalheads, this upmarket joint serves only burgers and beer. But what burgers! These masterpieces range from the superlative Smoke on the Water with its signature Jack Daniels glaze to the fiery Hell Awaits Burger, featuring habanero dressing. The hungriest of diners will meet their match in the 666g monster Number of the Beast (399kr).

Ceviche
PERUVIAN €€

(Taste of Peru; www.tasteofperu.se; Gustaf Daléns-gatan 2; mains 119-179kr; ⊘ 11am-6pm Mon-Fri, to 4pm Sat; 🚇 5, 6, 10, 13 Vågmästareplatsen) Well worth the short trip across the river, the city's only Peruvian eatery is found on the 1st floor of a market hall. Sate your cravings for ceviche (five types!), and the weekday specials – *aji de gallina* (chicken in a creamy yellow sauce), *seco de carne* (beef stew) and *arróz con mariscos* (seafood rice) are all present and correct.

Trattoria la Strega
ITALIAN €€

(📋 031-18 15 01; www.trattorialastrega.se; Aschebergsgatan 23B; mains 135-245kr; ⊘ 5pm-late Tue-Fri, from 4pm Sat & Sun; 📋; 🚇 1, 2, 3, 7, 10 Vasaplatsen) A genuine rustic trattoria in the middle of Gothenburg, La Strega has a limited but beautifully executed menu of regularly changing dishes, complemented by wines from different Italian regions. Feast on the likes of black-truffle risotto, buckwheat pasta with Savoy cabbage and entrecôte with chestnut ragu, and leave room for the organic gelato.

Simba
AFRICAN €€

(www.restaurangsimba.se; Sankt Eriksgatan 3; mains 149-240kr; ⊘ 4-10pm Tue-Thu, till late Fri & Sat; 🚇 5, 10 Lilla Bommen) Tuck into the likes of *domoda* (tender lamb with peanut butter) or springbok steak, or mop up *wat* (stew) with *injera* (spongy Ethiopian pancake) under the watchful eyes of the tribal masks surrounding you.

Hemma Hos
TAPAS €€

(📋 031-13 40 90; Haga Nygata 12; mains 139-169kr; ⊘ 11.30am-mdnight; 🚇 1, 3, 5, 6, 9 Hagakyrkan) With a smooth black bar and comfortable tables, this Haga restaurant-bar manages to be both urbane and relaxed. Its selection of traditional Swedish *husmanskost* – your basic comfort food, like meatballs with potatoes and lingonberries – makes it a popular lunch stop, and there is a good variety of wine by the glass.

⭐ Thörnströms Kök
SCANDINAVIAN €€€

(📋 031-16 20 66; www.thornstromskok.com; Teknologgatan 3; mains 325-355kr, 4-course menu 675kr; ⊘ 6pm-1am Mon-Sat; 📶; 🚇 7 Kapellplatsen) Specialising in modern Scandinavian cuisine, chef Håkan shows you how he earned that Michelin star through creative use of local, seasonal ingredients and flawless presentation. Feast on the likes of rabbit with pistachios, pickled carrots and seaweed; don't miss the remarkable milk-chocolate pudding with goat's-cheese ice cream. A la carte dishes are available if a multi-course menu overwhelms you.

⭐ Smaka
SWEDISH €€€

(📋 031-13 22 47; www.smaka.se; Vasaplatsen 3; mains 175-285kr; ⊘ 5-11pm; 📶; 🚇 1 Vasaplatsen) For top-notch Swedish *husmanskost*, like the speciality meatballs with mashed potato and lingonberries, it's hard to do better than this smart yet down-to-earth restaurant-bar. Mod-Swedish options might include hake with suckling pig cheek or salmon tartar with pickled pear.

Koka
SWEDISH €€€

(📋 031-701 79 79; www.restaurangkoka.se; Viktoriagatan 12C; 3-/5-/7-course meals 480/680/880kr; ⊘ from 6pm Wed-Sat; 🚇 1, 2, 3, 7, 10 Vasaplatsen) Stylish Koka is distinguished by its smart, contemporary decor – blond wood, clean lines, mood lighting – and a dedication to conjuring up inspired dishes from the seasonal ingredients of Sweden's west coast. Brace yourself for the likes of mackerel with gooseberries, pork with blackcurrant and chervil ice cream.

Magnus & Magnus
MODERN EUROPEAN €€€

(📋 031-13 30 00; www.magnusmagnus.se; Magasinsgatan 8; 4-/6-course menu 495/745kr; ⊘ from 6pm Mon-Sat; 🚇 1, 2, 5, 6, 9 Domkyrkan) Ever-fashionable Magnus & Magnus serves inspired and beautifully presented modern European dishes in an appropriately chic setting. It's an unpretentious place in spite of its popularity, with pleasantly down-to-earth waitstaff. The menu tantalises with its lists of ingredients (pork belly, king crab, melon, feta cheese) and the courtyard draws Gothenburg's hipsters in summer.

Magazzino
ITALIAN €€€

(www.magazzino.se; Magasinsgatan 3; mains 179-269kr; ⊘ 5-11pm; 📶; 🚇 1 Domkyrkan) Expect to wait for a table at this perennially popular Italian restaurant on a pedestrian stretch. With Italians in the kitchen you can expect authentic cuisine, plus some gourmet additional ingredients like pasta with pecorino cheese infused with truffle oil. The interior is lined with giant photos of Italian film stills, with moody lighting and a boisterous atmosphere.

Puta Madre MEXICAN €€€
(☑ 031-711 88 38; www.putamadre.se; Magasinsgatan 3; mains 205-265kr; ⊙ 6pm-midnight Mon-Thu, 5pm-2am Fri & Sat; ☐ 1, 3, 5, 6, 9 Domkyrkan) This tribute to a Mexican brothel madam serves fresh, imaginative takes on classic Mexican dishes, such as *chile en nogada* (stuffed chilli), fish tacos, shrimp and crab enchiladas and jicama salad. And haven't you always wanted to toast your friends with a 'Rusty Puta'?

🍷 Drinking & Nightlife

While Kungsportsavenyn brims with beer-downing tourists and after-work locals, there are some savvier options – in summer, seek out a perch on a sun-soaked terrace and watch the street life go by.

Clubs have minimum-age limits ranging from 18 to 25, and many have a cover charge on popular nights.

★**Champagne Baren** WINE BAR
(www.forssenoberg.com; Kyrkogatan; ⊙ 5-11pm Tue-Thu, 4pm-midnight Fri & Sat; 🔊; ☐ 1 Domkyrkan) What's not to like? This champagne bar has an idyllic setting on an inner courtyard with uneven cobbles, picturesque buildings and plenty of greenery. Along with glasses of bubbly, there are platters of cheese, oysters and cold cuts. Very popular with the boho-chic set. You can expect some cool background beats, as well as occasional live jazz.

NOBA Nordic Bar BAR
(www.noba.nu; Viktoriagatan 1A; ⊙ 4pm-1am Mon-Thu, to 3am Fri & Sat, 5pm-1am Sun; ☐ 1, 2, 3, 7, 10 Viktoriagatan) With ye olde maps of Scandinavia on the walls and a glassed-over beer patio with birch tree stumps for stools, this bar takes its Nordic beers very seriously. From Iceland's Freja to Denmark's Kärlek, you name it, they've got it. The free-flowing whiskies liven up the scene on weekends.

Greta's GAY
(☑ 031-13 69 49; Drottninggatan 35; ⊙ 9pm-3am Fri & Sat; ☐ 1, 3, 4, 5, 6, 9 Brunnsparken) Decked out with Greta Garbo memorabilia, Greta's is Gothenburg's dedicated gay club, featuring flamboyant Tiki parties, DJs and other kitsch-a-licious fun on Friday and Saturday nights.

Ölhallen 7:an BEER HALL
(Kungstorget 7; ⊙ 11am-midnight Sun-Tue, to 1am Wed-Sat; ☐ 3, 4, 5, 7, 10 Kungsportsplatsen) This well-worn Swedish beer hall – the last remaining from its era – hasn't changed much in over 100 years. It attracts an interesting mix of bikers and regular folk with its homey atmosphere and friendly service. The illustrations lining the walls are Liss Sidén's portraits of regulars in the old days.

Cafe Santo Domingo BAR
(www.cafesantodomingo.se; Andra Långgatan 4; ⊙ 9am-late; ☐ 1, 3, 5, 6, 9 Järntorget) Cafe–record shop serving mean espressos by day turns into a bar with a great array of beers and rowdy live-music sets by night.

Notting Hill PUB
(www.nottinghill.se; Nordhemsgatan 19A; ⊙ 4pm-midnight Mon-Thu, to 2am Fri & Sat; ☐ 1, 3, 5, 6, 9 Järntorget) This friendly and pretty local

KVARNBYN: CREATIVE OUTSKIRTS

The tiny, creative hub of Kvarnbyn, a district of Mölndal 8km south of Gothenburg, has long attracted architects, designers and artists looking to escape the high rents and pressures of the city. Here, a brooding landscape of roaring rapids gripped by grain mills and historic factories (Mölndal means valley of the mills) has been transformed into a dynamic yet low-key cultural centre.

The district's nexus is the smart, interactive Mölndals Museum (p136). Located in an old police station, the museum showcases 10,000-strong collection of local nostalgia.

The district also hosts some noteworthy cultural events. On a Saturday in mid- to late April, Kvarnbydagen (p140) sees local artists and designers open their studios to the public. In September Kulturnatt (p140) features open studios and art installations, as well as dance and music performances.

To reach Kvarnbyn from Gothenburg, catch a Kungsbacka-bound train to Mölndal station, then bus 756 or 752 to Mölndals Museum.

pub between the Haga and Linné districts – on a corner crammed with appealing drinking establishments – looks like it could've dropped in from the Cotswolds. There's a respectable selection of tipples, British and Swedish pub fare (meatballs, fish and chips) and football on the big screen.

Barn   BAR
(www.thebarn.se; Kyrkogatan 11; ⊙ 5pm-late Mon-Sat, from 2pm Sun; 🛜; 🚋 1 Domkyrkan) As the name suggests, this bar is all roughly hewn wood and copper taps, and the beer/wine selection is guaranteed to get you merry. Excellent cocktails – vouched for by local bartenders. The burgers make fantastic stomach-liners, too.

Nefertiti   CLUB
(www.nefertiti.se; Hvitfeldtsplatsen 6; ⊙ hours vary; admission 120-220kr; 🚋 1, 5, 6, 9, 11 Grönsakstorget) Named rather incongruously after an Egyptian goddess, this Gothenburg institution is famous for its smooth live jazz and blues, as well as club nights spanning everything from techno and deep house to hip hop and funk and a weekly soul night.

☆ Entertainment

Widely recognised as Sweden's premier music city, Gothenburg has a lively music scene, as well as one of the country's top opera houses. Check out www.goteborg.com to find out what's on. There are also several annual music festivals, including Way Out West (p140) which takes place in August and draws music fans from all over Europe.

Pustervik   LIVE MUSIC, THEATRE
(www.pusterviksbaren.se; Järntorgsgatan 12; 🚋 1, 3, 5, 9, 11 Järntorget) Culture vultures and party people pack this hybrid venue, with its heaving downstairs bar and upstairs club and stage. Gigs range from independent theatre and live music (anything from emerging singer-songwriters to Neneh Cherry) to regular club nights spanning hip hop, soul and rock.

Göteborgs Konserthuset   CLASSICAL MUSIC
(Concert Hall; ☎ 031-726 53 10; www.gso.se; Götaplatsen; tickets 100-360kr; ⊙ closed summer) Home to the local symphony orchestra, with top international guests and some sterling performances.

GöteborgsOperan   OPERA
(☎ 031-13 13 00; www.opera.se; Christina Nilssons Gata; tickets 100-850kr; 🚋 5, 10 Lilla Bommen)

Designed by architect Jan Izikowitz, the opera house is a striking contemporary glass building with a sloped roof overlooking Lilla Bommen harbour. Performances include modern classics such as *Phantom of the Opera* as well as contemporary dance by up-and-coming artists.

Nya Ullevi   STADIUM
(☎ 031-368 45 00; www.gotevent.se; Skånegatan) The city's outdoor stadium hosts rock concerts and sporting events.

Scandinavium   CONCERT VENUE
(☎ 031-368 45 00; https://gotevent.se/arenor/scandinavium/; Valhallagatan 1) An indoor concert venue near Nya Ullevi stadium.

Göteborgs Stadsteatern   THEATRE
(☎ 031-708 71 00; www.stadsteatern.goteborg.se; Götaplatsen; tickets from 110kr) Stages theatre productions in Swedish.

Folkets Bio   CINEMA
(☎ 031-42 88 10; www.hagabion.se; Linnégatan 21) For independent and art-house offerings.

Biopalatset   CINEMA
(☎ 08-56 26 00 00; www.sf.se; Kungstorget) Multiscreen Biopalatset screens mainstream blockbusters.

🛍 Shopping

Gothenburg is right up with Stockholm when it comes to shopping. For idiosyncratic small shops selling everything from handmade jewellery to organic honey, head to the Haga district. At the other end of the scale are designer boutiques and national chains on 'Avenyn' boulevard. For one-stop shopping head to central Nordiska Kompaniet, a hub of Swedish and international brands.

Nordiska Kompaniet   DEPARTMENT STORE
(www.nk.se; Östra Hamngatan 42; ⊙ 10am-8pm, to 6pm Sat, 11am-5pm Sun; 🚋 3,4, 5, 7, 10 Kungsportsplatsen) A local institution since 1971, the four floors of this venerable department store host the likes of Tiger, RedGreen, NK Boutique and Mayla amid its mix of Swedish and international designers.

DesignTorget   HOMEWARES
(www.designtorget.se; Vallgatan 14; ⊙ 10am-7pm Mon-Fri, to 5pm Sat, noon-4pm Sun; 🚋 1, 2, 5, 6, 9 Domkyrkan) Cool, affordable, brightly coloured designer kitchenware, jewellery and more from both established and up-and-coming Scandi talent.

J. Lindeberg
CLOTHING

(www.jlindeberg.com; Korsgatan 17; ⊙11am-6pm Mon-Fri, to 5pm Sat; ⧉1, 6, 9, 11 Domkyrkan) This established Stockholm designer offers slick knitwear, casual shirts and those perfect autumn/winter coats for the discerning gent.

Butik Kubik
CLOTHING

(www.butikkubik.se; Tredje Långgatan 8; ⊙noon-8pm Tue-Fri, to 6pm Sat; ⧉1, 6 Prinsgatan) Run by two young designers, this basement shop is a great place to check out local, bright, flowery threads.

Fanny Michel
FASHION & ACCESSORIES

(www.fannymichel.se; Korsgatan 2; ⊙11am-6pm Mon-Fri, to 5pm Sat, noon-4pm Sun; ⧉1, 6, 9, 11 Domkyrkan) Awash with lace, hats, scarves and other accessories. There's an outlet in Haga too.

Velour by Nostalgi
CLOTHING

(www.velour.se; Magasinsgatan 19; ⊙11am-6.30pm Mon-Fri, to 5pm Sat, noon-4pm Sun; ⧉1, 6, 9, 11 Domkyrkan) Revamped flagship store of local label. Stocks slick, stylish streetwear for guys and girls.

Bengans Skivor & Café
MUSIC

(⧉031-14 33 00; www.bengans.se; Stigbergstorget 1; ⊙10am-6.30pm Mon-Fri, 10am-4pm Sat, noon-4pm Sun; ⧉3, 9,11 Stigbergstorget) Gothenburg's mightiest music store is set in an old cinema, complete with retro signage and an indie-cool cafe.

Shelta
SHOES

(⧉031-24 28 56; www.shelta.eu; Andra Långgatan 21; ⊙noon-6.30pm Mon-Fri, to 5pm Sat; ⧉3, 9, 11 Masthuggstorget) Pimp your style with limited-edition and must-have sneakers and streetwear from big and lesser-known labels.

Systembolaget
DRINKS

(Kungsportsavenyn 18; ⊙10am-7pm Mon-Fri, to 3pm Sat; ⧉3, 4, 5, 7, 10 Valand) Handy central branch for all your alcohol-related needs.

ⓘ Information

EMERGENCY

Emergency	⧉112
Non-Emergency Police	⧉11 414
Sweden country code	⧉46

MEDICAL SERVICES

For 24-hour medical information, phone 1177.
Apotek Hjärtat (⧉0771-45 04 50; Nils Eriksongatan; ⊙8am-10pm) Late-night pharmacy inside the Nordstan shopping complex.

Sahlgrenska Universitetssjukhuset (⧉031-342 00 00; www.sahlgrenska.se; ⧉1) Major hospital about 5km northeast of central Gothenburg, near the terminus at the end of tram line 1.

MONEY

Banks with ATMs are readily available, including inside the Nordstan shopping complex and along Kungsportsavenyn.

Forex (www.forex.se) Foreign-exchange office with branches at Centralstationen, Kungsportsavenyn 22, Kungsportsplatsen, Landvetter Airport and Nordstan shopping complex.

POST

Postal services are mainly provided by kiosks, newsagents, petrol stations and supermarkets – look for the blue-and-yellow postal symbol.

TOURIST INFORMATION

Cityguide Gothenburg (www.goteborg.com/apps) Info on the city's attractions, events and more, available as an Android and iPhone app. City map available offline.

RFSL Göteborg (⧉031-788 25 10; www.rfsl.se/goteborg; Stora Badhusgatan 6; ⊙6-9pm Wed) Comprehensive information on the city's gay scene, events and more.

Tourist Office (www.goteborg.com; Nils Eriksongatan; ⊙10am-8pm Mon-Fri, to 6pm Sat, noon-5pm Sun) Branch office inside the Nordstan shopping complex.

Tourist Office (⧉031-368 42 00; www.goteborg.com; Kungsportsplatsen 2; ⊙9.30am-8pm late Jun–mid-Aug, shorter hours rest of year) Central and busy; has a good selection of free brochures and maps.

ⓘ Getting There & Away

AIR

Göteborg Landvetter Airport (www.swedavia.se/landvetter; ⧉Flygbuss) is located 25km east of the city. It has daily flights to/from Stockholm Arlanda and Stockholm Bromma airports, as well as weekday services to Umeå and several weekly services to Borlänge, Falun, Visby and Sundsvall.

Direct European routes include Amsterdam (KLM), Brussels (SAS), Copenhagen (SAS and Norwegian), Frankfurt (Lufthansa), Berlin (Air Berlin), Helsinki (Norwegian and SAS), London (British Airways and Ryanair), Munich (Lufthansa), Oslo (Norwegian) and Paris (Air France and SAS).

BOAT

Gothenburg is a major ferry terminal, with several services to Denmark and Germany.
Stena Line (Denmark) (p331)

GOTHENBURG & THE SOUTHWEST GOTHENBURG

Stena Line (Germany) (www.stenaline.se; Elof Lindälusgata 11; foot passenger one-way/return from 500kr; 🚋3 Jaegerdorffsplatsen)

For a special view of the region, jump on a boat for an unforgettable journey along the **Göta Canal** (www.gotakanal.se/en). Starting in Gothenburg, you'll pass through Sweden's oldest lock at Lilla Edet, opened in 1607. From there the trip crosses the great lakes Vänern and Vättern through the rolling country of Östergötland and on to Stockholm.

BUS

Västtrafik (🖉0771-41 43 00; www.vasttrafik. se) and **Hallandstrafiken** (🖉0771-33 10 30; www.hlt.se) provide regional transport links. If you're planning to spend some time exploring the southwest counties, a monthly pass or a *sommarkort* offers cheaper travel in the peak summer period (from late June to mid-August).

The bus station, **Nils Ericson Terminalen**, is next to the train station and has excellent facilities including luggage lockers (medium/large up to 24 hours 70/90kr). There's a Västtrafik information booth here, providing information and selling tickets for all city and regional public transport within the Gothenburg, Bohuslän and Västergötland area.

Swebus (🖉0771-21 82 18; www.swebus express.com) operates frequent buses to most major towns and cities; non-refundable advance tickets work out considerably cheaper than on-the-spot purchases. Services include:

Copenhagen (from 239kr, 4¾ hours, four daily)

Halmstad (from 109kr, 1¾ hours, five to seven daily)

Helsingborg (from 139kr, 2¾ hours, five to eight daily)

Malmö (from 119kr, 3½ to four hours, seven to nine daily)

Oslo (from 229kr, 3½ hours, five to 10 daily)

Stockholm (from 159kr, 6½ to seven hours, four to five daily)

CAR & MOTORCYCLE

The E6 motorway runs north–south from Oslo to Malmö just east of the city centre. There's also a complex junction where the E20 motorway diverges east for Stockholm.

International car-hire companies have desks at Göteborg Landvetter Airport and near the central train/bus stations.

Avis (www.avisworld.com)

Europcar (www.europcar.com)

Hertz (www.hertz-europe.com)

TRAIN

All trains arrive at and depart from Centralstationen, Sweden's oldest railway station and a heritage-listed building. The main railway lines

in the west connect Gothenburg to Karlstad, Stockholm, Malmö and Oslo. In the east, the main line runs from Stockholm via Norrköping and Linköping to Malmö. Book tickets online via **Sveriges Järnväg** (SJ; www.sj.se) or purchase from ticket booths at the station.

Luggage lockers (medium/large up to 24 hours 70/90kr) are available at Centralstationen.

ℹ️ Getting Around

TO/FROM THE AIRPORT

Flygbuss (🖉0771-51 52 52; www.flygbussarna. se; one-way/return adult 95/185kr, child 79/155kr) runs to Landvetter Airport from Nils Ericson Terminalen every 15 to 20 minutes from 4.20am to 9pm and from the airport to the city between 5am and 11.30pm. Discounts are available for online bookings.

The fixed taxi rate with **Taxi Göteborg** from the city to the airport is 453kr.

BICYCLE

Cyclists should ask at the tourist office for the free map *Cykelkarta Göteborg,* covering the best routes.

Styr & Ställ (www.goteborgbikes.se; per season 75kr) is Gothenburg's handy city-bike system. It involves buying a 'season pass' which then gives you unlimited access to bicycles stationed across the city. With the pass, all journeys under half an hour are free, making this ideal for quick trips. (There's a small fee for longer journeys.) You can also download directly onto your smart phone the app allbikesnow.com, which has a a city map showing all the bike locales, plus how many bikes are free at any given time.

Cykelkungen (🖉031-18 43 00; www. cykelkungen.se; Chalmersgatan 19; per day/wk 200/700kr; ⊙10am-6pm Mon-Fri) is a reliable spot for longer-term bike hire.

PUBLIC TRANSPORT

Buses, trams and ferries run by **Västtrafik** (p148) make up the city's public-transport system; there are Västtrafik information booths selling tickets and giving out timetables inside **Nils Ericson Terminalen**, in front of the train station on **Drottningtorget** as well as at **Brunnsparken**.

The most convenient way to travel around Gothenburg is by tram. Colour-coded lines, numbered 1 to 13, converge near Brunnsparken (a block from the train station). Trams run every few minutes between 5am and midnight; some lines run a reduced service after midnight on Friday and Saturday.

A city **transport ticket** costs 29/22kr per adult/child. One- and three-day **travel cards** (90/180kr, from Västtrafik information booths, 7-Eleven minimarkets or Pressbyrån newsagencies) can work out much cheaper. Holders of the **Göteborg City Card** (p140) travel free.

Västtrafik also has a handy app, Västtrafik To Go, which allows you to buy tickets on your phone.

TAXI

Taxi Göteborg (☑ 031-65 00 00; www.taxi goteborg.se) is one of the larger taxi companies.

Taxis can be picked up outside Centralstationen, at Kungsportsplatsen and on Kungsportsavenyn.

AROUND GOTHENBURG

Southern Archipelago

☑ 031 / POP 5000

Gothenburg's archipelago is divided into two sections, northern and southern. The northern archipelago is more accessible – you can drive there – and therefore more developed. To get more of a taste of remote island life, head to the car-free paradise of the southern archipelago. Though it's easy and quick to reach from Gothenburg, it feels worlds away.

There are nine major islands and numerous smaller ones. Brännö is the most popular for overnight stays.

❶ Getting There & Away

Styrsöbolaget (☑ 0771-41 43 00; www.styrs obolaget.se) runs an excellent 16-destination passenger-only ferry network. Most ferries leave from Saltholmen, reached by tram 11 (or 9 in summer) from central Gothenburg (about 35 minutes).

M/S Walona (☑ 031-711 34 50; www.vinga. org; adult/child round-trip 250/150kr; ☉10am Tue-Sat Jul-Aug) runs ferries to Vinga daily in summer from Stenpiren in Gothenburg.

Mid-June to mid-August you can take a ferry directly from Stenpiren in Gothenburg to Styrsö and Vrångö. Boats leave Stenpiren at 10.50am, 11.50am, 12.08pm and 12.25pm, returning from Vrångö about every half-hour from 3.30pm to 5pm (confirm schedules online with **Västtrafik**).

Tickets can be bought as you board the ferries.

Brännö

POP 790

Brännö's beaches and outdoor dance floor are its biggest attractions. The dancing brings crowds to the island on weekend nights from July to mid-August.

From the church in the centre of the island, day trippers can follow the cycling track through the woods towards the west coast. A 15-minute walk from the end of the track leads you to a stone causeway and the island **Galterö** – a strange treeless landscape of rock slabs, ponds, deserted sandy beaches and haunting bird calls.

✵ Festivals & Events

Dans på Brännö brygga   DANCE
(Dance at Brännö brygga; http://brannoforeningen.se/ kulturevenemang/dans-pa-branno-brygga/;   Husvik, Brännö; ☉7-11pm Sat Jul–mid-Aug) FREE Every Saturday night in July through mid-August, join the locals and other enthusiasts dancing on Brännö's outdoor dance floor, right by the Husvik ferry dock.

⊨ Sleeping & Eating

Pensionat Baggen   B&B €€
(☑ 031-97 38 80; www.brannovardshus.se; Husviksvägen 52; s/d/f 750/1290/1495kr; ⊠Husvik) Get away from it all at this simple, friendly place about halfway between the two ferry docks. There are 10 comfy rooms (seven doubles, one single and one family-size) and a sumptuous breakfast buffet complete with fresh bread from its very own bakery. There are also sleek modern rooms at the inn (*värdshus*) ranging from 1390kr to 1690kr.

Brännö Värdshus   SWEDISH €€
(www.baggebranno.se; Husviksvägen 52; mains 149-295kr, summer weekday lunch 189kr; ☉11am-11pm; ⊠Husvik) With the same owners as Pensionat Baggen, Brännö Värdshus houses a cosy restaurant, cafe and bakery and serves excellent meals, unsurprisingly emphasising seafood. In summer there's a weekday set-menu lunch (11am to 4pm), and regular live jazz and folk gigs in the evenings.

Note that the restaurant is about a 15-minute walk from the Husvik ferry station – no cars allowed on the island.

❶ Getting There & Away

Västtrafik (p148) ferries leave from Saltholmen in Gothenburg (take tram 11, or tram 9 in summer) at least hourly. There are two stops on the island, Rödsten (30 minutes) and Husvik (one hour). Fares are adult/child 29/22kr one-way.

You can book a ticket with **Västkustlinjen** (www.vastkustlinjen.se/dans-pa-branno-brygga; round-trip from 350kr) for the Saturday night **dance experience**.

Other Islands

Vinga ISLAND

(☎ 031-711 34 50; www.vinga.org; adult/child round-trip 250/150kr; ⊗ day tours 10am Tue-Sat Jul-Aug; ⛴; ☑ M/S Walona) Tiny Vinga has an impressive rocky landscape and good swimming, and has been home to a lighthouse since the 17th century. The writer, composer and painter Evert Taube was born here in 1890 – his father was the lighthouse-keeper. There's scarcely anything on the island except the lighthouse, a telegraph station and the Taube Museum (admission 50kr, includes all three). At the ferry dock is a small kiosk for snacks. Bring a picnic and enjoy scampering across the smooth, weather-beaten rocks.

Styrsö ISLAND

(☑ 282) In the central part of the archipelago, Styrsö has two village centres (Bratten and Tången, both with ferry terminals). Bratten was a herring processing factory for decades, then later became a fashionable bathing resort in the 1860s. (There's still a cafe in one of the resort buildings.) Tången is a fishing community with a couple of cafes and access to hiking trails. Walk up to Stora Rös, the archipelago's highest point and a World War I lookout, for great views.

Vrångö ISLAND

(☑ 281) The island of Vrångö is the southern-most of the islands that are inhabited year-round. The ferry docks at Mittvik, on the east side; it's about a 10-minute walk to the west coast, where there's a good swimming beach. The northern and southern ends of the island are part of an extensive nature reserve laced with walking trails. There's a good cafe as well as a fish smokery near the ferry dock.

Marstrand

☑ 0303 / POP 1349

A quick and rewarding day trip from Gothenburg, Marstrand is a well-known summer retreat, and has been since King Oscar II and company started taking the waters here in the 1880s. Before that, the island enjoyed fame as the herring capital of Europe, and (though the herring come and go) its seafood is still a major draw.

Solitude-seekers beware: dozens of visitors shuffle off and on the ferry linking the mainland to Marstrand island every 15 minutes. But it's easy to ditch the crowds if you

follow signs to the nature trail ('naturstig'), which leads around the rocky edges to the far side of the island for epic views and secluded sunbathing nooks.

◎ Sights

Carlstens Fästning FORTRESS

(www.carlsten.se; adult/child 95/50kr; ⊗ 11am-3pm Apr-May, 11am-5pm Jun & Aug, 10.30am-6.30pm Jul, 11am-3pm Sat & Sun Sep-Oct; ⛴; ☑ Marstrand) Looming over town, Carlstens Fästning is a fortress built in the 1660s after the Swedish takeover of Marstrand and Bohuslän. Marstrand's ice-free port was key to trade, so King Karl X Gustav built the fortress to defend it. The port continued to be fought over for decades. Carlstens has also been a prison, known for especially brutal conditions. Admission includes a guided tour. It's worth walking up even if you don't go in: the views of the archipelago are stunning.

🛏 Sleeping & Eating

Hotell Nautic HOTEL €€

(☎ 0303-610 30; www.nautichotell.se; Långgatan 6; s/d from 1295/1595kr; 🤖; ☑ Marstrand) Friendly, casual Hotell Nautic has a beachy feel and bright, simple rooms decked out in blues and creams. A couple have balconies with great sea views. A family-size room (2590kr) sleeps up to four.

Grand Hotel Marstrand HISTORIC HOTEL €€€

(☎ 0303-603 22; https://grandmarstrand.se/en/; Rådhusgatan 2; r from 2300kr; ☺ 🤖; ☑ Marstrand) Built in 1892, this pretty hotel in the town's central square has 23 old-fashioned but stylish rooms, some with views and balconies, traditional ceramic stoves, Persian rugs and period wallpaper. The highly regarded restaurant serves dinner nightly (mains 245kr to 345kr); book ahead.

Arvidsons Kiosk och Fisk SEAFOOD €

(Hamngatan 22; mains 93-100kr; ⊗ 10am-8pm Jun-Aug; ☑ Marstrand) Grab an order of fish and chips with aioli – it even comes in a fake-newsprint paper cone – from this seafood shop right next to the ferry dock.

★ Johan's Krog SWEDISH €€€

(☎ 0303-612 12; www.johanskrogmarstrand.se; Kungsgatan 12; mains 245-345kr; ⊗ 7pm-2am) Johan tantalises with the likes of cod loin in shellfish sauce with a scallop-lemon confit, mussels with fennel, or pan-seared sole with beets and mushrooms, all served in a pretty, flower-strewn, glassed-in balcony space.

ℹ Information

The **tourist office** (☑ 0303-600 87; www. marstrand.se; Hamngatan 33; ⊙ 10am-6pm Mon-Fri, 11am-5pm Sat & Sun Jun-Aug) is opposite the ferry terminal. Lots of info on Marstrand and the surrounding areas.

ℹ Getting There & Away

From Gothenburg's Nils Ericson bus terminal, take the frequent **Marstrands Expressen** (☑ 0771-41 43 00; www.vasttrafik.se; one-way 68kr, 1hr) bus directly to Marstrand's passenger-only ferry terminal.

The ferry crosses over to the island every 15 minutes (29kr, five minutes). The return trip is free. Bus tickets include the price of the ferry. If you're driving, leave your car in the paid parking lot near the ferry dock.

BOHUSLÄN

Bohuslän is a fascinating corner of Sweden. Its distinctive rocky coastline is home to some 8000 weather-beaten, sun-baked islands and islets and probably an equal number of adorable red wooden fishing huts and harbour shopfronts. The landscape resembles few other parts of the world – maybe for that reason, the area is a favourite among artists. Don't forget your camera.

Bohuslän Coast

Dramatic, stark and irrepressibly beautiful, the Bohuslän Coast is one of Sweden's natural treasures. The landscape here is a grand mix of craggy islands and rickety fishing villages caught between sky and sea. Island-hopping is a must, as is lounging on broad, sun-warmed rocks and gorging on the region's incredible seafood.

ℹ Getting There & Away

If you're heading north from Gothenburg, stop at the **tourist office** (☑ 0303-833 27; www.bast kusten.se; Kulturhuset Fregattan, Stenungsund; ⊙ 9am-6pm Mon-Fri, 11am-3pm Sat) in Stenungsund to pick up brochures and maps of the surrounding area.

Transport connections are generally good – the E6 motorway runs north from Gothenburg to Oslo via the larger towns of Stenungsund, Ljungskile, Herrestad, Munkedal and Tanumshede, passing close to Strömstad before crossing the Norwegian border. Local trains run frequently from Gothenburg to Strömstad, via much the same towns as the E6 route.

ℹ Getting Around

Using public transport to get to some of the Bohuslän Coast's remoter islands or quiet corners can be a bit of a fool's errand, particularly out of peak season. The coast is best suited to independent exploration on your own two or four wheels, but if you're reliant on buses and boats, it's best to use the Travel Planner feature on the Västtrafik (p148) website to avoid long connection times.

Tjörn
☑ 0304 / POP 15,050

A large bridge swoops from Stenungsund (on the Swedish mainland) to the island of Tjörn, a magnet for artists thanks to its striking landscapes and cutting-edge watercolour museum. Sailors are equally smitten, with one of Sweden's biggest sailing competitions, the **Tjörn Runt** (www.stss.se), taking place here in August.

Skärhamn and Rönnäng, in the southwest, are the island's main settlements. Skärhamn's proudest feature is the superb **Nordiska Akvarellmuseet** (☑ 0304-60 00 80; www.akvarellmuseet.org; Södra Hamnen 6, Skärhamn; adult/child 100kr/free; ⊙ 11am-6pm mid-May–mid-Sep, shorter hours rest of year), a sleek waterside building housing changing exhibits by regional and international artists. The five ultra-modern cubes right over the water are guest cabins for the artistically inclined or those looking for a quiet retreat.

✖ Eating

Don't miss the chance to try some legendary seafood while you're here.

★ Magasinet Härön   SEAFOOD €€€
(☑ 0304-66 40 20; www.magasinetharon.com; mains 199-239kr; ⊙ 11.30am-4pm & 5pm-late mid-Jun–mid-Aug) The summer home and restaurant of Gothenburg chef Mats Nordström, within a stone's throw of the sea in an 1847 fisherman's *magasinet* (depot), this seafood star is located at the northwestern end of Tjörn. The menu showcases fresh fish, mussels and shrimp, all served with the care Nordström became known for in his decade at Gothenburg's Wasa Allé.

Take the frequent passenger-only ferry *St Olaf II* from Kyrkesund to get here.

ℹ Getting There & Away

The Tjörn-Express bus runs up to six times on weekdays from Gothenburg's bus terminal to Tjörn, calling at Skärhamn, Klädesholmen and

ROCK CARVINGS UNVEILED

Bohuslän's Bronze Age dwellers did not have a written language, but they were prolific rock carvers and, like all humans since the beginning of time, possessed of the need to leave their mark on the world – to record their beliefs, rituals, triumphs and tragedies – in this case, by etching them into granite slabs.

Many of these 3000-year-old rock carvings (*hällristningar*) survive to this day. The Tanum plain, around Tanumshede, is particularly rich in carvings, and the entire 45-sq-km area has been placed on the Unesco World Heritage List. At the time of carving, the sites would have been close to the water, as the sea was 15m higher.

The interactive **Vitlycke Museum** (☑ 0525-209 50; www.vitlyckemuseum.se; ☉ 10am-6pm daily mid-Apr–Aug; ℗ ♿; ☐ 870, 945) FREE is an excellent introduction to the carvings, explaining their origins, offering interpretations of what each particular carving meant, and delving into the typical daily life of the carvers.

From the museum, a series of paths and boardwalks runs through pine forest to the most important of the rock-carving grounds, though dozens of lesser sites are scattered throughout the area. Cross the road to reach the splendid 22m **Vitlycke Rock**, which forms a huge canvas for 500 carvings of 'love, power and magic'. You may spot some of Sweden's most famous rock-art images, including *The Lovers* – a male and female figure, joined; a horned god riding a chariot; a whale; a grieving woman; a man running away from a giant snake; and a fertility goddess.

Further south is **Aspeberget**, the site with the heaviest concentration of carvings. You can tell that Bronze Age lives were dominated by two things: boats, and violence in the shape of men with hefty axes.

Towards the coast lies the third largest site, **Litsleby**. A nautical theme prevails, but the boats are eclipsed by the huge image of a (very obviously male) god, believed to be Odin, brandishing a spear. You may also spot dogs, a pair of bare feet and a spearman on horseback.

In case you're wondering, the carvings are all red not because 3000-something-year-old paint is remarkably well preserved but because modern-day archaeologists wanted to make the images easier to see and study. (The museum describes the still-controversial nature of this decision and why it was made.)

To get to Vitlycke by public transport, take bus 870 or 945 from Tanumshede bus station to Hoghem. From there it's a five- to 10-minute walk. Regional buses on the Gothenburg–Uddevalla–Strömstad route also stop at Tanumshede.

Rönnäng. Bus 355 from Stenungsund crosses the island to Rönnäng.

Orust & Mollösund

☑ 0304 / POP 15,160

Sweden's third-biggest island, Orust boasts lush woodlands and some breathtakingly pretty fishing villages. It also has a thriving boat-building industry, with over half of Sweden's sailing craft made here.

Supercute Mollösund, at the southwest edge of Orust, is the oldest fishing village on the Bohuslän Coast. There's a gorgeous harbour and several scenic walking paths for a gentle pick-me-up.

◉ Sights

Käringön ISLAND

(🚢 381) This picture-perfect island boasts plenty of good swimming holes, some complete with floats and trampolines for the enjoyment of those frolicking in the water. The plenitude of flat, broad rocks makes Käringön an ideal location for picnicking on a summer's day. Regular ferry 381 runs roughly hourly from Tuvesvik (on the northwestern coast of Orust island); check up-to-date timetables at www.vasttrafik.se.

🛏 Sleeping & Eating

Tofta Gård HOSTEL €

(☑ 0304-503 80; www.toftagard.se; Stockenvägen 25, Ellös; s/d/tr 450/650/725kr, breakfast 90kr; ☉ Apr-Oct; reception 9-11am & 4-7pm; ℗ @ 🛜; ☐ 371, 977) This is an outstanding STF hostel near Stocken on the island's west, about 5km from the larger village of Ellös. It's located in an old farmhouse and surrounding little cottages in a blissfully bucolic setting, with good walking, swimming and canoeing nearby. There's free laundry, an excellent breakfast spread, a sauna and two wood-fired hot tubs (book ahead). Catch buses in Henån.

Mollösunds Wärdshus   HOTEL €€
(☑ 0304-211 08; www.mwhus.se; Kyrkvägen 9; s/d from 1150/1295kr; ☺ Easter-Dec; ☎) Mollösunds Wärdshus is an upmarket 19th-century inn featuring 10 well-turned-out rooms with funky wallpaper, and a slinky, sun-soaked terrace for lazy wining and dining on local fish and seafood. Rooms with balconies are worth the extra splurge. Enquire here about island-hopping, adrenalin-pumping RIB boat tours.

Emma's Café, Grill & Vinbar   SEAFOOD €€
(☑ 0304-211 75; www.cafeemma.com; Hamnvä-gen 4; mains 155-189kr; ☺ 11am-midnight Jun–mid-Aug) An obvious hub of local social life, Emma's occupies the red house right on the harbour and consists of a small, welcoming hostel (doubles from 700kr) above a cosy ca-fe-restaurant serving hearty dishes created from local (mostly fishy) and organic ingre-dients – anything from open shrimp sand-wiches to exceptional fish soup.

ℹ️ Information

Orust's **tourist office** (☑ 0304-33 44 94; www.orust.se; Ängsvägen 5, Henån; ☺ 10am-6pm Mon-Thu, 10am-5pm Fri, 10am-2pm Sat Jul-Aug; 10am-5pm Wed, Thu & Fri rest of year) is in the town of Henån.

ℹ️ Getting There & Away

A bridge connects Orust to Tjörn, its southern neighbour. Local buses run here frequently from Uddevalla.

Lysekil

☑ 0523 / POP 14,521

With its air of faded grandeur, the 19th-century spa resort of Lysekil feels oddly like an English seaside town. It pampers summer visitors less than other Bohuslän towns do, but there's something strangely refreshing about this unfussed attitude.

⊙ Sights & Activities

Havets Hus   AQUARIUM
(www.havetshus.se; Strandvägen 9; adult/child 120/70kr; ☺ 10am-6pm mid-Jun–mid-Aug, hours vary rest of year; 🚼) Havets Hus is an excellent aquarium with sea life from Gullmarn, Swe-den's only true fjord, which cuts past Lysekil.

Peer at such cold-water beauties as wolffish, lumpsuckers, anglerfish, cranky-looking flatfish, rays, and ethereal jellyfish; watch a magnified shark's embryo grow; walk through an underwater tunnel; and learn about the pirate history of the area.

Fiskebäckskil   ISLAND
(☑ 847) Passenger/cyclist-only ferry 847 (25kr) crosses the Gullmarn fjord roughly hourly to Fiskebäckskil, of the cute cobbled streets and wood-clad houses. The interior of its **church** recalls an upturned boat, with votive ships and impressive ceiling and wall paintings. Fiskebäckskil is also reachable by road from the E4 and Tjörn.

Stångehuvud
Nature Reserve   NATURE RESERVE
FREE Out at the tip of the Stångenäs pen-insula, the Stångehuvud Nature Reserve, crammed with coastal rock slab, is worth a stop for its secluded bathing spots and the wooden lookout tower.

Seal Safaris   CRUISE
(☑ 0523-66 81 61; adult/child 220/110kr; ☺ 1pm Jul–mid-Aug) Seal safaris – which take you out onto the archipelago to watch seals lounging in the sun – last 1½ hours and leave from near the aquarium; buy tickets at Havets Hus.

🛏️ Sleeping & Eating

Siviks Camping   CAMPGROUND €
(☑ 0523-61 15 28; www.sivikscamping.nu; tent/RV sites from 280/310kr; ☺ end Apr–mid-Sep; 🅿) Built on large pink-granite slabs by a sandy beach 2km north of town, Siviks is the best-located campground in the area and particularly popular with RVs.

Strand Hostel & Hotell   HOSTEL, HOTEL €€
(☑ 0523-797 51; www.strandflickorna.se; Strand-vägen 1; hostel dm/s/d from 350/850/950kr, hotel s/d 1095/1440kr; 🅿☎) Not far from Havets Hus, this large, rambling wooden house resembles a mansion from the Deep South, and you can almost see the guests sip-ping bourbon on the porch. All of the pretti-ly wallpapered rooms are en suite, even the hostel rooms, though the hotel rooms (some with sea views) are rather plusher.

Old House Inn   INTERNATIONAL €€
(www.theoldhouseinn.se; Kungsgatan 36; mains 159-299kr; ☺ noon-late; ☑) The menu of this quaint restaurant on the little main square runs the gamut from pulled-pork sandwiches to pastas, while its chilli-chocolate pannacotta targets

those with a sweet tooth. Live music most nights in summer.

★ Brygghuset SEAFOOD €€€
(☑ 0523-222 22; www.brygghusetkrog.com; Fiskebäckskilsvägen 28; mains 195-315kr; ⊙noon-midnight; [P]) Across the estuary from the Fiskebäckskil ferry terminal, this celebrated waterfront restaurant is lauded for its superb fish dishes that taste so fresh that the fish may as well have just leapt out of the harbour onto your plate. At lunchtime, have your herring eight ways – count 'em! – at the self-service buffet or grab a seafood soup.

❶ Information

Tourist Office (☑ 0525-130 50; http://vastsverige.com/lysekil; Strandvägen 9; ⊙9.30am-5pm Mon-Fri, to 3pm Sat & Sun Jul–mid-Aug) Offers information on various summer boat tours, including island-hopping swimming trips and fishing jaunts.

❶ Getting There & Away

Express buses 840 and 841 run hourly from Gothenburg to Lysekil via Uddevalla (148kr, one hour, 50 minutes). You can also take one of the regular passenger ferries from Fiskebäckskil, just south of Lysekil (15 minutes).

Smögen

☑ 0523 / POP 1329

Another seaside star, Smögen sports a buzzing waterside boardwalk, rows of rickety fishermen's houses, and steep steps leading up into a labyrinth of lovingly restored cottages and pretty summer gardens.

Dubbed **Smögenbryggan** and famous throughout Sweden as a hip, youthful destination, the boardwalk heaves with bars and shops around the harbour; head in early or out of season if you're seeking solitude. Fishing boats unload their catches of prawns, lobsters and fish at the harbour.

◉ Sights

Hållö ISLAND
(☑ 0706-91 36 33; www.hallofarjan.se; round-trip adult/child 100/50kr; ⊙ferry 9.30am-4.45pm mid-Jun–mid-Aug; 🛥) This small, rocky, windswept island is home to a historic lighthouse and a number of bird species. Its otherworldly landscape is great for photographers, as is the view coming to and from Smögen harbour on the ferry. There's a hostel where those who want to feel completely remote can stay the night. From Smögen harbour,

the Hållö ferry leaves every half-hour or so from 9.30am in summer.

Smögen Fish Auction MARKET
(www.smogens-fiskauktion.com; Fiskhall; ⊙8am Mon-Fri, plus 4pm Thu) Fishing boats unload their catches of prawns, lobsters and fish at the Smögen harbour. You can score some über-fresh shellfish if you get to the small fish auction early enough; the big one happens online these days.

Nordens Ark ZOO
(☑ 0523-795 90; www.nordensark.se; Åby säteri; adult/child 250/100kr; ⊙10am-5pm Apr-Oct, to 7pm mid-Jun–mid-Aug, to 4pm rest of year; [P]🐾; 🚌 Västtrafik) Snow leopards, wolves and lynxes prowl Nordens Ark, a well-conceived safari park 12km northeast of Smögen. It shows off animals and plants from countries with a similar climate to Sweden's and has breeding programs for critically endangered species, such as the Amur tiger and Amur leopard. A 3km path allows visitors a glimpse of the wild beasts as it runs past the spacious enclosures, and guided tours are available daily in peak season (included in entry price).

🛏 Sleeping

Makrillvikens Vandrarhem HOSTEL €
(☑ 0523-315 65; www.makrillviken.se; Makrillgatan; r from 700kr, breakfast 80kr; [P]) Makrillvikens Vandrarhem, in the former yellow spa bathing house with smashing views of the archipelago, is a sterling, hugely popular budget choice affiliated with SVIF (Sveriges Vandrarhem i Förening; Swedish Hostel Association) – 500m from the boardwalk crowds, bathing spots just metres from your room and an old seaside sauna for guest use. For more watery action, there are canoes for hire. Book ahead!

Utpost Hållö CABIN €€
(☑ 0703-53 68 22; www.utposthallo.se; d/q/f 1000/1300/1600kr; ⊙mid-May–Aug) Treeless, rocky Hållö feels remote and raw. The lovely red and white-trimmed cabins of the Utpost Hållö are perched on broad granite slabs within 100m of the sea and the lighthouse. It's a great place to take in the ocean, birds and crisp blue skies. Hållö färjan (ferry) runs here from Smögenbryggan, while Hållöexpressen goes to and from Kungshamn.

Hotel Smögens Havsbad HOTEL €€€
(☑ 0523-66 84 50; www.smogenshavsbad.se; Hotellgatan 26; s/d from 1145/1690kr; [P]🏊📶) The

KLÄDESHOLMEN

The 'herring island' of Klädesholmen, to the far south of Tjörn and reachable via a bridge, is one of the west coast's most flawless spots. A mash-up of red and white wooden cottages, its activity is fairly subdued due to the departure of the herring (there were once 30 processing factories here, today just a handful). The tiny **herring museum** (☑0304-67 33 08; Sillgränd 8; ⊙3-7pm Jul–mid-Aug) FREE tells you all you need to know about Sweden's enduring love for its favourite fish.

The row of slick cubic buildings that compose the floating boutique **Salt & Sill** (☑0304-67 34 80; www.saltosill.se; s/d from 1790/2290kr; 🐾) hotel houses 23 light, bright, contemporary rooms – all clean lines and plasma-screen TVs, each featuring the hues of its namesake herb or spice. A floating sauna is available for pampering purposes. The attached **restaurant** (mains 195-355kr; ⊙noon-9pm Jul-Sep, call ahead other times) is a draw all its own.

Västtrafik (p148) buses run frequently to the island. Note that parking on the tiny streets is very limited.

great wooden pile that is Hotel Smögens Havsbad has what you might say is a rather tacked-on-looking prosthetic extension that is (thankfully for guests) beautiful on the inside, with light Scandi-style rooms, many with sea views. The on-site restaurant celebrates local seafood, with dishes like wolffish with blue-mussel froth and sautéed new potatoes.

🍴 Eating & Drinking

Hallo Bar   SEAFOOD €
(Fiskhamnsgatan 32; dishes from 85kr; ⊙11.30am-10pm) Right above the water, this friendly restobar serves small plates of seafood dishes (so you can really go to town here!), as well as beautifully battered fish and chips and overflowing prawn sandwiches.

Barn   CAFE
(www.thebarn.se; Sillgatan; mains 120-195kr; ⊙9am-11pm daily Jun-Aug) Arguably the nicest cafe for miles around, the Barn (formerly Coffee Room) serves burgers and fries, salads and sweets in a cozy candlelit room or outside on its pretty covered terrace.

Hamnen 4   SEAFOOD €€€
(☑0523-708 50; www.hamnen4.se; Sillgatan 14-16; mains 165-275kr; ⊙5pm-3am Mon-Fri, noon-3am Sat) As you walk along the boardwalk, you're likely to be lured into this waterside spot by the bewitching smells emanating from the grill. Hamnen 4 woos fish-lovers with its coley with blue mussels and brown-butter cod, but carnivores are also well catered for with expertly seared steaks and hamburgers. The well-stocked bar keeps the sea salts entertained into the wee hours.

ℹ️ Information

The **tourist office** (☑0523-66 55 50; www.vastsverige.com/sotenas; Bäckevikstorget 5; ⊙11am-7pm mid-May–mid-Aug) is in Kungshamn, just across the bridge.

ℹ️ Getting There & Away

Bus 841 runs regularly from Gothenburg to Torp, where you switch to the 860 to Smögen (185kr, 2¼ to 2½ hours, five daily). From Lysekil, take bus 850 and switch to 860 in Hallinden (68kr, 1¼ hours, five daily).

Fjällbacka

☑0525 / POP 859

Film star Ingrid Bergman spent her summer holidays at Fjällbacka (the main square is named after her), though you can bet that in her day the waterfront wasn't utterly clogged up with sun-worshipping crowds and the main street wasn't chock-a-block with classic Chevvies and Pontiacs on fine summer days. Despite that, the tiny town is utterly charming, its brightly coloured houses squashed between steep cliffs and placid sea.

A block off the waterfront, steep wooden staircases lead to the top of the Vetteberget cliff for unforgettable 360-degree views of the village, the sea and the skerries, and several paths cross the rocky plateau for longer strolls.

🏃 Activities

From July to mid-August, Vadero Express runs 1½-hour island boat trips, including a tour that takes in the local seal colony (per person 375kr; 3pm). Boats depart from Ingrid Bergmanstorg.

The **tourist office** (☑0525-611 88; www.
fjallbackainfo.com; Ingrid Bergmanstorg; ☺mid-
Jun–Aug) can advise on boat trips to the popular, rocky island of Väderöarna.

🛏 Sleeping & Eating

Badholmens Vandrarhem   HOSTEL €€
(☑0525-321 50; www.hamburgsundsbokning.se;
s/d/tr 925/1050/1375kr; ☺Apr-Oct) On a teeny
little island just off the harbour, Badholmens
Vandrarhem is a basic, friendly hostel reached
by a causeway. Four plain bunk-bedded huts
named after creatures of the deep look out to
sea, and there's a cafe, a laundry, a sauna and
hot tub for guests nearby. Just behind the huts
is a great spot for sunbathing and diving.

★ Stora Hotellet
Bryggan   BOUTIQUE HOTEL €€€
(☑0525-310 60; www.storahotellet-fjallbacka.se;
Galärbacken; s/d/ste from 1490/1990/2750kr;
@) Stora Hotellet is a whimsical hotel offering a trip 'around the world in 23 rooms'.
It was originally owned by a ship's captain
who decorated it with exotic souvenirs. He
named each room after his favourite ports
and explorers (and girls!), and each tells its
own story. Extras include five dining venues
that range from tapas bar to fine dining.

Bryggan Fjällbacka   SEAFOOD €€€
(☑0525-76 50 20; www.storahotelletbryggan.se;
Ingrid Bergmanstorg; lunch mains 125-165kr, dinner
mains 265-365kr; ☺cafe 11am-10pm, restaurant
6pm-late) With its killer waterside location,
laid-back Bryggan Fjällbacka gives you multiple dining options: the informal Bryggan Cafe
& Bistro, where you can grab an open shrimp
sandwich, salad and cold beer; the refined
Restaurant Matilda, where you may feast on
such fare as grilled scallops and seared tuna
steak; a tapas bar and a grill-bar. There's boutique accommodation to boot.

ℹ Getting There & Away

The best way to reach Fjällbacka from Gothenburg is either to take bus 871 to Håby and then
switch to bus 875 (186kr, 2¼ hours in total, two
daily), or else to take a train to Dingle station,
then transfer to Hamburgsund-bound bus 875 to
Fjällbacka (189kr, 2½ hours, two to three daily).

Strömstad

☑0526 / POP 6288
A resort, fishing harbour and spa town,
Strömstad is laced with ornate wooden
buildings echoing those of nearby Norway.

There are several fantastic Iron Age remains
in the area, and some fine sandy beaches at
Capri and Seläter. Boat trips run to the most
westerly islands in Sweden, popular for cycling and swimming.

⊙ Sights & Activities

Koster Islands   ISLAND
(www.kosteroarna.com; adult/child round trip
130/100kr) Boat trips run from Strömstad's
north harbour to the beautiful cluster of forested Koster Islands every 30 minutes from
July to mid-August, less frequently at other
times. Tiny North Koster is hilly and has
good beaches. Larger South Koster is flatter and better for cycling, with bike-rental
facilities, numerous restaurants scattered
about and two large beaches at Rörvik and
Kilesand. Trips are booked through the tourist office.

Skee Kyrka   CHURCH
(☺by appointment) FREE Open by appoint-
ment only (contact the tourist office), the
Romanesque stone Skee Kyrka is about 6km
east of Strömstad and has a 10th-century
nave. There's also a painted wooden ceiling and an unusual 17th-century reredos
with 24 sculptured figures. Nearby lie Iron
Age graves, a curious bell tower and a mid-
Neolithic passage tomb (c 3000 BC).

Stone-Ship Settings   ARCHAEOLOGICAL SITE
(Blomsholm; ☺24hr) FREE One of Sweden's
largest, most magnificent stone-ship settings (an oval of stones, shaped like a boat)
lies 6km northeast of Strömstad. There are
49 stones in total, with the stem and stern
stones reaching over 3m in height; the site
has been dated to AD 400 to 600. Across the
road is a huge site containing approximately 40 Iron Age graves. The tourist office can
help with transport. Alternatively, there's a
gorgeous walking path from the north of
town.

Strömstads Museum   MUSEUM
(www.stromstadsmuseum.se; Södra Hamngatan
26; ☺11am-4pm Tue-Fri) FREE Housed in an
old power station, this museum displays local photography and objects from nautical
history.

Selin Charter Boat Tours   CRUISE
(www.selincharter.se; tours from 200kr; ☺Jun-
Aug) Boat tours heading out to Ursholmen,
Sweden's most westerly lighthouse, and seal
safaris are on offer here, as well as mackerel
fishing (June) and lobster safaris (autumn).

Trips depart from Strömstad's southern harbour.

🛏 Sleeping & Eating

Strömstad Camping   CAMPGROUND €
(☎ 0526-611 21; www.stromstadcamping.se; Udde-vallavägen; sites 340kr, 2-bed cabins from 600kr; ⊙ mid-Apr–Aug; 🛜) In a lovely, large park at the southern edge of town, the campground has shady cabins and tiny camping pods for rent. It packs in the RVs in summer, but the modern facilities are able to handle the crowds. Bonus: there's a swimming beach just down the hill.

★ Emma's Bed and Breakfast   B&B €€
(☎ 0916-65 046; www.emmasbedandbreakfast.se; Kebal 2; r from 1195kr; 🅿🛜) A 10-minute walk from central Strömstad, this stately house, dating back to 1734, sits at the edge of a golf course amid quiet wooded grounds. The rooms are bright and airy and the friendly hostess whips up a full Scandinavian spread at breakfast time.

Heat   THAI, SUSHI €€
(www.heat.nu; Ångbåtskajen 6; mains 149-269kr, weekday lunch 99kr; ⊙ 11.30am-11pm Mon-Sat, from noon Sun) Dockside Heat packs some authentic, erm, heat with its Thai curries. Though we're normally wary of places that claim to offer two separate cuisines, the sushi here is as good as the dishes from Siam: the samurai sushi rolls stand out, and if you're in a group the 'deluxe sashimi' is a worthy splurge.

Rökeri i Strömstad   SEAFOOD €€€
(☎ 0526-148 60; www.rokerietistromstad.se; Torksholmen; lunch mains 150-189kr, dinner mains 209-359kr; ⊙ 11.30am-5pm & 6pm-late Jun-Aug, shorter hours rest of year) This family-run dockside restaurant dishes out deep bowls of fish soup, catch of the day and seafood-filled baguettes at lunch. Dinner is more refined; the smokehouse platter is a real treat. However, continents may drift before you get served when the restaurant is busy. The adjacent smokehouse is a great place to pick up slabs of gravadlax for a picnic.

❶ Information

The **tourist office** (☎ 0526-623 30; www.vastsverige.com/stromstad; Ångbåtskajen 2; ⊙ 9am-8pm Mon-Sat, 10am-7pm Sun Jun-Aug, shorter hours rest of year) sits just opposite the boat landing for the Koster Islands.

WORTH A TRIP

RESÖ

This tiny island, 10km south of Strömstad, is reachable via an appealing narrow road that winds its way through the forest and crosses a couple of bridges. There's a cute, crowded harbour and several great swimming beaches, a grocery store for picnic supplies, a flea market on summer weekends, and a charming summertime restaurant, **Lexö på Resö** (☎ 0525-250 00; Hamnholmen; pizzas 115-159kr, mains 155-220kr, herring buffet 145kr; ⊙ noon-midnight mid-Jun–mid-Aug), whose outdoor tables have killer views over the water. It's a place to immerse yourself in the favourite Swedish summer pastime of taking it easy.

❶ Getting There & Away

Buses and trains both use the train station near the southern harbour. **Västtrafik** (p148) runs bus 871 to Gothenburg (180kr, 2¼ hours, three to four daily). Direct trains connect Strömstad to Gothenburg (190kr, 2¼ to three hours, one to two hourly).

Color Line ferries run from Strömstad to Sandefjord in Norway (2½ hours).

DALSLAND

Dalsland is often described as 'Sweden's lake district' and boasts hundreds of crystal-clear lakes. The region is sparsely populated – about seven people for every square kilometre – but is a magnet for active, outdoors-loving people, especially kayakers. You can paddle north from the town of Ed on the fjordlike Stora Le lake all the way to Norway, passing verdant islands and quiet woodlands.

Walkers can enjoy miles of quiet trails and, in the later summer, may even be lucky enough to find mushrooms or berries along the way. Several companies in the area hire out kayaks, canoes and camping equipment.

❶ Getting There & Away

Mellerud is on the main Gothenburg–Karlstad train line, and **Swebus Express** (p148) buses between Gothenburg and Karlstad stop here once daily (except Saturday) in either direction. Local bus 720 runs a circular route to/from transport hub Mellerud via Upperud, Håverud and Skållerud.

Håverud

📞 0530 / POP 150

An intriguing triple transport pile-up occurs at tiny Håverud, where a 32m aqueduct carries the Dalsland Canal over the river, a railway passes above the aqueduct and a road bridge crosses above them both.

The area around the aqueduct is a chilled-out spot, with folks strolling along the sides of the canal or sitting with a beer and watching the water gush out from between the lock gates as boats navigate their way up the canal.

◉ Sights & Activities

About 3km south of the aqueduct is **Upperud**, home to the savvy **Dalslands Museum & Konsthall** (📞 0530-300 98; www.dalslandskonstmuseum.se; Upperud; ⊙ 11am-5pm Sun mid-Mar–mid-Nov, daily Jul; **P**) **FREE**. Pop in for a compact collection of local art, woodwork (including a shell-shocked wooden cat), ceramics, ironware and Åmål silverware, as well as thought-provoking photography exhibitions. The small sculpture park in the grounds features an anarchic wooden tower by eccentric artist Lars Vilks. The on-site Bonaparte cafe (so-called because Napoleon's niece Christine once lived there) combines yummy coffee and snacks with soothing lake views.

Another few kilometres south at **Skållerud** is a beautiful, shiny-red, 17th-century wooden **church** (⊙ 9am-7pm Sat & Sun Apr-Oct), with well-preserved paintings and baroque fittings.

Atmospheric **Högsbyn Nature Reserve** **FREE**, about 8km north of Håverud near Tisselskog, has woodland walks and a shallow bathing spot. Best of all are its impressive Bronze Age **rock carvings** *(hällristningar)*: 50 overgrown slabs feature animals, boats, labyrinths, sun signs, and hand and foot marks. The M/S *Dalslandia* does a 40-minute stop here on its trip between Håverud and Bengtsfors. Visits can be arranged through the tourist office.

Kanalmuséet MUSEUM
(www.kanalmuseet.se; adult/child 40kr/free; ⊙ 10am-6pm Jun-Aug, 11am-4pm May-Jun & Sep) The Tardis-like Kanalmuséet initiates you into the history of the Dalsland Canal (completed back in 1868), with its clever aqueduct designed by engineer Nils Ericsson – a necessity because the ground in this region made it impossible to build a lock to bypass the Håverud rapids.

Dalsland-West Värmland Railway RAIL
(📞 0531-106 33; www.dvvj.se; adult/child 360/180kr, boat & train combo ticket 430kr) Ride a historic train into the Dalsland countryside, taking in the sights and crossing the railway bridge over Nils Ericson's ingenious aqueduct spanning the canal in Håverud. The train ride can be combined with a return trip on turn-of-the-century canal boat M/S *Storholmen* along the canal to Långbron and Bengtsfors. You can also return via M/S *Dalslandia*.

'DOING' THE DALSLAND CANAL

The scenic Dalsland Canal crosses the eastern half of the Dalsland region, linking a series of narrow lakes between Vänern and Stora Le and providing a watery playground 250km long for boat enthusiasts and kayakers during the summer months.

If you wish to captain your own boat, you can rent a Nimbus 2600 from **Dalslands Kanal AB** (📞 0530-447 50; www.dalslandskanal.se; per week 14,995kr) (weekly rental only) and chug gently through tranquil rural scenery, negotiating locks en route. Want to be a passenger? **M/S Storholmen** (📞 070-541 06 33; www.storholmen.com; boat & train combo ticket 430kr, boat Håverud-Bengtsfors 325kr, children half-price; ⊙ 10.50am Tue, Thu & Sat mid-Jun–Aug) and **M/S Dalslandia** (📞 070-665 96 03; www.dalslandia.com; tickets from 205kr; ⊙ 10.50am Mon, Wed & Fri Jul-Aug) run short passenger trips along the canal from Håverud.

Want to paddle in glorious solitude? There are 10 locations along the Dalsland Canal network where you can rent kayaks and canoes and all necessary equipment and get advice on routes, including **Bootshaus** (📞 0531-125 40; www.bootshaus.se; Bengtsfors; per day/week from 220/1100kr, r from 400kr), where you can also find accommodation. Not challenging enough? Then join the **Dalsland Kanot Maraton** (www.kanotmaraton.se) endurance race that sees competitors racing their canoes over a gruelling 55km course here in mid-August.

🛏 Sleeping & Eating

STF Hostel Håverud   HOSTEL €
(☎0530-302 75; Museivägen 3; s/d 325/450kr;
Ⓟ🛜) The STF hostel could use a coat of
paint but it has a winning location overlooking the canal. Its attic-like rooms are pleasant but can feel a bit like a pressure cooker
in summer. Book ahead.

Håfveruds Rökeri & Brasseri   SEAFOOD €€
(Dalslands Centre; mains 165-250kr; ⊙noon-9pm)
Post-industrial Håfveruds Brasseri, based in
an old paper mill, and with shaded lockside
tables, serves everything from smoked salmon with new potatoes to hamburgers. The
attached smokery is the place to stock up on
fishy goodies or to grab a shrimp baguette.

ℹ Information

The well-stocked **tourist office** (☎0530-189
90; www.haverud-upperud.se; Dalslands Center;
⊙10am-7pm Jul–mid-Aug, shorter hours rest
of year) can organise joint boat and train jaunts
along the Dalslands Canal, fishing licences and
canoe hire.

ℹ Getting There & Away

Västtrafik (p148) buses run frequently to
Håverud and surrounding sights.

VÄSTERGÖTLAND

Home to Sweden's film-industry hub of
Trollhättan, Västergötland is a pleasant
mix of stylish manor houses, royal hunting
grounds and cultural attractions. The province is bordered by Sweden's two largest
lakes, Vänern and Vättern, and Göta Canal
tours abound. Castle buffs and opera lovers flock to Läckö Slott in summer, and the
woods are perfect for elk spotting, berry
picking or simply strolling.

ℹ Getting There & Away

There are good links by bus and train from Gothenburg to most cities in Västergötland. **Västtrafik** (p148) has a useful online travel planner.

Vänersborg
☎0521 / POP 21,699

Vänersborg, at the southern outlet of Vänern
lake, was once known as 'Little Paris', a nickname most likely applied by someone who
had never seen the real thing. The one piece
of information you'll take away from a visit

here is just how much the Swedish royal
family enjoys hunting elk. The area is home
to the royal hunting museum, as well as a
nature reserve where walking trails provide
excellent chances of stumbling across an elk
in the wild – try finding that in Paris!

◎ Sights & Activities

Hunneberg & Hanneberg
Nature Reserve   NATURE RESERVE
(🚌62) Described by Linnaeus as an 'earthly
paradise', the Hunneberg & Hanneberg Nature Reserve covers two dramatic, craggy
plateaus 8km east of town. There are 50km
of walking trails here that are certainly
worth exploring. The deep ravines and pri-
meval forest also make great hiding places
for wild elk, and this area has been a favourite royal hunting ground for over 100 years.

Transport links are tedious – your best
bet is to catch the frequent bus 62 from the
town square to Vägporten, then walk 2km
uphill.

Kungajaktmuseet Älgens Berg   MUSEUM
(☎0521-27 00 40; www.algensberg.com; Hunneberg 121; adult/child 80/40kr; ⊙10am-6pm
Jun-Aug, 11am-4pm Tue-Sun Sep-Nov & Feb-May,
11am-4pm Tue-Fri Dec-Jan) Kungajaktmuseet
Älgens Berg, the royal hunting museum,
is at the entrance to the Hunneberg &
Hanneberg Nature Reserve, and tells you
everything you could ever wish to know
about elk.

Elk-Spotting Safaris   TOUR
(☎0521-135 09; info@visittv.se; adult/child
395/250kr; ⊙tours 5-11pm or 6-11pm Mon &
Thu Jul & Aug) The Kungajaktmuseet runs
elk-spotting tours leaving from either the
Trollhättan train station or Vänersborg tourist office. Tours must be booked in advance
through the tourist office.

🛏 Sleeping

Hunnebergs Vandrarhem   HOSTEL €
(☎070-326 83 77; www.hunnebergsgard.se; Ber-
gagårdsvägen 9B, Vargön; s/d from 350/550kr;
⊙reception open 4-7pm; Ⓟ; 🚌62) In a big old
manor house near the cliffs of Hunneberg
(7km east of the centre), this is a large, well-
equipped SVIF hostel. Take bus 62 from the
town square to Vägporten, then walk 500m.

Ronnums Herrgård   HOTEL €€
(☎0521-26 00 00; www.ronnums.se; Vargön; s/d
from 1095/1195kr; Ⓟ🛜) Good enough for
Nicole Kidman, this stately mansion is set in

GOTHENBURG & THE SOUTHWEST VÄNERSBORG

gorgeous grounds, out towards Hunneberg. Rooms are seriously elegant, and the oak-floored suites are particularly special; modern touches such as iPod docks complement the lavish surroundings. Look out for special online rates, and if you feel like a gastronomic treat, the restaurant is one of the region's best.

ℹ Information

The helpful **tourist office** (☑ 0521-135 09; www.visittrollhattanvanersborg.se; Järnvägsbacken 1C; ⊙ 9am-6pm Mon-Fri, 10am-3pm Sat & Sun) is located at the train station.

ℹ Getting There & Away

Local buses run from the town square, while long-distance services stop at the train station. Local buses 61, 62 and 65 run roughly half-hourly between Vänersborg and Trollhättan (29kr, 20 minutes). Express bus 600 runs several times daily to Trollhättan, continuing to Gothenburg (132kr, 50 minutes).

SJ trains to Gothenburg (132kr, 50 minutes) run at least once hourly.

Trollhättan

☑ 0520 / POP 46,457

'Trollywood', as it's colloquially known, is home to Sweden's film industry. A number of local and foreign flicks have been shot in and around the town, including Lebanese-Swedish director Josef Fares' Oscar-nominated *Jalla! Jalla!* (2000) and Danish director Lars von Trier's *Dancer in the Dark* (1999), *Dogville* (2002) and *Manderlay* (2005). In the right weather, Trollhättan itself has the air of a surreal film set: looming warehouses, foggy canals, crashing waterfalls and a futuristic cable car all give it a bizarre and thrilling edge. The locks and canals have been the town's lifeblood for centuries, and Trollhättan has made the most of its industrial heritage, with red-brick warehouses housing everything from crowd-pleasing museums to the odd art installation.

◎ Sights

Innovatum Science Center   MUSEUM
(www.innovatum.se; adult/child 90/50kr; ⊙10am-5pm daily Jul-Aug, 11am-4pm Tue-Sun rest of year; ⊞) Innovatum Science Center, next door to the Saab Bilmuseum, is a fantastic science centre with all sorts of wacky interactive gadgets for kids of all ages – from weird skateboards you sit on, gyroscopes, whirl-pool machines, a machine that allows you to control a ball with your brain waves to over-sized Lego blocks for little ones. Why wasn't physics fun like this when we were kids?

Slussområde   PARK
Take a wander southwest of the town center to Slussområde, a lovely waterside area of parkland and ancient lock systems. Here you'll find cafes and the **Kanalmuseet** (free entry), which runs through the history of the canal as well as exhibiting over 50 model ships.

Saab Bilmuseum   MUSEUM
(☑0520-289 443; http://saabcarmuseum.se; Åkerssjövägen 18; adult/child 100/50kr; ⊙10am-5pm daily Jul-Aug, 11am-4pm Tue-Sun rest of year) Saab Bilmuseum is a must for car fanatics and Swedish design buffs. At this warehouse-showroom, gleaming Saab car models range from the first made (a sensational 1946 prototype) and the Sonnet Super Sport, of which only six were made between '55 and '57, to the futuristic Aero X – the Bio-Power Hybrid Concept that's the first car in the world to run on bioethanol and produce no emissions whatsoever.

Waterfall   WATERFALL
(www.fallochsluss.se; Slussområde; ⊙3pm daily Jul & Aug, 3pm Sat May, Jun & Sep) Northeast near the Hojum power station crowds gather on the bridge in anticipation of a mighty cascade of unleashed water. Normally the water is diverted through the power station, but at set times the sluice gates are opened and 300,000L per second thunders through. For an even more magnificent sight, wait for the night-time **illuminated waterfall**, which usually occurs during the Waterfall Days festival in mid-July.

Galleri Nohab Smedja   GALLERY
(☑0520-28 94 00; Åkerssjövägen 10; ⊙10am-5pm late Jun–Aug, shorter hours rest of year) FREE Galleri Nohab Smedja, an old smithy's workshop now used for temporary art exhibitions, such as metal art by local and international smiths, is managed by Innovatum Science Center. The gallery is opposite the museum, just behind the tourist office.

Innovatum Linbana   CABLE CAR
(per person 20kr; ⊙9am-5pm mid-Jun–Aug, shorter hours rest of year) The Innovatum Linbana sweeps you over the canal to the hydroelectricity area, giving you a great overview of the city's locks and waterways. Once you're

on the far side of the canal, follow the stairs down to the river, where you'll find one of Sweden's most unusual industrial buildings, the potent-looking **Olidan power station**, which supplied much of the country's electricity in the early 20th century.

☞ Tours

Canal Tours   BOATING
(☑0520-321 00; www.stromkarlen.se; Slussområde; adult/child 240/80kr; ☺departs noon & 12.30pm mid-Jun–mid-Aug) Two- to three-hour canal tours on the M/S *Elfkungen* leave at noon from the Slussområde or at 12.30pm from the pier behind the Scandic Swania Hotel (Storgatan 47) in central Trollhättan. Buy tickets on board.

✯ Festivals & Events

Waterfall Days   MUSIC
(www.vastsverige.com/fallensdagar; ☺mid-Jul) **FREE** A thumping three-day celebration held in mid-July with live bands, circus performances, fireworks and some impressive waterworks.

🛏 Sleeping

Gula Villan   HOSTEL €
(☑0520-129 60; www.svenskaturistforeningen. se; Tingvallavägen 12; s/d 300/420kr; 🅿🛜) The cheery STF hostel, in a pretty old yellow villa, is about 200m from the train station. The walls are on the thin side, but there's a good communal vibe and breakfast and bikes are available.

First Hotel Kung Oscar   HOTEL €€
(☑0520-47 04 70; www.kungoscar.se; Drottninggatan 17; s/d from 980/1180kr; 🅿🛜) Comfortable, contemporary business hotel – all charcoals and creams with bold splashes of colour, in an enviable central location. Complimentary dinner, a lavish breakfast spread and the helpfulness of the staff seal the deal, but get here early to snag one of the prized parking spots.

✗ Eating & Drinking

Cafe Gillet   SWEDISH €
(☑0520-42 44 40; www.cafegillet.se; Storgatan 22; sandwiches 40-55kr; daily lunch 75kr; ☺10am-8pm Mon-Thu, to 6pm Fri, to 4pm Sat; ♿) This pleasant cafe inhabits a cute yellow wooden house in a park, with patio seating in the summer. Cakes, pastries and sandwiches are excellent, and there's a good-value lunch menu on weekdays (lasagne, quiche, etc).

Strandgatan   EUROPEAN €€
(www.strandgatan.com; Strandgatan 34; mains 95-159kr; ☺10am-11pm Sun-Thu, to midnight Fri & Sat; 🛜) Trendy canalside bistro that sells everything from filled paninis, Greek salad and nachos to quiches, fish and chips, muffins and good coffee.

★ Albert Hotell   SWEDISH €€€
(☑0520-129 90; www.alberthotell.se; Strömsberg; mains 265-395kr; ☺11.30am-2pm Mon-Fri & 6-10pm Mon-Sat; 🅿🛜) This marvellous restaurant-hotel combo is based in a splendid 19th-century wooden villa. Superb, modish Nordic dishes might include steak with bone marrow or red tuna from Vänern lake and crème brûlée with local strawberries. The hotel itself offers 27 contemporary rooms (singles/doubles from 1200/1400kr), as well as a vintage suite. It's an easy 10-minute walk across the river from central Trollhättan.

Majo Bar   BAR
(www.majobar.se; Polhemsgatan 6; ☺5-11pm Tue-Thu, to 1am Fri & Sat) One of a handful of nightlife options, this stylish tapas bar has an extensive selection of beer and cocktails, imbibed to the accompaniment of local and international DJ talent on weekends.

ℹ Information

The main **tourist office** (☑0520-135 09; www. visittv.se; Åkerssjövägen 10; ☺10am-6pm Mon-Fri, 11am-5pm Sat & Sun, closes earlier Sep-May) is about 1.5km south of the town centre, next to the museum cluster. There's also a small info kiosk on Strandgatan behind the Scandic Swania hotel (same hours and info).

ℹ Getting There & Away

To reach the attractions in Trollhättan from the train station or the Drottningtorget bus station, walk south along Drottninggatan, then turn right into Åkerssjövägen, or take town bus 21 – it runs most of the time.

Local buses 61, 62 and 65 run from the Drottningtorget bus station to Vänersborg and bus 1 connects the town to Lidköping.

From the train station, a couple of blocks north of the city centre, trains run to Gothenburg (132kr, 38 minutes) at least once hourly.

Lidköping

☑0510 / POP 25,644

It might be short on wow factor, but cheery Lidköping – set on Vänern lake – is deeply likeable. Its handsome main square, Nya

DON'T MISS

SLEEPING IN A LIGHTHOUSE

Balanced atop the windswept skerries of the Bohuslän Coast, perched at the country's southernmost tip or acting as sturdy wardens of Gotland's sandy shores: the *fyr* (lighthouses) of southern Sweden are as varied as they are beautiful.

Staying in a lighthouse is one of southern Sweden's quintessential experiences, as you find yourself amid pristine and unique surroundings on the edge of civilisation. The following are a few of the best options:

Utpost Hållö (p154)

Stora Karlsö (p243)

Smuygehuk (☑ 0410-245 83; www.smygehukhostel.com; Smyge Fyrväg 194; s/d 375/520kr; ⊙ mid-May–mid-Sep; P)

Stadens Torg, is dominated by the curious, squat old courthouse and its tower (it's actually a replica – the original burnt down in 1960). A previous fire in 1849 destroyed most of the town, but the cute 17th-century houses around Limtorget still stand.

Lidköping's finest attractions lie some distance out of town, but are easily reached by local bus.

◎ Sights

★ **Läckö Slott**   CASTLE
(☑ 0510-103 20; www.lackoslott.se; Läckö; adult/child 100kr/free; garden only 50kr; parking 30kr; ⊙ 10am-6pm mid-Jun–Aug; tours in English 10.30am, 12.30pm, 2.30pm & 4.30pm; P ♿; ☐ 132) An extraordinary example of 17th-century Swedish baroque architecture, Läckö Slott lies 23km north of Lidköping. There's been a castle here since 1298; Count Magnus Gabriel de la Gardie acquired it in 1615 and made substantial improvements. Admission includes 40-minute guided tours, with access to the most interesting rooms, including the representative apartments, the count's private chambers, the Banquet Hall where guests enjoyed 55-course meals, and the chamber with the German double-headed eagle, perhaps intended as mockery of the enemy.

Husaby Kyrka   CHURCH
(Husaby; ⊙ 8am-8pm Mon-Fri, 9am-8pm Sat & Sun; ☐ 116, 228) FREE Husaby (15km east of Lidköping) is inextricably linked to Swedish history. Legend has it King Olof Skötkonung (d1022), the country's first Christian king, was baptised in a nearby spring by the English missionary Sigfrid. (Some dispute the exact timing and location.) Husaby Kyrka dates from the 12th century, but the base of the three-steeple tower may be that of an

earlier wooden structure; traces of an Iron Age village were found here. Inside are striking medieval paintings and thousand-year-old rune stones.

Kinnekulle   MOUNTAIN
(http://hikingkinnekulle.com/en/welcome.html) FREE The 'flowering mountain' Kinnekulle (306m), 18km northeast of Lidköping, features unusually diverse geology and plant life, including mighty ancient oaks. It's also home to rare creatures, including the greater crested newt and short-horned grasshopper. There are numerous short nature trails, or you can backpack the entire 45km-long **Kinnekulle vandringsled** (walking trail). The tourist office provides a map and the informative *Welcome to Götene and Kinnekulle* brochure.

Take road 44 northeast from Lidköping, then follow signs. Local trains and buses run to Källby, Råbäck and Hällekis, with access to the trail.

Vänermuseet   MUSEUM
(www.vanermuseet.se; Framnäsvägen 2; adult/child 40kr/free; ⊙ 10am-5pm Mon-Fri, 11am-4pm Sat & Sun) Vänermuseet boasts a 20-cu-metre aquarium, home to all manner of aquatic wildlife from its namesake lake, Europe's third largest (5650 sq km). A variety of other exhibits highlight the lake's nature and culture.

⌹ Sleeping

STF Vandrarhem Lidköping   HOSTEL €
(☑ 0510-664 30; www.lidkopingsvandrarhem. com; Gamla Stadens Torg 4; dm/s/d/tr 250/380/590/750kr; ⊙ reception open 8-10am & 4-6pm; 🛜) Just a couple of minutes' walk from the train station, this large yellow hostel sits in a tree-shaded spot in the old town.

Rooms are spartan but spacious, bathrooms institutional-looking but spotless, and you can cook up a storm in the guest kitchen while washing your dirties in the laundry room.

★ **Hotell Läckö**   HOTEL €€
(📞 0510-230 00; www.hotellacko.se; Gamla Stadens Torg 5; s/d/ste 895/1195/1795kr; 📶) Our favourite in town is this old-school, family-run charmer. The spacious rooms boast high ceilings, solid wooden furniture and crisp linen, while breakfast is served on dainty antique porcelain. There's a cosy little reading room with comfy leather armchairs, and quirky touches like bright bed-curtains, four-poster beds and whimsical hanging millinery.

Naturum Vanerskargarden   HOTEL €€
(📞 0510-48 46 60; http://naturum.lackoslott.se/; Läckö; s/d from 1290/1590kr, f 1990kr; 📶) 🖉 Imagine that you can see a castle overlooking a tranquil lake from your window. Actually, you don't have to: the 15 stylish rooms above Naturum are practically on top of Läckö Slott and the archipelago of Vänern lake, the on-site cafe is fabulous and the design of the futuristic nature centre lives up to its eco-credentials.

✖ Eating

Mellbygatans Ost &
Delikatesser   SWEDISH €€
(📞 0510-280 80; www.mellbygatansdelikatesser. com; Mellbygatan 10; mains 169-249kr; ⊙11am-3pm Mon-Fri & 6-11pm Tue-Sat; 🅿) A block from the main square, this sweet cafe and deli has been delighting locals with its fresh, changing menu for years, and has expanded its restaurant side and its house-brewed beer. You might be greeted with the likes of cheese and courgette pie with onion marmalade, pulled-pork sandwiches, and smoked-salmon salad.

★ **Restaurang Sjöboden**   SEAFOOD €€€
(📞 0510-104 08; www.sjoboden.se; Spikens Fiskehamn, Spiken; mains 270-310kr; ⊙5-10pm early Jun–Sep; 🚌132) Three kilometres south of Läckö Slott is the turnoff to the tiny village of Spiken, home to this unmissable harbourside restaurant. Feast on the best and freshest things pulled from Vänern lake along with locally sourced produce, either à la carte or as part of a three- or four-course menu (545/655kr).

❶ Information

The **tourist office** (📞 0510-200 20; www.lacko kinnekulle.se; Nya Stadens Torg; ⊙10am-3pm Mon-Fri Jan-Apr & mid-Sep–Dec; 10am-4pm Mon-Fri & 10am-2pm Sat May-Jun & mid-Aug–Sep; 10am-6pm Mon-Fri, 10am-3pm Sat, 11am-3pm Sun Jul–mid-Aug) is situated in the old courthouse on the main square.

❶ Getting There & Away

Town and regional buses stop on Nya Stadens Torg. Bus 1 runs roughly hourly between Trollhättan and Lidköping (102kr).

The train station is centrally located off Rörstrandsgatan. Trains go frequently to Gothenburg (202kr, five daily, 1¾ hours).

HALLAND

Sea, sun and surf are the name of the game in Halland, with the populations of the most desirable beach destinations often tripling during the summer months. The long whitesand beaches at Tylösand and Varberg are ideal for lounging, swimming and all manner of watersports. Firmly on dry land, there are an imposing fortress and museums to explore.

Halmstad

📞 035 / POP 66,124

Danish until 1645, Halmstad served as an important fortified border town. Its street plan was laid out by the Danish king Christian IV after a huge fire wiped out most of the buildings in 1619 (apart from a few merchants' houses along Storgatan). He also awarded Halmstad its coat of arms: you'll see the three crowns and three hearts motif dotted all over the place.

These days, the town's main draw is the beaches in the suburb of Tylösand, 8km southwest of the centre. It's a popular summer hang-out and party spot, with a huge hotel and lots of open-air bars.

⊙ Sights & Activities

Woman's Head   SCULPTURE
FREE Picasso's *Woman's Head* is down by the river, in Picassoparken off Strandgatan.

Halmstad Slott   CASTLE
(lansstyrelsen@n.lst.se; Aschebergsgatan 1) Halmstad Slott was built by King Christian IV of Denmark in the early 1600s, when Halland was still under Danish rule. It was where

Halmstad

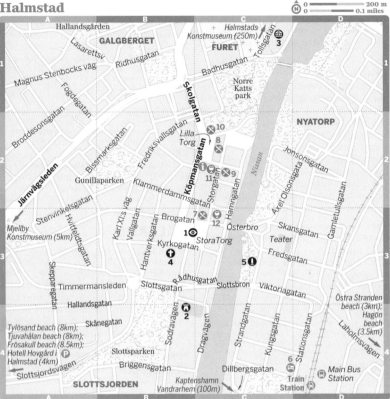

Halmstad

◎ Sights

⬜ Sleeping

⊗ Eating

⊕ Drinking & Nightlife

the Danish king met with Sweden's Gustav II Adolf in 1619 to sort out their issues over decadent meals. (It didn't last.) The castle has since been visited by many Scandinavian royals over the years, including Queen Christina in 1645. The castle is open twice yearly for guided tours in early summer: email for details.

Mjellby Konstmuseum   MUSEUM
(☎035-13 71 95; www.mjellbykonstmuseum.se; Mjällby; adult/child 80kr/free; ◷11am-5pm Jul–mid-Aug, from noon rest of year; ♿; ☐300) The main focus of Mjellby Konstmuseum, 5km west of town, is a changing exhibition of works by the Halmstad Group – six local artists who pushed the boundaries with French cubism in the 1920s and surrealism in the 1930s, influenced by Magritte and Dali. Not only were their pieces controversial at the time, but these six artists collaborated with each other on various projects.

Europa and the Bull   FOUNTAIN
In Stora Torg, the main square, stands Carl Milles' sculptural fountain *Europa and the*

Bull, with the characteristically buff mermen with somewhat scary faces.

St Nikolai Kyrka CHURCH
(www.svenskakyrkan.se/halmstad/st-nikolai-kyrka; Kyrkogatan 4; ⊘ 8.30am-6pm Jun-Aug, to 3pm Sep-May) **FREE** Medieval attractions in Halmstad include the lovely 14th-century church St Nikolai Kyrka. Frequent music events are held here in summer; check the schedule online.

Halmstads Konstmuseum MUSEUM
(☑035-16 23 00; www.hallandskonstmuseum.se; Tollsgatan; ⊘ closed for renovations until 2019) **FREE** Besides the modest permanent collection of works by the Halmstad Group, Halmstads Konstmuseum hosts some impressive temporary exhibitions, including a number of important regional and national artists. It's currently closed for an extensive rebuild.

★ **Beaches** BEACH
FREE Packed with tanned sun worshippers in the summer, Blue Flag–designated Tylösand, 8km southwest of town, is Halmstad's most popular beach area, with a perpetual party vibe courtesy of the nearby Hotel Tylösand, bars and restaurants. From here, head to the signposted Tjuvahålan smuggler's cove to search for pirate treasure, or walk north to Frösakull for some peace and quiet.

East of central Halmstad, the shallow, calm waters of Östra Stranden are particularly family friendly, while nudists can bronze their behinds at secluded Heden, near Hagön further south of town.

🛏 Sleeping

Kaptenshamn Vandrarhem HOSTEL, HOTEL €
(☑035-12 04 00; www.halmstadvandrarhem.se; Stuvaregatan 8; s/d hostel from 450/600kr, hotel from 1050/1400kr, hostel breakfast 80kr; P 🛜) This hostel-hotel is in a pleasant brick building about 100m south of the train station and then west on Dillbergsgatan by the river. Rooms are fairly basic, but spacious and quiet, and friendly staff, a leafy back patio and a nearby playground jazz things up.

Hotell Hovgård i Halmstad HOTEL €€
(☑035-12 35 77; www.hovgard.se; Gamla Tylösandsvägen 102; s/d/tr from 1290/1440/1990kr; P 🛜; 🚌30) Appealing family-run hotel halfway between Halmstad and Tylösänd. The rooms are decked out in soothing creams, with the odd wrought-iron bedstead, the

breakfast buffet is excellent and guest bicycles are available so that you can cycle from the hotel to the beach.

Tylebäck RESORT €€
(☑035-19 18 00; www.tyleback.com; Kungsvägen 1; sites from 250kr, s/d hostel from 750/950kr, hotel 1295/1490kr; P 🛜; 🚌10, 30) Accommodation to suit all travellers – camping, hostel, hotel – is offered at Tylebäck, in Tylösand, with sleek, modern cabins in an attractive forested setting.

Best Western Plus Grand Hotel HOTEL €€
(☑035-280 81 00; www.grandhotel.nu; Stationsgatan 44; s/d 1095/1250kr; P 🛜🐾) Across from the train station, this hotel in a 1905 building has 108 well-kept rooms decorated in traditional style with the odd modern touch. There's a decent restaurant and bar, too.

Hotel Tylösand HOTEL €€€
(☑035-305 00; www.tylosand.se; Tylöhusvägen; s/d incl spa from 1450/1950kr; P 🛜🐾; 🚌10, 30) Plusses: ideal if you're into beaches, clubbing, spa treatments, good breakfasts and/or Roxette (it's part-owned by Per Gessle). It's a large, upmarket complex on the beach, with a newly renovated spa and tons of art. Fusses: can be noisy, the windows only open a little, and rooms in the older buildings feel miles away from the lobby and spa area.

🍴 Eating

Indian Kitchen INDIAN €
(www.indiankitchenhalmstad.se; Nygatan 8; mains 85-145kr, lunch 79kr; ⊘11am-10pm; 🌱) Authentic Indian restaurant specialising mostly in northern Indian dishes. Dishes of the day are a good deal; we're particularly fond of the Goan fish curry and Achari lamb.

Skånskan BAKERY €
(Storgatan 40; sandwiches from 65kr; ⊘9am-8pm Mon-Fri, 10am-5pm Sat, noon-5pm Sun) This is a good old-fashioned bakery with cafe attached. As well as chunky sandwiches, there's a tempting stock of chocolates and cakes to crank up the calories.

Spis & Deli DELI €€
(www.spisdeli.se; Tyghusgatan 4; mains 105-170kr; ⊘10am-7pm Mon-Fri, 9am-5pm Sat, noon-4pm Sun; 🌱) Half health-food shop, half deli, Spis is all about eco-friendly, organic food. As you might have guessed, that's good news for vegans and vegetarians, who'll find a few items to sate them among the wraps, salads, meatless burgers and energy smoothies.

★ **Pio & Co** EUROPEAN €€€
(☑ 035-21 06 69; www.pio.se; Storgatan 37; mains 245-355kr; ☺ from 6pm Mon-Fri, from 5.30pm Sat, from 5pm Sun) Award-winning Pio is an up-market brasserie with an extensive menu of both Swedish and continental favourites – think Halland pork with roasted garlic and potatoes au gratin, cod loin with horserad-ish sauce, and potatoes with roe.

🍷 Drinking & Nightlife

Harrys PUB
(☑ 035-10 55 95; Storgatan 22; ☺ 5pm-midnight Sun-Fri, from noon Sat) American-style pub complete with a great alfresco terrace and the likes of pulled-pork sandwiches, falafel burgers and baby back ribs to back up your beer.

Bulls Pub PUB
(☑ 035-14 09 21; Bankgatan 5; ☺ 5-11pm Mon-Thu, noon-2am Fri & Sat, 3-11pm Sun) Popular English bar in a former fire station, with live music on weekends and light meals.

ℹ Information

The well-stocked **tourist office** (☑ 035-12 02 00; www.destinationhalmstad.se; Köpmans-gatan 20; ☺ 10am-7pm Mon-Fri, to 5pm Sat, to 2pm Sun) is right in the town centre.

ℹ Getting There & Away

From the **train station** (☑ 035-18 34 51; www.sj.se; Stationsgatan), regular trains between Gothenburg (215kr, 1¼ hours, twice hourly) and Malmö (185kr, 1½ to 1¾ hours) stop in Halmstad and call in at Helsingborg (138kr, one hour) and Varberg (122kr, 32 minutes).

Swebus Express (www.swebusexpress.com) buses run from the **main bus station** (Stations-gatan) to Malmö (165kr, 2¼ hours, six daily), Helsingborg (105kr, one hour, six daily) and Gothenburg (136kr, 1¾ hours, seven daily).

ℹ Getting Around

Local **Hallandstrafiken** (www.hallandstrafiken.se) buses 10 and 30 run half-hourly (hourly in the evenings) from the main square (Stora Torg) to the clubs and beaches at Tylösand.

Varberg

☑ 0340 / POP 27,602
The 19th-century bathing resort of Varberg lies by the side of a 60km stretch of beautiful white-sand beaches: its population triples in the summer months. The town's sights,

restaurants and hotels are largely clustered around its other main attraction, Varberg Fortress.

◉ Sights

Getterön Nature Reserve NATURE RESERVE
(☑ 0340-875 10) FREE Getterön Nature Re-serve, just 2km north of the town, has abun-dant bird life (mostly waders and geese) that attracts twitchers.

Varberg Fortress CASTLE
(Hallands Kulturhistoriska Museum; Varbergs fäst-ning; www.museumhalland.se; adult/child 100kr/free; ☺ 10am-6pm daily mid-Jun–mid-Aug) Var-berg's star attraction is this imposing me-dieval prison fortress overlooking the sea. Its museum is home to the 14th-century Bocksten Man, a garrotted, impaled and drowned murder victim, dug out of a peat bog at Åkulle in 1936. His 14th-century cos-tume is the most perfectly preserved medi-eval clothing in Europe and his full head of red-blond hair is intact. You can also delve into the still-unsolved mystery of King Karl XII's murder.

Grimeton Radio Station MUSEUM
(☑ 0340-67 41 90; www.grimeton.org; Grimeton; adult/child 120kr/free; ☺ tours in English 1pm & 3pm daily Jun-Aug) Built in the 1920s and now on the Unesco World Heritage List, Grimeton Radio Station is a monument to early technological advances. Once part of the interwar transatlantic communication network, it's now the world's only surviving long-wave radio station. The site is about 10km east of Varberg and is open in con-junction with tours during summer.

🏃 Activities

Fahlén Surfshop SURFING, KITESURFING
(☑ 0340-837 50; www.fahlensurf.se; Birger Svenssons väg 38; ☺ 10am-2pm Tue-Sun Jun-Aug) A few minutes' walk north from the train station, these guys cater to all your surfing, kitesurfing, windsurfing and paddleboard-ing needs with equipment rental and water-sports courses. Two hours of paddleboard-ing instruction costs 500kr, while an eight-hour introduction to kitesurfing will set you back 2500kr.

Nudist Beaches BEACH
Varberg has three nudist beaches just a short walk south from the fortress along the Strandpromenaden. Don't expect white sand; these beaches all consist of large,

smooth rocks, all with easy access to the water. Beaches are segregated by gender: the first two, Kärringhålan and Skarpe Nord, are women-only beaches; a few minutes further south is Goda Hopp, the men's bathing spot.

Apelviken   SURFING
(☑0340-67 70 55; www.apelviken.se) Apelviken, 2km south of Varberg, is Sweden's best spot for windsurfing and kitesurfing. At the southern end of Apelviken, **Surfcenter** (☑0340-64 13 00; www.apelviken.se/Aktiviteter/155/Surfcenter; surfboards per 2/4/6 hrs 200/300/400kr; ⊙noon-6pm Mon-Sat) rents boards and also gives surfing and windsurfing lessons from late May to August.

Kallbadhuset   SPA
(www.kallbadhuset.se; Otto Torels gata 7; adult/child 70/35kr; ⊙10am-5pm (to 8pm Wed) Jun–mid-Aug, 1-6pm rest of year) After you've finished sunbathing next to all the bronzed Nordic bodies at Kallbadhuset, a Moorish-style outdoor bathhouse on stilts above the sea, have a dip in the bracing waters. There's a sauna, and sunbathing areas (nudity is the norm) divided into male and female sections, with steps leading down into the water (facing away from the beach).

🛏 Sleeping & Eating

⭐**Fästningens Vandrarhem**   HOSTEL €
(☑0340-868 28; www.fastningensvandrarhem.se; Varbergs fästning; dm/s/d 295/545/590kr, breakfast adult/child 120/85kr) Within Varberg Fortress, this SVIF hostel can lock you up inside its single and double prison cells. If that's too 'authentic' an experience, opt for one of the large, bright rooms in surrounding buildings. Breakfast is extra in high season, and bicycles can be rented for 120kr.

Getteröns Camping   CAMPGROUND €
(☑0340-168 85; www.getteronscamping.se; sites/cabins from 280/455kr; ⊙May–mid-Sep; 🅿) On a sandy beach on the Getterön peninsula, tent spaces sit cheek by jowl with caravan spots and rows of self-contained summer cabins. It does get busy during high season, when most cabins are available only on a weekly basis.

⭐**Hotell Gästis**   HOTEL €€€
(☑0340-180 50; www.hotellgastis.nu; Borgmästaregatan 1; s/d from 1495/1795kr; 🅿🛜🏊) This one-of-a-kind hotel is bursting with quirky details including an elevator shaft covered in pulp-fiction covers and the basement Lenin Baths (open to non-guests), featuring hot and cold pools, a massage area and an anachronistic giant candlelit Jacuzzi. Cosy rooms come with shelves full of books, and a dinner buffet is included.

⭐**Vin & Skafferi Hus 13**   SWEDISH €€€
(☑0340-835 94; www.hus13.se; Varbergs fästning; mains 195-325kr; ⊙noon-3pm Tue-Sat, from 5pm Mon-Sat) Next door to the fortress hostel, this friendly wine bar and restaurant dishes up great lunches for 165kr (freshly fried mackerel, meatballs), with more sophisticated gourmet dishes – veal with hazelnuts, hake with beets and capers – tantalising diners' tastebuds in the evenings. Watch tourists stream up to the *fästning* from the pleasant outdoor patio.

ℹ Information

The well-stocked **tourist office** (☑0340-868 00; www.visitvarberg.se; Brunnsparken; ⊙10am-7pm Mon-Sat, to 9pm Thu, 11am-4pm Sun) is in the centre of town.

ℹ Getting There & Away

Stena Line (www.stenaline.se; Färjeläget Hamnen) ferries run twice daily between Varberg and the Danish town of Grenå; the ferry dock is next to the town centre.

From the **train station** (Östra Hamnvägen), regular services run to Halmstad (120kr, 36 minutes, twice hourly), Gothenburg (119kr, 45 minutes, twice hourly) and Malmö (235kr, 2½ hours, hourly).

Malmö & the South

Best Places to Eat

➡ Bastard (p178)

➡ Namu (p177)

➡ Mat & Destillat (p185)

➡ Wägga Fisk &
Delikatessrökeri (p205)

➡ Ebbas Fik (p188)

Best Places to Stay

➡ Saltsjobad (p195)

➡ Story Hotel Studio Malmö
(p176)

➡ Hotell Oskar (p184)

➡ Ohboy Hotell (p176)

➡ Quality Hotel View (p176)

Why Go?

It's no wonder that so many artists call southern Sweden home – the light seems softer, the foliage brighter and the shoreline more dazzling.

Skåne (Scania) was Danish property until 1658 and still openly flaunts its uniqueness – the heavy *Skånska* dialect, a wealth of half-timbered houses and the region's hybrid flag – a Swedish yellow cross on a red Danish background. Marvellous, multicultural Malmö, Skäne's largest and Sweden's third largest city is today linked to Copenhagen by the Öresund bridge, a marvel of modern engineering.

South of Malmö, Viking heritage abounds, while to the north, elegant and erudite Lund, is Sweden's answer to Cambridge. Cliffs dominate Skåne's northwestern coast, while its east is a gentler affair with sandy beaches and its medieval showpiece, Ystad.

Northeast of Skåne, forested Blekinge *län* (county) was the seat of Sweden's 17th-century sea power; beautifully preserved baroque Karlskrona is the jewel in its crown.

When to Go
Malmö

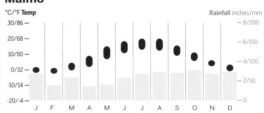

Jul & Aug Warmest and busiest months; tourists flock to the coast and the fabulous Malmö Festival.

May & Sep Cool, clear and peaceful. Autumn weather is ideal for apple harvesting and hikes.

Nov–Feb Expect the country's mildest winter, although it tends to be wet with snow inland.

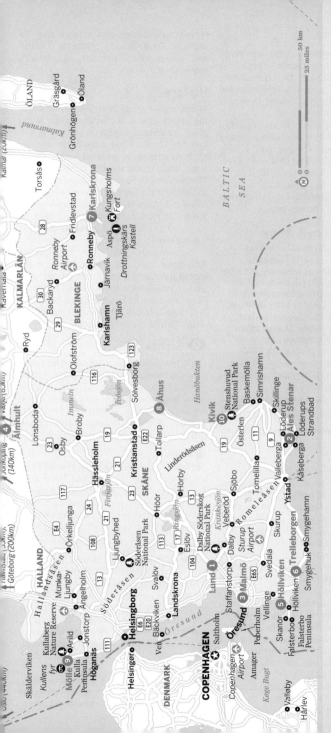

Malmö & the South Highlights

1 Kulturen (p183)
Wandering around Lund's outdoor museum complex.

2 Ales Stenar (p196)
Contemplating the mysteries of this megalithic stone ship.

3 Ribersborgs kallbadhus (p175) Throwing yourself, nude, into the sea at this historic ocean bath in Malmö.

4 IKEA Museum (p201) Learning how one man's vision can change the world.

5 Fotevikens Museum (p191) Hanging out with Vikings, near Höllviken.

6 Trelleborgen (p192) Marvelling at the pre-science ingenuity of our ancestors.

7 Marinmuseum (p203) Visiting national maritime museum in Karlskrona.

8 Absolut Experience Center (p198) Learning how vodka is made, then drinking some, in Åhus.

9 Ladonia (p190) Travelling internationally to this quirky micronation then riding an Icelandic horse.

10 Kiviks Musteri (p198) Picking apples in these sweet-smelling orchards near Kivik.

SKÅNE

Skåne (Scania) is Sweden at its most continental. Connected to Denmark by bridge, its trademark mix of manors, gingerbread-style abodes and delicate, deciduous forests are a constant reminder that central Europe is just beyond the horizon.

Dominating the scene is metropolitan Malmö, defined by its cosmopolitan culture and twisting tower. Further out, velvety fields, sandy coastlines and stoic castles create one of Sweden's most bucolic landscapes.

Add to this the fact that Skåne is often dubbed Sweden's larder and you have yourself one scrumptious Scandi treat.

ℹ️ Getting There & Away

Skåne is well serviced by road, rail and sea.

The E6 motorway runs north from outside Malmö along the province's western coast, while the E22 and E4 run almost parallel to each other (but about 50km apart) from the southwest of the province, across its centre to the northeast.

SJ Rail (🔲 0771–75 75 75; www.sj.se) and provincial transport operator **Skånetrafiken** (p189) operate a comprehensive network of regional trains and buses connecting most towns of any size.

There are international ferry ports at Helsingborg, Malmö, Trelleborg and Ystad.

There are airports, albeit small ones, at Malmö and Ystad.

Malmö

🔲 040 / POP 328,494

Sweden's third-largest city is a place where old meets new: from its proud castle and showpiece squares Stortorget and Lilla Torget, in the heart of Gamla Staden (the 'Old Town'), to the cosmopolitan promenades of Västra Hamnen's vibrant redeveloped waterfront. Here, Scandinavia's tallest building twists its way skyward, gazing down over the vast Öresund bridge – both are modern engineering marvels reflecting multicultural Malmö's progressive outlook.

'The bridge', connecting the city to coolcat Copenhagen's downtown and busy international airport, has helped forge a dynamic urban conglomeration. This, and the fact that Germany is just a short hop across the Baltic, helps explain why more than 150 nationalities call Malmö home.

It's no wonder then that Malmö is so fabulously worldly – Middle Eastern markets, Italian coffee culture, edgy international eateries and cruisy, chic bars counter its intrinsic Nordic reserve, while its classical and contemporary fine-arts and theatre scenes are thriving.

History

Malmö really took off in the 14th century with the arrival of the Hanseatic traders, when grand merchants' houses were erected, followed by churches and a castle. The greatest medieval expansion occurred under Jörgen Kock, who became the city's mayor in 1524. The town square, Stortorget, was laid out then, and many of the finest 16th-century buildings still stand. After the city capitulated to the Swedes in 1658, Malmö found its groove as an important commercial centre and its castle was bolstered to protect trade.

More recently, Malmö has traded in its 20th-century heavy industries, including car and aircraft manufacture, for cleaner, greener companies, particularly in the service, financial and IT sectors. Since its founding in the late 1990s, the university has also helped define the city, creating a thriving student population.

⊙ Sights

The city's major sights are all within easy strolling distance of the city centre. A good place to start your exploring is at the historic heart: the charming Lilla Torg square. There are also walking-, cycling- and boat-tours available (the latter in summer only); make enquiries at Travel Shop (p181).

⭐ **Gamla Staden**   AREA
(Old Town) Focusing on the area around **Stortorget** (the town square) and lively **Lilla Torget** (the little square) Malmö's Old Town is a gorgeous warren of cobblestone streets, half-timbered houses and bold facades that feel like they'd be more at place in Hamburg.

⭐ **Västra Hamnen**   AREA
(Western Harbour) Located about 2.5km northwest of the Old Town, buzzing, bayside Västra Hamnen represents the modern face of Malmö. It's a popular spot to stroll, sip coffee and browse boutiques, but mostly people come to marvel at the Öresund Bridge (p175) and ogle the Turning Torso (p174) twisting its way skyward: it's beautiful and an engineering marvel, but one can't help feel it's out of place here.

Follow the seafront in a southerly direction for 2km and you'll come to Ribersborgs Kallbadhus (p175) and its eponymous beach; both are local institutions.

OUTSTANDING MALMÖ ARCHITECTURE

The northwest harbour redevelopment is home to the **Turning Torso** (p174), a striking skyscraper that twists through 90 degrees from bottom to top–it doesn't actually rotate, but appears to do so, with the top floor's orientation being at a 90-degree angle to the building's foundation. Designed by Spaniard Santiago Calatrava, the 190m-high building is Sweden's tallest.

For vintage veneers, head for the statue of King Karl X Gustav in the centre of Stortorget and spin around (clockwise from the northwestern corner) to see the following buildings. **Kockska Huset** (Frans Suellsgatan 3), dating from 1524, is the robust former residence of one-time mayor and politician Jörgen Kock, who's governance led Malmö into a period of great prosperity. It's said Gustav Vasa stayed within its walls. The **Länsresidenset i Malmö** (Govenor's Residence; Stortorget 1) is a rather grand affair built in a Renaissance style. Its original foundations, laid in the 1600s lie beneath its present exterior, dating to 1849. Next door, the **Rådhuset** (city hall) was originally built in 1546 but has since been altered. At the southeastern corner of the square, the city's oldest pharmacy, **Apoteket Lejonet** (p175), flaunts an exquisite art-nouveau interior, with carved wooden shelves, antique medicine bottles and a glass-plated ceiling. Founded in 1571, the business originally occupied **Rosenvingeskahuset** on Västergatan.

Just off Östergatan, **St Gertrud Quarter** is a cute cluster of 19 buildings from the 16th to 19th centuries, with the mandatory mix of cobbled walkways, restaurants and bars. Across the road, **Thottska Huset** (St Gertrud Quarter) is Malmö's oldest half-timbered house (1558). It's now a restaurant, so peek inside.

★**Moderna Museet Malmö** MUSEUM
(☑040-685 79 37; www.modernamuseet.se/malmo; Gasverksgatan 22; ⊙11am-6pm Tue-Sun) FREE Architects Tham & Videgård chose to make the most of the distinct 1901 Rooseum, once a power-generating turbine hall, by adding a contemporary annexe, complete with a bright, perforated orange-red facade. Venue aside, the museum's galleries are well worth visiting, with the permanent exhibition including works by Matisse, Dalí and Picasso.

★**Malmö Museer** MUSEUM
(☑040-34 44 23; www.malmo.se/museer; Malmöhusvägen 6; adult/child 40kr/free; ⊙10am-5pm; ♿) Located within the vast Malmöhus Slott (p173), operating under the broad banner (and one low admission fee) of the Malmö Museer are three main museums within a museum: the Malmö Konstmuseum, Stadsmuseum (p175) and a large and unexpected **Aquarium** complete with an impressive nocturnal hall, wriggling with everything from bats to electric eels. There are gift shops and cafes inside all the museums, and plenty for kids, but be prepared for lots of walking, narrow staircases and cobblestones.

The excellent Teknikens och sjöfartens hus is part of the collection but not located within the castle walls: it's about 300m to the west.

★**Teknikens och sjöfartens hus** MUSEUM
(Technology and Maritime Museum; ☑040-34 44 38; Malmöhusvägen 7A; adult/child 40kr/free; ⊙10am-5pm) A short distance to the west of Malmöhus Slott (p173), the Technology and Maritime museum is home to aircraft, vehicles, a horse-drawn tram, steam engines, and the amazing 'U3' walk-in submarine. The submarine was launched in Karlskrona in 1943 and decommissioned in 1967. Upstairs, a superb hands-on experiment room will keep kids (of all ages) suitably engrossed. Admission includes access to all the museums of the Malmö Museer conglomeration.

★**Kungsparken** PARK
(King's Park) Since 1872, the 34,000-sq-metre King's Park in the shadow of Malmöhus Slott (p173) has been delighting Malmö's residents and visitors with its magnificent collection of more than 130 mature trees from around the world, as well as ponds, an organic vegetable garden and a fountain. It's a great spot for a picnic when the weather is fine. For those partial to a flutter, Malmö's only casino, the Cosmopol (p180), is within the park bounds.

Malmö Konstmuseum MUSEUM
(☑040-34 44 37; Malmöhusvägen 6; adult/child 40kr/free; ⊙10am-5pm) Within the walls of Malmöhus Slott (p173), under the banner of Malmö Museer, you'll find this superb collection of Swedish furniture and handicrafts, plus

Malmö

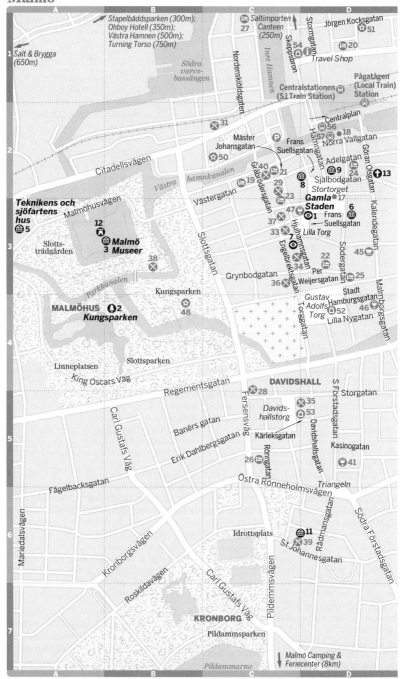

Salt & Brygga (650m)

Stapelbäddsparken (300m); Ohboy Hotell (350m); Västra Hamnen (500m); Turning Torso (750m)

Saltimporten Canteen (250m)

27

Jörgen Kocksgatan

51

20

Travel Shop

Skeppsbron

54

Stormgatan

Södra varvs-bassängen

Nordenskiöldsgatan

Inre Hamnen

Pågatågen (Local Train) Station

Centralstationen (SJ Train Station)

Citadellsvägen

31

Mäster Johansgatan

Frans Suellsgatan

Centralplan

56

57

18

Norra Vallgatan

Adelgatan

Göran Olssongatan

50

Västra hamnkanalen

40

21

19

Grönbrödersgatan

29

23

8

9

24

Själbodgatan

Stortorget

13

Teknikens och sjöfartens hus

5

Malmöhusvägen

12

Slotts-trädgården

3

Malmö Museer

Västergatan

Gamla Staden

17

47

37

1

Frans Suellsgatan

6

Kalendegatan

Slottsgatan

33

7

Lilla Torg

Hjulhamnsgatan

38

Parkkanalen

Engelbrektsgatan

34

22

45

Söderaren

Grynbodgatan

36

Per Weijersgatan

25

Kungsparken

48

MALMÖHUS

2

Kungsparken

Gustav Adolfs Torg

Torggatan

Stadt Hamburgsgatan

52

46

Malmborgsgatan

Lilla Nygatan

Linneplatsen

Slottsparken

King Oscars Väg

Regementsgatan

DAVIDSHALL

28

Fersensväg

Davids-hallstorg

35

53

S Förstadsgatan

Storgatan

Carl Gustafs Väg

Banérs gatan

Kärleksgatan

Davidshallsgatan

Kasinogatan

Erik Dahlbergsgatan

26

Romgatan

Östra Rönneholmsvägen

41

Fågelbacksgatan

Triangeln

Mariedalsvägen

Kronborgsvägen

Carl Gustafs Väg

Idrottsplats

11

39

St Johannesgatan

Rådmansgatan

Södra Förstadsgatan

Roskildavägen

KRONBORG

Pildemmsvägen

Pildammsparken

Malmö Camping & Feriecenter (8km)

Pildammarna

a vast collection of 20th-century Nordic art. The admission fee includes access to the castle and the other museums in the collection.

Malmö Chokladfabrik
MUSEUM

(Chocolate Museum; ☏040-45 95 05; www.malmo chokladfabrik.se; Möllevångsgatan 36; adult/child 100/50kr; ☺10am-6pm Mon-Fri, to 3pm Sat) 🍴 Watch heavenly cocoa concoctions being made, wander through the mini museum and devour the finished product at the chocolate-scented cafe. Dating from 1888, Malmö Chokladfabrik produces famously organic chocolates that have won several international chocolatiers' awards. The tours take around an hour and include an audiovisual presentation and a 20% discount in the choc shop.

Sankt Petri Kyrka
CHURCH

(☏040-27 90 43; www.svenskakyrkanmalmo.se; Göran Olsgatan 4; ☺10am-6pm) FREE This red-brick Gothic beast is Malmö's oldest church, built in the early 14th century. Protestant zealots whitewashed the medieval frescoes in 1555, but the original wall paintings in the Krämarekapellet have been successfully restored. There's a magnificent altarpiece dating from 1611 and a votive ship in the south aisle, dedicated to all who died at sea in WWII.

Malmöhus Slott
CASTLE

(☏040 34 44 37; Malmöhusvägen 6; adult/child 40kr/free; ☺10am-5pm, tours 3pm Wed-Sun Jul-Sep) FREE Erik of Pomerania built the first fortress here in 1436 but it was destroyed between 1534 and 1536 during a popular uprising in Skåne. After this rebellion, Denmark's King Christian III had the castle rebuilt in a Danish Gothic/Renaissance style, but his castle was devastated by fire in 1870. It lay in ruins until the 1930s when the Functionalist, factory-like red-brick buildings were added to what remained of the main building and the intact gun towers, and Malmo Museer (p171) was born.

Form/Design Center
ARTS CENTRE

(☏040-664 51 50; www.formdesigncenter.com; Lilla Torg 9; ☺11am-5pm Tue-Sat, noon-4pm Sun) FREE Ingeniously more of a shopping (p180) arcade disguised as a museum, the Form/Design Center is still an impressive showcase of design, architecture and art, featuring a central cobbled courtyard around which historic half-timbered houses have been converted into galleries and boutiques selling Scandi-cool art, fashion, crafts, toys and homewares and displaying ever-changing

Malmö

exhibitions. Pore over design magazines in the cafe and pick up one of the bicycle maps designed to guide you to design and architectural hot spots in the city.

Malmö Konsthall   GALLERY
(☑ 040-34 12 86; www.konsthall.malmo.se; St Johannesgatan 7; ☺ 11am-5pm daily, to 9pm Wed; P) FREE Malmö Konsthall, south of central Malmö, is one of Europe's largest contemporary-art spaces, with exhibitions spanning both Swedish and foreign talent. The museum cafe **Smak** (☑ 040-50 50 35; www.smak. info; mains 80-145kr; ☺ 11am-5pm) serves an excellent weekend brunch.

Turning Torso   NOTABLE BUILDING
(www.turningtorso.se; Lilla Varvsgatan 14) In the lovely Västra Hamnen (p170) area, you can't miss the eye-boggling Turning Torso, a futuristic skyscraper that twists through 90 degrees from bottom to top. Designed by Spaniard Santiago Calatrava and completed in 2005, it's the tallest building in Scandinavia, at 190m. As the building is almost completely residential, it has no observation deck, but there are conference rooms on the top two floors, which are occasionally opened to the public.

Stadsmuseum
MUSEUM

(City Museum; ☎040-34 44 37; Malmöhusvägen 6; adult/child 40kr/free; ⏱10am-5pm) The City Museum is chock full of exhibits on the history of Malmö and the Skåne region. Admission includes access to all the other museums in the Malmö Museer (p171) collection.

Apoteket Lejonet
HISTORIC BUILDING

(☎077-145 04 50; Stortorget 8; ⏱9am-6pm Mon-Fri, 10am-3pm Sat) At the southeastern corner of Stortorget, the city's oldest pharmacy (still in business) flaunts an exquisite art-nouveau interior, with carved wooden shelves, antique medicine bottles and a glass-plated ceiling.

🏃 Activities

Mostly flat, Malmö is very much bike- and pedestrian-friendly city. A number of outfitters rent bikes, including many hotels and hostels. For a fun way to explore the city, hire a paddle boat or an electirc boat (www.bookaboat.se) and hit the canals.

★ Ribersborgs kallbadhus
SWIMMING

(☎040-26 03 66; www.ribersborgskallbadhus.se; Limhamnsvägen; adult/child 65kr/free; ⏱9am-8pm Mon, Tue & Thu, to 9pm Wed, to 6pm Fri-Sun May-Sep, shorter hours rest of year) Ribersborg is a fetching sandy beach backed by parkland, about 2km west of the town centre. Off the beach, at the end of a 200m-long pier, is an open-air naturist saltwater pool, with separate sections for men and women, and a wood-fired sauna dating from 1898. There is also a pleasant cafe.

★ Stapelbäddsparken
SKATING

(☎020-34 45 00; www.stpln.se; Stapelbäddsgatan 3; ⏱10am-5pm Mon-Fri; ♿) **FREE** Swing by this intense urban jungle near the Turning Torso, at the northwestern harbour redevelopment, to gasp at skaters – local and international – sliding, flying and occasionally tumbling from dizzying heights. Check out www.bryggeriet.org for more details on the city's vibrant skateboarding scene.

Folkets Park
PLAYGROUND

(www.malmofolketspark.se; Norra Parkgatan 2A; ⏱park 7am-9pm Mon-Fri, 8am-9pm Sat & Sun, to 11pm Jun-Aug, attractions noon-7pm May–mid-Aug, shorter hours rest of year; ♿) **FREE** Family-friendly Folkets Park boasts pony rides, a fun fair, mini golf, a wading pool (transformed into an ice rink in winter), a reptile house and (phew, something for the grown-ups) – a beer garden. Entrance is free, but some attractions have a minimal cost.

City Boats Malmö
BOATING

(☎0704-71 00 67; www.cityboats.se; Amiralsbron, Södra Promenaden; per 30/60min 100/150kr; ⏱11am-7pm May-Aug) To scoot round Malmö's canals in a pedal boat, head to City Boats Malmö, just east of Gustav Adolfs Torg.

👉 Tours

Malmö By Foot
WALKING

(☎0708-43 50 20; www.malmobyfoot.com; 1¼hr tour 80kr; ⏱11am & 12.45pm Jul & Aug) A guided walk covering the history of Malmö from the Middle Ages to today. Tours in Swedish go twice a day from Sankt Petri Kyrka. Book online, by phone or through the tourist office. Customised tours in English are available for groups of 10 or more.

Malmö Bike Tours
CYCLING

(☎0708-46 25 40; www.malmobiketours.se; 2hr tour adult/child 350/250kr, rental day/week 150/650kr) Starting from Stortorget, Malmö Bike Tours runs two-hour and 3½-hour cycling trips around the city, covering major landmarks and lesser-known neighbourhoods. It also rents bicycles if you'd rather tour on your own. Book online, by phone or through the tourist office.

BRIDGING THE GAP

Opened in 2000, the **Öresund Bridge** (www.oresundsbron.com; motorcycle/car/minibus 265/520/1040kr) is Europe's longest cable-tied road and rail bridge, measuring 7.8km from Lernacken (on the Swedish side, near Malmö) to the artificial island of Peberholm (Pepper Island), south of Saltholm (Salt Island). From the island, a further 3km of undersea tunnel finally emerges just north of Copenhagen airport.

Local commuters pay via an electronic transmitter, while tolls for everyone else are payable by credit/debit card or in euros, Danish or Swedish currency at the Lernacken toll booths.

An alternative option is to catch a commuter train to Copenhagen (118kr), an easy 35-minute trip from Malmö and a good excuse to explore Denmark's so-hip capital. Regular passport checks have been suspended but you'll need to have your passport with you as random customs controls and inspections are commonplace.

Rundan BOATING

(☑040-611 74 88; www.stromma.se; Norra Vallgatan 60; adult/child from 140/70kr; ⊙10.30am-9pm Apr-Sep, shorter hours rest of year; 🚹) To experience Malmö by water, visit Rundan, opposite Centralstationen. Fifty-minute boat tours of the canals run regularly from April to September. They also run a small cafe on the quayside where you can pick up coffee and cake to take along on the trip.

✹ Festivals & Events

★Malmö Festival MUSIC

(www.malmofestivalen.se; ⊙mid-Aug) Malmö's premier annual event – with an average of some 1.5 million visitors – is the weeklong Malmö Festival. The mostly free events include theatre, dance, live music, fireworks and sizzling food stalls.

Malmo Pride LGBT

(www.malmopride.com; ⊙late Sep) Called the Regnbågsfestivalen (Rainbow Festival) until 2016, Malmö Pride celebrates LGBT diversity with exhibitions, films, workshops and parties, culminating in a pride parade.

🛏 Sleeping

Malmö Camping & Feriecenter CAMPGROUND €

(☑040-15 51 65; www.firstcamp.se/malmo/; Strandgatan 101; sites from 320kr, 2-bed cabins from 795kr; 🅿🛜🏊) By a little beach, this campground is in the shadow of the Öresund (p175) bridge, about 5km southwest of the centre of town: take bus 4 from Gustav Adolfs Torg (16kr).

STF Vandrarhem Malmö City HOSTEL €

(☑040-611 62 20; www.svenskaturistforeningen. se; Rönngatan 1; dm/d from 295/700kr; @🛜) Don't be put off by the exterior: this is a sparkling hostel right in the city centre with a bright and airy communal kitchen and an outdoor patio. Staff are enthusiastic and helpful.

★Story Hotel Studio Malmö BOUTIQUE HOTEL €€

(☑040-616 52 00; www.storyhotels.com/studio malmo/; Tyfongatan 1; d/ste from 990kr; 🌤🛜) If you love Swedish design, make a beeline for the fabulous, fresh and funky Story Hotel, one of Malmö's newest offerings. Exposed concrete walls, heavy red curtains, plush sofas, ocean views and sumptuous suites all tempt you to stay in...at least for a sleep-in. All rooms have queen or king beds, muted tones and raindrop showers. Most have wonderful views.

Go for the 'Large Ocean Room' (from 1590) if you can.

★Quality Hotel View HOTEL €€

(☑040-37 41 00; www.nordicchoicehotels.com/ hotels/sweden/malmo/quality-hotel-view/; Hyllie Stationstorg 29; d from 975kr; 🅿🌤🛜) For the location and price, you really can't go past the soaring heights of Malmö's most typically international hotel, with large rooms (many with bath-tubs), a superb breakfast buffet, great views and an excellent location directly atop Hyllie subway station putting you midway between Copenhagen airport and central Malmö. Access is everything.

★Ohboy Hotell BOUTIQUE HOTEL €€

(☑046-40 856 06; www.ohboy.se; Lilla Varvsgatan 24; ⊙d from 1050kr; 🛜) 🚲 Malmö's newest and quirkiest hotel is this concrete whopper designed by cyclists, for cyclists. There's a foldable bike in every room, pump and wash stations on-site, a rooftop terrace and garden and a variety of compact living solutions including lofts with additional hammock bedding and apartments. While it won't be to everyone's tastes, those who love it will love it a lot.

Located in the vibrant Västra Hamnen (p170) area and you can pick up a free bike from Malmö By Bike (p182; included in your room) on your way from Centralstation.

★Hotel Noble House HOTEL €€

(☑040-664 30 00; www.hotelnoblehouse.se; Per Weijersgatan 6; s/d from 995/1195kr; 🌤@🛜) The rooms of this low-cost Best Western have been recently re-furbished and feature parquet floors and a variety of tasteful design themes, with smart wallpaper and colourful accents. For comfort, price and location the hotel is an excellent choice.

Scandic Hotel St Jörgen HOTEL €€

(☑040-693 46 00; www.scandichotels.com; Stora Nygatan 35; s/d from 950/995kr; 🅿@🛜) A sleek, minimalist foyer reflects the contemporary, well-equipped and spacious rooms at this friendly, upmarket chain. Most rooms have bath-shower combos and look out onto Gustav Adolfs Torg. There are a few windowless 'cabin' rooms. Book online for the best rates.

Best Western Hotel Royal HOTEL €€

(☑040-664 25 00; www.bestwestern.se; Nora Vallgatan 94; s/d from 850/950kr; 🅿@🛜) This small hotel has rooms spread over a historic 16th-century building and its modern counterpart. Either choice is a sound one, with excellent facilities, although the modern rooms are more spacious. Rooms have parquet floors and earthy-toned decor. Comfortable chairs and sofas add to the appeal, while the breakfast buffet is right up there with Best Western's best.

Comfort Hotel Malmö
HOTEL €€
(☑040-33 04 40; www.nordicchoicehotels.com/hotels/sweden/malmo/comfort-hotel-malmo/; Carlsgatan 10C; s/d from 895/1000kr; P@☎) Not the right choice if you want an intimate place to propose: there are 293 rooms here, making it one of the largest hotels in the city. That said, the aesthetically revamped rooms are bright, airy and contemporary with massive black-and-white photos (with a music theme) covering an entire wall. The facilities are excellent and include a gym.

Hotel Duxiana
HOTEL €€
(☑040-607 70 00; www.malmo.hotelduxiana.com; Mäster Johansgatan 1; d/ste from 1095/2190kr; P@☎) Close to Centralstation, ubersleek Hotel Duxiana is one for the style crew. In a palate of white, black and gun-metal grey, design features include Bruno Mattheson sofas and seriously heavy-duty luxury hotel bedding. Single rooms are small but comfy, while the decadent junior suites feature a claw-foot bath-tub facing the bed.

Mäster Johan Hotel
HOTEL €€
(☑040-664 64 00; www.masterjohan.se; Mäster Johansgatan 13; r/ste from 995/1895kr; P@☎) Just off Lilla Torg, Mäster Johan is one of Malmö's better hotels. Rooms are huge by European standards, with bright carpets, large bathrooms and comfortable beds, but what was once elegant and high end, despite being immaculately maintained, is looking dated and a little gaudy. Breakfast is served in a glass-roofed courtyard and multilingual front-desk staff do their job well.

★Mayfair Hotel Tunneln
BOUTIQUE HOTEL €€€
(☑040-10 16 20; www.mayfairtunneln.com/en/; Adelgatan 4; s/d from 1325/1825kr; P☎) Central, classical and stylish, this boutique hotel in a heritage-listed building in the heart of Gamla Staden is great for history lovers. Rooms are bright and comfortable and a hearty breakfast spread is served in the hotel's vaulted cellar. With lots of staircases, nooks and narrow corridors it's not a great choice for mobility-impaired guests.

✗ Eating

Malmö isn't short on dining experiences, whether it's vegan grub enjoyed in a left-wing hang-out or designer supping on contemporary Nordic flavours. For atmosphere, head to the restaurant-bars on Lilla Torg. If you would rather eat with the locals, head to Davishall, where some of the best restaurants are located tucked away in the side streets.

The **Möllevångstorget Produce Market** (☺8am-5pm Mon-Sat) is great for fresh produce.

★Surf Shack
BURGERS €
(☑0761-76 40 18; www.surfshacksmash burgers.com; Västergatan 9a; burgers from 70kr; ☺10.30am-8pm Mon-Thu, to 11pm Fri-Sun; ✓) Enjoy a surfing-dude theme and a menu of top-range burgers, including a vegie option of tofu and black beans, 'no roll' (wrapped in lettuce) and healthy extra toppings like avocado, feta and grilled mushrooms. There are also sodas and shakes, including double chocolate and peanut butter if you are determined to sink that board.

Slottsträdgårdens Kafé
CAFE €
(☑040-30 40 34; www.slottstradgardenskafe.se; Malmöhusvägen 8; sandwiches from 70kr; ☺11am-5pm Apr-Sep) ✓ There is no better way to enjoy summertime Malmö than to settle down under a white umbrella at this quaint cafe, tucked in the middle of the Slottsträgården. Savour the aromas of fennel, herbs and baking while enjoying a delicious sandwich or square of rhubarb crumble with organic vanilla ice cream.

Falafel No 1
FELAFEL €
(☑040-84 41 22; www.falafel-n1.se; Österportsgatan 2; felafel from 65kr; ✓) Malmö residents are so fond of felafel that it even features in songs by local rapper Timbuktu. Falafel No 1 (also known as the Orient House) is a long-standing favourite. Enjoy your chick-pea treat with fresh salad, tomatoes, hot sauce and pickles: delicious!

Dolce Sicilia
ICE CREAM €
(☑040-611 31 10; www.dolcesicilia.se; Drottningtorget 6; ice cream from 30kr; ☺noon-5pm Mon, 11am-7pm Tue-Sun) ✓ Head to Dolce Sicilia, run by certified Sicilians, for fresh, organic, Italian-style gelato with flavours ranging from chilli chocolate to liquorice or forest berry.

★Namu
FUSION €€
(☑040-12 14 90; www.namu.nu; Landbygatan 5; mains 109-225kr; ☺11.30am-2pm & 5-11pm Tue-Thu,

to 1am Fri & Sat) Brainchild of *Masterchef Sweden* winner Jennie Walldén, Namu (meaning 'tree') serves up artfully prepared Korean dishes adapted according to the availability of seasonal local ingredients and presented in surroundings that merge Scandinavian design elements and traditional Korean styling beautifully. The result: a cultural and culinary synergy that fans of either genre won't want to miss.

★**Saltimporten Canteen** SWEDISH €€
(☑070-651 84 26; www.saltimporten.com; Grimsbygatan 24; dagens lunch 95kr; ☺noon-2pm Mon-Fri) This wonderfully minimalist open canteen housed in the old Salt Importing Warehouse, now a haven of creative and design offices, has polished concrete floors and a design palette that emphasizes its harbour views. Each day there's a different set lunch menu, and that's it – and it's almost always executed perfectly.

★**Mrs Saigon** VIETNAMESE €€
(☑040-788 35; www.mrs-saigon.se; Engelbrektsgatan 17; mains 90-130kr; ☺11.30am-3pm & 5.30-11pm Tue-Sat, noon-3pm Mon; ☎) Famed for her superb signature rice-noodle soup spiced with coriander, onion, basil and lime and served with chicken, beef or tofu, Mrs Saigon does her best to impress, and if the throngs of regular locals are any indication, she does. Other Vietnamese specialities include crispy shrimp rolls, homemade fish balls and stir-fried chicken flavoured with curry, lime leaves, lemongrass and chilli.

★**Bastard** EUROPEAN €€
(☑040-12 13 18; www.bastardrestaurant.se; Mäster Johansgatan 11; mains 95-185kr; ☺5pm-midnight Tue-Thu, to 2am Fri & Sat) ☝ This hipster restaurant with possibly the best and hipster-est name anyone has ever thought to call a restaurant is about as close as you'll get to a gastropub in Sweden. It serves predominantly small and share plates, ranging from gourmet meat platters to blackened grilled chicken for two or pizza with snails. The bar is a popular choice with well-heeled locals.

★**Eatery Social Taqueria** MEXICAN €€
(☑040-20 75 00; www.eaterysocial.se/en/; Dag Hammarskjölds Torg 2; small plates 70-165kr; ☺5pm-midnight Mon-Sat, noon-4pm Sun; ☑) This fun, boutique *taqueria* belonging to Swedish celebrity chef Marcus Samuelsson's stable serves the best Tex Mex small plates you'll get this side of Tijuana. All the favourites are there: tacos, quesadillas, tostadas, tequila!

Atmosfär SWEDISH €€
(☑040-12 50 77; www.atmosfar.com; Fersensväg 4; mains 130-185kr; ☺11.30am-11pm Mon-Fri, to 2am Sat; ☎) This classy neighbourhood restaurant changes its menu regularly depending on what's in season, but you can depend on flavourful, innovative combinations such as salads topped with young nasturtium leaves and pike with a fennel, leek and lobster sauce, that offer excellent value for the price. The cocktails (from 105kr) are similarly irresistible. Elderflower fizz, anyone?

Izakaya Koi IZAKAYA €€
(☑040-757 00; www.koi.se; Lilla Torg 5; mains 135-220kr; ☺kitchen noon-10pm Mon-Sat) On heaving Lilla Torget, Koi attracts crowds with excellent cocktails, sushi and other Asian-inspired nibbles. You'll find Malmö's trendsetters in the upstairs lounge, mingling on the dance floor or perched on white leather banquettes looking gorgeous well into the early hours.

Mrs Brown SWEDISH €€
(☑040-97 22 50; www.mrsbrown.nu; Storgatan 26; mains 165-185kr; ☺noon-3.30pm & 5-10.30pm Mon-Fri, 6-10.30pm Sat; ☑) ☝ Demure little Mrs Brown is the kind of neighbourhood place you dream will open up near you. The open kitchen churns out modern Scandinavian home cooking using local and organic ingredients such as Greenland prawns in chilli sauce. Service is attentive but not overbearing and the

dining room is decorated in a minimalist fashion that is both comforting and modish.

Salt & Brygga   BISTRO €€

(☑040-611 59 40; www.saltobrygga.se; Sundspromenaden 7; mains lunch 98-135kr, dinner 175-225kr; ☺11am-2pm & 5-11pm Mon-Fri, 12.30-4pm & 5-11pm Sat; 🔊) 🥢 With an enviable view overlooking the Öresund bridge and the small harbour, this stylish slow-food restaurant presents updated Swedish cuisine with a clear conscience. Everything is organic (including the staff's uniforms), waste is turned into biogas and the interior is allergy-free. Flavours are clean and strictly seasonal.

★ Johan P   SEAFOOD €€€

(☑040-97 18 18; www.johanp.nu; Hjulhamnsgatan 5; mains 225-375kr, 4-course set menu 695kr; ☺11.30am-11pm Mon-Fri, noon-11pm Sat, 1-10pm Sun) Old-timer Johan P continues to enthral diners with its fresh-off-the-boat seafood. Choose your fishy favourite from the market-style counter out back or go for the set menu. There are lovely bisques, *moules meunière* (mussels cooked in wine) and chilled shellfish platters. For snacks, Basque-style *pintxos* (tapas) are available.

Årstiderna i Kockska Huset   SWEDISH €€€

(☑040-23 09 10; www.arstiderna.se; Frans Suellsgatan 3; mains 235-325kr; ☺11.30am-midnight Mon-Fri, 5pm-midnight Sat) This top-notch restaurant serves meals in the vaults beneath Kockska Huset (p171). Food is up-scale Swedish and the atmosphere is classic with crisp-white tablecloths and quietly professional service. When the restaurant is busy, the chatter of your fellow diners reverberating off the vaulted cellar roof can be bothersome.

🍷 Drinking & Nightlife

★ Far i hatten   BAR

(☑040-615 36 51; www.farihatten.se; Folkets Park; ☺5pm-1am Mon-Fri, from 11.30am Sat & Sun, shorter hours winter) Smack bang in the middle of Folkets Park (p175), Far i hatten is a popular summer hang that transforms from smart casual cafe by day into an illuminated alfresco wonderland of an evening. There's a massive beery patio and even a ping-pong table!

★ Lilla Kafferosteriet   CAFE

(☑040-48 20 00; www.lillakafferosteriet.se; Baltzarsgatan 24; sandwiches from 55kr; ☺8am-7pm Mon-Fri, 10am-5pm Sat, 11am-5pm Sun) 🥢 Have a mosey around the warren of atmospheric rooms here before you select your table, or head out to the pretty patio. This is a serious-about-coffee cafe with freshly ground (Fairtrade) beans, plus plenty of sweet and savoury goodies. You may just stay for a while; it's that kind of place.

Bee Kök & Bar   GAY & LESBIAN

(☑031-13 38 39; www.beebar.se; Södra Förstadsgatan 36; ☺11.30am-11pm Mon-Thu, til 1am Fri & Sat, 1-11pm Sun) From the outside Bee looks pretty much like she's still in the closet, but when you walk in, there's a definite fun and free LGBT vibe in the air – which might be the reason why this sister's web profile says she's 'straight' friendly. Find out for yourself: Bee is about 600m north of Triangeln station.

Söder om Småland   BAR

(☑040-616 01 12; www.soderomsmaland.se; Claesgatan 8; ☺5pm-1am Wed-Sat) Depending on how you feel about the whole hipster thing, you'll either love or loathe this very hipstery joint, whose name means 'South of Småland'. The decor is fresh and clean, the beers, IPAs and the occasional live music, random and eclectic. If it's handsome, hairy vikings you seek, search no more.

Grand Öl & Mat   BAR

(☑040-12 63 13; www.grandolomat.se; Monbijougatan 17; ☺10pm-3am Fri & Sat May-Sep) Billed as a meeting place for food, drinks, culture and events, the Grand is a popular late-night weekend venue in summer, with regular cross-genre live performances and DJs, then reverts to more of a cafe-restaurant vibe in the winter months.

Mello Yello   BAR

(☑040-30 45 25; www.melloyello.se; Lilla Torg 1; ☺3.30pm-1am Mon-Fri, from noon Sat & Sun) Located on Lilla Torg, with nice nibbles and an almost always animated atmosphere. Mello Yello serves decent though pricey burgers to go with its impressive cocktail list and occasional live music and DJs.

Victors   COCKTAIL BAR

(☑040-12 76 70; www.victors.se; Lilla Torg 1; ☺11.30am-1am Mon-Thu, til 2am Fri & Sat, til midnight Sun) Appealing to a 30-something and older crowd, Victors does glam cocktails on Lilla Torg with light late-night snacks available to accompany your tipple.

Pickwick Pub   PUB

(☑040-23 32 66; www.pickwickpub.se; Stadt Hamburgsgatan 12; ☺4-10.30pm Mon-Thu, to 1.30am Fri & Sat, to 9.30pm Sun) Friendly, traditional pub with Chesterfield chairs and a cosy fireplace.

☆ Entertainment

★ Malmö Live
CONCERT VENUE

(🖰 040-34 35 00; www.malmolive.se/en; Dag Hammarskjölds Torg 4; ☉ varies by performance) Opened in 2015, Malmö Live is a world-class concert hall and home to the Malmö Symphony Orchestra.

★ Slagthusets Teater
PERFORMING ARTS

(Slaughterhouse Theatre; 🖰 040-611 80 90; www.slagthus.se; Jörgen Kocksgatan 7A; ☉ varies by performance) This former slaughterhouse is a multipurpose venue that hosts anything from concerts to DJs, plays and conferences. Check the website to see what's on when.

Casino Cosmopol
CASINO

(🖰 020-21 92 19; www.casinocosmopol.se; Slottsgatan 33, Kungsparken; ☉ 1pm-4am) One of four legal casinos in Sweden and located in the lovely Kungsparken (p171).

Inkonst
LIVE PERFORMANCE

(🖰 040-30 65 97; www.inkonst.com; Bergsgatan 29; ☉ 11pm-3am) This multifunction cultural hang-out serves up some brilliant club nights, pumping out anything from underground UK grime and garage to hip hop and rhythm and blues. It also stages theatre and dance performances.

Kulturbolaget
LIVE MUSIC

(🖰 040-30 20 11; www.kulturbolaget.se; Friisgatan 26; ☉ varies) Some pretty big names have performed here, but even if there's no one playing, 'KB' has a kicking bar and nightclub (usually Friday and Saturday).

🛍 Shopping

The hot spots for up-and-coming designers and vintage threads are the streets around Davidshallstorg, south of Gamla Staden. Close to here is Triangeln, one of the city's better shopping malls, which has an excellent range of national and international stores and boutiques.

You'll also find a diverse range of shops in the vibrant Västra Hamnen area.

★ Julmarknad i city
MARKET

(Gustav Adolfs torg) For 30 days leading up to 23 December, Malmö's Christmas markets warm the hearts of all who visit. Sip on some mulled wine and they'll warm your insides too!

Form/Design Center
DESIGN

(🖰 040-664 51 50; www.formdesigncenter.com; Lilla Torg 9; ☉ 11am-5pm Tue-Sat, noon-4pm Sun) This is your one-stop shop for all things Scandi-design related: books, homewares, gifts, cards and souvenirs. It's a great place to get gifts for your friends back home – they'll love you for it.

Gustus Butik & Galleri
ART

(www.gustus.se; Lilla Torg 9; ☉ 11am-6pm Mon-Fri, to 4pm Sat & Sun; 🕾) This delightful shop and gallery showcases primarily Swedish and Danish artists; the upstairs gallery is set in an atmospheric beamed room that dates back over 400 years. Although the exhibition changes every three months, the art here is generally contemporary, including sculpture in various mediums including wood, glass and ceramics. The shop sells unusual jewellery, prints, glassware and similar.

Prices are reasonable; the owner is committed to providing young talented artists a commercial outlet for their work.

Malmö Modern
HOMEWARES

(🖰 040-30 00 86; www.malmomodern.se; Skeppsbron 3; ☉ 11am-6pm Mon-Fri, to 3pm Sat) Scandinavian design really does have that certain something. Check out the homewares, fabrics, clocks, clothes and all sorts of idiosyncratic and thought-provoking dust collectors for your shelves back home.

Love Street Vintage
VINTAGE

(Kärleksgatan 15; ☉ noon-6pm Tue-Fri, to 4pm Sat) A glorious packed-to-the-rafters shop selling everything from beaded bags to denim jackets, boas, jewellery and '50s-style crockery.

Formargruppen
ARTS & CRAFTS

(🖰 040-780 60; www.formargruppen.se; Engelbrektsgatan 8; ☉ 11am-6pm Mon-Fri, to 4pm Sat) Representing a collective of Swedish artists, artisans and designers, this central shop-gallery stocks striking wares, from ceramics and pottery to jewellery and textiles.

ℹ Information

DANGERS & ANNOYANCES

There's been some degree of media hype about crime being on the rise but, by world standards, Malmö remains a safe place for travellers to visit. Exercise the usual precautions.

➡ It's not uncommon to see large groups of men conglomerating in squares and around station areas, day and night.

➡ At night, use your common sense when walking in the area around Triangeln subway or in dimly lit lanes between Gamla Staden to Västra Hamnen.

MEDICAL SERVICES

You can call the dentist and doctor on duty on 🖰 1177.

Akutklinik (☑ 1813; Eentrance 36, Södra Förstadsgatan 101) Emergency ward at the general hospital.

Apotek Gripen (☑ 0771-45 04 50; Bergsgatan 48; ⊙ 8am-10pm) After-hours pharmacy.

TOURIST INFORMATION

In 2017 Malmö closed its tourist-information offices due to increasing numbers of visitors sourcing their own information on the web or using the number of touch-screen tourist-information kiosks located around town. The official homepage (www.malmotown.com) is still operational but is mainly a placeholder with links to other sites.

Travel Shop (☑ 040-33 05 70; www.travel shop.se; Carlsgatan 4A; ⊙ 9am-5pm Mon-Fri, 10am-3pm Sat & Sun) North of Malmö Centralstationen, sells tickets for bus and train companies, as well as offering a wide range of tours, bike rental (per 24 hours 150kr) and help with accommodation. There's also an official touch-screen Tourist InfoPoint located here.

Visit Skåne (www.visitskane.com) Provincial tourist board for the Skåne region.

ⓘ Getting There & Away

AIR

Most visitors arriving in Malmö by air will fly into Denmark's **Copenhagen Airport** (☑ 32 31 32 31; www.cph.dk; Lufthavnsboulevarden, Kastrup; Ⓜ Lufthavnen, Ⓢ Københavns Lufthavn) for its vast network of connections to Europe, North America and Asia and it's excellent transport connections to downtown Malmö.

Malmö Sturup Airport (☑ 010-109 45 00; www.swedavia.com/malmo; Malmö-Sturup) is a relatively small international and domestic terminal with limited facilities. Located some 33km southeast of Malmö, it's serviced primarily by **SAS** (☑ 0770-727 727; www.sas.se), with up to eight daily flights to/from Stockholm Arlanda, and low-cost domestic carrier **BRA** (☑ 0771-44 00 10; www.flygbra.se), with daily flights to Stockholm Bromma and a number of domestic destinations, including Visby on Gotland.

BUS

Malmö is easy to reach via bus from other major towns and cities in Sweden. The excellent Resrobot website (www.kopbiljett.resrobot.se) has the nation covered for fares and timetables.

Skånetrafiken (p189) operates Skåne's regional bus and train networks (the latter known as Pågatågen).

All local (around town) and regional buses depart from the **bays** (p182) outside Centralstation's main and west exits. Take bus 146 if you're heading to the ferries departing from Trelleborg (75kr, 40 minutes) and bus 100 for Falsterbo (75kr, one hour). Both services run once or twice hourly.

Most bus companies offer easy online ticketing, but if you'd like to ask a service representative or pay in cash, stop in to **Travelshop**.

Swebus (☑ 0771-21 82 18; www.swebus.se) operates regular direct services to Stockholm (from 279kr, 8½ hours, two to four daily), Jönköping (from 219kr, 4½ hours, four daily), Gothenburg (from 119kr, 3¼ hours, up to four daily) and Oslo (Norway; from 259kr, eight hours). Cheaper fares are often available online during spot sales.

Eurolines (www.eurolines.com) runs a daily service to/from London.

The **long-distance** (Norra Vallgatan 58) bus stop is in front of (and over the canal from) Malmö Centralstation.

CAR & MOTORCYCLE

Several car-hire companies, including **Avis** (☑ 0770-82 00 82; www.avis.com) and **Hertz** (☑ 0771-51 52 52; www.hertz.com), are represented at Sturup airport.

Parking in the city is expensive: typical charges start at 20kr per hour or 160kr per 24 hours. Most hotels also charge for parking. The most central large-scale parking lot is the **Bagers plats carpark** (per hr/day 25/180kr; ⊙ 24hr).

TRAIN

Pågatågen (local trains) operated by **Skåne-trafiken** (p189) run regularly to Helsingborg (118kr, from 40 minutes), Landskrona (99kr, 30 minutes), Lund (63kr, 10 minutes), Simrishamn (118kr, 1½ hours), Ystad (99kr, 50 minutes) and other towns in Skåne. Bicycles are half-fare but are not allowed during peak times except from mid-June to mid-August.

SJ Rail (p170) operates several trains per day to/from Gothenburg (from 206kr, 2½ hours) and Stockholm (417kr, 4½ hours, hourly) also servicing many intermediary stations in central Sweden.

Baggage lockers at Malmö Centralstation start at 30kr per 24 hours.

Local operator **Snälltåget** (☑ 0771-26 00 00; www.snalltaget.se/en; Norra vallgatan 34) stepped in to start up a new and alternative night train to Berlin, when Deutsche Bahn pulled their service in 2015. A bed in a six-berth sleeper car (three departures a week in each direction) costs 399kr and the carriages are delightfully old-worldy. If you don't want to share, you can rent the whole compartment for 1999kr – a great deal if you're travelling with two or three friends. At the time of writing the service was only operational from May to September, but check the website for detailed timetables and updates.

ⓘ Getting Around

Most of Malmö's sights can be easily reached by foot, though the city has an extensive network of public buses and trains which can be useful for more thorough explorations of the city.

In 2010 the Citytunneln opened giving Malmö three new subway stations – Malmö Centralstation, Triangeln and Hyllie – allowing for through travel from Malmö to Copenhagen airport and quick and convenient access to Malmö's outer-lying suburbs, including the bustling Triangeln shopping district and the up-and-coming Hyllie area. Rail is the most convenient way to reach these two areas.

The **Skånetrafiken** (p189) public transport system operates in zones, with a single journey within the city costing 25kr. The **local & regional** bus bays are outside Malmö Centralstation.

Aside from **Flygbussarna** (🖉 0771-51 52 52; www.flygbussarna.se; ⊙ customer service line 8am-11pm) you can't buy public transport tickets onboard buses or trains, but they can be conveniently purchased using the Skånetrafiken app for your smartphone, at ticket machines or at the **Skånetrafiken** (p189) offices at Centralstaion and Triangeln station. Cheaper one- and three-day passes (p182) are available.

Malmö is extremely bike-friendly: both **Travel Shop** (p181) and **Rundan** (p176) offer rentals, or you can get free rentals if you stay at the city's unique **Ohboy Hotell** (p176) using the **Malmö by Bike** (www.malmobybike.se; 24-/72hr rental 65/180kr) service. Malmö by Bike has stations located around the city; go to its website or download the app to rent bikes.

Malmö's taxis have been known to overcharge visitors. Two reputable operators are **Taxi Skåne** (🖉 040-33 03 30; www.taxiskane.com) and **Taxi 97** (🖉 040-97 97 97; www.taxi97.se).

PUBLIC TRANSPORT PASSES

If you are planning on travelling around Malmö by public transport, consider buying a 24- or 72-hour Timmarsbijett (65/165kr) offering unlimited public transport (buses and trains) within the service area for the duration of the ticket. And yes, Skånetrafiken inspectors check tickets vigilantly.

TO/FROM MALMÖ STURUP AIRPORT

Flygbussarna runs regular scheduled shuttles to/from **Malmö Sturup Airport** (p181) and Centralstation (adult/child one way 115/95kr) roughly every 40 minutes on weekdays, with six services on Saturday and seven on Sunday. Tickets can be purchased at a ticket machine at the bus stop, online, or on the bus, but it's cheaper to purchase online and tickets can only be purchased onboard with a credit card, no cash.

A taxi to/from the airport will set you back around 500kr.

TO/FROM COPENHAGEN AIRPORT

Up to four trains per hour run from the airport to/from Malmö Centralstation (Dkr89/118kr, 35 minutes) and beyond. Ensure that you have your passport as trains are occasionally stopped and inspected by visa and customs officials on the Swedish side.

All of the main car-rental providers have offices at the airport and it can sometimes be cheaper to rent your car from here than in Malmö, but beware: crossing the **Öresund Bridge** (p175) in both directions might be an experience, but it isn't exactly cheap (standard vehicle 520kr).

Getting a taxi across the bridge will set you back a cool 800kr – you're better off getting the train.

Lund

🖉 046 / POP 118,542

Founded by the Danes around 1000 AD, Lund is the second-oldest city in Sweden. Surrounded by copses of beech trees and with an impressive architectural legacy, it just might be the loveliest. Lund's magnificent, medieval old town – centred upon its strikingly beautiful cathedral, around which Sweden's oldest, most prestigious university (c1666) radiates – is up there with the best.

Once the seat of the largest archbishopric in Europe, the city today has a much more low-key, out-of-the-limelight vibe, which helps make it feel so special. The beauty of its old bones and a throng of engaged youth drive a lively arts and culinary scene.

Just a few hundred metres from the station, the old town's endlessly photogenic lanes reveal a clutch of impressive museums, cafes and bars spilling over the cobbles, and soft, leafy parks.

Lund is an essential day trip from Malmö and an excellent base for stays in Skåne.

⊙ Sights

For a relatively small town, Lund has an impressive number of noteworthy sights, including the grand total of four museums, ranging from a huge open-air museum to a gloomy crypt (part of the archeological museum) complete with skeletons dating from the Middle Ages. On a lighter note, there are also numerous galleries and small, special-interest museums and archives dotted around town, many attached to university departments; the tourist office can provide more information.

★**Lunds domkyrka**   CATHEDRAL
(🖉 046-35 87 42; www.lundsdomkyrka.se; Kyrkogatan; ⊙ 8am-6pm Mon-Fri, 9.30am-5pm Sat, 9.30am-6pm Sun) Lund's twin-towered Romanesque cathedral is magnificent. Try

Lund

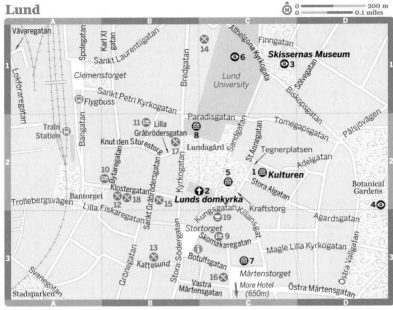

Lund

◎ Top Sights

1 Kulturen	C2
2 Lunds domkyrka	C2
3 Skissernas Museum	C1

◎ Sights

4 Botanical Gardens	D2
Drottens kyrkoruin	(see 13)
5 Historiska Museet	C2
6 Lund University	C1
7 Lundskonsthall	C3
8 Universitetshuset	B2

⬚ Sleeping

9 Hotel Ahlström	C3

10 Hotell Oskar	B2
11 Winstrup Hostel	B2

⊗ Eating

12 Crêperiet	B2
13 Gattostretto	B3
14 Govindas	C1
15 Klostergatans Vin & Delikatess	B2
16 Malmstens Fisk & Köj	C3
17 Mat & Destillat	B2
Saluhallen	(see 16)
18 St Jakobs Stenugnsbageri	B2

◉ Drinking & Nightlife

19 Café Ariman	C3

to pop in at noon or 3pm (plus 1pm on Sunday and holidays) when the marvellous astronomical clock strikes up 'In Dulci Jubilo' (a traditional Christmas carol) and the wooden figures at the top whirr into action. Within the crypt, you'll find Finn, the mythological giant who helped construct the cathedral, and a 16th-century well, carved with comical scenes.

★**Kulturen**   MUSEUM
(☑046-35 04 00; www.kulturen.com; Tegnerplatsen; adult May-Aug 120kr, Sep-Apr 90kr, child free; ⊙10am-5pm May-Aug, noon-4pm Tue-Sun Sep-

Apr; ♿) Kulturen, opened in 1892, is a huge open-air museum filling two whole blocks. Its 30-odd buildings include everything from the meanest birch-bark hovel to grand 17th-century houses. Permanent displays encompass Lund in the Middle Ages, vintage toys, ceramics, silver and glass (among many others); ask about guided tours in English. The popular outdoor cafe flanks several rune stones.

★**Skissernas Museum**   ARTS CENTRE
(Sketch Museum; ☑046-222 72 83; www.skissernas museum.se; Finngatan 2; adult/child 80/60kr;

SKÅNELEDEN TRAIL

The Skåneleden trail has Skåne covered, and by covered we mean more than 1000km of groomed walking trails, broken down into five sub-trails with a total of 89 sections. It's up hill and down dale, alongside babbling brooks, through golden fields past sparkling lakes into green forests, charming medieval villages and onto sandy shores! To see what the hype is all about and choose which bits you want to walk, log on to the trail's comprehensive website: www.skaneleden.se.

⊙ noon-5pm Tue & Thu-Sun, to 9pm Wed) The exhibition rooms here, with their visual feast of paintings and sculpture, are designed for maximum impact and art immersion. Several sculptures and installations are huge, including the 6m-high *Women by the Sea* by Ivar Johnsson. Formerly a private collection, it includes works by some of the world's greats, including Joan Miró, Henri Matisse, Raoul Dufy, Sonia Delaunay and Fernand Léger. A sculpture park includes pieces by Henry Moore.

Lundskonsthall   GALLERY
(⏲ 046-35 52 95; www.lundskonsthall.se; Mårtenstorget 3; ⊙ noon-5pm Wed, Fri, Sat & Sun, to 8pm Tue & Thu) FREE This contemporary art space has cutting-edge exhibitions, including Tate Modern–style installations and other forms of creative art.

Lund University   UNIVERSITY
(www.lunduniversity.lu.se; Sandgatan) Lund University is ranked as one of the world's top 100 universities and is one of Europe's oldest institutions for education. It's buildings are scattered about the city making it largely 'barrier-free' with the lines between campus and Lund's old town delightfully blurred.

Universitetshuset   HISTORIC BUILDING
(University House; cnr Kyrkogatan & Paradisgatan) The main university building, topped by four sphinxes representing the original faculties, looks a little bit like the White House. It's often spectacularly and colourfully illuminated at night.

Drottens kyrkoruin   MUSEUM
(⏲ 046-14 13 28; Kattesund 6A; ⊙ 9am-6pm Mon-Thu, 10am-6pm Fri & Sat) FREE Subterranean Drottens kyrkoruin contains the foundations of an 11th-century church, as well as a grisly collection of skeletons that build a picture of the Middle Ages through their diseases and amputations!

Historiska Museet   MUSEUM
(History Museum; ⏲ 046-222 79 44; www.luhm.lu.se; Kraftstorg; 60kr; ⊙ 11am-4pm Tue-Fri, noon-4pm Sun) Behind the cathedral, the Historiska Museet has a large collection of pre–Viking Age finds, including a 7000-year-old skeleton. It's joined with **Domkyrkomuseet**, which explores the history of the Church in the area; the rooms filled with countless statues of the crucified Christ are supremely creepy.

Botanical Gardens   GARDENS
(⏲ 046-222 73 20; www.botaniskatradgarden.se; Östra Vallgatan 20; ⊙ 6am-9.30pm) FREE The 8-hectare Botanical Gardens, east of the town centre, feature around 7000 species and nine climate zones. The tropical greenhouses are open from 11am to 3pm.

🛏 Sleeping

Curiously, despite the number of students here (and the number of visiting parents...) there's not a surplus of accommodation, particularly in the budget range. There are, however, some beautiful, high-end hotels which are worth the investment if such things make you happy. The Lund Tourist Center (p186) can also assist with arranging a private room from 300kr per person, plus a 50kr booking fee.

Winstrup Hostel   HOSTEL €
(⏲ 0723-29 08 00 08; www.winstruphostel.se; Winstrupsgatan 3; dm 395kr, breakfast 95kr, towel purchase 70kr; 🛜) The dorm accommodation here is imaginatively designed for added privacy; beds are essentially cubby hole–style spaces, accessed by a respective short ladder. The whole place has a sparkling contemporary look.

★**Hotell Oskar**   BOUTIQUE HOTEL €€
(⏲ 046-18 80 85; www.hotelloskar.se; Bytaregatan 3; s/d from 995/1195kr; @🛜) Tucked away in a petite 19th-century townhouse, this central hotel has superb rooms reflecting sleek Scandi design. It's also well equipped, with DVD players, kettles and stereos, plus it has a pretty back garden. The adjacent cafe is handy for coffee and cake.

More Hotel   APARTMENT €€
(www.themorehotel.se/en/Lund; Kastanjegatan 18; studios from 895kr; P 🛜) This smart aparthotel occupying a former railway shed has a variety of self-contained studios and apartments

that are spacious and modern. It's popular with families visiting their kids at university and offers excellent value. Long-stay rates are available.

Hotel Ahlström HISTORIC HOTEL €€
(✏046-211 01 74; www.hotellahlstrom.se; Skomakaregatan 3; s/d without bathroom from 695/875kr, r with bathroom from 995kr; 🖤) Lund's oldest hotel is friendly and affordable, and on a quiet, central street. Rooms have parquet floors, cool white walls and washbasins (most bathrooms are shared). Breakfast is brought to your door. On the downside, some readers have complained of a whiff of drains.

🍴 Eating & Drinking

⭐**St Jakobs Stenugnsbageri** BAKERY €
(✏046-13 70 60; www.stjakobs.se; Klostergatan 9; baked goods 20-55kr; ⊙8am-6pm Mon-Fri, to 4pm Sat, to 3pm Sun) Mouth-watering is the only way to describe the selection of stone-baked breads, knotted cardamom rolls, melt-in-your-mouth coconut-lemon towers and crisp sugar cookies overflowing from the countertops and baking trays at St Jakobs. During the summer you're likely to see an enormous bowl of strawberries at the centre of it all, served with fresh cream, of course.

⭐**Govindas** VEGETARIAN €
(✏046-12 04 13; Bredgatan 28; lunch 70kr; ⊙11.30am-3.30pm Mon-Fri, closed Jul; 🌶) 🍃 In a quiet, leafy cobbled courtyard, vegetarian Govindas is a hit with kronor-conscious students and anyone craving a spicy curry and cool raita. Much of the produce is organically grown by the charming owner.

Crêperiet FRENCH €
(✏072-362 85 30; www.creperiet.nu; Klostergatan 14; crêpes 65-105kr; ⊙7am-9pm Mon-Sat, to 8pm Sun; 🍴) This laid-back stop, with its handful of tables and stripped-back decor, produces superb *galettes* with an imaginative combo of ingredients including creamed spinach, brie, sundried tomatoes and walnuts, plus the safe standards of cheese, ham and crème fraiche. The sweet crêpes go way beyond the ubiquitous Nutella, with choices such as Rosseau with cinnamon, apples, ice cream and a generous splash of Calvados.

Saluhallen FOOD HALL €
(www.lundssaluhall.se; Mårtenstorget; small plates 40-95kr; ⊙10am-6pm Mon-Wed, to 7pm Thu & Fri, 9.30am-3pm Sat) This mouth-watering market hall sells reasonably priced grub, from fresh fish and piping-hot pasta to Thai, kebabs and croissants. In addition to its storefront offerings, six smart-casual restaurants are housed in its annexe.

Café Ariman CAFE
(www.ariman.se; Kungsgatan 2B; ⊙11am-midnight Mon, to 1am Tue, Wed & Thu, to 3am Fri & Sat, 3-11pm Sun) Head to this hip, grungy hang-out for cathedral views, strong coffee and fine cafe fare such as ciabattas, salads and burritos. It's popular with left-wing students: think nose-rings, dreads and leisurely chess games. From September to May, DJs hit the decks on Friday and Saturday nights.

Malmstens Fisk & Köj SEAFOOD €€
(✏046-12 63 54; www.malmstensfisk.se; Saluhallen, Mårtenstorget; mains 145-205kr; ⊙11.30am-6pm Mon-Wed, to 7pm Thu, to 10pm Fri & Sat) Locals swear the seafood here is the best in town. Tucked into a classy corner in the gourmet market, the menu is reassuringly brief, depending on what is fresh that day. If you're just a tad peckish, go for a simple starter such as mussels in white wine with parsley or the signature Malmstens fish soup with bread and aioli.

Gattostretto ITALIAN €€
(✏046-32 07 77; www.gattostretto.se; Kattesund 6A; lunch 90kr, mains 139-205kr; ⊙11.30am-9pm Mon-Sat) Located over medieval ruins and co-run by an affable Roman chef, this breezy cafe-restaurant serves a tasty slice of *dolce vita*. Guzzle down proper Italian espresso and a slice of *torta rustica* (a 'rustic pie' stuffed with meat, cheese and vegetables), or long for Rome over hearty *ragù* (meat sauce) pasta or tri-coloured bruschetta.

Klostergatans Vin & Delikatess EUROPEAN €€
(✏046-14 14 83; www.klostergatan.se; Klostergatan 3; dinner mains 125-249kr; ⊙11am-3pm & 5-9pm Mon-Thu, to 11.30pm Fri, noon-4pm Sat.) A French-style wine bar and delicatessen, ideal for a quick bite or for a longer meal, complete with crisp white tablecloths and a glass of the house wine. The menu definitely has a Gallic influence, using local ingredients. Its adjacent sister bakery, Patisseriet, has lovely cakes, coffees and sandwiches.

⭐**Mat & Destillat** SWEDISH €€€
(✏046-12 80 00; www.matochdestillat.se; Kyrkogatan 17; mains 129-279kr; ⊙noon-midnight Mon-Sat; 🍴) This high-end experimental kitchen and cocktail bar is turning heads on the Scanian culinary circuit for its artful, inventive

locavore dishes offering modern twists on Swedish classics. It's also a popular spot for classy cocktails with superb bar snacks.

❶ Information

Lund Tourist Centre (☎ 046-35 50 40; www.lund.se; Botulfsgatan 1A; ⓧ 10am-6pm Mon-Fri, to 2pm Sat) Located at the southern end of Stortorget, with an excellent range of information about Lund. It can help with sourcing accommodation if you're stuck for a bed for the night and can provide you with a handy map of town, as well as a map that shows bicycle routes.

❶ Getting There & Away

Lund is just 21km northeast of Malmö by road or rail. Frequent trains and buses make the journey between the two cities.

It takes just 15 minutes from Lund to Malmö by train (63kr) and some trains run to Copenhagen Airport in less than 35 minutes (147kr). Other direct services include Kristianstad (118kr, 50 minutes) and Karlskrona (241kr, 2½ hours).

All long-distance trains operated by **SJ Rail** (p170) from Stockholm or Gothenburg en-route to Malmö, stop in Lund.

FlixBus (☎ 0850-51 37 50; www.flixbus.se) operates daily services to Gothenburg (49kr, 3¾ hours) and Stockholm (from 299kr, eight hours).

Flygbuss (☎ 0771-77 77 77; www.flygbussarna.se) operates services to Malmö's Sturup Airport.

Helsingborg

☎ 042 / POP 106,388

At its heart, Helsingborg boasts a showcase of rejuvenated waterfront restaurants, lofty castle ruins and lively cobblestone streets, which in summer, thrive to the beat of a banging cultural drum: Helsingborg is a proud patron of theatre and the arts, and lovers of either discipline will find like-minded people here.

Perhaps this longing for creative expression stems from the fact that its strategic position on the Öresund, a mere 4km from Denmark, saw Helsingborg battled over with ferocious regularity during the many Swedish–Danish wars, until in 1710 Danish invaders were finally defeated just outside the city.

In this historical context it's easier to get a sense of the brazen statement the architects of Helsingborg's wealth of flouncy, turreted, buildings might have been making, and a happy denouement that today, almost 15 million passengers traverse the waterway shared by the city and its Danish counterpart Helsingør, with friendly, seasoned nonchalance.

◉ Sights

★ Fredriksdal museer och trädgårdar
MUSEUM

(Fredriksdal Museum and Gardens; ☎ 042-10 45 00; www.fredriksdal.se; off Hävertgatan; adult/child May-Sep 70kr/free, Oct-Mar free; ⓧ 10am-6pm May-Sep, shorter hours rest of year; P ♿) One of Sweden's best open-air museums, based around an 18th-century manor house (not open to the public), the houses and shops you see here once graced the streets of central Helsingborg; they were moved here, brick by brick, in the 1960s. Thankfully, this is no contrived theme park; the whole place is charming and there's plenty of scope for souvenir shopping at the art and craft workshops. There are also herb, rose and vegetable gardens and blissfully leafy grounds.

★ Dunkers Kulturhus
MUSEUM

(☎ 42 10 74 00; www.dunkerskulturhus.se; Kungsgatan 11; exhibition prices vary; ⓧ 8am-6pm Mon-Fri, from 10am Sat & Sun) Just north of the transport terminal, the crisp white Dunkers Kulturhus houses an interesting town museum (free) and temporary exhibitions (admission varies), plus a concert hall, an urbane cafe and a design-savvy gift shop and school of the arts. The building's creator, Danish architect Kim Utzon, is the son of Sydney Opera House architect Jørn Utzon.

Toy World
MUSEUM

(☎ 042-453 97 00; www.toyworld.se; Kullagatan 12; 60kr; ⓧ noon-5pm Wed-Fri, til 4pm Sat & Sun; P ♿) We think you'll be hard-pressed to find an adult who won't also enjoy this dinky collection of toys and games from around the world – there's something to whisk almost everyone back to the carefree days of youth. The admission price includes a small toy – kids love it!

Kärnan
RUINS

(☎ 042-10 50 00; www.helsingborg.se/karnan; Slottshagsgatan; adult/child 50kr/free; ⓧ 10am-6pm Jun-Aug, closed Mon rest of year) Dramatic steps and archways lead up from Stortorget to the square tower Kärnan (34m), all that remains of the medieval castle. The castle became Swedish property during the 17th-century Danish-Swedish War, and was mostly demolished once the fighting stopped. The tower was restored from its derelict state in 1894, and the view is regal indeed.

Sofiero
GARDENS

(☎ 042-10 25 00; www.sofiero.se; Sofierovägen; adult/child 100kr/free; ⓧ park 10am-6pm, palace &

Helsingborg

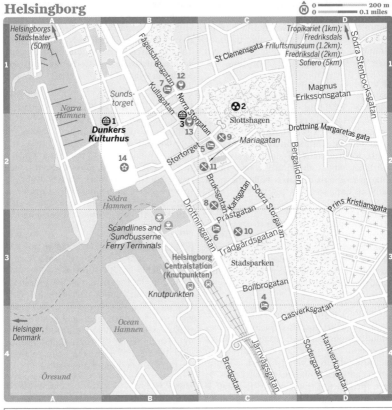

Helsingborg

orangery 11am-6pm; P ♿) Located about 5km north of Helsingborg, Sofiero is an impressive former royal summer residence and park with wonderful rhododendrons (best seen in full bloom in May and June) and occasional big-name summer gigs, the likes of Bob Dylan.

🛏 Sleeping

★ **Elite Hotel Mollberg** HOTEL €€
(☎042-37 37 00; www.elite.se/helsingborg/mollberg; 18 Stortorget; d/ste from 846/1272kr; 🛜) This grand old dame has been lovingly maintained and updated although it has changed management many times over the

MALMÖ & THE SOUTH HELSINGBORG

years. The current team runs a tight ship, which means great-value rooms and the chance to experience a wonderful historic hotel without suffering through painfully out-of-date decor or ridiculously overpriced rates. The Mollberg is a happy medium.

★ V Hotel HOTEL €€
(☑ 042-14 44 20; www.vhotel.se; Fågelsångsgatan 1; s/d from 995/1395kr; P @ ⓩ) Trendy and urbane, this hipster hotel sets the tone from the get-go with velvet cushions, modern bookshelves and brass candlesticks decorating the lobby. Rooms are similarly chic and stylish, although they do vary considerably: some are swing-a-cat size, while the most luxurious has a spa.

Comfort Hotel Nouveau HOTEL €€
(☑ 042-37 19 50; www.nordicchoicehotels.se/hotell/sverige/helsingborg/comfort-hotel-nouveau/; Gasverksgatan 11; d from 895kr; ⓩ) This good-value, central hotel is popular with a younger crowd for it's quirky, stylish rooms, including Scandi-design elements.

Hotel Maria HOTEL €€
(☑ 042-24 99 40; www.hotelmaria.se; Mariagatan 8A; s/d from 900/1150kr; P @ ⓩ) Tucked away behind Olsons Skafferi restaurant, Hotel Maria is utterly inspired, with each room flaunting a different historical style. Themes include national romantic, art deco and '70s disco. Beds are divinely comfy, the staff is friendly and there's a tapas bar downstairs.

Hotell Linnéa HOTEL €€
(☑ 042-37 24 00; www.hotell-linnea.se; Prästgatan 4; d from 650kr; P @ ⓩ) Linnéa is super-central and has a pretty, small courtyard for catching the rays, as well as a cosy library. The carpeted, mildly corporate-looking rooms are spacious and well equipped with kettle and minibar.

✖ Eating

Globetrotter FUSION €
(☑ 042-37 18 00; www.theglobetrotter.se; Stortorget 20; small plates 35-85kr; ⓧ 5-10pm Sun-Thu, to 1am Fri & Sat; ⓩ) These beautifully presented gastro-Asian tapas and mains hit the spot and, combined with the mood music and superb Stortorget people-watching potential from the terrace, make it hard to get a table at weekends.

★ Ebbas Fik CAFE €€
(☑ 042-28 14 40; www.ebbasfik.se; Bruksgatan 20; mains 85-169kr; ⓧ 9am-6pm Mon-Fri, to 4pm Sat; ⓩ) It's still 1955 at this kitsch-tastic cafe, complete

with jukebox (1kr), retro petrol pump and hamburgers made to Elvis' recipe. You can also buy '50s memorabilia here, ranging from vinyl records to Enid Blyton books (in Swedish!). The extensive cafe menu also includes sandwiches, baked potatoes, Coca-Cola floats and American-style pie.

Via 95 BISTRO €€
(☑ 042 13 21 00; www.via95.se; 95 Drottninggatan; mains 145-325kr; ⓧ 11am-10pm) While Via 95 could equally be listed under 'Drinking' for its wonderful waterfront outlook that on a sunny day lends itself to that, it's a top spot to go for 'after work' (5pm to 9pm) small plates: mussels, calamari, buckets of shrimp (prawns). The dinner menu features steak, seafood and burgers all done well and/or well done. Did we mention the cocktails?

Olsons Skafferi ITALIAN €€
(☑ 042-14 07 80; www.olsonsskafferi.se; Mariagatan 6; mains 129-259kr; ⓧ 11am-5.30pm & 7.30-11pm Mon-Sat; ⓩ) Olsons is a super little spot, with alfresco seating on the pedestrian square right in front of Mariakyrkan. It doubles as an Italian deli and cafe, with rustic good looks, spangly chandeliers and pasta that would make Bologna proud. Be sure to finish things off in proper Italian fashion with Vino Santo and *cantuccini* (almond biscotti). Lunch is more economical.

Merry Widow HUNGARIAN €€€
(☑ 042-21 45 22; www.hungarian-restaurant.com; 29 Bruksgatan; mains 185-305kr; ⓧ 6-10pm Mon-Sat) For something a little out of the ordinary, this fabulously authentic restaurant serves hearty Hungarian fare – and when we say hearty we mean portion sizes are on the food-coma-inducing end of the scale. We're talking pork medallions, goulash and of course, schnitzel. Vegetarians will want to keep walking.

ⓘ Drinking & Entertainment

Bara Vara BAR
(☑ 042-24 52 52; www.baravara.eu; Fågelsångsgatan 2; ⓧ 11.30am-2pm & 5.30pm-1am Tue-Fri, 6pm-1am Sat; ⓩ) This very fashionable bar with outside seating, uber-stylish decor and a great wine list is also a reputable though pricey restaurant.

Madame Moustache BAR
(☑ 042-14 79 50; www.madamemoustache.se; Norra Storgatan 9; ⓧ 5pm-1.30am Thu-Sat) If you like your bars with atmosphere you can't go past this classic in a historic half-timbered building; sitting rooms are suitably 'period' with chintzy furniture, shelves of antiquated

books, museum-piece wirelesses and similar. It's complemented by a streetside courtyard centred on a bubbling fountain.

Tivoli CONCERT VENUE

(✆ 042-18 71 71; www.thetivoli.nu; Kungsgatan 1; ⊙ 11pm-late Wed-Sat) Down by the harbour, the Tivoli is Helsingborg's most enduring and multi-purpose venue: sometimes nightclub, sometimes live house, almost always at the heart of the weekend's best events. Check the website for what's on when.

ℹ Information

At time of writing the local tourist office had recently closed and was not planning to reopen.

Friendly staff now roam the area's key attractions and there's an automated information point at Helsingborg Centralstation. Otherwise, you can use the city-wide free wi-fi to log on to www.visithelsingborg.com and chat with a live representative or find the location of the nearest roaming tourist information officer. Neat idea!

ℹ Getting There & Away

Helsingborg is a major hub. The waterfront **Knutpunkten** complex is where ferries, buses and **SJ Rail** (p170) trains arrive and depart.

BOAT

Knutpunkten (Drottninggatan) is the terminal for the **Scandlines** (✆ 042-18 61 00; www.scandlines.se) car ferry to Helsingør. There are five different boats, three have the Scandlines mark, while the other two are branded HH ferries. The one-way journey for a car under 6m, including driver, is 480kr. As a foot passenger, the fare is adult/child 36/22kr.

Sundbusserne (✆ +45 53 73 70 10; www.sundbusserne.se; adult/child 38/24kr), a Danish line, also operates from the terminal, using smaller, passenger-only ferries (adult/child 45/30kr)

BUS

Helsingborg Bus Terminal is located on the ground level of **Knutpunkten**.

Skånetrafiken (✆ 0771-77 77 77; www.skanetrafiken.se) operates local and regional bus services throughout the Skåne region.

Swebus (p181) runs north to Gothenburg, continuing on to Oslo, and south to Malmö. It also operates services northeast to Stockholm via Jönköping and Norrköping. Fares to Stockholm start at 469kr (7½ hours), to Gothenburg 139kr (three hours) and to Oslo as low as 249kr (seven hours) if you book in advance.

TRAIN

Underground platforms in **Knutpunkten** (p189) serve regular **SJ Rail** (p170) services to destinations including Stockholm (from 523kr, five hours), Gothenburg (343kr, 2¼ hours), Lund (99kr, 30 minutes), Malmö (118kr, 40 minutes) and Kristianstad (118kr, 1½ hours).

ℹ Getting Around

Bike hire is available at **Travelshop** (✆ 042-12 70 20; www.travelshop.se; Knutpunkten; bike rental per day/week 120/550kr; ⊙ 9.30am-7pm), located at the bus station at Knutpunkten.

Skanetrafiken (p189) local buses cost 25kr per ride. A variety of ticket options are available.

Taxi Helsingborg (✆ 042- 217 217; www.taxi-helsingborg-217217.se) can help when you need a taxi, or download the MyTaxi app.

Kulla Peninsula

Skåne's wind-battered northwest coast is a seductive brew of golden light, artisan studios and sleepy villages set against the backdrop of steep cliffs, rolling fields and lush green forests. If elves and faeries did exist, you'd find them here for sure. A short distance from Malmö and an even shorter hop from Helsingborg, the Kulla Peninsula feels half a world away.

There's not much to do here but 'be', but that's half the appeal. Ask any of the local artists and they'll tell you that this is a special, intimate place that gives you the opportunity to get to know yourself or another better. Bring a book, your favourite snuggly clothes and leave your troubles behind.

ℹ Getting There & Away

Rte 111 runs from Helsingborg for about 37km to the tip of the peninsula, beyond Mölle.

Skånetrafiken operates regular bus services to these little towns making them easy to get to even though you'll feel world's away when you're there.

Höganäs

✆ 042 / POP 25,847

Gateway to the Kulla Peninsula, the coal-mining town of Höganäs (21km north of Helsingborg) harbours a handful of arty sites that are worth seeing – most notably Sweden's best-known pottery factory. Most visitors stop by on their way to Mölle, 12km further north, and the eastern coast of the Kulla peninsula.

◉ Sights

Höganäs has an interesting posse of public art, liberally sprinkled around town. Two of the most entertaining works are a family of

MALMÖ & THE SOUTH KULLA PENINSULA

pigs on Storgatan and a levitating dog on Köpmansgatan.

Höganäs Museum & Konsthall MUSEUM

(🖉042-34 13 35; www.hoganasmuseum.se; Polhemsgatan 1; adult/child 60kr/free; ⊘1-5pm Tue-Sun, closed Jan) Art lovers should head to this fascinating museum where the highlight is a brilliant collection of witty, exquisitely humane sculptures from home-grown artist Åke Holm.

🛍 Shopping

Fabriksbutik Höganäs
Saltglaserat CERAMICS

(🖉042-32 76 55; www.saltglaserat.com; Bruksgatan 36; ⊘10am-6pm Mon-Fri, 11am-4pm Sat & Sun Jun-Aug, shorter hours rest of year) This is Sweden's most famous pottery factory, established in 1835. Its trademark brown salt-glazed pottery is a veritable national icon and its famous Höganäskrus (little jug) is mentioned in the opening line of August Strindberg's novel *Natives of Hemsö*.

🛈 Getting There & Away

Skånetrafiken (p189) bus 220 goes from Höganäs to Helsingborg (63kr, 40 minutes) while bus 223 runs to Arild (47kr, 20 minutes).

Mölle

🖉042 / POP 629

The steep, picket fence–pretty village of Mölle is the Kulla Peninsula's main tourist centre, boasting one of Sweden's loveliest historic castle estates just outside town, a good selection of accommodation and dining options and general photogenic appeal.

Five kilometres east of Mölle, the fishing village (and artists' colony) of Arild lays on the charm with its petite pastel houses, teeny-tiny harbour and supporting cast of roses, hollyhocks and coastal nature reserves.

Mölle also enjoys a scandalous past: in the 19th century it was one of the first seaside resorts to encourage mixed bathing, much to the horror of the country…and to the delight of racy Berliners, who flocked here on a now-defunct rail link from the German capital.

◉ Sights & Activities

★ Kullens Fyr LIGHTHOUSE

(🖉0705-82 23 72; www.kullensfyr.se; Italienska vägen 323; adult/6-12yr 30/15kr; ⊘11am-5pm mid-Jun–mid-Aug, weekends only mid-Aug–Nov) It's worth a visit to what's arguably Scandinavia's oldest lighthouse (there's been a light of some kind here for more than 1000 years)

on the Kullaberg Peninsula, if only to appreciate its dramatic clifftop position. The lighthouse remains a crucial navigational beacon in heavily trafficked waters – its 1000-watt beam is visible for 27 nautical miles.

★ Krapperups Slott HISTORIC BUILDING

(🖉042-34 41 90; www.krapperup.se; Krapperups Kyrkovägen 13; ⊘11am-5pm Jun-Aug, 11am-5pm Sat & Sun Feb-May & Sep-Dec; 🅿🖼) FREE While you'd never guess from its name, Krapperups Slott is one of Sweden's oldest and loveliest estates located 5km south of Mölle. The manor has an exterior inlaid with giant white stars representing the coat of arms of the Gyllenstierna family, who lived here for centuries. It is also home to an exquisite garden. Hour tours of the building (100kr) can be arranged in advance. The grounds also house an art gallery and local museum, a cafe and a gift shop.

★ Royal Republic of Ladonia PUBLIC ART

(www.ladonia.org) In 1996 Swedish artist Lars Vilks built two sculptures, the driftwood Nimis and its younger concrete sibling Arx, on a beach in the Kullaberg National Park on the Kulla Peninsula's northern side. Created without permission, their existence sparked several court cases between Vilks and the county council, not to mention the odd fire and chainsaw attack. Crafty Vilks founded Ladonia at the site, effectively turning his works into protected 'national monuments'. Consult the website for the scoop.

Kullaberg Nature Reserve NATURE RESERVE

(www.kullabergsnatur.se; Kullaberg) This magnificent nature reserve occupies the tip of the Kulla Peninsula and houses Scandinavia's brightest lighthouse, Kullens fyr, the light of which can be seen from 50km away. The reserve offers a dramatic spectacle of plunging cliffs, windswept vegetation and incredible sunsets, and a number of hiking trails crisscross the area, leading to ancient caves, tide pools and secluded swimming spots.

The reserve's website is a good place to get an idea of the available activities.

Kullabergs Islandshäster HORSE RIDING

(🖉042-33 52 44; www.kullabergsislandshastar. com; Himmelstorpsvägen 48-7; rides from 600kr) A novel way of exploring the area around Mölle is on an Icelandic horse, one of the world's gentlest, most smooth-gated equine breeds. Kullabergs Islandshäster organises 1½- and 2½-hour horseback trips (600/750kr) on the Kulla Peninsula, or there's a four-hour lunch expedition to Mölle (1150kr).

Kullabergsguiderna ADVENTURE SPORTS
([☑]073-988 10 77; www.kullabergsguiderna.se;
Italienska vägen 323; [☺]daily Jul–mid-Aug, less frequently rest of year; [♿]) This company organises a wide range of activities. You can go on
a one-hour caving expedition (adult/child
150/50kr) with experienced guides (starting from Naturum at the Kullaberg Nature
Reserve) or opt for abseiling (200kr) down
the primordial cliffs. Alternatively, why not
take to the seas with a porpoise safari (adult/
child 395/265kr)?

[🛏] Sleeping & Eating

First Camp Mölle CAMPGROUND €
([☑]042-34 73 84; www.firstcamp.se/molle; Mölle-
hässle; powered sites from 275kr, 4-person cabins
from 590kr; [P]) This friendly campground is
a good bet. It's 2km southeast of Mölle, and
you can hire bikes here for exploring the
area (60kr per day).

Strand Hotell HOTEL €€
([☑]042-34 61 00; www.strand-arild.se; Stora Vägen
42, Arild; d from 1250kr; [P][@][🛜]) A civilised option in picture-perfect Arild that oozes old-
world appeal. Four of the elegant rooms in
the old building boast balconies with sea
views, while the modern annexe features
long, narrow rooms with terraces and sea
views for all. There's a fine in-house restaurant here, too.

★Hotel
Rusthållargården HISTORIC HOTEL €€€
([☑]042-34 65 30; www.rusthallargarden.com; Utsikten 1, Arild; d from 1950kr; [P][@][🛜][🏊]) [✎] This
lovely hotel in Arild, 5km east of Mölle, has
been managed by the same family since
1904 and is housed in a charming white-
and-blue-trimmed farm building that dates
back to 1675. Rooms in the main building
are comfortable and quaint – think flowered
wallpaper and wooden floors – and half
have sea views. There's a swimming pool
and an excellent, mostly organic, breakfast.

★Flickorna Lundgren På Skäret CAFE €
([☑]042-34 60 44; www.fl-lundgren.se; Skäretvä-
gen 19; pastries from 35kr; [☺]10am-6pm Jun-Aug,
to 8pm mid-Jul–mid-Aug; [P]) Signposted off
the main road between Arild and Jonstorp,
this is a huge, justifiably famous cafe in a
gorgeous garden setting. Grab a large plate
of pastries and your copper kettle, and lose
yourself in a cloud of flowers. It's wildly popular, so be prepared for crowds during the
peak months of July and August.

[ℹ] Information

Naturum Kullaberg ([☑]042-34 70 56; Italienska
vägen 323; [☺]11am-4pm) can word you up on
the area's flora, fauna and geology and arrange
guided walks in the **Kullaberg Nature Reserve**.

[ℹ] Getting There & Away

From Höganas **Skånetrafiken** (p189) bus 222
runs every other hour to Mölle (47kr, 20 minutes) and vice versa.

Falsterbo Peninsula

Looking a bit like a turkey's head but usually
described as a fish tail (on a map), this windswept peninsula 30km south of Malmö lures
a steady stream of sun-lovers to its sandy
beaches in the summer months. It also has
a healthy following of ornithologists drawn
to its impressive posse of feathered friends.

Casually known as the Swedish Riviera,
Falsterbo's long, white-sand beach with its
colourful beach huts is popular with Sca-
nians, particularly Malmö weekenders. A
sense of serenity is enhanced by a ban on jet
skis and motorboats here. Just north of the
beach, the twinned towns of Skänor and Falsterbo are where you'll find most amenities
and accommodation.

Vikings can be found on the opposite coast,
north of the town of Höllviken, while at the
tip of the peninsula, the hook-shaped island of
Måkläppen is a nature reserve, off-limits to the
public from March to October.

[◉] Sights

★Fotevikens Museum HISTORIC SITE
([☑]040-33 08 00; www.fotevikensmuseum.se; Mu-
selvägen 24, Höllviken; adult/child 110/40kr; [☺]10am-
4pm Jun-Aug, shorter hours rest of year; [P][♿]) If you
mourn the passing of big hairy men in long-
boats, find solace at the fascinating Foteviken
Viking Reserve, an evocative 'living' reconstruction of a late–Viking Age village. Around
22 authentic reconstructions of houses have
been built, near the site
of the Battle of Foteviken (1134). Amazingly,
the reserve's residents live as the Vikings did,
eschewing most modern conveniences and
adhering to old traditions, laws and religions
– even after the last tourist has left.

Bärnstensmuseum MUSEUM
(Swedish Amber Museum; [☑]040-45 45 04; www.
brost.se; Södra Mariavägen 4, Höllviken; adult/child
25/10kr; [☺]11am-5pm mid-May–end Sep, shorter
hours rest of year; [P]) There's something a little

macabre about this unique museum, which shows ancient insects trapped in sticky resin from 40 million years ago, forever preserved in pieces of beautiful amber stone. The museum is on the southern outskirts of Höllviken, just off the coast road towards Trelleborg.

Falsterbo Museum MUSEUM
(⌨ 040-47 22 42; www.falsterbomuseum.se; Sjögatan 12, Falsterbo; adult/child 40/10kr; ◷ 10am-6pm mid-Jun–Aug) Little Falsterbo Museum, at the southern tip of the peninsula, is a pleasing jumble: a small Naturum, old shops and smithies, WWII mines and the remains of a 13th-century boat.

🛏 Sleeping & Eating

Falsterbo Resort CAMPGROUND €
(⌨ 040-602 40 20; www.falsterboresort.se/en/; Reuterswärds-vägen, Falsterbo; powered sites/ cabins from 220/1000kr; ◷ Apr-Sep; P) This super-friendly campground is a couple of kilometres from Falsterbo in an idyllic spot close to the beach; the renovated camping cabins are of a high standard.

Skanörs Gästgifvaregård HOTEL €€€
(⌨ 040-47 56 90; www.skanorsgastis.com; Mellangatan 13, Skanör; r from 1695kr; P ☎) This lovely private hotel in Skanör has plushly decorated and eminently comfortable rooms combined with an impressive restaurant (which also offers cookery classes).

Da Aldo ITALIAN €
(⌨ 040-47 40 26; www.aldo.se; Mellangatan 47, Skanör; gelato from 30kr, piadine 70kr; ◷ 8.30am-10pm) Calabrian expat Aldo makes sublime gelato here on Skanör's main street using strictly Italian ingredients and no added egg, cream or butter. Lunch options, from frittata and salads to *piadine* (Italian flatbread sandwiches) and stuffed aubergine, are well priced and equally authentic. As for the coffee...*buonissimo!*

★ Skanörs Fiskrögeri SEAFOOD €€€
(⌨ 040-47 40 50; www.rogeriet.se; Hamnvagen 1, Skanör; mains 218-393kr; ◷ noon-9pm Jun-Aug, til 8pm Thu-Sun Apr, May & Sep) By the harbour, this marine-chic restaurant is a must for seafood lovers, as its harbourside location and white smokehouse chimneys attest. The fish soup is exquisite and there's a gourmet seafood deli for stocking that beachside picnic. Open seasonally from April to September; check the website for specific opening hours of the restaurant and deli, which vary slightly.

ℹ Information

You'll find **Falsterbo Strandbad Turistcenter** (⌨ 040-42 54 54; Strandbadsvägen 30, Falsterbo; ◷ 10am-6pm Mon-Fri, to 2pm Sat & Sun mid-Jun–mid-Aug, shorter hours rest of year) by the beach.

ℹ Getting There & Away

Skänor-Falsterbo is 31km south of Malmö, following the E6 motorway and Rte 100.

Bus 100 (75kr, one hour) regularly shuttles back and forth between Malmö and Falsterbo, stopping in Höllviken (63kr, 35 minutes). It departs from the bays in front of Malmö's Centralstation.

Trelleborg

⌨ 0410 / POP 43,913

Trelleborg is home to a truly extraordinary (although reconstructed) sight: a 9th-century, wooden, Viking ring fortress. The city is also known for its beautiful gardens, palm-flanked main avenue and excellent shopping.

Trelleborg is the main gateway between Sweden and Germany, with frequent ferry services.

◉ Sights

★ Trelleborgen HISTORIC SITE
(⌨ 0410-73 30 21; www.trelleborgen.se; Västra Vallgatan 6; visitors centre adult/child 30kr/free; ◷ 10am-4pm Jun-Aug, 1-5pm Mon-Thu rest of year; P ♿) FREE Trelleborgen is a 9th-century Viking ring fortress, discovered in 1988 off Bryggaregatan (just west of the town centre). A quarter of the palisaded fort and a wooden gateway have been recreated, as has a Viking farmhouse and a medieval house built within the walls. A small museum showcases finds from the archaeological digs, including Viking jewellery, grooming implements and a 10th-century skull illustrating the ancient trend of teeth filing.

Axel Ebbe Konsthall GALLERY
(⌨ 0410-73 30 56; Hesekillegatan 1; 30kr; ◷ noon-4pm Wed-Sun mid-Jun–Aug) By the town park, Axel Ebbe Konsthall features nude sculptures by Scanian Axel Ebbe (1868–1941). For a preview, check out the fountain Sjöormen (literally 'the sea monster') in Storatorget.

Trelleborgs Museum MUSEUM
(⌨ 0410-73 30 50; museum@trelleborg.se; Östergatan 58; 30kr; ◷ noon-4pm Tue-Sun) Just east of the town centre, this museum covers a wide range of themes, including a 700-year-old settlement discovered nearby.

🛏 Sleeping & Eating

Night Stop
MOTEL €

(☑ 0410-410 70; www.hotelnightstop.com; Östergatan 59; s/d/tr 300/400/500kr; 🅿 🛜) Simple and functional with shared bathrooms, Night Stop has the cheapest beds in town. Open 24 hours, it's about 500m from the ferry. Turn right along Hamngatan after disembarking. Breakfast costs 50kr.

Hotel Dannegården
HOTEL €€

(☑ 0410-481 80; www.dannegarden.se; Strandgatan 32; r from 1175kr; 🅿 @ 🛜) Trelleborg's most beautiful slumber spot is this old sea captain's villa. Run with quiet confidence, rooms here are discreetly luxurious, the breakfast is generous and the staff is pleasant. Extras include a reputable restaurant, a sauna and spa, plus gorgeous gardens.

Vattentornet Café & Bistro
CAFE €

(☑ 0410-254 84; Stortorget 2; sandwiches from 45kr; ⊙ 9am-6pm Mon-Thu, to 8pm Fri & Sat, 11am-4pm Sun) On the ground floor of the splendid 58m-high water tower (1912), selling sandwiches, cakes and other yummy snacks; try to snag an outdoor table in the fabulous courtyard here with its thought-provoking murals.

Restaurang & Pizzeria Istanbul
TURKISH €

(☑ 0410-44 44 44; Algatan 30; mains 75-145kr; ⊙ 11am-11pm) This bustling place has a huge menu of pasta, pizza, salad and kebabs, plus pricier local fish and meat dishes.

ℹ Information

Trelleborg Tourist Center (☑ 0410-73 33 20; www.trelleborg.se/turism; Kontinentgatan 2; ⊙ 9am-6pm Mon-Fri, 10am-4pm Sat, 10am-2pm Sun) is located directly opposite the ferry terminal.

ℹ Getting There & Away

Trelleborg is 32km south of Malmö on the E6 motorway and 48km west of Ystad.

Skånetrafiken (p189) bus 190 runs from Ystad to Trelleborg (87kr, one hour) and bus 146 runs to to Malmö (64kr, 50 minutes). You can also catch trains to Malmö (75kr, 35 minutes) and Helsingborg (110kr, 1½ hours).

Stena Line (☑ 031-85 80 00; www.stenaline.com) ferries connect Sweden to Germany with sailings to Sassnitz (from 190kr, twice daily each way) and Rostock (from 315kr, two or three daily) from the **Stena Line Ferry Terminal**.

TT-Line (☑ 0450-28 01 81; www.ttline.com) ferries also make the link, shuttling to Travemünde

(from 310kr) and Rostock (from 450kr) three to four times daily.

Fares vary by sailing and capacity: check online for the best rates and to make bookings.

Ystad
☑ 0411 / POP 29,338

Medieval market town Ystad has an intoxicating allure thanks to its half-timbered houses, rambling cobbled streets and the frequently haunting sound of its nightwatchman's horn. Fans of crime novels may recognise Ystad as the setting for the best-selling Inspector Wallander crime thrillers.

Ystad was Sweden's window to Europe from the 17th to the mid-19th century, with new ideas and inventions – including cars, banks and hotels – arriving here first. Now a terminal for ferries to Poland and the Danish island of Bornholm, the port area's transitory feel thankfully doesn't spread to the rest of city. Once you start to explore you might find the place will work its magic and you'll want to linger longer.

⊙ Sights

Half-timbered houses are scattered round town, especially on Stora Östergatan. Most date from the latter half of the 18th century, although **Pilgrändshuset** (☑ 0411-147 31) on the corner of Pilgrand and Stora Östergatan is Scandinavia's oldest half-timbered house and dates from 1480. Take a peek, too, at the facade of beautiful **Änglahuset**, on Stora Norregatan, which originates from around 1630.

★ Cineteket
MUSEUM

(☑ 0411-57 70 57; www.ystad.se/cineteket; Elis Nilssons väg 8; adult/child 60kr/free; ⊙ 10am-4pm Mon-Thu, Sat & Sun mid-Jun–Aug, hours vary rest of year) Fans of crime thrillers most likely know the name Henning Mankell (b 1948), author of the best-selling Inspector Wallander series. The books are set in the small, seemingly peaceful town of Ystad. The gloomy inspector paces its medieval streets, solving gruesome murders through his meticulous police work...but at a cost to his personal life, which is slowly and painfully disintegrating. Cineteket runs guided tours (by appointment; adult/child 120/70kr) of the adjoining **Ystad Studios**, from May to September.

★ Klostret i Ystad
MUSEUM

(☑ 0411-57 72 86; www.klostret.ystad.se; St Petri Kyrkoplan; adult/child 40kr/free; ⊙ noon-5pm Tue-Fri, noon-4pm Sat & Sun) Klostret i Ystad,

Ystad

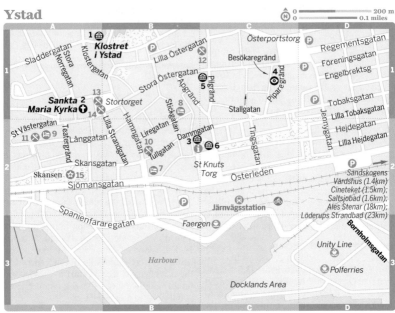

Ystad

in the Middle Ages Franciscan monastery of Gråbrödraklostret, features local textiles and silverware. The monastery includes the 13th-century deconsecrated Sankt Petri Kyrkan (now used for art exhibitions), which has around 80 gravestones from the 14th to 18th centuries. Admission also includes entry to Ystads Konstmuseum.

★ **Sankta Maria Kyrka** CHURCH
(📞0411-692 00; Stortorget 2A; ⊙10am-6pm Jun-Aug, to 4pm Sep-May) FREE Among the church's highlights are a fabulously ornate 17th-century baroque pulpit, an elaborate pipe-organ, chandeliers and excellent acoustics. It's from the church's clock tower that the town's

nightwatchman famously sounds his horn – a tradition that's been upheld since 1250.

Per Helsas Gård ARTS CENTRE
(Besökaregränd 3; ⊙11am-5pm Jun-Aug, shorter hours rest of year) Housed in one of Ystad's most iconic (and magnificent) half-timbered buildings, dating from the 1500s and set around a courtyard. The central cobbles here are flanked by craft workshops, art galleries and a cafe.

Ystads Konstmuseum MUSEUM
(📞0411-57 72 85; www.konstmuseet.ystad.se; St Knuts Torg; adult/child 40kr/free; ⊙10am-5pm Mon-Fri, noon-4pm Sat & Sun Jul & Aug, shorter

hours rest of year) FREE Included in the same ticket as Klostret i Ystad is the Ystads Konstmuseum with its savvy collection of southern Swedish and Danish art, including works by the great Per Kirkeby.

Charlotte Berlins Museum MUSEUM
(✆0411-188 66; www.charlotteberlinsmuseum.se; Dammgatan 23; adult/child 20kr/free; ☺noon-5pm Mon-Fri, to 4pm Sat & Sun Jun-Aug, tours hourly from 11am) For fetching interiors, pop into Charlotte Berlins Museum housed in a late-19th-century, middle-class abode.

🛏 Sleeping

Travellers with their own wheels can select from the B&B and cabin options along the scenic coastal roads on either side of town. In recent years Ystad has become a bit of a hot spot for destination weddings, honeymoons and general romance, so you'll find a selection of year-round luxe boutique properties here too.

★ Sekelgården Hotel HOTEL €€
(✆0411-739 00; www.sekelgarden.se; Långgatan 18; s/d from 995/1395kr; P@🖙) A romantic family-run hotel in a superb half-timbered house (1793); staying here is a bit like staying with your (affluent) country cousins. Rooms are set around a delightful garden and are all different, although typically decorated with a combination of William Morris–style wallpaper and pastel paintwork combined with colourful quilts, rugs and fabrics.

Hotell Klara B&B €€
(✆0702-94 52 55; www.ystadhotell.se; Stickgatan 17; s/d from 795/895kr; 🖙) Next to a large playground, so a good option for families with tots, the half-timbered building contrasts sharply with the 12 modern and crisply renovated apartments with their well-equipped kitchenettes and small dining space.

★ Saltsjobad SPA HOTEL €€€
(✆0411 136 30; www.ysb.se; Saltsjöbadsvägen 15; d/ste from 1400/2250kr; P❄🖙🏊) One of the

finest hotels and day spas in Skåne is here in Ystad, right on the beach. Generous guest rooms and suites furnished in chic styles all feature downy bedding, lots of natural light and big bathrooms. The on-site amenities, from the swimming pool to the restaurant and treatment rooms, are all first class.

Hotell Continental HISTORIC HOTEL €€€
(✆0411-137 00; www.hotelcontinental-ystad.se; Hamngatan 13; s/d from 1490/1690kr; P@🖙) On the site of the old customs house, the Continental is reputedly Sweden's oldest hotel, dating from 1829. It's loaded with old-world charm (think grand chandeliered foyer and marble staircase), but its rooms are more business-style with light wood furnishings, parquet floors and smart, if small, slate grey and cream bathrooms.

🍴 Eating

Upperllerner EUROPEAN €€
(✆0411-78 800; www.uppellerner.se; Stortorget 11; mains 90-195kr; ☺5-11pm Mon-Fri, 8pm-late Sat & Sun) A brick-clad dining space combined with subtle lighting creates a soothing rustic ambience for enjoying mainly meat and fish dishes, including classics such as steak tartare and a gut-busting mixed grill. There's terrace seating overlooking the square.

Store Thor INTERNATIONAL €€
(✆0411-185 10; www.storethor.se; Stortorget 18; mains 110-190kr; ☺11.30am-4pm & 5pm-late Mon-Sat) Store Thor was described as one of Ystad's best restaurants by Kurt Wallander in the movie *Täckmanteln*. It occupies the monastic arched cellar of the old town hall (1572). Nibble on such tapas as jalapeño peppers with cheese, tuck into succulent grilled meats or enjoy the cognac raw-spiced salmon with dill-stewed potatoes. The square-side terrace is a hit with summertime night owls.

Bröderna M BISTRO €€
(✆0411-191 99; www.brodernam.se; Hamngatan 11; mains 75-180kr; ☺11.30am-11pm Mon-Fri, from

---

THE NIGHTWATCHMAN'S HORN

Ever since 1250 a nightwatchman has blown his bugle through the little window in the clock tower of Ystad's **Sankta Maria Kyrka** (every 15 minutes from 9.15pm to 3am). The tradition was apparently introduced to help thwart fires, a hazardous side effect of the flammable thatched-roof houses. If a blaze started, the watchman would blow his horn repeatedly, which was a signal for locals to rush to the scene and extinguish the blaze. It was a serious role: if the nightwatchman had the audacity to doze off while on duty, he was unceremoniously beheaded. These days, the nightwatchman continues to take his ancient role seriously, though it is no longer likely (or legal) that he'll lose his head if his alarm doesn't go off!

DON'T MISS

ALES STENAR

Ales Stenar ([☎] 0411-57 76 81; www.visitskane.com/classic-attractions/ales-stones; Löderup; admission free, tours adult/child 20/10kr; ⊙24hr) [FREE] has all the mystery of England's Stonehenge, with none of the commercial fanfare. The 67m-long oval of stones, shaped like a boat, was probably constructed around AD 600 for reasons unknown. Limited excavations at the site have revealed no bones; it's possible that this wasn't a grave but a ritual site, with built-in solar calendar (the 'stem' and 'stern' stones point towards the midsummer sunset and midwinter sunrise).

The enigmatic ship is in the middle of a raised field, with an uncannily low and level 360-degree horizon. In the summer, a diminutive roadside tourist office provides information and runs tours.

Free to visit and always open, Ales Stenar lies 19km east of Ystad at Kåseberga. It's badly served by public transport, although bus 392 from Ystad runs daily in summer. At other times, take bus 570 from Ystad to Valleberga kyrka, and then walk 5km south to Kåseberga.

noon Sat & Sun) Relaxed and contemporary, Bröderna M serves up Ystad's best pizza, ranging from classic margheritas to thin-crust topped with prosciutto, rocket and pecorino. Main dishes are solid bistro fare: steak with red-wine sauce or fish soup.

Host Morten CAFE €€
([☎] 0411-134 03; Gåsegränd; mains 85-160kr; ⊙11am-5pm Mon-Fri, 11am-3pm Sat, 12.30-5pm Sun) Plunge into that Henning Mankell novel at this fabulous cafe – serving light meals such as filled baked potatoes, focaccias and piled-high salads – or pluck a book from one of the shelves and plan to stay awhile. In summer the 18th-century cobbled courtyard is a delight, especially when there's live music.

Bryggeriet SWEDISH €€
([☎] 0411-699 99; www.ystadbryggeriet.se; Långgatan 20; mains 140-210kr; ⊙11.30am-9pm Tue-Fri, to 10pm Sat, to 7pm Sun) Unique Bryggeriet is a relaxed meat-leaning restaurant-pub in an old brewery. The courtyard is an excellent spot to linger over a well-cooked meal and Ystad Färsköl, a beer brewed on the premises. The chocolate truffle with raspberry sorbet comes plumply recommended.

★ **Sandskogens Värdshus** EUROPEAN €€€
([☎] 0411-23 73 00; www.villastrandvagen.se/en/; Strandvägen 1; 5-course set menu 595kr (with wine 795kr); ⊙5-11pm Mon-Sat) Under the tutelage of one of Sweden's most highly regarded chef's, Daniel Müllern, this restaurant serves up exquisite five-course dinners served in an historic mansion (where you can also stay if you choose). The regularly changing menu is posted online. Dress to impress and bring someone special.

🍷 Drinking & Entertainment

There is a collection of pubs and bars, with sunny outdoor patios conducive to the imbibing of alcohol, dotted around the area between Stortorget and the bus station.

Ystads Teater THEATRE
([☎] 0411-57 77 98; www.ystadteater.se; Sjömansgatan 13; ticket prices vary) The extraordinary Ystads Teater dates back to 1894; its repertoire spans operas, musicals, tango and big-band gigs. Guided tours (usually in Swedish) of the building take place daily from late June to August. Contact the tourist office for details.

🛈 Information

Ystads Turistbyrå ([☎] 0411-57 76 81; www.ystad.se; St Knuts Torg; ⊙9am-7pm Mon-Fri, 10am-6pm Sat & Sun mid-Jun–mid-Aug; 🛜) is located just outside the train station and has free internet access.

🛈 Getting There & Away

Ystad is 60km southeast of Malmö on the E65 motorway, and 45km southwest of Simrishamn via Rte 9.

Ystad is a popular ferry port. **Unity Line** ([☎] 0411-55 69 00; www.unityline.se; adult one way from 418kr) and **Polferries** ([☎] 040-12 17 00; www.polferries.se; adult one way 353kr) operate daily crossings between Ystad and Swinoujscie (Poland). Fares start at around 353kr and the journey takes approximately 6½ hours.

Faergen ([☎] +45-702 315 15; www.faergen.dk; adult one way from 200kr) runs frequent ferries and catamarans between Ystad and Rønne, on the Danish island of Bornholm. Fares start at 200kr and it takes under 90 minutes to get across.

Skånetrafiken (p189) bus 190 runs from Ystad to Trelleborg (87kr, one hour) via Smygehuk. Bus 570 to Simrishamn (69kr, 40 minutes) via

Löderup runs hourly in the summer. Buses depart from outside Ystad train station.

SJ Rail (p170) and **Skånetrafiken** (p189) operate regular trains between Ystad and Malmö (99kr, 50 minutes), Lund (111kr, 1¼ hours) and Simrishamn (69kr, 40 minutes).

Simrishamn

📞 0414 / POP 6527

Summer holidaymakers mill around Simrishamn harbour, licking ice creams or waiting for the ferry to the Danish island of Bornholm.

Simrishamn is the largest city in the sparsely populated southeastern tip of Skåne, in the area known as Österlen, an alluring pocket of waving wheat fields, tiny fishing villages and glorious apple orchards. Everything moves at a slow, seductive speed: cycling is the best way of fitting in with the tempo.

◎ Sights & Activities

Quaint pastel-hued houses line **Lilla Norregatan** and the nearby **Sankt Nikolai Kyrka** dates to the 1400s.

The region is great for cycling and there are a variety of routes to choose from, ranging from a 66km spin covering major food highlights to the 136km-long Österlen Trail. The Simrishamn tourist office has free biking maps, or contact **Österlenguiderna** (📞 0414-68 46 00; www.osterlenguiderna.se; Hoby 2314, Borrby), which rents bikes and runs organised tours.

Glimmingehus   CASTLE

(📞 0414-186 20; Hammenhög 1; adult/child 60kr/free; ⊙ 10am-6pm Jun-Aug, shorter hours rest of year; 🅿) Located 12km southwest of Simrishamn, the striking, five-storey Glimmingehus dates from the early 1500s and is one of the best-preserved medieval castles in Sweden. Features include an all-encompassing moat and 11 resident ghosts! Guided tours in English are at 3pm daily in July and August (less frequently the rest of the year). In summer there's a stellar cafe and a program of medieval events and activities: contact the castle for details.

Regional bus 576 runs from Simrishamns station to Glimmingehus (25kr, 20 minutes), but you must phone to reserve the bus (operated by a local taxi company) at least two hours in advance on 📞 0771-77 44 99. Make enquiries at the station if you need help.

Autoseum   MUSEUM

(📞 0702-03 94 20; www.autoseum.se; Fabriksgatan 10; adult/child 100/60kr; ⊙ 11am-5pm daily Jul & Aug,

11am-5pm Sat & Sun Apr-Jun, Sep & Oct) Rev-heads shouldn't miss Sweden's largest auto museum with its booty of classic cars, bikes and buggies, plus the more recent addition of a music section with old gramophones and similar.

🛏 Sleeping & Eating

Accommodation in the area is geared more towards the many cyclists and nature lovers passing through: there are plenty of hostel beds and campsites, but you won't find any luxury, full-service hotels here.

STF Vandrarhem Simrishamn   HOSTEL €

(📞 0414-105 40; www.simrishamnsvandrarhem.se; Christian Barnekowsgatan 10C; s/d from 495/595kr; ⊙ Apr-Nov; 🅿 @ 🛜) Tucked away near Simrishamn hospital, this hostel comes highly recommended. It offers spotless, homely lodgings with bathroom and TV in every room.

★ Sjöbacka Gård   B&B €€

(📞 0414-310 66; www.sjobacka.se; Gislöv 1832, Skillinge; s/d from 764/864kr; 🅿 🛜) This fine accommodation is located in the countryside about 11km southwest of Simrishamn. The B&B occupies an atmospheric Scanian farmhouse complete with fireplace, antiques, heaving bookshelves and a gorgeous cobblestone courtyard with pots of flowers and fragrant herbs. There is occasional live music here in summer.

If you don't have your own wheels, to get here from Simrishamn, take bus 577 bound for Borrby and get off at stop 'Grosshög' (25kr, 15 minutes), then walk south along Kaptensgatan for about 350m until you reach the next main intersection. From here, it's another 300m or so, heading west.

Hotell maritim   BOUTIQUE HOTEL €€

(📞 0414-41 13 60; www.engaffelkort.se; Hamngatan 31; s/d from 1050/1450kr; 🅿 @ 🛜) The old blue building by the harbour is a wonderful boutique hotel with stylish decor, lashings of white linen and sea views. It's also home to a fine restaurant (mains 255kr to 310kr) specialising in fish dishes.

★ Gärdens Café & Vedugn   PIZZA €€

(📞 0414-161 61; Storgatan 17; pizza from 120kr; ⊙ 11am-10pm Mon-Sat, noon-8pm Sun; 🚲) Head for the outside terrace with its mini maze, riot of flowers and pretty tiled tables. A former cafe (the cinnamon rolls still sell out fast), the thin crispy-base pizzas are Neapolitan authentic and fabulous. Try the white pizza with its earthy topping of potatoes, caramelised onions, cheese and baby spinach.

MALMÖ & THE SOUTH ÅHUS

WORTH A TRIP

KIVIK

North of Simrishamn, the sleepy hamlet of Kivik is known for apples and ancient burial cists (quite the contrast). It's hard to go past delights like apple cake, apple butter, apple cider and apple brandy, all of which you can sample, as well as exploring the orchards themselves, at **Kiviks Musteri** (☑0414-719 00; www.kiviksmusteri.se; Karakåsvägen 45, Kivik; ☉10am-6pm Jun-Aug, shorter hours rest of year; P⛟) [FREE].

After that, it's worth supplementing your horticultural and culinary pursuits with a dose of history at the ancient burial ground of **Kungagraven** (King's Grave; ☑0414-703 37; Bredarörsvägen 18, Kivik; adult/child 30kr/free; ☉10am-6pm mid-May–Aug; P), Sweden's largest Bronze Age grave, believed to have once been a site of human sacrifice. While the displays within are replicas, it's still a great place to gain perspective on Sweden's long historical lineage.

Kivik is also the gateway village for visits to the scenic, seaside **Stenshuvud National Park** (☑0414-708 82; www.stenshuvud.se; Naturum Stenshuvud). When you're in the park, consult the experts at **Naturum** (Visitor Centre; ☑0414-708 82; ☉11am-4pm mid-Aug–Sep, shorter hours rest of year) for information about flora, fauna, walking trails and swimming spots.

If you're not full of apple cake and cider, you might wish to pop in to **Kivik Strand & Logi Café** (☑0414-711 95; www.kivikstrand.se; Tittutvägen, Kivik; d hostel/hotel from 890/990kr; ☉Apr-Oct; P🛜) for espresso and key lime pie – otherwise, it's a cosy place to spend the night. **STF Vandrarhem Hanöbris** (☑0414-700 50; www.hanobris.se; Bokekullsvägen 2, Kivik; r hostel/hotel from 695/895kr; ☉Apr-Oct; P@🛜) also has decent, though basic, lodgings.

The easiest way to explore Kivik (19km north of Simrishamn) and the national park is by car, but you can also get here via **Skånetrafiken** (p189) bus 3 from Simrishamn (38kr, 30 minutes).

ⓘ Information

Simrishamns Turistbyrå (☑0414-81 98 00; www.visitystadosterlen.se; Varvsgatan 2; ☉9am-7pm Mon-Fri, 10am-6pm Sat & Sun Jul & Aug, 9am-5pm Mon-Fri rest of year) has information on the whole of Österlen and can help with accommodation, ferry crossings and journeys to Kivik and the Stenshuvud National Park.

ⓘ Getting There & Away

Simrishamn is 40km northeast of Ystad and 56km south of Åhus.

Skånetrafiken (p189) operates scheduled rail services between Simrishamn and Ystad (69kr, 40 minutes) onwards to Malmö (118kr, 1½ hours).

Bus 3 goes to Kivik (38kr, 30 minutes).

Åhus

☑044 / POP 9950

The small coastal town of Åhus (about 18km southeast of Kristianstad) is a popular summer spot thanks to its long sandy beach.

The surrounding area is also known for its eels: the Eel Coast runs south from Åhus, and this delicacy is served up boiled, fried, smoked, grilled or cooked on a bed of straw at restaurants and at autumn Eel Feasts throughout the region.

If eels aren't your thing (don't knock it 'til you've tried it), Åhus is also known for its ice cream and vodka.

⦿ Sights & Activities

⭐**Absolut Experience Center**   DISTILLERY
(☑044-28 80 00; www.absolut.com; Köpmannagatan 23; ☉10am-5pm Mon-Fri, til 2pm Sat) Åhus is home to the Absolut Vodka distillery, where half a million bottles are produced daily. Free tours run six times daily on weekdays from late June to the end of August (call ahead or check online for times). The tour bus departs from outside the factory entrance, 400m southwest of Åhus Turistbyrå. At all other times, tours must be booked in advance.

Upzone   HEALTH & FITNESS
(☑033-41 17 41; www.upzone.se; Fädriften 2; adventures 195-395kr; ☉Mar-Nov) Upzone is an awesome (and incredibly challenging) warren of rope ladders, swings, elevated gang planks, suspension bridges and walkways built in the treetops. The idea is to run (and jump and swing and climb) through the course as fast as you can. One for fitter folks who'll have loads of fun. Couch potatoes will want to run and hide.

Sleeping

STF Vandrarhem Åhus HOSTEL €
(☑044-24 85 35; www.cigarrkungenshus.se; Stavgatan 3; hostel dm/s/d from 250/325/500kr, B&B per person from 400kr; ☺Mar-Nov; Ⓟ@) Very close to the harbour is STF Vandrarhem Åhus, an agreeable youth hostel and B&B based in a 19th-century cigar factory.

Åhus Seaside HOTEL €€
(☑044-28 93 00; www.ahusseaside.com; Kantarellvägen 1; d from 895kr) You can't go past the waterfront position of this old-school seaside resort, which at the time of writing was in the process of transforming itself into a new-school seaside resort. Check out the website to see where it's at – you'll likely nab a retro beachfront bargain if progress comes slowly. The property has two wings...it's the waterfront one that you're after.

Drinking & Nightlife

Le Bardo BAR
(☑076-806 73 23; www.ahusseaside.com/le-bardo/; Ankvägen 18; ☺5pm-1am Jun-Aug) At Åhus Seaside, by the pier, this place gets packed on a summer night with drinkers, diners and folks who want to dance the night away.

ℹ Information

Åhus turistbyrå (☑044-13 47 77; Torget 15) Well-stocked tourist office with enthusiastic staff who can assist with accommodation queries and help you find the best spots to swim.

ℹ Getting There & Away

Åhus is 18km southeast of Kristianstad on the Baltic coast.

Skånetrafiken (p189) bus 551 runs several times an hour between Kristianstad and Åhus (55kr, 30 minutes).

Kristianstad

☑044 / POP 83,191

Kristianstad is a handsome town with elegant squares, an exquisite cathedral, quirky street sculptures and a sprinkling of eye-catching 18th- and 19th-century buildings.

Known as the most Danish town in Sweden, its construction was ordered by the Danish king Christian IV in 1614. Its rectangular street network still follows the first town plan, although the original walls and bastions have long gone (aside from the Bastionen Konungen rampart, which has been restored).

A major transport hub and a gateway to Skåne's southern coast, the city is also the region's administrative and political centre.

◉ Sights

★**Trefaldighetskyrkan** CHURCH
(Holy Trinity Church; ☑044-780 64 00; Västra Storgatan 6; ☺8am-4pm) 🆓 One of the finest Renaissance churches in Scandinavia, Trefaldighetskyrkan was completed in 1628 when Skåne was still under Danish control. The light-filled interior has many of its original fittings, including wonderfully carved oak pews and an ornate marble and alabaster pulpit.

Bastionen Konungen HISTORIC SITE
(Östra Boulevarden) One of Kristianstad's 10 original bastions (fortifications) dating from the late 1700s is now an outdoor information point and museum of sorts, with historical artifacts, including old canons, dotted around.

Regionmuseet Kristianstad MUSEUM
(Kristianstad Regional Museum; ☑044-13 52 45; www.regionmuseet.se; Stora Torg; ☺11am-5pm Jun-Aug, from noon Tue-Sun Sep-May) 🆓 Originally intended as a palace, the building ended up being used as an arsenal. It now houses local-history exhibits and art, handicrafts and silverware displays. **Café Miro** (☑044-13 60 97; Östra Storgatan 27B, Stora Torg; sandwiches & snacks 35-75kr; 🍴) 🌿 serves great organic lunches, with herbs and flowers picked from the owner's garden.

Filmmuseet MUSEUM
(☑044-13 57 29; Östra Storgatan 53; ☺noon-5pm Mon-Fri Jul–mid-Aug, noon-5pm Sun only rest of year) 🆓 Swedish filmmaking began in Kristianstad, so it's appropriate that Filmmuseet, one of Sweden's few film museums, is based here. That said, the presentation of its collection is modest at best.

Sleeping & Eating

★**Bäckaskog Slott** HISTORIC HOTEL €€
(☑044-530 20; www.backaskogslott.se; Barumsvägen 255, Kiaby; s/d cottage from 495/795kr, castle from 1195/1800kr; Ⓟ@🛜) This dreamy castle sits between two lakes 15km northeast of Kristianstad. Built as a monastery in the mid-13th century, it's a stunning spot, with different tiers of accommodation available in various wings and cottages in the grounds. Plus there is a well-priced restaurant. Bus 558 (25kr, 20 minutes) from Kristianstad bus station to Arkelstorp stops near the castle.

Kristianstad

N 0 ——— 100 m
0 ——— 0.05 miles

Best Western Hotel Anno 1937
HOTEL €€

(☎ 044-12 61 50; www.hotelanno.se; Västra Storgatan 17; s/d from 1095/1345kr; P @ 🛜) A rustic beam here, a 17th-century wall there: this hotel has a pleasing sense of pervading history. Opposite the cathedral, its pale-toned rooms are a bit dull, but the amenities are good and include a sauna.

First Hotel Christian IV
HISTORIC HOTEL €€

(☎ 044-20 38 50; www.firsthotels.com; Västra Boulevarden 15; s/d from 995/1275kr; P @ 🛜) With parquet floors and stucco ceilings, Hotel Christian IV is certainly grand, if a little worn around the edges. The beautiful turn-of-the-century building was once a bank; one of the vaults is still a place of value: it's home to a vast wine cellar.

La Finestra Italiana
ITALIAN €

(☎ 044-20 97 20; www.lafinestraitaliana.se; Vastra Storgatan 30; pasta from 70kr, pizza 75-110kr; ⊙ 11am-4pm Tue-Fri, to 9pm Sat & Sun) Look for the yellow awning and head for the outside terrace (weather permitting), as the interior space is bar-stool style and you may be elbowed into a corner by the takeaway crowd. The pizzas and pasta dishes taste pretty authentic for being this far north. Italian espresso is also available.

Conditori Duvander
SWEDISH €

(☎ 044-21 94 18; www.conditoriduvander.se; Hesslegatan 6; light meals 65-95kr; ⊙ 7.30am-7pm Mon-Fri, 10am-8pm Sat, 10am-5pm Sun) This historic restaurant and patisserie has a belle-époque feel with its marble columns, arched windows, potted palms and classic tilework. Equally enticing for a (Fairtrade) coffee and cake or a light lunch with choices such as salads, wraps and pasta plus daily specials.

Kippers Källare
MEDITERRANEAN €€

(☎ 044-10 62 00; www.kippers.se; Östra Storgatan 9; mains 145-225kr; ⊙ noon-3pm & 6-11pm Tue-Sat) Sporting a 17th-century arched cellar, this is the most atmospheric restaurant in town. Spanish-style tapas take up much of the menu, but there are more substantial dishes including suckling pig and burgers.

ℹ Information

Kristianstad Tourist Center (☎ 044-13 53 35; www.kristianstad.se/turism; Stora Torg; ⊙ 10am-5pm Mon-Fri, to 2pm Sat-Sun)

ℹ Getting There & Away

Kristianstad is 80km northeast of Lund via the E22 motorway and 60km southwest of Karlshamn, further along the E22.

SJ Rail (p170) has regular train services to Karlshamn (113kr, 40 minutes) and Lund (118kr, 1¼ hours) onwards to Malmö (111kr, 1½ hours) or Helsingborg (also 111kr, 1½ hours).

Skånetrafiken (p189) operates buses to Ystad (93kr, 1¾ hours) and Simrishamn (81kr, 1½ hours) while **Svenska Buss** (p204) has one daily service to Stockholm (420kr, 9¾ hours). The **bus station** (Västra Boulevarden) is next to the train station.

ÅLMHULT: IKEA MUSEUM

When in 1958, a 27-year-old businessman by the name of Ingvar Kamprad opened a hulking furniture store in the little town of Älmult (population: 8,955), people thought he was stark raving bonkers. And when you visit Älmhult and imagine what it was like in 1958, you'll understand why. Sweden didn't even have supermarkets then! If you look around you now, you'll probably see a 'something' in your room that got there because Ingvar the entrepreneur had a vision.

Kamprad's store grew into the global base of a Swedish brand that is known the world over: that's right, IKEA! The store (which closed in 2012) was spared from demolition and re-imagined as the world's first IKEA Museum (☎0476-44 16 00; www.ikeamuseum. com; Ikeagatan 5, Älmhult; adult/child 60/40kr; ☺10am-7pm; P), opened in June 2016. It's well worth a visit so you can learn straight from the horse's mouth how IKEA shaped the future. There's an obligatory resturant selling real-deal IKEA *köttbullar* (Swedish meatballs) and a shop with museum-only products, but if you need a hard-core IKEA fix, there's a megastore up the road.

Trains run almost hourly from Malmö to Älmhult (143kr, 1¼ hours) so it's an easy day trip if you don't fancy spending the night. But because Älmhult really is a little town in the middle of nowhere, the purpose-built IKEA Hotell (☎0476-64 11 00; www.ikeahotell. se; Ikeagatan 1, Älmhult; s/d from 495/995kr; P☎), opposite the museum, is another world first – allowing visitors even more time to shop. Clever IKEA.

At time of writing, Ingvar, aged 91, is still going strong, although he retired at 87 and handed the hotseat at the head of his empire to his youngest son. In 2017 Kampar's estimated net worth was in the vicinity of US$42 billion.

The moral of the story is: the next time someone says you're nuts for following your dreams, don't pay them too much attention – you just might change the world.

If you need a taxi when you're in town, try **Taxi Kurir Kristianstad** (☎044-21 52 70; www. taxikurir.se).

BLEKINGE

With its long coastline and safe harbours, Blekinge province's past and present are faithfully fastened to the sea. Sweden and Denmark once squabbled over the area, a trump card in power games over the Baltic. It's the only historical county in Sweden other than Gotland whose historical borders (covering 3039-sq-km) are exactly the same as the present-day administrative area. It might be Sweden's second-smallest province, but that doesn't mean its historical significance has been forgotten.

Today, the jewel in Blekinge's crown is the Unesco-lauded naval town of Karlskrona, famed for its wealth of baroque architecture. The region's second-largest town, Karlshamn, was the last part of the homeland many thousands of 19th-century emigrants saw before they sailed off to new lives in America.

Beyond these urban centres a low-key landscape of fish-filled rivers and lakes, brooding forests and a stunning archipelago – perfect for reading books or lazy island-hopping – awaits.

ⓘ Getting There & Away

The E22 motorway from Malmö and Lund runs through Blekinge län, passing through Karlshamn and Karlskrona before heading it's way north just inland from the Baltic coast.

SJ Rail (p170) operates regular services between Malmö and Karlshamn (178kr, two hours) which continue on to Karlskrona (241kr, 2¾ hours).

Karlskrona has a small airport and daily ferry sailings to Gdynia, Poland, while Karlshamn also has daily ferry connections to Klaipeda, Lithuania.

Karlskrona

☎0455 / POP 66,262

This handsome military-base town is included on the Unesco World Heritage list for its impressive collection of 17th- and 18th-century naval architecture, which could best be described as being in the Danish Baroque style.

It was the failed Danish invasion of Skåne in 1679 that sparked Karlskrona's conception, when King Karl XI decided that a southern

Karlskrona

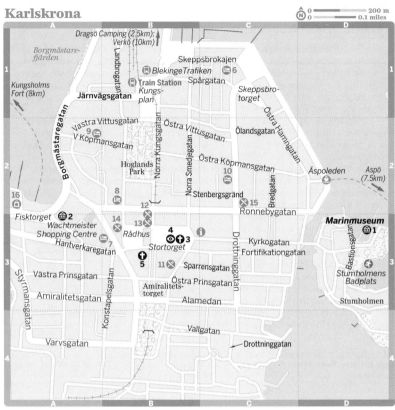

Karlskrona

naval base was needed for better control over the Baltic Sea. Almost immediately, it became Sweden's third-biggest city – hard to imagine today, given it's now so delightfully compact and quiet.

Much of the town still has military ties, so for many sights you'll only be granted admission if you join a tour.

◎ Sights

★ **Drottningkärs kastell** · FORT
(☎0455-33 93 00; Drottningskär, Aspö; ⊙noon-9pm Jun-Aug, noon-5.30pm Fri-Sun Sep-May; ⊛) Bristling with cannons, this fortified tower on the island of Aspö was described by Admiral Nelson of the British Royal Navy

as 'impregnable'. You can visit the tower on an Äspoleden (p204), a free car ferry that operates up to twice hourly in July and August from Handelshamnen, north of the Marinmuseum.

★ **Marinmuseum** MUSEUM
(www.marinmuseum.se; Stumholmen; adult/child 100kr/free; ⊙10am-6pm Jun-Aug, shorter hours rest of year; P) The striking Marinmuseum is the national naval museum. Dive in for reconstructions of a battle deck in wartime, a hall full of fantastic figureheads, piles of model boats, and even some of the real thing – such as a minesweeper, the HMS *Västervik* and Sweden's royal sloop. There is also a pleasant restaurant (mains from 100kr).

★ **Kungsholms Fort** FORT
(Tjurkö; adult/child 230/100kr; ⊙May-Sep) Karlskrona's star is the extraordinary offshore Kungsholms Fort, with its curious circular harbour, established in 1680 to defend the town. The fort can only be visited on two-hour guided boat tours which must be booked through Karlskrona Turistbyrå (p204) or at the Marinmuseum. Highly recommended.

Stortorget SQUARE
Karlskrona's monumental square, Stortorget, was planned to rival Europe's best. Alas, the funds ran out, resulting in a somewhat odd mix of grand architectural gestures and humble stand-ins. Dominating the square are the courthouse, along with the baroque church Fredrikskyrkan and Trefaldighetskyrkan, which was inspired by Rome's Pantheon.

Blekinge Museum MUSEUM
(☎0455-30 49 85; www.blekingemuseum.se; Borgmästaregatan 21; adult/child 80kr/free; ⊙10am-6pm Jun-Aug, noon-5pm Tue-Sun rest of year) This evocative museum explores the local fishing, boat-building and quarrying trades. The most captivating part is Grevagården, an impressively preserved 18th-century abode crammed with thousands of vintage objects, from fans and fashion to bizarre wax models of syphilis-plagued faces. Topping it off is a petite baroque garden and an inviting cafe.

Fredrikskyrkan CHURCH
(☎0455-33 47 00; Stortorget 3; ⊙11am-4pm Mon-Fri, 9.30am-2pm Sat) FREE This striking, somewhat mesmerising baroque church on the main square is included under the broad World Heritage listing of Karlskrona's architecture. At the time of writing it was closed indefinitely for extensive restoration.

Trefaldighetskyrkan CHURCH
(Trinity Church; ☎0455-33 47 00; Stortorget; ⊙11am-4pm Mon-Fri, 9.30am-2pm Sat) FREE Inspired by Rome's Pantheon, this gorgeous church built between 1697 and 1709 looks somehow out of place on the vast and juxtaposing Stortorget.

🏃 **Activities**

Pick a sunny summer afternoon for an hour-long cruise or perhaps kayak around Karlskrona's sparkling archipelago, comprising almost 1000 rocky islands. Cruises are just one of the many tour options available through Karlskrona Turistbyrå (p204). Details are available on its home page, including information about tours of the naval shipyard at Lindholmen and walking tours of the city's museums and heritage lanes.

Stumholmens Badplats BEACH
(Stumholmen) This pleasant bathing spot on the island of Stumholmen is a 1km walk from Karlskrona's main square.

🛏 **Sleeping**

Dragsö Camping CAMPGROUND €
(☎0455-153 54; www.dragso.se; Dragsövägen; sites/d/2-bed cabins from 250/500/575kr; ⊙Apr–mid Sep; P) This large, good-looking campground, 2.5km northwest of town, is situated on a scenic bay. Facilities include boat and bicycle hire, plus a Karlskrona-themed minigolf course. Bus 7 stops about 1km short of the campground.

STF Vandrarhem
Trossö Karlskrona HOSTEL €
(☎0455-100 20; www.karlskronavandrarhem.se; Drottninggatan 39; dm/s/d from 170/290/380kr; 🌐) Modern, clean and friendly, this central hostel has a laundry, a TV room, a backyard for kids to play in and handy parking across the street.

Clarion Collection
Hotel Carlscrona HOTEL €€
(☎0455-36 15 00; www.hotelcarlscrona.se; Skeppsbrokajen; s/d from 1095/1345kr; P🌐) Handy for the train station, this chain hotel combines original rustic beams and slinky furniture in the bar, and navy blues, greys and handsome wooden furnishings in its stately rooms. An added bonus is an included mid-afternoon snack and nightly evening meal.

First Hotel Ja HOTEL €€
(☎0455-555 60; www.firsthotels.se; Borgmästaregatan 13; s/d from 895/1075kr; P@🌐) Karlskrona's top slumber spot boasts fashionable rooms with stripey wallpaper and decorative fabrics.

Hotel perks include a sauna, a bar-restaurant and a breakfast buffet served in a pleasant atrium. There are also several more decorative 'Ladies Rooms', exclusively for women.

Hotell Aston   HOTEL €€
(☑ 0455-194 70; www.hotellaston.se; Landbrogatan 1; s/d from 895/1095kr; P 🛜) Third-floor Hotell Aston and its sister, Hotell Conrad, are both smart, central options. Aston has spacious rooms, with simple, modern furnishings (but six flights of stairs). Serves an excellent breakfast.

Hotell Conrad   HOTEL €€
(☑ 0455-36 32 00; www.hotelconrad.se; Västra Köpmansgatan 12; s/d from 790/945kr; 🛜) An old-fashioned hotel that takes up three buildings, with decorations based on the era of the buildings: '70s, '80s and 'culture' from the late 1700s. Comfortable rooms and an exceptionally good buffet breakfast. It's the sister property to Hotell Aston.

🍴 Eating

Dining options in Karlskrona are generally better than other small cities in southern Sweden, with a decent selection of restaurants serving Swedish cuisine (plenty of seafood) and a smattering of world flavours.

If you're self-catering you'll find supermarkets and the Systembolaget liquor store in the Wachtmeister Galleria (www.wachtmeistergalleria.se; Borgmästaregatan 13; ⊙ 9am-6pm) shopping centre, along with casual dining options.

Lennarths Konditori   BAKERY €
(☑ 0455-31 03 32; Norra Kungsgatan 3; cakes from 30kr; ⊙ 8am-6pm Mon-Sat) Old-school bakery with a fantastic tubular retro ceiling, two outdoor terraces, and calorific treats. Try the delectable (if unfortunately named) *munk;* think doughnut meets apple strudel.

★ Nya Skafferiet   DELI €€
(☑ 0455-171 78; www.nyaskafferiet.se; Rädhusgatan 9; buffet 100kr, light meals 125-180kr; ⊙ 9am-6pm Mon-Fri, to 3pm Sat) This is a worldly Mediterranean cafe right behind the main square. There is a superb lunch buffet, as well as a well-stocked deli offering a bounty of cheeses, charcuterie, breads and excellent coffee. If you've not yet tried *köttbullar* (Swedish meatballs), here's a good place to start: order them off the à la carte menu.

Restaurang Montmartre   ITALIAN €€
(☑ 0455-31 18 33; www.montmartre.se; Ronnebygatan 18; pizza 89-125kr, mains 119-249kr; ⊙ 4-11pm Mon-Fri, from 1pm Sat & Sun) The atmospheric Montmartre evokes a French bistro with its wine-red drapes, tasselled lampshades and oil paintings. The menu hops over the border, however, with excellent pastas and 36-plus choices of pizza.

Nivå Bar & Stek   INTERNATIONAL €€
(☑ 0455-103 71; www.niva.nu; Norra Kungsgatan 3; mains 165-275kr; ⊙ 5-11pm Mon-Thu, 4pm-1am Fri, noon-1am Sat) Just off Stortorget, this steakhouse has a variety of light, well-priced dishes (nachos, burgers, salads), as well as heartier meals from the grill and some vegie options. It's also a popular evening bar; the doors stay open until at least 1am.

2 Rum & Kök   EUROPEAN €€€
(Två Rum & Kök; ☑ 0455-104 22; www.2rok.se; Södra Smedjegatan 3; fondue for 2 from 318kr, mains 225-295kr; ⊙ 5-10.30pm Mon-Sat) This gourmet spot is best known for its magnificent fondue, with flavours ranging from French to barbecue.

ℹ Information

Karlskrona Turistbyrå (☑ 0455-30 34 90; www.visitkarlskrona.se; Stortorget 2; ⊙ 9am-7pm Jun-Aug, shorter hours rest of year) Internet access, tour bookings and super-helpful staff who get lots of practice communicating face-to-face with curious visitors. Great range of interesting, inexpensive and well-timed tour options.

ℹ Getting There & Away

Karlskrona is 56km east of Karlshamn and 135km south of Kalmar, the gateway to Öland.

Blekingetrafiken (☑ 0455-56 00; www.blekingetrafiken.se) operates public transport in the local area while SJ Rail offers frequent direct train services to Karlshamn (99kr, one hour) and Kristianstad (172kr, 1½ hours), Lund (241kr, 2½ hours) and Malmö (241kr, 2¾ hours).

Svenska Buss (☑ 0771-67 67 67; www.svenskabuss.se) runs daily services to/from Stockholm (420kr, nine hours).

Stena Line (☑ 031-85 80 00; www.stenaline.com) ferries to Gdynia, Poland, start at 389kr. The journey takes about 9½ hours and boats depart from Verkö, 10km east of Karlskrona. Fares vary dramatically; check prices and book online for the best deals.

The free **Äspoleden** (www.trafikverket.se/aspoleden) car ferry shuttles between Karlskrona and the island of Äspo between 6am to midnight, at least hourly.

All buses depart from the bays adjacent to Karlskrona Centralstation.

Ronneby (☑ 010-109 54 00; www.swedavia.com) airport is 33km west of Karlskrona and has limited regular domestic connections.

For local taxis, call **Zon Taxi** (☑ 0455-230 50; www.zontaxi.se) or book online through the website.

Karlshamn

☑ 0454 / POP 32,130

You'd never guess that quiet Karslhamn, with its quaint cobbled streets, old wooden houses and art-nouveau architecture, was once so wicked. Alcoholic drinks, tobacco, snuff and playing cards were produced in great quantities here and it was a major 19th-century smugglers' den. It was also the port from where, in the 19th century, thousands of Swedes bade Sweden farewell and set sail for new lives in America.

○ Sights & Activities

★**Karlshamns Museum** MUSEUM
(☑ 0454-148 68; www.karlshamnsmuseum.se; Vinkelgatan 8; 20kr; ⊙ 1-5pm Tue-Sun Jun-Sep, 1-4pm Mon-Fri rest of year) The 'culture quarter' museum has interesting information about Karlshamn's history of producing tobacco and *punsch* (strong alcoholic punch), as well as a replica of the city's liquor factory (**Punchmuseet**, admission 20kr), complete with barrels, bottles and machinery. Beautiful 18th-century houses include the manor and merchant house Skottsbergska Gården and **Holländarhuset** (Dutchman's house).

Skottsbergska Gården HISTORIC BUILDING
(☑ 0454-148 68; www.karlshamnsmuseum.se; Drottninggatan 91; 20kr; ⊙ 1-5pm Tue-Sun Jun-Sep, 1-4pm Mon-Fri rest of year) This magnificent former mansion and merchant house is filled with antiques and valuable paintings. It falls under the Karlshamns Museum banner but a separate admission fee is charged.

Kreativum Science Center MUSEUM
(☑ 0454-30 33 60; www.kreativum.se; Strömmavägen 28; adult/child 150/115kr; ⊙ 11am-4pm Fri-Sun; ▣) This hands-on science museum, touching on all of the major scientific disciplines through fun activities and exhibits, is great for families. Its primary appeal will be for kids aged under 16, but parents will find some of the exhibits rewarding too.

It's located about 3km north of the station, on the far side of the E22.

★**Kallbadhuset Karlshamn** SWIMMING
(☑ 0705-98 42 66; http://kallbad.com/; Östersjön; 100kr; ⊙ 2-9pm Tue, 8am-5pm Wed-Sun) There's nothing more invigorating than immersing yourself in the frigid ocean. This architecturally impressive modern bathhouse, perched on stilts above the sea, replete with sauna (the idea is you warm up first, then cool down in the ocean) and terrace.

🛏 Sleeping & Eating

Hotell Bode HOTEL €
(☑ 0454-315 00; www.hotellbode.se; Fogdelyckeg 28; r from 895kr; 🖀) No two rooms are alike at this cosy, private hotel which is a sound, central choice provided you don't mind the lack of lift or the majority of rooms having shared showers (all rooms have en-suite toilets). Newly renovated rooms with private showers are available.

First Hotel Carlshamn HOTEL €€
(☑ 0454-890 00; www.firsthotels.com; Varvsgatan 1; s/d from 995/1195kr; ▣ @ 🖀) Rooms at this riverside hotel are spotlessly clean and comfortable, if not a little bit stuck in 1994. The best offer harbour views and private tubs.

★**Wägga Fisk &**
Delikatessrökeri SEAFOOD €€
(☑ 0454-190 35; www.delikatessrokeri.se; Saltsjöbadsvägen 44; dagens lunch 125kr, mains 115-175kr; ⊙ 9am-6pm Mon-Fri, 9am-2pm Sat, 11am-3pm Sun) This bright and cheery seafood restaurant sits on a picturesque harbour about 2.5km from the centre of town – a pleasant 30-minute stroll. Choose from the delicious array of seafood from the deli-style counter, then head to the terrace and enjoy seamless maritime views while your dish is prepared.

★**Gourmet Grön** BUFFET €€
(☑ 0454-164 40; www.karlshamn.gourmetgron.se; Biblioteksgatan 6; lunch buffet 100kr; ⊙ 11.30am-2pm Mon-Fri; ▮) 🍴 This waterside award-winner serves healthy, tasty buffets with an emphasis on organic and vegie food, offering excellent value.

ℹ Information

Karlshamn Tourist Centre (☑ 0454-812 03; www.karlshamn.se; Pirgatan 2; ⊙ 10am-7pm Mon-Fri) can help with information and bookings.

ℹ Getting There & Away

Karlshamn is 59km east of Kristianstad on the E22 motorway and almost exactly that distance west of Karlskrona, also on the E22.

SJ Rail's (p170) frequent services between Malmö and Karlshamn (178kr, two hours) continue on to Karlskrona (241kr, 2¾ hours).

DFDS Seaways (☑ 0454-336 80; www.dfds seaways.se) sails once a day between Karlshamn and Klaipėda (Lithuania; one way from 660kr, 14 hours).

The Southeast & Gotland

Best Places to Eat

➡ Gröna Stugan (p223)

➡ Bolaget (p238)

➡ Krakas Krog (p243)

➡ Pescadores (p215)

➡ Restaurant Solbacken (p217)

Best Places to Stay

➡ Vox Hotel (p215)

➡ Slottshotellet (p222)

➡ Hotell Västanå Slott (p216)

➡ Hotel St Clemens (p237)

➡ Kosta Boda Art Hotel (p225)

Why Go?

Southeastern Sweden is a treasure trove of stoic castles, story-book villages and mystical islands. Carved by the epic Göta Canal, Östergötland boasts lovable, lakeside Vadstena, home to a hulking Renaissance castle, and candy-crazed Gränna.

Småland sparkles with its ethereal forests, preserved pastel towns and show-off Kalmar castle. Snoop through Astrid Lindgren's childhood home in Vimmerby, check out Jönköping-Huskvarna's cool retro museums or try blowing glass in the villages of the so-called 'Glasriket' region.

Offshore Öland has a beguiling mix of windmills, wild animals, windswept coastlines and Iron Age archaeological sites. Not surprisingly, much of the island sits on the Unesco World Heritage list. The jewel in Southeastern Sweden's crown is the island of Gotland, a mesmerising spectacle of rune-scattered landscapes, medieval churches, sandy beaches and the magical, magnificent Hanseatic walled city of Visby, where we'll forgive you for thinking you've stepped back in time.

When to Go
Visby

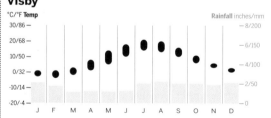

Jun–Aug Visitors are drawn by warm days, canal boat trips and Gotland's medieval week.

May & Sep Weather less predictable but often as nice as summer.

Dec Christmas markets abound across Småland.

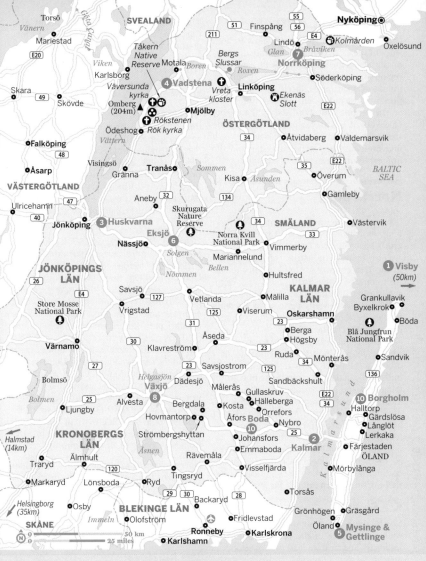

The Southeast & Gotland Highlights

1 Visby Sankta Maria domkyrka (p235) Climbing the stairs behind the cathedral for stunning views in Visby.

2 Kalmar Slott (p221) Making your every storybook castle dream come true.

3 Husqvarna Fabriksmuseum (p214) Walking down memory lane in this retro Huskvarna museum.

4 Vadstena Slott (p212) Recounting the lives of kings at this Renaissance fortress.

5 Mysinge Hög (p232) Visiting extraordinary Iron Age grave fields in Southern Öland.

6 Eksjö Museum (p217) Exploring the history of this picturesque wooden Eksjö.

7 Industrilandskapet (p208) Wandering the re-

imagined post-industrial landscapes of Norrköping.

8 Utvandrarnas Hus (p219) Tracing journeys between Sweden and the USA.

9 Glass Factory (p225) Browsing Boda's collection of art glass, or blowing your own.

10 Solliden Palace (p231) Smelling the roses at the royal summer-palace gardens.

ÖSTERGÖTLAND

Östergötland county harbours gems on both sides of the Göta Canal, which threads diagonally across the region. Along its banks, the region's main towns are mostly 19th-century industrial heartlands, laced with some impressive post-industrial conversions.

The region's west, bordered by the mighty Lake Vättern, is a treat of flat, lush countryside steeped in ancient history. This is where you'll find Sweden's rune-stone superstar and the unmissable medieval town of Vadstena.

Norrköping

✒ 011 / POP 139,363

It's hard to imagine Norrköping (norr-sher-ping) as it would've been 20 years ago – a grotty has-been past its use-by-date.

Norrköping's industrial identity began in the 17th century but took off in the late 19th century when textile mills and factories sprang up alongside the swift-flowing Motala *ström*. Seventy per cent of Sweden's textiles were once made here, the last mill shutting shop in the 1970s.

Forward planning and Sw dish design smarts stepped in at the right time to cleverly redevelop the city's defunct historical mills and canals into a hip posse of cultural hang-outs and Manhattan-style lofts against a backdrop of fringing waterfalls and locks. As Stockholm grapples with a high cost of living and little room for growth, nearby cities like Norrköping are on the radar.

While parts of town have already reverted to their working-class roots, the proliferation of construction sites indicates Norrköping's transformation is far from over.

◎ Sights

Norrköping's main sights are within easy walking distance of the centre. Pedestrian walkways and bridges lead past magnificent former factory buildings and around the ingenious system of locks and canals. The most thunderous waterfall is Kungsfallet, near the islet Laxholmen. Within the area are several interesting museums, all with free admission.

★ **Arbetets Museum**   MUSEUM
(Museum of Work; ✒ 011-18 98 00; www.arbetets museum.se; Laxholmen; ☉ 11am-5pm Wed-Mon, to 8pm Tue May-Sep) FREE The innovative Arbetets Museum documents working life.

There's one permanent display about Alva Carlsson, a typical worker in the former cotton mill, and temporary exhibitions focusing mainly on gender issues, human rights or multiculturalism. The seven-sided building, completed in 1917 and dubbed the 'flatiron', is a work of art in itself.

★ **Norrköpings konstmuseum**   GALLERY
(Norrköping Art Gallery; ✒ 011-15 26 00; www. norrkoping.se/konstmuseet; Kristinaplatsen 6; ☉ noon-4pm Tue-Sun, to 8pm Wed Jun-Aug) FREE Overlooking leafy Vasaparken, the city's impressive art gallery boasts a collection of important early-20th-century works, including modernist and cubist gems as well as one of Sweden's largest collections of graphic art.

Kolmårdens djurpark   ZOO
(Kolmården Wildlife Park; ✒ 010-708 70 00; www. kolmarden.com; Kolmården; adult/child 429/379kr; ☉ 10am-7pm mid-Jun–mid-Aug; P; 🚌 433) Opened in 1965, Scandinavia's largest zoo attracts some 750,000 visitors a year who come to visit its 750-odd residents from all climates and continents. Features include a safari park and a separate Tropicarium (✒ 011-39 52 50; www.tropicarium.se; adult/child 120/80kr; ☉ 10am-4pm) with its motley crew of spiders, sharks, alligators and snakes. The zoo also puts on dolphin shows which may concern some visitors, as animal welfare groups claim keeping dolphins in enclosed tanks is harmful for these complex animals.

Kolmården lies 35km north of Norrköping, on the north shore of Bråviken. Take bus 433 from Norrköping (83kr, 40 minutes).

Norrköpings stadsmuseum   MUSEUM
(Norrköping City Museum; ✒ 011-15 26 20; www. norrkoping.se/stadsmuseet; Holmbrogränden 2; ☉ 11am-4pm Tue-Sun) FREE Stadsmuseum delves into the town's industrial past, with still-functioning machinery, a great cafe and dynamic temporary exhibitions.

🛏 Sleeping

Norrköping has some good budget options and plenty of reasonably priced midrange accommodation – there's surprisingly not much by the way of high-end boutique lodging here...yet.

Abborrebergs Veranda   HOSTEL €
(✒ 073-385 44 00; www.abborreberg.se; Abborreberg Friluftsgård 2; dm/s/d from 275/325/525kr; ☉ Apr–mid-Oct; P; 🚌 116) Stunningly situated in a coastal pine wood 7km east of town,

Norrköping

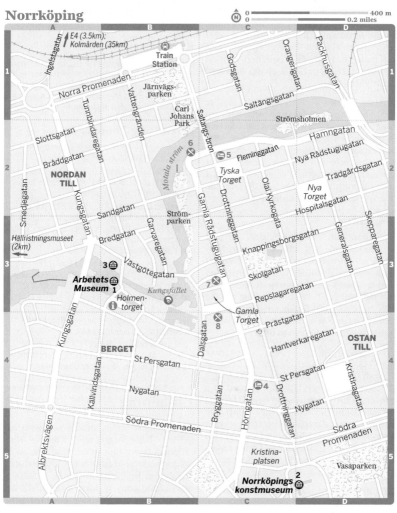

Norrköping

◎ Top Sights
1 Arbetets Museum	B3
2 Norrköpings konstmuseum	D5

◎ Sights
3 Norrköpings stadsmuseum	B3

🛏 Sleeping
4 Hotell Hörnan	C4
5 Strand Hotell	C2

🍽 Eating
6 Bryggeriet	B2
7 Fiskmagasinet	C3
8 Lagerqvist	C4

this sterling hostel offers accommodation in huts scattered through the surrounding park. The associated ice-cream parlour is always a hit. Take bus 116 to Lindö (42).

★ **Strand Hotell** BOUTIQUE HOTEL **€€**
(☑011-16 99 00; www.hotellstrand.se; Drottninggatan 2; s/d from 995/1295kr, apt 2100kr; @ 🛜)
A real gem in the heart of town, the Strand

takes up the 2nd floor of a gorgeous 1890 building overlooking the Motala river and Drottninggattan. It has operated as a hotel since the 1930s, and the furniture and fabrics make the most of the building's existing features, such as cut-glass chandeliers and big bay windows.

Hotell Hörnan   HOTEL **€€**
(☑ 011-16 58 90; www.hotellhornan.com; cnr Hörngatan & Sankt Persgatan; r with/without bathroom from 865/665kr; ❄ ☎) These spacious rooms offer good value. Glossy parquet floors, comfortable chairs, colourful rugs and scarlet drapes contrasting with dazzling white linen equal a contemporary, comfortable look. Pick up the key to your room in the adjacent pub.

✖ Eating

Restaurants are one-part cuisine, one-part service and one-part atmosphere and Norrkoping's industrial bones have given it umpteen opportunities to create inspiring dining spaces where young restaurateurs can ply their craft – without forking out the kind of rents you'd find in similar spaces in cities like London or New York. The result is lots of fun places for you to dine.

Fiskmagasinet   SEAFOOD **€€**
(☑ 011-13 45 60; www.fiskmagasinet.se; Skolgatan 1; lunch 90kr, mains 135-285kr; ☺ 11.30am-2pm & 5-10pm Mon-Fri, noon-10pm Sat) Housed in a converted 19th-century *snus* (snuff) factory, urbane Fiskmagasinet combines an intimate bar with a casually chic dining room serving savvy seafood dishes like grilled scampi with mashed potato, truffle and port-wine reduction, as well as cheaper Swedish classics.

Lagerqvist   EUROPEAN **€€**
(☑ 011-10 07 40; www.restauranglagerqvist.se; Gamla Torget 4; mains 125-285kr; ☺ 5-11pm Tue-Sun) This perennially popular restaurant-pub has a great summer garden courtyard and snug vaulted cellar. Meat dishes are the speciality, with innovative sides such as green beans with truffle butter. There are also platters for sharing.

Bryggeriet   SWEDISH **€€€**
(☑ 011-10 30 20; www.gamlabrygg.se; Sandgatan 1; mains 195-298kr; ☺ 4-10pm Mon-Fri, to 11pm Sat & Sun) Enjoy a dreamy position overlooking the water. The menu here includes finely crafted game dishes with fillet of deer and wild boar, while lunch is more along the lines of posh burgers and pasta. The atmos-

phere is elegant – don't turn up in thongs (flip-flops).

ⓘ Information

Experience Norrköping (☑ 011-15 50 00; www.upplev.norrkoping.se/en/; Källvindsgatan 1; ☺ 10am-6pm daily Jul–mid-Aug, shorter hours rest of year) Runs free one-hour walking tours of the industrial area in summer.

ⓘ Getting There & Away

Norrköping is 43km northeast of Linköping on the E4 and 61km southwest of Nyköping.

Regional buses depart from the bays next to the train station, while the long-distance buses leave from the bays opposite.

Swebus Express (☑ 0771-21 82 18; www.swebus.se) has frequent services to Stockholm (from 149kr, 2¼ hours), Jönköping (from 219kr, 2½ hours), Gothenburg (from 299kr, five hours) and Kalmar (from 269kr, four hours).

Norrköping is on the main **SJ Rail** (p186) railway line with regular services to Stockholm (206kr, 1½ hours), Malmö (206kr, 3¼ hours), Nyköping (75kr, one hour) and Linköping (65kr, 25 minutes).

Sweden's third-largest airport, **Stockholm Skavsta** (p329) is 60km away.

Local **Norrköping Airport** (☑ 011-15 37 22; www.norrkopingairport.com) has direct flights from Copenhagen, Munich and Helsinki.

Linköping

☑ 013 / POP 112,013

Most famous for its mighty medieval cathedral, Linköping fancies itself as Norrköping's more upmarket rival. Its most infamous claim to fame is the 'bloodbath of Linköping'. Following the Battle of Stångebro (1598), many of King Sigismund's defeated Catholic army were executed here, leaving Duke Karl and his Protestant forces in full control of Sweden.

While quite the modern, industrial city today (manufacturer Saab is the major employer), pockets of its past survive in its churches, castle and museums and in the picture-perfect streets around Hunnebergsgatan and Storgatan.

◎ Sights & Activities

★**Ekenäs Slott**   CASTLE
(☑ 073-650 24 20; www.ekenasslott.se; Ekenäs Slott 1; tours adult/child 80/40kr; ☺ guided tours on the hour 1-3pm Tue-Sun Jul, Sat & Sun Jun & Aug; ℗) Built between 1630 and 1644, this is one

of the best-preserved Renaissance castles in Sweden. Features include three spectacular towers, a moat, and furnishings from the 17th to 19th centuries. It's located 20km east of Linköping; you'll need your own transport to get here.

★ **Gamla Linköping**   AREA
(☎013-12 11 10; www.gamlalinkoping.info; Tunnbindaregatan 1; P🚻) FREE Located 2km west of the city, this is one of the biggest living-museum villages in Sweden. It's a gorgeous combo of cobbled streets, picket-fenced gardens and around 90 19th-century houses. Just 300m through the forest is **Valla Fritidsområde**, a recreation area with domestic animals, a children's playground, minigolf, small museums and vintage abodes.

Linköpings domkyrka   CHURCH
(Linköping Cathedral; ☎013-20 50 60; Sankt Petersgatan; ☉9am-6pm) FREE Made from blocks of hand-carved limestone, the enormous *domkyrka* was the country's largest and most expensive church in the Middle Ages. Its foundations were laid around 1250 and its 107m spire and vast interior still impress. Inside, the contemporary stained-glass windows may also catch your eye; they're the work of famous British stained-glass artist Brian Clarke.

There are organ concerts on Thursday in summer.

★ **Kinda Canal Cruises**   CRUISE
(☎070-637 17 00; www.rederiabkind.se; half-day cruises from 515kr; ☉May-Oct) While it's upstaged by the Göta Canal, Linköping boasts its own canal system, the 90km Kinda Canal. Opened in 1871, it has 15 locks, including Sweden's deepest. Cruises include evening

sailings, musical outings and wine-tasting trips. For a simple day excursion, from late June to early August, the *M/S Kind* leaves Tullbron dock at 10am on Tuesday, Thursday and Saturday, and travels to Rimforsa (return by bus or train).

🛏 Sleeping & Eating

Park Hotel   HOTEL €€
(☎013-12 90 05; www.fawltytowers.se; Järnvägsgatan 6; s/d from 1145/1345kr; P@🛜) Close to the train station and somewhat disturbingly billed as Sweden's 'Fawlty Towers', this smart family-run establishment resembles that madhouse in appearance only (yes, there's an elk head at reception). The public spaces sport chandeliers and oil paintings, and clean, parquet-floored rooms are crisply modern. You have to love the Swedish sense of humour.

Hotell du Nord   HISTORIC HOTEL €€
(☎013-12 98 95; www.hotelldunord.se; Repslagaregatan 5; s/d from 695/895kr; P🛜) Located across from the beautiful Järnvägsparken, Hotell du Nord is appropriately leafy and tranquil. The main dusky-rose 19th-century building looks like a doll's house, staff are friendly and the rooms are light filled and welcoming (those in the aesthetically challenged rear building are freshly renovated and larger). There's a patio for outdoor summer breakfasts.

Café Berget   BAKERY €
(☎013-13 18 11; www.cafeberget.com; Klostergatan 38; cakes from 35kr; ☉10am-6pm Mon-Fri, to 4pm Sat) Up a narrow set of stone stairs you'll find a sunny terrace, resplendent with flowers and ivy, which serves as the doorstep to this glorious little bolt-hole bakery. Café Berget serves

---

BERGS SLUSSAR

Bergs Slussar, 12km northwest of Linköping, is one of the most scenic sections of the Göta Canal: there are seven locks with a height gain of 19m – very impressive in canal terms! The nearby ruin **Vreta kloster**, Sweden's oldest monastery, was founded by Benedictine monks in 1120. While it's worth a look, the adjacent 13th-century **abbey church** is actually more interesting.

The **Bergs Slussar Tourist Office** (p212) occupies the same building as the beautifully located **Bergs Slussar Vandrarhem** (☎013-603 30; www.bergsslussar.com/vandrarhem; Oscars Slussar 2; dm 295kr; ☉May-Aug), right by the locks, where you can also play minigolf and hire bikes to ride along the canal.

You'll find a couple of cafes and restaurants out this way, including **Kanalkrogen** (☎013-600 76; www.kanalkrogen.nu; Loggvägen 2, Vreta Kloster; mains 198-279kr; ☉11.30am-6pm Mon-Sat), with a great range of meals and lockside views.

Buses 521 and 522 run regularly from Linköping.

up classic Swedish baked goodies – vanilla cream hearts and blueberry tartlets – as well as coffee, tea and sandwiches, in lovingly restored rooms in this 1905 building.

★ **Stångs Magasin** SWEDISH €€€
(☑ 013-31 21 00; www.stangsmagasin.se; Södra Stånggatan 1; lunch 115kr, mains 145-505kr; ⊙ 11.30am-2pm Mon-Fri, 6pm-midnight Tue-Fri, 5pm-midnight Sat Jul & Aug; ☎) In a 200-year-old warehouse down near the Kinda Canal docks, this elegant award-winner fuses classic Swedish cuisine with continental influences – think stuffed trout with beet aioli. There is an extensive wine list and a sommelier on hand to help you choose.

❶ Information

Bergs Slussar Tourist Office (☑ 013-190 00 70; Oscars Slussar 2; ⊙ 9.30am-5pm May-Aug) This small tourist office is located near the locks.

Visit Linköping (☑ 013-190 00 70; www.visitlinkoping.se; Storgatan 15; ⊙ 10am-6pm Mon-Fri, to 4pm Sat, to 6pm Sun) For brochures, maps and good advice.

❶ Getting There & Away

Linköping is 43km southwest of Norrköping and 50km east of Vadstena.

Östgöta Trafiken (☑ 0771-21 10 10; www.ostgotatrafiken.se) operates scheduled regional buses to Vadstena (150kr, 1¼ hours), which leave from outside the train station.

Swebus Express (p210) runs frequently to Jönköping (from 169kr, 1½ hours), Gothenburg (from 149kr, four hours) and north to Norrköping (from 59kr, 45 minutes). These long-distance buses depart from **Linköping Fjärrbussterminal** (Linköping Long-distance Bus Terminal; ☑ 070-318 41 09; Järnvägsgatan; ☎), 500m northwest of the train station.

Linköping is on the main north–south **SJ Rail** (p186) line between Malmö (206kr, three hours) and Stockholm (also 206kr, 1¾ hours). Frequent

❶ BUS TICKETS

You cannot pay cash on the bus throughout Östergötland. The best way to pay for your ticket is to buy a **Resekortet** travel card, which you can then load with a minimum of 100kr. Go to www.osgotatrafiken.se for a list of sales agents and venues where you can purchase the card.

regional trains run north to Norrköping (from 85kr, 25 minutes).

Linköping City Airport (☑ 013-18 10 30; www.linkopingcityairport.se; Åkerbogatan) is only 2km east of town. There's no airport bus, but taxi company **Taxibil** (☑ 013-14 60 00; www.taxibil.se) charges around 180kr for the ride into town.

Vadstena

☑ 0143 / POP 5646

Sublimely situated beside Lake Vättern, Vadstena is a legacy of both church and state power, and today St Birgitta's abbey and Gustav Vasa's castle compete with each other for admiration.

The atmosphere in the old town, with its wonderful cobbled lanes, intriguing small shops and wooden buildings, makes it an especially satisfying place to end a day of touring along the Göta Canal.

Vadstena really is a wonderfully quiet and pretty lakeside town with a hell of a lot of charm. There's something about the place that, if you've come for a day trip, you will wish you were spending the night. To prevent disappointment, book a night in advance.

◉ Sights

Both the old courthouse **rådhus** (road house), on the town square, and **Rödtornet** (Sånggatan) are late-medieval constructions.

★ **Vadstena Slott** CASTLE
(☑ 0143-62 16 00; www.vadstenaslott.com; Slottsvägen; tours adult/child 90/70kr; ⊙ 11am-6pm Jun-early Aug, to 4pm rest of year) Overlooking the lake, and considered one of the finest early Renaissance buildings in the Nordic region, construction commenced on Vadstena Slott, the family project of the early Vasa kings, in 1545. View their gloomy portraits inside, along with a modest historical display. The furnished upper floors are the most interesting, and be sure to visit the chapel, with its incredible 17-second echo! There are guided tours (in English, adult/child 130/90kr) from mid-July to mid-September; call ahead for times.

★ **Motala Motor Museum** MUSEUM
(☑ 0141-564 00; www.motormuseum.se; Platensgatan 2, Motala; adult/child 100/45kr; ⊙ 10am-8pm) If you're a rev-head or just a lover of beautiful machines, this vehicle museum in a lovely lakeside spot is a must for its staggering collection of more than 300 vehicles

of all makes, shapes, sizes and eras, from the humble to the extravagant.

★ Sancta Birgitta Klostermuseet
MUSEUM

(☑ 0143-100 31; www.klostermuseum.se; La-sarettsgatan; adult/child 80/40kr; ⊙ 10.30am-5pm Jul–mid-Aug, 11am-4pm Jun & rest of Aug) The Sancta Birgitta Klostermuseet is in Bjälboät-tens Palats (a royal residence that became a convent in 1384) and tells the story of St Bir-gitta's roller-coaster life and those of all her saint-and-sinner children. Artefacts include the coffin that carried her back from Rome.

Rökstenen
MONUMENT

(Rök) Sweden's most famous rune stone, the 9th-century Rökstenen, is near the church at Rök (just off the E4 on the road to Heda and Alvastra, 25km from Vadstena). It's a monumental memorial stone raised to commemorate a dead son and features the longest runic inscription in the world. It's an ancient, intricate verse so cryptic that schol-ars constantly scrap over its interpretation. The outdoor exhibition and stone are always open.

Buses are virtually nonexistent, though the scenic flatlands around Vättern make for perfect cycling.

Vadstena klosterkyrka
CHURCH

(Vadstena Abbey Church; ☑ 0143-298 50; La-sarettsgatan 5; ⊙ 9am-8pm Jul, to 7pm Jun & Aug) 'Of plain construction, humble and strong', the church was built in response to one of St Birgitta's visions. After its consecration in 1430, Vadstena became *the* top pilgrim-age site in Sweden. Step inside for medieval sculptures and carved floor slabs.

🛏 Sleeping & Eating

Pensionat Solgården
B&B €

(☑ 0143-143 50; www.pensionatsolgarden.se; Strågatan 3; s/d from 540/790kr; ⊙ May-Sep; P 🛜) Set in a classic 1905 wooden house, this family-run hotel boasts lovingly dec-orated rooms; some have private bath-rooms and all have an art/artist connection. They're each *very* different – check the pho-tos on the website to choose your favourite (number 25 is particularly grand).

Vadstena Klosterhotel
HISTORIC HOTEL €€

(☑ 0143-315 30; www.klosterhotel.se; Lasarettsga-tan 5; r from 1475kr; P @ 🛜) History and luxury merge at this wonderfully atmospheric hotel in St Birgitta's old convent. The bathrooms are a wee bit dated, but the medieval-style

rooms are great, with chandeliers and high wooden beds. Most boast lake views. The hotel also has simpler rooms with shared bathrooms and showers in a nearby cottage (singles/doubles 790/990kr).

Rådhuskällaren
INTERNATIONAL €€

(☑ 0143-121 70; www.radhuskallaren.com; Rådhus-torget; mains 145-270kr; ⊙ noon-10pm Wed-Sat, to 6pm Sun) Under the old courthouse, this affa-ble 15th-century cellar restaurant dishes out simple but satisfying burger, pasta and fish meals. Its outdoor area is a favourite after-noon drinking spot in summer.

★ Restaurant Munkklostret
EUROPEAN €€€

(☑ 0143-130 00; www.klosterhotel.se; Lasaretts-gatan 5; mains 198-295kr; ⊙ noon-11pm daily Jun-Aug, from 6pm rest of year; P 🛜) The Vad-stena Klosterhotel's ravishing restaurant is the best dining spot in town. Seasonal, succulent steak, lamb, game and fish dishes are flavoured with herbs from the monas-tery garden, and served in the monks' old dorms.

❶ Information

Vadstena Turistbyrå (☑ 0143-315 70; www.vadstena.se; Storgatan 31; ⊙ 10am-2pm Mon-Sat, longer hours in summer) Has plenty of local info on Lake Vättern.

❶ Getting There & Away

Vadstena is 58km north of Gränna on the E4 and 51km west of Linköping.

Only buses run to Vadstena – take bus 610 to Motala (for trains to Örebro), or bus 661 to Mjölby (for trains to Linköping and Stockholm). **Blåklints Buss** (☑ 0142-121 50; www.blaklints-buss.se) runs one to three services daily from the Viking Line Terminal in Stockholm to Vads-tena (250kr).

Cykelaventyr (☑ 076-831 48 25; www.cykelaventyr.se; Kanalvägen 17, Borensberg) in Motala (15km north of Vadstena) has bikes for rent (165kr per day).

SMÅLAND

The province of Småland isn't small at all, but occupies some 29,400-sq-km of dense forests, glinting lakes and bare marsh-lands from the Baltic Sea coast, deep into the Swedish interior. In fact, it's so big that its broken up into five smaller counties or *län*: Kalmar, Östergötland, Jönköpings, Kronobergs and Halland, of which Kalmar is the largest and Östergötland the most populous.

Historically, Småland served as a buffer between the Swedes and Danes who were forever having territorial tussles. Today, it's known for its Glasriket 'Kingdom of Glass' (think Orrefors and Kosta Boda glassware), the scenic Lake Vänern towns of Jönköping-Huskvarna, Gränna and Vadstena, and as the jump-off point for island explorations to Öland (from Kalmar, with its magnificent castle) and Gotland (from Oskarshamn, with its hulking ferries).

From nature to history and culture, Småland has a lot to offer – plan for a few days here if you can.

❶ Getting There & Away

Self-driving is the best way to explore this large and diverse province.

The E4 motorway flanks Småland's western border, while the E22 hugs the Baltic Coast, it's eastern extent. The area is criss-crossed with many county roads, where you'll see plenty of trees, lots of lakes and maybe even a moose.

SJ Rail (p186) operates services along the Malmö–Stockholm main line and some local branch lines which pass through Småland's western frontier, but for the eastern Baltic Coast you're limited to local and long-distance buses.

Jönköping-Huskvarna

📝036 / POP 87,758

On the southern shore of lovely Lake Vättern lies Jönköping (yern-sher-ping), Småland's most populous municipality. The city also goes under the name Jönköping-Huskvarna, sharing the limelight with its lakeside neighbour, home of the almost-eponymous manufacturer Husqvarna, whose excellent museum traces the company's history making everything from guns to motorbikes, sewing machines and robot lawnmowers.

Museum buffs will love it here – the city has plenty of quirky exhibitions to educate and enthral. Few would know it, but the world owes much to Jönköping, birthplace of the humble safety match. Of course, there's a match museum to word you up on this undervalued necessity, a collection of retro radios, a kid-friendly science museum and a superb collection of the work of renowned fairy-tale illustrator John Bauer at the county museum.

Well-priced accommodation, decent dining options and ease of access mean that Jönköping-Huskvarna warrants your attention for at least a day or two.

◉ Sights

★**Husqvarna Fabriksmuseum**　　MUSEUM
(📝036-14 61 62; www.husqvarnamuseum.se; Hakarpsvägen 1; adult/student 70/50kr, child under 12yr free; ⊙10am-5pm Mon-Fri May-Sep, to 3pm Oct-Apr, noon-4pm Sat & Sun year-round) Square-jawed men going hunting while their wives snuggle up to sewing machines: the Husqvarna Fabriksmuseum conjures up a vivid 1950s world and while that world might not be a picture of gender equality today, it is nonetheless intrinsic to our histories. This atmospheric museum in Huskvarna charts the company's rise as an arms manufacturer before diverting into more wholesome developments such as motorbikes, microwaves and sewing machines. It's got a wonderfully authentic feel – fans of retro design could spend hours here.

★**Upptech**　　MUSEUM
(📝036-10 60 77; www.upptech.se; Västra Holmgatan 34a; adult/child 80/60kr; ⊙10am-4pm Sat & Sun; 🅿🚼) Jönköping's science museum makes for an interesting and fun day out for inquisitive adults, though it's definitely geared towards the younger generation. The impressive 1.7-sq-km of hands-on exhibits includes a Lego Mindstorm area (programmable Lego bots!) and a miniature electric-car driving course for youngsters. Although the language is predominantly Swedish, most exhibits are quite hands-on in approach and challenge the visitor to 'figure things out'. If you get stuck, staff speak beautiful English.

Jönköpings Läns Museum　　MUSEUM
(📝036-30 18 00; www.jkpglm.se; Dag Hammarskjöld plats 2; ⊙10am-5pm Mon-Fri, 11am-3pm Sat & Sun) **FREE** Visiting and permanent exhibitions cover local history and contemporary culture, but the best reason for coming here is to see the haunting fantasy works of artist John Bauer (1882–1918). In his short life, the local artist produced an illuminating and haunting body of work, predominantly illustrations, inspired by his time in the forests around Jönköping and Lake Vänern.

Tändsticksmuseet　　MUSEUM
(📝036-10 55 43; www.matchmuseum.se; Tändsticksgränd 27; adult/child 50kr/free, Nov-Feb free; ⊙10am-5pm Mon-Fri, to 3pm Sat & Sun Jun-Aug, shorter hours rest of year) Apparently 'the only match museum in the world', Tändsticksmu-

seet, in an old match factory, deals with this practical Swedish invention. It's quite an eye-opener: the industry was initially based on cheap child labour, workers frequently suffered from repulsive 'phossy jaw', and it was common knowledge that phosphorus matches were good for 'speeding up inheritance and inducing abortions'.

Smedbyn i Huskvarna   STREET
(www.smedbyn.se; Smedbygatan 5a; ⊙ 10am-5pm; P) This atmospheric little lane of Falu-red houses converted into primarily private galleries and craft boutiques, all selling their wares, makes for an interesting stroll (and shop).

🛏 Sleeping & Eating

⭐ **STF Vandrarhem Huskvarna**   HOSTEL €
(✆ 036-14 88 70; www.hhv.se; Odengatan 10; hostel dm/s/d per person from 230/440/590kr, hotel s/d from 895/995kr; @ 🛜) Standards are high at this sizeable year-round property which is divided into a hostel (shared facilities) and hotel wing. A bunch of fresh, new hotel rooms have just been completed. All rooms (including dorms) are bright and stylish and have a TV. An impressive breakfast buffet is an additional 75kr. For hostel rooms, linen/towels cost 80kr, as does cleaning.

Elite Stora Hotellet   HOTEL €€
(✆ 036-10 00 00; www.elite.se; Hotellplan; s/d from 895/995kr; P @ 🛜) The Elite is Jönköping's harbourside show-stopper. Rooms are historic hotel chic, with either pastel, Carl Larsson–inspired undertones or a more contemporary combo of black-and-white photographs and natural hues. There's a sauna, a pool table and a slinky restaurant, as well as a banquet hall fit for royalty.

⭐ **Vox Hotel**   BOUTIQUE HOTEL €€€
(✆ 036-770 00 00; www.voxhotel.se; Lantmätargränd 2; d/ste from 895/2595kr) This bright and colourful 143-room hotel overlooking Lake Vättern is very cool. From its modern adaptions of classic Scandinavian furniture to bold colour schemes and mosaic-tiled bathrooms, you're bound to want to stay in. Even more so if you book one of the hotel's impressive two-room suites with lake-view balconies. Budget rooms (without window) are available and breakfast is killer.

Kafé Braheparken   VEGAN €
(✆ 036-12 60 20; www.kafebraheparken.se; Kyrkogatan 16; dagens lunch 98kr, mains 62-85kr;

BUNN & ÖREN

The beautiful lakes of Bunn and Ören, and their dark forests, inspired local artist John Bauer to paint his trolls and magical pools (you can see his work at Jönköpings Läns Museum). In summer you can take a boat tour to the lakes, departing from Bunnströms badplats, 2.5km from Gränna.

⊙ 11am-5pm Mon-Fri; ✍) 🍃 Really tasty organic vegan dishes and a generous lunchtime buffet with tofu 'cheese', hummus and more green crunchy veg than you can shake a carrot stick at, plus a hot special. Also sells delicious pies, cakes and cookies.

⭐ **Pescadores**   SEAFOOD €€
(✆ 036-12 20 01; www.pescadores.se; Svavelsticksgränd 23; menus 359-519kr, mains 105-289kr; ⊙ 11.30am-2pm & 5-10pm Tue-Sun) A family-run fish restaurant located in one of the quirky brick buildings that once belonged to the match-making empire. The father and son owners were previously commercial crayfishermen, so they know their stuff. The menu features all the classics, from fresh, fresh fish and chips to gravlax and mussel soup. It's the perfect spot to see how Swedes do seafood.

Mäster Gudmunds Källare   EUROPEAN €€
(✆ 036-10 06 40; www.mastergudmund.se; Kapellgatan 2; set lunch 79kr, mains 149-249kr; ⊙ 11.30am-2pm & 6-10pm Mon-Fri, noon-10pm Sat, to 5pm Sun) This much-loved restaurant sits in a 17th-century cellar, with beautiful vaulted ceilings and excellent-value lunch sets. Evening mains are mainly meaty and fishy local dishes, with a few nods to French and Italian fare: something for everyone.

ℹ Information
Destination Jönköping (✆ 036-10 50 50; www.jkpg.com; Södra Strandgatan 13b; ⊙ 9.30am-5pm Mon-Fri, to 3pm Sat & Sun) Located in the Juneporten complex at the train station.

ℹ Getting There & Around
Jönköping is 119km north of Växjö on Rte 30 and 60km west of Eksjö along Rte 40.

The long-distance bus station is next to the train station.

Swebus Express (p210) operates daily services to Gothenburg (from 99kr, 2¼ hours), Stockholm (from 139kr, 4½ hours), Helsingborg (from 219kr, three hours) and Malmö (from 279kr, 4¼ hours).

Jönköping is on a regional **SJ Rail** (p186) line; you'll need to change trains in either Nässjö (71kr, 35 minutes) or Falköping (110kr, 45 minutes) to get to or from larger centres.

Jönköping Airport (☑ 036-31 11 00; www.jonkopingairport.se) is located about 8km southwest of the town centre and offers low-cost domestic flights with **Nextjet** (☑ 0771-90 00 90; www.nextjet.se), limited connections to Lufthansa's international network via Frankfurt, as well as daily charter flights to holiday destinations.

Buses are operated by **Länstrafiken** (p220) and depart opposite Juneporten on Västra Storgatan.

Take local bus 1 or 101 to get to Huskvarna (43kr, 25 minutes), or go by less frequent train (43kr, five minutes).

If you need a cab, try **Taxi Jönköping** (☑ 036-34 40 00; www.taxijonkoping.se).

Gränna

☑ 0390 / POP 2553

Little lakeside Gränna draws regular crowds in the sunny months of spring and summer when the scent of sugar hangs about the place and shops overflow with the village's trademark red-and-white peppermint *polkagris* (rock candy). On weekends and in school holidays, you'll find traffic flow grinds to a halt as carloads craving candy search for parking spots on the elevated main street and motorhomes roll their way down the hill to Lake Vättern and the ferry to Visingsö, for which Gränna is the gateway port.

If you're travelling with kids, or in a motorhome, or a lover of camping life, you'll probably love Granna too. If not, you might find the village a tad touristy and out of the way, despite its quaint appeal and friendly locals.

⊙ Sights & Activities

Grenna Museum – The Andrée Expedition – Polar Centre   MUSEUM
(☑ 036-10 38 90; www.grennamuseum.se; Brahegatan 38-40; adult/child 50/20kr; ⊙10am-6pm daily mid-May–Aug, to 4pm Sep–mid-May; ℗) This unique and impressive museum describes the disastrous attempt of Salomon August Andrée to reach the North Pole by

balloon in 1897. It's riveting stuff, particularly the poignant remnants of the expedition: cracked leather boots, monogrammed handkerchiefs, lucky amulets, and mustard paper to ward off those polar winds.

Grenna Polkagriskokeri   FACTORY
(☑ 0390-100 39; www.polkagris.com; Brahegatan 39; ⊙8am-9pm Mon-Fri, 9am-8pm Sat & Sun) Several sweet-makers in Gränna have kitchens where you can watch the town's trademark red-and-white peppermint *polkagris* (rock candy) being made, but this place, directly opposite Turistbyrå Gränna, is the best known. The hard candy is made from an original 19th-century recipe comprising only sugar, water, vinegar and natural peppermint oil.

Grenna Ballongresor   BALLOONING
(☑ 0390-305 25; www.flyg-ballong.nu; Jönköpingsvägen 71; 1hr flight 1/2 people 3500/5500kr; ⊙reception 10am-2pm) Take to the skies in a hot-air balloon for a one-hour scenic trip over the lakes and the patchwork of forests and fields.

🛏 Sleeping & Eating

Strandterrassen   HOSTEL €
(☑ 0390-418 40; www.strandterrassen.se; Amiralsvägen 55; dm from 260kr; ℗🖢) This hostel offers simple, bright, clean rooms in long wooden cabins, as well as a cafe. Breakfast is an additional 85kr and linen and towel hire will set you back another 90kr. It's right on the water near the Gränna–Visingsö Ferry.

★Hotell Västanå Slott   HISTORIC HOTEL €€€
(☑ 0390-107 00; www.countrysidehotels.se/en/hotel/vastana-castle; Västanå 1; d from 2200kr; ℗🖢) Originally built as a palace in 1590, then owned by Count Per Brahe in the 17th century, Västanå Slott, located 6km south of Gränna, became Sweden's first Manor House hotel in 1948. It remains decorated according to its 18th-century past, with chandeliers, brooding oil paintings and suits of armour, and decadent guest rooms perfect for staying in: some rooms have deep copper tubs.

Hotel Amalias Hus   BOUTIQUE HOTEL €€€
(☑ 0390-413 23; www.amaliashus.se; Brahegatan 2; s/d from 1350/1890kr; ℗@🖢) Once owned by Amalia Eriksson, the creator of Granna's famous peppermint rock, this hotel is one for lovers of classic country style. Beautifully restored rooms are individually styled and feature downy beds, antique furniture and

lacy drapes. Deluxe rooms and suites have Jacuzzis. It's a good choice if you enjoy the play of luxury, ceremony and old-fashioned service.

Fiket BAKERY €
(☎0390-100 57; www.fiket.se; Brahegatan 57; light meals 65-130kr; ⊙8.30am-6pm Mon-Sat, 10am-4pm Sun) The pick of Gränna's eateries is this time-warp bakery-cafe, complete with retro jukebox, chequered floor and record-clad walls. Tackle tasty grilled baguettes, quiches, salads and pastries, either indoors or on the breezy balcony.

❶ Information

Turistbyrå Gränna (Gränna Tourist Office; ☎036-10 38 60; www.jkpg.com/sv/granna; Brahegatan 38; ⊙10am-6pm daily mid-May–Aug, to 4pm Sep–mid-May) Has knowledgeable, helpful staff who can tell you where the best spots to go for walks, swims and hikes can be found, and help you find a place to stay.

❶ Getting There & Away

Gränna is 32km north of Jönköping-Huskvarna on the E4 motorway. Continuing north on the E4, the next major town is Linköping, 95km away.

Local bus 101 runs hourly from Jönköping to Gränna (71kr, one hour). Bus 120 runs several times Monday to Friday from Gränna to the mainline train station in Tranås (71kr, one hour).

Daily **Swebus Express** (p106) destinations include Gothenburg, Jönköping, Linköping, Norrköping and Stockholm. Swebus Express services stop 3km outside Gränna, from where you can catch bus 121 into town or walk (30 minutes).

Eksjö

☎0381 / POP 17,129

Compact Eksjö (eh-qua), located almost in the very centre of Småland, is one of the most exquisitely preserved wooden towns in Sweden.

The area south of today's town square was razed to the ground in a blaze in 1856, paving the way for the beautiful neoclassical buildings you see today, while the area to the north survived the fire. It's buildings date back to the 17th century and include Eksjö's two excellent museums. Both sides will have you swooning over the jumble of candy-coloured houses and flower-filled courtyards.

On weekends and in summer, when there always seems to be something going on, the little town is popular with day trippers. Outside the busy times, it's blissfully quiet and a lovely, central place to base yourself for a night or two if you have aspirations to explore Småland.

◉ Sights & Activities

★**Eksjö Museum** MUSEUM
(☎0381-361 60; www.eksjomuseum.se; Österlånggatan 31; 50kr; ⊙1-5pm Tue-Fri, 11am-3pm Sa & Sun) Award-winning Eksjö Museum tells the

---

VISINGSÖ

Across the water and 6.2km west of Gränna is the peaceful island of Visingsö. Home to Sweden's largest oak forest, it's a great place to cycle, relax and enjoy the peace and tranquillity of nature. There's also a 17th-century church, a small castle and an aromatic herb garden.

The **Gränna–Visingsö Ferry** (☎036-10 37 70; adult/child 50/25kr) runs half-hourly in summer (less frequently the rest of the year). Return tickets for foot passengers are 50kr per adult, and 25kr for those aged between six and 15 years; a bicycle is 50kr and a car plus driver is 180kr.

For information on where to explore, contact **Turistbyrå Gränna** before setting out or **Tourist Visingsö** (☎036-10 38 89; www.visingso.net; Hamnen, Visingsö; ⊙10am-5pm daily May-Aug, shorter hours rest of year) at the harbour when you arrive. The latter can also assist with bike hire (from 80kr per day).

There are plenty of camping spots on the island, but if you need more of a roof over your head, **Visingsö Vandrarhem** (☎0390-401 91; www.visingso-vandrarhem.se; Fredängen, Visingsö; dm/s/d per person 200/400/600kr, breakfast 85kr; ⊙May-Oct) is a lovely, low-cost option.

If you're just coming for the day and are looking for a bite, pop in to **Restaurant Solbacken** (☎0390-400 29; www.restaurang-solbacken.se; Hamnen, Visingsö; mains 125-229kr; ⊙10am-3pm Mon-Thu, to 8pm Fri & Sat, to 6pm Sun) 🍴.

THE GÖTA CANAL

Not only is the Göta Canal Sweden's greatest civil-engineering feat, idling along it on a boat or cycling the towpaths is one of the best ways to soak up Central Sweden's lush and lilting countryside.

The canal connects the North Sea with the Baltic Sea, and links the great lakes Vättern and Vänern. Its total length is 190km, although only around 87km is human-made – the rest is rivers and lakes. Built between 1802 and 1832 by a burly team of some 60,000 soldiers, it has provided a hugely valuable transport and trade link between Sweden's east and west coasts.

The canal has two sections: the eastern section from Mem (southeast of Norrköping) to Motala (north of Vadstena on Vättern); and the western section from Karlsborg (on Vättern) to Sjötorp (on the shores of Vänern). The system is then linked to the sea by the Trollhätte Canal, in Västergötland. Along these stretches of the canal are towpaths, used in earlier times by horses and oxen pulling barges. Nowadays they're the domain of walkers and cyclists.

A variety of operators offer four- to six-day cruises along the length of the canal between Stockholm and Gothenburg as well as shorter, cheaper and more popular half- and full-day trips on each lake and along sections of the canal. Schedules and pricing changes seasonally, and special events sailings (sometimes including a meal and entertainment) are often held.

Your best planning resources are the many local *turisybyrå* (tourist offices) and the official website: www.gotakanal.se.

town's story from the 15th century onward. The top floor is devoted to local Albert Engström (1869–1940), renowned for his burlesque, satirical cartoons. Eksjö was once known as the 'Hussar Town', and the region's long-standing military connections are also explored at the museum. The town hosts a **tattoo** (www.eksjotattoo.se; ⊙ Aug) in early August, complete with plenty of military pomp and circumstance.

Skurugata Nature Reserve NATURE RESERVE
(Skurugata) The Skurugata Nature Reserve, 13km northeast of Eksjö, is centred on a peculiar 800m-long fissure in the rocks. Its sides tower to 56m, yet in places the fissure is only 7m wide. In times past, the ravine was believed to harbour trolls and thieves. The nearby hill of **Skuruhatt** (337m) offers impressive forest views. You'll need your own transport to get here.

Höglandsleden HIKING
(www.swedishtouristassociation.com/trails/hoglandsleden/) Try some berry picking or just enjoy woodland tranquillity on the well-maintained Höglandsleden trail, a 440km trail with a large looped section, which passes through the Skurugata Nature Reserve; ask the Eksjö Infocenter for details and maps.

🛏 Sleeping & Eating

★**Eksjö Camping** CAMPGROUND €
(📞 0381-395 00; www.eksjocamping.se; Prästängsvägen 5; sites from 195kr, 2-/4-bed cabins from 375/595kr; 🅿 🛜) This friendly nook by picturesque Lake Husnäsen, about a kilometre east of town, has a restaurant and cafe with a big outdoor terrace and even minigolf. There's also a hostel with dorm beds (from 300kr) and a clutch of cosy camping cabins.

Hotell Vaxblekaregården B&B €€
(📞 0381-140 40; www.vaxblekaregarden.com; Arendt Byggmästares-gata 8; s/d from 995/1195kr; @🛜) Set in a converted 17th-century wax-bleaching workshop, this boutique number features stylish, pared-back rooms with wooden floorboards, Carl Larsson-inspired wallpaper and wrought-iron bedheads. The lounge-laced backyard hosts barbecues and live-music gigs on Saturday evening from mid-June to mid-August.

Lennarts Konditori BAKERY €
(📞 0381-61 13 90; www.lennartskonditori.se; Norra Kyrkogatan 6b; light meals 70-120kr; ⊙ 7am-7pm Mon-Fri, 10am-5pm Sat & Sun) This traditional Swedish *konditori* (bakery-cafe) is about as old-school as they come, dating from 1947. With an outdoor terrace and views of Eksjö's

lovely main street, Lennarts is the go-to for cakes, crêpes, quiche and coffee.

Sunrise MONGOLIAN €€
(📞0381-121 20; www.sunrise-eksjo.se; Norra Storgatan 19; mains 118-208kr; ☉11.30am-9pm Mon-Sat, 1-8pm Sun; 🍴) The Mongolian barbecue (adult/child 208/108kr) at this authentic restaurant is the star turn here, prepared fresh on the griddle with a selection of 12 sauces, plus a vegetarian option. A wide range of other pan-Asian dishes, including more vegie options, are available.

ℹ️ Information

Eksjö Infocenter (📞0381-361 70; www.visit eksjo.se; Norra Storgatan 29; ☉8am-8pm daily Jul–mid-Aug, 10am-6pm Mon-Fri & 10am-2pm Sat rest of year) Can arrange English-language guided town tours or audio guides for 40kr and 45kr, respectively, from Monday to Saturday from late June to early August. Bicycle hire (65/230kr per day/week) is also available.

ℹ️ Getting There & Away

Eksjö is a middle child, located 60km east of Jönköping and 60km west of Vimmerby.

Local bus 325 runs to Nässjö (43kr, 25 minutes) where you can connect with **SJ Rail's** (p186) tiny *länståg* (regional train) service to Jönköping (71kr, 35 minutes) and the network beyond, or get bus 351 (71kr, one hour) direct to Jönköping.

Växjö

📞0470 / POP 89,500

A venerable old market town, pretty Växjö (vek-hwa), in Kronobergs *län*, is today a growing city and an important stop for Americans seeking their Swedish roots. An annual festival commemorates the mass 19th-century emigration from the area, which is well documented in the insightful emigration museum.

Vaxjö's glass museum, packed with gorgeous works of art and plenty of history, is another highlight, as are its waterfront parklands, historic church and laid-back vibe.

⊙ Sights

Enquire at the tourist office about guided summer walking tours (50kr, 5.30pm Tuesday and Thursday) around town.

★**Smålands Museum** MUSEUM
(📞0470-70 42 00; www.kulturparkensmaland. se; Södra Järnvägsgatan 2; adult/child 90kr/free; ☉10am-5pm Tue-Fri, to 4pm Sat & Sun) Among the varied exhibits at Sweden's oldest provincial museum is a truly stunning exhibition about the country's 500-year-old glass industry, with objects spanning medieval goblets to cutting-edge contemporary sculptures. It even houses a Guinness World Record collection of Swedish cheese-dish covers – 71 in total. There's a great cafe and the ticket price covers the adjacent Utvandrarnas Hus.

★**Utvandrarnas Hus** MUSEUM
(House of Emigrants; 📞0470-70 42 00; www. utvandrarnashus.se; Vilhelm Mobergs gata 4; adult/ child 90kr/free; ☉10am-5pm Tue-Fri, to 4pm Sat & Sun) Utvandrarnas Hus boasts engrossing displays on the emigration of more than one million Swedes to America (1850–1930) and includes a replica of Vilhelm Moberg's office and original manuscripts of his famous emigration novels. Entry price also covers admission to the neighbouring Smålands Museum.

Växjö Konsthall MUSEUM
(Växjö Art Gallery; 📞0470-414 75; www.vaxjo.se/ konsthall; Västra Esplanaden 10; ☉noon-6pm Tue-Fri, to 4pm Sat & Sun) FREE Växjö's art gallery showcases contemporary work by local and national artists; expect anything from minimalist ceramics to mixed-media installations.

🛏️ Sleeping & Eating

Växjö Vandrarhem HOSTEL €
(📞0470-630 70; www.vaxjovandrarhem. nu; Brandts väg 11, Evedal; dm/s/d from 200/495/595kr; ☉reception 5-8pm Jun-Aug; 🅿️@🛜) Located at the lakeside recreation area of Evedal, 6km north of Växjö, this former spa hotel dates from the late 18th century. All rooms have washbasins, and there's a big kitchen, a laundry and a wonderful lounge in the attic. You can also hire canoes and bikes.

★**B&B Södra Lycke** B&B €€
(📞0706-76 65 06; www.sodralycke.se; Hagagatan 10; s/d from 500/800kr; 🅿️🛜) This charming B&B in an atmospheric mid-19th-century family house is in a residential area 10 minutes' walk southwest from the centre via Södra Järnvägsgatan (check online for a map). There are three rooms and an appealingly overgrown garden complete with vegetable plot, wildflowers, greenhouse and black hens.

THE SOUTHEAST & GOTLAND VÄXJÖ

Växjö

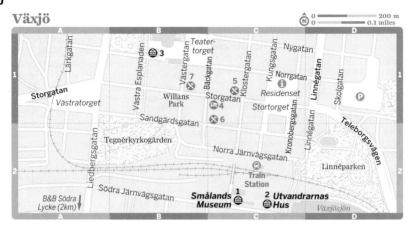

Växjö

Clarion Collection Cardinal   HOTEL €€

(☏0470-72 28 00; www.nordicchoicehotels.com/hotels/sweden/vaxjo/clarion-collection-hotel-cardinal/; Bäckgatan 10; s/d from 895/1095kr; P@🖧) A jump up in quality, the central Cardinal offers simple, stylish rooms with Persian rugs and the odd antique touch. There's also a small fitness centre, a bar and a restaurant serving modern Nordic cuisine. Note that, as with all Clarion Collection hotels, a buffet dinner (as well as breakfast) is generously included in the room price.

Bröd & Sovel   BAKERY €

(☏0470-470 75; www.pmrestauranger.se/sv/brod-sovel/; Storgatan 12; baked goods from 55kr; ⊙7.30am-7pm Mon-Fri, 9am-5pm Sat, noon-7pm Sun; P) This bakery, lauded throughout Swedish culinary circles, offers a vast array of buttery pastries, creamy cakes, freshly made sandwiches and homemade sweets. At the very least pick up half a dozen of the chocolate-covered macadamia nuts to go – you'll be back for more...

★ Kafe de Luxe   INTERNATIONAL €€

(☏0470-74 04 09; www.kafedeluxe.se; Sandgärdsgatan 19; mains from 140-245kr; ⊙11am-midnight Mon-Thu, to 2am Fri & Sat, 10am-1am Sun; 🍴) An urban-boho vibe, great music (live at weekends) and '50s- to '60s-style decor, including an adjacent candy-coloured ice-cream parlour, contribute to the special feel of this place. The burgers are renowned, as is the eclectic dinner menu with its French-inspired dishes such as entrecôte with a classic *Béarnaise* sauce and its innovative vegie choices: nettle gnocchi, anyone? Occasional DJs.

PM & Vänner   SWEDISH €€€

(☏0470-70 04 44; www.pmrestauranger.se; Storgatan 22; restaurant tasting menu 995kr; mains 209-365kr; ⊙11.30am-1.30pm Mon-Sat, plus 6-10pm Wed-Sat) A stylish bistro complete with black-and-white tiled floors and wicker chairs, serving up new-school Swedish flavours with global twists. Local produce sparkles in dishes ranging from grilled cod with summer chanterelles to Småland veal.

ⓘ Information

Vaxjo turistbyrå (☏0470-73 32 80; www.vaxjoco.se; Stortorget, Residencet; ⊙9.30am-6pm Mon-Fri & 10am-2pm Sat Jun-Aug) Located on the main square.

ⓘ Getting There & Away

Växjö is 80km west of Nybro on Rte 25 and 120km south of Jönköping on Rte 30.

Småland Airport (☏0470-75 85 00; www.smalandairport.se) is 9km northwest of Växjö and is serviced by low-cost carriers **Ryanair** (☏0900-20 20 240; www.ryanair.com) and **BRA** (www.flygbra.se). **Växjö Taxi** (☏0470-135

00; www.vaxjotaxi.se) will get you to the airport from the centre of town for around 250kr.

Jönköpings Länstrafiken (JLT; ☑ 0771-444 333; www.jlt.se; ☺7.30am-6pm Mon-Fri) runs daily buses to Jönköping (198kr, 1¾ hours) while **Kronoberg Länstrafiken** (☑ 0470-72 75 50; www.lanstrafikenkron.se) shuttles back and forth to Kosta, in the Glasriket (94kr, one hour). Buses depart from the train station.

SJ Rail (p186#) trains connect Växjö to Kalmar (164kr, 1¼ hours), Malmö (216kr, two hours) and Jönköping (198kr, 1¾ hours).

Kalmar

☑0480 / POP 66,571

Sheltered from the wild Baltic Sea by the island of Öland, Kalmar's maturity and medieval charm are immediately evident. The classy, compact city claims one of Sweden's most spectacular castles, within which the Kalmar Union of 1397, which united the crowns of Sweden, Denmark and Norway, was signed.

Dominating the landscape from its ever so slightly elevated position overlooking the Kalmar Strait, the fortress possesses all the elements a storybook castle should have, including opulent interiors even more spectacular than its robust turreted armour. The castle is reason alone to visit the city.

Other local assets include Sweden's largest gold hoard, from the 17th-century ship *Kronan*, and the cobbled streets of its immaculately preserved Old Town. But the main reason people come by Kalmar – many of them totally unaware of the treasures that lie beyond the motorway – is to cross the whopping 6km-long Öland bridge, to the mystical island of Öland, beyond.

◉ Sights

★**Kalmar Slott**   CASTLE

(☑0480-45 14 90; www.kalmarslott.se; Kungsgatan 1; adult/child 120/100kr; ☺10am-6pm daily Jul–mid-Aug, shorter hours rest of year; ⊕) Fairy-tale turrets, a drawbridge, a foul dungeon and secret passages…Kalmar Slott has everything that a proper castle should. This dominant Renaissance stronghold was once the most important building in the land and is appropriately fortified outside and sumptuously furnished inside. You're free to wander around the castle as you please, but the engaging and fun hour-long guided tours (at least one a day, at 11.30am) included in your admission fee really help you appreciate the significance of this magnificent relic.

Of the many highlights to be discovered, King Erik's chamber is a real scene-stealer – Erik's rivalry with his brother Johan was so great that he installed a secret passage in the loo! There's also a superb suspended ceiling in the Golden Hall; mesmerising wall-to-wall and floor-to-ceiling marquetry in the Chequered Hall; an elaborate bed, stolen as war booty then carefully vandalised so that no Danish ghosts could haunt it; and a delightful chapel, one of Sweden's most wanted for weddings. Visiting exhibitions add to the whole experience.

★**Kalmar läns museum**   MUSEUM

(Kalmar County Museum; ☑0480-45 13 00; www. kalmarlansmuseum.se; Skeppsbrogatan; adult/up to 19yr 100kr/free; ☺10am-4pm Mon-Fri, 11am-4pm Sat & Sun; ℗) The highlight of this fine museum, in an old steam mill by the harbour, are finds from the 17th-century flagship *Kronan*. The ship exploded and sank just before a battle in 1676, with the loss of almost 800 men. It was rediscovered in 1980, and more than 30,000 wonderfully preserved items have been excavated so far, including a spectacular gold hoard, clothing and musical instruments.

World of Dinosaurs   MUSEUM

(☑0480-49 57 00; www.aworldofdinosaurs.com; Tingby gård; adult/child 175/125kr; ☺11am-5pm Sat & Sun; ℗⊕) Kids go gaga for the massive monsters of the past in this gargantuan indoor Dino Museum about 10km west of Kalmar. While it's not quite Jurassic Park and some of the Sauropod's feel distinctly plasticky, the museum's redeeming feature is its collection of more than 100 authentic skeletons and an impressive bunch of convincing full-scale dino models to cower beneath.

Krusenstiernska Gården   GARDENS

(☑0480-41 15 52; www.krusenstiernskagarden. se; Stora Dammgatan 11; tours adult/child 40/15kr; ☺11am-5pm) Krusenstiernska Gården is a 19th-century middle-class home around 500m from the entrance to Kalmar Slott that seems to be delightfully stuck in a warp of time. From May to September, tours of the house are held at noon, 1pm and 2pm, but entry to the beautiful gardens and cafe is free, anytime.

Kalmar Konstmuseum   MUSEUM

(☑0480-42 62 82; www.kalmarkonstmuseum.se; Stadsparken; adult/child 50kr/free; ☺11am-5pm; ℗) The striking Kalmar Konstmuseum can be found in the park near Kalmar Slott.

Kalmar

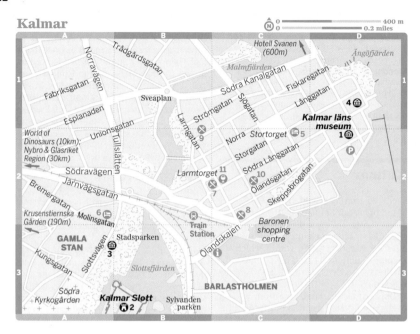

While it doesn't have a permanent collection, its striking galleries usually host one or two visiting contemporary exhibitions at any given time.

Kalmar Sjöfartsmuseum
MUSEUM

(☎0480-158 75; www.kalmarsjofartsmuseum.se; Södra Långgatan 81; adult/child 50/20kr; ⊙11am-4pm daily mid-Jun–mid-Sep; 🚻) Ah-har, me hearties! Salty sea dogs should line up for this eccentric collection of seafaring memorabilia, with bottled ships, foghorns and all manner of things made out of knots and armadillos.

🛏 Sleeping

★Hotell Svanen
HOTEL €

(☎0480-255 60; www.hotellsvanen.se/en/; Rappegatan 1; dm/d from 195/575kr; P) This smart budget hotel, surrounded by water, is excellent value considering the overall quality of its rooms, range of options (like bike and canoe rentals), bright, clean, common areas, and overall good vibes. Room types range from dorms to private, freshly renovated, 'extra comfort rooms' with smart styling and downy beds. There's free parking and all guests can use the communal kitchen.

Calmar Stadshotell
HOTEL €€

(☎0480-49 69 00; www.ligula.se/en/profilhotels/calmar-stadshotell/; Stortorget 14; d from 895kr; P 🛜) There's been a hotel on this site since 1741 but the current building dates from 1906. It's a classic hotel that has big old bones and brand new clothes – there's nothing old-fashioned about the relatively plain Jane styling. Service, however, is from another era, when the guest was treated like royalty – and why shouldn't you be? You're a long way from home.

★ **Slottshotellet** HOTEL €€
(☑0480-882 66; www.slottshotellet.se; Slottsvägen 7; r/ste from 1395/1795kr, annexe s/d 795/995kr; 🅿@🛜) This wonderfully cosy, romantic hotel is housed in four buildings in a gorgeous green setting near Kalmar Slott. Most rooms have antique furniture with textured wallpaper, crystal chandeliers and oriental rugs. Across the road, a budget wing, sporting a white minimalist look in stark contrast to the fluffy main wing, has crisp, clean rooms from 995kr.

🍴 Eating & Drinking

★ **Ming Palace** CHINESE €
(☑0480-166 86; www.mingpalacekalmar.se/en/; Fiskaregatan 7; buffet lunch/dinner from 108/145kr; ⊙11am-8pm Mon-Sat, to 8pm Sun) The daily lunch buffet at this friendly, central Cantonese restaurant (with retro booths) is always heaving with patrons. There's a wide range of dishes (including tofu and vegies, and salt and pepper squid) that are constantly topped up while the counter is kept clean by hawk-eye staff who swoop in to tidy any spills. It's delicious and great value all-you-can-eat.

Da Ernesto ITALIAN €€
(☑0480-241 00; www.ernestokalmar.se; Södra Långgatan 5; pizzas 120-165kr, mains 210-320kr; ⊙5-11pm Mon-Fri, noon-midnight Sat, 1-10pm Sun; 🍴) Run by a real-deal Neapolitan, this Italian cafe, restaurant and bar attracts scores of people with its baristi and extensive menu including pastas, Neapolitan-style pizzas and heavy, Italian seafood and meat dishes (all the favourites). Dine in or take away.

Restaurang Källaren Kronan SWEDISH €€
(☑0480-41 14 00; www.kallarenkronan.com; Ölandsgatan 7; mains 135-295kr; ⊙noon-2pm & 6-10pm Tue-Sun) Six cellars have been transformed into a high-calibre experience, with meals served under a cosy vaulted ceiling. There's even a 1660s menu, with mains such as salmon poached in wine with crayfish and root vegetables. Otherwise, the menu is replete with Swedish classics including meatballs and gravlax.

★ **Gröna Stugan** EUROPEAN €€€
(☑0480-158 58; www.gronastuganikalmar.se; Larmgatan 1; mains 185-295kr; ⊙5-11pm Mon-Sat,

to 9pm Sun; 🍴) Located in an unassuming sage-green building complete with round windows reminiscent of a ship, this gem of a restaurant serves up beef tartar, whole witch flounder and New Zealand lamb – gorgeous on the plate and even better to eat. Leave space for the blueberry pancakes with raspberry panna cotta. Vegetarians are catered for.

★ **Lilla Puben** PUB
(☑0480-42 24 22; www.lillapuben.se; Larmgatan 24; ⊙5pm-1am Tue-Sat) Thirsty? This bar is almost obscenely decorated with shelf after shelf of every imaginable brand of beer, some 700 varieties, as well as a choice of 120 whiskies.

ℹ Information

Kalmar Turism (☑0480-41 77 00; www.kalmar.com; Ölandskajen 9; ⊙9am-9pm Mon-Fri, 10am-5pm Sat & Sun Jun-Aug, shorter hours rest of year) Does an excellent job of promoting the city. You'll find colourful chests with drawers full of brochures and maps popping up in unexpected locations around town.

ℹ Getting There & Away

Kalmar is 109km east of Växjö via Rte 25 and 75km south of Oskarshamn via the E22 motorway. It's 40km to Borgholm via the 6km long Öland bridge.

Swebus Express (p210) operates daily services to Norrköping (from 309kr, four hours) and Stockholm (from 359kr, 6½ hours). All buses depart from the terminal at Centralstation.

SJ Rail (p186) trains run every hour or two between Kalmar and Alvesta (195kr, 1¼ hours), where you can connect with services to Stockholm, Malmö and Gothenburg. Direct trains also run to Linköping (224kr, three hours), with connections to Stockholm.

Kalmar Airport (☑480-45 90 00; www.kalmarairport.se) is located 6km west of town. **SAS** (☑08-797 4000; www.flysas.com) flies several times daily to Stockholm Arlanda, but if you've been staying in town and are feeling adventurous, check the airport website for last-minute deals on charter flights to destinations in Europe.

Glasriket

With its hypnotic glass-blowing workshops, the so called 'Kingdom of Crystal' is an attempt to revive the fading Swedish art of glass blowing, which began in Kosta in 1742. With the closure of major factories in

Boda (2008) and Orrefors (2013), the 'Glasriket' banner seeks to unify the remaining glass-blowing and crystal workshops which are spread out over a broad area around the villages of Kosta, Boda, Orrefors and Nybro. It's a niche market and a difficult task.

Kosta, with its full-scale factory, is the epicentre of the revival, but it's become a bit of an outlet shopping paradise, frequented by the busload. Glass-lovers will want to augment their shopping trip with a visit to at least one of the smaller *glasbruks* – each has something to offer.

The region is also popular with Americans tracing their ancestors: many emigrated from the area at the end of the 19th century.

Kosta is the hub of the Glasriket region and the only town with a full-scale glassworks, but it seems to have become more about sales and less about art. Historically, there were thriving industries in the towns of Orrefors, Kosta and Boda. The Kosta glassworks eventually became Kosta Boda and in 1989 merged with the Orrefors glassworks to form Orrefors Kosta Boda.

❶ Getting There & Away

Apart from the main routes, bus services around the area are practically nonexistent. The easiest way to explore is with your own transport (beware of elk). Bicycle tours on the unsurfaced country roads are excellent; there are plenty of hostels, and you can camp almost anywhere, except near the military area on the Kosta–Orrefors road.

Kalmar Länstrafik (p230) bus 139 runs from Nybro to Orrefors and Målerås from mid-June to mid-August only and calls at a few of the glass factories. The service operates four times per day on weekdays and once on Saturday.

Year-round bus services connect Nybro and Orrefors (40kr, 25 minutes) and Kosta is served by regular bus 218 from Växjö (85kr, one hour).

Buses and trains run from Emmaboda to Nybro (49kr, 15 minutes) and Kalmar (75kr, 30 minutes); trains also run to Karlskrona (86kr, 45 minutes), Växjö (55kr, 35 minutes) and Alvesta (85kr, 50 minutes), from where there are direct services to Gothenburg and Stockholm.

Kosta

🕿 0478 / POP 884

The little town of Kosta is where Glasriket first fired up, way back in 1742. It's a crucial stop for those exploring the area, which will either be something you're very interested

in, or not at all. In fact, if you just have a passing interest in glass and glass blowing and you're not sure which of the Glasriket villages to visit – Kosta is the one-stop shop.

Most visitors to the village – which today feels a bit like a glass-blowing theme park – will either take a tour of the Kosta Glassworks factory or head to the Kosta Glascenter, where you can witness glass-blowing firsthand, or try it yourself.

Otherwise, there's a fancy hotel, a variety of discount and high-end shopping outlets and not much else.

◉ Sights

Unlike the other towns of the Glasriket, where many glass-blowers are going it on their own or establishing new brands, most of Kosta's sights, dining and accommodation options are monopolised by the Orrefors Kosta Boda company, which owns both the Orrefors and Kosta Boda brands.

★**Kosta Glassworks** FACTORY
(🕿 0478-345 00; www.kostaboda.se/en/about-kosta-boda/glassworks; Stora vägen 96; ☉ shops 10am-6pm Mon-Fri, to 5pm Sat & Sun, glass-blowing demonstrations 9am-3.30pm Mon-Fri, 10am-4pm Sat & Sun) The site of one of Sweden's original glassworks, established in 1742, the Kosta Boda complex continues to reel in coachloads of visitors. It's touristy, but the combination of gallery, glass-blowing demonstrations, eateries, and discount retail offerings, combined with the stunning Kosta Boda Art Hotel make it an attractive package. Book and begin 30-minute guided tours of the facility (50kr) from the Kosta Boda Art Gallery.

Kosta Boda Art Gallery GALLERY
(🕿 0478-345 29; www.kostaboda.se/en/about-kosta-boda/kosta-boda-art-gallery; Stora vägen 96; ☉ 10am-5pm Mon-Fri, to 4pm Sat & Sun) The factory's own gallery has some stunning pieces but feels at times like a front for its nearby retail outlets. You can see even more exquisite pieces in the rooms and common areas of the Kosta Boda Art Hotel, which is like an extension of the gallery itself.

Kosta Glascenter WORKSHOP
(🕿 070-684 61 91; www.kostaglascenter.se; Stora vägen 96; ☉ 10am-6pm Mon-Fri, to 5pm Sat & Sun; ℗) **FREE** Not to be confused with the Kosta Glassworks, but within its grounds, the Kosta Glascenter offers demonstrations, workshops and classes in glass blowing with a variety of local artists. And there are plenty

THE GLASSWORKS

Boda

Once one of the largest crystal manufacturers in the world, the glassworks here closed in 2008.

Glass Factory (☑0471-024 93 60; www.theglassfactory.se; Storgatan 5, Boda glasbruk; adult/child 60kr/free; ☺10am-6pm Mon-Fri, 11am-5pm Sat & Sun May-Sep, 11am-4pm Wed-Sun Oct-Apr; P) Occupying the site of the former glassworks, the project contains a glass-art glass collection of more than 30,000 pieces. Watch craftspeople at work then try your hand at blowing glass.

Orrefors

The most significant factory closure happened here in 2012, when company executives laid off more than 130 staff and decided to smash surplus inventory rather than flood the market with discounted 'high art' pieces.

Målerås (☑0481-314 00; www.maleras.se; Industrigatan 20, Malerås; ☺10am-6pm Mon-Fri, to 5pm Sat & Sun) About 8km northwest of Orrefors in Målerås, this brand is the collaboration of acclaimed glass-blower Mats Jonasson and four other talented artists. Try your hand blowing glass in the hot shop.

Orrefors Park (☑070-999 60 40; www.facebook.com/orreforspark/; Bruksområdet 1; ☺11am-6pm; P) Adjacent to the former factory, this kick-starter project is a first step at renewing the village. There's a museum, workshops and a garden with a dual purpose.

Carlos R Pebaqué (☑0481-321 17; www.carlosartglass.com; Glasblasarvärgen 8, Gullaskruv; ☺11am-6pm Mon-Fri, to 5pm Sat, to 4pm Sun) This Uruguayan-born artist creates extraordinary vases in his one-man studio, at Gullaskruv, located 6km northwest of Orrefors. Highly recommended.

Nybro

The area around nearby Pukeberg's former factories is under transformation after being heavily contaminated from years of industry. The Swedish Environmental Protection Agency has poured 58 million kronor into restoring the area.

Nybro Glasbruk (☑0481-428 81; www.nybro-glasbruk.se; Herkulesgatan 2; ☺10am-4pm Mon-Sat, from noon Sun; P) A small workshop and boutique which is known for its offbeat designs.

Pukeberg Glasbruk (www.pukeberg.se; Pukebergarnasvägen; ☺10am-5pm Mon-Fri, to 2pm Sat, noon-4pm Sun; P) A tale of industrial transformation, this lovely but unfortunately named complex has galleries and workshops and is home to the new Swedish School of Glass.

of outlets where you can buy one-off pieces made on the premises.

🛏 Sleeping & Eating

Kosta Lodge　　　　　　　　　LODGE €€
(☑0478-59 05 30; www.kostalodge.se; Stora vägen 2; r/cabin from 995/1295kr; P🏊) Affiliated with the Kosta Boda Art Hotel and Kosta Glassworks, this sprawling Falu-red lodge, with its own mini-lake, clutch of charming, rustic cabins and a Vegas-in-Sweden-style pool area with two pools and wood-fired Jacuzzi tubs, is the lower cost, grassroots-but-high-end alternative to staying in the arty-farty hotel. A pool entry fee applies (adult/child 100/50kr).

★**Kosta Boda Art Hotel**　　　HOTEL €€€
(☑0478-348 30; www.kostabodaarthotel.com; Stora vägen 75; s/d from 1295/2590kr; P❄🎏🏊) One of the only truly luxury hotel offerings in Småland, the Art Hotel showcases the famed glass and crystal brand's creations in unusual ways – like its designer glass bar. Each of the 102 decadent hotel rooms also features Kosta glasswork and textiles designed by local artists. Outdoors, you'll find the finest private swimming pool for miles.

BOND WAS HERE...

Although the entry price to the **James Bond Museum** (☑ 0481-129 60; www.007museum.com; Emmabodavägen 20, Nybro; adult/child 150/75kr; ☉10am-5pm Mon-Fri, 10am-2pm Sat; ℗) is a little steep, Bond fans will enjoy this quirky museum of James Bond memorabilia, the product of one man's lifetime obsession with 007. Located in Nybro, the complex includes a diverse collection of artifacts from cars to aircraft and even a Venetian gondola! Check out the website for the lowdown on the museum's creator!

Even if you don't stay the night, drop in to scope out the lobby, and have a drink at the bar or a meal at the hotel's Linnéa Art Restaurant.

Linnéa Art Restaurant SWEDISH €€€
(☑ 0478-348 40; www.kostabodaarthotel.com; Stora vägen 75; buffet 245kr, mains 189-325kr; ☉noon-3.30pm) This swish restaurant within the Kosta Boda Art Hotel serves up a delicious lunchtime buffet prepared from local seafood and produce. Of an evening, things get decidedly classier when the lights go down – dress to be seen. Reservations are recommended.

🛍 Shopping

Kosta Outlet SHOPPING CENTRE
(☑ 070-161 08 72; www.kostaoutlet.se; Stora Vägen 77; ☉10am-8pm) This sprawling outlet store doesn't just hawk glassware – there's a huge clothing outlet on the top floor with a wide range of gear at reasonable prices and a large food court.

ℹ Information

There's a Glasriket Pass (100kr) allowing free admission into 'hot shops' and museums, and discounts on purchases. It's a good deal if you want to try glass blowing and buy some pieces, but skip it if you're just browsing.

Oskarshamn

☑ 0491 / POP 27.006

Oskarshamn is a busy but otherwise unremarkable port city. The main reason people come here is to leave here – taking the regular car ferries to Gotland and Öland or seasonal cruises to the mythical, mystical, off-the-beaten-track island of Blå Jungfrun.

That's not to say Oskarshamn isn't a pleasant, attractive little town – it is: but while you're waiting for the boat, there's really not much to do here but daydream about the next phase of your adventurous voyage.

Oskarshamn's **Kulturhuset** (Cultural Hall; ☑ 0491-880 40; Hantverksgatan 18-20; adult/child 90kr/free; ☉10am-4pm May-Aug, shorter hours rest of year; ℗) houses two interesting museum collections with a single admission. Döderhultarmuseet features around 200 works by home-grown artist Axel Petersson 'Döderhultarn' (1868–1925), who captured local characters and occasions in vigorous and often amusing woodcarvings. The Sjöfartsmuseet showcases local maritime exhibits.

🛏 Sleeping & Eating

Best Western Sjofartshotellet HOTEL €
(☑ 0491-76 83 00; www.sjofartshotellet.se; Sjöfartsgatan 13; d from 795kr; ℗🐾) This simple little chain hotel has wonderfully friendly staff, free limited parking and spotlessly clean, simple rooms decorated in a nautical theme. The included breakfast spread is nicely presented.

Restaurang Cecil CHINESE €€
(☑ 0491-187 50; www.restaurangcecil.se; Lilla Torget 2; mains 78-155kr; ☉11am-9pm; 🍽) The delightfully named Cecil restaurant has friendly, English-speaking staff who serve up decent Chinese meals in delightfully retro, little bit kitsch, but spotlessly clean premises off the main square. The best thing is that it has booths and 'banquets' for one – a good value option that is usually reserved for parties of two or more. Service is respectful and efficient.

ℹ Information

Attraktiva Oskarshamn (☑ 0491-770 72; www.oskarshamn.se; Hantverksgatan 3; ☉9am-5pm Mon-Fri, 10am-3pm Sat & Sun) This tourist office is located in the big shopping plaza on the main square. Follow the signs.

ℹ Getting There & Away

Oskarshamn is 75km north of Kalmar on the E22 motorway and 69km south of Västervik.

Destination Gotland (p234) operates a fleet of huge car ferries from its terminal near the train station, daily in winter and twice daily in summer. Passenger-only fares start as low as

495kr, but prices vary wildly due to demand and other factors: get a real-time quote online.

M/S Solsund (📞 0499-449 20; www.olands-farjan.se; Skeppsbron) operates two ferries each day to Byxelkrok, on Northern Öland (adult/child 150/100kr), from June to August. Boats depart from the ferry terminal off Skeppsbron – follow the signs. A limited number of spots for vehicles are available, starting at 450kr. The usually smooth journey takes 2¼ hours.

Trains no longer run to Oskarshamn Central-station, but most buses stop there.

Kalmar Länstrafik (p230) operates regular bus services from Oskarshamn to Kalmar (102kr, 1¼ hours).

Swebus Express (p210) has daily buses from Kalmar that stop in Oskarshamn en route to Stockholm (5¼ hours, from 339kr).

The closest **SJ Rail** (p186) station is in Berga, 25km west of town with connections to Linköping and Nässjö. Local buses connect Oskarshamn with Berga (68kr, 30 minutes).

Västervik

📞 0490 / POP 36,438

Västervik is a breezy, busy, summer holiday town with quaint cobbled streets, some semblance of nightlife, sandy beaches just east of town and 5000 islands on its doorstep. Yup, 5000. Don't try to see them all – that would just be silly. But a popular option is to take a cruise and at least see some of them.

Harried by the Danes in its early years, the town bloomed into a major shipbuilding centre between the 17th and 19th centuries. Today, it's a popular domestic holiday destination and an absolute delight if you can time your visit to that sweet spot either side of the Swedish school holidays when the weather is warm and the crowds are at bay.

In mid-July, Västervik welcomes thousands of excited Swedes for one of the nation's best-known song festivals.

◎ Sights & Activities

St Petri Kyrka   CHURCH
(📞 0490-842 45; Östra Kyrkogatan 67) This stunning church is a dramatic mass of spires and buttresses that seem to point forever upwards, which seems fitting if St Petri (St Peter) is the one guarding the pearly gates.

Västerviks Museum   MUSEUM
(📞 049-211 77; www.vasterviksmuseum.se; Kulbacken 2; adult/child 50kr/free; ⊙ 10am-4pm Mon-Fri, 1-4pm Sat & Sun Jun-Aug, closed Sat rest of year) Displays at this museum, just north of the

Västervik

Västervik

◎ Sights
1 St Petri Kyrka...A3
2 Västerviks Museum B1

◎ Activities, Courses & Tours
3 Västerviks Skärgårdsturer.................B3

◎ Sleeping
4 Hotel Fängelset B4
5 Västerviks Stadshotell B3

◎ Eating
6 Restaurang Smugglaren B3

tourist office, cover the town's history. You'll also find **Unos Torn**, an 18m-high lookout tower with archipelago views.

★ **Västerviks Skärgårdsturer**   CRUISE
(📞 070-265 09 01; www.vasterviksskargardsturer.se; tours from adult/child 110/60kr; ⊙ mid-Jun–end Aug) Reasonably priced archipelago

BLÅ JUNGFRUN NATIONAL PARK

The Blå Jungfrun National Park encompasses a 1km-long granite island also known as 'Witches' Mountain' because, according to ancient folklore, this is where witches (continue to) gather on Maundy Thursday to meet the devil and talk shop. Charming. It's hard to imagine this by any stretch as you're gazing upon the fantastic scenery, gnarled trees, bird life and the big blue sea. But easier to picture when you come across the curious and somewhat creepy stone maze, Trojeborg.

In 2014 a team of archaeologists visiting the island discovered evidence of ancient human life, similar to what has been found on nearby Öland and Gotland, including evidence of ritual practices that may lend credence to the myths about the island's pagan ties. It's said that if you remove a stone from Blå Jungfrun, you'll be cursed for eternity! Would you risk it?

To get here without your own boat or broomstick, local launch M/S Solkust (☑ 0491-77 072; www.solkustturer.se; adult/child 280/140kr; ⊘ mid-Jun–Aug) has summer sailings to the island that allows passengers about 3½ hours to explore. Contact Attraktiva Oskarshamn (p226) for the scoop.

tours depart from Skeppsbrokajen daily from mid-June to the end of August. Buy tickets directly at the Skärgårdsterminalen pier kiosk, at the Västervik Tourist Office or via the website. For a full day of touring on the archipelago, bikes can be rented on the island of Hasselö and from Handelsboa at Hasselö Sand.

🛏 Sleeping & Eating

Västerviks Stadshotell   HISTORIC HOTEL **€€**
(Best Western; ☑ 0490-820 00; www.stadshotellet.
nu; Storgatan 3; s/d from 1050/1350kr; P @ 🛜)
Major renovations added another floor to this elegant central hotel under the Best Western umbrella. Rooms are spacious and modern, plus there's a sauna, spa and gym. The breakfast buffet is particularly lavish.

Hotel Fängelset   HOTEL **€€**
(☑ 076-136 89 66; www.hotellfangelset.se; Fängelsetorget 1; d from 990kr, s without bathroom from 570kr; P @ 🛜) Housed in a magnificent building, this former prison (until 2007) has a lingering institutional feel, with rooms in the cells (with bars still on the windows). Space is tight, even in the doubles, where the bathrooms are similarly cell-size. The quirkiness continues with the on-site craft brewery – you can taste the results in the bar.

★ Restaurang Smugglaren   EUROPEAN **€€€**
(☑ 0490-213 22; www.smugglaren.se; Smugglaregränd 1; mains 250-345kr; ⊘ 6-11pm Mon-Sat) In a cosy wooden building tucked down an alley off Strandvägen, Smugglaren dresses up Swedish classics such as beef with lingon-

berries or salmon tournedos. Model ships, paraffin lamps and the odd elk head crank up the eccentricity.

❶ Information

Västervik Tourist Office (☑ 0490-875 20; www.vastervik.com; Stora Torget 4; ⊘ 10am-6pm Mon-Fri, to 2pm Sat May-late Jun, shorter hours rest of year)

❶ Getting There & Away

Västervik is 55km east of Vimmerby and 105km southeast of Linköping.

SJ Rail (p186#) operates frequent trains between Västervik and Linköping (173kr, 1¾ hours).

Kalmar Länstrafik (p230) operates regular buses to Vimmerby (85kr, one hour), Oskarshamn (93kr, one hour) and Kalmar (119kr, 2½ hours).

Buses leave from outside the train station, which is located at the eastern edge of the town centre.

Destination Gotland (p234) operates ferries to Visby on Gotland from the **Skärgårds Ferry Terminal** from late June to early August: prices vary wildly. Get quotes and book online.

Vimmerby

☑ 0492 / POP 15,600

Vimmerby is the birthplace of Astrid Lindgren and home to one of Sweden's favourite drawcards – a theme park based on the Pippi Longstocking books. Almost everything in town revolves around the strongest girl in the world – there's little escape!

Even if you didn't grow up on these stories as a child or don't know much about Pippi, you might be surprised by how much you'll grow to like her, or be engaged by the history of the author, how Pippi came to be in the world and how she changed over the years. A brand new museum traces her evolution on film.

Trust your instincts, if none of the above appeals, Vimmerby won't impress in person. If the above makes your inner-child sing a little, you're going to love exploring the town that gave the world a storybook hero whose adventures have been translated into no fewer than 64 languages.

☉ Sights

★ Astrid Lindgrens Näs   MUSEUM
(☑0492-76 94 00; www.astridlindgrensnas.se; Prästgårdsgatan 24; adult/child 170kr/free, tours 95/50kr; ☉10am-6pm mid-Jun–end Aug, 11am-4pm Wed-Sun rest of year; P🚼) Astrid Lindgrens Näs is a fascinating cultural centre set on the farm in which Lindgren, author of the world-bestselling Pippi Longstocking books, grew up. There's a permanent exhibition about the writer's life and temporary exhibitions inspired by Lindgren's stories and legacy. The real highlight are the 30-minute guided tours of Lindgren's faithfully restored childhood home. Book in advance.

Filmbyn Småland   MUSEUM
(☑0708-20 97 45; www.filmbyn.se/en/; Spilhammarvägen 4, Mariannelund; adult/child 175/150kr; ☉10am-6pm Jun-Aug) This 2017 museum in Mariannelund (20km west of Vimmerby) explores the history of film in Småland with a definite angle on Pippi's adventures on celluloid. We're talking about Sweden's favourite Pippi Longstocking here, created by author Astrid Lindgren in 1944, if you weren't in the know. Since her 1969 feature film debut, 13-episodes of a TV series were made for Swedish TV and she has appeared in a variety of other animated incarnations from around the world.

Astrid Lindgrens Värld   AMUSEMENT PARK
(☑0492-798 00; www.alv.se; Vimmerby; adult/child 405/295kr; ☉10am-6pm daily Jun-Aug, to 5pm Sat & Sun Sep; P🚼) In Astrid Lindgrens Värld, actresses dressed as Pippi (complete with gravity-defying pigtails) sing and dance their way around the 100 buildings and settings (you read that right) from Astrid Lindgren's Pippi Longstocking books – it's

a theme park for rebels, kids, the young at heart and die-hard Pippi Longstocking fans. Prices drop outside peak season as there are fewer activities and theatre performances. The park is 1.5km from central Vimmerby – about 15 minutes' walk.

⊨ Sleeping

Vimmerby Vandrarhem   HOSTEL €
(☑0492-100 20; www.vimmerbyvandrarhem.nu; Järnvägsallén 2; dm/tw from 175/520kr; P@) This cheerful hostel, based in a fine wooden building, is right near the train station. A variety of simple rooms are available and there's a lovely garden and barbecue area.

Astrid Lindgrens Värld
Campground   CAMPGROUND €
(☑0492-798 00; www.alv.se; Astrid Lindgrens Värld; sites/4-bed cabins from 395/1895kr; ☉mid-May–Aug; P) These sites and simple cabins are on the premises of the Astrid Lindgrens Värld theme park.

❶ Information

Vimmerby Turistbyrå (☑0492-310 10; www.vimmerby.com; Rådhuset 1; ☉9am-6pm Mon-Fri, to 2pm Sat & Sun Jun-Aug, shorter hours rest of year) Faces the main square.

❶ Getting There & Away

Vimmerby is 60km east of Eksjö on Rte 40 and 55km west of Västervik.

All bus and train services depart from the Resecentrum, downhill past the church from Stora Torget.

Kalmar Länstrafik (p230) runs bus services to Västervik (85kr, one hour) while **SJ Rail** (p186) runs local trains south to Kalmar (108kr, two hours) and north to Linköping (159kr, 1½ hours). There is a station at Astrid Lindgrens Värld.

ÖLAND

☑0485 / POP 25,021

Like a deranged vision of Don Quixote, Öland is *covered* in old wooden windmills. Symbols of power and wealth in the mid-18th century, they were a must-have for every aspiring Man about Town and the death knell for many of Öland's oak forests. Today 400 or so remain, many lovingly restored by local windmill associations.

At 137km long and 16km wide, the island is Sweden's smallest province. Once a regal hunting ground, it's now a hugely popular

Öland

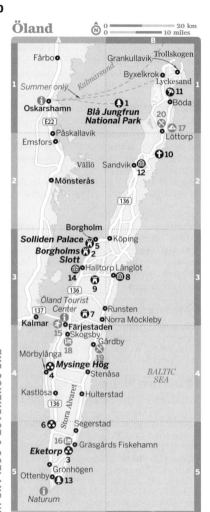

N 0 ———— 20 km
0 ———— 10 miles

There are no bicycle lanes on the bridge between Öland and Kalmar, so cyclists should exercise caution! Bicycles aren't allowed on the bridge in summer – instead there's free Cykel-buss or Cykelfärjeservices to get you across (roughly hourly; enquire at the tourist office in Kalmar). If you fancy pedalling your way across Öland, check **Cykla på Öland** (www.cyklap-aoland.se; Träffpunkt Öland 102) for cycling routes and other handy information.

From mid-June to mid-August, **M/S Solsund** (p226) sails twice daily from Byxelkrok (north-west Öland) to Oskarshamn on the mainland, 60km north of Kalmar. One-way tickets cost adult/child 150/100kr and a limited number of spots are available for vehicles, starting at 450kr. The journey takes 2¼ hours.

Silverlinjen (⌨ 0485-261 11; www.silverlinjen. se) runs one to two daily direct buses from Öland to Stockholm (from adult/child 320/220kr, 6½ hours), calling at Kalmar; reservations are essential.

Kalmar Länstrafik (KLT; ⌨ 010-21 21 000; www.klt.se) buses connect all the main towns on the island to Kalmar; they run every hour or two to Borgholm (56kr, one hour) and Mörbylånga (40kr, one hour). A few buses per day run to Byxelkrok and Grankullavik (both 96kr, around

summer destination for Swedes – the royal family still has a summer pad here. The island gets around two million visitors annually, mostly in July. Around 90% of them flock to the golden shores fringing the northern half of the island to bask and bathe. Behind the beaches, fairy-tale forests make for soulful wanders.

⊙ Getting There & Away

The 6km-long Öland bridge links the island with the mainland, at Kalmar.

2¼ hours), in the far north of the island. Services to the south are poor, with some improvement May to August.

ℹ Getting Around

Having the freedom of your own wheels to explore the diverse landscapes of this long, ancient island will make all the difference. Public transport is limited.

The island is excellent for cycling due to its long sunny days and lack of hilly terrain. That said, Öland is bigger than you might think, so if you want to see the north and the south and you have limited time, you'll really need a car.

Borgholm

🔊 0485 / POP 3071

Öland's 'capital' and busiest town, Borgholm has a pleasant centre 'grid' of pedestrian streets lined with shops and restaurants that can get packed out in midsummer. The most dramatic (and satisfying) sight is the enormous ruined castle on its outskirts.

⊙ Sights

★**Solliden Palace** PALACE
(Sollidens Slott; 🔊 048-51 53 56; www.sollidens slott.se; adult/child 105/80kr; ⊙11am-6pm May-Sep) Sweden's most famous 'summer house', Solliden Palace, 2.5km south of Borgholm town centre, is still used by the Swedish royals. Its exceptional gardens are open to the public and are well worth a wander. The idyllic cafe is ideal for a post-garden break.

★**Borgholms Slott** CASTLE
(🔊 0485-885 00; www.borgholmsslott.se; adult/child 95/60kr; ⊙10am-6pm Jun-Aug) Northern Europe's largest ruined castle, Borgholms Slott, looms just south of town. This epic limestone structure was burnt and abandoned early in the 18th century, after life as a dyeworks. There's a great museum inside and a nature reserve nearby, as well as summer concerts, children's activities and a cafe.

Guided tours are recommended but must be booked in advance and aren't cheap at 400kr per person.

VIDA Museum & Konsthall MUSEUM
(🔊 0485-774 40; www.vidamuseum.com; Landsvägen; adult/child 80kr/free; ⊙10am-6pm daily Jul–early Aug, shorter hours rest of year; P) VIDA Museum & Konsthall is a strikingly modern museum and art gallery in Halltorp, about 9km south of Borgholm. Its finest halls are

devoted to two of Sweden's top-class glass designers.

🍴 Sleeping & Eating

Ebbas Vandrarhem & Trädgårdscafé HOSTEL €
(🔊 0485-103 73; www.ebbas.se; Storgatan 12; dm/s/d from 300/375/580kr; ⊙May-Sep; 🛜) Look for the classic 1950s Morris Minor 1000 out front here. Five of the lemon-yellow rooms overlook the gorgeous rose-laced garden, and four the bustling Borgholm main street. There's a kitchen for self-caterers...or just pop downstairs to the cafe for decent hot and cold grub (lunch 100kr), served until 9pm in summer.

★**Hotell Borgholm** HOTEL €€€
(🔊 0485-770 60; www.hotellborgholm.com; Trädgårdsgatan 15-19; s/d from 1295/1535kr; ✱ @ 🛜) Cool grey hues, bold feature walls, pine-wood floors and smart functionalist furniture make for stylish slumber at this urbane hotel. Rooms are spacious, with those on the top floor being especially chic. Owner Karin Fransson is one of Sweden's top chefs, so a table at the restaurant here is best booked ahead (tasting menu with/without wine 2260/1295kr).

Robinson Crusoe EUROPEAN €€
(🔊 0485-44 477; www.robinsoncrusoe.se; Hamnvägen 1; lunch buffet 160kr, mains 135-260kr; ⊙noon-10pm Apr-Sep) Slouch back on the plush, purple terrace sofas for a cocktail or an excellent coffee, or make a date for the daily buffet. The setting is sublime, overlooking the bobbing boats in Borgholm harbour.

ℹ Information

Ölands Turistbyrå (🔊 0485-890 00; www.oland.se/en; Storgatan 1; ⊙9am-6pm Mon-Fri, to 5pm Sat, 10am-4pm Sun) Located down by the marina end of Storgatan.

ℹ Getting There & Away

Borgholm is 40km northeast of Kalmar, across the 6km long Ölandsbron.

Northern Öland

The north of the island has a wild beauty and is home to some of Öland's best beaches – soft white sand and fewer crowds. It's relatively undeveloped up here, so this is definitely where to come if you're looking to get away. Camping in the region in the shoulder season (the months of April to May and September to October) can feel blissfully isolated.

⦿ Sights

Lyckesand
BEACH

One of the island's best beaches, known for it's long stretches of fine white sand and calm waters.

Källa kyrka
CHURCH

(Källa-hagaby Gamla vägan 15) This atmospheric church, at a little harbour about 36km northeast of Borgholm, off Rd 136, is a fine example of Öland's medieval fortified churches. The broken **rune stone** inside shows the Christian cross growing from the pagan tree of life.

Sandvikskvarn
HISTORIC BUILDING

(🖉 0485-261 72; www.sandvikskvarn.se; Stenhuggarvägen 3, Löttorp; adult/child 20kr/free; ⊙ noon-8pm daily May-Sep, to 10pm mid-Jun–mid-Aug; 🅿) At Sandvik on the west coast, about 30km north of Borgholm, this Dutch-style windmill is one of the largest in the world. In summer, you can climb its seven storeys for good views across to the mainland. The rustic restaurant serves the local speciality, *lufsa* (baked pork and potato; 75kr); and there's an adjacent pizzeria (with pizzas from 80kr).

🛏 Sleeping & Eating

Accommodation options up here are few and far between but you can pitch a tent in plenty of enchanting spots.

Neptuni Camping
CAMPGROUND €

(🖉 0485-284   95; www.neptunicamping.se; Småskogsvägen; sites 200kr, cabins from 450kr; 🅿) This campground just north of Löttorp is a wild and grassy place with good amenities.

Lammet & Grisen
SWEDISH €€

(🖉 0485-203 50; www.lammet.nu; Löttorp; dinner buffet 250kr; ⊙ from 4.30pm; 🅿👶) Just 10km south of Böda, come here for all-you-can-eat buffet evenings, with whole spit-roasted lamb and pork on the menu, plus live entertainment. The restaurant is particularly family-friendly and you can get discounts by booking your table online.

❶ Getting There & Away

Kalmar Länstrafik (p230) operates very limited transport connections and the bus routes and timetables are reasonably difficult to interpret for the uninitiated. A few buses per day run to Byxelkrok and Grankullavik (both 96kr, around 2¼ hours), in the far north of the island.

You'll have a much better time of it riding a rental bike or self-driving your way around the region.

Southern Öland

Most of Öland's southern frontier has made it onto Unesco's World Heritage list. Its treeless, limestone landscape is hauntingly beautiful and littered with the relics of human settlement and conflict. Besides linear villages, Iron Age fortresses and tombs, this area is also a natural haven for plants and wildlife.

Fortresses, a zoo and a charming farm village are southern Öland's star attractions. The largest settlement is Färjestaden (Ferry Town), although the town lost its purpose somewhat after the bridge was built (despite recent efforts to rejuvenate the old jetty).

South of Färjestaden, the entire island is a Unesco World Heritage site, lauded for its unique agricultural landscape, its continuous use from the Stone Age to today, and being peppered with runic stones and ancient burial cairns.

⦿ Sights

★ Mysinge Hög
ARCHAEOLOGICAL SITE

The biggest single monument amid the ancient grave fields of Mysinge and Gettlinge is Bronze Age tomb Mysinge hög, 4km east of Mörbylånga, from where there are views of almost the whole World Heritage site.

★ Eketorp
ARCHAEOLOGICAL SITE

(🖉 0485-66 20 00; www.eketorp.se; Eketorp; adult/child 80kr/free; ⊙ 11am-5pm daily May, Jun & late Aug, 10.30am-6pm Jul–mid-Aug; 🅿👶) If you can't picture how the ring forts looked in their prime, take a trip to Eketorp. The site has been partly reconstructed to show typical fortified villages in medieval times. Children will love the scampering pigs, and the fort is particularly fun when there are re-enactment days – phone for details. Excavations at the site have revealed more than 26,000 artefacts, including 3 tonnes of human bones; some of the finds are on display at the little **museum** inside.

There are free daily tours in English from late June to the end of August (11.15am, 1.15pm and 2.15pm). The fort is 6km northeast of Grönhögen; there are several buses (summer only) from Mörbylånga.

Ismantorp
FORTRESS

(☑010-223 80 00) The vast Ismantorp fortress, with the remains of 88 houses and nine mysterious gates, is deep in the woods, about 20km northeast of Ölands Djurpark. Drive north to Rälla and take a right on Högsrumsvägen; keep following this road for about 10km to reach the fortress. It's an undisturbed fortress ruin, illustrating how the village's tiny huts were encircled by the outer wall. The area, just south of the Ekerum–Långlöt road, can be visited at any time.

Gråborg
FORTRESS

(Borg) The largest Iron Age ring fort in the country, Gråborg was built as the Roman Empire was crumbling. Its impressively monumental walls measure 640m around, even though much of the stonework was plundered for later housing. After falling into disuse, the fort sprang back to life around 1200, when the adjacent St Knut's chapel (now a ruin) was built. The Gråborg complex is about 8km east of Färjestaden; note that you need your own transport to get here.

Gettlinge
ARCHAEOLOGICAL SITE

The ancient grave field of Gettlinge, together with similar site Mysinge, stretches for kilometres on the ridge alongside the main Mörbylånga–Degerhamn road. The fields include burial sites and standing stones from the Stone Age to the late Iron Age.

Stora Alvaret
NATURE RESERVE

Birds, insects and flowers populate the striking limestone plain of Stora Alvaret. Birdwatching is best in May and June, which is also when the Alvar's rock roses and rare orchids burst into bloom. The plain occupies most of the inland area of southern Öland, and can be crossed by road from Mörbylånga or Degerhamn.

Himmelsberga
MUSEUM

(☑0485-56 10 22; www.himmelsbergamuseum.com; Himmelsberga; adult/child 80/60kr; ☉11am-5.30pm daily Jun–mid-Aug, shorter hours rest of year) This is the best open-air museum on Öland; basically a traditional farming village on the east coast at Långlöt, its quaint cottages are fully furnished. There's hay in the mangers and slippers by the door; it's so convincing you'd swear the inhabitants just popped out for a minute. Extras include a dinky cafe and modern art gallery.

🛏 Sleeping & Eating

Outside Borgholm, island accommodation is sparse but there are a few quaint B&Bs and caravan parks, usually chock-full of RV groups in the summer. Outside the busy months, camping in the area is bliss.

Vandrarhemmet Ölands Skogsby
HOSTEL €

(☑0485-383 95; www.vandrarhskogsby.se; s/d per person 180/320kr; ☉mid-Apr–Sep; P⊛🛜) This charming STF hostel claims to be Sweden's oldest (it dates from 1934). It's based in a flowery old wooden house 3km southeast of Färjestaden. The Färjestaden–Mörbylånga bus 103 (30kr) runs past at least five times daily.

Mörby Vandrarhem & Lågprishotell
HOSTEL €

(☑0485-493 93; www.morbyhotell.se; Bruksgatan; hostel s/d from 350/550kr, hotel s/d from 695/895kr; ☉May-Aug; P⊛🛜♿) In the small village of Mörbylånga, this place has a mixture of hostel- and hotel-style accommodation. The big, anonymous building is a bit hospital-like, but there's a pool and plenty of space, with a park and beaches nearby, as well as bikes for hire.

Gammalsbygårdens Gästgiveri
B&B €€

(☑0485-66 30 51; www.gammalsbygarden.se; Gammalsby 114; s/d from 795/895kr; P⊛) This country farmhouse sits on the hauntingly beautiful southeastern coast, 5km north of Eketorp. The picture-perfect lounge is complemented by cheerful rooms with whitewashed walls and cosy floor heating. A couple of rooms have private balconies. The restaurant serves fish, venison, lamb and heavenly desserts. Booking ahead is essential.

Gärdby Kafe
CAFE €

(☑0485-330 06; Gärdby; snacks from 65kr; ☉10am-5pm Mon-Fri, to 4pm Sat & Sun) Detour to this heart-warming cafe, which dates from the 1920s and oozes old-fashioned charm with its dazzling, white, stripped-back tearooms and expansive garden with well-weathered sculptures and randomly placed tables and chairs. Savoury snacks, traditional sweets, locally produced deli items and superb coffee are on offer.

ℹ Information

The bridge from Kalmar lands you on the island just north of Färjestaden, where the staff of the well-stocked **Öland Tourist Center** (☑0485-890 00; www.olandsturist.se; Träffpunkt Öland 102; ☉9am-7pm Mon-Fri, to 6pm Sat, to 5pm Sun Jul–mid-Aug) in the Träffpunkt Öland complex can book island accommodation (for a small fee), as well as organise themed packages, including cycling, spa and gourmet getaways.

There is also a small history and nature exhibit here at **Naturum** (☑ 0485-66 12 00; www. ottenby.se; ⊙ 10am-6pm daily Jul–mid-Aug), where you can ask questions about the local flora and fauna.

❶ Getting There & Away

To make the most of your time on the island, you need at least a bike. Even better would be a car with a bike on bike racks and if there's more than one in your party...two bikes! If you can make that happen, don't hesitate. Ask at the **Öland Tourist Center** (p233) if you need help making arrangements.

Bus services to the south are complicated and infrequent although there is some improvement over the summer season. Most locals drive or ride bikes – so as they say, 'When in Öland, do what the Ölanders do...'.

GOTLAND

☑ 0498 / POP 57,203

Gotland is the largest island in the Baltic sea (2994-sq-km in diameter), situated off Sweden's southeastern coast. Archaeological finds have revealed that the history of human life on the island predates the Christian

tradition, stretching back some 8000 years. Sparsely populated and barely developed, considering its long history of occupation, the charm of the island is its tranquil, almost haunting, beauty.

Gotland's capital Visby, with its intact city walls, is a medieval marvel, magnificent in its authenticity. From the hilltop behind its striking cathedral, overlooking the Baltic, you could easily believe you were somewhere in the Mediterranean, or if you've an active imagination, that you've slipped way back in the annals of time. Come for Medieval Week, when everyone dresses the part, and it's even easier to believe.

Outside Visby, wheels are essential for exploring the island's diverse landscapes – sandy shores, grassy meadows, secluded coves and historical hamlets.

❶ Information

Information on the island abounds:
➡ www.gotland.com/en/
➡ www.destinationgotland.com
➡ www.gotland.net
➡ www.guteinfo.com

❶ Getting There & Away

AIR

Gotlands Flyg (☑ 0771-44 00 10; www. gotlandsflyg.se) offers daily flights between Visby and Stockholm Bromma year-round, and between Visby and Malmö from June to September. Prices start at 392kr one way; book early for discounts, and enquire about standby fares.

NextJet (☑ 0771-90 00 90; www.nextjet.se) operates daily flights from Stockholm Arlanda to Visby (June to September). Prices start at 495kr one way.

BOAT

Destination Gotland (☑ 0771-22 33 00; www. destinationgotland.se; Korsgatan 2, Visby) operates year-round car ferries between Visby and both Nynäshamn (three hours, one to six times daily) and Oskarshamn (three to four hours, one or two daily). Seating is reserved and private cabins with two plank sofas, a writing desk, TV and bathroom with shower and toilet are available for the roughly three-hour journey. Cabins accept four passengers, so if you want one for yourself, you have to pay the fee for four people. Pets are allowed on-board so to avoid a dog-smelly ride, request an allergy-friendly cabin.

Gotlandsbåten (www.gotlandsbaten.se; Färjeleden 2, Visby) runs ferries from Västervik

Gotland

Ⓝ 0 ———— 30 km
  0 ———— 15 miles

↑ Nynäshamn (130km) Gotska Sandön (38km) Äjkesvik
Kappelshamnsviken FÅRÖ Sudersand
Kappelshamn Fårö Fårösandviken Sundersandviken
Lickershamn Irevik 148 Fårösund
Lummelunda Lärbro Farösund
Oskarshamn (110km) 149 148 Tingstäde Slite
Snäck 147 Vitviken
Vibble Visby Aminne
Tofta 140 142 Roma 146
Strand Gnisvärd 145 Kräklingbo
Västergarn 143 Katthammarsvik
Lilla Karlsö Klinteham Ljugarn
Ethelhem Östersjön
Stora Karlsö Stånga 144 Garde
Hemse Horte
Nisseviken Ronehamn
Grötlingbo 142
Burgsviken Gansviken BALTIC
Burgsvik SEA
Holmhällar

to Visby (three hours, one or two daily) from June to August. Regular one-way adult tickets for the ferry start at 295kr, but from mid-June to mid-August there is a far more complicated fare system; some overnight, evening and early-morning sailings in the middle of the week have cheaper fares.

With each carrier, transporting a bicycle costs around 60kr; a car usually starts at 375kr, although tiered pricing operates in summer. Advance reservations are *strongly* recommended.

ℹ Getting Around

There are more than 1200km of roads in Gotland, typically running from village to village through picture-perfect landscapes. Cycling on these is heavenly, and bikes can be hired from a number of places in Visby. The forested belt south and east of Visby is useful if you bring a tent and want to take advantage of the liberal camping laws.

Many travel agents and bike-hire places on the island also rent out camping equipment. In Visby, hire bikes from **Gotlands Cykeluthyrning** (📞 0498-21 41 33; www.gotlandscykeluthyrning. com; Skeppsbron 2; bikes adult/child per day from 120/80kr, per week from 600/400kr; ⊙ 9am-6pm Jun-Aug, shorter hours rest of year) at the harbour. It also rents tents (100/500kr per day/week), or you can hire the 'camping package': two bikes, a tent, a camping stove and two sleeping mats (per day/week 370/1850kr), which is a brilliant way to see the island, and great value.

Kollektiv Trafiken (📞 0498-21 41 12; www. gotland.se/kollektivtrafiken; single ride 80kr) runs buses to all corners of the island. The most useful routes, which run up to seven times daily, operate between Visby and Klintehamn (on the southwest coast), Burgsvik (in the far south) and Fårösund (in the north, with bus connections to Fårö). A one-way ticket will not cost more than 80kr (to bring a bike on-board add 40kr), but enthusiasts will find a monthly ticket good value at 760kr.

For car hire, try **Avis** (📞 0770-82 00 82; www. avis.com) or **Europcar** (📞 08-462 4848; www. europcar.com/location/sweden) for longer term rentals from the airport or snag a cheap deal by the marina with island operator **Visby Harbour Car Rental** (Visby Gästhamn Holmen 1; ⊙ Aug & Sep).

Visby

📞 0498 / POP 23,576

Gotland's picturesque, medieval capital, Visby, is a delight in every way. Even if you saw nothing else of the wealth of fascination the island has to offer, a stroll among Visby's tangle of cobbled lanes, lined with painted cottages sprouting colourful wildflowers from cracks in their pavement, will not be forgotten quickly.

You'll have your finger on the shutter at almost every turn, snapping scenes that could come straight from a storybook – hauntingly beautiful ruined Gothic churches, the astounding, mostly intact 12th-century ramparts surrounding the Old Town, and the truly magnificent Saint Maria Cathedral

Visby swarms with summer holidaymakers. For many, Medieval Week means the chance to don all manner of fancy garb and parade around as knights, queens, peasants and strumpets, dining, drinking and dancing against a Unesco World Heritage backdrop – surprisingly convincing and fun! Others will prefer to visit during quieter times to ponder Visby's charms, undistracted.

◉ Sights & Activities

The town, with its 12th-century wall of 40 towers, is a noble sight – savour it for a few hours while walking around the perimeter (3.5km). Also take time to stroll around the Botanic Gardens and the narrow roads and picturesque lanes just south of here. Pick up a map and the *Welcome to World Heritage Visby* booklet to help guide you around the town.

Gotlands Turistbyrå (p239) organises free two-hour tours at 11am daily from June to August, departing outside the tourist office. No reservations are necessary.

⭐**Gotlands Museum** MUSEUM (📞 0498-29 27 00; www.gotlandsmuseum.se; Strandgatan 14; incl Konstmuseet adult/child 120kr/ free; ⊙ 11am-4pm Tue-Sun; 🚼) Gotlands Museum is one of the mightiest regional museums in Sweden. While highlights include amazing 8th-century, pre-Viking picture stones, human skeletons from chambered tombs and medieval wooden sculptures, the star turn is the legendary Spillings treasure horde. At 70kg it's the world's largest booty of preserved silver treasure.

⭐**Visby Sankta Maria domkyrka** CATHEDRAL (Visby Saint Maria Cathedral; www.visbydf.se; Norra Kyrkogatan 2; ⊙ 9am-9pm Jul & Aug, to 5pm rest of year) Visby's church ruins contrast with the stoic and utterly awe-inspiring Sankta Maria *kyrka*. Built in the late 12th and early 13th centuries and heavily touched up over the years, its whimsical towers are topped by baroque cupolas. Soak up the beautiful

THE SOUTHEAST & GOTLAND VISBY

Visby

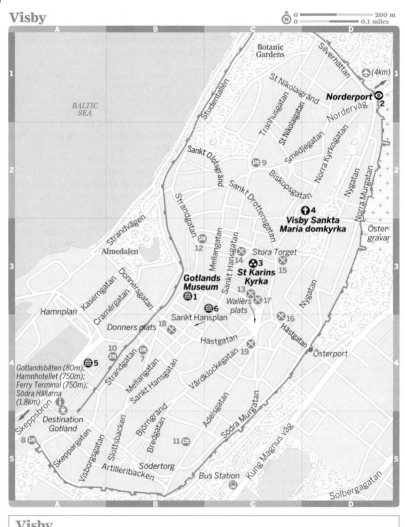

Visby

stained-glass windows, carved floor slabs and ornate carved reredos. The cathedral is used for intimate music concerts in summer. The best place to view the cathedral is from behind – climb all those stairs up the hillside for astounding views.

★ **St Karins Kyrka**   RUINS
(Stora Torget) One of the most stunning of Visby's medieval churches, it's often used for performances. In winter, local children skate on an artificial ice rink within the stone walls. Can you imagine?

★ **Norderport**   LANDMARK
The northern gate of Visby's city wall is a good entry point if you're short on time. Follow the wall in a southwesterly direction until you find the tallest rampart, that's Langa Lisa (six storeys high), and then continue on past the Maiden tower and the Love gate (holding someone special's hand?) until you reach the gunpowder store called Kruttornet – that's the oldest section of the ramparts, built around 1150.

Södra Hällarna   NATURAL FEATURE
(South Cliffs; Färjeleden) Formerly a military station, the southern cliffs are a wonderful spot to gaze out over the Baltic towards the mainland, or look back at the walled city behind you. There are walking paths you can mill about on.

Konstmuseet   MUSEUM
(☑ 0498-29 27 75; www.gotlandsmuseum.se/konstmuseet; Sankt Hansgatan 21; adult/child 80kr/free, incl Gotlands Museum adult/child 120kr/free; ☉ noon-4pm Tue-Sun) The Konstmuseet has a small permanent collection that primarily focuses on Gotland-inspired, 19th- and 20th-century art. More exciting are the temporary exhibitions, which often showcase contemporary local artists.

Fenomenalen   MUSEUM
(☑ 0498-26 34 71; www.fenomenalen.se; Skeppsbron 4; 70kr; ☉ noon-4pm Tue-Sun Aug-Dec; P) Appropriate for Gotland, Visby's quaint and informative science museum focuses more on the origins of science through hands-on historical artifacts and simple experiments rather than attempting to dazzle with all-out modern technology. Great for kids, especially on a rainy island day.

Östergravar   HISTORIC SITE
The grassy area outside the city wall known as the East Graves is a popular spot for

---

AT A GLANCE: VISBY CITY WALL

➡ Built: 1150-1200s

➡ Average height: 11m

➡ Length: approximately 3.5km

➡ Number of turrets: 27

➡ Materials: locally quarried limestone

---

jousts during Medeltidsveckan – and a great spot for photographers.

Österport   LANDMARK
This former city-wall gate near Östergravar is a good way to enter the city, as it puts you at the higher elevations, allowing you to walk your way down the hill and see the best views first.

Gotland Gokart   AMUSEMENT PARK
(☑ 0700-635 700; www.gotlandgokart.se; Broväg 110; 1/2 circuits 230/350kr; ☉ 2-5pm Mon-Sun; 🚗) Kids and adults alike love doing circuits (about eight minutes of action) at this outdoor go-kart park.

★☆ Festivals & Events

Medeltidsveckan   CULTURAL
(Medieval Week; www.medeltidsveckan.se; ☉ Aug) Weeklong medieval festival held throughout the streets of Visby, with axe throwing, archery, live music and feasting.

🛏 Sleeping

Fängelse Vandrarhem   HOSTEL €
(☑ 0498-20 60 50; www.visbyfangelse.se; Skeppsbron 1; dm/s/d 300/450/750kr; 🛜) This hostel offers beds year-round in the small converted cells of an old prison. It's in a handy location, between the ferry dock and the harbour restaurants, and there's an inviting terrace bar in summer. Reception is open from 9am to 2pm, so call ahead if you are arriving outside these times.

★ **Hotel St Clemens**   HOTEL €€
(☑ 0498-21 90 00; www.clemenshotell.se; Smedjegatan 3; r/ste from 1295/2195kr; P 🛜 🐾) Located at the southeastern corner of the botanical garden, this family-run hotel is just a stone's throw away from the vine-covered ruins of the ghostly St Clemens kyrka. It takes up five historical buildings and has two gardens and a summery floral theme in the rooms.

Hotel Stenugnen HOTEL €€

(☎0498-21 02 11; www.stenugnen.nu; Korsgatan 6; s/d from 1000/1350kr; P⎸ 🛜) At this inviting small hotel, bright, whitewashed rooms are designed to make you feel as if you're sleeping in a yacht, and the location is practically on top of the medieval wall. Plenty of rainy-day distractions are provided for kids and the homemade bread is just delicious. Cheaper doubles come with shared bathrooms in the annexe.

Värdshuset Lindgården HOTEL €€

(☎0498-21 87 00; www.lindgarden.com; Strandgatan 26; s/d 1250/1450kr; @) This is a sound central option, with guest rooms (completely renovated to a high standard in 2016) featuring neutral tones, woodsy surfaces and a splash of color for good measure. Rooms are set facing a soothing garden beside a popular restaurant. Dine outdoors and listen to music in the romantic courtyard in summer.

Hotel Villa Borgen BOUTIQUE HOTEL €€

(☎0498-20 33 00; www.gtsab.se; Adelsgatan 11; s/d/apt from 1050/1195/2000kr; @🛜) This place has attractive rooms with lashings of white linen, pale grey walls and scarlet cushions. Accommodation is set around a pretty, quiet courtyard, and the intimate breakfast room with French doors and stained glass contributes to the boutique feeling. There's also a self-contained apartment that can sleep six.

★ Clarion Hotel Wisby HISTORIC HOTEL €€€

(☎0498-25 75 00; www.clarionwisby.com; Strandgatan 6; s/d from 1880/2190kr; P⎸@🛜🏊) Top of the heap in Visby is the luxurious, landmark Wisby. Medieval vaulted ceilings and sparkling candelabras contrast with eye-catching contemporary furnishings. The gorgeous pool (complete with medieval pillar) occupies a converted merchant warehouse. Don't miss the 11th-century chapel, just inside the entrance. The Kitchen & Table restaurant receives rave reviews from readers.

✖ Eating

Visby has plenty of eating options; more so per capita than any other town in Sweden. The majority are located around the main square, Stora Torget, but explore the backstreets and you'll find tucked-away cafes where you can sit in a flower-filled garden. Be sure to try the traditional *saffranspankaka* (a saffron-based pancake topped with berries and cream).

★ Lilla Bjers Farm Pub GASTROPUB €€

(☎0498-65 24 40; www.lillabjers.se; Lilla Bjers 410; ⊙noon-3pm & 5pm-midnight) About 7km southwest of Visby, Lilla Bjers is an award-winning farm eatery with a great outdoorsy feel, locavore food (as local as homegrown can be!), chilled beer and cider, and wholesome good vibes.

Visby Crêperie & Logi CRÊPES €

(☎0498-28 46 22; www.creperielogi.se; Wallérs plats; galettes from 98kr, crêpes from 45kr; ⊙11am-midnight Mon-Sat, to 4pm Sun May-Aug; ⎸🍴) Cheapish, cheerful and a hit with the boho-arty crowd, this lovable corner bolthole serves scrumptious savoury *galettes* and sweet crêpes, ranging from a moreish lamb, chèvre, honey, rocket and almond combo to a wicked chocolate composition further enhanced with white-chocolate chunks and ice cream. The recommended tipple is cider, with 10 varieties to choose from.

★ Surfers ASIAN €€

(☎0498-21 18 00; www.surfersvisby.se; Södra Kyrkogatan 1; small plates 90-120kr; ⊙5pm-2am) Not your normal Chinese restaurant abroad, the speciality here is Szechuan finger food designed to share and ranging from Chinese dumplings to traditional twice-cooked pork. There's plenty of heat in the dishes, which are complemented by the other Surfers' speciality: zingy cocktails (from 100kr) made with fresh fruit and juice – they're good for you. Honest.

★ Bolaget FRENCH €€

(☎0498-21 50 80; www.bolaget.fr; Stora Torget 16; mains 190-260kr; ⊙5-10pm Mon & Tue, 11.30am-2pm & 5-10pm Wed-Fri, 1-10pm Sat; 🛜) Take a defunct Systembolaget shop, chip the 'System' off the signage, and reinvent the space as a buzzing, French bistro-inspired hot spot (fried frog legs, anyone?). Staff members are amiable and the summertime square-side bar seating is perfect for a cool break.

Amarillo INTERNATIONAL €€

(☎073-416 80 86; www.amarillovisby.se; Schweitzergränd 5b; mains 110-165kr; ⊙5-11pm Tue-Thu, to midnight Fri & Sat; 🛜) This is a relaxed, unpretentious place with distressed wood panelling, stylish artwork and a menu of small tapas-style dishes with Pacific, Swedish and Mexican influences. Expect tasty bites such as shrimp tacos, pork buns and scallops, with sides including dill and Parmesan fries and cheesy cornbread. There is an excellent range of craft and imported beers too, including several available on tap.

Jessens Saluhall & Bar
SWEDISH €€

(☑ 0498-21 42 14; www.saluhallochbar.se; Hästgatan 19; mains 125-175kr; ☺ 11am-6pm Mon-Thu, to 8pm Fri, to 4pm Sat) Although the seating area here is very plain diner-style, the fact that this venue doubles as a deli and sells fresh seafood and meat means that the ingredients are top quality. Daily specials are chalked up on a board and generally include the perennially popular fish soup. Meat is sourced locally, with lamb and beef dishes generally taking centre stage.

Vinäger
CAFE €€

(☑ 0498-21 11 68; www.vinager.se; Hästgatan 34; tapas 65kr, mains 135-210kr; ☺ 11am-5pm & 6-10pm) Sporting a slick, ethno-chic interior, this hip cafe-bar puts the emphasis on fresh food, whether it's pumpkin ravioli, red-pepper salad or sinfully good carrot cake. The outdoor restobar cranks up the X factor with a dazzling white, glam alfresco lounge for enjoying those super-smooth cocktails.

Bakfickan
SEAFOOD €€

(☑ 0498-27 18 07; www.bakfickanvisby.se; Stora Torget; mains148-278kr; ☺ 11am-10pm Mon-Fri, noon-10pm Sat & Sun; ☎) White-tiled walls, merrily strung lights and boisterous crowds define this foodie-loved bolt-hole, where enlightened seafood gems might include *toast skagen* (shrimps, dill and mayonnaise), pickled herrings on Gotland bread or Bakfickan's fish soup. Delicious!

ℹ Information

Gotlands Turistbyrå (☑ 0498-20 17 00; www.gotland.info; Donners Plats 1; ☺ 8am-7pm daily summer, 9am-5pm Mon-Fri & 10am-4pm Sat rest of year) The tourist office is conveniently located at Donners Plats and can help with accommodation and advise on what is going on during your stay. It also organises free tours during the summer months.

ℹ Getting There & Away

The **airport** (Visby Flygplats 8; ☑ 010-109 52 00; www.swedavia.com/visby; Visby Flygplats 8) is 4km northeast of Visby, with regular year-round flights (p234) to Stockholm. In the summer months there are also flights to other destinations, including Malmö and Gothenburg. Catch a taxi into town (around 200kr); there is an airport bus during summer.

Car ferries (p234) operate in the summer between Visby and destinations including

Nynäshamn (three hours, one to six times daily), Oskarshamn (three to four hours, one or two daily) and Västervik (three hours, one or two daily). Prices start at 275kr.

Buses depart from the **bus station** (www.gotland.se/busstationsflytt; Kung Magnus Väg; ☺ 7am-10pm Mon-Fri, to 8pm Sat, 8am-4pm Sun) on Kung Magnus Väg; destinations include Klintehamn, Burgsvik and Fårösund. A one-way ticket costs a maximum of 80kr (plus 40kr to bring a bike onboard).

Northern Gotland

North of Visby, Gotland is all about the beaches – you'll find some of the province's most secluded coves and white sandy stretches on the island of Fårö, linked to the mainland by a quick, free and regular car ferry as well as more medieval ruins, *raukar* and remnants from Gotland's military past.

Further afield, the Gotska Sandön National Park, accessible only by ferry or private boat, offers the chance to get Robinson Crusoe–like in the big blue Baltic Sea.

◉ Sights & Activities

★ Gotska Sandön
NATIONAL PARK

(☑ 0498-24 04 50; www.gotskasandon.se) Isolated Gotska Sandön, with an area of 37 sq km, is an unusual island with lighthouses at its three corners, 30km of beaches, sand dunes, pine forest and a church. There's a fantastic network of trails right around the island. Contact **Gotska Sandön Accommodation** (☑ 0498-24 04 50; www.sandoresor.se; campsite/dm/cabin from 30/500/2200kr; ☺ mid-May–early Sep) to book the basic but rustic beds that are available on the island: bring all supplies with you.

Gotska Sandön Ferries (p241) run from Fårösund and Nynäshamn three to four times weekly when operating (895/1095kr return from Fårösund/Nynäshamn).

★ Blå Lagunen
LAGOON

(Blue Lagoon; Blå Lagunen, Läbro) This remote, flooded, former quarry really does have that tropical azure water, but it has two drawbacks: it's steep, deep and not great for kids; and in summer it feels as busy as Bondi (or Biarritz, or Ipanema) on a scorcher of a day.

★ Bungemuseet
MUSEUM

(☑ 0498-22 10 18; www.bungemuseet.se; Bunge Hägur 119; adult/child 100kr/free; ☺ 11am-6pm daily Jul–mid-Aug, 10am-5pm Jun & late Aug, 11am-5pm early Sep) Step back in time at the

THE SOUTHEAST & GOTLAND NORTHERN GOTLAND

Bungemuseet, an open-air museum with 17th- to 19th-century houses, picture stones dating from AD800 and a historic playground. It's near Gotland's northeastern tip, about 1km south of where the Fårö ferry departs.

Tjelvars grav   HISTORIC SITE

(Boge) Located about 42km east of Visby you'll find this fascinating and definitely thought-provoking scene of Bronze Age standing stones arranged in the shape of a ship. Who came up with the idea to memorialise their dead in such a way and how did they do it? The mind boggles.

Bro Kyrka   CHURCH

(☑ 0498-22 27 00; Bro) If you're heading northeast, visit the remarkable Bro church, which has several 5th-century picture stones in the south wall of the oratory, beautiful sculptures and interior lime paintings.

Bungenäs   AREA

(www.bungenas.se; ⊗ May-Sep) FREE Formerly a military base (and part of the adjoining land still is used by the military), this bizarre and wonderful collection of unexpected buildings by the water has been turned into a cafe, event space and accommodation. Bring your swimmers if the weather is fine – there's a jetty and a nice spot to jump in for a dip.

It's about a 1.5km walk from the car park to where the action is.

Jungfrun   NATURAL FEATURE

Outside the little village of Lickershamn (tee hee) on the west coast of the island, you'll find these eroded limestone *raukar*, some of which are a whopping 12m high. The largest of them is called the Jungfrun maiden and has all sorts of spooky stories attached to it.

Lummelunda Grottan   CAVING

(☑ 0498-27 30 50; www.lummelundagrottan.se; Lummelunda Lummelundsbruk 520; adult/child 140/70kr) This limestone grotto, south of Lummelunda on the island's west coast, is Gotland's largest. The best way to experience the cave is on a three-hour tour (900kr) with a guide – places fill up fast and the temperature down there gets to a chilly 8°C, so be sure to book in advance and rug up before you descend.

🍴 Sleeping & Eating

Lummelunda Hostel   HOSTEL €

(☑ 0498-27 30 43; www.lummelundavandrarhem. se; Nyhamn; r without bathroom 500kr, cabins with/without bathroom 900/700kr; ⊗ May-Sep; 🅿) This rustic-style accommodation near the Lummelunda Grottan has a choice of doubles in the main building, plus cabins that range from very basic (bathroom and kitchen in the main house) to fully equipped with small terraces.

Kappelshamns Fritidsby   LODGE €€

(☑ 0498-22 70 09; www.kappelshamn.com/en; Flenvikevägen 82, Lärbro; d from 550kr; 🏊) On the far north of the island, near the fishing hamlet of Kappelshamn, you'll find these delightful and secluded cottages with their own little pool just 150m from the water. In low season, the place is as idyllic as you can get, and even in peak season, its small enough that you won't be troubled by the constant shrieks of excited kids.

Tjauls Gård   B&B €€

(☑ 0736-15 57 53; www.tjaulsgard.se; Lummelunda Tjauls 188; r incl breakfast 995kr; 🅿🛜) This homely farmhouse is a great place to stay, with a spa and the option of horse riding, bike hire and off-road-motorbiking tours (owners are keen bikers). Rooms are spacious and comfortable.

⭐ Fabriken Furillen   HOTEL €€

(☑ 0498-22 30 40; www.furillen.com; Rute Furilden, Läbro; r from 2145kr; ⊗ Jun-Sep; 🅿❄🛜🐕) ⦿ In the unlikely setting of an old limestone factory in a remote eastern corner of the island, this extraordinary hotel combines a raw industrial environment with cutting-edge Scandinavian design. There are even hermit huts for those really wanting to get away from it all, with hand-built Hästens beds and a copy of Thoreau's *Walden*. The restaurant (mains from 295kr) is Michelin-chef standard and uses only local products and produce.

Sjalso Bageri   BAKERY €

(☑ 0498-27 09 09; www.sjalsobageri.se; Själsö Själsövägen 10) This popular bakery in Sjalso village, outside Visby (about 3km north of the airport), bakes amazing fresh loaves, which you can buy on their own or have them transformed into delicious fresh sandwiches. There's also a range of tasty pastries and baked goods.

Lickershamnskrogen   SWEDISH €€

(☑ 0498-27 24 25; www.lickershamnskrogen.se; Stenkyrka Lickershamn, Tingstäde; mains 159-295kr; ⊗ 8am-9pm May-Aug) Near the Jungfru trailhead at Lickershamn, this place serves both local and Med-style dishes and tapas. There's also a hut selling smoked fish.

ℹ️ Getting There & Around

You'll need your own wheels (two or four) to really explore the area. Cars *and* bikes can be hired in Visby, or you can rent bikes in most villages of any size on the mainland, or when you reach Fårö.

Kollektiv Trafiken runs limited bus services from Visby to Fårö – a one-way ticket costs a maximum of 80kr (plus 40kr to bring a bike onboard). Get timetables from **Gotlands Turist-byrå** (p239) in Visby.

The free, yellow Fårö ferry ply the waters between Gotland and Fåro. Just drive up and wait your turn. Sailings are regular and it only takes minutes to cross, but you should expect around 30 minutes to make the crossing, including waiting, loading and unloading.

Fårö

This island, once home to Ingmar Bergman, has magnificent *raukar* formations; watch the sunset at Langhammarshammaren if you can. At the island's eastern tip, the rocks by Fårö lighthouse are laced with fossils. British troops who fought in the Crimean war are buried at Ryssnäs in the extreme south; obey signs posted along roads here, as this area is still used for military exercises. The beaches here are some of the island's finest and the isolated fishing villages are unspeakably picturesque.

It's hard to imagine a better way to absorb the area than by cycling up to Fårö and following the bike trails around the beautiful, windswept little island.

⊙ Sights & Activites

⭐ **Bergmancenter**   ARTS CENTRE
(☑ 0498-22 68 68; www.bergmancenter.se; Fårö Svens 1118; ☺ 10am-6pm summer, noon to 4pm May & Sep; ℗) **FREE** The Bergmancenter,

honouring Sweden's most famous film director, the late Ingmar Bergman, a Fårö local, was inaugurated in 2014 and hosts exhibits, lectures, workshops and screenings, as well as a library and cafe. It's free to take a look around the centre but prices vary for screenings and special events.

Helgumannens Fiskeläge   HISTORIC SITE
(Helgumannen Fishing Village) It's worth making the trek to this isolated fishing village just to contemplate the remoteness of life out here and the beauty of real isolation.

Fårö Islandshästar   HORSE RIDING
(☑ 070-690 04 32; fia@faroislandshastar.se) Hardy, docile Icelandic horses are a popular riding breed, with short or longer treks on offer for both children and adults. Email for pricing.

🛏️ Sleeping & Eating

⭐ **Crêperie Tati**   CRÊPES €
(☑ 070-203 89 24; Fårö Broskogs; crêpes from 50kr) Folks line up 20-deep for the tasty sweet and savoury crêpes served at this boho/hippy/cowboy/hipster ranch with its quirky collectibles and small garden out back. We're not sure if the queue is so much about the quality of the crêpes or the cool environs, or that there's just nowhere else to eat for miles.

In the evening when it's wearing its **Kutens Bensin** (www.kuten.se; Fårö Broskogs) hat, people come for the music.

ℹ️ Information

There's an information signboard near each side of the ferry crossing, but if you want to speak to someone, you'll need to contact **Gotlands Turistbyrå** (p239) in Visby before you set out.

ℹ️ Getting There & Around

The frequent yellow Fårö ferry between Fårösund (northeastern tip of Gotland) and Fårö is free for cars, passengers and cyclists.

INGMAR BERGMAN

The wild, mysterious landscape of Fårö is not easily forgotten, as anyone who has visited can testify. The tiny island just off the northern tip of Gotland particularly haunted Ingmar Bergman (1918–2007), the legendary Swedish director, who first visited Fårö in 1960 while scouting locations for *Through a Glass Darkly*. Bergman ended up living and working on Fårö for 40 years, shooting seven films there, and he is now buried on the island.

Learn about his life and works at the impressive, modern **Bergmancenter**, or, if you're a total film buff, time your visit to the popular **Bergman Week** (www.bergman veckan.se) festival.

THE SOUTHEAST & GOTLAND FÅRÖ

The crossing takes about five minutes, but you should allow for about half an hour from start to finish, including waiting and loading times.

From May to September, **Gotska Sandön Ferries** (🅙 0498-24 04 50; ☺ mid-May–early Sep) run to gorgeous Gotska Sandon island from Fårösund.

Southern Gotland

The towns of Hemse and Burgsvik are two of the larger commercial centres in the sprawling south. There are good beaches on both the east coast, where Ljugarn is the go-to for sandy shenanigans, and the west, where the Ekstakusten coast road around Karlsö offers breathtaking scenery of the offshore Karlsö islands.

The ragged cape of Gotland's southernmost tip feels as isolated and remote as its north, and if you're here long enough to experience the dramatic and polarised beauty of each, you'll be almost qualified to call yourself a Gotlander – but not quite. Locals say you have to last a few harsh winters here to cut your teeth first.

◉ Sights

★ Stora Karlsö   NATURE RESERVE
(www.storakarlso.se) This remote island nature reserve is home to extensive bird life including thousands of guillemots and razorbills, as well as the maculinea arion (large blue butterfly). For nature-lovers, it's well worth the travel time needed to get there. You can visit the island as a day trip (with 3½ hours ashore) or stay overnight.

From Klintehamn harbour, catch a ride on the passenger-only **Klintehamn-Stora Karlsö Farje** (www.storakarlso.se/resa-till-stora-karlso/turlista-och-priser/) to the nature reserve one to three times daily from May to early September (adult/six to 15 years return 345/155kr, 30 minutes).

★ Gothem kyrka   CHURCH
(🅙 0498-300 01; Gothem Prästgården 929) On the east coast, 34km from Visby, Gothem church is one of the most impressive in Gotland; the nave is decorated with friezes dating from 1300.

Ljugarn   AREA
Ljugarn is a small east-coast seaside resort. There are impressive *raukar* formations at Folhammar Nature Reserve, 2km north. Southwest of Ljugarn and the village of Alskog, the imposing Garde church has four

extraordinary medieval lychgates and an upside-down medieval key in the door; the original 12th-century roof is still visible.

Romakloster   RUINS
(🅙 0498-501 23; admission free, guided tour per group 800kr; ☺ 10am-6pm daily May-Sep, shorter hours rest of year) **FREE** Heading southeast from Visby on Rte 143, 6km southwest of the town Dalhem on your way to Ljugarn, pull over to check out this 12th-century Cistercian monastery ruin, a kilometre from the main road. Summer theatre performances here cost around 250kr – tickets available from Gotlands Turistbyrå (p239). The 18th-century manor house is also impressive.

Öja kyrka   CHURCH
(Öja) Just north of Burgsvik, Öja church dates from 1232 and has Gotland's highest church tower (67m). It has a magnificent cross, and the wall and ceiling paintings are remarkably detailed. Look for the inscribed stone slabs under the covered shelter just outside the churchyard.

Lojsta träsk   LAKE
(Lojsta Lakes) Stop off at Lojsta to see the deepest lakes in Gotland, the remains of an early medieval fortress and a fine church.

🏃 Activities

Dalhem Steam Railway   RAIL
(www.gotlandstaget.se; Hesselby Jernvagsstation; adult/child 50/30kr; ☺ 11.15am-3.45pm Wed, Thu & Sat Jul-early Aug, Sun only Jun & rest of Aug) This early-20th-century steam engine operates a limited timetable from June through August along a 6.5km stretch of track between the outposts of Hesselby (in Dalhem) and Roma. Hesselby station also houses a fascinating railway-themed museum.

Truffle-Hunting Safaris   OUTDOORS
(www.tryffelsafari.se; ☺ Oct & Nov) Truffle-hunting safaris in the Ljugarn area are a unique way for foodies to discover more about this delicacy and local produce in general. Check the website for package prices, which include a five-star dinner (featuring truffles, of course) and accommodation at **Smakrike Krog & Logi** (🅙 0498-49 33 71; www.smakrike.se; Claudelins väg 1, Ljugarn; mains 245-345kr; ☺ noon-4pm & 5.30-10pm mid-Jun–Aug; 🅿 ☏) 🍴.

🛏 Sleeping & Eating

As with the north, accommodation is spread out over a diverse area and many lodgings are some distance from any services.

★**Warfsholm** HOTEL €

(☑0498-24 00 10; www.warfsholm.se; Klinte Varvsholm 612; sites 100kr, s/d from 490/690kr; ☺hotel May-Sep, apt & cottages year-round; P ☎) Enticing Warfsholm has several accommodation options, plus a beautiful waterside location, a pleasant restaurant and a cosy bar. There are rooms in the atmospheric 19th-century main house, as well as apartments and cottages in the grounds.

★**STF Stora Karlsö** HOSTEL €€

(☑0498-24 05 00; www.storakarlso.se; hostel s/d 200/500kr, old lighthouse r from 800kr; ☺May-Aug) At the island of Stora Karlsö off the coast of Gotland, you can stay in rooms still decorated with the antique furniture left by the lighthouse-keeper. There's a small restaurant if you don't fancy cooking and it's a fantastic place to birdwatch or go fossil hunting. The island is reachable by two to three ferries daily.

Djupvik Hotel HOTEL €€€

(☑0498-24 42 72; www.djupvikhotel.com; Eksta Bopparve; r incl breakfast from 2390kr; P ✳ @ ☎ ✉) A hotel for the ultimate in pampering, with a fabulous remote setting near the rocky shores of the Ekstakusten nature reserve and every amenity, including free yoga sessions and bikes, for serious de-stressing. The restaurant also serves excellent locavore cuisine.

Katthamrsviks Rokeri SEAFOOD €€

(☑0498-523 75; www.katthammarsviksrokeri.se; Jacob Häggs vägan 54; mains 85-210kr; ☺11am-5pm) You can't get more fishy than this local institution that catches, smokes, grills, pickles and prepares all manner of ocean bounty.

★**Krakas Krog** SWEDISH €€€

(☑0498-530 62; www.krakas.se; Kräklings 223, Katthammarsvik; mains 280-345kr; ☺4-10pm Wed-Sun early Jun–Sep) The owners of Krakas Krog make a point of sourcing their ingredients from Gotland's fields, woods and sea, including frogs' legs direct from the garden. Meals are served on the porch and in the petite dining room. The menu is replete with local delicacies: eggs with morels and beets, turkey in truffle broth or Baltic Sea turbot with sage butter.

ⓘ Getting There & Around

Wheels are essential here. If you didn't bring your own bike or car over with you on the ferry, or if you came by plane, there's likely to be bikes available at your accommodation or in the nearest village. But that doesn't help you get there in the first place: Visby is the only place you'll have any luck renting a car.

Limited and infrequent bus services are provided by **Kollektiv Trafiken** (p235). Destinations include Klintehamn and Burgsvik – a one-way ticket costs a maximum of 80kr (plus 40kr to bring a bike onboard). Get timetables from **Gotlands Turistbyrå** (p239) in Visby.

THE SOUTHEAST & GOTLAND SOUTHERN GOTLAND

Jämtland & the Bothnian Coast

Best Places to Eat

➡ Hemmagastronomi (p265)

➡ Tant Anci & Fröcken Sara (p256)

➡ Innefickan Restaurang & Bar (p248)

➡ Matildas (p254)

➡ Lörruden (p255)

Best Places to Stay

➡ Treehotel (p265)

➡ U&Me Hotel (p262)

➡ Eriksgårdens Fjällhotell (p251)

➡ Hotell Fjällgården (p249)

➡ Lilla Hotellet (p259)

Why Go?

The north of Sweden seems to have it all. There are endless pristine forests where the odds of encountering elk, reindeer and bear are high and the hiking is splendid. There are jagged mountains that provide Sweden's best skiing in winter and host the best mountain biking in summer, along with every other mountain sport you can imagine.

On the other hand, you are never too far from the bright lights of civilisation: you can go lake-monster spotting in Östersund, party with locals and visit quality museums in the student towns of Gävle, Umeå and Luleå, or just enjoy the laid-back rhythm of life in the pretty coastal towns, rich in historical sights and medieval churches. Slow down even further by lingering in the tiny fishing villages and sampling the fresh catch, or strike out for Höga Kusten's remote islands and wonder why the Swedes invented *surströmming* (fermented herring).

When to Go
Sundsvall

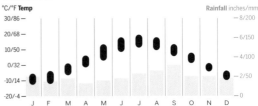

Mar & Apr Days are longer and warmer, but still plenty of snow for snow sports.

Jul The best time for hiking and island-hopping with long days.

Aug Fill your belly with crayfish on Höga Kusten's islands.

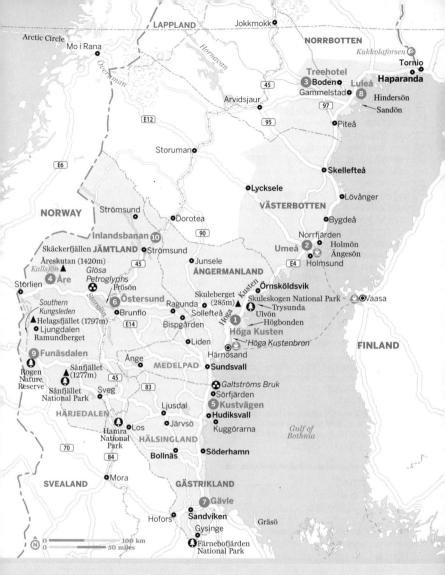

Jämtland & the Bothnian Coast Highlights

1 Höga Kusten (p256)
Travelling along the coastline, and sampling *surströmming*.

2 Umeå (p260) Visiting the superb museums and sculpture park.

3 Treehotel (p265) Staying in a spaceship or bird's nest at this incredible remote hotel.

4 Åre (p249) Skiing, biking, rafting or zorbing at Sweden's outdoor-adventure capital.

5 Kustvägen (p257) Driving the scenic coastal road.

6 Östersund (p246) Searching for Storsjöodjuret, the legendary lake monster.

7 Gävle (p252) Looking the straw goat as attempts are made to burn it down.

8 Luleå (p264) Visiting Sweden's largest church town at Gammelstad.

9 Funäsdalen (p250) Hiking the wilderness on one of the town's 'gem hikes'.

10 Inlandsbanan (p249) Riding this scenic train from Östersund, north to Lappland or south to Mora.

JÄMTLAND

Jämtland has been attracting visitors for more than 1000 years, originally with pilgrims following in the footsteps of St Olav on trails to Nidaros in Trondheim, Norway. These days hikers, hunters and outdoors enthusiasts pull on their boots to explore the wonderful, sparsely populated natural environment, while gold medal–winning ski racer and local boy Ingemar Stenmark put Swedish skiing on the map in the 1970s, generating huge interest in resorts such as Åre and Funäsdalen. Jämtland's countless lakes and rivers pull in fishers, kayakers and canoeists, while if you're into exploring, you'll have to keep your eyes open for reindeer wandering the roads. It's not all about the outdoors though, with Östersund selected as a Unesco-designated city of gastronomy and some top-notch remote restaurants attracting the attention of gourmets. With so much to do, Jämtland is an enthralling place to visit.

❶ Getting There & Away

Östersund's airport has daily connections to Stockholm.

There are trains from Stockholm to Östersund via Gävle, and in summer Inlandsbanan trains come south from Gällivare in Lappland, and north from Mora.

If you've got wheels, which will be useful if you want to explore Jämtland, head west on the E14 at Sundsvall on the Bothnian Coast (377km from Stockholm) to get to Östersund.

Östersund

✍ 063 / POP 49,806

This pleasant town by Lake Storsjon, in whose chilly waters is said to lurk a rarely sighted monster, is a relaxed and scenic gateway town for further explorations of Norrland. It's remote enough that if you are approaching by car, you can expect to see almost as many reindeer as cars. The town dates from 1786 and was a lucrative trading centre.

Today, its appeal lies in its air of relaxation: in summer, people flock to the terrace bars and cafes of this Unesco-designated 'city of gastronomy', or wander the pedestrianised shopping streets in the stroll-friendly centre. One of the best ways to appreciate Östersund is to take the footbridge across to the adjacent island of Frösön and gaze back at the city in profile, ideally around sunset. Seen in that light, this fun-loving university town is hard to resist.

◎ Sights

★ Mus-Olles Museum   MUSEUM

(✍ 0640-220 60; www.musolles.com; Sjövik 453, Ytterån; adult/child 100kr/free; ⊙ 8am-4pm late Jun-late Aug; ℗) If you're into collections of stuff, this is the place to come, about 34km northwest of Östersund and a kilometre north of the E14. Per-Olov Nilson was a charismatic collector extraordinaire who first opened his museum in 1906. He hoarded more than 150,000 objects, including 25,000 related to packaging, then formed a trust, which now operates the museum, to run things once he passed on (in 1955). This fascinating museum, including a cafe and various buildings, is on Per-Olov's old property.

★ Jamtli   MUSEUM

(www.jamtli.com; Museiplan; adult/child 70kr/free, entry late June–late Aug free; ⊙ 11am-5pm daily late Jun-late Aug, Tue-Sun rest of year; ℗ ♿) Jamtli, 1km north of the centre, consists of two parts. The open-air museum, comprising painstakingly reconstructed wooden buildings, complete with enthusiastic guides wearing 19th-century period costume; and the indoor museum, home to the **Överhogdal Tapestries**, the oldest of their kind in Europe – Christian Viking relics from AD 1100 that feature animals, people, ships and dwellings. Another fascinating display is devoted to Storsjöodjuret (the lake monster), including taped interviews with those who've seen it, monster-catching gear and a pickled monster embryo.

Moose Garden   ANIMAL SANCTUARY

(✍ 070-363 60 61; www.moosegarden.com; Orrviken 215, Orrviken; adult/child 140/90kr; ⊙ tours 11am & 1pm late Jun–mid-Aug; ℗) Head to Moose Garden, 16km southwest of Östersund, to get up close and personal with the King of the Forest – or at least, some tame ones. You get to learn all about the moose, pat one and get as many photos as you like. There is also accommodation here in the form of Moose Lodges (from 690kr).

Storsjöhyttan   FACTORY

(✍ 063-13 36 30; www.storsjohyttan.com; Sjötorget 5; ⊙ 10am-5pm Mon-Thu, to 4pm Fri, 11am-3pm Sat) At Sweden's first Économusée (a concept originating in Quebec), you can observe the three masters of glass at work as they

Östersund

Östersund

◎ Sights
1 Badhusparken A1
2 Storsjöhyttan.......................................A2

◉ Activities, Courses & Tours
3 S/S Thomée A2

◉ Sleeping
4 Clarion Hotel Grand Östersund...........B1
5 Hotel Emma B2
6 Hotel Jämteborg A3

◎ Eating
7 En Liten Röd...B1
8 Innefickan Restaurang & Bar..............B2
9 Wedemarks Konditori & Bageri..........B2

◎ Drinking & Nightlife
10 Jane Doe...B2
11 Jazzkoket B3

Frö, the pagan god of fertility, worshipped by the Vikings originally resident here.

Just across the footbridge, outside Landstingshuset and near the Konsum supermarket, is Sweden's northernmost **rune stone**, which commemorates the 1050 arrival of Austmaður or 'East Man', the first Christian missionary on Frösön.

🛏 Sleeping

Hotel Jämteborg   HOTEL €
(☑ 063-51 01 01; www.jamteborg.se; Storgatan 54; hostel d/tr from 590/690kr, B&B s/d/tr 590/790/890kr, hotel s/d from 1095/1250kr; ℗ 🛜) Just imagine: you're travelling with friends that you're all on different budgets. Hotel Jämteborg comes to the rescue, with its catch-all combo of hostel beds, B&B rooms and hotel rooms in several adjacent buildings. The cheerful hotel rooms come in cream and crimson, defying Sweden's 'earth tones only' rule. The hostel is only open from June to August.

★ Hotel Emma   HOTEL €€
(☑ 063-51 78 40; www.hotelemma.com; Prästgatan 31; s/d from 720/895kr; ℗ 🛜) The individually styled rooms at super-central Emma nestle in crooked hallways on two floors, with homey touches such as squishy armchairs and imposing ceramic stoves; some rooms have French doors facing the courtyard. The breakfast spread is a delight. Reception hours are limited, so call ahead if arriving late or early.

transform white-hot melted putty into original, striking creations. Immerse yourself in different glassmaking techniques and the history of glass, or take some glassy goodies home with you.

Badhusparken   BEACH
(www.vinterparken.se) The waterfront park is the town's most popular stop for sunbathing and a brisk swim. In winter the lake turns into Sweden's largest ice-skating rink (rent your skates here; 160kr per day) and you also can swim in the specially cut hole in the ice further south along the waterfront before making a spirited dash to the nearby mobile sauna and spa (140kr).

Frösön   ISLAND
Large and peaceful Frösön island sits just across the bridge from central Östersund, reachable by road and by footbridge from Badhusparken. The island takes its name from

STORSJÖODJURET – THE LAKE MONSTER

Just imagine…you're sitting by Storsjön lake at dusk when you notice a dark shadow rise out of the water. Could it be just ripples in the wake of a passing boat? Perhaps a couple of elk swimming? Or maybe it's the head of Storsjöodjuret – the monster that dwells somewhere in the dark waters of the 91m-deep lake.

Sightings of the only monster of its kind in Sweden were made as early as 1635, when the description of a strange animal with a black serpentine body and catlike head first appeared in a folk tale. The Frösö Runestone does, in fact, depict a serpent-like creature and the Lake Monster has had such a grip on the public imagination that in 1894 a hunt for it was organised by a special committee put together by King Oscar II. However, the Norwegian whalers specially hired for the job came back empty-handed. Every summer there are claims of new sightings, and the monster was granted protected status as an 'endangered species' in 1986, only for it to be revoked in 2005.

Through the Östersund tourist office you can book a spot on the popular two-hour monster-spotting cruise aboard the 1875 **S/S Thomée** (☑063-14 30 00; www.ostersund. se/thomee; adult/child 100/50kr; ☺Jun-early Sep) steamship.

Clarion Hotel Grand Östersund   HOTEL €€
(☑063-55 60 00; www.nordicchoicehotels.se; Prästgatan 16; s/d from 1050/1250kr; P🅿🛜❄) Östersund's most luxurious option has an excellent restaurant featuring sophisticated northern Swedish and international cuisine, and the plushest of the rooms come with their very own marbled hallways. It's in an excellent location on the Stortorget central square.

Wedemarks Konditori & Bageri   CAFE €
(☑063-51 03 83; http://wedemarks.se; Prästgatan 27; snacks 60-80kr; ☺8am-10pm Mon-Fri, 10am-5pm Sat, 11am-4pm Sun; 🛜) This glorious cafe has been sweet-toothing its customers since 1924; this is the place to try a slice of typical Swedish delights such as the traditional Princess layer cake with its topping of bright green marzipan. If you are in a savoury mood, go for a succulent vegie or beef sandwich or shrimp-filled baked potato.

En Liten Röd   INTERNATIONAL €€
(☑063-12 63 26; www.enlitenrod.se; Brogränd 19; mains from 175kr; ☺5-10.30pm Mon-Sat; 🛜) Tucked away in a backstreet, this place dates from the '70s, and although the decor hasn't changed too much since then, it still has a classy dress-for-dinner feel. The speciality is fondue with a choice of classic Swiss-style cheese, meat, seafood and, yes, creamy dark chocolate. More traditional dishes include pepper steak, beef bourguignon and pasta.

★**Innefickan Restaurang & Bar**   FUSION €€€
(☑063-12 90 99; www.innefickan.se; Postgränd 11; mains from 210kr; ☺5pm-late Tue-Sun) With a cosy cellar ambience – all exposed brick and contemporary art pieces – Innefickan packs a great deal of creativity into its succinct menu. Try the carpaccio with wasabi and coriander; the veal with chanterelles and pumpkin purée is expertly seared, and rhubarb is transformed into something far greater than the raw material in this place's capable hands.

🍷 Drinking & Nightlife

★**Jazzkoket**   PUB
(☑063-10 15 75; http://jazzkoket.se; Prästgatan 44; ☺5pm-midnight Tue-Thu, 11.30am-2am Fri, 11.30am-1am Sat) Jazzkoket wears many hats and changes them often: she can be a relaxed loosen-your-tie-after-work venue, and a sultry, stormy bacchanale on weekend nights, when her walls reverberate with the sounds of live jazz and rock. The menu's a bit hit-and-miss, but the charcuterie and cheese platters from local producers are a sure bet.

Jane Doe   BAR
(☑063-10 01 39; www.janedoebar.se; Prästgatan 44; ☺3pm-2am Tue-Sat, 9pm-2am Sun) If you were born to be bad and you're after 'food, drinks and rock'n'roll', Jane Doe is the place to go. If you're hungry, the Smokin' Hot Jane burger (165kr) is sure to hit the spot, but if you want to knock a few back, there's beer, wine, cider and plenty of harder stuff to choose from. Jane also does takeaway.

ℹ Information

Tourist Office (☑063-701 17 00; www.visit ostersund.se; Rådhusgatan 44; ☺9am-5pm

Mon-Fri, 10am-3pm Sat & Sun) Efficient office opposite the town hall.

ℹ Getting There & Away

The **airport** (☑ 063-19 30 00; www.swedavia. se/ostersund; Frösön) serving both Östersund and Åre is on Frösön island, 11km west of the town centre. The airport bus leaves regularly from the bus station (adult/child90/45kr).

SAS flies to Stockholm. During the ski season, the airport receives charter flights from London Heathrow, Manchester, Amsterdam and Copenhagen.

Daily bus 45 runs north at 7.15am from Östersund to Gällivare (532kr, 11¼ hours) via Arvidsjaur (460kr, seven hours) and Jokkmokk (574kr, 9½ hours) and south to Mora (284kr, 5¼ hours, two daily) from the **bus station** (☑ 0771-10 01 10; http://ltr.se; Gustav III Torg; ⊘ 6am-10.30pm Mon-Fri, 6.30am-7.30pm Sat, noon-10pm Sun).

In summer, the daily 7.05am **Inlandsbanan** (p334) train heads north to Gällivare (1378kr, 14½ hours) and one heads south to Mora (596kr, six hours). SJ departures include two trains daily to Stockholm (701kr, five hours) via Uppsala, and up to six daily trains heading west to Åre (146kr, 1¼ hours).

Åre

☑ 0647 / POP 1417

Beautifully situated in a mountain valley by the shores of Åresjön lake, Åre is Sweden's most popular skiing resort and visitors invade the village during the December-to-May skiing season. Things don't drop off much for summer though, as this small village is taking on the mantle of the adventure capital of Sweden. In July, Åre hosts the Åre Bike Festival and the hard-core Åre Extreme Challenge that has its competitors running, paddling and cycling for glory. Besides traditional sports, winter and summer bring a bewildering array of mountain-related activities that you can try your hand at, such as dog-sledding, snowmobile safaris, paragliding, white-water rafting and hill-carting. There's even a chocolate factory to help with après-adventure recovery.

◉ Sights & Activities

★ Kabinbanan   CABLE CAR, VIEWPOINT
(adult/child 150/110kr; ⊘ 10am-4pm daily late Jun-late Sep) Taking you almost to the top of Mt Åreskutan, this gondola is worth taking for the awesome views alone. The seven-minute ride departs from behind Åre's main square and whisks you up to a viewing platform

(1274m) complete with Åre's most expensive cafe. Hike up to the peak from there.

Åre Bergbana   FUNICULAR
(adult/child 60kr/free) This lovely old mountain railway was completed in 1910 and was one of the first ski lifts in Åre. These days, the funicular is run by SkiStar during winter and Hotel Fjällgården keeps it operating in the evenings and at other times to get guests to the hotel. The trip takes seven minutes and is included for hotel guests.

Åre Chokladfabrik   FACTORY
(Åre Chocolate Factory; ☑ 0647-155 80; https:// arechokladfabrik.se; Björnänge 801; ⊘ 10am-5pm) It's hard to drive past this place at the eastern end of town on the E14. These guys have been producing hand-made chocolates, truffles and caramels since 1991, and if you want to see why they've been so successful, drop by and try some of the chocolate up for tasting. It's seriously good stuff!

★ Åre Bike Park   MOUNTAIN BIKING
(http://bikingare.com) In summer the slopes of Mt Åreskutan become an enormous playground dedicated to downhill biking. More than 30 trails span 40km of track, ranging from beginner to extreme (the trails are graded using the same system as ski slopes). The Kabinbanan cable car, the Bergbanan funicular, the VM6 and Hummelliften chairlifts are fitted with bike racks.

Mt Åreskutan   SKIING
(www.skistar.com/are; 1-day ski pass 425kr) The combined Åre, Björnen and Duved ski area boasts 38 ski lifts, 100 pistes and 1000 vertical metres of skiable slopes, with runs suitable for all abilities. Åre and Björnen are linked by trails and lifts, while Duved is 10km west. The ski season is between December and mid-April, though skiing conditions are best from February, when daylight hours increase.

⇌ Sleeping

Hotell Fjällgården   HOTEL €€
(☑ 0647-145 00; www.fjallgarden.se; s/d from 745/1390kr; 🅿 🛜) Among the trees and with great views at the top of Åre's funicular since 1910, this is as much an activity centre as hotel. On top of all the outdoor activities, there's a top restaurant and après-ski bar, often including live music. Rooms run from simple skier rooms to suites – and the hotel keeps the funicular running to get you here.

★ Copperhill Mountain Lodge　　LODGE €€€
(☑0647-143 00; https://copperhill.se; Åre Björnen; r from 1440kr; P ☎) Beautifully constructed of wood and stone with copper accents, this lodge looks down on Åre from its lofty mountain perch. Its stylish, contemporary rooms are grouped according to precious metals; Gold Suites at the top, Brass, Zinc, Copper, Silver...you get the idea. The spa, Niesti Restaurant, and library and Fireside Lounge & Bar just add to the ambience.

Holiday Club　　HOTEL €€€
(☑0647-120 00; www.holidayclubresorts.com/en/resorts/are; Åre station; r from 1690kr; P ☎ ⛳) This massive new family-friendly place is between Åre station and the lake and super-convenient to everything. Apart from all the outdoor adventures, you'll find an adventure pool, spa, gym, bowling and a top-notch restaurant in Grow and an O'Learys sports bar. Open year-round, there's everything from well-fitted-out hotel rooms to suites to apartments.

✕ Eating & Drinking

Broken　　AMERICAN €€
(☑0647-506 33; http://broken-are.com; Torggränd 4; mains from 115kr; ⊙noon-11pm) Just off the main square, this American-style diner is where all the hungry bikers and skiers converge to replenish burned calories by hoovering down Philly cheese steak, fajitas the size of your head, rib platters and jumbo hamburgers, all washed down with frozen margaritas.

Vinbaren Åre　　BAR
(http://vinbaren-are.com; Stationsvägen; ⊙4pm-late Nov-Apr & Jun-Aug) Its vast wine list spans the world, and you have to get here early to get a seat, as the skiing clientele packs this place to the rafters in the evenings. The tapas don't let the side down either: think fish tacos, cheese fondue, pulled pork and mini burgers.

ℹ Information

Tourist Office (☑0647-163 21; www.visitare.com; St Olafsväg 33; ⊙10am-6pm Mon-Fri, to 3pm Sat & Sun; ☎) Inside the public library in the train station building. Plenty of info on the area, including maps of hiking trails and brochures on outdoor activities.

ℹ Getting There & Away

Bus 155 runs east to Östersund (185kr, two hours, one or two daily). Bus 157 runs west to Duved (30kr, 10 minutes, up to 10 daily) and

bus 571 connects Duved to Storlien (110kr, 30 minutes, daily).

Åre has east-bound trains for Östersund (155kr, 1¼ hours, six daily) and to Stockholm (from 822kr, from seven hours, five daily). To get to Trondheim, Norway (296kr, 2½ hours, two daily), change at Storlien (98kr, 45 minutes, two daily).

Funäsdalen

☑0684 / POP 890

Funäsdalen is a small, narrow mountain resort village nestled along a single road at the northern end of Funäsdalssjön lake. It's an attractive place, dominated by the impressive peak Funäsdalsberget, which towers above the village and is accessed by a new cable car. The village and surrounding area are popular with hikers, skiers, mountain bikers, fishermen and other outdoor-sports enthusiasts. Beyond Funäsdalen, Rte 84 leads uphill to diminutive Tänndalen and further west to Norway, while the highest road in Sweden leads north to beautiful Ljungdalen village, surrounded by mountains.

◉ Sights & Activities

Härjedalens Fjällmuseum　　MUSEUM
(☑0684-164 25; www.fjallmuseet.se; Rörovägen 30; adult/child 150kr/free; ⊙11am-5pm mid-Jun–late Sep; P ♿) Härjedalens Fjällmuseum has displays covering the South Sami, who still herd their reindeer in from the nearby Mittådalen and Brändåsen villages, and settlement of this area by local farmers and miners. The adjacent Fornminnesparken open-air section features 19th-century buildings from this area.

FunäsGondolen　　CABLE CAR
(www.funasdalenberghotell.se; adult/child 140/100kr; ⊙10am-3pm Jul-Sep & winter; ♿) The FunäsGondolen whisks its passengers to the top of Mt Funäsdalsberget (directly above the village). It's not a massive mountain nor a lengthy gondola, but the 360-degree panoramic views make a trip to the top worthwhile. There's skiing in winter and Café Toppstugan at the top, waiting with coffee and waffles.

★ Funäsdalen Gem Hikes　　HIKING
(www.funasfjallen.se) The tourist office has published a pocket hiking guide (89kr) for around Funäsdalen, with 30 'gem hikes' and nine 'culture walks'. The hikes range in length from gentle rambles taking an hour or two, to full-on full-day treks taking 10 to

WILDERNESS CRUISE

The remote mountains and fells of Jämtland and Härjedalen are responsible for some of the most exciting back-to-nature cooking in Sweden. But to taste it, you have to travel the extra mile...

Fäviken Magasinet (☑ 0647-401 77; http://favikenmagasinet.se; per person 3000kr) This intimate 16-seat, five-table mountain restaurant has one of Sweden's finest culinary reputations, drawing strictly on seasonal Jämtland produce and traditions such as drying, pickling and salting. There are also divine double rooms here for 2500kr, including breakfast. It's at Fäviken, 15km east of Åre at Järpen, turn north. Book well ahead for both the restaurant and accommodation.

Havvi i Glen (☑ 070-600 64 76; www.havviiglen.se; Glen 530, Åsarna; mains 195-265kr, tasting menu 1395kr) A proud standard-bearer for the Slow Food Sápmi movement, Havvi i Glen initiates you into the richness of mountain Sami cuisine, with game, mushrooms and berries featuring prominently on its seasonal menu. Expect the likes of thinly sliced reindeer steak with blueberry chutney, smoked Arctic char with sea buckthorn, and cloudberry sorbet. The website provides directions and opening hours.

12 hours. There are all sorts of tips and information on each hike.

🛏 Sleeping

Funäsdalen Berg & Hotell　　　　HOTEL €€
(☑ 0684-214 30; www.funasdalenberghotell.se; Strandvägen 2a; hostel dm/d from 280/550kr; P 🛜 ♨) This is the go-to accommodation in Funäsdalen: a large, modern hotel with attractive hotel rooms in three levels of fanciness, plus hostel beds, overlooking the lake. It's open all year and has a good restaurant (the daily lunch buffet draws the locals), pool and spa. Just across the road from the gondola.

★ Eriksgårdens Fjällhotell　　　HOTEL €€
(☑ 0684-210 06; http://eriksgarden.se; Vintergatan 3; s/d from 775/950kr; P 🛜) Eriks has got things covered in Funäsdalen, with Eriks Villa budget rooms and the hotel with standard and premium rooms only 50m away. The rooms are fine, but it's the facilities, including Eriks Kitchen & Bar restaurant, the sports bar, night club and spa that will really make your visit.

ℹ Information

Tourist Office (☑ 0684-155 80; www.funasdalen.se; Rörosvägen 30; ⊙ 10am-5pm; 🛜) Inside Funäsdalen's Härjedalens Fjällmuseum; can advise on and arrange all manner of outdoor activities.

ℹ Getting There & Away

Härjedalingen (https://harjedalingen.se) runs daily buses between Stockholm and Funäsdalen (489kr, eight hours).

Bus 623 Runs from Funäsdalen to Tänndalen (33kr, 10 minutes).

Bus 613 Operates between Ljungdalen and Åsarna (204kr, 1¾ hours), where you can transfer to bus 164 to Östersund (155kr, 1½ hours) or else catch the Inlandsbanan train.

Bus 164 Runs from Funäsdalen via Åsarna to Östersund (269kr, 3½ hours).

THE BOTHNIAN COAST

ℹ Information

The lovely Bothnian Coastline runs 850km from Gävle in the south to Haparanda, on the border with Finland, in the north. It's truly the long and winding road, with the E4 highway doing the distance, marked with attractive cities and towns at manageable driving distances, at places where rivers from the mountains to the west come down to meet the Gulf of Bothnia. There are lively student cities at Gävle, Umeå and Luleå, plus timber towns such as Sundsvall and Skellefteå and gorgeous islands and coastlines at Höga Kusten and Kustvägen. Your visit will be all the more enjoyable with time up your sleeve and your own wheels.

ℹ Getting There & Away

There are airports at Sundsvall, Umeå, Skellefteå and Luleå with regular connections to Stockholm and some to other centres. Some receive charter flights at various times of the year.

Trains from Stockholm head up the Bothnian Coast, stopping at Gävle, Hudiksvall, Sundsvall, Härnösand, Umeå, Luleå and points in-between. From Boden, near Luleå, trains head northwest to Kiruna in Swedish Lappland and on to Narvik in Norway.

Buses head all the way up the coast to Haparanda on the Finnish border.

The E4 motorway runs 1024km from Stockholm up the Bothnian Coast to Haparanda.

Gävle

026 / POP 71,033

Infamous among certain naughty youngsters because its name sounds a lot like a Swedish swear word, Gävle (Yerv-luh) is a lively university town that's been a prosperous industrial centre since the late 19th century, when it exported local timber and iron. Founded in 1446, Gävle is officially Norrland's oldest town, but not much of its original incarnation remains due to a devastating fire in 1869. A vibrant culinary scene and a host of oddball attractions in and around town appeal to a motley crew of beachgoers, would-be arsonists, whisky connoisseurs and trainspotters, and make Gävle linger-worthy for a day or three.

Coffee-lovers may be surprised to hear that Gevalia Coffee, nowadays a subsidiary of Kraft Foods, was started by Victor Theodore Engwall in Gävle in 1853.

☉ Sights & Activities

★ **Mackmyra Whisky** DISTILLERY
(026-54 18 80; www.mackmyra.se; Kolonnvägen 2; ☉restaurant 11am-9pm Sat) Mackmyra Svensk Whisky, established in 1999 as the first Scandinavian malt-whisky distillery, offers tasting sessions that must be booked in advance via the website. You'll find the distillery, warehouse, and visitor center with restaurant just outside Gävle.

Joe Hillgården MUSEUM
(www.joehill.se; Nedre Bergsgatan 28; ☉10am-3pm Jun-Aug) FREE One of the old houses in Gamla Gefle is a museum marking the birthplace of Joel Hägglund, who moved to the USA, changed his name to Joe Hill and became a legendary labour-union organiser. Hill was wrongly convicted of a murder and executed in Utah in 1915. Some of his folk songs form part of the memorial here.

Gamla Gefle HISTORIC SITE
(www.facebook.com/gamlagefle) A fire in 1869 wiped out most of the old wooden buildings that formed the town's core. Today the little cluster that survived the fire is preserved in the rickety area that is Gamla Gefle, just

south of the river. There are lovely cobblestoned streets, colourful houses adorned with bright flower boxes in summer, and a feeling of community pride on display.

Sveriges Järnvägsmuseet MUSEUM
(Swedish Railway Museum; www.trafikverket.se/jarnvagsmuseum; Rälsgatan 1; adult/under 19yr 100/60kr; ☉10am-5pm Jun-Aug; P⛽) Inside Gävle's former engine shed, this excellent museum traces the history of the railway in Sweden through seriously hands-on displays. Besides numerous old locomotives and carriages that you can clamber inside (including the 1859 hunting coach belonging to King Karl XV), there are collections of miniature trains, an X2000 simulator, toy railways, and a small railway for kids to ride. To get here, walk to the southern end of Muréngatan, and then follow the cycle path to the museum.

Länsmuseum Gävleborg MUSEUM
(www.lansmuseetgavleborg.se; Södra Strandgatan 20; ☉11am-6pm Tue-Fri, noon-4pm Sat & Sun) FREE The county museum, Länsmuseum Gävleborg, has beautifully designed exhibitions on regional culture through the ages, from prehistory to the 'golden era' (mid-19th century) to modern times, with the life stories of key figures in Gävle's history. It has undergone extensive renovations that had it closed for over a year, reopening in late 2017.

Sveriges Fängelse Museum MUSEUM
(Swedish Prison Museum; http://sverigesfangelsemuseum.se; Hamiltongatan 3; adult/student 80/40kr; ☉noon-4pm Wed-Sun, daily Jul & Aug) Duck into underground dungeons, check out ye olde instruments of retribution, peer into the windowless 'punishment' cells and enjoy the tableaux of slatterns and miscreants getting merry inside one of Sweden's first penitentiaries.

Walking Tour WALKING
The tourist office has pieced together a lovely two-hour walk (5km) around 24 hot spots in Gävle, including impressive buildings, statues, fountains and the park. Pick up the map and hot-spot explanation sheet at the office before you go.

🛏 Sleeping

★ **Gefle Vandrarhem** HOSTEL €
(Gävle Youth Hostel; 026-62 17 45; www.geflevandrarhem.se; Södra Rådmansgatan 1; dm/s/d 220/395/480kr; ☉mid-Jan–early Dec; P🐾) Set in one of Gamla Gefle's old-style wooden

Gävle

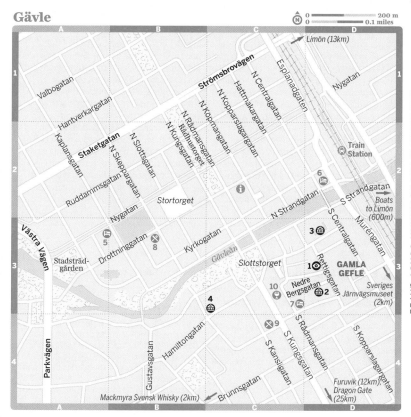

0 ___ 200 m
0 ___ 0.1 miles

Limön (13km)

Train Station

Boats to Limön (600m)

Stortorget

Stadsträd-gården

Slottstorget

GAMLA GEFLE

Sveriges Järnvägsmuseet (2km)

Nedre Bergsgatan

Mackmyra Svensk Whisky (2km)

Furuvik (12km); Dragon Gate (25km)

buildings around a flowering courtyard, this quiet hostel with good guest kitchen is popular with travellers of all ages. Breakfast buffet costs 75kr. It's about a 10-minute walk from the station, has free wi-fi and there are laundry facilities available.

Elite Grand Hotel Gävle   HOTEL €€
(☑026-400 73 00; www.elite.se; Kyrkogatan 28; s/d from 750/950kr; P🖥) This beautifully restored art-deco hotel, in a massive building that originally opened as a hotel in 1901, has a lot going for it, not least its super-central location and bright, contemporary decor. The restaurant and bar are superb, overlooking the Gävle river.

Best Western Hotel City Gävle   HOTEL €€
(☑026-61 26 00; www.hotelcity.nu; Nygatan 8; s/d from 995/1195kr; P🖥) The name might sound a tad sterile, but the Hotel City Gävle more than does the business with attractive rooms, a good location and a hearty buffet

Gävle

◎ Sights

⌂ Sleeping

✗ Eating

🍷 Drinking & Nightlife

breakfast. It's hard to go wrong here, with a good on-site restaurant, plus plenty more nearby.

THE GÄVLE GOAT

Gävle's most famous resident is the 13m-tall straw Gävle Goat – a giant version of the traditional Yule Goat. It's been making an appearance at Slottstorget in early December since 1966 and every year attempts are made to burn it down. Bets are made locally and internationally as to whether the goat will go down before Christmas or before New Year's Eve.

Since this seasonal vandalism really, erm, gets their goat, city authorities have attempted to prevent the goat's untimely demise, using tricks such as treating it with flame-retardant chemicals, spraying it with water to create a covering of ice, and even getting Swedish Home Guard to protect it (1993). This has not deterred would-be vandals: in 1976, parties unknown drove a car into it; in 2001, an American was arrested after he approached the goat brandishing a lighter – he claimed that he thought burning down the goat was a quaint local tradition; and in 2005, security cameras captured the image of two arsonists dressed as Santa and a gingerbread man shooting a flaming arrow at it. The only time the goat was burned down 'legally' was during the shooting of the Swedish film *Black Jack* in 1990, when the director paid the hefty 100,000kr fine (the cost of building the goat) for the privilege.

In 2016, the goat didn't last a day, destroyed by an arsonist just hours after its 50th birthday!

✖ Eating & Drinking

Cafe Pazzo   ITALIAN €
(✎ 026-10 34 00; www.pazzo.se; Drottninggatan 6; mains 89-129kr; ⊙ 11am-9pm) This self-styled 'bistro' cooks up large portions of pizza and pasta as well as lighter bites (including foccacia, salads, grilled sandwiches). There's nice outside seating for when things have warmed up.

★ Matildas   FUSION €€
(✎ 026-62 53 49; www.matildas.nu; Timmermansgatan 23; mains from 170kr; ⊙ 5pm-late Tue-Sat) The menu at this small, stylish bistro is short, sweet and seasonal, with a real depth of flavour to the dishes, wonderful attention to presentation and a relaxed ambience. Feast on lobster tacos, oysters paired with champagne, crispy pork belly and homemade black pudding with lingonberry. The home-brewed beer, served by the delightful owners, goes down very smoothly.

Bishop's Arms   PUB
(✎ 026-65 25 75; www.bishopsarms.com/Gavle/Presentation; Södra Kungsgatan 7; ⊙ 4pm-midnight Mon-Fri, 1pm-1am Sat, 4-10pm Sun) It's rather like drinking in an antiques shop, albeit one with the widest selection of beers and microbrews in town. Conversation-friendly ambience, too.

❶ Information

Tourist Office (✎ 026-17 71 17; www.visitgavle.se; Drottninggatan 22; ⊙ 8am-5pm Mon-Fri, 10am-2pm Sat) This very efficient office has brochures aplenty on the city and surrounding area.

❶ Getting There & Away

Long-distance bus services leave from behind the train station. For Ybuss departures, take a 'Busstaxi' from the train station to Gävlebro. **Ybuss** (www.ybuss.se) runs daily to Sundsvall (250kr, 2¾ to 3¼ hours, three to six daily) and Umeå (415kr, 6½ to 7½ hours, three daily). **SGS Bussen** (https://sgsbussen.se) serves Stockholm (160kr, two hours, five to seven daily).

There are numerous daily services to Stockholm (from 165kr, 1½ to 2¼ hours) via Uppsala (from 109kr, 45 minutes to 1¼ hours) and Sundsvall (from 106kr, 2¼ hours). One or two trains run to Kiruna (from 745kr, 14¼ hours), via Luleå (from 755kr, 10 hours), and three to Östersund (from 285kr, 3½ hours).

Hudiksvall
✎ 0650 / POP 15,015

Hudiksvall is one plucky little town. Not only has it survived 10 major fires that left it in piles of ashes, but it also weathered a Russian rampage in 1721 – check out the cannonball pockmarks on Jacobs Kyrka just southwest of the town centre. Hudiksvall's cute harbour, surrounded by red wooden fishermen's storehouses (Möljen), has a sedate appeal, as does the grander Fiskarstan district, further along Hamngatan. Hudiksvall is a pleasant little place to hang out and enjoy the laid-back atmosphere of this part of the Bothnian Coast.

⊙ Sights

★ Hälsinglands Museum   MUSEUM
(☑ 0650-196 01; www.halsinglandsmuseum.se;
Storgatan 31; ⊙ noon-4pm Mon & Sat, 10am-4pm
Tue-Fri) `FREE` The Hälsinglands Museum covers local history, culture and art, including
a recreated cottage interior with traditional
painted furniture and costumes from the
region. Highlights are the eerily illuminated
medieval church art, including a particularly striking Madonna carved by local artist
Haaken Gulleson, the Malsta rune stone
from around AD 1000, engraved with the
Helsinge runic script, and changing contemporary art exhibitions.

Jacobs Kyrka   CHURCH
(⊙ 10am-4pm) Just southwest of the centre,
the unusually ornate Jakobs Kyrka dates
from 1672. The exterior is still pockmarked
from the 18th-century Russian cannonball
onslaught, though if you think that the citizens of Glada Hudik haven't had a good
clean out since then, the cannonball by the
steps to the pulpit is, in fact, a replica.

Fiskarstan   HISTORIC SITE
Beyond Möljen, along Hamngatan and a
couple of blocks up from it, is Fiskarstan
(Fishermen's Town), consisting of partially
preserved, elegantly wood-panelled merchants' yards and winter dwellings of local
fishermen, dating back to the early 19th century. It's a good spot to take a wander.

🛏 Sleeping & Eating

★ Strandpiren Hotell   HOTEL €€
(☑ 0650-104 44; http://strandpiren.se; Sjötullsga-
tan 15; s/d 880/1080kr; P 🞐) This lovely new
place is right on the water about 1km east
of the railway station. Rooms are fresh and
exquisite, there's a great bar and restaurant,
and the terrace actually overhangs the sea.
This is a top place to stay, made a lot better
if you've got your own wheels.

Quality Hotel Statt   HOTEL €€
(☑ 0650-150 60; www.choicehotels.com; Storgatan
36; s/d 780/1080kr; P ✳ 🞐 🛋) Timber barons spent their time carousing in this 19th-
century hotel fronting a lovely open park
along Storgatan in the middle of town. It's
recently joined the Quality Hotel brand and
meets all their requirements, so you can expect fairly standard stuff. You can carry on
the carousing tradition at O'Leary's on-site
bar and work off your hangover in the pool/
sauna/gym.

★ Lörruden   SEAFOOD €€
(☑ 060-370 98; http://sillmans.se/loran; Lörud-
den 173; mains from 165kr; ⊙ noon-10pm Tue-Sat,
to 9pm Sun-Mon) Lörruden's restaurant sits
amid red fishing cottages right by the water and has a devoted following of Sundsvall
customers due to the chefs' passion for locally sourced ingredients. Dishes such as the
hearty fish stew and seafood lasagne really
stand out, and the perch with chanterelles
and truffle purée made us moan out loud
with pleasure.

★ Skatans Cafe & Krog   SWEDISH €€
(www.skatanscafe.se; Skatan 192; mains from 125kr;
⊙ 11am-9pm Jun-late Aug) Superlative marina-
side restaurant in the village of Skåtan, serving up fresh fishermen's offerings, as well
as a bounty of smoked prawns and gravlax from its very own smokery. Ship-shape
rooms upstairs in sailor stripes are the best
place to stay along the Coastal Road.

Sigges Bistro & Bar   SWEDISH €€
(☑ 0650-333 33; www.facebook.com/siggeshudik;
Hamngatan 6; mains from 125kr; ⊙ 6pm-late Tue-
Sat) A fantastic setting on the waterfront,
a well-executed menu that runs the gamut
from herring platters with all the trimmings
to homemade cheeseburgers and Caesar salads, and on-the-ball waiting staff make this
the place of choice for Hudik's young, trendy
crowd. On weekends the bar pumps bass as
a small nightclub.

ℹ Information

Tourist Office (☑ 0650-191 00; www.
hudiksvall.se/turism; Storgatan 33; ⊙ 10am-
4pm Mon-Fri) Just up from the museum, the
tourist office has helpful bilingual staff.

ℹ Getting There & Away

The bus station is next to the main train station,
by the harbour. **Ybuss** (☑ 060-17 19 60; www.
ybuss.se) travels to Gävle (152kr, 1½ hours to
two hours), Stockholm via Uppsala (251kr, 3¾ to
five hours, two to three daily) and Umeå (341kr,
5¼ hours).

Trains run to Sundsvall (from 57kr, 50 minutes), Gävle (from 105kr, 1¼ hours) and Stockholm (from 255kr, 2¾ hours).

Sundsvall

☑ 060 / POP 51,350

Once a pre-Viking trading post on the island
of Härnön, Härnösand was burned to the
ground three times in the 1700s: once when

drunken churchgoers set the place on fire by accident, once by schoolboy pranksters, and once when Russian Cossacks flattened it in 1721. Härnösand's Storatorget (main square) is lined with attractive, neoclassical, 18th-century buildings, and its pretty harbour fills up with yachts in July when Härnösand celebrates summer with its Stadfest.

⊙ Sights

Murberget   MUSEUM
(☑0611-886 00; www.murberget.se; Varvsallén; ◎10am-5pm) FREE This thorough open-air museum features more than 80 wooden buildings from Ångermanland from the 18th century onwards. Among the traditional farmhouses, 19th-century inn, smithy, church and school in the style typical of this part of Norrland, you'll find Rysstugan, the only building to survive the marauding Russians in 1721. The museum is a 30-minute walk from the town centre, or take bus 2 or 52 from Nybrogatan near the Rådhuset.

Länsmuseet Västernorrland   MUSEUM
(☑0611-886 00; www.murberget.se; Varvsallén; ◎10am-5pm) FREE Part of the Murberget complex, this excellent museum features permanent exhibitions, such as historic photographs of the region and Sami handicraft. Of equal interest are its temporary offerings that change regularly and often include Sami art exhibitions. There's also a cafe and shop on-site. Take bus 2 or 52 from Nybrogatan.

🛏 Sleeping & Eating

STF Mitti Härnösand   HOSTEL €
(☑0611-243 00; www.mittiharnosand.com; Franzengatan 14; hostel dm/s/d from 150/300/400kr; ◎reception 8-10am & 3-7pm; P🛜🐾) Directly across the street from the cathedral, the restored, rambling wooden building that dates from 1846 (the same as the cathedral!) is the original of the two hostel locations for STF Mitti Härnösand. Dorm rooms are simple, but do the business, and private rooms are available. Reception is at Köpmangatan 7.

First Hotel Stadt   HOTEL €€
(☑0611-55 44 40; www.firsthotels.se; Skeppsbron 9; s/d/ste from 840/890/1400kr; P🛜) The top spot to stay in town is this refined harbourside hotel that is part of the First Hotels chain and offers standard Scandinavian-modern rooms. A good breakfast is included, there's a decent restaurant and bar, and the hotel reception is one of the town's Information Points.

★Kanal Café & Restaurang   SWEDISH €€
(☑0611-106 66; www.kanalcafeet.se; Storgatan 18; mains from 109kr; ◎11am-9pm Mon-Thu, to 10pm Fri & Sat) This compact cafe, only a couple of minutes' walk from the central square, has a loyal local following thanks to lunchtime dishes, such as hot-smoked salmon with house mayo, dinner delights that include steak with Jack Daniel's whisky-pepper sauce and tapas platters made for sharing.

★Tant Anci & Fröcken Sara   CAFE €
(☑060-785 57 00; http://tantanci.se; Bankgatan 15; mains from 79kr; ◎10am-10pm Mon-Thu, to 8pm Fri, 11am-5pm Sat; 🚲) 🌱 Humongous bowls of soup or salad are the speciality at this frilly organic cafe, where you can also get hearty sandwiches, giant bowls of pasta and pastries.

ℹ Information

Information Point (www.harnosand.se; Skeppsbron 9) The tourist office on Storatorget has closed and the job has been handed to a few Information Points about town. The best and easiest to access is at reception at **First Hotel Stadt** on the waterfront, a few minutes' walk from the square. It's open 24/7 (as is reception).

ℹ Getting There & Away

Ybuss (www.ybuss.se) runs daily to Sundsvall (98kr, 45 minutes), Gävle (299kr, 3¾ hours) and Stockholm (362kr, 5½ to seven hours). Heading north they run to Umeå (249kr, three to 4¼ hours).

The station is on the mainland, a 10-minute walk from the central square. Trains run to Sundsvall (from 76kr, 45 minutes), Gävle (from 235kr, three to four hours) and Stockholm (from 375kr, 3¼ to 4¾ hours). Heading north they run to Umeå (from 235kr, two to 2½ hours).

Höga Kusten

Cross the Höga Kustenbron, the spectacular suspension bridge over the Ångerman river – Norrland's answer to the Golden Gate Bridge and one of the longest in the world (1867m) – and you find yourself amid some of the most dramatic scenery on the Swedish coastline. The secret to the Höga Kusten's (High Coast's) spectacular beauty is elevation; nowhere else on the coast do you find such a mountainous landscape, with sheer rocky cliffs plunging straight down to the sea, as well as lakes, fjords and dozens of tranquil islands, covered in spruce and pine forest. The region is recognised as a

KUSTVÄGEN

If you're driving between Hudiksvall and Sundsvall, the 75km-long **Kustvägen** (Coastal Road; www.kustvagen.se) is a much lovelier alternative to the E4. Narrow, winding and largely unpeopled, Kustvägen meanders through forest and past secluded beaches and tiny former fishing communities.

Coming from Hudiksvall, get off the E4 at Jättendal and go straight into the easily spotted **tourist office** (☑0652-161 75; www.upplevnordanstig.se; Landsvägen 1; ☺11am-6pm Mon-Fri, noon-4pm Sat & Sun). It has excellent maps, advice and English-speaking staff. From there, follow the road east to **Mellanfjärden** on the coast before it turns north to **Sörfjärden**. From the northern end of the beach, a gorgeous walking path skirts the forested peninsula. Further north, a tiny road branches off east to **Oxsand**, a village with appealing bathing spots. Another turn-off further along takes you to **Galtströms Bruk**, where there's a miniature railway for children and the small but lovely **Vitsand Beach**, just a stroll through the forest, with flat slabs of waterside rock perfect for sunbathing.

Further north still, **Skatan** is a picture-perfect village with a small yacht marina, and **Skatans Cafe & Krog** (p255) that serves mostly fishy delights; there are ship-shape rooms upstairs should you wish to linger. At the northern end of the Kustvägen there's a T-junction; the eastern branch leads you to Lörruden, well worth some of your time, while the western one takes you back to the E4 via Njurundabommen. **Lörruden restaurant** (p255) sits amid red fishing cottages right by the water.

geographically unique area and was listed as a Unesco World Heritage site in 2000.

Höga Kusten stretches from north of Härnösand to Örnsköldsvik, and it's a wonderful area for scenic drives along narrow, twisty roads, though you can't really say that you know the Höga Kusten without visiting its tranquil islands.

🏃 Activities

The **Höga Kusten Leden** (High Coast Trail) is 129km long and runs the entire length of the Höga Kusten, starting at the northern end of the Höga Kustenbron (the bridge) and finishing at the summit of Varvsberget, the hill overlooking Örnsköldsvik. The trail is divided into 13 sections, each between 15km and 24km in length, with accommodation at the end of each section consisting mostly of rustic cabins. Buses running along the E4 stop at either end of the trail, as well as by the Lappuden, Ullånger, Skoved, Skule Naturum and Köpmanholmen villages along the way, close to the different sections of the trail. The trail is well signposted, but it's best to pick up a detailed booklet and map at the tourist office (p258) in the Hotell Höga Kusten.

Parts of the trail involve an easy ramble, whereas other sections will challenge you with steep, uneven ground. Take food and plenty of drinking water with you.

The trail takes in some of the most beautiful coastal scenery in Sweden, from rocky coastline and sandy coves to lush countryside, dense evergreen forest and deep ravines, including **Slåtterdalskrevan**, a 200m-deep canyon in **Skuleskogen National Park**, through which part of the trail passes. The 26-sq-km park, which lies between Docksta and Köpmanholmen, is a Unesco World Heritage site due to its wealth of fauna and flora: the park is home to lynx, roe deer, mink and other shy animals, as well as all four of Sweden's game birds: the black grouse, willow grouse, capercallie and hazel hen.

A recommended detour from the trail is north of Docksta, towards Norrgällsta (1.4km), where you can either hike up Mt Skuleberget or take the **Höga Kusten Liften chairlift** (☑070-232 73 36; www.facebook.com/hogakustenliften; Norrgällsta 112; per person 120kr; ☺11am-5pm Jun-Aug) to the top to appreciate the all-encompassing view. The **Skuleberget cave** is another popular attraction – it was once a hideout for bandits. Other worthwhile diversions include Dalsjöfallet (1.5km from the main trail), a **waterfall** that lies halfway between the Skuleberget and Gyltberget mountains, and **lake Balestjärn**, with its crystal-clear waters, in the middle of the small peninsula to the north of Köpmanholmen.

🛏 Sleeping & Eating

There are places to stay at Härnösand and the Hotel Höga Kusten at the southern end of the High Coast, at small villages throughout the area, and at Örnsköldsvik at the northern end.

Be prepared if you are heading out on hikes or to islands without much in the way of facilities. Otherwise, you'll find places to eat throughout the Höga Kusten.

★ **First Hotel Statt** HOTEL €€
(☑ 0660-26 55 90; www.firsthotels.com; Lasarettsgatan 2, Örnsköldsvik; r from 820kr; P 🛜) In Örnsköldsvik, at the northern end of Höga Kusten, this place is a good spot to use as a base for your explorations. It's an old building, but the rooms are modern and spacious and a good breakfast is included. There's no dinner restaurant, but it's central and there are plenty of eating spots to choose from.

Hotel Höga Kusten HOTEL €€
(☑ 0613-72 22 70; www.hotellhoga-kusten.se; Hornöberget; r from 1095kr; P 🛜) You'll have to be on the ball to book a room at Sweden's first wind-powered hotel, at the southern end of the Höga Kusten. It's just on the northern side of the bridge and also hosts the tourist office in reception. There's a good restaurant and cafe, but you'll need to book early if you're keen to stay.

ℹ Information

Naturum (☑ 0613-70 02 00; www.naturum hogakusten.se; ☉ 10am-5pm Apr-late Jun, 9am-7pm late Jun–mid-Aug, 10am-5pm mid-Aug–Sep) Off the E4, north of the village of Docksta, has exhibitions on the formation of the Höga Kusten and stocks brochures on the area. Adrenalin junkies can tackle the four via-ferrata routes of varying difficulty (www.viaferrata.se; from 395kr per person) along the flanks of Skuleberget mountain (285m) behind the visitor centre between May and October.

Tourist Office (☑ 0771-265 00 00; www.hogakusten.com; ☉ 9am-7pm Jun-Aug) Inside Hotel Höga Kusten, just north of Höga Kustenbron suspension bridge, this place can help you with information on exploring the region. It's open year-round and has a detailed map of the scenic byways, boat timetables and a pamphlet on the Höga Kusten Trail.

ℹ Getting There & Around

Höga Kusten is to the north of Härnösand and south of Örnsköldsvik. The E4 passes through on its way up the coast, but if you're keen to explore, you'll need to get off it, best with your own set of wheels. Both towns also have stations on the main train line that runs up the Bothnian Coast, as well as bus stations.

Höga Kusten can be tricky to explore if you're relying solely on public transport. The three main islands can be reached by a combination of buses and boats in summer only; arm yourself with bus and boat timetables in advance to plan the multi-legged journey. As for the coast itself, buses reach few of the remote fishing villages, so you're better off with your own set of wheels. That's unless, of course, you wish to walk the Höga Kusten Leden.

Härnösand

☑ 0611 / POP 17,556

Your first views of central Sundsvall may be one of the most pleasant (or mind-boggling) surprises of your visit to the Bothnian coast. The city was a well-off timber town exporting to the world when it was burned to the ground in 1888, after a spark from a steamboat set the town brewery alight. The central city was levelled in half a day. Civic leaders, finding that the town's timber barons were actually over-insured, then decided that their city should be rebuilt in stone and brick, buildings separated by wide avenues.

WORTH A TRIP

HÖGBONDEN

A tiny island in the southern part of Höga Kusten, Högbonden is only 15 minutes by boat from the villages of Bönhamn and Barsta. It's famous for its 100-year-old lighthouse – its only building – atop the highest point of the rocky plateau that soars above the island's tree line. Högbonden is bisected by a narrow gorge, and its rugged cliffs lend themselves to exploration. Your only option is to come here as a day tripper and don't forget to bring a picnic.

The **M/S Ronja ferry** (www.hkship.se; one way/return 100/150kr) to Högbonden departs Barsta between late June and mid-August at 10am, noon, 2pm and 5pm daily, returning at 10.45pm, 12.45pm, 2.45pm and 5.45pm, while the Bönhamn–Högbonden service runs at 10.30am, 12.30pm, 2.30pm and 5.30pm, returning at 10.15am, 12.15pm, 2.15pm and 5.15pm. There are reduced services from Barsta from early May to late June and from mid-August to early October.

This new start produced a construction boom and incredibly ornate stone buildings, all built within a decade of the fire, that stand to this day.

Sundsvall's main appeal lies less in any one specific sight than in the Bothnian Coast's most cosmopolitan city as a whole, complete with highly strollable boulevards and a clutch of great restaurants.

⊙ Sights

★ Stenstan Visitor Centre   MUSEUM
(☑ 060-658 58 00; http://stenstanvisitorcenter.se; Storatorget; ⊘ 10am-6pm Mon-Fri, 10am-4pm Sat, noon-4pm Sun) FREE This incredibly high-tech multimedia museum shares space with the tourist office at the Stadhus on the central square of Storatorget. Besides showing films of the 1888 fire and its aftermath, it features touch-screen tables and picture frames that allow you to follow the reconstruction of central Sundsvall through old photos, and information on each rebuilt building such as the background of the architect and original drawings. The centre's technology is now being exported to museums around the world.

Kulturmagasinet   MUSEUM
(www.sunsvall.se/kulturmagasinet; Sjögatan; ⊘ 10am-7pm Mon-Thu, to 6pm Fri, 11am-4pm Sat & Sun) FREE Down near the harbour, Kulturmagasinet is a magnificent restoration of some old warehouses and now contains the town library and **Sundsvall Museum**, which has engaging exhibits on the history of Sundsvall, natural history and geology. There's a permanent art exhibition upstairs featuring 20th-century Swedish artists and superb temporary exhibitions.

Alnö Gamla Kyrka   CHURCH
(⊘ noon-6pm mid-Jun–mid-Aug) This magnificent church, a mixture of 12th- and 15th-century styles, sits 2km north of the bridge (at Vi) on Alnö island, just east of Sundsvall. The upper wall and ceiling paintings, likely done by one of Albertus Pictor's pupils, have survived intact. Even better is the late-11th-century carved wooden **font** across the road; the upper part combines Christian and Viking symbolism, while the lower part shows beasts that embody evil. Catch bus 1 to Vi, then walk 1km north.

⛏ Sleeping

★ Lilla Hotellet   HOTEL €
(☑ 060-61 35 87; www.lilla-hotellet.se; Rådhusgatan 15; s/d 750/900kr; ☜) In a stone building

designated a historical monument (since it was built the year after the great fire), this small family-run hotel has a great location and a friendly vibe. The eight spacious rooms with high ceilings have interesting architectural details, such as ceramic tile stoves. Throw in a good breakfast and this is a really good budget option.

Elite Hotel Knaust   HOTEL €€
(☑ 060-608 00 00; www.elite.se; Storgatan 13; s/d from 830/1100kr; P ☜) In a striking 19th-century building on Sundsvall's main pedestrian drag, this opulent hotel is full of old-world charm. Besides the grand, lobby-dominating (and much photographed) marble staircase, the rooms are decorated in classic Scandinavian style and have high ceilings. The breakfast buffet is excellent.

✕ Eating & Drinking

Udda Tapas Bar   TAPAS €
(☑ 073-098 66 07; www.uddasundsvall.se; Esplanaden 17; tapas 40-85kr; ⊘ 5-11pm Mon-Thu, to 2am Fri & Sat) Head for the roof terrace of this congenial bar on summer evenings to savour the likes of clams with lemongrass, smoked reindeer with Dijon mustard, lamb tacos and yellow beets with honey and feta, along with a glass of wine or a local brew. DJs kick it up a notch on weekends.

Invito Ristorante Italiano   ITALIAN €€
(☑ 060-15 39 00; www.invitobar.se; Storgatan 6-8; pizzas from 149kr, mains from 189kr; ⊘ 11am-2pm & 5-11pm Mon-Fri, 5pm-1am Sat) In a great location on Storgatan, Invito has plush indoor seating, plus outdoor dining for when things warm up. On offer are a variety of top pizzas, plus main courses such as fish casserole with salmon, cod, mussels and shrimp (219kr) and pappardelle pasta with beef fillet (229kr) – all paired with suggested wines.

★ Oscar Matsal & Bar   BAR
(☑ 060-12 98 11; www.oscarmatsal.se; Bankgatan 11; ⊘ 11am-2pm Mon-Fri & 5-10pm Mon-Thu, to 3am Fri & Sat) The hottest watering hole in town with retro decor triples as a sophisticated bistro and a nightclub where you can knock back Tom Collinses while checking out the latest live band.

ⓘ Information

Tourist Office (☑ 060-658 58 00; www.visitsundsvall.se; Storatorget; ⊘ 10am-6pm Mon-Fri, 10am-4pm Sat, noon-4pm Sun) Inside the Stadhus, the tourist office shares its space with the Stenstan Visitor Centre.

❶ Getting There & Away

Sundsvall-Timrå Airport (Midlanda Airport; ☑070-522 03 12; www.sdlairport.se) is 21km north of Sundsvall; flights serve Gothenburg, Stockholm and Visby (summer only). Charter flights head out to places including Crete, Mallorca and Gran Canaria.

Buses depart from the Sundsvall bus station, near Kulturmagasinet. **Ybuss** (p255) runs to Gävle (from 257kr, 2¾ to 3¾ hours) and Stockholm (320kr, 4½ to six hours). Länstrafiken Västerbotten buses 10 and 100 run to Umeå (320kr, 5¼ hours) via other coastal towns.

Trains run west to Östersund (from 279kr, 2½ hours) and south to Gävle (from 106kr, 2¼ hours) and Stockholm (from 325kr, 3½ to five hours). The station is just east of the town centre on Landsvagsalen, which is a continuation of Köpmangatan.

Ulvön
☑0660

The largest island in the Höga Kusten archipelago, Ulvön is famous for its regatta (mid-July) and for the production of *surströmming*. It's possible to purchase the noxious (or delightful, depending on your outlook) stuff in the shops at Ulvöhamn, the island's one-street village and main port. A cycle path leads through the picturesque fishermen's settlement with traditional red-and-white wooden houses drowning in colourful flower blossoms in summer, past the tiny 17th-century chapel decorated with colourful murals, and onwards to the preserved 17th-century fishing village of Sandviken in the northern part of the island.

◉ Sights

Ulvö Museum   MUSEUM
(☑070-860 22 40; www.ulvomuseum.com; adult/youth 40/20kr; ☉11am-4pm Jun-Aug) This lovely little museum sits on Ulvöhamn's main street in an old building where Swedish author Ludvig Nordström lived when working there in 1905. The museum focuses on the village's herring fishing history, including the salting houses and the memorable characters who came to prominence. The population hit a high of 340 in 1910.

🛏 Sleeping & Eating

★ Ulvö Hotell   HOTEL **€€**
(☑0660-22 40 09; www.ulvohotell.se; Ulvö Hamngata 105; r from 1075kr; ☎🏊) Ulvö Hotell, with its superb restaurant, bar and pool area, makes a great place to stay on the island. The rooms feature a cream-and-charcoal colour scheme

and quality furnishings. Located at the eastern end of the village, its restaurant is popular with day trippers and has a seasonal menu featuring local ingredients.

UlvöByn Café & Bistro   SWEDISH **€€**
(☑070-309 28 84; http://ulvobyn.se; Ulvö Hamngata 142; mains from 155kr; ☉10am-10pm Jun-Aug, plus weekends & holidays) Ulvöhamn's top cafe is about halfway along the street and caters for everybody with plates such as *Stekt strömming på spisbröd* (fried herring on crisp bread; 75kr) through to full main courses. It's a very convivial atmosphere with both outdoor and indoor seating, plus friendly service.

❶ Getting There & Away

MF Ulvön & MF Minerva (☑070-651 92 65; http://en.mfulvon.se; return adult/6-19yr 150/90kr) Between mid-June and mid-August, ferries leave Köpmanholmen for Ulvöhamn (adult/six to 19 years 150/90kr return, 1½ hours, six daily), three of them stopping at Trysunda on the way. From late May to mid-June and mid-August to mid-September, reduced services call at Ulvöhamn twice daily and at Trysunda once or twice daily. Both destinations are served daily the rest of the year.

M/S Kusttrafik (☑0613-105 50; www.hkship. se; one way/return 150/225kr) Ferry to Ulvön leaves Ullånger for Ulvöhamn via Docksta daily at 9.30am, returning from Ulvöhamn at 3pm, between June and August.

Umeå
☑090 / POP 121,030

Umeå has claims to fame on several counts: it was the European Capital of Culture in 2014; it has the second-largest art gallery in Sweden; it's home to Europe's greatest museum collection of vintage guitars; and it is the former residence of Stieg Larsson, author of *The Girl with the Dragon Tattoo*. Its location, a mere 400km below the Arctic Circle, means it is also popular with Northern Light seekers.

A youthful college town, Umeå has a long and fascinating history. The town was founded in 1622, and was home to the indigenous Sami people whom visitors can learn about on a couple of excellent museums. Aside from its grand slam of cultural sights, Umeå has a superb choice of restaurants and bars, plenty of green spaces, and great shopping. It makes an excellent stopover on your way further north, as well as a destination in its own right.

Umeå

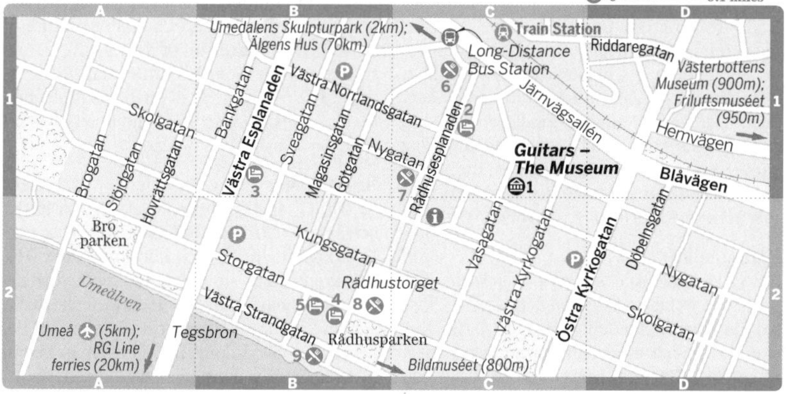

(Map of Umeå with labels)

Umedalens Skulpturpark (2km); Älgens Hus (70km); Train Station; Long-Distance Bus Station; Riddaregatan; Västerbottens Museum (900m); Friluftsmuséet (950m); Skolgatan; Brogatan; Skjolsgatan; Hovrättsgatan; Bankgatan; Västra Esplanaden; Sveagatan; Västra Norrlandsgatan; Magasinsgatan; Götgatan; Nygatan; Rådhusesplanaden; Järnvägsallén; Hemvägen; Guitars – The Museum; Blåvägen; Bro parken; Kungsgatan; Storgatan; Vasagatan; Västra Kyrkogatan; Östra Kyrkogatan; Döbelnsgatan; Nygatan; Umeälven; Rådhustorget; Västra Strandgatan; Skolgatan; Umeå (5km); RG Line ferries (20km); Tegsbron; Rådhusparken; Bildmuséet (800m)

0 ———— 200 m
0 ———— 0.1 miles

⊙ Sights & Activities

★ **Västerbottens Museum**   MUSEUM
(☐ 090-16 39 00; www.vbm.se; Helena Elizabeths väg, Gammliavägen; ⊙ 10am-5pm, to 9pm Wed; **P** ⛵) **FREE** The star of the Gammlia museum complex, the engrossing Västerbottens Museum traces the history of the province from prehistoric times to today. Exhibitions include an enormous ski-through-the ages collection starring the world's oldest ski (5400 years old), and an exploration of Sami rock art and shaman symbols. There are excellent temporary exhibitions as well as regular workshops and activities for children. There is also a superb cafe specialising in organic fare. Take bus 2 or 7 or walk 1km from the station.

★ **Guitars – The Museum**   MUSEUM
(☐ 090-580 90; www.guitarsthemuseum.com; Vasagatan 18-20; adult/student 150/100kr; ⊙ noon-6pm Mon-Sat) If you're into the six-string, then this result of two brothers' lifelong hobby, a huge collection of vintage guitars, is for you. Want to see a 1959 Les Paul Standard, identical to the one on which Keith Richards played the 'It's All Over Now' riff? They've got it. Or perhaps a 1958 Gibson Flying V, made famous by ZZ Top?

★ **Älgens Hus**   ANIMAL SANCTUARY
(☐ 0932-500 00; www.algenshus.se; Västernyliden 23, Bjurholm; adult/child 130/65kr; ⊙ noon-6pm Tue-Sun mid-Jun–mid-Aug; ⛵) This moose park, 70km west of Umeå along Rte 92, near Bjurholm, is your chance to meet the (tame) King of the Forest face to face. In Swedish, these are elk, but English-speakers know these giants as moose. There's a museum, video explanations of a year in the life of a moose, and even a small dairy where the ultra-rare moose cheese is produced; at 6000kr per kilogram, this is the most expensive cheese you'll ever taste.

Umedalens Skulpturpark   SCULPTURE
(www.umedalenskulptur.se; Umedalen; ⊙ 24hr) For more than two decades, eminent Swedish and international artists have exhibited their works in Umedalsparken, 5km west of the centre of Umeå. Through those years, Balticgruppen, the owner of the compound, has purchased 44 sculptures that form the permanent collection that can be seen today. Take bus 1 to the Glädjens gränd stop. The park is in the grounds of a former psychiatric hospital, built in 1930. Go anytime, but guided tours must be pre-booked – see the website for details.

Umeå

Friluftsmuséet
MUSEUM

(www.vbm.se; Gammliavägen; ⊙10am-5pm; ⊕) **FREE** Part of the Gammlia museum complex, this open-air historic village presents ye olde church, a smokehouse, a windmill, a 17th-century gatehouse and traditional Sami dwellings. Decked out in period costume, staff demonstrate traditional homestead life. Play games from the olden days, meet the sheep and chickens, or else take the kids for a spin in a horse-drawn carriage (daily noon to 2pm).

Bildmuséet
GALLERY

(www.bildmuseet.umu.se; Östra Strandgatan 30b; ⊙11am-8pm Tue, to 6pm Wed-Sun) **FREE** Close to the Umeå Academy of Fine Arts, this state-of-the-art modern art museum is part of Umeå University, housed in an acclaimed building at the Umeå Arts Campus by the shores of the Umeälven river. It produces and shows contemporary international art, photography, architecture, design and other forms of visual culture.

Umeå Walking Tour
WALKING

(⊙daily 4pm, late Jun–mid-Aug) **FREE** A free daily guided walking tour of Umeå departs the tourist office at 4pm in summer, taking one to 1½ hours. No need to book – tours are in English on Wednesdays and Saturdays.

🛏 Sleeping

STF Vandrarhem Umeå
HOSTEL €

(☑090-77 16 50; www.umeavandrarhem.com; Västra Esplanaden 10; dm/s/d from 250/425/850kr; 🛜) This efficient hostel has rooms of varying quality: try to nab a space in one of the newer rooms with beds, as opposed to the dorms with bunks. It's in a great location, at the edge of the town centre, and the facilities (kitchen, laundry) are very handy for self-caterers. Bed linen, towels and the buffet breakfast cost extra.

★ U&Me Hotel
HOTEL €€

(☑090-206 64 60; http://umehotel.se; Storgatan 46; r from 800kr; 🛜) This new-concept hotel in central Umeå is super cool. You'll spot the massive white building from miles away, and the hotel is on floors six to 13. Below is the city's continental indoor square and cultural hub known as Väven. This is where you'll check in on tablets, have breakfast at the bakery and cafe, and even issue your own room key.

★ Stora Hotellet Umeå
BOUTIQUE HOTEL €€

(☑090-77 88 70; www.storahotelletumea.se; Storgatan 46; s/d/ste from 1000/1150/6000kr; P 🛜) First opened as a hotel in 1895, Stora Hotellet had major renovations to coincide with the city being named European Capital of Culture in 2014. The six categories of rooms have names such as Superstition, Adventure and Mystique, and if you're after a bit of historical ambience, this is a top place to stay. The hotel's restaurant, Gotthards Krog, is superb.

Hotel Aveny
HOTEL €€

(☑090-13 41 00; https://ligula.se/profilhotels/hotel-aveny; Rådhusesplanaden 14; r/ste from 1285/2885kr; P 🛜) 🌿 Not only does Hotel Aveny take its eco-credentials seriously, it also has a playful techno-sleek decor scheme, vivid with all the colours of the neon rainbow. Rooms are modern and comfortable; suites contain spas and rain showers. The Scottish pub and Italian restaurant on the premises are a nice bonus.

🍴 Eating

Umeå is fast becoming somewhat of a culinary hot spot and exciting new restaurants are opening up all the time. Restaurants run the gamut from inexpensive Asian noodle bars to retro art cafes plus, of course, there are the high-end sophisticated venues that specialise in classic Swedish game dishes from the north, with reindeer and elk as the star turns.

★ Två Fiskare
SEAFOOD €€

(☑090-765 70 20; www.tvafiskare.se; Storgatan 44; mains from 95kr; ⊙10am-6pm Mon-Fri, to 4pm Sat) This place takes fish very seriously indeed. Not only does it sell it fresh; it also prepares a handful of exquisite seafood and fish dishes daily for those in the know. Crabcakes, fish soup, smoked salmon...the dishes will depend on what is flapping fresh that day. Undecided? Then opt for the classic fish and chips, served in newspaper, the traditional way.

Lottas Krog
PUB FOOD €€

(☑090-12 95 51; www.lottas.nu; Nygatan 22; mains from 179kr; ⊙3pm-midnight Mon-Thu, 2pm-1am Fri, noon-1am Sat; 🛜) You may have to elbow your way to the bar to order your pint at this longtime favourite local haunt; but the atmosphere is worth the wait, with a cosy, pubby atmosphere and plenty of Swedish craft beers on offer. The food here is gastropub with excellent burgers and sweet potato fries.

Vita Björn
SWEDISH €€

(☑070-549 63 45; www.vitabjorn.nu; Kajen 12; mains from 139kr; ⊙11am-9.30pm May-Sep) Perch yourself on the sunny deck of this boat-restaurant and choose from a casual international menu of caesar salad, vegie burgers, baked salmon and beef tenderloin. For us, however, it gets no better than that simple, moreish Swedish delight – fresh grilled herring.

★ **Koksbaren**   SWEDISH €€€
(📋 090-13 56 60; www.koksbaren.com; Rådhusesplanaden 17; mains from 255kr; ⊘5-11pm Mon-Sat; 🕿) Expect stunning culinary combinations at this sophisticated restaurant on the corner near the train station. Virtually everything is made here, including the ketchup and the 'smoked' mayonnaise. The speciality is dry cured steaks with a choice of rib eye, sirloin or filet mignon. The bright yet classy dining area adds to the agreeable eating experience. Reservations are definitely recommended.

Rex Bar och Grill   INTERNATIONAL €€€
(📋 090-70 60 50; www.rexumea.com; Rådhustorget; mains from 225kr; ⊘11am-2pm & 5-11pm Mon-Thu, 11am-2am Fri & Sat; 🕿) This popular upmarket bistro, bar and nightclub (at weekends) has northern Swedish cuisine meeting international brasserie in a convincing explosion of flavours. Choose the northern menu (bleak roe, smoked Arctic char and reindeer steak) or opt for Iberico pork cheek or grilled courgette with morels. Alternatively, stop by for the American-style pancake-and-mimosa weekend brunch. To avoid disappointment, be sure to make dinner reservations on weekend.

ℹ Information

Tourist Office (📋 090-16 16 16; www.visit umea.se; Rådhusesplanaden 6a; ⊘10am-6pm Mon-Fri, 10am-4pm Sat, 11am-3pm Sun) Centrally located with helpful staff who can advise on places to stay and what's going on.

ℹ Getting There & Away

Umeå is an excellently connected city with a comprehensive network of bus, trains, boats and flights.

Departures include three daily trains to Stockholm (from 550kr, 6½ hours), while the north-bound trains to Luleå (315kr, 5½ hours) stop in Boden, from where there are connections to Kiruna (685kr, 7½ to 8½ hours) and Narvik (in Norway; 452kr, 11 hours).

The **long-distance bus station** (📋 090-70 65 00; Järnvägsallén 2; ⊘ticket office 7am-6pm Mon-Fri, 9am-3pm Sat, 11am-6pm Sun) is directly opposite the train station. Ybuss runs

services south to Gävle (395kr, 6½ to 7½ hours) and Stockholm (450kr, 9¼ to 10 hours), stopping at all the coastal towns.

Buses 20 and 100 head up the coast to Haparanda (368kr, 6½ to 7¾ hours) via Luleå (340kr, four to five hours) and Skellefteå (197kr, two to 2½ hours).

Local buses leave from Vasaplan on Skolgatan.

Wasaline (📋 090-18 52 14; www.wasaline. com; Blå Vagen 4, Holmsund) operates ferries between Umeå and Vaasa (Finland) once or twice daily (360kr one way, four hours, Sunday to Friday) from Holmsund, 20km south of Umeå. A bus to the port leaves from near the tourist office an hour before RG Line's departures.

Umeå Airport (📋 01-109 50 00; www. swedavia.com/umea; Flygplatsvägen) is 5km south of the city centre. SAS and Norwegian fly daily to Stockholm's Arlanda and Bromma, Braathens Regional Aviation (formerly Malmö Aviation) to Gothenburg and Stockholm, and Direktflyg to Östersund and Luleå.

Airport buses run to the city centre (45kr, 20 minutes).

Skellefteå

📋 0910 / POP 71,750

Historically an industrial city with the nickname 'Gold Town' thanks to its gold mining industry, these days, Skellefteå mines for copper. There's plenty to keep visitors busy though, including one of the country's most atmospheric *kyrkstad* (church towns), a top contemporary art museum, and Sweden's oldest wooden bridge. The central city is pleasant enough, but most of the sights of interest are a 20-minute walk west of the centre.

Locals are proud of their region's natural environment, so if you're into hiking, fishing, paddling or exploring islands – there are a lot of interesting islands in Skellefteå's archipelago – consider spending a few days here and discussing your options at the tourist office.

◉ Sights

★ **Bonnstan**   HISTORIC SITE
(Brännavägen) During the Protestant reformation in Sweden in the 16th century, church attendance was demanded of all parishioners, and later in 1861, a regulation ordering it was introduced. Church towns built up to house those who lived too far away to attend church on a day trip. Skellefteå's Bonnstan, a *kyrkstad* (church town), was one of 47 in the Norrbotten and Västerbotten counties and has been well preserved. There are 114 dark buildings containing 376 rooms. It's

fascinating stroll through these legally protected streets.

Lejonströmsbron   BRIDGE

(Lejonström bridge) This is the oldest wooden bridge in Sweden, completed in 1837, and until 2006, at 207m in length, it was also the longest. It was a toll bridge at first, and in 1868, an interesting law was introduced creating a speed limit – horses or carts ridden or driven faster than a pedestrian incurred a fine of five *riksdaler*. These days, cars take turns passing over the bridge in different directions. It's a popular sight among Swedish visitors.

Museum Anna Nordlander (MAN)   GALLERY

(Skellefteå Art Museum; ☑ 0910-73 55 21; http://skellefteamuseum.se; ☺10am-4pm Tue-Sun) FREE This municipal contemporary art museum is dedicated to the life and work of Anna Norlander (1843–1879), a well-known painter born in Skellefteå. She was one of the first women to study at the Royal Academy of Arts in Stockholm and later continued her studies in Brussels and Paris. As well as works by Norlander, it features a strong list of changing exhibitions.

🛏 Sleeping & Eating

★ Stiftsgården   HOSTEL, HOTEL €

(☑ 0910-72 57 00; www.stiftsgarden.se; Brännavägen 25; hostel s/d from 290/480kr, hotel s/d from 950/1200kr; P 🐾) Across the road from Landskyrka, this church-run place spread across green fields is home to a hotel and, in an annexe, Skellefteå's STF hostel. The thimble-size, whitewashed rooms are simple yet comfortable, while the hotel rooms are all creams and light wood furnishings. The grand yellow building hides an award-winning gourmet restaurant (three-course meals 425kr). Reception keeps short hours.

Quality Hotel Skellefteå Stadshotell   HOTEL €€

(☑ 0910-71 10 60; www.nordicchoicehotels.no; Stationsgatan 8; r from 1020kr; P 🐾) Central to town and only a couple of minutes' walk from the shops and restaurants, this place has standard-quality hotel rooms. It's not huge on character, but you know what you're getting. There is complimentary coffee and Swedish waffles at reception, a hearty breakfast is included in the rates and you're guaranteed a friendly welcome.

Nygatan 57   SWEDISH €€

(☑ 0910-134 44; www.nygatan57.se; Nygatan 57; lunch mains from 99kr, dinner mains from 175kr; ☺11am-1.30pm Mon-Fri, 5-10pm Mon-Sat) You know a place is trendy when it's known solely by its street address, and this indoor-outdoor bistro's popularity is down to the quality of its dishes using local produce. This is a Swedish Lapland menu with dishes such as baked char from Vilhelmina (295kr) and pork from Kåge in beer confit (259kr).

❶ Information

Tourist Office (☑ 0910-45 25 10; www.skelleftea.se; Trädgårdsgatan 7; ☺10am-7pm Mon-Fri, to 4pm Sat, noon-4pm Sun; 🐾) On the corner of the pedestrianised Nygatan and the central square.

❶ Getting There & Away

The main train line doesn't run through Skellefteå. If you're using trains, the train station is 52km west at Bastuträsk.

Buses 20 and 100 depart for Luleå (158kr, 2½ hours) and Umeå (177kr, two to 2½ hours).

There are daily flights between Stockholm's Arlanda Airport and Skellefteå (SFT). There are bus connections for all arrivals and departures. The airport is 15 minutes away.

Luleå

☑ 0920 / POP 74,800

Luleå is the capital of Norrbotten, chartered in 1621, though it didn't become a boom town until the late 19th century when the Malmbanan railway was built to transport iron ore from the Bothnian Coast to Narvik (Norway). The town centre moved to its present location from Gammelstad, 9km to the northwest, in 1649 because of the falling sea level (8mm per year), due to postglacial uplift of the land.

A laid-back university town and an important high-tech centre, Luleå claims more than its fair share of top-notch restaurants for a town its size, as well as an enticing archipelago of islands off its coast and a sparkling bay with a marina.

◉ Sights

★ Gammelstad   HISTORIC SITE

(☑ 0920-45 70 10; www.lulea.se/gammelstad) FREE The Unesco World Heritage–listed Gammelstad, Sweden's largest church town, was the medieval centre of northern Sweden. The 1492-built stone **Nederluleå church** has a reredos worthy of a cathedral and a wonderfully opulent pulpit. It has 420 wooden houses (where the pioneers stayed during weekend pilgrimages) and six church stables remaining.

Guided tours (80kr) leave from the Gammelstad tourist office at 11am, 1pm and 3pm (mid-June to mid-August). Bus 9 runs hourly from Luleå; disembark at the Kyrkbyn stop.

Norrbottens Museum   MUSEUM

(☑ 0920-24 35 02; http://norrbottensmuseum.se; Storgatan 2; ☉ 10am-4pm Mon-Fri, noon-4pm Sat & Sun; ⚐) **FREE** Besides the extensive displays on the history of Norrbotten, Norrbottens Museum is worth a visit for the Sami section alone, with its engrossing collection of photos, tools, and dioramas depicting traditional reindeer-herding Sami life, as well as a nomad tent for kids. The little ones will love the recreated 19th-century playrooms.

Teknikens Hus   MUSEUM

(www.teknikenshus.se; University Campus; adult/ under 4yr 70kr/free; ☉ 10am-4pm mid-Jun–Aug; ⚐; ☒ 4, 5) Curious minds of all ages will love the gigantic educational playground that is Teknikens Hus, within the university campus 4km north of town. It has hands-on exhibitions about everything from hot-air balloons and rocket launching to the aurora borealis. Take bus 4 or 5 to Universitetsentrén.

🛏 Sleeping

Citysleep   HOSTEL €

(☑ 0920-42 00 02; www.citysleep.se; Skeppsbrogatan 18; dm 500kr; 🛜) The only budget digs in central Luleå don't come more anonymous than this: book online to get the door code, since there's no reception, then let yourself into a featureless room with two-tiered beds. There is reasonably good in-room ventilation and a large guest kitchen. Quite a few rules here, so you'll need to study the website carefully.

★ Clarion Sense   HOTEL €€

(☑ 0920-45 04 50; www.clarionsense.se; Skeppsbrogatan 34; s/d/ste from 1095/1295/3595kr; 🛜☒) Top dog in Luleå's sleeping scene is the super-central, ultra-modern Clarion Sense. Popular with the business set (and anyone who's not averse to a bit of pampering), it offers generously proportioned rooms, all classic charcoals and creams with contemporary bold splashes of colour. The fitness centre and sauna seal the deal.

Elite Luleå   HOTEL €€

(☑ 0920-27 40 00; www.elite.se; Storgatan 15; s/d from 750/950kr; 🅿✳🛜) One of Luleå's most sumptuous hotels, the grand Elite is

HULKOFFGÅRDEN

This lovely lodge (☑ 0922-320 15; www. hulkoff.se; Korpikylä 197; s/d 850/1500kr; 🅿🛜) is a yellow farmhouse, 35km north of Haparanda along Rte 99, amid the most peaceful countryside imaginable and with wonderfully welcoming proprietresses. Next door, its restaurant is the best in the area, with northern Swedish specialities made from organic, locally sourced ingredients. The reindeer meat and beef comes from the farm and fish out of the river.

more than a hundred years old, with classically decorated and beautifully refurbished rooms. All bathrooms are decked out in Italian marble and the plusher suites come with whirlpool tubs as well. Bargains are to be had on weekends and the breakfast buffet is extensive.

★ Treehotel   BOUTIQUE HOTEL €€€

(☑ 0928-104 03, 070-572 77 52; www.treehotel.se; Edeforsväg 2 A, Harads; r 4700-7200kr; 🅿) 🌿 A spaceship suspended in the trees. A mirror cube reflecting sunlight and surrounding spruces. A giant bird's nest...The seven tree rooms that make up Sweden's most mind-boggling, award-winning lodgings sit just off Rte 97, about halfway between Luleå and Jokkmokk, in the midst of pristine forest. There are saunas and spas to relax stiff muscles after hiking, kayaking or dog-sledding.

🍽 Eating & Drinking

★ Bastard Burgers   BURGERS €€

(http://bastardburgers.se; Stationsgatan 29; burgers from 109kr; ☉ 11am-8pm Mon-Thu, to 9pm Fri & Sat, noon-5pm Sun) Could possibly do with a name change, but Bastard Burgers is a big hit with locals in Luleå. While the signature burger is known as The Bastard, it goes international with the New York Original Streetburger, the Berlin Cheesedog (65kr) and the Chicago Beefdog (65kr). This is where it's at, with some top beers on offer too.

★ Hemmagastronomi   FUSION €€

(☑ 0920-22 00 02; www.hemmagastronomi.se; Norra Strandgatan 1; tapas from 75kr; ☉ 10am-10pm Mon-Sat) Is it a bakery? Is it a deli? Is it a bar? Is it a bistro? Hemmagastronomi wears many hats and we love them all. Come for a leisurely lunch, or for a bit of romance in

DON'T MISS

LULEÅ ARCHIPELAGO

This extensive offshore archipelago contains more than 1700 large and small islands, most of them uninhabited and therefore perfect for skinny-dipping, berry picking, camping wild...we can go on! The larger islands, decorated with classic red-and-white Swedish summer cottages, are accessible by boat from Luleå. Facilities are limited, so most visitors come as picnicking day trippers. Here's our island-in-a-nutshell top five:

Sandön The largest permanently inhabited island, and the easiest to access from Luleå, features an attractive beach in Klubbviken bay and a walking path running across pine moors.

Junkön It's distinguishing feature is a 16th-century windmill; fishers catch herring and whitefish here in summer.

Småskär Covered in Siberian spruce and part of a bird sanctuary. The fishing harbour in Kyrkviken was probably used as early as the 1500s.

Kluntarna The all-in-one island, with holiday cottages and all the different bits of scenery you'll find on the other islands – pine forest, seabird colonies and fishing villages.

Brändöskär Bleakly beautiful, lashed by the wind and waves in the outermost archipelago.

Regular boats depart from Södra Hammen in Luleå from late June to mid-August, with a reduced service running until mid-September; check online timetables at www.botten viken.se. Fares are 50kr to Klubbviken and 110kr to all the other islands.

the evening under dimmed lights over soft-shell-crab tapas and seafood platters, complemented by the wide-spanning wine list.

Kitchen & Table   FUSION €€
(☑ 0920-45 04 50; www.kitchenandtable.se; Skeppsbrogatan 34; mains from 165kr; ⊙ 5-11pm Mon-Thu, to 1am Fri & Sat) The local Luleå specials here are great – expect lots of fabulous local produce including vendace roe, *surströmming*, Arctic char, venison, cloudberries, black grouse and almond potatoes. And this place is a clear winner when it comes to sheer ambience, with huge windows drinking in the bay views.

Cook's Krog   SWEDISH €€
(☑ 0920-20 10 25; www.cookskrog.se; Storgatan 17; mains from 169kr; ⊙ 5pm-late Mon-Sat) Still *the* choice for discerning carnivores, Cook's Krog is Luleå's top spot for steak, reindeer and other Norrbotten specialities. It's next to the Quality Hotel Luleå.

Bishop's Arms   PUB
(☑ 0920-27 40 30; www.bishopsarms.com/Lulea; Storgatan 15; ⊙ 4pm-late) With book-filled nooks, the Luleå version of this pseudo-English pub chain is one of the town's most popular watering holes, spilling out onto Storgatan on good-weather days. Whisky-lovers can sample more than 200 kinds of the amber stuff.

ℹ Information

Tourist Office (☑ 0920-45 70 00; www.lulea. nu; Skeppsbrogatan 17; ⊙ 10am-6pm Mon-Fri,

to 4pm Sat & Sun) Inside Kulturens Hus, a block down from Storgatan.

ℹ Getting There & Away

There are overnight trains to Stockholm (840kr, 14 to 15 hours) via Gävle (same price, 11¾ to 12½ hours) and Uppsala (same price, 14 hours). Two daily trains connect Luleå with Narvik (Norway; 485kr, 7¼ to 8¼ hours) via Kiruna (295kr, 3¾ to 4¼ hours) and Abisko (472kr, 5½ to 6½ hours).

Buses 20 and 100 run north to Haparanda (190kr, 2½ hours) and south to Umeå (320kr, four to five hours), stopping at all the coastal towns. Bus 44 connects Luleå with Gällivare (325kr, 3½ to 4½ hours) and Jokkmokk (245kr, three hours) up to five times daily.

Luleå Airport (☑ 010-109 48 00; www. swedavia.se/lulea) is 10km southwest of the town centre. There are daily flights to Stockholm and Gothenburg. Bus 4 connects it to the city centre.

Haparanda

☑ 0922 / POP 4850

Haparanda was founded in 1821 across the river to compensate for the loss of Finnish Tornio, an important trading centre, to Russia in 1809. When both Sweden and Finland joined the EU, the two towns declared themselves a single Eurocity. Still, Sweden drew the short straw: Tornio got the art galleries and the vibrant nightlife, and what did Haparanda get? The world's northernmost IKEA. Not to worry though, it's easy enough to stroll across the border.

There's plenty here for outdoors enthusiasts, with islands out in the Haparanda Archipelago, activities such as fishing and rafting on the Torne River, and some excellent hiking and ski trails. This is the eastern extreme for Sweden, with the Torne River acting as the Sweden–Finland border from Haparanda all the way north as far as Pajala (175km).

◉ Sights & Activities

Museum of Tornio Valley
MUSEUM
(📞+358 50 597 1559; www.tornio.fi/museo; Torikatu 4, Tornio; adult/child €5/free; ⊙11am-6pm Tue-Thu, to 3pm Fri-Sun) This museum, only a 200m walk from Haparanda's Tourist Office and into Finland, showcases Tornio Valley culture and history on both sides of the Swedish–Finnish border. There's lots of pictorial and film material, plus exhibits on cross-border marriages, trade and smuggling. Keep in mind that the entrance fee is in euros and there's a one-hour time difference as you wander over to this interesting Haparanda–Tornio collaboration of a museum.

Kukkolaforsen
CULTURAL CENTRE
(www.kukkolaforsen.se) Located 15km north of Haparanda on Rte 99, Kukkolaforsen is a scenic spot where the Torneälv River is covered with the white crests of the Kukkolaforsen rapids, and in summer, you can watch locals hunt for whitefish using medieval dip nets from rickety-looking wooden jetties that poke out into the river. There's a 5m-high, wrought-iron statue of a dip-net fisherman that pays homage to the old fishing methods. Finland is oh so close on the other side of the river.

Haparanda Archipelago National Park
NATIONAL PARK
This gorgeous national park covers the Swedish side of the islands and is to the west of the Finnish Perämeri National Park. There are two relatively large islands, Sandskär and Seskar Furö, and a number of smaller islands and reefs. There are ringed and grey seals, plus numerous bird species. Regular boat trips head out to the islands of the national park from Haparanda – check for the latest at the tourist office.

Tornio Golf Course
GOLF
(📞+358 16 431 711; http://torniogolf.fi; adult/junior €45/25; ⊙summer) This golf course might have its pro shop in Finland, but we feel justified listing it here as a fair bit of the course is in Sweden! In fact, on Hole 6, players tee off in Sweden and the green is in Finland, so with

the one-hour time difference, this could be the longest time-taking Par 3 in the world.

Haparanda Hiking Trail
HIKING
Head to the Tourist Office and pick up a map for this 9km hike starting at a parking area off the E4, about 1.5km west of Haparanda. It's well organised, with interesting flora and fauna, hay meadows, marshes, barns and even a lookout tower for spotting wildlife. In winter it becomes a cross-country ski trail.

🛏️ Sleeping & Eating

There are a couple of decent options on the Swedish side of the border and more on the Finnish side. The Haparanda-Tornio Tourist Office can help with making bookings.

River Motell & Vandrarhem
HOSTEL €
(📞0922-611 71; www.rivermotell.com; Strandgatan 18; r from 475kr; 🅿🛜) More or less right on the river in Haparanda, this motel has attractive rooms that are a bargain for the price, a guest kitchen, a terrace and a sauna. The cheapest rooms have shared bathrooms, but if you're happy to fork out a tad more, en-suite bathrooms are very good.

★Haparanda Stadshotell
HOTEL €€
(📞0922-614 90; www.haparandastadshotell.se; Torget 7; s/d from 1060/1295kr; 🅿🛜) First opened in 1900, this large, dignified hotel is the architectural focus of the town in the central square, south of the E4. Rates include breakfast. Its Gulasch Baronens Pub is open Monday to Saturday 4pm to 10pm with a bistro menu.

IKEA
SWEDISH €
(Norrskensvägen 5; mains from 25kr; ⊙10am-7pm) Ironically, IKEA is actually one of the better places to eat out in Haparanda, as it offers Swedish standards such as meatballs and mash for as little as 25kr (to give you stamina for more flat-packed-furniture shopping!).

ℹ Information

Haparanda-Tornio Tourist Office (📞0922-262 00; www.haparandatornio.com; Krannigatan 5; ⊙8am-7pm Mon-Fri, 7am-3pm Sat, 10am-4pm Sun) Haparanda's tourist office is shared with Tornio (on the Swedish side!) in the bus station just across from IKEA.

ℹ Getting There & Away

Buses 20 and 100 run south to Luleå (178kr, 2½ hours) and Umeå (356kr, 6½ to 7¾ hours), while bus 53 connects Haparanda to Kiruna (395kr, six hours). Trains don't come this far.

Lappland &
the Far North

Best Places to Eat

➡ SPiS (p282)

➡ Martin Bergmans Fisk
(p271)

➡ Icehotel Restaurant (p284)

➡ Hans På Hörnet (p276)

➡ Ájtte Museum Restaurant
(p278)

Best Places to
Stay

➡ Icehotel (p284)

➡ Lapland Lodge (p275)

➡ Bed & Breakfast Gällivare
(p279)

➡ Hotell Akerlund (p278)

➡ Lilla Hotellet (p271)

Why Go?

Lappland is Europe's last true wilderness. With a grand mountain range, endless forest and countless pristine lakes as your playground, it's your chance to be a true explorer. Its great swathes of virgin land are dotted with reindeer – this is Sami country still, and your chance to delve into the reindeer herders' centuries-old way of life.

Travelling in the far north of Sweden can draw you into an unusual rhythm. The long, lonely stretches between towns are often completely deserted apart from the ever-present reindeer, often found wandering down the roads. Extreme natural phenomena are at their strongest here – in summer you'll be travelling under the perpetual light of the midnight sun; in winter, under the haunting wraiths that are the northern lights. During the colder months, Lappland is a different country: a white wilderness traversed by huskies and snowmobiles, and punctuated with colourful Sami winter markets.

When to Go
Kiruna

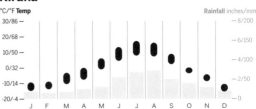

Jan & Feb Kiruna Snow Festival, Sami Winter Market in Jokkmokk, and the northern lights.

Mar & Apr Warmer, longer days perfect for snowmobiling, dogsledding and ice-driving.

Jul & Aug Hit the trails in the national parks during the warmest and driest months.

Lappland & the Far North Highlights

1 Aurora Sky Station
(p284) Watching the northern lights from Abisko's epic viewing deck.

2 Icehotel (p284)
Spending a night in Jukkasjärvi's spectacular ice dwelling.

3 Jokkmokk (p277)
Checking out Sami crafts and reindeer races at the Jokkmokk Winter Market.

4 Kungsleden (p286)
Tackling Sweden's legendary 450km-long hiking trail.

5 Arvidsjaur (p275)
Driving on frozen lakes and going snowmobiling or husky sledding.

6 Inlandsbanan (p280)
Riding Lappland's scenic train north to Gällivare.

7 Vildmarksvägen
(p270) Driving Sweden's

most beautiful road from Strömsund to Vilhelmina.

8 Silvermuseet (p276)
Viewing the largest collection of Sami silver creations in Arjeplog.

9 Padjelanta Trail (p290)
Trekking in the Laponia World Heritage area.

10 Kebnekaise (p283)
Making the climb up Sweden's highest peak (2111m).

Strömsund

☎ 0670 / POP 3589

Located 100km north of Östersund along the E45, Strömsund is seen as the southern entry point to Lappland – it is also the starting point for the Vildmarksvägen (Wilderness Rd; Rte 342). It's the first town of any size north of Östersund, but there's not much to keep you here. There are extensive waterways popular with kayakers and fishing enthusiasts.

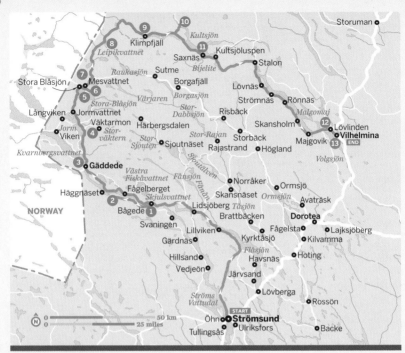

Driving Tour
The Vildmarksvägen

START STRÖMSUND
END VILHELMINA
LENGTH 370KM, EIGHT TO 10 HOURS

Strömsund marks the beginning of the most spectacular drive in Sweden. The Vildmarksvägen (Wilderness Rd; Rte 342) is only open in summer, normally from the start of June until mid-October. Pick up a detailed map and brochure at the Strömsund tourist office.

Head north out of Strömsund through through dense evergreen forest, stopping by one of many pristine lakes. If you're lucky, you may spot a bear, wolverine, elk or lynx.

Ninety-two kilometres northwest, you reach a worthwhile detour just south of **1 Bågede**. A rocky track leads towards the impressive 43m **2 Hällsingsåfallet**, a powerful waterfall that tumbles into an 800m-long canyon. Near the Norwegian border, another 40km west, is **3 Gäddede**, the only village with a petrol station. At Gäddede, you can arrange a spelunking tour of the **4 Korallgrotan** (Coral Cave) – Sweden's

longest cave, 11km north of **5 Stora Blåsjön**, a lake 50km north of Gäddede.

Before reaching the lake, turn off to the **6 Mountain Moose Moosepark**, a good stop for elk-viewing. Just past the lake, a road leads to **7 Ankarede**, a centuries-old meeting place for the local Sami, who gather at its 1898 chapel for midsummer celebrations.

Beyond Stora Blåsjön village, Rte 345 climbs up onto the vast, boulder-strewn, desolate **8 Stekkenjokk plateau**, snow covered even in summer, before descending to the tiny village of **9 Klimpfjäll**. A turn-off 13km east leads to the late-18th-century Sami church village at **10 Fatmomakke**, where you'll find traditional Sami *kåtor* (wooden dwellings) and log cabins.

Twenty kilometres further east, you reach the fishers' paradise of **11 Saxnäs**, a small village set in a scenic spot between lakes.

Another 89km brings you to the Vildmarksvägen/E45 junction. If you get here early enough, you can grab a meal ast the excellent **12 Martin Bergmans Fisk** smokery before driving the final 3km south to **13 Vilhelmina** for a well-earned rest.

Ströms Hembygdsförenings   MUSEUM
(🖵 0670-100   16;   www.hembygd.se/strom;
🕑 10am-4pm Mon-Fri Jun-Aug) **FREE** Wander
around the 20 old buildings that make up
this outdoor community museum down by
the water. On site, Cafe Tomten serves up
coffee, tea and snacks.

Vilseledaren   GUIDES
(🖵 076-145 48 91; http://vilseledaren.se; Stora Blåsjön
595) These are the guys to contact regarding
adventuring along the Vildmarksvägen. Based
in Stora Blåsjön, near the Norwegian border,
they can take you caving in the Korallgrottan,
Sweden's longest cave, hiking to the hidden
river of Bjurälven, and even on a beaver safari.
Check out the website.

Hotel Nordica   HOTEL €€
(🖵 0670-61 10 00; www.hotelnordica.se; Ramselevägen 6; s/d from 1095/1195kr; 🅿 🛜) Standard rooms in sedate creams inside a squat
red building. The antler-festooned restaurant makes a good pit stop for the weekday
evening buffet (99kr).

❶ Information

Tourist Office (🖵 0670-164 00; www.
stromsund.se; Ramselevägen 6; 🕑 10am-6pm
Mon-Fri, to 3pm Sat) Inside Hotel Nordica, it
has brochures and info on the Vildmarksvägen
(Wilderness Rd).

❶ Getting There & Away

Bus 45 passes through daily in both directions on
the Gällivare–Jokkmokk–Arvidsjaur–Sorsele–
Östersund route.

Inlandsbanan trains (p280) stop in summer,
one in each direction each day. The station is at
Ulriksfors, 4km to the southeast.

Vilhelmina
📋 0940 / POP 3657

The attractive little town of Vilhelmina was
named in 1804 after the queen, Frederika
Dorotea Vilhelmina av Baden. The town
of Dorotea, 55km to the south down the
E45, also got one of her names. Vilhelmina's original name was Volgsjö, Vualtjere in
Sami, and it was an important site for the
Sami people when they travelled north each
spring. The area gets cold in winter – Mal-
govik, 20km to the northwest, still holds the
record for Sweden's coldest temperature, a
frigid -53°C in 1941.

The town sprawls along the E45 and there
are interesting places to stop, even if you
aren't staying.

◉ Sights

Kyrkstaden   HISTORIC BUILDING
(Storgatan) The main attraction of Vilhelmina is its colourful restored church town. Its
30-plus cottages were built when the church
was consecrated in 1792 and parishioners
from distant villages were required to attend
services from afar. These days you'll find
Kyrkstaden buildings being used for a Sami
handicraft shop, an old-style general store,
an art gallery and a hostel.

Risfjells Sameslöjd   MUSEUM, GALLERY
(🖵 0940-152 05; www.sameslojd.se; Volgsjövägen
46; 🕑 10am-5pm Mon-Fri, 11am-2pm Sat) Part
Sami-handicraft store, part museum, Risfjells
Sameslöjd is a good place to pick up leatherwork, woodwork or a knife by husband-and-
wife artisan team Sven-Åke and Doris Risfjell.
They are happy to explain the difference between North and South Sami *duodji* (handicrafts; the Risfjells are South Sami) and show
you the vintage *duodji* in their small museum
on the main road through town.

🍴 Sleeping & Eating

STF Vilhelmina/Kyrkstaden Hostel   HOSTEL €
(🖵 0940-398 87; www.swedishtouristassociation.
com/facilities/stf-vilhelminakyrkstaden-hostel/;
Tingsgatan 1; 2-/4-bed cottages from460/600kr; 🛜)
Open year-round, this great little selection of
cottages is actually in the Kyrkstaden (church
town). There are one- to four-bed cottages, all
with their own kitchen and toilet, some with
showers and television. The services building
makes up for what's not there. It's a very picturesque spot, and is often the scene of cultural events. Reception is at the tourist office.

★ Lilla Hotellet   HOTEL €€
(🖵 0940-150 59; www.lillahotellet.vilhelmina.
com; Granvägen 1; s/d 790/1090kr; 🛜) Calling
itself the Little Hotel with the Big Heart,
this homey, appealing little place really is a
pleasure. Everything is bright and friendly,
including the staff, cute spa, restaurant and
bar. The summer dinner buffet (180kr) is excellent. Rooms are spacious and bright – if
you're into Elvis, ask for Room 9.

★ Martin Bergmans Fisk   SEAFOOD €€
(🖵 0940-250 90; http://mbergmansfisk.se; mains
from 110kr; 🕑 9am-7pm) This smokery at the
junction of E45 and the Vildmarksvägen,
3km north of Vilhelmina, is so popular that
even the Inlandsbanan train stops twice a
day to let passengers off to eat. The specialty
is platters of salmon, done three ways and

served with potato salad. Pizza and a few other dishes are also available.

❶ Getting There & Away

Vilhelmina's South Lapland Airport (www.south laplandairport.com) is 10km to the southeast of town and has daily connections to Stockholm.

Bus 45 passes through daily in both directions on the Gällivare–Jokkmokk–Arvidsjaur–Sorsele–Östersund route.

Inlandsbanan trains (p280) stop in summer, one heading in each direction each day.

Storuman
📋 0951 / POP 2207

At the intersection of the E45, running south–north up through Lappland, and the Blåvägen (E12), that runs southeast–northwest from Umeå on the Bothnian Coast right through to Norway's Atlantic coast, Storuman is an attractive little town sitting on the edge of a beautiful lake. By nature of the town's position, most visitors are just passing through, but if you've got some time on your hands, there are some interesting places to explore. Check out the Luspholmen islands in the lake, reached by causeway, Sweden's largest wooden church, and Utsikten, the hill above town that reveals marvellous views on a good day.

Built in 1885, with seating for 2000 over two floors, **Stensele Kyrka** (📋 0951-265 00; www.svenskakyrkan.se/stensele; ⊙ 7am-4pm Mon-Fri, 9am-5pm Sat & Sun) [FREE] is Sweden's biggest wooden church. A seat was originally provided for every man, woman and child in the parish. It's 5km east of Storuman.

The scenic, 2000km-long **Blåvägen** (Blue Highway; www.blavagen.nu; aka E12) runs from Norway's Atlantic coast all the way to the shores of Russia's Lake Onega. In Sweden, you can follow it from the Norwegian border to Hemavan, Tärnaby, Storuman and out to the coast at Umeå.

🛌 Sleeping & Eating

Storumans Bad & Camping CABIN €
(📋 0951-143 00; www.campingstoruman.se; Lokgränd 3; site/cabin from 250/550kr; ⊙ Jun-Aug; 🅿 🛜) This efficient place is down by the lake and has everything required, including a services building with kitchen, showers, sauna and laundry. The cabins are very popular and there's plenty to do for families, with a tennis court, paddle boats and minigolf. The Storuman tourist office is at reception.

Hotell Toppen HOTEL €€
(📋 0951-777 00; www.hotelltoppen.se; Blåvägen 238; s/d from 995/1195kr; 🅿 🛜) Right on the main street, you can't miss Hotell Toppen as the Wildman statue is out front. This place has decent rooms, plus a good restaurant, pub and bar. The restaurant is one of Storuman's top spots to eat, with an appropriately game-heavy menu and a bargain weekday lunch buffet (95kr). There's occasional live music in the bar.

★ Hembygdsgården Cafe & Museum CAFE €
(Hembygdsgård; snacks from 30kr; ⊙ noon-4pm & 6-10pm Jun-Aug) Head to the Storuman tourist office to get directions here or you'll never find it. On one of the islands out in the lake, reached by a causeway, you'll find this absolutely delightful cafe and museum. Pick from what has been made for the day, such as apple cake, homemade bread and biscuits, then go upstairs to peruse the museum.

❶ Information

Tourist Office (📋 0951-143 10; www.storuman.se/turist; Lokgränd 3; ⊙ 9am-5pm Jun-Aug) At Storumans Bad & Camping, this place is very efficient, with maps and brochures.

❶ Getting There & Away

Bus 45 runs daily on the Gällivare–Jokkmokk–Arvidsjaur–Sorsele–Storuman–Östersund route along the E45.

SAMI FOREST STAY

To experience the life of the forest Sami, visit **Båtsuoj Sami Camp** (📋 070-253 51 87, 070-642 31 66; www.batsuoj.se; Gasahed 1, Slagnäs; short tour/long tour/overnight stay 290/690/1100kr), where Tom and Lotta Svensson practise their traditional livelihood full time. You can watch the reindeer get lassoed, stay overnight on reindeer skins inside a *kåta* (typical forest Sami log hut), learn about Sami shamanic practices, eat grilled reindeer and sip coffee cooked over a wood fire. Book visits in advance.

The camp is near the village of Gasa, 17km north of the village of Slagnäs (30km east of Sorsele, 53km west of Arvidsjaur on the E45). Follow the red hand-painted signs that point north.

Bus 31 runs northwest to Tärnaby (169kr, 1¾ hours) and southeast to Umeå (265kr, 3½ hours) on the E12.

Twice-weekly Lapplandspilen buses (www.lapplandspilen.se) ply the route between Hemavan and Stockholm via Storuman.

In summer, **Inlandsbanan trains** (p280) stop here daily, heading north to Gällivare and south to Östersund.

Hemavan & Tärnaby

⏱ 0954 / POP 704

These twin resorts are way out in the mountains, 130km northwest of Storuman on the Blåvägen (E12), not far from the Norwegian border.

Tärnaby, an elongated one-street village that sits on the shores of Gäutan lake, is known as the birthplace of double Olympic gold-medallist skier Ingemar Stenmark. Hemavan, its smaller counterpart 18km north, is the southern entry point to the 500km Kungsleden trail that passes through the Vindelfjällens Nature Reserve, and both are popular bases for fresh-air fiends. There's everything from excellent hiking and skiing to checking out holy mountains, from descending steep slopes on mountain bikes in a shower of mud and scree to sedate pedalling around lakes.

◉ Sights & Activities

★ Atoklimpen
MOUNTAIN

Atoklimpen (1006m), a monolithic, bare mountain 35km west of Tärnaby, has been regarded as holy by the Sami for centuries. Evidence of sacrificial sites and encampments with hearths is scattered across the area, and dates back to the 15th century; a 3km trail leads up to the top.

Ski Areas
SNOW SPORTS

(www.hemavantarnaby.com; day ski pass 410kr) Tärnaby and Hemavan offer decent downhill skiing and the day ski passes are valid at both resorts. There's a good mix of runs for all abilities at the two, though Tärnaby's are more extensive and there are opportunities for night skiing. If that's not challenging enough, experienced skiers can go off-piste or arrange heli-skiing trips at the tourist office.

If snowboarding, jumps and tricks are more your bag, there's a fun park in the area also.

Cykel och Fiskecenter Hemavan
MOUNTAIN BIKING

(www.cykelochfiskecenter.se; Renstigen 1, Hemavan; ⊙ 9am-5pm Mon-Fri, 10am-2pm Sat) Head here for outdoor gear. Besides leasing mountain bikes,

Lucas' great store has it all if you're heading out into the wilderness or going to walk the Kungsleden. The seasons are covered, with backpacks, fishing, cycling gear, cross-country skis and all levels of outdoor clothing. Next to the hostel in Hemavan.

Drottningsleden
HIKING

(Queen's Trail) This spectacular, yet not too demanding, 9km trail (four to six hours) takes in splendid views of Norwegian peaks before descending to Naturum in Hemavan. Follow signs to a turn-off 15km north of Tärnaby along the main road. You can hike in reverse from Hemavan for more of an uphill challenge. Get a map from the tourist office.

🛏 Sleeping & Eating

STF Hemavan Hostel
HOSTEL €

(⏱ 0954-300 02; www.svenskaturistforeningen.se/hemavan; r from 460kr; P @ ⊠ ⚡) A sprawling complex of a hostel, STF Hemavan is perpetually busy with hikers. The separate blocks are each equipped with a kitchen, and while the rooms are a tad bland, the facilities (cafeteria, swimming pool, obstacle course, lively bar upstairs in the main building) are top notch. Many use this place at the start or finish of their Kungsleden hike.

★ Tärnaby Fjällhotell
HOTEL €€

(⏱ 0954-104 20; www.tarnabyfjallhotell.com; Östra Strandvägen 16; s/d from 1000/1300kr; P 🛜) This appealing ski lodge sits just off the main road. Rooms are bright and comfortable, with nice touches such as reading lights; bigger rooms offer more space to throw your gear around. The hunting lodge–style restaurant invests heavily in local, seasonal ingredients, and there are 360-degree views of the surrounding mountains from the sauna.

Sånninggården
SWEDISH €€

(⏱ 0954-330 00; www.sanninggarden.com; Klippen 225; mains from 180kr; ⊙ 11am-9pm) At the tiny village of Klippen, about 6km north of Hemavan, the cheery dining room inside the barnlike Sånninggården has a deceptively rustic feel. This is where Sweden's gourmets come to feast on such local delicacies as reindeer steak, Arctic char fillet with *Västerbottens ost* (crumbly cheese), and pheasant fillet with chanterelle pie.

ℹ Information

Tourist Office (⏱ 0954-104 50; www.hemavantarnaby.com; Strandvägen 1; ⊙ 9am-5pm) On the Blåvägen (Blue Hwy) that runs through Tärnaby, this is the tourist office for both villages. Handy booklets on hiking and biking routes available.

Vindelfjällen Naturum (📞 0954-380 23; www.vindelfjallen.se; ⏰ 9am-6pm) Next to Hemavan's entrance to the Kungsleden and under a huge golden ball that can be spotted from afar, the Naturum (National Park visitors centre) features exhibits on local flora and fauna. Staff can advise on trekking and day hikes in the area.

ℹ️ Getting There & Away

Hemavan Tärnaby Airport (www.hemavantarnaby airport.se) is at Hemavan village and has daily connections with Stockholm-Arlanda Airport.

Bus 31 runs the Hemavan–Tärnaby–Storuman (192kr, 2¼ hours) and –Umeå (275kr, 5¼ hours) route.

Buses 31 and 320 run between Tärnaby and Hemavan (41kr, 36 minutes).

Sorsele

📞 0952 / POP 1277

While the riverside township of Sorsele that sits on the E45 may be small, the municipality of Sorsele is anything but. It stretches east to west for 200km and is 50km wide, including the free-flowing Vindelälven and wild expanses of the Vindelfjällen Nature Reserve. This is popular country for outdoors enthusiasts and hikers, fishers and winter sports people who flock here throughout the year.

Sorsele township is a good base, but to head into the Vindelfjällen Nature Reserve, you'll want to travel 88km northwest up the dead-end road to Ammarnäs, one of the exit/entry points for the Kungsleden. Inlandsbanen trains stop in Sorsele twice daily in summer, one heading in each direction, and the Inlandsbanen museum is here.

⭕ Sights & Activities

Inlandsbanemuseet   MUSEUM

(Stationsgatan 19; ⏰ 9am-6pm) **FREE** The Inlandsbanemuseet, inside the Sorsele train-station building, tells the story of the 1289km railway and how it was built between Kristinehamn in the south and Gällivare in the north – from the first dreams of the late 1800s right through to the present day. It's a pleasant little museum, but you won't find a lot of information in English. There are lots of intriguing old photos though, covering over 100 years of railway history.

Älvkungen   BOATING

(📞 070-229 90 55; www.facebook.com/Alvkungen; per person from 200kr; ⏰ summer only) Take a ride on the Vindelälven in this boat that was built in 1921. Popular in summer, it drops in to little islands and you can swim if the weather is right. Book through the tourist office or the River Hotel. Departures are often timed to match with Inlandsbanan train arrivals. It's moored just past the fire station.

🛏️ Sleeping

Sorsele River Hotel   HOTEL €€

(📞 0952-121 50; www.sorseleriverhotel.se; Hotellgatan 2; s/d 995/1295kr; 🅿️ 🛜) Sorsele's riverside hotel is a pleasant place in the centre of town and makes a good base for exploring the surrounding wilderness areas. Reception will help you book various activities such as boat trips, fishing, dogsledding and snowmobiling. The hotel also offers a superb weekday lunch buffet (89kr) that is popular with locals, and often has a dinner buffet (150kr) too.

ℹ️ Information

Tourist Office (📞 0952-140 90; www.sorsele.se; Stationsgatan 19; ⏰ 9am-6pm) Inside the Sorsele train-station building with the museum and a nice little cafe, this place has plenty to offer, especially to keen fishers.

ℹ️ Getting There & Away

Bus 45 passes through daily in both directions on the Gällivare–Jokkmokk–Arvidsjaur–Sorsele–Östersund route.

Bus 341 runs from Sorsele to Ammarnäs (115kr, 1¼ hours).

Inlandsbanan trains (p280) stop in summer, one heading in each direction each day.

Ammarnäs

📞 0952 / POP 87

Tiny Ammarnäs, nestling in a river valley hemmed in by the Ammarfjället mountains, has been used by Sami herders for centuries. Even now, a good proportion of the population makes their living from reindeer husbandry.

Ammarnäs is one of the main entry points for the Vindelfjällen Nature Reserve. Hikers can tackle the wildest part of the Kungsleden from here or else embark on easier day hikes, such as the 8km jaunt to the top of Mt Kaissats (984m) that runs from Stora Tjulträsk at the western end of the village.

This is a one-way-in, one-way-out spot, 88km northwest of Sorsele. While you'll spot many hikers, an incredible number of fishers turn up to fish the Vindelån and tributaries for trout, grayling and char.

☉ Sights & Activities

Vindelfjällen
Nature Reserve   NATURE RESERVE
The largest natural reserve in Sweden and
one of the largest protected areas in Europe,
covering 5628 sq km, the Vindelfjällen Nature Reserve is named after the Vindelän, a
hotspot for outdoors enthusiasts. Activities
include hiking, horseback riding, dogsledding,
cross-country skiing, snowmobiling , hunting,
fishing and more. The main entry points for
visiting the reserve are Ammarnäs, 88km
northwest of Sorsele, and Hemavan, 148km
northwest of Storuman. You'll find a Naturum
(visitors centre) in both these towns.

Walking Trails   HIKING
The Naturum and tourist office have put together a map with 10 loop hiking trails in the
Ammarnäs region, ranging from two hours to
three days in duration. They can also provide
information on huts for overnight hikes. Drop
by for the map (70kr) and advice.

⊨ Sleeping

Ammarnäsgården   HOTEL, HOSTEL €
(⊠0952-600   03;   http://ammarnasgarden.se;
Tjulträskvägen 1; hostel s/d 350/570kr, hotel s/d
950/1390kr; ⊙1Jun-30Sep; P ☒) The only hotel
in Ammarnäs also runs the adjoining youth
hostel, in a picturesque location. There's a sauna and pool, and the hotel's restaurant serves
reindeer stew, fish and elk burgers. It has
beautiful views out over the Tjulån.

★ Guide Center   CABINS €€
(⊠073-084   70   33;   http://ammarnasguide.se;
Smedvägen 11; cottages per week from 6500kr;
P ☎) This all-stop shop should be your first
port of call in Ammarnäs. We've listed its
cottages, but it also has cabins and flats, and
runs a bistro, bar and coffee shop. It organises all activities in the region. In summer
it can sort out fly-fishing, mountain biking,
horse riding, bird safaris and more; in winter, snowmobiling, ice fishing and snowshoeing. Check out the great website.

❶ Information

Tourist Office (⊠0952-600 00; www.ammarnas
fjallen.com; Ammarnäsgården; ⊙9am-5pm
mid-Jun–Sep) The tourist office and the Naturum
share the same space and act as a visitors centre
for the area. Pick up maps and advice here.

❶ Getting There & Away

Bus 341 runs between Sorsele and Ammarnäs
(119kr, 1¼ hours).

Arvidsjaur

⊠0960 / POP 6529
If you've come from another town along the
E45, Arvidsjaur, with its busy, bustling main
street, will seem like a virtual metropolis.
Established several centuries ago as a Sami
marketplace and meeting spot, Arvidsjaur is
home to a number of Sami families who still
make a living from reindeer herding.

Between December and April dozens of
test drivers from different car companies
descend on the town to stage their own
version of *Top Gear* – putting fast machines
through their paces on the frozen lakes. This
is also hiking, hunting and fishing country;
outdoor enthusiasts use Arvidsjaur as a base
for all sorts of activities.

☉ Sights & Activities

★Lappstaden   HISTORIC BUILDING
(Lappstadsgatan; tours 50kr; ⊙tours 6pm mid-Jun–
mid-Aug) **FREE** The first church was built in Arvidsjaur in 1607, and church-attendance laws
(urged by zealous priests and enforced by the
monarchy) imposed a certain amount of pew
time upon the nomadic Sami. To make their
church visits manageable, they built small,
square cottages with pyramid-shaped roofs
(gåhties) for overnighting. Eighty *gåhties* are
preserved here, just across Storgatan from the
modern church.

Steam Train   RAIL
(adult/child 220/110kr) From mid-July to early
August an immensely popular 1930s steam
train makes return evening trips to Slagnäs
on Friday and Saturday, departing at 5.45pm
and returning around 10pm. It stops along
the way at Storavan beach for a barbecue
and swim. Book through the tourist office.

⊨ Sleeping & Eating

★ Lapland Lodge   HOTEL €€
(⊠0960-137   20;   www.laplandlodge.se;   Östra
Kyrkogatan 18; B&B s/d/f 690/850/950kr, hotel s/d
1490/1890kr; P ☎) Next to the church, this
friendly place offers a range of room configu-
rations in a top location near the main street.
Contemporary comforts sit amid antique style
accented with old wooden skis, antlers and
snowshoes. An outdoor hot tub and sauna are
available, and snowmobile, ice-driving and
husky-sledding tours run in winter.

Rent Your Own Island   CABIN €€
(⊠070-573 37 36; http://natursafari.se; Piteva-
gen 41, Abborrträsk; per day/week 1600/9800kr)

DON'T MISS

WINTER FUN

Arvidsjaur really comes into its own in winter. On the high-octane side of things, snow-mobiles whiz along the 600km or so of snowmobile tracks around the town, teams of huskies carry passengers through the snow and driving enthusiasts grapple with the steering wheels of BMWs, Audis and Porsches on special ice tracks marked on frozen lakes. The operators below can help you tap into the snowy thrills:

Snowmobile Adventures (☑ 0960-137 20; www.laplandlodge.se; Östra Kyrkogatan 18) Based at Lapland Lodge, these guys have four levels of trips – beginner, advanced, mountain safaris and extreme safaris. A two-hour starter tour costs 1090kr. A six-hour pro-rider safari will knock you back 5090kr. Check out your options online.

Sports Cars on Ice (☑ 0960-137 20; www.laplandlodge.se; Östra Kyrkogatan 18; 3-hr ice driving 5900kr) These guys, also based at Lapland Lodge, organise ice driving (three to six hours) in an Audi TT Quattro so you can be like all those other test drivers in town who are working.

Nymånen Dogsledding (☑ 070-625 40 32; www.nymanen.com; per person from 1250kr) 🏃 Go dog-sledding with one of the largest Siberian-husky kennels in Lappland, certified eco-friendly by Nature's Best.

There are not too many opportunities to rent your own island with a log cabin, sauna, outdoor hot tub, boat transportation and fishing licence in Lappland. The cabin has two double and three single beds at the perfect spot to get away from it all. The hot tub costs extra. It's available year-round, but email for up-to-date details.

★ **Hans På Hörnet** CAFE €
(http://hanspahornet.blogspot.se; Storgatan 21; mains from 59kr; ⊘ 8.30am-5.30pm Mon-Fri, 10am-3pm Sat) This very local spot has a popular buffet lunch (90kr), and also serves up inexpensive salads, sandwiches and pies. This is the place to try *palt*, a Swedish meat-filled dumpling.

Afrodite GREEK €€
(☑ 0960-173 00; Storgatan 10; mains from 70kr; ⊘ 11am-10pm) The Goddess of Love tempts diners with 'Greek-inspired' dishes, so expect to see chicken souvlaki alongside reindeer and smoked moose pizzas in this vaguely Mediterranean set-up with fake marble busts. The food is good though, and the locals know it.

ⓘ Information

Tourist Office (☑ 0960-175 00; www.arvidsjaur.se; ⊘ 10am-6pm Mon-Fri & 10am-4.30pm Sat & Sun Jun-Aug) On Storgatan, the town's main road. Staff are helpful.

ⓘ Getting There & Away

Arvidsjaur Airport (☑ 0960-173 80; www.ajr.nu), 11km east of the centre, has daily connections to Gällivare and Stockholm-Arlanda with

Nextjet (www.nextjet.se). It also has direct winter connections with Stuttgart, Frankfurt-Hahn, Munich and Hanover with FlyCar (www.fly-car.de).

Arvidsjaur is connected by daily Inlandsbanan trains in summer to Östersund (728kr, 8¼ hours), Gällivare (420kr, 5¾ hours) and Jokkmokk (265kr, 3½ hours).

The bus station is at Västlundavägen, in the town centre.

Useful bus routes include:

Bus 45 South to Östersund (440kr, 7¼ hours); north to Gällivare (311kr, 3¾ hours) via Jokkmokk (215kr, 2¼ hours)

Bus 104 To Arjeplog (130kr, one hour).

Arjeplog

☑ 0961 / POP 1977

Sitting 85km northwest of Arvidsjaur, the tiny Sami town of Arjeplog (Árjepluovve, in Sami) sits on the Silvervägen (Silver Rd; E95), surrounded by prime fishing country of 8700 lakes (each local has their favourite). Arjeplog's star attraction is its excellent silver museum – silver was found here in the 1620s and a mining industry was established from those days. The town sits on Lake Hornavan, Sweden's deepest lake (221m), known for its scenic beauty. This is a cute little place, and a good base for exploring the surrounding area.

⊙ Sights & Activites

★ **Silvermuseet** MUSEUM
(Silver Museum; ☑ 0961-145 00; www.silvermuseet.se; Torget 1; adult/child 80kr/free; ⊘ 9am-

7pm summer) Housed in what used to be a nomad school, the tour de force at Arjeplog's Silvermuseet is the vast collection of Sami silver objects – the most extensive of its kind – including belt buckles, ornate spoons and goblets, and collars that would traditionally have been passed down from mother to daughter. You may also spot a *dássko*, a special bag for a silver spoon, used by the Southern Sami; shaman drums; and 2000-year-old skis worn by Sami hunters.

Fjällflygarna Heli-hike   HIKING
(✆ 0961-230 40; www.fjallflygarna.se; Adolfström 158) Includes a helicopter flight from Adolfström (73km northwest of Arjeplog) to a mountain top, a 6km self-guided hike down to a wilderness restaurant featuring local delicacies, and a boat trip back to Adolfström. It's surprisingly reasonable – 1180kr per person for two; 700kr per person for four. Talk to the Arjeplog tourist office – book at least one day ahead.

🛏 Sleeping & Eating

Hornavan Hotell   HOTEL €€
(✆ 0961-77 71 00; www.hornavanhotell.se; Västra Skeppsholmen 3; s/d from 775/995kr; P 🤶) With glorious views out over the lake and slick rooms, a gym, indoor hot tub and sauna, this is a top spot to lay your head in Arjeplog year-round. The hotel, about 500m from the centre, also features one of the top restaurants in town.

Hotel Lyktan   HOTEL €€
(✆ 0961-612 10; www.hotellyktan-arjeplog.se; Lugnetvägen 4; s/d 750/950kr; P 🤶) The most central place to stay in Arjeplog has been revamped and moved upmarket, shedding its basic hostel rooms and introducing appealing doubles with shiny wooden floors and discreet splashes of colour. Facilities include a pool table, sauna and gym. The hotel also runs a hostel from May to October. Check the website for details.

★ Arjeplog Vilt & Kafé   SWEDISH €
(✆ 0961-100 01; Torget 1; snacks from 50kr; ⊙ 10am-5pm Mon-Thu, 9am-4pm Fri, 11am-3pm Sat & Sun) This place has it all, from snacks to dried salmon, reindeer pelts, sausages and souvenirs for sale. Don't miss the special Kaffetåren, a local Sami favourite that involves putting dried reindeer meat, sliced boiled reindeer tongue and cheese into a cup of coffee (75kr). It's surprisingly palatable! Open year-round, this is where the locals go.

ℹ Information

Tourist Office (✆ 0961-145 00; www. arjeploglapland.se; Torget 1; ⊙ 10am-1pm & 2-4pm Mon-Fri, 10am-2pm Sat & Sun) Helpful office inside the Silvermuseet.

ℹ Getting There & Away

Buses 17 and 26 run between Arjeplog and Arvidsjaur (130kr, one hour) with bus 26 continuing on to Skellefteå (252kr, 3¼ hours).

Bus 104 runs between Arjeplog and Jäkkvikk (105kr, 1¼ hours) for the Kungsleden.

Jokkmokk

✆ 0971 / POP 2790

The capital of Sami culture, and the biggest handicraft centre in Lappland, Jokkmokk (meaning 'river bend' in Sami) not only has the definitive Sami museum but also is the site of a huge annual winter market gathering. Just north of the Arctic Circle, it's a tranquil place and the only town in Sweden that has a further-education college that teaches reindeer husbandry, craft making and ecology using the Sami language. Jokkmokk is a jumping-off point for visiting the four national parks that are part of the Laponia World Heritage Area and makes a great base for all manner of outdoor adventures year-round.

◎ Sights & Activities

★ Ájtte Museum   MUSEUM
(✆ 0971-170 70; www.ajtte.com; Kyrkogatan 3; adult/child 80/40kr; ⊙ 9am-6pm) This illuminating museum is Sweden's most thorough introduction to Sami culture. Follow the 'spokes' radiating from the central chamber, each dealing with a different theme – from traditional costume, silverware, creatures from Sami folk tales and 400-year-old painted shamans' drums, to replicas of sacrificial sites and a diagram explaining the uses and significance of various reindeer entrails. The beautifully showcased collection of traditional silver jewellery features heavy collars, now making a comeback among Sami women after a long absence.

★ Sameslöjdstiftelsen Sami Duodji   GALLERY
(✆ 0971-128 94; www.sameslojdstiftelsen.com; Porjusvägen 4; ⊙ 10am-5.30pm) **FREE** This centrally located Sami gallery and crafts centre is your one-stop shop for diverse, authentic Sami handicrafts of the highest quality: from leatherwork, clothing in Sami colours and silver jewellery to bone-inlaid wood carvings

and Sami knives in reindeer-antler sheaths. Most items are available for purchase.

Jokkmokk Guiderna CANOEING, SNOW SPORTS
(☎ 0971-122 84; www.facebook.com/jokkmokk guiderna) ⚑ Canoe rental and hiking/canoe tours by a Nature's Best ecotourism operator. It also excels at multiday dogsledding expeditions in Sarek National Park in winter.

Laponia Adventures OUTDOORS, SNOW SPORTS
(☎ 070-547 97 10; www.laponiaadventures.com) These guys specialise in guided trips and activities in the Laponia World Heritage Area, such as winter ski expeditions and Kungsleden hiking trips. They also provide route planning, transport into the park areas and luggage storage.

⚑ Festivals & Events

★ Jokkmokk Winter Market CULTURAL
(www.jokkmokksmarknad.se) Winter travellers shouldn't miss the annual Sami Winter Market, held the first Thursday through Saturday in February. The oldest and biggest of its kind, it attracts some 30,000 people annually; it's like a yearly party for Sami traders to make contacts and see old friends, while visitors can splurge on the widest array of Sami *duodji* (handicrafts) in the country.

🛏 Sleeping & Eating

Arctic Camp Jokkmokk CABIN €
(☎ 0971-123 70; http://arcticcampjokkmokk.se; 2-/4-bed cabin 440/1015kr; P 🖥 🛋) This camping and holiday village 3km east of the centre is perfect for families.There's a sauna and hot tub, heated outdoor pools for summer, plus a restaurant and shop. The 57 cottages of various sizes all have full kitchen equipment, toilet, shower and television; laundry facilities are available. Did we mention the water slide?

★ Hotell Akerlund HOTEL €€
(☎ 0971-100 12; http://hotelakerlund.se; Herrevägen 1; s/d from 1195/1395kr; P 🛜) This pleasant central hotel rises above a slightly shabby outward appearance – it's coming up to 100 years as an inn – by having a very sharp lobby and rooms. After changing ownership and its name (formerly Hotel Gästis) in 2015, it underwent extensive renovations and is a top place to stay. The attached restaurant is shaped like a Sami *kåta* (hut).

Hotel Jokkmokk HOTEL €€
(☎ 0971-777 00; www.hoteljokkmokk.se; Solgatan 45; s/d from 960/1155kr; P 🛜) Overlooking picturesque Talvatis on the south side of town, Jok-

kmokk's nicest hotel has thoroughly modern, if unmemorable, rooms, a superb tiled sauna in the basement and another by the lake (for that refreshing hole-in-the-ice dip in winter). The large restaurant, shaped like a Sami *kåta*, appropriately serves the likes of elk fillet and smoked reindeer with juniper-berry sauce.

★ Ájtte Museum Restaurant SWEDISH €€
(www.ajtte.com/besoka/restaurang-ajtte; Kyrkogatan 3; lunch buffet 90kr, mains from 95kr; ⊙ 9am-6pm) This Sami restaurant makes it possible to enhance what you've learned about the local wildlife by sampling some of it – from *suovas* (smoked and salted reindeer meat) to reindeer steak and grouse with local berries. The weekday lunchtime buffet is very popular and serves home-style Swedish dishes.

Café Gasskas CAFE €€
(☎ 070-365 97 48; www.gasskas.se; Porjusvägen 7; mains from 175kr; ⊙ 4-10pm Mon-Fri) This friendly coffee shop turned gourmet spot delights resident and visiting palates with a succinct menu of local game and fish (think elk burger, grilled Arctic char and reindeer steak with all the trimmings). Café Gasskas has been keeping erratic opening hours of late, so try your luck.

🛍 Shopping

Jokkmokk is the best location in Sweden to pick up impressive Sami creations, from contemporary fashion to knives, silver jewellery and more. The museum shop is good, as are a couple of galleries in town.

Jokkmokks Tenn DESIGN
(☎ 0971-554 20; www.jokkmokkstenn.se; Järnvägsgata 19; ⊙ 7.30am-4.30pm Mon-Thu, to 1pm Fri) Head into this metalworks studio where artisans are making Sami-inspired jewellery, goblets, cups and vases out of pewter (tin and copper), silver and gold. This is pure Lappland-designed and Lappland-made; you can watch pieces being fashioned – and then purchase them!

ℹ Information

Tourist Office (☎ 0971-222 50; www.destinationjokkmokk.se; Stortorget 4; ⊙ 9.30am-6.30pm Mon-Fri, 10am-5pm Sat & Sun) Very helpful staff. Stocks numerous brochures on activities and tours in the area.

ℹ Getting There & Away

In the summer only, daily **Inlandsbanan trains** (p280) head south to Östersund (993kr, 12 hours) via Arvidsjaur (129kr, 3¾ hours) at 9.14am, and north to Gällivare (154kr, 2¼ hours) at 6.18pm.

Buses arrive and leave from the bus station on Klockarvägen.

Bus 45 Connects Jokkmokk with Östersund (507kr, 9¾ hours) via Arvidsjaur (215kr, 2¼ hours). Also heads north to Gällivare (142kr, 1½ hours).

Bus 44 Runs to Luleå (237kr, 2¾ hours) via Gällivare (142kr, 1½ hours).

Gällivare

✆0970 / POP 18,425

Gällivare (Váhtjer in Sami) and its northern twin, Malmberget, are surrounded by forest and dwarfed by the bald Dundret hill. After Kiruna, Malmberget (Ore Mountain) is the second-largest iron-ore mine in Sweden. And as with Kiruna, the area's sustaining industry is simultaneously threatening the town with collapse into a great big pit, so buildings are gradually being shifted to sturdier ground. Gällivare's biggest attractions are ore-oriented, and even if you don't descend into the subterranean gloom, a visit to Malmberget casts a melancholy spell – many of its houses have been abandoned in anticipation of their imminent destruction.

The strong Sami presence in Gällivare is reflected in its monuments. The bronze statue opposite the church, by local sculptor Berto Marklund, is called *Tre seitar* (*seite* being a Sami god of nature) and symbolises the pre-Christian Sami religion. The nearby granite sculpture *Same*, by Allan Wallberg, depicts a sitting Sami in North Kaitum costume.

◉ Sights & Activities

**Laponia Visitor
Centre Gällivare** CULTURAL CENTRE
(✆0970-166 60; https://laponia.nu; ◷9am-5pm Mon-Fri) **FREE** Upstairs in the train station and looked after by the tourist office, this lovely exhibition about Sami culture, specifically life in autumn, is well worth visiting. The displays and videos are very insightful and the place has been beautifully set up. If the door isn't open, the helpful staff in the tourist office will unlock it for you.

LKAB Iron-Ore Mine MINE
(360kr; ◷tours 9.30am & 1.30pm daily mid-Jun–mid-Aug) Descend into the bowels of the earth to marvel at the immense, noisy trucks labouring in the darkness of the underground LKAB iron-ore mine. Malmberget (the whole town!) is being phased out for mine expansion and won't be here by 2032.

Cultural Trail WALKING
The tourist office has put together a map and explanation booklet for a 1½- to two-hour walk (6km) around the cultural sights of Gällivare. Included are the church, statues, the city's oldest building erected in 1747, the old Gällivare Homestead area and views of Castle Fjällnäs, built to house the mining company manager. Pick up a map and hit the road.

Gällivare & Dundret Tour TOURS
(adult/child 350/170kr) Dundret (823m) is a nature reserve with excellent views of the town, Malmberget and the Aitik copper mine, and a favourite spot for viewing the midnight sun. The tourist office organises three-hour tours (from 10pm early June through to the end of July) from the train station that take you through the past, present and future of Gällivare, and include refreshments.

🛏 Sleeping & Eating

★Bed & Breakfast Gällivare B&B €
(✆0970-156 56; www.bbgellivare.se; Laestadiusvägen 18; s/d/tr/q 585/685/980/1100kr; ☏🅟🛜) Marita's is a lovely spot atop a small hill, about an 800m (15-minute) walk north of the station. This two-storey B&B is her pride and joy and Marita loves chatting with her guests. Bathroom facilities are shared, but there's a generous buffet included in the reasonable rates, good wi-fi and free parking outside.

Gällivare Camping CAMPGROUND €
(✆0970-100 10; www.gellivarecamping.com; Kvarkbacksvägen 2; sites 180kr, dm/s 250/280kr, 2-/4-bed cabins 700/800kr; 🅟🛜) This year-round campground shares a lovely riverside spot with the *hembygdsområde*, an old homestead. Cabins are set up more like apartments, with excellent, modern facilities. Campers and hostel guests have access to the service building with kitchen, TV, shower, sauna and laundry room.

Sofias Kök SWEDISH €
(✆0970-554 50; www.sofiaskok.se; Storgatan 19; lunch buffet 95kr, mains from 80kr; ◷10am-9pm Mon-Thu, 9.30am-3am Fri, noon-3am Sat, 1-9pm Sun) A very local spot for a good-value lunch buffet and Swedish standards such as chunky pea soup. In the evening you can nurse a pint with the local barflies.

Nittaya Thai THAI €€
(✆0970-176 85; http://nittayathairestaurant.se; Storgatan 21; mains from 110kr; ◷10am-9pm

THE MIDNIGHT SUN

Northern Sweden's most spectacular attractions are its natural phenomena. In summer, beyond the Arctic Circle, the sun does not leave the sky for weeks on end. You can see the midnight sun just south of the Arctic Circle as well (Arvidsjaur is the southernmost point in Sweden where this occurs), due to the refraction of sunlight in the atmosphere. The midnight sun can be seen on the following dates in the following places:

TOWN	MIDNIGHT SUN
Arvidsjaur	20/21 Jun
Arjeplog, Haparanda	12/13 Jun to 28/29 Jun
Jokkmokk	8/9 Jun to 2/3 Jul
Gällivare	4/5 Jun to 6/7 Jul
Kiruna	28/29 May to 11/12 Jul
Karesuando	26/27 May to 15/16 Jul
Treriksröset	22/23 May to 17/18 Jul

Mon-Thu, to 10pm Fri, 1-10pm Sat & Sun; 🍽) Authentic Thai cuisine in attractive surroundings. The changing weekday lunch buffet (90kr) is a crowd-pleaser, and the curries and stir-fried dishes off the menu are good too.

ℹ Information

Tourist Office (📞 0970-166 60; www.gellivare lapland.se; Central Plan 4; ⊙7.30am-9pm daily late Jun-Aug, 9am-5pm Mon-Fri rest of year) Inside the train station. Organises mine and midnight-sun tours. Baggage storage available.

ℹ Getting There & Away

Gällivare Lapland Airport is 7km east of the city and has flights to/from Stockholm-Arlanda.

The **Inlandsbanan** (Inland Railway; www. inlandsbanan.se; ⊙mid-Jun–mid-Aug) train runs south to Östersund (507kr, 11¼ hours, one daily at 7.50am) via Jokkmokk (154kr, 1½ hours) and Arvidsjaur (420kr, 4½ hours).

Other departures include the westbound train to Narvik (360kr, 4¾ to 5¼ hours) via Kiruna (147kr, one to 1¼ hours) and Abisko (175kr, three hours), and the eastbound train to Luleå (258kr, 2½ to three hours).

Regional buses depart from the train station.

Bus 10 To Malmberget; departs from directly opposite the Gällivare church.

Bus 45 Runs to Östersund (483kr, 11 hours) via Jokkmokk (also covered by bus 44, 142kr, 1½ hours) and Arvidsjaur (311kr, 3¾ hours).

Bus 44 Runs via Jokkmokk to Luleå (310kr, 3½ to 4¾ hours).

Bus 52 To Kiruna (180kr, 1¾ to two hours).

Kiruna

📞 0980 / POP 22,900

Scarred by mine works, the 'current' Kiruna may not be the most aesthetically appealing city, but it's a friendly place with the highest concentration of lodgings and restaurants in the northwestern corner of Sweden. Its proximity to great stretches of hikeable wilderness and the proliferation of winter activities make it an excellent base.

The citizens of Kiruna (Giron in Sami) have for many years had to live with the news that their city is on the verge of collapsing into an enormous iron mine. Fortunately a solution is under way: the building of a new city 3km to the east, largely funded by the mining company. Although just about the entire existing central city will be demolished, both the historic church and clock tower will be moved. To see what the new city will look like in 2033, check out the excellent model, plans and pics at the tourist office.

⦿ Sights

Kiruna Kyrka   CHURCH
(Gruvvägen 2; ⊙9am-5.45pm) Consecrated in 1913, the Kiruna *kyrka* was built to look like a huge Sami *kåta* (hut) and is particularly pretty against a snowy backdrop. A landmark, it's slated to survive the town's move to the east.

LKAB Iron-Ore Mine   MINE
(www.kirunalapland.se; Kiruna; adult/student 360/260kr) Kiruna owes its existence to the world's largest iron-ore deposit, 2km into the ground, and the action happens as far as 1545m below the surface. A visit here

Kiruna

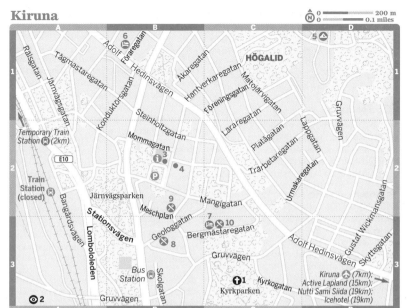

consists of being bussed to a closed-off section of a mine tunnel, where you can hear mind-blowing stats and view truly giant mining equipment, such as the mills used to crush ore. Tours leave from the tourist office daily between June and August and with advance booking the rest of the year.

Tours

A City on the Move GUIDED TOUR
(☏070-578 04 98; www.kirunastorytelling.se; adult/youth 450/250kr; ⏱10am & 2pm Mon-Fri) This 2½-hour guided tour by minibus takes visitors through 'the move', visiting the oldest parts of town that are due to disappear and the new centre of Kiruna, 3km to the east. The starting point is Kiruna tourist office; you'll need to pre-book.

Active Lapland SNOW SPORTS
(☏076-104 55 08; www.activelapland.com; Solbacksvägen 22; tours from 1250kr) This experienced operator offers 2½-hour dog-sled rides (1250kr), rides under the northern lights (highly recommended), and airport pick-ups by dog sleigh (5400kr). They'll even let you drive your own dog-sled (3200kr).

Kiruna Guidetur OUTDOORS
(☏0980-811 10; www.kirunaguidetur.com; Vänortsgatan 8) These popular all-rounders organise

Kiruna

anything and everything from overnighting in a self-made igloo, snowmobile safaris and cross-country skiing outings in winter, to overnight mountain-bike tours, rafting and quad-biking in summer. Book via the website, or visit the shop on the main square.

Festivals & Events

Snöfestivalen ART, CULTURAL
(Kiruna Snow Festival; www.snofestivalen.com) In the last week of January, this festival is focused on

snow sculpting. The tradition began in 1985 as a space-themed snow-sculpture contest to celebrate the launching of a rocket from nearby space base, Esrange. It now draws artists from all over to create ever more elaborate and beautiful shapes. The festival also features Sami reindeer-sled racing and other activities.

🛏 Sleeping

As the largest town in northern Lappland, Kiruna is the obvious destination for many. In accordance, there is an excellent choice of accommodation. Book ahead in January, when the annual Kiruna Snow Festival takes place.

★ SPiS Hotel & Hostel   HOSTEL €
(☑ 0980-170 00; www.spiskiruna.se; Bergmästaregatan 7; dm/d from 305/535kr, hotel s/d 995/1195kr; P 🛜) This catch-all hotel-and-hostel combo features modern hotel rooms and cosy dorms in central Kiruna. There's a deli, bakery and top-quality restaurant as part of the complex, plus a handy communal guest kitchen and an even handier supermarket just a few minutes' stroll away. Look for the orange building.

Camp Ripan   CAMPGROUND, HOTEL €
(☑ 0980-630 00; www.ripan.se; Campingvägen 5; sites 150kr, cabins from 1100kr; P 🛜 🏊) This large and well-equipped campground has hotel-standard chalets and stylish rooms with Sami-inspired art – in addition to its caravan and tent sites. The Aurora Spa is popular and so is the outdoor pool, when things warm up. There's also a small shop and a top-notch restaurant.

★ Hotel Arctic Eden   BOUTIQUE HOTEL €€
(☑ 0980-611 86; www.hotelarcticeden.se; Föraregatan 18; s/d 1000/1300kr; P 🛜 🏊) At Kiruna's fanciest lodgings the rooms are a chic blend of Sami decor and modern technology; there's a plush spa and indoor pool, and the friendly staff can book all manner of outdoor adventures. A Sami-inspired, family-owned place, it has a fine restaurant and an excellent handicraft store. Part of the complex, the Arctic Thai & Grill is flooded with customers.

✖ Eating

There is plenty of cuisine choice here, but if you can, try to taste some Sami-inspired dishes, like smoked and salted reindeer meat and grouse with local berries, which you can find in several local restaurants. Fish and seafood dishes are also great choices, with fresh trout, salmon and perch regularly showing up on

menus. There are two good-sized supermarkets located centrally in town.

Café Safari   CAFE €
(☑ 0980-174 60; www.cafesafari.se; Geologgatan 4; cakes/sandwiches from 45/75kr; ⏱ 8am-6pm Mon-Fri, 10am-4pm Sat; ✏) This is a long cafe serving treacle-thick coffee, outstanding cakes (try the pecan pie), scrummy sandwiches, quiche and baked potatoes – and even Bubbies mochi ice-cream from Honolulu!

★ SPiS   SWEDISH €€
(☑ 0980-170 00; www.spiskiruna.se; Bergmästaregatan 7; mains from 185kr) With a top deli and bakery, breakfast and lunch buffets, and a quality dinner menu, SPiS is considered the best place to eat in Kiruna. The restaurant has won numerous awards and its four-/five-course menus (565/755kr) with wine pairings are the way to go. The Meat Locker has amazing options including the 500g entrecôte (495kr).

★ Camp Ripan Restaurang   SWEDISH €€
(☑ 0980-630 00; www.ripan.se; Campingvägen 5; lunch buffet weekday/weekend 100/125kr, dinner mains from 175kr; ⏱ 11am-2pm & 6-9.30pm Mon-Fri, noon-2pm & 6-9.30pm Sat & Sun; P 🛜 ✏) The lunch buffet is good value, but the real draw is the Sami-inspired à la carte menu featuring local, seasonal produce. The restaurant, located at the local campground, hosts regular culinary events, like a four-course meal with drinks accompanied by a spellbinding northern lights slide show, as well as cookery demos.

Landströms Kök & Bar   SWEDISH €€
(☑ 0980-133 55; www.landstroms.net; Föreningsgatan 11; mains from 175kr; ⏱ 6-11pm Mon-Thu, to 1am Fri & Sat) Take a stylish, monochrome interior, throw in some reindeer steak, haloumi burgers, racks of lamb, and crayfish sandwiches, and add a concise, well-chosen wine menu and beers that span the world, and you've got a winning recipe for a perpetually buzzy bistro.

ℹ Information

Tourist Office (☑ 0980-188 80; www.kiruna lapland.se; Lars Janssonsgatan 17; ⏱ 8.30am-6pm Mon-Fri, to 4pm Sat & Sun) Inside the Folkets Hus visitor centre; has internet access and can book various tours.

ℹ Getting There & Away

Kiruna Airport (☑ 010-109 46 00; www. swedavia.com/kiruna), 7km east of the town, has flights to Stockholm (two to three daily), as well as several weekly flights to Luleå and Umeå. The **airport bus** (one way 110kr) is timed to meet

Stockholm flights and runs between the tourist office and the airport during peak season.

Kiruna station has been closed and torn down. The 'Temporary Station' is a make-do affair a couple of kilometres to the north of the old station. There is a daily overnight train to Stockholm (from 696kr, 17½ hours) that departs at 4pm. Other destinations include Narvik (Norway; 227kr, 3½ to 3¾ hours) via Abisko (199kr, 1½ to two hours), Luleå (385kr, 4¼ hours) and Gällivare (139kr, 1¼ hours).

Buses depart from the centrally located **bus station** (☑ 980-124 00; www.ltnbd.se/kiruna; Hjalmar Lundbohmsvägen 45; ⊙7am-4pm Mon-Fri).

Bus 91 Runs to Narvik (Norway; 320kr, 2¾ hours) via Abisko (210kr, 1¼ hours) and Riksgränsen (240kr, two hours).

Bus 50 To Jukkasjärvi (48kr, 30 minutes).

Bus 10 & 52 To Gällivare (195kr, 1¾ hours).

Nikkaluokta & Kebnekaise

Tiny Nikkaluokta, 66km west of Kiruna, is a popular entry point to the Kungsleden. It's also the starting point for those wishing to hike or climb Sweden's highest mountain, Kebnekaise (2111m); the views of the surrounding peaks and glaciers are incredible on a clear day.

Basically, there is nothing in Nikkaluokta except a bus stop, a huge car park and Nikkaluokta Sarri AB, with cabins, camping, a cafe and a small shop. From there, it is a 19km walk west to STF (Swedish Tourist Association) Kebnekaise Fjällstation, from where you can join the Kungsleden, climb Kebnekaise, or just enjoy some time out in the wilderness.

In July and August the marked **Kebnekaise Hike** up the western flank of Sweden's highest mountain is usually snow-free and no technical equipment is required to reach the southern summit (9km each way; five to seven hours one way) from the Kebnekaise mountain station. The summit has a sheer drop on both sides – take a good map and check weather forecasts.

🛏 Sleeping & Eating

★**STF Kebnekaise Fjällstation** LODGE €
(☑ 0980-550 00; www.svenskaturistforeningen. se/kebnekaise; dm/d/q 420/1550/2100kr; ⊙mid-Feb–early May & mid-Jun–mid-Sep; ☎) This large, attractive mountain lodge nestles at the foot of Mt Kebnekaise, a 19km walk west from Nikkaluokta. A popular entry point to the Kungsleden, it has equipment rental and

a gear shop, a sauna and an excellent restaurant serving meals from locally sourced ingredients. The oldest part of the lodge, with fireplaces and characterful bunk rooms, dates to 1907.

Nikkaluokta Sarri AB CABIN, CAMPING €
(☑ 0980-550 15; http://nikkaluokta.com; cabins s/d from 450/650kr; 🅿 ☎) Sitting alone at the end of the road at Nikkaluokta, this place has cabins, camping, a cafe, a small shop and a gallery. It also operates snowmobile transport to the Kebnekaise mountain station in winter, and boat transfers 6km up Ladtjojavri in summer. Check out the excellent website. This friendly place is all there is at Nikkaluokta.

🛈 Getting There & Around

It's a 66km drive west from Kiruna to Nikkaluokta. A four-person taxi will cost about 1400kr.

Bus 92 runs between Nikkaluokta and Kiruna (110kr, 70 minutes, two daily).

Kallax Flyg helicopters (☑ 0980-810 00; www.kallaxflyg.se; adult/2-11yr 850/500kr) transports hikers twice daily (8.30am and 5pm) between Nikkaluokta and Kebnekaise, from late June to late August and daily until late September (8.30am). Can drop off hikers in the wilderness upon request.

Jukkasjärvi

☑ 0980 / POP 548

The tiny village of Jukkasjärvi is 20km east of Kiruna, 200km north of the Arctic Circle, and is surrounded by lakes, fir trees and reindeer. It is also home to one of Sweden's most famous attractions: the extraordinary Icehotel. Aside from this blockbuster of a sight, though, this tiny village is well worth a stroll. The only road, Marknadsvägen, passes by some simple rustic homes that are still owned by local families (some of whom are somewhat bemused by the village's Icehotel fame). The street eventually peters out when it reaches the historic wooden church. It is remarkable that this village has remained charmingly unchanged, despite its fame as one of the most extraordinary holiday destinations in the world.

◉ Sights

Nutti Sámi Siida MUSEUM
(☑ 0980-213 29; www.nutti.se; Marknadsvägen 84; adult/child 150/75kr; ⊙10am-5pm mid-Jun–Aug, tours 10am & 3pm; ♿) Next to the church, Nutti Sámi Siida is a reindeer yard that you can tour with a Sami guide to learn about reindeer

farming and traditional Sami housing. You can pick up excellent Sami *duodji* (handicrafts), chow down on Sami food at Café Sápmi and arrange a stay at the nearby Reindeer Lodge. It's well worth a visit.

Jukkasjärvi Kyrka   CHURCH

(Marknadsvägen; ⊙9am-6pm) This is the oldest church in Lappland (1608). The brightly painted altarpiece by Uppsala artist Bror Hjorth, cut out in teak, depicts scenes with revivalist preacher Lars Levi Laestadius. In the centre of the birch organ above the entrance hangs a shaman's drum, merging the Sami sun symbol with the Christian cross. The organ has three sounds: birdsong, drum, and reindeer hooves. Rather gruesomely, under the floor lie the mummified remains of villagers who died here in the 18th century.

🛏 Sleeping & Eating

★ **Icehotel**   ICE HOTEL €€€

(☑0980-668 00; www.icehotel.com; Marknadsvägen 63; s/d/ste from 2400/3300/5400kr, cabins from 2000kr; ⊙Dec-Apr; P🛜) Every winter, from December onwards, the Icehotel seems to grow organically from ice blocks taken from the Torne river, while international artists flock from all over to carve the ice sculptures that make its frozen rooms masterpieces. Snuggle up between reindeer furs on a bed of snow and ice in the igloo-like 'cold rooms'; thankfully, the bathrooms are heated...

★ **Icehotel 365**   HOTEL €€€

(☑0980-668 00; www.icehotel.com; Jukkasjärvi; ste from 5500kr; P🛜) Opened in 2016 and adjacent to the Icehotel site by the river, the big plus here is that it's open year-round. Even in summer, guests have an 'ice experience' with frigid rooms full of ice sculptures, and an ice bar. Insulated to keep the cold in during summer, Icehotel 365 forms part of the original Icehotel in winter.

Reindeer Lodge   CABIN €€€

(☑0980-213 29; www.nutti.se; Paksuniemivägen 188; per adult incl meals from 1650kr) 🍃 Reindeer Lodge comprises five cosy two-person cabins in the woods, on the banks of the Torne river. Located 3km away from Jukkasjärvi, they feature a wood-heated sauna and a fully equipped kitchen cabin. In winter, the isolated location is good for viewing the northern lights and a small timber dining room serves elk, reindeer and Arctic char.

★ **Icehotel Restaurant**   SWEDISH, FUSION €€€

(☑0980-66 800; www.icehotel.se; Marknadsvägen; mains from 175kr, set menus from 595kr; ⊙11.30am-2.30pm & 6-10pm; ✎) Though the dining room and cocktail bar are both warm and traditional, the gourmet treat that is the Icehotel Restaurant has the novelty of dishes served on plates made from Torne river ice. This unique place excels when it comes to fusion dishes, such as reindeer steak with shiitake mushrooms and decadent, moreish chocolate souffles with cloudberry puree.

❶ Getting There & Away

Bus 501 runs four times daily between Kiruna and Jukkasjärvi (45kr, 30 minutes).

Abisko

☑0980 / POP 85

Easy access to spectacular scenery makes Abisko (Ábeskovvu in Sami) one of the highlights of any trip to Lappland. The 75-sq-km Abisko National Park spreads out from the southern shore of scenic lake Torneträsk. It's framed by the striking profile of Lapporten, a 'gate' formed by neighbouring hills that serves as the legendary gate to Lappland. This is also the driest part of Sweden and consequently has a relatively long hiking season. In winter, people come to see the northern lights; in summer they come to hike and to see the midnight sun.

Across the highway from the STF Turiststation, the **Aurora Sky Station** (www.aurora skystation.se; ⊙9pm-1am Dec-Mar, 9.30am-4pm Jun-Sep & 10pm-1am Tue, Thu & Sat mid-Jun–mid-Jul) chairlift takes you up Mt Nuolja (1164m), where you can enjoy epic views from the deck of the Panorama Café. In summer this is a prime spot from which to see the midnight sun – the lift is open 10pm to 1am three days per week in June and July. In winter, come to view the northern lights – it's open 9pm to 1am, December to March.

🏃 Activities

Hiking is the big draw here – trails are varied in both distance and terrain, and while most people come here to tackle part (or all) of the 450km-long Kungsleden, there are plenty of shorter rambles.

Excellent day hikes include the 8km hike to the Kårsa rapids, over the Ábeskoeatnu river and then along the left fork of the signposted Kårsavagge (Gorsavággi in Sami) trail through birch and pine forest, and the great 14km, four-hour return hike along the Paddus nature trail, past an STF reconstruction of a traditional Sami camp. It leads to Báddosdievvá, a former Sami sacrificial site with awesome views of Lapporten and lake Törnetrask.

Longer hikes include the trip to the Gorsajökeln glacier, staying overnight at the STF hut at the heart of the Kårsavagge valley, west of Abisko (15km each way), and the 39km-long Rallarvägen (Navvy Rd) to Riksgränsen, running parallel to the railway line and used by railway construction workers in the early 20th century. A good side venture from Rallarvägen is the 10km return trip to the enormous boulders and impressive rock formations of Kärkevagge (Geargevággi) valley from Låktatjåkka (short train/bus ride from Abisko). Trollsjön (Rissájáurre), the 'Sulphur Lake', is at the end of the valley, its clear blue waters named after the colour of burning sulphur.

For hikes in this area, employ maps *Fjällkartan BD6* or *Calazo Kungsleden* (120kr), both available at the STF lodge and Naturum.

Sleeping

★ **STF Abisko Turiststation & Abisko Mountain Station** HOSTEL €
(☑ 0980-402 00; www.abisko.nu; hostel dm/tw 295/885kr, hotel d 1540kr; ⊘ year-round; P 🖿 🖿) This 350-bed place overlooking Torneträsk lake is a massive hiker destination. There's huge demand for the excellent facilities: guest kitchens, a basement sauna, a supply shop and an excellent restaurant. There are single and twin rooms in the main building, two- and four-bed rooms in the Youth Hostel

Keron (shared shower and toilet) and cabins with private facilities for self-caterers.

Abisko.net HOSTEL €
(☑ 0980-401 03; www.abisko.net; Lapportsv 34A; dm/d from 250/600kr; P 🖿) This friendly backpackers' delight is spread over two buildings, with comfortable doubles and dorms with wide bunks, sharing guest kitchens and a wonderful sauna. Brothers Tomas and Andreas keep a large team of sled dogs; dog-sledding, snowmobiling, ice-fishing, snowshoe tours and northern lights tours are all available here. Cross under the railway tracks 150m east of Abisko Östra station.

ℹ️ Information

Naturum (☑ 0980-788 60; www.national parksofsweden.se; ⊘ 9am-6pm Tue-Sat early Jul-Sep & Feb-Apr) Effectively the national park visitors centre, the Naturum has detailed exhibitions, a reference library, maps and booklets for sale and extensive information on the Kungsleden. Helpful staff are happy to answer questions and make suggestions based on the amount of time you have.

ℹ️ Getting There & Away

Abisko has two train stops: Östra station puts you in the centre of tiny Abisko village, 2km to the east and outside of the national park, while Abisko Turiststation is across the highway from the Naturum, inside the national park.

Trains run to Kiruna (125kr, 1¼ hours) and to Narvik (120kr, 1¾ hours).

Buses stop at Abisko Östra (main village) and Abisko Turiststation – the start of the Kungsleden – five minutes apart. Bus 91 runs east

---

ℹ️ CHASING THE NORTHERN LIGHTS

The otherworldly lights of the aurora borealis, named after the Roman goddess of dawn and the Greek term for the north wind, have captivated the imagination of the people of the north and travellers alike for centuries. The celestial spectacle of the streaks in the sky – from yellowish-green to violet, white and red – are caused by the collision of energy-charged sun particles with atoms in the Earth's magnetic field, and are visible in the north of Sweden between October and March.

Don't expect to see the northern lights every day; all depends on weather conditions, and if it's cloudy the lights aren't visible. One of Lappland's best spots for aurora borealis viewing is Abisko's **Aurora Sky Station**, away from the village's light pollution and vastly aided by Abisko's dry climate.

Nutti Sámi Siida (☑ 0980-213 29; www.nutti.se; Jukkasjärvi) 🖿, the **Icehotel** and most tour agencies in Kiruna, Abisko and elsewhere in Lappland organise northern lights tours, often combined with other outdoor activities. **Lights Over Lapland** (☑ 0760-754 300; www.lightsoverlapland.com; 3hr photography tours 1195kr, 4-day expeditions 18,500kr) teaches you how to capture this otherworldly shining for posterity.

to Kiruna (175kr, 1¼ hours) and west to Narvik (Norway; 185kr, 1½ hours).

It's a 94km drive from Kiruna to Abisko, taking about an hour in summer driving conditions.

Riksgränsen

ℐ 0980 / POP 84

A tiny ski-resort town tucked just inside the border with Norway, over 200km north of the Arctic Circle, Riksgränsen is the only place in Sweden where you can ski into Norway and back approaching midsummer.

In the early 1900s there was so much snow and life was so hard that the 500 residents were forced to move away. The 1902 completion of the Ofotenbanan railway linking Kiruna and Narvik in Norway set things in motion, though. Some 26 years later the Swedish Ski Club started making overnight trips to the area, and once the first ski lift was installed in 1952, Riksgränsen took off. And it's not just for winter-sports enthusiasts. Riksgränsen is also popular for winter testing of pre-production cars by a number of European manufacturers.

With a total of six lifts, Riksgränsen is a very popular **ski resort** (http://riksgransen.se; day pass adult/child 375/295kr; ☺Feb–Jun) offering everything you'd expect. There's rental gear, a sports shop, ski school, guided tours and heliskiing. One thing skiers won't be used to though, is midnight sun skiing offered on specific dates in May from 10pm to 12.30am. The Scandinavian Big Mountain Championships are held here each May.

🛏 Sleeping

★ **Meteorologen Ski Lodge**   HOTEL €€€
(ℐ 0980-641 00; www.riksgransen.se; Riksgränsvägen; s/d from 1500/2500kr; ℗ 🕸) Lovingly restored, this intimate timber building with just 14 exquisite rooms was built in 1903 and spent its early years as the area's customs house. It's now a cosy lodge with a homey atmosphere, featuring a restaurant serving mostly Swedish standards, and a lively bar.

Hotell Riksgränsen   HOTEL €€€
(ℐ 0980-400 80; www.riksgransen.se; Riksgränsvägen 15; d/tr/ste from 3290/4690/9900kr; ☺mid-Feb–Jun; ℗ 🕸) The hotel features top-quality skier rooms for two to four people, excellent single and double rooms, plus a number of suites. It's within a couple of hundred metres of the lifts and the train station, and also has Restaurang Lapplandia, the après-ski bar Grönan, and the sports shop. There are also apartments in the same building as the hotel.

🛈 Getting There & Away

Trains stop in Riksgränsen on the way from Kiruna to Narvik, as does bus 91.

It's about a 90-minute drive northwest from Kiruna (131km).

Kungsleden

Kungsleden (King's Trail) is Sweden's most important hiking and skiing route. It runs for around 450km from Abisko in the north to Hemavan in the south, through Sami herding lands consisting of spectacular mountainous wilderness that includes Sweden's highest mountain, Kebnekaise (2111m), fringed with forests, speckled with lakes and ribboned with rivers.

The route is split into five mostly easy or moderate sections, with Svenska Turistföreningen (STF: Swedish Tourist Association) **mountain huts** (www.swedishtouristassociation. com; dm from 360kr, sites 100kr; ☺late Feb–early May & late Jun–mid-Sep), each manned by a custodian, spaced out along the route. They are 10km to 20km from one another (first come, first served), and there are four STF mountain lodges and two hostels en route. Many of the mountain huts sell provisions (check which ones on the website), and kitchen facilities are provided, but you'll need your own sleeping bag and there's no electricity. The section between Kvikkjokk and Ammarnäs is not covered by the STF, so you'll need to be prepared to camp.

Insect repellent is a must in summer to avoid becoming a walking mosquito buffet, and be prepared for changeable weather.

Abisko to Kebnekaise

From Abisko it's 86km to Kebnekaise Fjällstation (around five days of hiking), and 105km to Nikkaluokta if you're leaving the trail at Kebnekaise (around seven days).

This, the most popular section of the Kungsleden, runs through the dense vegetation of Abisko National Park, mostly following the valley, with wooden boardwalks over the boggy sections and bridges over streams. The highest point along the trail is the Tjäkta Pass (1150m), with great views over the Tjäktavagge valley.

There are five STF huts along the trail: Abiskojaure (in a lovely lakeside setting), Alesjaure (with a sauna and a great view from the mountain ridge), Tjäkta (before Tjäkta Pass), Sälka and Singi. The STF has mountain lodges at Abisko (p285) and Kebnekaise (p283).

LAPPLAND & THE FAR NORTH RIKSGRÄNSEN

Kebnekaise to Saltoluokta

This section is 52km (four to six days) from Kebnekaise Fjällstation and 38km from Singi to Saltoluokta.

South of Singi, 14km from Kebnekaise, this quieter section of the trail runs through peaceful valleys and beech forest. Row yourself 1km across Teusajaure lake and then cross the bare plateau before descending to Vakkotavare through beech forest.

A bus runs from Vakkotavare to the quay at Kebnats, where there's an STF ferry across Langas lake to Saltoluokta Fjällstation. STF has a mountain lodge at Saltoluokta (p290), and four huts en route, at Singi, Kaitumjaure, Teusajaure and Vakkotavare.

Saltoluokta to Kvikkjokk

This section is 73km, or four to six days of hiking. From Saltoluokta, it's a long and relatively steep climb to Sitojaure (18km, six hours), where you cross a lake using the boat service run by the hut's caretaker, followed by a boggy stretch with wooden walkways. At Aktse (an excellent base for side trips into Sarek National Park), on the shores of Laitaure lake, you are rewarded with expansive views of the bare mountainous terrain, before you cross the lake using the rowboats provided and pass through pine forest to reach Kvikkjokk.

STF has a lodge at Kvikkjokk (p290), and huts at Sitojaure, Aktse and Pårte.

Kvikkjokk to Ammarnäs

This is the wildest and most difficult section of the park, recommended for experienced hikers only. It stretches for 157km, or seven to 10 days of hiking. Bring your own tent, as accommodation is very spread out.

Take the boat across Saggat lake from Kvikkjokk before walking to Tsielejåkk, from where it's 55km to the next hut at Vuonatjviken. Then cross Riebnesjaure lake and another one from Hornavan to the village of Jäkkvikk, from where the trail runs through Pieljekaise National Park. From Jäkkvikk it's only 8km until the next hut, followed by another stop at the village of Adolfström. Cross Iraft lake before making for the cabins at Sjnjultsie. Here the trail forks: either take the direct 34km route to Ammarnäs or take a 24km detour to Rävfallet, followed by an additional 20km to Ammarnäs.

Ammarnäs to Hemavan

This section is 78km, or four to six days' hiking. Much of the southern section of the Kungsleden runs through Vindelfjällens Nature Reserve. This trail is the easiest of the five sections, mostly consisting of a gentle ramble through beech forest and wetlands, and over low hills. There's a long, steep climb (8km) through beech forest between Ammarnäs and Aigert, but at the top you are rewarded with an impressive waterfall.

To reach Syter, cross the wetlands using the network of bridges, stopping at the hut by Tärnasjö lake for a spell in the sauna. The hike up to Syter peak (1768m) from Syter hut is greatly recommended and the view on the way down to Hemavan, taking in Norway's Okstindarnas glaciers, is particularly spectacular.

STF has a hostel at Hemavan (p273), and five huts en route at Aigert, Serve, Tärnasjö, Syter and Viterskalet.

ⓘ Getting There & Away

The Kungsleden is reasonably straightforward to access from its most popular entry points, but if you're aiming for a remoter part of the trail, you may have to contend with limited (or, outside peak season, practically nonexistent) bus services.

Frequent trains stop at Abisko en route from Kiruna to Narvik (Norway). Inlandsbanan trains stop at Storuman (for Hemavan), Sorsele, Arvidsjaur (for Arjeplog), Jokkmokk and Gällivare in summer.

There are bus routes to other starting points along the Kungsleden:

Kiruna–Nikkaluokta Bus 92 (110kr, 70 minutes, two daily)

ⓘ KUNGSLEDEN MAPS

The best maps for each section of the Kungsleden are:

Abisko–Kebnekaise Fjällkartan BD6 or Calazo Kungsleden

Kebnekaise–Saltoluokta Fjällkartan BD8 or Calazo Kebnekaisefjällen

Saltoluokta–Kvikkjokk Fjällkartan BD10 or Calazo Sarek & Padjelanta

Kvikkjokk–Ammarnäs Fjällkartan BD14 (north) and BD16 (south) or Calazo Kvikkjokk-Ammarnäs

Ammarnäs–Hemavan Fjällkartan AC2 or Calazo Ammarnäs-Hemavan

Gällivare–Ritsem via Kebnats and Vakko-tavare Bus 93 (200kr, 3¼ hours, daily)

Jokkmokk–Kvikkjokk Buses 47 and 94 (178kr, 2¼ hours, daily)

Arjeplog–Jäkkvik Bus 104 (105kr, 1¼ hours, daily on weekdays)

Sorsele–Ammarnäs Bus 341 (119kr, 1¼ hours, one to three daily)

Umeå–Hemavan via Tärnaby Bus 31 (275kr, 5¼ hours, one to three daily)

Kallax Flyg helicopters (p283) transport hikers twice daily between Nikkaluokta and Kebnekaise from late June to late August and daily until late September, while **Fiskflyg** (www.fiskflyg.se; Strömgatan 43, Porjus; adult/child under 7yr 1250/625kr) has helicopter flights from Kvikkjokk. Drop-offs in wilderness locations of your choice can also be arranged.

Karesuando

📞 0981 / POP 310

The one-elk town of Karesuando (Gárasavvon in Sami), 260km above the Arctic Circle, is the northernmost church village in Sweden, and it feels that way: utterly remote and lonely. This Sami reindeer-herder community revels in the romance of extremes: the midnight sun shines here from late May to mid-July, but in winter the temperature hits -50°C. Karesuando's frontier feel is reflected in the four languages spoken by the locals (sometimes all at once): Swedish, Finnish, Northern Sami and Norwegian.

If it's all just too quiet and nothing much is open, cross the bridge to Finland's marginally more happening Kaaresuvanto. Alternatively, if you've got your own wheels, make tracks towards Kiruna or south along the wonderfully unpeopled Rte 99 that skirts the Finnish border en route to Pajala.

◉ Sights

Karesuando Knives   FACTORY

(Karesuando Kniven; www.karesuandokniven.com; Råstogatan 2; ⊙9am-3pm Mon-Fri) FREE This small operation on the west side of town makes genuine knives and axes shaped by centuries of Sami traditions, using raw materials that include reindeer hide, horn, bone, curly birch and wool. The blades are stainless steel and made in Sweden. Check out the factory and small shop.

Laestadius Pörte   MUSEUM

A short walk west of the tourist office is Laestadius Pörte, the compact log cabin that was home to Lars Levi Laestadius, his wife and their 14 children between 1826 and 1849.

Vita Huset   MUSEUM

(White House; ⊙7am-3pm Mon-Fri) Vita Huset is a folk museum in a former policemen's residence, with evocative photos depicting Finn civilians fleeing the retreating German forces in 1944, their cattle in tow. Dozens were rescued by Olga Raattamaa, a local from Kummavuopio depicted in one of the photos. She rowed the refugees across the river to safety in Sweden and they were then de-loused in this very building.

🛏 Sleeping & Eating

There was very little in the way of places to sleep at the time of research, but the tourist office assures us that the Arctic Star Hotel will be up and open year-round in Karesuando from 2018. Also, the Davvi Arctic Lodge is an option on the Finnish side of the river.

Karesuando Camping   CAMPGROUND €

(📞070-605 11 24; Laestadiusvägen 153; sites/cabins 230/500kr; ⊙Jun-Aug; ℗) Pitch your tent down by the river, or park yourself up inside a Sami-style *kåtor* (traditional dwelling), or choose a simple cabin at this place about a kilometre east of town.

Arctic Lunch & Grill   FAST FOOD €

(mains 45-75kr; ⊙11am-6pm) The only place to chow down in Karesuando, west of the tourist office and near the petrol station. Burgers or Asian-style fry-up: the choice is yours.

ℹ Information

Tourist Office (📞0981-202 05; www.karesuando.se; ⊙10am-5pm Mon-Fri) By the bridge to Finland in the Eurosando building, with regional info, souvenirs and a coffee shop.

ℹ Getting There & Away

Bus 50 runs between Karesuando and Kiruna (249kr, three hours).

There is a petrol station here.

Pajala

📞 0978 / POP 1958

Tiny riverside Pajala, 100km above the Arctic Circle, was made famous in the hugely popular Swedish novel and film *Popular Music*, and is a place with deeply rooted Torne Valley culture, where the locals speak Tornedalsfinska (Torne Valley Finnish).

In winter it hosts charter flights from the UK full of happy families on day trips to visit Santa's Winter Village. If you're passing through, you can be excused for thinking

TRERIKSRÖSET – WHERE THREE LANDS MEET

Treriksröset, the spot marking the meeting point of Sweden, Norway and Finland, lies 100km northwest of Karesuando.

If driving, cross the bridge from Karesuando to the Finnish Kaaresuvanto, and take the E8 route northwest to **Kilpisjärvi** (110km). Alternatively, walk across the bridge and take the daily bus departing Kaaresuvanto (1¾ hours, one daily at 2.35pm, plus another one at 4.25pm from June to mid-September) and then hike the 11km woodland trail from the northern side of the village to the small **Goldjärvi lake**, where a yellow concrete 'bell' marks the spot.

To shorten your hike to just 3km each way, hop aboard the **M/S Malla** (☑ 358-400 66 93 92; www.mallalaiva.com), which – if it has at least four passengers – sails from Kilpisjärvi to Koltaluokta, an old Sami residence (€28 return, 45 minutes, 10am, 2pm and 6pm Finnish time late June to early August). The boat waits at Koltaluokta for two hours.

Check up-to-date bus timetables at www.matkahuolto.fi and don't forget that Finland is one hour ahead of Sweden!

it looks a bit like a big truck stop, but it is a pleasant enough place to break up the journey.

⊙ Sights

Santa's Winter Village   VILLAGE
(www.santaswintervillage.se) Alf Andersson's Santa's Winter Village is so popular that charter flights arrive for the day from the UK with families ready to experience a Lappland Santa experience 100km above the Arctic Circle. There's snowmobiling, dogsledding, reindeer, and Santa's big cabin where he reads children's letters and plans Christmas (in a top secret location of course!).

Laestadius Pörtet   MUSEUM
(☑ 0978-758 80; www.laestadiusfriends.se; Laestadiusvägen 36; 65kr; ⊙10am-6pm mid-Jun–mid-Aug) This was the home of fiery preacher Lars Levi Laestadius from 1849 until his death 12 years later. Here you'll find many personal objects and an exhibition dedicated to his life and work. Laestadius (1800–1861) was a Sami pastor in the Swedish state Lutheran church in Lappland. He founded the Laestadian pietist revival movement to help his Sami congregations, who were being ravaged by alcoholism. Laestadius Days are celebrated each year, usually in July.

🛏 Sleeping & Eating

Smedjan Hotel   HOTEL €€
(☑ 0978-108 15; www.hotellsmedjan.se; Fridhemsvägen 1; s/d from 790/890kr; P 🛜) This all-purpose place right on Rte 99 has all the bases covered, with decent rooms, a restaurant that usually has buffet offerings for breakfast (included in room rates), lunch (89kr) and dinner (95kr), a bar, and – if your timing is right – live music. Pizza is also on the menu. Lots of room here, so there's free parking outside.

Thai Dan Sai   THAI €
(☑ 072-731 30 77; www.thaidansai.se; Medborgarvägen 3; mains from 89kr; ⊙11am-9pm Tue-Thu, to 2am Fri, 4pm-2am Sat) The lovely proprietor from northern Thailand has been winning many local and visiting fans with her fiery curries, stir-fried dishes and oodles of noodles. The lunch buffet for 90kr is a top deal.

ℹ Information

Tourist Office (☑ 073-823 93 98; www.pajalaturism.se; Tornedalsvägen 12; ⊙10am-5pm Mon-Fri summer only) Helpful little office, one street in from the main roundabout that has Smedjan Hotel on the corner. Call if you need help outside opening hours.

ℹ Getting There & Away

Bus 55 links Pajala and Luleå (281kr, 3½ hours).

Bus 53 runs south to Haparanda (248kr, three to 3½ hours) and northwest to Kiruna (248kr, 2¾ to three hours).

Pajala's airport, opened in 1999 to debunk the town's reputation as the most inaccessible municipality in Sweden, receives flights from Luleå.

Laponia World Heritage Area

Established in 1996, the vast Laponia World Heritage Area covers 9400 sq km, comprising the mountains, forests and marshlands of four national parks – Padjelanta, Sarek, Stora Sjöfallet and Muddus – and two nature reserves, Sjaunja and Stubba.

Unusually for a World Heritage Area, it's recognised both for its cultural and natural wealth. Laponia encompasses ancient reindeer-grazing grounds of both the mountain and the forest Sami, whose settlements and herds of around

50,000 reindeer are located here. The Sami still lead relatively traditional lives, following the reindeer during their seasonal migrations. The mountain Sami winter in the forests, where there is lichen for their herds, and move into the mountains in summer, while their forest counterparts follow their herds through the forests year-round.

While much of Lappland's World Heritage Area is inaccessible to visitors, the Kungsleden passes through, and the Padjelanta Trail is also extremely popular.

The magnificent Naturum Laponia, on Viedásnjárgga Headland in Stora Sjöfallet National Park (92km off the E45) is the main visitors centre – though it's a long drive to get there. Laponia Visitors Centre (p279) Gällivare is at the train station and its equivalent in Jokkmokk is the Ájtte Museum (p277). There are also visitors centres in Porjus and Kvikkjokk.

Stora Sjöfallet National Park   NATIONAL PARK
(Stuor Muorkke National Park) Mountainous and thickly forested Stora Sjöfallet National Park is the northernmost part of the World Heritage Area. It is dominated by Áhkká (2105m), known as the 'Queen of Lappland' and crowned with 10 glaciers. The Kungsleden passes through Stora Sjöfallet at the eastern end of the park, and at its western end is Ritsem, from where you can head out on the Padjelanta Trail. Naturum Laponia, the World Heritage area's main visitor centre, is at the eastern end of the park.

Sarek National Park   PARK
Sarek National Park, central in the World Heritage Area, is for experienced and well-kitted-out trekkers only. Named after Sarektjåhkká (2098m), and full of sharp peaks and huge glaciers, the park is rich in wildlife such as bears, wolverines and lynxes. There are no tourist facilities; where trails exist they are often washed out or in poor repair, there are rivers to cross, and the extremes of terrain can be exacerbated by volatile weather conditions. Talk to locals before heading out.

★ Padjelanta Trail   HIKING
The popular 139km-long Padjelantaleden (Padjelanta Trail) can be hiked in seven to 10 days (use Fjällkartan BD10 and Fjällkartan BD7). You'll need a boat ride at both ends – to/from Ritsem at the northern end and to/from Kvikkjokk at the southern end. There are huts along the length of the trail where hikers can sleep and cook, some selling provisions.

At the northern end (by Akkajaure), you can start at either of the STF huts, Vaisaluokta or Áhkká (the latter is easier). STF also runs the Såmmarlappa, Tarrekaise and Njunjes huts at the southern end of the trail, and STF Kvikkjokk Fjällstation. To reach the northern end of the trail, take bus 93.

🛏 Sleeping & Eating

Parts of the World Heritage Area are more accessible than others. There are good huts and lodges along the Kungsleden and Padjelanta trails, and options in Kvikkjokk and Stora Sjöfallet villages. If you're not heading out hiking, stay in Jokkmokk or Gällivare, where there are plenty of choices.

★ STF Saltoluokta Fjällstation   LODGE €
(☑ 0973-410   10;   www.swedishtouristassociation. com/facilities/stf-saltoluokta-mountain-station; dm/ s/d from 345/545/760kr; ☺ Mar-Apr & mid-Jun–mid-Sep; 🛜) This popular mountain station, established in 1912, is on the Kungsleden southeast of Stora Sjöfallet. Numerous guided wilderness tours are available, including kayaking, fishing and a hike up Lulep Gierkav (1139m) for great views. Take bus 93 (to Ritsem), get off at Kebnats, then take a boat in summer or follow the marked trail in winter.

STF Kvikkjokk Fjällstation   LODGE €
(☑ 0971-210   22;   http://kvikkjokkfjallstation.se; dm/s/d from 365/695/960kr; ☺ mid-Feb–May & mid-Jun–Oct; 🅿🛜) This picturesque mountain lodge at Kvikkjokk is a good spot to stay for Kungsleden walkers and for those starting or finishing the Padjelanta Trail. It sits on the banks of a roaring river and has a restaurant serving breakfast, lunch and dinner, as well as fully equipped guest kitchens. Equipment rental and sauna are available.

❶ Getting There & Away

Muddus National Park and Stubba Nature Reserve are easy to get to, sitting on both sides of the E45, that connects Jokkmokk and Gällivare.

You'll have to take a **boat** (☑ 070-205 31 93; www.battrafikikvikkjokk.se), then walk or use a **helicopter** (p288) from either Ritsem (bus 93 from Gällivare to Ritsem; 200kr, 3¼ hours, mid-June to mid-September) in the north, or Kvikkjokk (buses 47 and 94 connect Jokkmokk and Kvikkjokk; 178kr, 2¼ hours) in the south, to get into remote Padjelanta National Park. Most visitors are walking the Padjelanta Trail.

Kungsleden hikers walk through Sjaunja Nature Reserve, Stora Sjöfallet National Park and the south of Sarek National Park. Stora Sjöfallet, about 90km northwest of Porjus on the Porjus–Ritsem road, and Kvikkjokk, at the end of the Jokkmokk–Kvikkjokk road (118km), provide access.

Understand Sweden

Sweden Today

A generally prosperous and peaceful country, Sweden seems able to weather its storms rather easily. Of course, there are always internal tensions and occasional threats to smooth sailing, whether they're economic challenges or political battles. But, overall, a visitor to Sweden gets the sense that the system works quite well. The Swedish word *lagom* means not too much and not too little, but just right. Sweden strives to embody this concept. It's not perfect, but it's reassuringly consistent.

Best on Film

The Seventh Seal (1957) Ingmar Bergman pits mankind against Death in a cosmic chess game.
Let the Right One In (2008) Tomas Alfredson's icy, preteen take on the vampire romance is palpably set in Norrland.
Together (2000) Lukas Moodysson aims his lens at a Swedish commune in 1975.
I Am Curious (Yellow) (1967) Vilgot Sjöman's hugely influential political satire took swings at the young king.
Songs from the Second Floor (2000) Roy Andersson's bleak meditation on modern humanity.

Best in Music

Greatest Hits (ABBA; 1975) Pure pop gold and still Sweden's biggest musical export.
Robyn Is Here (Robyn; 1997) Two top-10 Billboard singles.
Writer's Block (Peter Bjorn and John; 2006) Indie rock band strikes a chord with an international audience.
Verkligen (Kent; 1996) Beloved alt-rock band from Eskilstuna.
Look Sharp! (Roxette; 1988) The pop duo's second album was a smash hit.
'Heartbeats' (José González; 2003) Swedish artist of Argentinean descent hits No. 1 with a song originally by (also Swedish) the Knife.

People & Immigration

Sweden's population is relatively small given the size of the country – its nearly 10 million people are spread across the third-largest country in Western Europe, creating one of the lowest population densities on the continent. Most Swedes live in the large cities of Stockholm, Gothenburg, Malmö and Uppsala. About 30,000 Finnish speakers form a substantial minority in the northeast, near Torneälven. The interior of Norrland is sparsely populated.

Swedish culture strongly values socially progressive ideas such as gender and racial equality, equal rights for gay people, a free press and free expression, transparency in government, environmental protection and workers' rights. At the same time, racial and religious tensions have increased in recent years, as the number of foreign-born Swedes has grown – state statistics show that crimes against Muslims jumped by nearly 90% between 2012 and 2015. Currently around 15% of the population was born outside Sweden.

Equality is a straightforward enough goal in a small, homogenous society, but Sweden's relatively sudden diversity has required some adjustment, and it hasn't always gone smoothly. Resistance to immigration by fringe groups and far-right political parties has led to some ugly clashes; demonstrations by white-supremacist and neo-Nazi groups have become increasingly visible. Prime Minister Stefan Löfven made a public statement against the rise of neo-Nazi movements in Sweden in 2017, calling on Swedes not to tolerate fascist views.

Sweden first opened its borders to mass immigration during WWII. At the time it was a closed society, and new arrivals were initially expected to assimilate and 'become Swedish'. But in 1975 parliament adopted a new set of policies that formally recognised the freedom to preserve and celebrate traditional native cultures.

Sweden has been a leader in welcoming immigrants and refugees from Middle Eastern and African countries. In 2014, the Swedish government announced that it would take unlimited numbers of Syrian refugees for permanent residence.

Political Leadership

The government is currently being steered by a coalition of the Social Democrats and the Green Party. The second-largest party are the Moderates, whose former leader Fredrik Reinfeldt was the previous prime minister. The far-right nationalist Sweden Democrats are the third-largest party in Parliament; other parties have been steadfastly unwilling to work with them.

In 2017, Social Democrat leader Stefan Löfven – prime minister since 2014 – faced outrage in the wake of a scandal surrounding an IT security breach. Though many expected his entire government to resign and for snap elections to be called, the prime minister instead reshuffled his cabinet and managed to maintain stability. But the near-disaster revealed a lack of confidence in the leadership.

Löfven said he would seek to continue as Sweden's prime minister during the 2018 general election. Views on immigration – whether it should be restricted or kept relatively open – are now the number one factor as Sweden's many political parties and coalitions grapple for power.

Strain on the System

Despite its middle-way steadiness over the long term, recently Sweden has seen changes in the economy and the political mood that have led some people to question their assumptions. For decades the country was viewed by left-leaning outsiders as an almost utopian model of a socialist state, a successful experiment that gave hope to progressives everywhere. This is still more or less true. Inevitably, though, as the country has grown, it has had to adjust to modern realities – both economic and socio-political – and some cracks have begun to appear in the facade.

Between 2012 and 2015, Sweden granted asylum to 101,925 refugees. The influx peaked in 2015, when Sweden took in nearly 163,000 new asylum-seekers. The following year, though the population grew by 140,000, only 29,000 were asylum-seekers, a result of the government's late-2015 decision to limit immigration, according to Sweden.se. Sweden has welcomed more refugees per capita in the wake of the Syrian Civil War than any other European country. This growth has caused some political leaders, particularly on the far right, to suggest the country's resources are being stretched too far. Still, a Eurobarometer survey from 2016 showed that 64 percent of Swedes have a positive view of immigration from outside the EU; the EU average is 34 percent.

POPULATION: **9.9 MILLION**

GDP: **$511 BILLION**

GDP PER CAPITA: **$56,319**

UNEMPLOYMENT: **7.4%**

ADULT LITERACY: **99%**

if Sweden were 100 people

89 would be Swedish
3 would be Finn & Sami (Lapp)
1 would be Yugoslav
1 would be Iranian
6 would be Other

belief systems
(% of population)

83 Church of Sweden

17 Other

population per sq km

SWEDEN   NORWAY   DENMARK

 ≈ 15 people

History

Sweden has a dramatic history whose earliest events – from geological uprisings to widespread religious conversions – can still be seen shaping the country today. Most people have at least a passing familiarity with stories of the Vikings and the Norse gods, but there are equally vivid tales of intrigue and drama throughout Sweden's development, in both the political and the royal spheres. Learning a little about the events that shaped the country's history will only add to a visitor's experience of it today.

The First Arrivals

In the grip of the last ice age Sweden was an inhospitable place, but perhaps less so than Siberia, where the first hunter-gatherers originated 10,000 to 6000 years ago. As the ice retreated, tribes from central Europe migrated into the south of Sweden, and ancestors of the Sami people hunted wild reindeer into the northern regions.

Between 1800 BC and 500 BC, Bronze Age cultures blossomed. Huge Bronze Age burial mounds, such as Kiviksgraven in Österlen, suggest that powerful chieftains had control over spiritual and temporal matters.

After 500 BC, the Iron Age brought about technological advances, demonstrated by archaeological finds of agricultural tools, graves and primitive furnaces, but as the climate worsened again, the downturn in agriculture coincided with the arrival of the Svea – powerful tribes who ended up settling much of Sweden. By AD 600, the Svea people of the Mälaren valley (just west of Stockholm) had gained supremacy, and their kingdom, Svea Rike, gave the country of Sweden its name: Sverige.

Top Five World Heritage Sites in Sweden

Hanseatic town of Visby (p235)

Naval port of Karlskrona (p201)

Gammelstad church village (p264), Luleå

Höga Kusten (p256)

Laponia (p289)

Vikings & Christians

Scandinavia's greatest impact on world history probably occurred during the Viking Age, when hardy pagan Norsemen set sail for other shores. The Swedish Vikings were more inclined towards trade than their Norwegian or Danish counterparts, but their reputation as fearsome warriors was fully justified. At home it was the height of paganism; Viking leaders claimed descent from Freyr, 'God of the World', and celebrations at Uppsala involved human sacrifices.

TIMELINE	**10,000– 6000 BC**	**1800–500 BC**	**500 BC**
	Ice sheets melt and hunter-gatherer tribes, the ancestors of the Sami, follow reindeer into a newly uncovered Sweden. An early human settlement is founded near Arjeplog.	*Hällristningar* (petroglyphs) illustrating Bronze Age beliefs appear in many parts of Sweden, such as Dalsland and Bohuslän. The sun, hunting scenes and ships are common themes.	The runic alphabet arrives, probably from the Germanic region. It is used to carve inscriptions onto monumental rune stones (there are around 3000 in Sweden) well into medieval times.

TRACING YOUR (SWEDISH) ANCESTORS

Around a million people emigrated from Sweden to the USA and Canada between 1850 and 1930. Many of their 12 million descendants are now returning in search of their roots.

Luckily, detailed parish records of births, deaths and marriages have been kept since 1686 and there are *landsarkivet* (regional archives) around the country. The national archive is Riksarkivet (www.riksarkivet.se), in Stockholm; its newly digitised system allows you to search the National Archives Database and to use SVAR, the Digital Research Room.

Utvandrarnas Hus (p219) in Växjö is a particularly good museum dedicated to the mass departure.

Also worth a look is *Tracing Your Swedish Ancestry,* by Nils William Olsson, a free do-it-yourself genealogical guide. Download the latest version from the New York Consulate-General of Sweden's website: www.swedenabroad.com/SelectImage/15063/tracingyour swedishancestry.pdf, or get it free from Amazon.com.

The Vikings sailed a new type of boat that was fast and highly manoeuvrable but sturdy enough for ocean crossings. Initial hit-and-run raids along the European coast were followed by major military expeditions, settlement and trade. The well-travelled Vikings settled part of the Slavic heartland, giving it the name 'Rus,' and ventured as far as Newfoundland, Constantinople (modern-day Istanbul) and Baghdad, setting up trade with the Byzantine Empire.

Christianity only took hold when Sweden's first Christian king, Olof Skötkonung (c 968–1020), was baptised. By 1160, King Erik Jedvarsson (Sweden's patron saint, St Erik) had virtually destroyed the last remnants of paganism.

Rise of the Swedish State

By the 13th century, royal power disintegrated over succession squabbles between the Erik and Sverker families, with medieval statesman Birger Jarl (1210–66) rising to fill the gap.

His son, King Magnus Ladulås (1240–90), granted numerous privileges to the Church and the nobility, including freedom from taxation. At the same time, he forbade the aristocracy from living off the peasantry when moving from estate to estate.

After deposing Magnus' eldest son, Birger (1280–1321), for fratricide, the nobility looked to Norway for their next ruler, choosing the infant grandson of King Haakon V. When Haakon died without leaving a male heir, the kingdoms of Norway and Sweden were united (1319).

The increasingly wealthy Church began to show its might in the 13th and 14th centuries, commissioning monumental buildings such as the

The leather jacket (complete with original blood-stains) that Gustav II Adolf was wearing when killed in battle, as well as his stuffed horse Streiff, can be seen in the Livrustkammaren in Stockholm.

98	c 800	1008	1252
The Svea tribe that effectively rules what is now Sweden is first mentioned by Tacitus; they are referred to as Suinoes.	Birka, founded on Björkö (an island in Mälaren lake), becomes a powerful Svea trading centre. Byzantine and Arab coins have been found here, confirming the existence of trade routes.	Sweden's first Christian king, Olof Skötkonung, is baptised at St Sigfrid's Well in Husaby, but worship continues in Uppsala's pagan temple until at least 1090.	The city of Stockholm is founded by king's statesman Birger Jarl, who has been running the country since 1229.

Domkyrka (Cathedral) in Linköping (founded 1250) and Scandinavia's largest Gothic cathedral in Uppsala (founded 1285).

However, in 1350 the rise of state and church endured a horrific setback when the Black Death swept through the country, carrying off around a third of the Swedish population.

The Birth & Death of a Union

The Black Death created a shortage of candidates for the throne. In 1364, the nobles installed Albrecht of Mecklenburg as their ruler but balked at his attempts to wield his own power. Their revolt was aided by Danish regent Margareta, and the resulting Union of Kalmar (1397) united Denmark, Norway and Sweden under one crown.

Erik of Pomerania, Margareta's nephew, held that crown until 1439, his rule marred by a constant struggle against the Hanseatic League – a group of well-organised merchants who established walled trading towns in Germany and maintained a strong presence in the young city of Stockholm.

Out of the chaos following Erik's deposition, Sten Sture the Elder (1440–1503) eventually emerged as 'Guardian of Sweden' in 1470, going on to fight and defeat an army of unionist Danes at the Battle of Brunkeberg (1471) in Stockholm.

In a move of retaliation that sounded the union's death knell, Christian II of Denmark invaded Sweden and killed the regent Sten Sture the Younger (1493–1520), adding a massacre in Stockholm's Gamla Stan to his list of accomplishments.

The Vasa Dynasty

The brutal 'Stockholm Bloodbath' sparked off an insurrection in 1520 under the leadership of the young nobleman Gustav Ericsson Vasa (1496–1560). Having failed to raise enough support, Gustav was fleeing for the Norwegian border when two exhausted skiers caught him up to tell him that the people had changed their minds. This legendary ski journey is celebrated every year in the Vasaloppet race between Sälen and Mora.

Gustav I ruled from 1523 to 1560, leaving behind a powerful, centralised nation state. He introduced the Reformation to Sweden and passed the power on to his descendants though the 1544 parliament act that made the monarchy hereditary.

After Gustav Vasa's death in 1560, bitter rivalry broke out among his sons. His eldest child, Erik XIV (1533–77), held the throne for eight years in a state of not-unjustified paranoia. After committing a trio of injudicious murders at Uppsala Slott, Erik was deposed by his half-brother Johan III (1537–92) and dispatched to the afterlife via poisoned pea soup at Örbyhus Slott.

Although not history textbooks, Vilhelm Moberg's four novels about 19th-century Swedish emigration are based on real people and bring this period to life. They're translated into English as *The Emigrants, Unto a Good Land, The Settlers* and *The Last Letter Home*.

1350s	1434	1439–70	1520
Following the Black Death scourge, St Birgitta (1303–73) founds a nunnery and cathedral in Vadstena, which becomes Sweden's most important pilgrimage site.	High taxation imposed by the Kalmar Union to fund wars against the Hanseatic League make Erik of Pomerania deeply unpopular; the peasantry rise in the Engelbrekt revolt.	Following the short-lived replacement of Erik of Pomerania, succession struggles begin again: two powerful Swedish families, the unionist Oxenstiernas and the nationalist Stures, fight for supremacy.	After granting a full amnesty to Sture followers, Christian II goes back on his word: more than 80 nobles and clergy are arrested, tried and butchered in the 'Stockholm Bloodbath'.

The last of the male Vasa rulers, 17-year-old Gustav II Adolf (1594–1632), proved to be a military genius, recapturing southern parts of the country from Denmark and consolidating Sweden's control over the eastern Baltic. He was killed in battle on 6 November 1632, a day remembered for centuries in Sweden as a moment of national trauma.

Gustav II Adolf's daughter Kristina was still a child in 1632, and her regent continued her father's warlike policies. In 1654 Kristina abdicated in favour of her cousin Karl X Gustav, ending the Vasa dynasty.

Rise & Fall of the Swedish Empire

The zenith and collapse of the Swedish empire happened remarkably quickly. During Karl XI's reign, successful battles were waged against Denmark and Norway, the latter resulting in the seizure of Bohuslän, Härjedalen and Jämtland, and the empire reached its maximum size when Sweden established a short-lived American colony in what is now Delaware.

Inheritor of this huge and increasingly sophisticated country was 15-year-old King Karl XII (1681–1718), an overenthusiastic military adventurer who spent almost all of his reign at war. Karl XII cost Sweden its Latvian, Estonian and Polish territory, with the Swedish coast sustaining damaging attacks from Russia, and he perished by a mystery sniper's hand in 1718.

KRISTINA, QUEEN OF CONTROVERSY

Queen Kristina (1626–89) lived an eccentric and eventful life. Her father, Gustav II, expecting great things from her, instructed that the girl be raised as a prince. He then promptly went off and died in the Battle of Lützen, leaving his six-year-old successor and his country in the hands of the powerful Chancellor Oxenstierna.

Kristina received a boy's education, becoming fluent in six languages and skilled in the art of war, and she took her oath as king, not queen, earning her the nickname 'Girl King'. Childish spats with Oxenstierna increased as she grew older. After being crowned queen in 1644, she defied him even when he had the country's best interests at heart.

In 1649 Kristina made public her desire not to marry, and named her beloved cousin Karl X Gustav her heir to the throne. Kristina's ever-erratic behaviour culminated in her abdication in 1654. Disguised as a man, she rode through Denmark on horseback; tense relations between the two countries would not have allowed her true self safe passage. Kristina ended up in Rome, where she converted to Catholicism – a scandalous act on the part of a daughter of Protestantism's champion. She is one of only four women to be buried in the basilica of St Peter's in Rome.

A strong female character known for her bisexuality, in modern times Kristina has become a lesbian icon, while her cross-dressing has made her a favourite of the transgender community.

1523	1527	1563–70	1618–48
Gustav Vasa becomes the first Vasa king after the Kalmar Union between Denmark, Sweden and Norway breaks up; he marches into Stockholm and is crowned on 6 June, now the country's national day.	Reformation parliament passes a law that transfers the property of the Church to the state and places the Church under the state's direct control (repealed in 2000).	During the Vasa brothers' reigns, there are wars against Lübeck and Poland, and the Danes try and fail to reassert sovereignty over Sweden in the Northern Seven Years War.	Devout Lutheran Gustav II Adolf intervenes in the Thirty Years War between Protestants and Catholics, invading Poland and defeating his cousin King Sigismund III, but dying in battle in 1632.

MURDER MOST MYSTERIOUS

Assassination has been a common enough cause of death for so many Swedish heads of state as to qualify as 'natural causes'. King Karl XII (1681–1718) was mysteriously shot dead while inspecting his troops during a winter siege in Trondheim, Norway. While Norwegians take credit for the killing, the theory that Karl XII had been shot by one of his own men, disgruntled because the king's many military losses cost Sweden its rank as a great power, has persisted among historians.

Less than a century later, in March 1792, King Gustav III was assassinated at a masked ball in the foyer of the Royal Opera House. The assassination – later the subject of a Verdi opera – was the result of a conspiracy hatched by nobles alarmed at the king's autocratic ways. His principal assailant, Jacob Johan Anckarström, was stripped of his lands and titles before being flogged and decapitated.

This trend of unsolved high-profile deaths has continued to the present day. In 1986, Social Democrat Prime Minister Olof Palme (1927–86) was shot dead by a mystery man as he walked home from the cinema with his wife on a frigid February night. Palme's wife, who behaved strangely throughout the murder investigation, eventually identified Christer Pettersson as the murderer. Pettersson was acquitted on appeal, as there was a great deal of doubt as to whether the murderer could have been accurately identified from a single glimpse on a dark night. Questions remain unanswered as to why the police investigation was so bungled and why strong leads weren't followed up, and conspiracy theories abound. Palme's murderer is still at large, though in recent years some evidence has emerged that implicates the South African secret service, which may have targeted Palme due to his strong anti-apartheid stance.

In 2003 Foreign Minister Anna Lindh (1957–2003) was fatally stabbed while shopping at the Nordiska Kompaniet department store in central Stockholm. Her murderer, Mia-jailo Mijailovič, was caught with the help of DNA evidence; the attack doesn't appear to have been politically motivated.

The Age of Liberty

In the 18th century, intellectual enlightenment streaked ahead and Sweden produced a number of celebrated writers, philosophers and scientists. Anders Celsius gave his name to the temperature scale, Carl Scheele discovered chlorine and Carl von Linné (Linnaeus) was the great botanist who developed theories about plant reproduction.

Gustav III (1746–92) was a popular and sophisticated king who granted freedom of worship and was surprisingly successful in the maritime battle in the Gulf of Finland against Russia in 1790. Still, his costly foreign policy earned him enemies in the aristocracy and ultimately led to his assassination.

1658	1697–1718	1789	1792
The last remaining parts of southern Sweden still in Danish hands are handed over at the Peace of Roskilde after Swedish troops successfully invade Denmark across the frozen Kattegatt.	Karl XII holds the throne. Russia, Poland and Denmark form an anti-Sweden alliance; the Swedish army is crushed by the Russians at Poltava in 1709 – a battle that ends Sweden's time as a superpower.	The coup d'etat mounted by Gustav III curtails parliamentary powers and reintroduces absolute rule.	At a masked ball in 1792, Gustav III is surrounded by conspirators and shot in the back of the head by Jacob Johan Anckarström, the captain of the king's regiment.

The rule of his son Gustav IV Adolf (1778–1837), forced to abdicate after getting drawn into the Napoleonic Wars and permanently losing Finland (one-third of Sweden's territory) to Russia, ended unrestricted royal power with the 1809 constitution.

More or less out of the blue, Napoleon's marshal Jean-Baptiste Bernadotte (1763–1844) was invited by a nobleman, Baron Mörner, to take the Swedish throne – which he did, along with the name Karl Johan. Judiciously changing sides, he led Sweden, allied with Britain, Prussia and Russia, against France and Denmark.

Sweden (Not) at War

Sweden declared itself neutral in 1912, and remained so throughout the bloodshed of WWI. Swedish neutrality during WWII was ambiguous: letting German troops march through to occupy Norway and selling iron ore to both warring sides certainly tarnished Sweden's image, leading to a crisis of conscience at home as well as international criticism.

On the other hand, Sweden was a haven for refugees from Finland, Norway, Denmark and the Baltic states; downed Allied air crew who escaped the Gestapo; and many thousands of Jews who escaped persecution and death.

Beyond the Wars

After WWII and throughout the 1950s and '60s, the Social Democrats continued with the creation of *folkhemmet* (the welfare state). The idea of a socially conscious society with financial security for all began with the coalition of 1936 between the Social Democrats and the Farmers' Party and introduced unemployment benefits, child care, paid holidays and much more. The standard of living for ordinary Swedes rose rapidly, with poverty virtually eradicated.

Sweden began to take an active (peaceful) role in world affairs in the second half of the 20th century, offering asylum to those fleeing from political oppression worldwide. Prime Minister Olof Palme (1927–86) was deeply involved in questions of democracy, disarmament and the developing world when he was assassinated on the streets of Stockholm in 1986.

In the last 30 years, Sweden has become an affluent country with a strong economy and one of the most comprehensive welfare systems in the world – though its systems are being tested by massive immigration. The country suffered greatly from economic recession and unemployment in the early '90s, and its export-led economy continues to be vulnerable to global economic depression. Cuts have had to be made to the welfare state over the last two decades, and many Swedes feel that the country's immigration policies add to the strain. They argue that the dramatic increase in population renders the existing welfare system

The Vikings, by Magnus Magnusson, is an extremely readable history book, covering the storied travellers' achievements in Scandinavia (including Sweden), as well as their wild deeds around the world.

Queen Kristina was immortalised in August Strindberg's 1901 play; her life was also chronicled in Veronica Buckley's biography *Christina, Queen of Sweden,* and she was fictionalised in the 1933 film *Queen Christina,* starring Greta Garbo.

1814	1921	1944	1953
After Napoleon's defeat, Sweden forces Denmark to swap Norway for Swedish Pomerania. The Norwegians object, and Swedish troops occupy most of the country, the forced union lasting until 1905.	In the interwar period, a Social Democrat–Liberal coalition government takes control and introduces reforms, including an eight-hour working day and universal suffrage for adults aged over 23.	Diplomat Raoul Wallenberg rescues nearly 100,000 Hungarian Jews from the SS by hiding them in Swedish 'neutral houses' in Budapest.	Dag Hammarskjöld is elected Secretary-General of the UN. Under his guidance, the UN resolves the 1956 Suez Crisis.

unsustainable – a view that has led to increased racial tension and more frequent demonstrations and counter-protests.

On the international front, Sweden opted to join the EU in 1995 by a very narrow margin and, while nonaligned militarily, Sweden's troops continue to take part in numerous NATO peacekeeping missions.

Emigration & Industrialisation

Industry arrived late in Sweden (during the second half of the 19th century), but when it did come it eventually transformed the country from one of Western Europe's poorest to one of its richest.

Significant Swedish inventions, including dynamite (Alfred Nobel) and the safety match (patented by Johan Edvard Lundstrom), coupled with efficient steel-making and timber exports and a thriving textiles industry, added to a growing economy and the rise of a new middle class.

Coupled with discontent in the countryside and exacerbated by famine early in the process, industrialisation led to enormous social changes – from mass emigration to the rapid growth of labour and social movements such as unionisation.

Political Shake-up

The Social Democrats, who held a majority of the government (and therefore shaped national policy, most notably the famous 'cradle to grave' welfare state) for most of the past 85 years, have begun to see their influence wane. The first big blow came in 2006, when the long-entrenched party lost its leadership position in the Swedish parliament. The centre-right Alliance Party (made up of four centre-right parties – the Moderates, the Liberals, the Christian Democrats and the Centre Party) won the election, with Prime Minister Fredrik Reinfeldt campaigning on a 'work first' platform. Reinfeldt's government lowered tax rates and trimmed certain benefits, hoping to jump-start the economy and reduce unemployment.

The 2010 election saw the Social Democrats' worst result since 1921: they won only slightly more than 30% of the seats in parliament. The Alliance Party won again (173 of the 349 seats), meaning Reinfeldt continued as prime minister. Unemployment remained high, though, and by 2012 the Social Democrats had regained some favour. In the September 2014 general election, Reinfeldt failed to secure a third term as prime minister; instead, Social Democrat leader Stefan Löfven stepped in, leading a coalition government with the Green Party.

In that election's most startling result, the far-right nationalist Sweden Democrats doubled their proportion of the vote, thereby becoming the third-largest party in parliament. This caused immediate friction as the other parties were unwilling to work with the Sweden Democrats.

In 1979, hundreds of Swedes called in sick to work on account of 'being gay' to protest homosexuality being treated as a medical disorder at the time.

In 2009, experts sought to establish the chemical composition of the bullet that killed King Karl XII and solve the 18th-century whodunnit once and for all. Sadly, permission to have his body exhumed was denied, as it had already been plucked from its resting place three times since 1917.

1995	2001	2014	2017
Reluctantly, Sweden joins the European Union.	Parliament votes 260 to 48 against abolition of the monarchy, even though the monarch ceased to have any political power in 1974.	Umea is named a European Capital of Culture, with the spotlight falling on northern Sweden and Sami art and culture.	Five people are killed and several injured when an Uzbek asylum-seeker with ties to ISIS hijacks a truck and drives it into a crowd outside a Stockholm department store.

Food & Drink

Sweden has come a long way from the days of all-beige fish and potato platters. Not only has immigration and EU influence introduced new flavours to the Swedish menu, a wave of bold young chefs has been experimenting with traditional Swedish fare and melding it with various other influences. The result is an exciting dining scene on par with some of the best food cities in Europe.

Classic Cuisine

Traditional Swedish cuisine is based on simple, everyday dishes known generally as *husmanskost* (basic home cooking). The most famous example of this, naturally, is Swedish meatballs. Other classic *husmanskost* dishes, largely built around seafood and potatoes, include various forms of pickled and fried herring, cured salmon, shrimp, roe and *pytt i panna* (potato hash served with sliced beets and a fried egg on top), which may be the ultimate comfort food. Open-face shrimp sandwiches are everywhere, piled high with varying degrees of art. The most thorough introduction to all the staples of Swedish cooking is the smörgåsbord, commonly available during the winter holidays.

One speciality food that not many visitors (and not all that many Swedes, either) take to immediately is *surströmming*. It's a canned, fermented Baltic herring opened and consumed ritually once a year, during late August and early September. It may be wrapped in *tunnbröd* (soft, thin, unleavened bread like a tortilla) with boiled potato, onions and other condiments, all washed down with ample amounts of *snaps* (a distilled alcoholic beverage, such as vodka or aquavit). *Surströmming* may be an acquired taste, but it has a legion of hard-core fans, mostly in northern Sweden. It even boasts its own festival in the village of Alfta. Cans of it make excellent souvenirs, as long as you wrap them well to avoid the truly nightmarish possibility of a leak into your suitcase. (And check with your airline first – flying with *surströmming* is not always allowed.)

The prevalence of preserved grub harks back to a time when Swedes had little choice but to store their spring and summer harvests for the long, icy winter. The landscape similarly influences menus in various parts of the country; you'll find regional specialities wherever you travel, from Västerbotten pie to saffron pancakes (both delicious!).

Wild game features strongly in Swedish cuisine, particularly in the northern part of the country. Traditional Sami cooking relies heavily on reindeer, whether cured, dried, roasted or preserved as sausage or jerky. Elk and moose are also fairly common. Particularly in Sami cooking, game is often served with rich sauces that incorporate wild berries.

Other northern specialities include *ripa* (ptarmigan) and Arctic char, a cousin of salmon and trout. The mild-flavoured char makes a seasonal appearance on menus all over Sweden in summer, and is absolutely worth a try, especially for the various inventive methods of preparing it. A chefs' favourite, the sturdy fish is a blank canvas that can handle all kinds of interesting treatments.

Speaking of berries, another uniquely Scandinavian taste is that of the *hjortron* (cloudberry). These grow in the marshes of Norrland and look a bit like pale raspberries, but their flavour is almost other-worldly, and Swedes consider them a delicacy. They're often served as a warm sauce over ice cream. If they strike your fancy, you'll find any number of places selling jars of cloudberry jam to take home. (There's also a sweet *hjortron* liqueur.)

Other traditional foods worth trying include *toast skagen* (toast with bleak roe, crème fraiche and chopped red onion), the classic *köttbullar och potatis* (meatballs and potatoes, usually served with lingonberry jam, known as *lingonsylt*), and *nässelsoppa* (nettle soup, traditionally served with hard-boiled eggs). Pea soup and pancakes are traditionally dished up on Thursday. Seafood staples include caviar, gravad or rimmad lax (cured salmon), and the ubiquitous *sill* (herring), eaten smoked, fried or pickled and often accompanied by Scandi trimmings such as capers, mustard and onion. Tucking into a plate of freshly fried Baltic herring with new potatoes and lingonberry sauce from an outdoor table overlooking the sea is a quintessential – and easily achieved – Swedish experience.

Swedes are devoted to their daily coffee ritual, *fika,* which inevitably also includes a pastry – often *kanelbullar* (cinnamon buns) or *kardemummabullar* (cardamom rolls). Almond paste (marzipan) is a common ingredient in pastries, such as the princess torte, a delicate cake with a lime-green marzipan shell commonly available at bakeries. Gourmet *konditori* (old-fashioned bakery-cafes) and cafes offer their own variations on all the standard cakes and cookies – best to sample several.

Contemporary Tendencies

Essentially, contemporary Swedish cuisine melds global influences with local produce and innovation: think baked wood pigeon with potato-and-apple hash or cauliflower 'cornet' with white chocolate and caviar. Locals have rediscovered the virtues of their own pantry. The result is an intense passion for seasonal, home-grown ingredients, whether apples from Kivik or bleak roe from Kalix. Equally important is the seasonality of food; expect succulent berries in spring, artichokes and crayfish in summer, and hearty truffles and root vegetables in the colder months.

Another growing obsession is a predilection for sustainable farming, small-scale producers and organic produce. Increasingly, restaurants and cafes pride themselves on serving organically grown and raised food, as well as actively supporting ethical, ecofriendly agricultural practices. Practically all the coffee served in big chain hotels is certified organic

ESSENTIAL FOOD & DRINK

Scandinavian cuisine, once viewed as meatballs, herring and little else, is now at the forefront of modern gastronomy. New Nordic cuisine showcases local produce, blending traditional techniques and contemporary experimentation.

Swedish menu essentials:

Coffee To fit in, eight or nine (OK, four) cups a day is about right; luckily, the region's cafes are a delight.

Reindeer & Game Expect to see reindeer and other delicious game on the menu, especially up north in Sami cooking.

Alcohol Beer is everywhere, and improving; but try a shot of *brännvin* (aquavit) with your pickled herring, too.

Fish Salmon and cod are ubiquitous and delicious, and smoked, cured, pickled or fried herring is fundamental. Tasty lake fish include Arctic char and pike-perch.

(labelled *krav* or *ekologisk*), for example, as is most of what you'll find alongside it on the breakfast buffet.

Not surprisingly, this newfound culinary savvy has affected the tourist trade. Gastro-themed itineraries and activities are on the rise, with everything from Gotland truffle hunts to west-coast lobster safaris, while numerous tourist boards stock culinary guides to their respective regions.

Festive Flavours

Around Christmas, many restaurants start offering a *julbord*, a particularly gluttonous version of Sweden's world-famous smörgåsbord buffet. Among the usual delicacies of herring, gravlax, meatballs, short ribs and *blodpudding* (blood pudding) are seasonal gems including baked ham with mustard sauce and *Janssons frestelse* (hearty casserole of sweet cream, potato, onion and anchovy). *Julmust* (sweet dark-brown soft drink that foams like a beer when poured) and *glögg* (warm spiced wine) are also Yuletide staples. The best accompaniment to a warm cup of *glögg,* available at kiosks everywhere in winter, is a *pepparkaka* (gingerbread biscuit) or a *lussekatt* (saffron bun).

During Sweden's short, intense summers, many people hit the countryside for lazy holidays and alfresco noshing. Summer lunch favourites include various *inlagd sill* (pickled herring) with *knäckebröd* (crispbread), strong cheese like the crumbly *Västerbottens ost,* boiled potatoes, diced chives and cream, strawberries, plus a finger or two of *snaps* and some light beer 'to help the fish swim down to the stomach'. Towards the end of summer, Swedes celebrate (or commiserate) its passing with *kräftskivor* (crayfish parties), eating *kräftor* boiled with dill, drinking *snaps* and singing *snapsvisor* (drinking songs).

For those with a sweet tooth, the lead-up to Lent means one thing: the *semla* bun. A wickedly decadent concoction of a wheat-flour bun crammed with whipped cream and almond paste, it was traditionally eaten on *fettisdagen* (Fat Tuesday). These days, it undermines diets as early as January.

Drinks

In the early days, when Stockholm was a rough port town full of stumbling sailors, alcohol taxes were levied according to where you happened to be when you fell down drunk or threw up. (These days, the same method can be used to decide which bars to frequent – or avoid.) Liquor laws and customs have changed a bit since then, motivated not least by Sweden's need to conform more closely to EU standards. But there are still a few guidelines to navigate when pursuing adult beverages in Sweden.

Öl (beer) is ranked by alcohol content; the stronger the beer, the higher its price and, generally speaking, the more flavour it has. Light beers (*lättöl;* less than 2.25%) and 'folk' beers (*folköl;* 2.25% to 3.5%) account for about two-thirds of all beer sold in Sweden; these can be bought in supermarkets. Medium-strength beer (*mellanöl;* 3.5% to 4.5%) and strong beer (*starköl;* over 4.5%) can be bought only at outlets of the state-owned alcohol store, Systembolaget, or in bars and restaurants. 'Systemet', as it's often called, is also the only place (other than bars and restaurants) to buy hard liquor or wine.

Much like North American domestic brews, the everyday Swedish beer produced by mass breweries like Falcon, Pripps and Spendrups is notable only for its lack of distinctive flavour. Happily, the range of good microbrews available has drastically improved in recent years. (Look for Jämtlands brewery's Fallen Angel bitter, anything from Nynäshamns Ångbryggeri or the Wisby line from Gotlands brewery.) Imports from the rest of Europe are also much easier to find than in pre-EU days. In bars and restaurants, domestic brews such as Spendrups cost anywhere from 50kr to 70kr a pint, imported beer closer to 75kr, and wine or mixed drinks around 98kr to 120kr. Pear and apple ciders are also common, frequently in light-alcohol or alcohol-free versions.

Sweden's trademark spirit is *brännvin,* of which Absolut Vodka is the most recognisable example. A particularly Scandinavian subsection of *brännvin,* called aquavit and drunk as *snaps,* is a fiery and strongly flavoured drink that's usually distilled from potatoes and spiced with herbs. (A small shot of aquavit is sometimes called a *nubbe,* and it's often accompanied by drinking songs.)

The legal drinking age in Sweden is 18 years; this applies to buying beer in grocery stores and any kind of alcohol in bars and restaurants. The minimum age to buy alcohol at a Systembolaget store is 20 years. Many bars and clubs impose higher age limits for admission.

The beverage you're most likely to encounter in Sweden isn't even alcoholic. Coffee is the unofficial national drink, with an ever-increasing number of cafes ditching the percolated stuff for Italian-style espresso. The daily ritual of coffee and a pastry *(fika)* is an easy and rewarding one to adopt during your visit. (Tea is also readily available.) And *saft* is cordial commonly made from lingonberries, blueberries or elderflowers, though the word can refer to ordinary apple or orange juice as well.

Practical Info

Where to Eat

Hotels and hostels offer *frukost* (breakfast) buffets that typically include yoghurt and cereal, several types of bread, pastries, crispbread and/or rolls, with *pålägg* (toppings) including butter, sliced cheese, boiled eggs, sliced meat, liver pâté, Kalles caviar (an iconic caviar spread), pickled herring, sliced cucumber and marmalade. Several coffee chains (Wayne's Coffee, Espresso House) dot the landscape, offering reliably decent cappuccinos and lattes along with breakfast pastries, salads and sandwiches.

A hearty lunch has long been a mainstay of the workforce, with cafes and restaurants usually serving a weekday lunch special (or a choice of several) called *dagens rätt* at a fixed price (typically 85kr to 125kr) between 11.30am and 2pm Monday to Friday. It's a practice originally supported and subsidised by the Swedish government with the goal of keeping workers happy and efficient, and it's still one of the most economical ways to sample top-quality Swedish cooking. The *dagens rätt* usually includes a main course, salad, beverage, bread and butter, and coffee or a light beer or soda.

For a lighter lunch, head to a *konditori*, where staples include substantial pastries and the delectable *smörgås* (open sandwich), an artfully arranged creation usually topped with greens, shrimp or salmon, roe, boiled egg and mustard-dill sauce. Most cafes and coffee shops these days serve hearty, good-value salads that include grains or pasta with lettuce and vegies in an enormous bowl (typically costing 85kr to 100kr).

Etiquette

For the most part, table manners in Sweden are the same as those in the rest of Europe. On very formal occasions, wait for the host to welcome you to the table before beginning to eat or drink. Aside from a proper *skål,* don't clink glasses (it's considered vulgar), and in formal settings refrain from sipping your wine outside of toasts until the host has declared that everyone may drink freely.

Make sure you're wearing clean socks when dining in someone's home, as you'll generally be expected to take off your shoes in the foyer. (It's not uncommon to bring along a pair of house shoes to change into.)

RESOURCES

Culinary Skåne (http://matupplevelser.skane.org/en) A network of restaurants and growers that produces a regional guide to produce, cuisine and epicurean events.

Swedish Institute (www.sweden.se) Provides a detailed discussion of Swedish food; follow the 'Lifestyle' tab.

Äkta Sylt (www.aktasylt.se) A website devoted to lingonberry jam, its preservation and marketing; in Swedish.

Vår Kokbok A classic Swedish cookbook from the '50s, akin to Betty Crocker's books in the US.

Swedes are typically quite punctual, so make an effort to arrive at the agreed-upon time rather than 'fashionably late'. (It's not unheard-of to arrive several minutes early and walk around the block until the appointed time, rather than risking a late arrival.) And don't go empty-handed; a bottle of wine or flowers will make the right impression.

Cheap Eats

Street snacks are the cheapest, quickest way to fill up in Sweden, particularly in cities but also on beaches, along motorways and in campgrounds. A snack kiosk with a grill is known as a *gatukök* (literally, 'street kitchen'). In the world of Swedish street food, hot dogs reign supreme – the basic model is called a *grillad korv med bröd,* grilled sausage with bread (hot dog in a bun), although you can also ask for it boiled *(kokt)*. Adventurous souls can request a mind-boggling variety of things done to the *korv,* chiefly involving rolling it up in flatbread with accompaniments from shrimp salad to mashed potatoes or coleslaw to fried onions. Kebab restaurants are another good bet for tasty, quick and cheap eats. And the range of available street foods continues to grow – it's now easier to find anything from churros to Thai.

Opening Times

Restaurants generally open from 11am to 2pm for lunch, and from 5pm until 10pm for dinner. Cafes, bakeries and coffee shops, as well as more casual restaurants, are likely to be open all day, from around 8am until 6pm.

Tipping

Tipping in Sweden has been described as 'totally random' – it's becoming a little more common, though it isn't expected outside of fine-dining restaurants. A service cost is always figured into the bill, but if you've had excellent service, a 10% to 15% tip is a suitable complement.

Self-Catering

Easily found in Swedish towns and villages, the main supermarket chains are ICA, Coop Konsum and Hemköp. Plastic carrier bags cost 5kr at the cashier.

Supermarkets across Sweden have prepared foods for quick snacks, but making your own meals is easy if you're hostelling or camping. Produce in standard supermarkets is fine but you'll be better off seeking out fresh, seasonal fruit and vegetables at market squares such as Hötorget in Stockholm as well as at rural farm shops and roadside stands.

Vegetarians & Vegans

Vegetarian and vegan restaurants and buffets are common in cities, and veg-friendly options exist in nearly all restaurants even in rural areas.

People & Culture

As is true of most places, Sweden's pop culture reflects its people's collective psyche – in this case, with an enthusiastic embrace of both the grim and the frivolous. Swedish humour is a quirky thing indeed; it can be easily overlooked by the untrained eye, or even misperceived as grumpiness. Swedish literature and cinema tend to favour a weighty, Gothic sense of drama blended with gallows humour and stark aesthetics – in other words, the opposite of its best-known pop music.

The National Psyche

Blonde, blue-eyed, cold and reserved: while these four elements may make up the prevailing stereotype of Swedes, the reality is, perhaps unsurprisingly, much more complex and contradictory. Dark hair, impish stature and random acts of friendliness are not as uncommon as you may think, while a widespread passion for travel and trends can make for curious locals and enlightening conversations.

Two vital concepts in the typical Swedish mindset are *lagom* and *ordning och reda*. *Lagom* means 'just right' – not too little, not too much. A good example is *mellanöl* (medium ale) – it's not strong, but it's not as weak as a light ale. An exception to *lagom* is the smörgåsbord.

Ordning och reda connotes tidiness and order: everything in its proper place in the world. A good example is the queuing system; almost every transaction in Sweden requires participants to take a number and stand in line, which everyone does with the utmost patience. An exception to *ordning och reda* is Stockholm traffic.

Lifestyle

Swedes are a friendly sort. *Var så god* is a common phrase and carries all sorts of expressions of goodwill: 'Welcome', 'Please', 'Pleased to meet you', 'I'm happy to serve you', 'Thanks' and 'You're welcome'. And Swedes are so generous with their use of 'Thank you' (*tack*) that language texts make jokes about it.

It wasn't until the 1930s that urban Swedes surpassed the number of rural Swedes, and even the most seasoned urbanites commonly retain a strong affinity with nature. The rural *sommarstuga* (summer cottage) is almost de rigueur, at least as an aspiration; there are around 600,000 second homes in Sweden, and no Swede doesn't want a little wooden cottage in the country or on an archipelago island. As it is, Sweden boasts the highest number of holiday cottages per capita in the world, and most of the people you'll run across in campgrounds on summer holidays are Swedes themselves, enjoying the natural wonders of their own country.

Another common sight that surprises and delights many visitors to Sweden is the large number of men pushing baby strollers. Gender equality has advanced further in Sweden than in most countries. The government has a Minister for Integration and Gender Equality, as well as the Office of the Equal Opportunities Ombudsman, the latter ensuring that all employers and institutions of learning actively promote gender equality and prevent sexual discrimination. Women make up nearly half of parliament members in the Riksdag and enjoy enviable child-care services, and both parents are assured of plenty of child-care leave from employers.

The NBC-TV sitcom *Welcome to Sweden* offered a goofball take on the many eccentricities of Swedish culture from an outsider's point of view; created by Greg Poehler, the two-season series followed the various misadventures of an American who quits his job in New York and moves to Sweden to be with his Swedish fiancée and her family.

Swedish Cinema

Sweden led the way in the silent-film era of the 1920s with such masterpieces as *Körkarlen* (The Phantom Carriage), adapted from a novel by Selma Lagerlöf and directed by Mauritz Stiller. In 1967 came Vilgot Sjöman's notorious *I Am Curious (Yellow)*, a subtly hilarious sociopolitical film that got more attention outside Sweden for its X-rating than for its sharp commentary (and its in-jokes about the king, which foreign audiences, unsurprisingly, failed to get).

With a few exceptions, though, one man has largely defined modern Swedish cinema to the outside world: Ingmar Bergman. With deeply contemplative films such as *The Seventh Seal, Through a Glass Darkly* and *Persona*, the beret-topped director explored human alienation, the absence of god, the meaning of life, the certainty of death and other light-hearted themes. Love him or not, it's basically impossible to discuss or think about Swedish cinema without considering Bergman and his influence.

More recently, the Swedish towns of Trollhättan and Ystad have become film-making centres, the former drawing the likes of wunderkind director Lukas Moodysson, whose *Lilja 4-Ever, Show Me Love* and *Tillsammans* have all been both popular and critical hits. Moodysson went through a dark phase for a few years but found himself back on the international-cinema radar with 2014's *We Are the Best!*, a thrilling and heart-warming movie about three high-school girls in 1980s Stockholm who form a punk band out of spite. It's based on a semi-autobiographical graphic novel by Moodysson's wife, Coco, called *Aldrig Godnatt* ('Never Goodnight'), and it's an excellent portrait of the texture of urban Swedish life in this period.

Lebanese-born Josef Fares *(Jalla! Jalla!, Kopps, Zozo, Leo)* is part of a new guard of second-generation immigrant directors. Alongside Iranian-born directors Reza Bagher *(Wings of Glass)* and Reza Parsa *(Before the Storm)*, Fares has turned a spotlight on the immigrant experience in Sweden. His uncharacteristically dark 2007 feature, *Leo*, also marked Fares' on-screen debut.

FEEL-BAD SWEDISH FILMS

The Swedish film industry is active and varied, but most people associate it with the godfather of gloom, Ingmar Bergman. Many filmmakers have followed in his grim footsteps:

➡ *Songs from the Second Floor* (Roy Andersson; 2000) A post-apocalyptic urban nightmare in surreal slow motion; it's not for everyone.

➡ *Lilya 4-Ever* (Lukas Moodysson; 2002) A grim tale of human trafficking.

➡ *Ondskan* (Evil; Mikael Håfström; 2003) Violence at a boys' boarding school.

➡ *Zozo* (Josef Fares; 2005) A Lebanese orphan makes his way to Sweden alone, then has culture shock.

➡ *Darling* (Johan Kling; 2007) Harsh economic realities bring together a shallow, privileged party girl and a sweet old man in an unlikely friendship.

➡ *Let the Right One In* (Tomas Alfredson; 2008) An excellent, stylish, restrained take on the horror-film genre that gets at what it's like to be a lonely preteen in a cold, hostile world.

Another Swedish award-winner is director Roy Andersson, once dubbed a 'slapstick Ingmar Bergman'. His film *Du levande* (*You, the Living*) scooped up three prizes (including best picture) at Sweden's prestigious Guldbagge Awards in 2008.

That year also saw the well-deserved success of Tomas Alfredson's odd, quietly unsettling teenage-vampire story, *Let the Right One In,* based on a best-selling Swedish novel. Its American remake was also well received.

But of course the big news in contemporary Swedish cinema has been the film version of Stieg Larsson's runaway hit series of crime novels, starting with *The Girl with the Dragon Tattoo* (2009). Starring Michael Nyqvist and Noomi Rapace, the Swedish trilogy was a huge commercial success, and the first installment has been remade in English by director David Fincher, with Daniel Craig as journalist Mikael Blomkvist, mostly on location in Sweden.

Jazz is huge among Swedes; for a primer, look for records by Lars Gullin, Bernt Rosengren and Jan Johansson.

Swedish Literature

Historically, the best known of Sweden's artistic greats have been writers, chiefly the poet Carl Michael Bellman (1740–95), influential dramatist and author August Strindberg (1849–1912) and children's writer Astrid Lindgren (1907–2002).

During WWII some Swedish writers took a stand against the Nazis, including Eyvind Johnson (1900–76) with his *Krilon* trilogy, completed in 1943, and poet and novelist Karin Boye (1900–41), whose novel *Kallocain* was published in 1940. Vilhelm Moberg (1898–1973), a representative of 20th-century proletarian literature and a controversial social critic, won international acclaim with *Utvandrarna* (The Emigrants; 1949) and *Nybyggarna* (The Settlers; 1956).

Contemporary literary stars include playwright and novelist Per Olov Enquist (b 1934), who achieved international acclaim with his novel *Livläkarens besök* (The Visit of the Royal Physician; 2003), in which King Christian VII's physician conspires with the queen to seize power.

Readers interested in deepest Norrland, with its strange and uniquely remote vibe, should investigate the work of the late Torgny Lindgren, particularly his novel *Pölsan* (Hash; 2004), or the short stories in *Merab's Beauty* (1989).

Mikael Niemi's (b 1959) novel *Populärmusik från Vittula* (Popular Music; 2003), a coming-of-age story of a wannabe rock star in Sweden's remote north, became an international cult hit, as well as a 2004 film directed by Iranian-born Swedish director Reza Bagher.

Nonfiction author Sven Lindqvist (b 1932) is recognised for his hard-hitting, sometimes controversial titles. His most famous offering is arguably *Utrota varenda jävel* (Exterminate All the Brutes; 1992), exploring the Holocaust-like devastation European colonists wrought on Africa. More recently, his book *Terra Nullius* (2005, translated into English in 2007) is a powerful, moving history of colonial Australia and the attempted destruction of Aboriginal culture.

A Man Called Ove (2013) is a novel about a grumpy old man in a Swedish suburb who struggles (comically) to deal with the changes modernity has brought to his country and, more importantly, to his parking area; the book was a surprise hit domestically for journalist and blogger Fredrik Backman and has been widely translated. It offers an insightful view of life in a modern Swedish apartment community.

Crime Fiction

The massive success of the Millennium Trilogy, by the late journalist Stieg Larsson (he was the second-best-selling author in the world for 2008), has brought new and well-deserved attention to Swedish crime fiction, which was already a thriving genre domestically. *The Girl with* the *Dragon Tattoo* (2005) – originally entitled *Män som hatar kvinnor* (Men Who Hate Women) – is the tip of the iceberg when it comes to this genre; Swedish crime writers have a long and robust history.

A few names to start with include Håkan Nesser, whose early novels *The Mind's Eye* (1993) and *Woman with Birthmark* (1996) have at last been translated into English; and Sweden's best-known crime-fiction writer, Henning Mankell, whose novels are mostly set in Ystad and feature moody detective Kurt Wallander. Johan Theorin's quartet of mysteries (starting with *Echoes from the Dead,* 2008) is set on the island of Öland. Other writers to seek out include Karin Alvtegen (dubbed Sweden's 'queen of crime'), Kerstin Ekman, Camilla Läckberg and Jens Lapidus.

Must-Reads

One of the best ways to get inside the mind of a country is to read its top authors. Some popular works by Swedish authors include *The Long Ships* (1954) by Frans Gunnar Bengtsson, *The Wonderful Adventures of Nils* (1906–07) by Selma Lagerlöf, *The Emigrants* series (1949–59) by Vilhelm Moberg, *Markings* (1963–64) by Dag Hammarskjöld, *Röda Rummet* (1879) by August Strindberg and *The Evil* (1981) by Jan Guillou.

Swedish Music

Any survey of Swedish pop music should probably start with ABBA, the iconic, extravagantly outfitted winner of the 1974 Eurovision Song Contest (with 'Waterloo'). You can immerse yourself in ABBA completely at the Stockholm museum (p53) dedicated to the group and its history.

More current Swedish successes are pop icon Robyn, indie melody-makers Peter Björn & John, and the exquisitely mellow José González, whose cover of the Knife's track 'Heartbeats' catapulted the Gothenburg native to international stardom.

Other artists of note include the Field, aka Alex Wilner, and Kristian Matsson, the singer-songwriter who goes by the Tallest Man on Earth, as well as home-grown stalwarts such as the massively popular Kent, the Hives, the Shout Out Louds and Håkan Hellström, who is much lauded for his original renditions of classic Swedish melodies.

Swedish songwriters and producers are sought-after commodities: Denniz Pop and Max Martin have penned hits for pop divas such as Britney Spears and Jennifer Lopez, while Anders Bagge and Bloodshy & Avant (aka Christian Karlsson and Pontus Winnberg) co-created Madonna's 2005 album *Confessions on a Dance Floor.* DJ Avicii wrote or contributed to a handful of international hits in the 2010s.

Multiculturalism

Over the past couple of decades, immigration has noticeably altered the make-up of the Swedish population. Around 15% of Swedes today are foreign-born, and that number is on the upswing as immigration continues to expand. (More than one million Swedish citizens in 2016 were foreign-born.) Swedish musician José González, celebrity chef Marcus Samuelsson and film director Josef Fares are testament to Sweden's increasingly multicultural composition. Some 200 languages are now spoken in the country, as well as variations on the standard – the hip-hop crowd, for example, speaks a mishmash of slang, Swedish and foreign phrases that's been dubbed 'Rinkeby Swedish' after an immigrant-heavy Stockholm suburb.

As hip-hop artist Timbuktu (himself the Swedish-born son of a mixed-race American couple) once told the *Washington Post,* 'Sweden still has a very clear picture of what a Swede is. That no longer exists – the blond, blue-eyed physical traits. That's changing. But it still exists in the minds of some people'.

ABBA is the fourth-best-selling musical act in history, after Elvis, the Beatles and Michael Jackson – the group has sold more than 380 million records worldwide.

A total of 60,343 people were granted Swedish citizenship in 2016, according to Statistics Sweden – substantially more than in any previous year. Many of the newcomers were UK citizens coming to Sweden in the wake of Brexit. The largest group of new citizens were from Somalia, followed by Syria, Iraq, Poland, Thailand and Afghanistan.

Religion

Christianity arrived fairly late in Sweden and was preceded by a long-standing loyalty to Norse gods such as Odin, Thor and their warlike ilk. Some of the outer reaches of Sweden, particularly in the far north, were among the last areas in Europe to convert to Christianity.

According to the country's constitution, Swedish people have the right to practise any religion they choose. Complete separation of church and state took effect in 2000; prior to that, Evangelical Lutheranism was the official religion. There are also about 100,000 members of Christian Orthodox churches, 20,000 Jews and an estimated 100,000 Muslims in Sweden.

Only about 10% of Swedes regularly attend church services, but church marriages, funerals and communions are still popular.

Sport

Football

Football (soccer) is the most popular sporting activity in Sweden. There are more than 3000 clubs with about a million members. The domestic season runs from April to early November. The national arena, Råsunda Stadium in Solna, a suburb in Stockholm's northwest, can hold up to 37,000 roaring spectators.

Two of Sweden's best-known Swedish football players are Gunnar Nordahl (1921–95), who helped Sweden win gold at the 1948 Olympics and went on to be the all-time top scorer at AC Milan, and Malmö-born Zlatan Ibrahimović (b 1981).

Ice Hockey

There are amateur ice-hockey teams in most Swedish communities. The national premier league, Elitserien, has 12 professional teams; there are also several lower divisions. Matches take place from autumn to late spring, up to four times a week in Stockholm, primarily at Globen arena.

Skiing

Alpine skiing competitions are held annually, particularly in Åre. Vasa-loppet, the world's biggest Nordic (cross-country) skiing race, takes place on the first Sunday in March.

Swedish skiing stars include four-time Olympic gold-medal-winner Gunde Svan and giant-slalom icon Ingemar Stenmark, who won a total of 86 races in the Alpine Ski World Cup.

Other Sports

Swedish men have excelled at tennis; superstars include Björn Borg, Mats Wilander and Stefan Edberg. Borg won the Wimbledon Championships in England five times in a row.

Golf is hugely popular, with more than 400 courses in the country. Sweden's Annika Sörenstam is ranked as one of the game's leading players.

Bandy, a team sport similar to ice hockey, is played on an outdoor pitch the size of a football field; watching a match is a popular winter social activity in many Swedish cities. (In Stockholm, they're held at Zinkensdamms Idrottsplats.)

Sailing is very popular, around Stockholm in particular, where yacht ownership is extremely common, as well as in smaller villages along both coastlines.

Environment

Sweden is often listed among the world's most ecofriendly, sustainable countries. Its scenic beauty and natural resources are a major part of what make the place such a rewarding destination, and Swedes tend to cherish what they have. Getting outdoors is a popular activity here and, relatedly, green practices such as recycling and conservation are the norm. Even in large cities, Swedes display a deep connection to and reverence for the natural world.

The Land

Geography

Physically, Sweden is long and thin – about the size of California, with a surface area of around 450,000 sq km. It's mostly forest (nearly 60% of the landscape) and is dotted with about 100,000 inland lakes. This includes Vänern, Western Europe's largest lake, at 5585 sq km. There's also 7000km of coastline, plus scads of islands – the Stockholm archipelago alone has around 24,000 of them. The largest and most notable islands are Gotland and Öland on the southeast coast.

From its position on the eastern side of the Scandinavian peninsula, Sweden borders Norway, Finland and Denmark – the latter a mere 4km to the southwest of Sweden and joined to it by a spectacular bridge and tunnel. The mountains along the border with Norway are graced with alpine and Arctic flowers, including mountain avens (with large, white, eight-petalled flowers), long-stalked mountain sorrel (an unusual source of vitamin C), glacier crowfoot, alpine aster and various saxifrages. Orchids grow on Öland and Gotland. Up north are forests of Scots pine, Norway spruce and firs; the southern part of the country is now mostly farmland.

> Sweden is a long, drawn-out 1574km from north to south, but averages only about 300km in width.

Geology

Between 500 and 370 million years ago, the European and North American continental plates collided, throwing up an impressive range of peaks called the Caledonian Mountains, which were as tall as today's

---

HOW'S THE WEATHER

Sweden has a mostly cool, temperate climate, but the southern quarter of the country is warmer than the rest. The average maximum temperature for July is 18°C in the south and around 14°C in the north. Long hot periods in summer aren't unusual, with temperatures soaring to over 30°C. The west coast is warmer than the east, thanks to the warming waters of the Gulf Stream.

The harsh Lappland winter starts in October and ends in April, and temperatures can plummet as low as -50°C. Snow can accumulate to depths of several metres in the north, making for superb skiing, but snow depths in the south average only 20cm to 40cm. It usually rains in winter in the far south (Skåne).

Norway's mountain ranges act as a rain break, so yearly rainfall is moderate. Swedish summers are generally sunny, with only occasional rainfall, but August can be wet.

Himalayas. Their worn-down stubs form the 800km-long Kjölen Mountains along the Norwegian border – among which is Kebnekaise (2106m), Sweden's highest mountain.

Parts of Skåne and the islands of Öland and Gotland consist of flat limestone and sandstone deposits, probably laid down in a shallow sea east of the Caledonian Mountains during the same period.

Lake Siljan, in the central south, marks the site of Europe's largest meteoric impact: the 3km-wide fireball hurtled into Sweden 360 million years ago, obliterating all life and creating a 75km ring-shaped crater.

Midnight Sun & Polar Night

Because the Earth is tilted on its axis, the polar regions are constantly facing the sun at their respective summer solstices, and are tilted away from it in winter. The Arctic and Antarctic Circles, at latitudes 66°32'N and 66°32'S respectively, are the southern and northern limits of constant daylight on the longest day of the year.

The northern one-seventh of Sweden lies north of the Arctic Circle, but even in central Sweden the summer sun is never far below the horizon. Between late May and mid-July, nowhere north of Stockholm experiences true darkness; in Umeå, for example, the first stars aren't visible until mid-July. Although many visitors initially find it difficult to sleep while the sun is shining brightly outside, most people get used to it.

Conversely, winters (especially in the far north) can be dark and bitterly cold, with only a few hours of twilight to break the long polar nights. During this period, some people suffer from seasonal affective disorder (SAD), which occurs when they're deprived of the vitamin D provided by sunlight. Its effects may be minimised by taking supplements of vitamin D (as found in cod-liver oil) or with special solar-spectrum light bulbs.

Swedish elk are slightly smaller than their closely related American relatives, called moose.

Wildlife

Thanks to Sweden's geographical diversity, it has a great variety of European animals, birds and plants. And its relatively sparse population means you're likely to see some in the wild.

Sweden's large carnivores – the bear, wolf, wolverine, lynx and golden eagle – are all protected species. Wolf hunting was banned in the 1970s, after the wolf population had been brought nearly to extinction, but in 2010 the Swedish parliament authorised a cull to bring the newly resurgent

SOMETHING FISHY...

Sprats and herring are economically important food sources. Among other marine species, haddock, sea trout, whiting, flounder and plaice are reasonably abundant, particularly in the salty waters of the Kattegatt and Skagerrak, but the Baltic cod is heading for extinction due to overfishing.

Indigenous crayfish were once netted or trapped in Sweden's lakes, but overfishing and disease have driven them to extinction.

Grey and common seals swim in Swedish waters, although overfishing has caused a serious decline in numbers. Common dolphins may also be observed from time to time.

The North and, particularly, the Baltic Seas are suffering severe pollution, and vast algae blooms, caused partly by nitrogen run-off from Swedish farms. As a result, herring, sprats and Baltic salmon contain higher than average levels of cancer-causing dioxins; the Swedish National Food Agency has recommended that children and women of child-bearing age eat Baltic fish no more than two or three times a year.

Overfishing of these waters is also a huge cause for concern, with cod and Norwegian lobster on the verge of extinction. Fishing quotas are determined by the EU as a whole, and there's been a constant struggle to achieve balance between sustainable fish stocks and consumer demand.

species' numbers back down. Most of the country's wolf population is in Dalarna and Värmland.

The Swedish Environmental Protection Agency (www.swedishepa.se) has detailed information on Sweden's policies regarding endangered animals.

The wolverine, a larger cousin of the weasel, inhabits high forests and alpine areas along the Norwegian border. There are an estimated 680 in Sweden, mostly in Norrbotten and Västerbotten.

Brown bears were persecuted for centuries, but recent conservation measures have seen numbers increase to about 3200. Bears mostly live in forests in the northern half of the country but are spreading south.

Another fascinating forest dweller is the lynx, which belongs to the panther family and is Europe's only large cat. Sweden's 1200 to 1500 lynx are notoriously difficult to spot because of their nocturnal habits.

Not all of Sweden's wild creatures are predatory, of course. The iconic elk (moose in the USA) is a gentle, knobby-kneed creature that grows up to 2m tall. Though they won't try to eat you, elk are a serious traffic hazard, particularly at night: they can dart out in front of your car at up to 50km/h.

Around 260,000 domesticated reindeer roam the northern areas under the watchful eyes of Sami herders. Like elk, reindeer can be a major traffic hazard.

Lemmings are famous for their extraordinary reproductive capacity. Every 10 years or so the population explodes, resulting in denuded landscapes and thousands of dead lemmings in rivers and lakes and on roads.

You can swim – and fish for trout and salmon – in the waters by Stockholm's city centre. (Check fishing regulations at the tourist office.)

National Parks

Sweden was the first country in Europe to set up a national park (1909). There are now 29, along with around 2600 smaller nature reserves; together they cover about 9% of Sweden. The organisation Naturvårdsverket oversees and produces pamphlets about the parks in Swedish and English, along with the excellent book *Nationalparkerna i Sverige* (National Parks in Sweden).

Four of Sweden's large rivers (Kalixälven, Piteälven, Vindelälven and Torneälven) have been declared National Heritage Rivers in order to protect them from hydroelectric development.

The right of public access to the countryside *(allemansrätten)* includes national parks and nature reserves.

Northern Sweden
Abisko Northern gateway to the Kungsleden hiking track.
Haparanda Skärgård Beaches, dunes and migrant bird life.
Muddus Ancient forests and muskeg bogs, superb birdwatching.
Padjelanta High moorland; great hiking.
Pieljekaise Moorlands, birch forests, flowering meadows and lakes.
Sarek Wild mountain ranges, glaciers, deep valleys; expert hiking.
Stora Sjöfallet Famous waterfall; hydroelectric development.
Vadvetjåkka Large river delta containing bogs, lakes, limestone caves.

Central Sweden
Ängsö Tiny island; meadows, deciduous forest, bird life, spring flowers.
Björnlandet Natural forest, cliffs and boulder fields.
Färnebofjärden Bird life, forests, rare lichens and mosses.
Fulufjället Contains Njupeskär, the country's highest waterfall at 93m.
Garphyttan An 111-hectare park; fantastic springtime flowers.
Hamra Only 800m by 400m; virgin coniferous forest.
Kosterhavet The sea and shores surrounding the Koster Islands.
Sånfjället Natural mountain moorland with extensive views.
Skuleskogen Hilly coastal area, good hiking.

AURORA BOREALIS

The aurora borealis, or northern lights, appear in many forms – pillars, streaks, wisps and haloes of vibrating light – but they're most memorable when they take the form of pale curtains, apparently wafting on a gentle breeze. Most often, the Arctic aurora is faint green, light yellow or rose-coloured, but in periods of extreme activity it can change to bright yellow or crimson.

The northern lights (norrsken) are caused by streams of charged particles from the sun and the solar winds, which are diverted by the Earth's magnetic field toward the polar regions.

Because the field curves downward in a halo surrounding the magnetic poles, the charged particles are drawn earthward here. Their interaction with atoms in the upper atmosphere (about 160km above the surface) releases the energy that creates the visible aurora. During periods of high activity, a single auroral storm can produce a trillion watts of electricity with a current of 1 million amps.

The best time to catch the northern lights in Sweden is from October to March.

Tresticklan Natural coniferous forest, fine bird life.
Tyresta Stockholm's own national park.
Töfsingdalen Wild and remote; boulder fields, pine forest.

Southern Sweden

Blå Jungfrun Island with granite slabs, caves, labyrinth.
Dalby Söderskog Forest, wildlife.
Djurö Bird life and deer on an archipelago.
Gotska Sandön Sandy isle featuring dunes, dying pine forest.
Norra Kvill An 114-hectare park; ancient coniferous forest.
Söderåsen Deep fissure valleys, lush forests; hiking and cycling.
Stenshuvud Coastal park; beaches, forest, moorland.
Store Mosse Bogs with sand dunes, bird life.
Tiveden Hills, forests, lakes, boulder fields, beaches.

Environmental Issues

Four of the national parks in Lappland – Muddus, Padjelanta, Sarek and Stora Sjöfallet – are Unesco World Heritage sites.

Ecological consciousness in Sweden is very high and reflected in concern for native animals, clean water and renewable resources. Swedes are fervent believers in recycling household waste. Most plastic bottles and cans can be recycled – supermarket disposal machines give 0.50kr to 2kr per item.

Two organisations that set standards for labelling products as ecologically sound are the food-focused KRAV (www.krav.se), a member of the International Federation of Organic Agriculture Movements, and Swan (www.svanen.se), which has a wider scope and certifies entire hotels and hostels.

Linked to environmental concerns is the challenge of protecting the cultural heritage of the Sami people. The harnessing of rivers for hydro-electric power can have massive (negative) impact on what has historically been Sami territory, whether by flooding reindeer feeding grounds or by diverting water and drying up river valleys. In general, the mining, forestry and space industries have wreaked havoc on Sami homelands.

Environmental Organisations

Naturvårdsverket (www.swedishepa.se) Useful website of the Swedish Environmental Protection Agency.
Svenska Ekoturismföreningen (www.ekoturism.org) Promotes environmentally friendly tourism.
Svenska Naturskyddsföreningen (www.naturskyddsforeningen.se) Excellent website on current environmental issues.

Design & Architecture

Swedish design is firmly integrated into daily life: functionality is key, although beauty and cleverness are equally important. It's rare to walk into a Swedish home or public space that isn't arranged for maximum efficiency and comfort, whether that means cute IKEA kitchen hooks or optical-illusion wallpaper. Of course, there are also plenty of aesthetic flourishes – bold-print fabrics, beautiful glassware, swoopy architectural details. But the core of Swedish design and architecture is simple structural elegance above all.

History

Sweden's architecture has a mostly classical sensibility, with some Romanesque and Gothic influences from the mainland. Sweden embraced the Renaissance in the 16th and 17th centuries, which is also evident in the nation's core historic architecture.

Magnificently ornate baroque architecture arrived (mainly from Italy) during the 1640s, while Queen Kristina held the throne. For good examples, visit Kalmar, a historical centre of power and the site of the eponymous union of Denmark, Norway and Sweden in 1397.

Kalmar's Domkyrkan (Cathedral), designed in 1660, and the adjacent Rådhus (Town Hall) – as well as Drottningholms Slott (1662) outside of Stockholm – were all designed by the court architect Nicodemus Tessin the Elder. Tessin the Younger designed the vast Kungliga Slottet (Royal Palace) in Stockholm after the original palace was gutted by fire in 1697.

Pre-Renaissance examples include the Romanesque Domkyrkan in Lund, consecrated in 1145 and still dominating the city centre with its two imposing square towers. Fine Gothic churches include Mariakyrkan in Sigtuna (completed in 1237) and Uppsala's Domkyrkan, consecrated in 1435. The island of Gotland, however, is your best bet in Sweden for ecclesiastical Gothic architecture, with around one hundred medieval churches scattered across the ancient landscape.

The 19th century brought urban and social upheaval, industrialisation and the influx towards urban areas. There followed the creation of a Swedish state, and in architecture, the National Romanticism movement –

Key Turn-of-the-Century Buildings in Stockholm

Fredrik Lilljekvist's Royal Dramatic Theatre ('Dramaten') (1908)

Ferdinand Boberg's Rosenbad (1902)

Ragnar Östberg's Stockholm City Hall (1911)

FROZEN ART & DESIGN

The Icehotel, in the small village of Jukkasjärvi just outside of Kiruna, not only started the global trend of ice hotels and bars but also has become a focus for collaboration among artists and designers from Sweden and around the world.

The hotel is made from both snow and ice, the superstructure built in a manner similar to rammed earth, with snow blown and compacted onto Gothic-arch-like steel forms that produce simple vaulted spaces. Artists then create suite interiors using a combination of malleable snow and chiselled or carved ice.

A wide range of artists come to the Icehotel. Regulars include fourth-generation stonemason Mats Nilson and younger designer Jens Thoms Ivarsson, but new artists are invited to design suites each year – it's never the same hotel twice.

an often-decorative classical free-style with Arts and Crafts influences. Known in Sweden as *Jugendstil,* it has strong similarities to the more continental art nouveau. Typical examples of this period include Central-badet in Stockholm and the artist Anders Zorn's home in Mora.

Following this period, abstracted and more international modernism took hold, and Stockholm's 1930 exhibition introduced modern design and the Swedish architects of the 20th century.

Key Architects

Standout architectural firms include the established Wingårdh, but emerging practices such as Elding Oscarson show a restrained international influence. Lund & Valentin in Gothenburg have, since 1952, been a good index of architectural tastes, as seen in their postmodern GöteborgsOperan (1994).

The transition to modernity was led by Erik Gunnar Asplund (1885–1940), Sweden's most important architect. Two perfect examples of his work are found in and around Stockholm: Stadsbiblioteket (the City Library; 1932) and, a bit outside of town, Skogskyrkogården (the Woodland Cemetery), where you'll find perhaps the greatest collection of work from the Swedish master; many of the pavilions are collaborations with the less prolific Sigurd Lewerentz (1885–1975).

Asplund was typical of the Swedish approach. He travelled widely as a young designer, returning to his homeland to make an architecture both of its time and true to Swedish tradition. His work contrasted with the more aggressive radical modernism of France and Germany, and set the tone for Finnish master Alvar Aalto.

Urban Landscapes

The post-industrial city of Malmö has become a hot spot of design and innovation. The old docks northwest of Gamla Staden (Old Town) were converted into ecologically focused housing for the new century. Its landmark Turning Torso (2005) – a twisting residential tower designed by Catalan architect Santiago Calatrava – is an arresting sight dominating the skyline.

FLATPACK FURNITURE THE WORLD OVER

Ingvar Kamprad was 17 years old when he created IKEA in the city of Älmhult, in the craft-focused province of Småland. He has gone on to become one of the world's richest men, and the company he started now has its own dedicated museum in the town where it was born.

The IKEA name (a combination of Kamprad's initials and those of the farm and village where he grew up) was officially registered in 1943. Initially selling pens, watches and nylon stockings, the company added furniture to its products four years later, which gradually evolved into the IKEA-designed flatpack creations so familiar today.

There was almost an early end to the Ikea empire when the first Stockholm shop and all its stock burned down in 1970. But, besides his devotion to work and obsession with cost cutting, Kamprad also seems to have thrived on adversity – Ikea bounced back.

Seeking to bring simple, good design to the whole world, in an affordable way, IKEA has had enormous influence. Cheap and innovative products were born out of Swedish modern design – the idea of the house as the starting point of good design, rather than the end.

The clean-cut company was rocked in 1994 by revelations that Kamprad once had links with a pro-Nazi party in Sweden (he later offered a public apology and expressed much regret for this time of his life).

The famously frugal Kamprad has now taken a back seat in terms of running the company, but ownership is still within the family. Control over the empire is now divvied up among Kamprad's three children and divided into a series of complex charity and trust entities. Today IKEA has stores in more than 50 countries, with several more planned; branches first opened in Australia in 1975, Saudi Arabia in 1983, the US in 1985, Britain in 1987, China in 1998 and Russia in 2000.

Close by is the Öresund bridge (Georg KS Rotne; 2000) connecting the two metropolitan areas of Malmö and Copenhagen. Malmö has become a commuter base for Danish residents in Copenhagen as a result of this remarkable piece of infrastructure – after it reaches the end of the bridge section the road and rail lines literally disappear into the water, to become a tunnel until it emerges next to Copenhagen airport. It's quite a sight from the air.

Within Stockholm, contemporary design and culture found a robust home in 1974 in Kulturhuset, a large modernist pavilion holding a wide range of cultural activities. Designed by Peter Celsing, it's like a big set of drawers offering their wares onto the large plaza outside, Sergels Torg; the *torg* (town square) is the modern heart of Stockholm, and standing at its centre is *Kristallvertikalaccent* (Crystal Vertical Accent), a wonderful, luminescent monument to modernity and glassmaking traditions. Designed by sculptor Edvin Öhrström, it was the result of a 1962 competition.

More recently, the planned suburb Hammarby Sjöstad, just south of Stockholm's centre, has taken shape as a sustainably built, eco-conscious neighbourhood. Its approach to mindful integration of infrastructure, transportation, public spaces and energy conservation has been widely influential in urban planning.

Glassmaking

The southern province of Småland has been Sweden's glassmaking headquarters for well over one hundred years. The cluster of glass-blowing factories – among them well-known brands Orrefors and Kosta Boda – has consolidated over time. A high point of glass design was in the 1960s, when traditional figurative forms meshed with abstracted patterning as young designers were given the chance to compete with more established figures. Since then, the glassmaking universe has been home to some of Sweden's most innovative artists, including Bertil Vallien, known for his mysterious, haunting faces inside glass blocks, and Ulrica Hydman-Vallien (his wife), with her distinctively painted glass bowls.

Contemporary design and architecture generally follow global trends, but the characteristically Swedish interests of nature and craft are evident when cruising through blogs such as the snappy Ems Designblogg (http://em. residence magazine.se).

The Sami

The only internationally recognised group of indigenous people in Scandinavia, the Sami migrated here following the path of retreating ice and have inhabited the far northern territory collectively known as Sápmi for thousands of years. They lived by hunting reindeer in the area extending from Norway's Atlantic coast to the Kola Peninsula in Russia.

Sápmi & Modern Sweden

By the 17th century, the depletion of reindeer herds had transformed the Sami's hunting economy into a nomadic herding economy. Until the 1700s, the Sami lived in *siida* (village units or communities), migrating for their livelihoods, but only within their own defined areas. Those areas were recognised and respected by the Swedish government until colonisation of Lappland began in earnest, and the Sami found their traditional rights and livelihoods threatened both by the settlers and by the establishment of borders between Sweden, Norway, Finland and Russia.

Who is a Sami?

Fewer than half of all Sami can actually read and speak Sami. The most common language is North Sami, spoken by around 18,000 of the 50,000 Sami speakers. Sami languages are mutually unintelligible: Kildin Sami speakers from Vilhelmina can communicate with Russia's Kola Sami but not Kiruna Sami.

In Sweden today, the stereotype of the nomadic reindeer herder has been replaced with the multifaceted reality of modern Sami life. According to the Sámediggi (Sami parliament) statutes, a Sami is a person who identifies as Sami, who either knows the Sami language or who has had at least one parent or grandparent who spoke Sami as their mother tongue.

The Sami population of Sápmi numbers around 100,000, out of whom around 45,000 live in Norway, 27,000 or so in Sweden, slightly fewer in Finland and some 2000 in Russia. These numbers are approximate, as a census has never taken place. Famous people of Sami descent include Joni Mitchell and Renée Zellweger.

Sami Language

Particularly precise when it comes to describing natural phenomena, the landscape and reindeer, Sami is not a single language. There are, in fact, 10 Sami languages spoken across Sápmi, which belong to the Finno-Ugrian language group and are not related to any Scandinavian language.

Sweden officially recognises the Sami languages as minority languages and international law decrees that Sami children are entitled to mother-tongue education in Sami. In practice, however, it hasn't always proved possible to find Sami-speaking teachers, and some municipalities feel that it costs too much to provide education in Sami.

The Centre for Sami Research (CeSam) in Umeå conducts research into Sami language and Sami language courses can be taken at Umeå and Uppsala universities.

Sami Religion & Mythology

Sami beliefs have traditionally revolved around nature, and Shamanism was widespread until the 17th century. The *noaidi,* or shamans, bridged the gap between the physical world and the spiritual world; when in a trance, it was thought that they could shape-shift and command natural phenomena.

YOIK

One of the cornerstones of Sami identity is the *yoik* (or *joik*), a form of self-expression that has traditionally provided a bond between the Sami and nature. The *yoik* is a rhythmic poem or song composed for a specific person, event or object to describe and remember their innate nature. Thus you can *yoik* anything you like, from a new pair of trainers to your beloved grandmother. The *yoiking* tradition was revived in the 1960s, and it's now performed in many different ways – including experimental *yoik* and hard *yoik*, pioneered by contemporary musicians.

Sami folklore features many myths and legends concerning the under-world. Forces of nature, such as the wind and the sun, play an important role in Sami myths and legends: Sápmi is said to have been created by a monstrous giant named Biogolmai, the Wind Man. Sami creation stories feature the Son of the Sun as their ancestor, while the Daughter of the Sun is said to have brought the Sami their reindeer.

In 1685 it was decided by the monarchy and the church that the Sami must be converted to Christianity. Idolatry trials were held, shaman drums burned and sacred sites desecrated. However, not all effects of Christianity were negative: Laestadianism helped to alleviate the poverty and misery of the Sami in 19th-century Lappland.

The Sami Information Centre in Östersund (www.samer.se) is a treasure trove of information on all aspects of Sami life – from history and present-day culture to politics and food.

'A Lapp Must Remain a Lapp'

From the 1800s onward, Sweden's policies regarding the Sami were tinted with social Darwinist ideas, deeming the Sami to be an inferior race fit only for reindeer husbandry. The nomadic Sami were prevented from settling lest they become idle and neglect their reindeer. A separate schooling system was set up, with Sami children denied admission to regular public schools. Under the *Nomad Schools Act* of 1913, they were taught in their family's tent (*lávvu*) for three years by teachers who moved between Sami settlements in summer. After three more years of limited schooling in winter, they were considered sufficiently educated without becoming 'civilised'.

Despite demands that nomad schools should meet the same stand-ards as regular Swedish schools, the situation did not improve until after WWII, when the Sami began to actively participate in the struggle for their rights, forming numerous associations and pressure groups.

Sami Government

The Sami in Sweden are represented by the Sámediggi (Sami parliament), comprising 31 members. Funded by grants from the government, it over-sees many aspects of Sami life, from representing reindeer-herding interests and promoting Sami culture to appointing the board of directors for Sami schools. While it acts in an advisory capacity to the Swedish government, the Sámediggi does not have the power to make decisions regarding land use.

The Swedish Sami also take part in the Sámiraddi, the unifying body for the Sami organisations across Sápmi and international Sami inter-ests. Sámiraddi is an active participant in the WCIP (World Council of Indigenous Peoples).

The red, blue, green and yellow of the Sami flag, designed by Norway's Astrid Båhl in 1986, correspond to the colours of the traditional Sami costume, the *kolt*, while the red and blue halves of the circle represent the sun and the moon, respectively.

Sami Rights & Today's Challenges

The Sami claim the right to traditional livelihoods, land and water, citing *usufruct* (age-old usage) and the traditional property rights of the Sami *siidas* (villages or communities), which are not formally acknowledged by Sweden. The Swedish state is yet to ratify the International Labour Organi-zation's Convention 169, which would recognise the Sami as an indigenous people with property rights, as opposed to just an ethnic minority.

While the Swedish state supports Sami efforts to preserve their unique reindeer-herding heritage, with an allowance of 300 to 500 reindeer per family, there is one condition: herding units, or *sameby,* may not engage in any economic activity other than reindeer herding. Currently, around 10% of Sweden's Sami are full-time reindeer herders.

In theory, the *Reindeer Husbandry Act* gives reindeer herders the right to use land and water for their own maintenance and that of their reindeer. In practice, a large chunk of land allocated to the herders for grazing is unsuitable for that purpose, and tourism and extractive industries such as mining also continue to pose a threat to that traditional Sami occupation.

Sami Duodji

Sami crafts combine practicality with beauty. 'Soft crafts', such as leatherwork and textiles, have traditionally been in the female domain, whereas men have predominantly pursued 'hard crafts', such as knife making, woodwork or silverwork.

Traditional creations include wooden *guksi* (drinking cups) or other vessels, made by hollowing out a burl and often inlaid with reindeer bone; knives, with abundantly engraved handles made of reindeer or elk antler and equally decorative bone sheaths; and silverwork – anything from exquisitely engraved spoons, belt buckles and brooches to earrings and pendants.

Designs differ depending on whether an item hails from northern or southern Lappland: northern knife sheaths are typically more steeply curved and decorated with patterns of stars and flowers, while southern craftsmen use abstract square patterns. Northern leatherwork and embroidery often feature cloth appliques, while southern Sami favour leatherwork combined with beadwork.

Recurring symbols are found in Sami silver jewellery. These include the sunwheel that graces women's belts; animal motifs that were once painted on sacred shaman's drums: beavers, reindeer, moose; and *komsekule*, silver filigree balls that once graced Sami collars but were then used as an anti-goblin charm when hung on children's cradles. The heavy silver collars worn by women often feature the Gothic letter 'M'. In the Middle Ages, such 'M's were a pilgrim sign that symbolised the Virgin Mary.

In the 1970s there was a revival of Sami handicraft; since then, genuine Sami work that uses traditional designs and materials has borne the Sámi Duodji trademark.

People of the Eight Seasons

For centuries, Sami life revolved around reindeer. Thus, the Sami year traditionally has eight seasons, each tied to a period of reindeer herding:

Gidádálvve (springwinter; early March to late April) Herds are moved from the forests to calving lands in the low mountains during the spring migration.
Gidá (spring; late April to late May) Calves are born. Leaves and grass are added to the reindeer's diet.
Gidágiesse (springsummer; end of May to Midsummer) Herds are moved to find more vegetation for calves and their mothers. Reindeer mostly rest and eat. Herders repair temporary homes.
Giesse (summer; Midsummer to end of August) Reindeer move to higher ground to avoid biting insects. Herders move them into corrals for calf marking.
Tjaktjagiesse (autumnsummer; end of August to mid-September) Reindeer build up fat for the winter. Some of the uncastrated males *(sarvss)* are slaughtered in specially designated corrals. Meat is salted, smoked and made into jerky.
Tjaktja (autumn; mid-September to mid-October) Reindeer mating season. The reindeer stay mostly in the low mountains, where they feed on roots and lichen.
Tjaktjadálvve (autumnwinter; mid-October to Christmas) Reindeer are divided into grazing groups *(sijdor)* and taken to winter grazing grounds in the forest. Surplus reindeer are slaughtered.
Dálvve (winter; Christmas to the end of February) Herders frequently move the reindeer around the forests to make sure the reindeer get enough lichen to eat.

Traditional Sami clothing, or *gákti,* comes with its own varied and distinctive headgear and is one of the most distinct symbols of Sami identity. The Sami can tell at a glance which part of Sápmi another is from, or whether the wearer is unaccustomed to wearing Sami garments.

Gällivare-based Visit Sápmi (https://visitsapmi.wordpress.com) pools resources from all over Sápmi and aims to connect travellers with specific aspects of Sami culture – from Sami tour companies to Sami culinary experiences and craftsmen.

Survival Guide

Directory A–Z

Accommodation

Sweden has a wide variety of accommodation that is generally of a very high standard. Book ahead in summer to secure the best prices.

The below room prices are for a double room in the summer season (mid-June through August); standard weekday prices during the rest of the year might be twice as high. Breakfast is normally included in hotel room prices, but usually costs extra in hostels.

€ less than 800kr

€€ 800kr–1600kr

€€€ more than 1600kr

Cabins & Chalets

Camping cabins and chalets (*stugor*) are common at campgrounds and scattered through the countryside. Most contain four beds, with two- and six-person cabins sometimes available. They're good value for small groups and families, costing between 350kr and 950kr per night. In peak summer season, many are rented out by the

week (generally for 1000kr to 5000kr).

The cheapest cabins are simple, with bunk beds and little else (bathroom and kitchen facilities are shared with campers or other cabin users). Chalets are generally fully equipped with their own kitchen, bathroom and even living room with TV. Bring your own linen and clean up yourself to save cleaning fees of around 500kr.

Pick up the catalogue *Campsites & Cottages in Sweden* from any tourist office, or check out www.camping.se.

Camping

Camping is wildly popular in Sweden, and there are hundreds of camping grounds all over the country. Most open between May and September. The majority are busy family-holiday spots with fantastic facilities, such as shops, restaurants, pools, playgrounds, beaches, walking trails, canoe or bike rentals, mini golf, kitchens and laundry facilities. Camping grounds are usually a combination of tent and/or RV

sites, primitive camping huts (duvet provided; bring your own sheets) and sometimes more luxurious cabins.

Camping prices vary (according to season and facilities) from around 250kr for a small site at a basic ground to 350kr for a large site at a more luxurious campground. Slightly cheaper rates may be available if you're a solo hiker or cyclist.

You must have a Camping Key Europe card to stay at most Swedish campgrounds. Buy one online at www.camping.se or pick it up at your first campground. One card (150kr per year) covers the whole family.

Hostels

Sweden has more than 450 hostels (*vandrarhem*), usually with excellent facilities – they're often more like budget hotels. Most hostels aren't backpacker hangouts but are used as holiday accommodation by Swedish families, couples or retired people. Another quirk is the scarcity of dormitories; hostels are more likely to have singles and doubles of almost hotel quality, often with en-suite bathrooms. About half are open year-round; many others open from May to September, some only from mid-June to mid-August in more remote locations.

Be warned: some Swedish hostels keep very short reception opening times,

BOOK YOUR STAY ONLINE

For more accommodation reviews by Lonely Planet authors, check out http://lonelyplanet.com/hotels/. You'll find independent reviews, as well as recommendations on the best places to stay. Best of all, you can book online.

generally from 5pm to 7pm, and 8am to 10am. The secret is to prebook by telephone – reservations are recommended in any case, as good hostels fill up fast. If you're stuck arriving when the front desk is closed, you'll usually see a number posted where you can phone for instructions. (Hostel phone numbers are also listed online with STF and SVIF.)

Sleeping bags are usually allowed if you have a sheet and pillowcase; bring your own, or hire them (50kr to 65kr). Breakfast is usually available (70kr to 95kr). Before leaving, you must clean up after yourself; cleaning materials are provided. Most hostels are affiliated with STF or SVIF, but there are other unaffiliated hostels also with high standards of accommodation.

STF

About 350 hostels are affiliated with **Svenska Turistföreningen** (STF; ☎070-695 21 16; www.svenskaturist foreningen.se; membership adult/child 295/150kr), part of Hostelling International (HI). STF produces a detailed online guide to its hostels on its website (in English). All STF hostels have kitchens.

Holders of HI membership cards pay the same rates as STF members. Nonmembers can pay 50kr extra per night (100kr at mountain lodges) or join up online or at a hostel. Prices quoted in our reviews are for STF members. Children under 16 pay about half the adult price.

SVIF

More than 150 hostels belong to **Sveriges Vandrarhem i Förening** (SVIF; ☎031-82 88 00; www.svif.se). No membership is required, and rates are similar to those of STF hostels. Most SVIF hostels have kitchens, but you sometimes need your own utensils. Details and booking can be found online, where

there's also a downloadable PDF listing all SVIF hostels and their phone numbers.

Hotels

Sweden is unusual in that hotel prices tend to fall at weekends and in summer (except in touristy coastal towns), sometimes by as much as 50%. We list the standard summer rates, as that's when most people will be visiting, but be aware that prices may be nearly double at other times of year. Many hotel chains are now also offering a variety of low rates for online booking. Hotel prices include a breakfast buffet unless noted in individual reviews.

There are a number of common midrange and top-end chains. Radisson and Elite are the most luxurious. Scandic is known for being environmentally friendly, and usually has great breakfast buffets. The top-end Countryside chain has the most characterful rooms, in castles, mansions, monasteries and spas.

Best Western (www.best western.se)

Countryside (www.countryside hotels.se)

Elite (www.elite.se)

First (www.firsthotels.com)

Nordic Choice (www.nordic choicehotels.se)

Radisson (www.radisson.com)

Scandic (www.scandichotels.com)

Sweden Hotels (www.sweden hotels.se)

Your Hotel Worldwide (www.yourhotelsworldwide.net)

Mountain Huts & Lodges

Most mountain huts (*fjällstugor*) and lodges (*fjällstationer*) in Sweden are owned by STF. There are about 45 huts and nine mountain lodges, mostly spaced at 15km to 25km intervals along major hiking trails, primarily in the Lappland region. Reception

hours are quite long as staff members are always on-site. Basic provisions are sold at many huts and all lodges, and many lodges have hiking equipment for hire.

STF mountain huts have cooking and toilet facilities (none has a shower, but some offer saunas). Bring your own sleeping bag. Huts are staffed during March and April and also from late June to early September. You can't book a bed in advance, but no one is turned away (although in the peak of summer this may mean you sleep on a mattress on the floor). Charges for STF or HI members vary depending on the season, and range from 360kr to 410kr in season, 150kr off-season (children pay half). Nonmembers pay 100kr extra. You can also pitch a tent in the mountains, but if you camp near STF huts you are requested to pay a service charge (members/nonmembers 100/200kr), which gives you access to any services the hut may offer (such as kitchen and bathroom facilities).

At the excellent STF mountain lodges, accommodation standards range from hostel (with cooking facilities) to hotel (with full- or half-board options), and overnight prices range from 350kr to around 1500kr. There are often guided activities on offer for guests, and usually a restaurant and shop.

PRIVATE ROOMS, B&BS & FARMHOUSES

Many tourist offices have lists of rooms in private homes, a great way of finding well-priced accommodation and getting to meet Swedish people. Singles/doubles average 550/750kr.

Along the motorways (primarily in the south), you may see 'Rum' or 'Rum & Frukost' signs, indicating informal accommodation (*frukost* means breakfast) from 350kr to 500kr per person.

The organisation **Bo på Lantgård** (☑035-12 78 70; www.bopalantgard.se) publishes a free annual booklet on farmhouse accommodation (B&B and self-catering), available from any tourist office. Prices range from 400kr to 1250kr per night, depending on the time of year, facilities and number of beds.

Customs Regulations

The duty-free allowance for bringing alcohol into Sweden from outside the EU is 1L of spirits or 2L of fortified wine, 4L of wine and 16L of beer. The tobacco allowance is 200 cigarettes, 100 cigarillos, 50 cigars or 250g of smoking tobacco. You must be at least 20 years old to bring in alcohol and 18 to bring in tobacco.

The limits on goods brought into Sweden with 'tax paid for personal use' from within the EU are more generous and somewhat flexible; tax is assessed on a case-by-case basis.

Going through customs rarely involves any hassles, but rules on illegal drugs are strictly enforced; you may be searched on arrival, especially if you're travelling from Denmark. Live plants and animal products (meat, dairy etc) from outside the EU, and all animals, syringes and weapons must be declared to customs on arrival. For the latest regulations, contact Swedish Customs (www.tullverket.se).

Discount Cards

CITY SUMMER CARDS

Gothenburg, Malmö, Stockholm and Uppsala have tourist cards that get you into their major attractions and offer parking, travel on public transport and discounts at participating hotels, restaurants and shops.

HOSTEL & STUDENT CARDS

A Hostelling International (HI) card means cheaper beds in STF hostels, mountain stations and cabins. You can join the STF and tourist offices in Sweden (membership adult/16 to 25yr/6 to 15yr/family 295/150/30/450kr); membership is good for one year.

The most useful student card is the International Student Identity Card (www.isic.org), which offers discounts on many forms of transport (including some airlines, international ferries and local public transport) and on admission to museums, sights, theatres and cinemas.

SENIORS

Seniors normally get discounts on entry to museums and other sights, cinema and theatre tickets, air tickets and other transport fares. No special card is required to receive this discount, but show your passport if you are asked for proof of age (the minimum qualifying age is generally 60 or 65 years).

Electricity

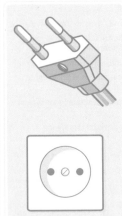

Type C
220V/50Hz

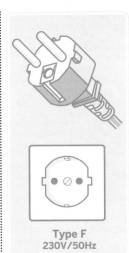

Type F
230V/50Hz

Embassies & Consulates

A list of Swedish diplomatic missions abroad (and links) is available at Sweden Abroad (www.swedenabroad.com). Most diplomatic missions are in Stockholm, although some neighbouring countries also have consulates in Gothenburg, Malmö and Helsingborg.

Food

The following price categories for listings refer to the average price of a main dish, not including drinks.

€ less than 100kr

€€ 100–200kr

€€€ more than 200kr

For more on Food in Sweden, see p301.

Health

You're unlikely to encounter serious health problems in Sweden. Travel health depends on your predeparture preparations, your daily health care while travelling, and how you handle any problem that does develop.

Insurance

Depending on the type of policy you choose, insurance can cover you for everything from medical expenses and luggage loss to cancellations or delays in your travel arrangements.

In Sweden, EU citizens pay a fee for all medical treatment (including emergency admissions), but showing an EHIC (European Health Insurance Card) form will make matters much easier. Enquire about the EHIC well in advance at your social-security office, travel agent or local post office. Travel insurance is still advisable, however, as it allows treatment flexibility and will also cover ambulance and repatriation costs.

If you do need health insurance, remember that some policies offer 'lower' and 'higher' medical-expense options, but the higher one is chiefly for countries that have extremely high medical costs, such as the USA. Everyone should be covered for the worst possible scenario, such as an accident requiring an ambulance, hospital treatment or an emergency flight home. You

may prefer a policy that pays health-care providers directly, rather than your having to pay on the spot and claim later.

Worldwide travel insurance is available at www.lonelyplanet.com/bookings. You can buy, extend and claim travel insurance online any time – even if you're already on the road.

Internet Access

Most hotels have free wi-fi, and some have computers and printers in the lobby or business centre. Nearly all public libraries offer free internet access, but often the half-hour or hour slots are fully booked in advance by locals, and certain website categories may be blocked. Many tourist offices offer a computer terminal for visitor use (usually free or for a minimal fee).

Internet cafes are rarely found in Sweden as the vast majority of Swedes have internet access at home.

Wireless internet access at coffee shops is nearly universal and usually free; ask for the password when you order. At bus and train stations and airports, you often have to sign up for an

account (usually free) to access the wi-fi.

LGBTI+ Travellers

Sweden is a famously liberal country; it was a leader in establishing gay and lesbian registered partnerships, and since 2009 its gender-neutral marriage law has given same-sex married couples the same rights and obligations as heterosexual married couples. The national organisation for gay and lesbian rights is **Riksförbundet för Sexuellt Likaberättigande** (RFSL; Map p58; ☑08-50 16 29 00; www.rfsl.se; Sveavägen 59; ☺10am-3pm or 4pm Mon-Fri, closed most of Jul & Aug; ⊠Rådmansgatan).

There are gay bars and nightclubs in the big cities, but ask local RFSL societies or your home organisation for up-to-date information. The *Spartacus International Gay Guide* (www.spartacusworld.com), published by Bruno Gmünder Verlag (Berlin), is an excellent international directory of gay entertainment venues, but it's best used in conjunction with more up-to-date listings in local papers; as elsewhere, gay venues in the region can

EMBASSIES & CONSULATES IN STOCKHOLM

COUNTRY	TELEPHONE	WEBSITE	ADDRESS
Australia	☑08-613 29 00	www.sweden.embassy.gov.au	8th fl, Klarabergsviaducten 63
Canada	☑08-453 30 00	www.sweden.gc.ca	Klarabergsgatan 23
Denmark	☑08-406 75 00	www.sverige.um.dk	Jakobs Torg 1
Finland	☑08-676 67 00	www.finland.se/fi	Gärdesgatan 9-11
France	☑08-459 53 00	www.ambafrance-se.org	Kommendörsgatan 13
Germany	☑08-670 15 00	www.stockholm.diplo.de	Skarpögatan 9
Ireland	☑08-54 50 40 40	www.embassyofireland.se	Hovslagargatan 5
Netherlands	☑08-55 69 33 00	www.nederlandwereldwijd.nl/landen/zweden	Götgatan 16a
Norway	☑08-58 72 36 00	www.norge.se	Skarpögatan 4
UK	☑08-671 30 00	www.britishembassy.se	Skarpögatan 6-8
USA	☑08-783 53 00	www.usembassy.gov/sweden	Dag Hammarskjölds väg 31

change with the speed of summer.

Another good source of local information is the free monthly magazine *QX*. You can pick it up at many clubs, shops and restaurants in Stockholm, Gothenburg, Malmö and Copenhagen (Denmark). The magazine's website (www.qx.se) has excellent information and recommendations in English.

One of the capital's biggest parties is the annual **Stockholm Pride** (www.stockholmpride.org/en; ☉late Jul or early Aug), a five-day festival celebrating gay culture. The extensive program covers art, debate, health, literature, music, spirituality and sport.

Legal Matters

If arrested, you have the right to contact your country's embassy, which can usually provide you with a list of local lawyers. There is no provision for bail in Sweden. Sweden has some of the most draconian drug laws in Western Europe, with fines and possible long prison sentences for possession and consumption.

Maps

Tourist offices, libraries and hotels usually stock free local town plans.

The best maps of Sweden are published and updated regularly by Kartförlaget, the sales branch of the national mapping agency, **Lantmäteriet** (☏026-63 30 00; www.lantmateriet.se); they can be bought at most tourist offices, bookshops and some youth hostels, service stations and general stores.

Motorists planning an extensive tour should get the *Motormännens Sverige Vägatlas* produced by Kartförlaget (275kr, often cheaper online), with town plans and detailed coverage

at 1:250,000 as far north as Sundsvall, then 1:400,000 for the remainder.

The best tourist road maps are those of Kartförlaget's *Vägkartan* series, at a scale of 1:100,000 and available from larger bookshops. Also useful, especially for hikers, is the *Fjällkartan* mountain series (1:100,000, with 20m contour interval); these cost around 135kr apiece and are available at larger bookshops, outdoor-equipment stores and STF mountain stations.

To purchase maps before you arrive, try **Kartbutiken** (Map p48; ☏08-20 23 03; www.kartbutiken.se; Mäster Samuelsgatan 54; ☉10am-6pm Mon-Fri, 10am-4pm Sat, noon-4pm Sun; ⬛T-Centralen).

Money

ATMs widely available. Credit cards accepted in most hotels and restaurants.

Opening Hours

Except where indicated, we list hours for high season (mid-June to August). Expect more limited hours the rest of the year.

Banks 9.30am to 3pm Monday to Friday; some city branches open to 5pm or 6pm.

Bars & Pubs 11am or noon to 1am or 2am.

Government Offices 9am to 5pm Monday to Friday.

Restaurants 11am to 2pm and 5pm to 10pm, often closed on Sunday and/or Monday; high-end restaurants are often closed for a week or two in July or August.

Shops 9am to 6pm Monday to Friday, to 1pm Saturday.

Photography

Camera supplies are readily available in all the large cities. Expert, a chain of electrical-goods shops, sells

a wide range of photography gadgets.

It's particularly important to ask permission before taking photos of people in Sami areas, where you may meet resistance. Photography and taking videos are prohibited at many tourist sites, mainly to protect fragile artwork. Photographing military establishments is forbidden. Observe signs, and when in doubt, ask permission.

Technical challenges include the clear northern light and glare from water, ice and snow, which may require use of a UV filter (or skylight filter) and lens shade; and the cold – most cameras don't work below -20°C.

Lonely Planet's Guide to Travel Photography, by Richard I'Anson, contains handy hints.

Post

Swedish postal service **Posten** (☏020-23 22 21; www.posten.se) has a network of around 3000 counter services in shops, petrol stations and supermarkets across the country. Look for the yellow post symbol on a pale-blue background, which indicates that postal facilities are offered.

If your postal requirements are more complicated (such as posting a heavy parcel), ask at the local tourist office. Package services are offered at certain office-supply stores.

Mailing letters or postcards weighing up to 20g within Sweden costs 7kr; it's 21kr to elsewhere in Europe and beyond. Air mail will take a week to reach most parts of North America, perhaps a little longer to Australia and New Zealand.

Public Holidays

Midsummer brings life almost to a halt for three days: transport and other services are reduced, and most shops and smaller tourist offices close, as do some attractions. Some hotels close between Christmas and New Year. Upscale restaurants in larger cities often close for a few weeks in late July and early August.

School holidays vary, but in general the kids will be at large for Sweden's one-week sports holiday (February/March), the one-week Easter break, Christmas, and from June to August.

Many businesses close early the day before and all day after official public holidays.

Nyårsdag (New Year's Day) 1 January

Trettondedag Jul (Epiphany) 6 January

Långfredag, Påsk, Annandag Påsk (Good Friday, Easter Sunday and Monday) March/April

Första Maj (Labour Day) 1 May

Kristi Himmelsfärdsdag (Ascension Day) May/June

Pingst, Annandag Pingst (Whit Sunday and Monday) Late May or early June

Midsommardag (Midsummer's Day) Saturday between 19 and 25 June

Alla Helgons dag (All Saints Day) Saturday, late October or early November

Juldag (Christmas Day) 25 December

Annandag Jul (Boxing Day) 26 December

Note also that Midsommarafton (Midsummer's Eve), Julafton (Christmas Eve; 24 December) and Nyårsafton (New Year's Eve; 31 December) are not official holidays but are generally nonworking days for most people.

Safe Travel

Sweden is a very safe country, but you should consider the following:

➡ In and around train stations in large cities

PRACTICALITIES

Weights and measures Sweden uses the metric system. Some shops quote prices followed by '/hg', which means per 100g. Watch out for *mil*, which Swedes may translate into English as 'mile' – a Swedish *mil* is actually 10km.

Newspapers Domestic papers (including the Gothenburg and Stockholm dailies and evening tabloids) are in Swedish only. A good selection of English-language imports is sold at major transport terminals, Press Stop, Pressbyrån and tobacconists – even in small towns.

Radio Try National Swedish Radio (variable stations around the country, see www.sr.se for a directory) for classical music and opera, pop and rock, and news.

TV National channels TV1 and TV2 broadcast mainly about local issues, mostly in Swedish. TV3, TV4 and TV5 have lots of shows and films in English.

(Gothenburg, Malmö and Stockholm), be aware of pickpockets.

➡ Only use taxis from reputable companies (we list several), and agree on a fare before you get in.

➡ If you're venturing out into the wilderness, make sure someone knows where you're going and when you expect to be back.

➡ Familiarise yourself with the 'new' Swedish bills and coins, as there may still be old (invalid) currency in circulation.

Telephone

Swedish phone numbers have area codes followed by a varying number of digits. Look for business numbers in the Yellow Pages (www.gulasidorna.se).

Public telephones are increasingly rare, although you may find them at transport hubs, including train and bus stations. They accept phonecards or credit cards. Telia phonecards (*telefonkort*) cost 50kr and 120kr (for 50 and 120 units, respectively) and can be bought from Telia phone shops and newsagents.

Time

Sweden is one hour ahead of GMT/UTC and is in the same time zone as Norway and Denmark as well as most of Western Europe. When it's noon in Sweden, it's 11am in London, 1pm in Helsinki, 6am in New York and Toronto, 3am in Los Angeles, 9pm in Sydney and 11pm in Auckland. Sweden also has daylight saving time: the clocks go forward an hour on the last Sunday in March and back an hour on the last Sunday in October.

Timetables and business hours are quoted using the 24-hour clock, and dates are often given by week number (1 to 52).

Toilets

Public toilets in parks, shopping malls, libraries, and bus or train stations are rarely free in Sweden, though some churches and most museums and tourist offices have free toilets. Pay toilets cost 5kr to 10kr, usually payable by coin or text message, except at larger train stations and department stores (where there's an attendant).

Tourist Information

Most towns in Sweden have centrally located tourist offices (*turistbyrå*) that provide free street plans and information on accommodation, attractions, activities and transport. Brochures for other areas in Sweden are often available. Ask for the handy booklet that lists addresses and phone numbers for most tourist offices in the country.

Most tourist offices are open long hours daily in summer; from mid-August to mid-June a few close down, while others have shorter opening hours – they may close by 4pm, and not open at all at weekends. Public libraries, hostels and large hotels are good alternative sources of information.

Travellers with Disabilities

Sweden is one of the easiest countries in which to travel in a wheelchair. People with disabilities will find transport services, ranging from trains to taxis, with adapted facilities – contact the operator in advance for the best service.

Public toilets and some hotel rooms have facilities for those with disabilities. Some street crossings have ramps for wheelchairs and audio signals for visually impaired people, and some grocery stores are wheelchair-accessible.

For further information about Sweden, contact **De Handikappades Riksförbund** (☑08-685 80 00; www. dhr.se), the national association for the disabled.

Also, contact the travel officer at your national support organisation; they may be able to put you in touch with tour companies that specialise in travelling with disabilities.

Download Lonely Planet's free Accessible Travel guide from http://lptravel.to/AccessibleTravel.

Visas

Americans don't need a visa to enter Sweden; some nationalities will need a Schengen visa, good for 90 days.

Citizens of EU countries can enter Sweden with a passport or a national identification card (passports are recommended) and stay indefinitely. *Uppehållstillstånd* (residence permits) are no longer required for EU citizens to visit, study, live or work in Sweden.

Non-EU passport holders from Australia, New Zealand, Canada and the US can enter and stay in Sweden without a visa for up to 90 days. Australian and New Zealand passport holders aged between 18 and 30 can qualify for a one-year working-holiday visa. For longer stays, you'll need to apply for a visitor's permit instead of an entry visa. These must be applied for before entering Sweden. An interview by consular officials at your nearest Swedish embassy is required – allow up to eight months for this process. Foreign students are granted residence permits if they can prove acceptance by a Swedish educational institution and are able to guarantee that they can support themselves financially.

Citizens of South Africa and many other African, Asian and some eastern European countries require tourist visas for entry to Sweden (and any other Schengen country). These are only available in advance from Swedish embassies (allow two months); there's a non-refundable application fee of €60 for most applicants. Visas are good for any 90 days within a six-month period; extensions aren't easily obtainable.

Migrationsverket (www. migrationsverket.se) is the Swedish migration board and handles all applications for visas and work or residency permits.

Volunteering

Historically, volunteering in Sweden was difficult for non-Swedish speakers, but that's changing. IVolontärbyrån (www.volontarbyran.org) is a nationwide organisation with a program that matches volunteers with opportunities, recently including English-speakers.

Work

Non-EU citizens require an offer of paid employment prior to their arrival in Sweden. They need to apply for a work permit (and residence permit for stays over three months), enclosing confirmation of the job offer, completed forms (available from Swedish diplomatic posts or over the internet), two passport photos and their passport. Processing takes six to eight weeks, and there's a non-refundable application fee of 2000kr (1000kr for athletes, performers and a few other job categories).

Australians and New Zealanders aged 18 to 30 years can qualify for a one-year working-holiday visa. Full application details are can be viewed online through Migrationsverket (www. migrationsverket.se).

Work permits are only granted if there's a shortage of Swedish workers (or citizens from EU countries) with certain in-demand skills; speaking Swedish may be essential for the job. Students enrolled in Sweden can take summer jobs, but these can be hard to find and such work isn't offered to travelling students.

Plenty of helpful information can be found online from the Arbetsförmedlinga (Swedish National Labour Market Administration; www. arbetsformedlingen.se).

Transport

GETTING THERE & AWAY

There is a good choice of flights to Sweden from most of the major cities in Europe. Trains also head here, many using Hamburg as a gateway to Scandinavia. Long distance buses also make the trip with connections from the UK via the Channel Tunnel. Flights, tours and rail tickets can be booked online at lonelyplanet.com/bookings.

Entering the Country

Sweden's main airport is Stockholm Arlanda. Entry is straightforward; most visitors simply need to fill out and hand over a brief customs form and show their passport at immigration.

Air

Sweden is well connected by air with four major international airports.

Airports & Airlines

Stockholm Arlanda (ARN; ☑10-109 10 00; www.swedavia.se/arlanda) links Sweden with major European and North American cities. **Göteborg Landvetter** (www.swedavia.se/landvetter; ☐Flygbuss) is Sweden's second-biggest international airport. **Stockholm Skavsta** (Nyköping Airport; NYO;☑0155-28 04 00; www.skavsta.se/en; General Schybergs Plan 22, Nyköping; ☐Flygbussarna) is located 100km south of Stockholm, near Nyköping, and is mainly used by RyanAir flights. **Sturup Airport** (☑010-109 45 00; www.swedavia.com/malmo; Malmö-Sturup) in Malmö serves the south of the country and is also a major international hub.

Continental Europe

Regional carrier Scandinavian Airlines System (SAS) offers numerous direct services between Stockholm and European capitals including Amsterdam, Brussels, Geneva, Moscow, Paris and Prague. Many services are routed via Copenhagen (Denmark). Similar routes leave from Gothenburg.

Air Berlin flies from Göteborg Landvetter to Berlin several times weekly; also from Landvetter, Air France goes to Lyon, and Lufthansa goes to Frankfurt and Munich.

Finnair has direct flights from Helsinki to Stockholm (around 15 daily) and Gothenburg (up to four services daily).

Ryanair has frequent flights from Stockholm Skavsta to Barcelona, Brussels, Düsseldorf, Frankfurt, Hamburg, Milan, Paris, Riga and Rome.

CLIMATE CHANGE & TRAVEL

Every form of transport that relies on carbon-based fuel generates CO_2, the main cause of human-induced climate change. Modern travel is dependent on aeroplanes, which might use less fuel per kilometre per person than most cars but travel much greater distances. The altitude at which aircraft emit gases (including CO_2) and particles also contributes to their climate change impact. Many websites offer 'carbon calculators' that allow people to estimate the carbon emissions generated by their journey and, for those who wish to do so, to offset the impact of the greenhouse gases emitted with contributions to portfolios of climate-friendly initiatives throughout the world. Lonely Planet offsets the carbon footprint of all staff and author travel.

UK & Ireland

Ryanair flies from London Stansted to Stockholm Skavsta and Malmö's Sturup Airport; Glasgow Prestwick to Stockholm Skavsta; London Luton to Västerås; and Shannon to Stockholm Skavsta.

Between London Heathrow and Stockholm Arlanda, several commercial airlines have regular daily flights, including SAS and British Airways.

SAS flies at least four times daily from Stockholm Arlanda to Manchester and Dublin via London or Copenhagen. SAS also flies daily between London Heathrow and Gothenburg.

British Airways flies twice weekly from Göteborg Landvetter to Birmingham and Manchester.

USA

Icelandair has services from Baltimore-Washington, Boston, New York, Minneapolis, Portland and Orlando via Reykjavík to Stockholm. SAS's North American hub is Newark Airport, with direct daily flights to/from Stockholm. SAS also flies daily from Chicago to Stockholm. Lufthansa has daily flights from Newark Airport to Stockholm.

Land

Direct access to Sweden by land is possible from Norway, Finland and Denmark (via the Öresund toll bridge).

Nettbuss Express (☑0771-15 15 15; www.nettbuss.se) Long-distance buses within Sweden and to Oslo (Norway) and Copenhagen.

Sveriges Järnväg (SJ;☑0771-75 75 99; www.sj.se) Train lines with services to Copenhagen and Oslo.

Swebus Express (☑0771-21 82 18; www.swebus.se) Long-distance buses within Sweden and to Oslo and Copenhagen.

Border Crossings

Border-crossing formalities within the EU are virtually nonexistent, although it is prudent to carry your passport if you plan on catching the train from Copenhagen (or Copenhagen airport) to Malmö as extra security measures are sometimes put in place.

Denmark
BUS

Swebus Express runs between Gothenburg and Copenhagen (229kr, 4½ hours, daily). Nettbuss Express runs regular buses on the same route. Both offer student, youth (under 26) and senior discounts.

CAR & MOTORCYCLE

You can drive from Copenhagen to Malmö across the Öresund bridge on the E20 motorway. Tolls are paid at Lernacken, on the Swedish side, in either Danish or Swedish currency (single crossing per car/motorcycle 520/265kr), or by credit or debit card.

TRAIN

Öresund trains operated by Skånetrafiken (www.skanetrafiken.se) run every 20 minutes from 6am to midnight (and once an hour thereafter) between Copenhagen and Malmö (one-way from 99kr, 45 minutes) via the bridge. The trains usually stop at Copenhagen airport. From Copenhagen, change in Malmö for Stockholm-bound trains.

Frequent services operate between Copenhagen and Gothenburg (407kr, four hours) and between Copenhagen, Kristianstad and Karlskrona.

Finland
BUS

Frequent bus services run from Haparanda to Tornio (20kr, 10 minutes). Tapanis Buss (www.tapanis.se) runs express coaches from Stockholm to Tornio via Haparanda twice a week (735kr, 15 hours). **Länstrafiken i Norrbotten** (☑0771-10 01 10; www.ltnbd.se) operates buses as far as Kaaresuando, from where it's only a few minutes' walk across the bridge to Kaaresuvanto (Finland).

There are also regular regional services from Haparanda to Övertorneå (some continue to Pello, Pajala and Kiruna) – you can walk across the border at Övertorneå or Pello and pick up a Finnish bus to Muonio, with onward connections from there to Kaaresuvanto and Tromsø (Norway).

CAR & MOTORCYCLE

The main routes between Sweden and Finland are the E4 from Umeå to Kemi and Rd 45 from Gällivare to Kaaresuvanto; five other minor roads also cross the border.

Germany
BUS

Flixbus runs direct daily services from Gothenburg to Berlin (766kr, 12 hours, daily), as well as through Jönköping (622kr, 19 hours).

TRAIN

Hamburg is the central European gateway to Scandinavia, with direct trains daily to Copenhagen and a few that go on to Stockholm. Direct overnight trains and Swebus Express buses run daily between Berlin and Malmö via the Trelleborg–Sassnitz ferry (www.berlin-night-express.com; from 450kr, nine hours).

Norway
BUS

Nettbuss runs from Stockholm to Oslo (from 379kr, 7½ hours, three daily) and from Gothenburg to Oslo (from 219kr, four hours, several daily). Swebus Express has the same routes with similar prices. In the north, buses run once daily from Umeå to Mo i Rana (eight hours) and from Skellefteå to Bodø (nine hours, daily except Saturday); for details, contact **Länstrafiken i Västerbotten** (☎0771-10 01 10; www. tabussen.nu) and **Länstrafiken i Norrbotten** (☎0771-10 01 10; www.ltnbd.se).

CAR & MOTORCYCLE

The main roads between Sweden and Norway are the E6 from Gothenburg to Oslo, the E18 from Stockholm to Oslo, the E14 from Sundsvall to Trondheim, the E12 from Umeå to Mo i Rana, and the E10 from Kiruna to Bjerkvik.

TRAIN

SJ trains run twice daily between Stockholm and Oslo (450kr to 1000kr, five hours), and at night to Narvik (800kr, about 20 hours). It is also possible to travel from Helsingborg to Oslo (856kr, seven hours, twice daily), via Gothenburg.

UK
TRAIN

Connections from the UK go through the Channel Tunnel to Continental Europe. Note that you usually have to book each section separately. From London, a 2nd-class single ticket (including couchette, 24 hours, several daily) costs around £300 to Stockholm. For reservations and tickets, contact **Deutsche Bahn UK** (☎08718 808066; www.bahn. co.uk).

Sea

Ferry connections are frequent to various destinations in Sweden from Finland, Poland, Germany and Norway. Most lines offer substantial discounts for seniors, students and children. Prices quoted are for single journeys at peak times (weekend travel, overnight crossings, mid-June to mid-August); other fares may be up to 30% lower.

Denmark
GOTHENBURG–FREDRIKSHAVN

Stena Line (☎031-704 00 00; www.stenaline.se) Three-hour crossing from Gothenburg to Fredrikshavn. Up to six ferries daily.

Stena Line (Denmark) (www. stenaline.se; Danmarksterminalen, Masthuggskajen; foot-passenger one-way from 200kr; 🚊3 Masthuggstorget) Nearest to central Gothenburg, the Stena Line Denmark terminal near Masthuggstorget (tram 3, 9 or 11) has around six daily departures for Frederikshavn in peak season (one-way/return from 500/1000kr; foot passenger from 200kr).

HELSINGØR–HELSINGBORG

This is the quickest route and has frequent ferries (crossing time around 20 minutes).

HH-Ferries (☎042-19 80 00; www.hhferries.se) A 24-hour service. Pedestrian/car and up to nine passengers 52/525kr. Pedestrians can bring bicycles along at no extra charge.

VARBERG–GRENÅ

Stena Line Four-hour crossing. Three or four daily. Pedestrian/ car and five passengers/bicycle 215/1005/253kr.

YSTAD–RØNNE

BornholmsTrafikken (☎0411-55 87 00; www.faergen.dk/ ruter/bornholmerfaergen.aspx) Conventional and fast services (1½ hours, 80 minutes, two to nine times daily). Car with five passengers from 1030kr.

Eastern Europe

Polferries (☎040-12 17 00; www.polferries.se; one-way adult 779kr) and **Unity Line** (☎0411-55 69 00; www. unityline.pl; one-way passenger 442kr) have daily Ystad–Swinoujscie (Poland) crossings. Polferries also runs Nynäshamn–Gdańsk (Poland).

Stena Line Operates ferries between Nynäshamn and Vent-

spils (Latvia) around five times per week.

Tallink (Map p48; ☎08-666 60 01; www.tallink.ee; Cityterminalen) runs the routes Stockholm–Tallinn (Estonia) and Kapellskär–Paldiski (Estonia).

Finland

Helsinki is called Helsingfors in Swedish, and Turku is Åbo.

Stockholm–Helsinki and Stockholm–Turku ferries run daily throughout the year via the Åland islands. These ferries have minimum-age limits; check before you travel.

STOCKHOLM–ÅLAND ISLANDS (MARIEHAMN)

Viking Line ships also go to Åland from Stockholm and Kapellskär two or three times daily.

Eckerö Linjen (☎0175-258 00; www.eckerolinjen.fi; passenger/ car 30/130kr) Runs to the Åland islands from Grisslehamn.

STOCKHOLM–HELSINKI

Tallink (Map p48; ☎08-666 60 01; www.tallink.ee; Cityterminalen) & **Silja Line** (Map p48; ☎08-22 21 40; www.silja.com) Around 15 hours. Ticket and cabin berth from about 1195kr.

Viking Line (Map p48; ☎08-452 40 00; www.vikingline. fi) Ticket and cabin berth from about 1000kr.

STOCKHOLM–TURKU

Silja Line (Map p48; ☎08-22 21 40; www.silja.com) Eleven hours. Deck place 138kr, cabins from 478kr; prices are higher for evening trips. From September to early May, ferries also depart from Kapellskär (90km northeast of Stockholm); connecting buses operated by Silja Line are included in the full-price fare.

Viking Line (Map p48; ☎08-452 40 00; www.vikingline.fi) Operates routes to Turku from Stockholm and, in high season, also from Kapellskär.

UMEÅ–VAASA

Wasaline (☎090-18 52 00; www.wasaline.com) Runs the

Umeå–Vaasa route. One-way foot passengers 330kr; cars 505kr.

Germany

TRELLEBORG–ROSTOCK & TRELLEBORG–TRAVEMÜNDE

TT-Line (www.ttline.com) Seven hours. Two to five daily. Car and up to five passengers Trelleborg–Rostock 500kr, Trelleborg–Travemünde 800kr. Berths are compulsory on night crossings.

Norway

There's a daily overnight **DFDS Seaways** (☑031-65 06 80; www.dfdsseaways.com) ferry between Copenhagen and Oslo (from €94 per passenger plus €85 per vehicle), via Helsingborg. Passenger fares between Helsingborg and Oslo (14 hours) cost from 1100kr, and cars 475kr, but the journey can't be booked online; you'll need to call.

A **Color Line** (☑0526-620 00; www.colorline.se) ferry between Strömstad and Sandefjord (Norway) sails two to six times daily (2½ hours) year-round. Tickets cost from €22; rail pass holders get a 50% discount.

GETTING AROUND

Transport in Sweden is reliable and easy to navigate. Roads are generally in good repair, and buses and trains are comfortable, with plenty of services on board and in stations. There's a good trip planner at https://rese planerare.resrobot.se.

Public transport is heavily subsidised and well organised. It's divided into 24 regional networks (länstrafik), but with an overarching Resplus system (www.samtrafiken.se), where one ticket is valid on trains and buses. Timetables can be accessed online.

Car Expensive but ideal if you want to explore smaller roads and remote places, especially ideal for camping and outdoor activities.

Bus More thorough coverage than trains, and often equally quick and cheap (if not more so).

Train Affordable and extensive; speed depends on whether the route is local, regional or express.

Air

Domestic flights link various towns and cities in Sweden and can be a fast, if not particularly cheap, way of getting around. There are 30-odd small regional airports located throughout the country.

Airlines in Sweden

Despite the large number of smaller airports, domestic airlines in Sweden tend to use **Stockholm Arlanda** (ARN; ☑10-109 10 00; www.swedavia.se/arlanda) as a hub. Flying domestic is expensive on full-price tickets, but discounts are available on internet bookings, student and youth fares, off-peak travel, return tickets booked in advance and low-price tickets for accompanying family members and seniors.

Airlines catering to domestic air travel include the following:

Braathens Regional Aviation (☑010 722 10 00; www.flygbra. se) Gothenburg, Stockholm, Malmö, Östersund, Halmstad, Kalmar, Ronneby, Sundsvall, Visby, Växjö, Ängelholm and Umeå.

SAS (☑0770-72 77 27; www. flysas.com) Arvidsjaur, Borlänge, Gällivare, Gothenburg, Halmstad, Ängelholm-Helsingborg, Hemavan, Hultsfred, Jönköping, Kalmar, Karlstad, Kiruna, Kramfors, Kristianstad, Linköping, Luleå, Lycksele, Malmö, Mora, Norrköping, Oskarshamn, Oskersund, Skellefteå, Stockholm, Storuman, Sundsvall, Sveg, Torsby, Trollhättan, Umeå, Vilhelmina, Visby, Västerås, Örebro and Örnsköldsvik.

Air Passes

Visitors who fly SAS to Sweden from the UK can add on a Visit Scandinavia/Nordic Airpass, allowing one-way travel on direct flights between any two Scandinavian cities serviced by SAS and its partner airlines. For the latest, call SAS at ☑800-221-2350 or check www.flysas.com.

Bicycle

Like most of Scandinavia, Sweden is an extremely bike-friendly country with a well-developed network of cycle paths in and around its towns and cities. There are also well-marked cycle routes around the country. Cycling is an excellent way to explore at your own pace and is a very common mode of transport for Swedes. Comprehensive cycling maps showing scenic trails are published by the Swedish Cycling Society and available in book shops. If you speak Swedish, check out the Cycling in Sweden website (www.routesnorth.com). Helmets are compulsory for all cyclists under age 15.

Boat

Canal Boat

Canals provide cross-country routes linking Sweden's main lakes. The longest cruises, on the Göta Canal from Söderköping (south of Stockholm) to Gothenburg, run from mid-May to mid-September, take at least four days and include the lakes between.

Rederiaktiebolaget Göta Kanal (☑031-80 63 15; www.gotacanal.se) operates three ships over the whole distance at fares from 12,295kr to 17,125kr per person for a four-day cruise, including full board and guided excursions.

Ferry

An extensive boat network and the five-day Båtluffarkortet (Boat Hiking Pass; 445kr, plus 20kr for card) open up the attractive Stockholm archipelago. Gotland is served by regular ferries from Nynäshamn and Oskarshamn, and the quaint fishing villages off the west coast can normally be reached by boat with a regional transport pass – enquire at the Gothenburg tourist offices.

Bus

There is a comprehensive network of buses throughout Sweden and you can travel on any of the 24 good-value and extensive *länstrafik* networks as well as on national long-distance routes. In general, travelling by bus is cheaper than by train.

Express Buses

Swebus Express (☑0771-21 82 18; www.swebus.se) has the largest network of express buses; in the north it operates as Ybuss. Generally, tickets for travel between Monday and Thursday, and tickets purchased over the internet or more than 24 hours before departure are cheaper; if you're a student

or senior, ask about fare discounts. **Svenska Buss** (☑0771-67 67 67; www.svenskabuss.se) and **Nettbuss** (☑0771-15 15 15; www.nettbuss.se) also connect many southern towns and cities with Stockholm; prices are often slightly cheaper than Swebus Express prices, but services are less frequent.

North of Gävle, regular connections with Stockholm are provided by several smaller operators, including **Ybuss** (☑060-17 19 60; www.ybuss.se), which has services to Sundsvall, Östersund and Umeå.

Regional Networks

The *länstrafik* bus networks are well integrated with the regional train system, with one ticket valid on any local or regional bus or train. Rules vary, but transfers are usually free if they are within one to four hours. Fares on local buses and trains are often identical, though prices can vary wildly depending on

when you travel and how far in advance you buy tickets.

Bus Passes

Good-value daily or weekly passes are usually available from local and regional transport offices, and many regions have 30-day passes for longer stays or summer travel. These can be bought online, from most newsagents, and from tourist information offices.

Car & Motorcycle

Sweden has good roads, and the excellent E-class motorways rarely have traffic jams.

Automobile Associations

The Swedish national motoring association is **Motormännens Riksförbund** (☑020-21 11 11; www.motormannen.se).

Bringing Your Own Vehicle

If you're bringing your own vehicle, you'll need vehicle

ROAD DISTANCES (KM)

	Gävle	Göteborg	Helsingborg	Jönköping	Kalmar	Karlstad	Kiruna	Linköping	Luleå	Malmö	Skellefteå	Stockholm	Sundsvall	Umeå	Uppsala	Örebro
Göteborg	520															
Helsingborg	690	220														
Jönköping	450	150	240													
Kalmar	560	350	290	215												
Karlstad	325	250	470	245	455											
Kiruna	1090	1645	1785	1540	1660	1420										
Linköping	365	280	365	130	235	230	1440									
Luleå	755	1300	1440	1210	1310	1080	342	1116								
Malmö	740	280	65	290	290	530	1835	415	1500							
Skellefteå	620	1185	1310	1075	1175	950	470	970	135	1360						
Stockholm	175	480	565	330	415	305	1265	205	930	620	795					
Sundsvall	215	765	890	670	770	540	875	575	540	955	405	390				
Umeå	485	1010	1140	935	1040	810	605	850	270	1230	135	660	270			
Uppsala	110	485	615	380	460	285	1195	250	860	665	725	70	320	590		
Örebro	235	285	450	200	350	115	1340	115	970	495	840	200	445	705	170	
Östersund	385	795	990	790	950	560	815	680	595	1075	470	560	185	370	490	590

registration documents, unlimited third-party liability insurance and a valid driving licence. A right-hand-drive vehicle brought from the UK or Ireland should have deflectors fitted to the headlights to avoid dazzling oncoming traffic. You must carry a reflective warning breakdown triangle.

Driving Licenses

An international driving permit is not necessary in Sweden; your domestic licence will do.

Hire

To hire a car you have to be at least 20 (sometimes 25) years of age, with a recognised licence and a credit card.

International rental chains have desks at Stockholm Arlanda and Göteborg Landvetter airports and bus stations, and offices in most major cities.

Avis (☑0770-82 00 82; www.avisworld.com)

Europcar (☑020-78 11 80; www.europcar.com)

Hertz (☑0771 21 12 12; www.hertz-europe.com)

Mabi Hyrbilar (☑08-612 60 90; www.mabi.se/english) National company with competitive rates.

Road Hazards

In the north, elk (moose, to Americans) and reindeer are serious road hazards; around 40 people die in collisions every year. Look out for the signs saying *viltstängsel upphör*, which mean that elk may cross the road, and for black plastic bags tied to roadside trees or poles, which mean Sami have reindeer herds grazing in the area. Report all incidents to police – failure to do so is an offence.

In Gothenburg and Norrköping, be aware of trams, which have priority; overtake on the right.

Road Rules

Drive on and give way to the right. Headlights (at least dipped) must be on at all times when driving. Seatbelts are compulsory, and children under seven years old should be in the appropriate harness or child seat.

The blood-alcohol limit in Sweden is 0.02% – having just one drink will put you over. Random checks are not unheard of. The maximum speed on motorways (signposted in green and called E1, E4 etc) is 120km/h, highways 90km/h, narrow rural roads 70km/h and built-up areas 50km/h. The speed limit for cars towing caravans is 80km/h. Police using hand-held radar speed detectors have the power to impose on-the-spot fines of up to 1200kr.

Hitching

Travellers who decide to hitch should understand that they are taking a small but potentially serious risk; consider travelling in pairs, and always let someone know where you're planning to go. Hitching isn't popular in Sweden and very long waits are the norm. It's prohibited to hitch on motorways.

Local Transport

In Sweden, local transport is always linked with regional transport (*länstrafik*). Regional passes are valid both in the city and on rural routes. Town and city bus fares are around 20kr, but it usually works out cheaper to get a day card or other travel pass.

Swedish and Danish trains and buses around the Öresund area form an integrated transport system, so buying tickets to Copenhagen from any station in the region is as easy as buying tickets for Swedish journeys.

Train

Sweden has an extensive and reliable railway network, and trains are almost always faster than buses, although not necessarily cheaper. (Exceptions include local commuter trains in large urban and suburban areas, which make frequent stops.)

Inlandsbanan (☑0771-53 53 53; www.inlandsbanan.se; Storsjöstråkket 19, Östersund) One of the great rail journeys in Scandinavia is this slow and scenic 1300km route from Kristinehamn to Gällivare. Several southern sections have to be travelled by bus, and the all-train route starts at Mora. It takes seven hours from Mora to Östersund (596kr) and 15 hours from Östersund to Gällivare (1378kr). A pass allows two weeks' unlimited travel for 1995kr.

Sveriges Järnväg (SJ; ☑0771-75 75 99; www.sj.se) National network covering most main lines, especially in the southern part of the country.

Tågkompaniet (☑0771-44 41 11; www.tagkompaniet.se) Operates excellent overnight trains from Gothenburg and Stockholm north to Boden, Kiruna, Luleå and Narvik, and the lines north of Härnösand.

Costs

Ticket prices vary depending on the type of train, class, time of day, and how far in advance you buy the ticket. Full-price 2nd-class tickets for longer journeys cost about twice as much as equivalent bus trips, but there are various discounts available for advance or last-minute bookings. Students, pensioners and people aged under 26 get a discount. When buying in advance, you pay more for the flexibility to change your ticket.

All SJ ticket prices drop from late June to mid-August. Most SJ trains don't allow bicycles to be taken onto trains (they have to be sent as freight), but some in southern Sweden do; check when you book your ticket.

Train Passes

The Sweden Rail Pass, Eurodomino tickets and international passes, such as Interrail and Eurail, are accepted on SJ services and most regional trains.

The Eurail Scandinavia Pass (www.eurail.com) entitles you to unlimited rail travel in Denmark, Finland, Norway and Sweden; it is valid in 2nd class only and is available for four, five, six, eight or 10 days of travel within a two-month period

ROUTE	OPERATOR
Frederikshavn–Gothenburg	Stena Line
Grenå–Varberg	Stena Line
Helsinki–Åland–Stockholm	Silja Line
Stockholm–Tallinn	Silja Line
Stockholm–Riga	Silja Line
Turku–Åland–Stockholm/Kappelskär	Silja Line
Turku/Helsinki–Stockholm	Viking Line

(prices start at US$303 for five days). The X2000 trains

require all rail-pass holders to pay a supplement of 75kr. The pass also provides free travel on Scandlines' Helsingør to Helsingborg route, and 20% to 50% discounts on the following ship routes. Some of the main rail routes across the country:

➡ Stockholm north to Uppsala–Gävle–Sundsvall–Östersund

➡ Stockholm west to Örebro–Karlstad–Oslo

➡ Stockholm west to Örebro–Gothenburg

➡ Stockholm south to Norrköping–Malmö–Copenhagen

Language

As a member of the North Germanic or Scandinavian language family, Swedish has Danish and Norwegian as the closest relatives. It is the national language of Sweden, spoken by the majority of residents (around 8.5 million). In neighbouring Finland it shares official status with Finnish and is a mandatory subject in schools, but it's the first language for only about 300,000 people or 6% of Finland's population.

The standard language or *Rikssvenska* reek·*sven*·ska (lit: kingdom-Swedish) is based on the central dialects from the area around Stockholm. Some of the rural dialects that are spoken across the country are quite diverse – for example, *Skånska* skawn·ska, spoken in the southern province of Skåne, has flatter vowels (and sounds a lot more like Danish), whereas *Dalmål* daal·mawl, spoken in the central region of Dalarna, has a very up-and-down sound.

Most Swedish sounds are similar to their English counterparts. One exception is fh (a breathy sound pronounced with rounded lips, like saying 'f' and 'w' at the same time), but with a little practice, you'll soon get it right. Note also that ai is pronounced as in 'aisle', aw as in 'saw', air as in 'hair', eu as the 'u' in 'nurse', ew as the 'ee' in 'see' with rounded lips, and ey as the 'e' in 'bet' but longer. Just read our coloured pronunciation guides as if they were English and you'll be understood. The stressed syllables are indicated with italics.

BASICS

Hello.	*Hej.*	hey
Goodbye.	*Hej då./Adjö.*	hey daw/aa·*yeu*
Yes.	*Ja.*	yaa
No.	*Nej.*	ney
Please.	*Tack.*	tak
Thank you (very much).	*Tack (så mycket).*	tak (saw *mew*·ke)
You're welcome.	*Varsågod.*	var·sha·*gohd*

Excuse me.	*Ursäkta mig.*	oor·*shek*·ta mey
Sorry.	*Förlåt.*	feur·*lawt*

How are you? *Hur mår du?*		hoor mawr doo
Fine, thanks. And you? *Bra, tack. Och dig?*		braa tak o dey
What's your name? *Vad heter du?*		vaad *hey*·ter doo
My name is ... *Jag heter ...*		yaa *hey*·ter ...
Do you speak English? *Talar du engelska?*		taa·lar doo *eng*·el·ska
I don't understand. *Jag förstår inte.*		yaa feur·*shtawr in*·te

ACCOMMODATION

Where's a ...?	*Var finns det ...?*	var fins de ...
campsite	*en camping-plats*	eyn *kam*·ping·plats
guesthouse	*ett gästhus*	et *yest*·hoos
hotel	*ett hotell*	et hoh·*tel*
youth hostel	*ett vandrar-hem*	et *van*·drar·hem

Do you have a ... room?	*Har ni ...?*	har nee ...
single	*ett enkelrum*	et *en*·kel·rum
double	*ett dubbelrum*	et *du*·bel·rum

How much is it per ...?	*Hur mycket kostar det per ...?*	hoor *mew*·ket *kos*·tar de peyr ...
night	*natt*	nat
person	*person*	*peyr*·shohn

SAMI LANGUAGES

Sami languages are related to Finnish and other Finno-Ugric languages. Five of the nine main Sami languages are spoken in Sweden, with speakers of each varying in number from 500 to 5000.

Most Sami speakers can communicate in Swedish, but relatively few speak English. Knowing some Sami words and phrases will give you a chance to access the unique Sami culture.

Fell (Northern) Sami

The most common of the Sami languages, Fell Sami is considered the standard Sami variety. It's spoken in Sweden's far north around Karesuando and Jukkasjärvi.

Written Fell Sami includes several accented letters, but it still doesn't accurately represent the spoken language – even some Sami people find the written language difficult to learn. For example, *giitu* (thanks) is pronounced 'geech-too', but the strongly aspirated 'h' isn't written.

Hello.	Buorre beaivi.
Hello. (reply)	Ipmel atti.
Goodbye.	
(to person leaving)	Mana dearvan.
(to person staying)	Báze dearvan.
How are you?	Mot manna?
I'm fine.	Buorre dat manna.
Yes.	De lea.
No.	Li.
Thank you.	Giitu.
You're welcome.	Leage buorre.

1	okta
2	guokte
3	golbma
4	njeallje
5	vihta
6	guhta
7	cieza
8	gávcci
9	ovcci
10	logi

DIRECTIONS

Where's the ...?	
Var ligger ...?	var li·ger ...
What's the address?	
Vilken adress är det?	vil·ken a·dres air de
Can you show me (on the map)?	
Kan du visa mig (på kartan)?	kan doo vee·sa mey (paw kar·tan)
How far is it?	
Hur långt är det?	hoor lawngt air de
How do I get there?	
Hur kommer man dit?	hoor ko·mar man deet

Turn ...	Sväng ...	sveng ...
at the corner	vid hörnet	veed heur·net
at the traffic lights	vid trafik-ljuset	veed tra·feek·yoo·set
left	till vänster	til ven·ster
right	till höger	til heu·ger

It's ...	Det är ...	de air ...
behind ...	bakom ...	baa·kom ...
far away	långt	lawngt
in front of ...	framför ...	fram·feur ...
left	till vänster	til ven·ster
near (to ...)	nära (på ...)	nair·ra (paw ...)
next to ...	bredvid ...	breyd·veed ...
on the corner	vid hörnet	veed heur·net
opposite ...	mitt emot ...	mit ey·moht ...
right	till höger	til heu·ger
straight ahead	rakt fram	raakt fram

EATING & DRINKING

What would you recommend?	
Vad skulle ni rekommendera?	vaad sku·le nee re·ko·men·dey·ra
What's the local speciality?	
Vad är den lokala specialiteten?	vaad air deyn loh·kaa·la spe·si·a·li·tey·ten
Do you have vegetarian food?	
Har ni vegetarisk mat?	har nee ve·ge·taa·risk maat
I'll have ...	
Jag vill ha ...	yaa vil haa ...
Cheers!	
Skål!	skawl

I'd like (the) ...	Jag skulle vilja ha ...	yaa sku·le vil·ya haa ...
bill	räkningen	reyk·ning·en
drink list	dricks listan	driks·lis·tan

LANGUAGE EATING & DRINKING

menu	menyn	me·*newn*
that dish	den maträtten	deyn *maat*·reten

Could you prepare a meal without ...?	Kan ni laga en maträtt utan ...?	kan nee *laa*·ga eyn *maat*·ret *oo*·tan ...
butter	smör	smeur
eggs	ägg	eg
meat stock	köttspad	*sheut*·spaad

SIGNS

Ingång	Entrance
Utgång	Exit
Öppet	Open
Stängt	Closed
Förbjudet	Prohibited
Toaletter	Toilets
Herrar	Men
Damer	Women

Key Words

bar	bar	bar
bottle	flaska	*flas*·ka
breakfast	frukost	*froo*·kost
cafe	kafé	ka·*fey*
children's menu	barnmeny	barn·me·*new*
cold	kylig	*shew*·lig
cup	kopp	kop
daily special	dagens rätt	*daa*·gens ret
dinner	middag	*mi*·daa
drink	dricka	*dri*·ka
food	mat	maat
fork	gaffel	*ga*·fel
glass	glas	glaas
hot	varm	varm
knife	kniv	kneev
lunch	lunch	lunsh
market	torghandel	*tory*·han·del
menu	meny/matsedel	me·*new*/*maat*·sey·del
plate	tallrik	*tal*·reek
restaurant	restaurang	res·taw·*rang*
snack	mellanmål	*me*·lan·mawl
spoon	sked	fheyd
teaspoon	tesked	*tey*·fheyd
with	med	me
without	utan	*oo*·taan

Meat & Fish

chicken	kyckling	*shewk*·ling
fish	fisk	fisk
herring	sill	sil
lobster	hummer	*hu*·mer
meat	kött	sheut
meatballs	köttbullar	*sheut*·bu·lar

salmon	lax	laks
tuna	tonfisk	*tohn*·fisk
venison	rådjur	*rawd*·yur

Fruit & Vegetables

blueberries	blåbär	*blaw*·bair
carrot	morot	*moh*·rot
fruit	frukt	frukt
mushrooms	svamp	svamp
potatoes	potatis	poh·*taa*·tis
raspberries	hallon	*haa*·lon
strawberries	jordgubbar	*yohrd*·gu·bar
vegetable	grönsak	*greun*·saak

Other

bread	bröd	breud
butter	smör	smeur
cake	kaka	*kaa*·ka
cheese	ost	ost
egg	ägg	eg
jam	sylt	sewlt
rice	ris	rees
soup	soppa	*so*·pa

Drinks

beer	öl	eul
coffee	kaffe	*ka*·fe
(orange) juice	(apelsin-) juice	(a·pel·*seen*·) djoos
milk	mjölk	myeulk
mineral water	mineral-vatten	mi·ne·*raal*·va·ten
red wine	rödvin	*reud*·veen
soft drink	läsk	lesk

sparkling wine	mousserande vin	moo·sey·ran·de veen
tea	te	tey
water	vatten	va·ten
white wine	vitt vin	vit veen

EMERGENCIES

Help!	Hjälp!	yelp
Go away!	Försvinn!	feur·shvin
Call ...!	Ring ...!	ring ...
a doctor	efter en doktor	ef·ter en dok·tor
the police	polisen	poh·lee·sen

It's an emergency!
Det är ett nödsituation! — de air et neud·si·too·a·fhohn

I'm lost.
Jag har gått vilse. — yaa har got vil·se

I'm sick.
Jag är sjuk. — yaa air fhook

It hurts here.
Det gör ont här. — de yeur ont hair

I'm allergic to (antibiotics).
Jag är allergisk mot — yaa air a·leyr·gisk moht

NUMBERS

1	ett	et
2	två	tvaw
3	tre	trey
4	fyra	few·ra
5	fem	fem
6	sex	seks
7	sju	fhoo
8	åtta	o·ta
9	nio	nee·oh
10	tio	tee·oh
20	tjugo	shoo·go
30	trettio	tre·tee
40	fyrtio	fewr·tee
50	femtio	fem·tee
60	sextio	seks·tee
70	sjuttio	fhu·tee
80	åttio	o·tee
90	nittio	ni·tee
100	ett hundra	et hun·dra
1000	ett tusen	et too·sen

(antibiotika). — (an·tee·bee·oh·ti·ka)

Where are the toilets?
Var är toaletten? — var air toh·aa·le·ten

SHOPPING & SERVICES

Where's the ...?	Var ligger ...?	var li·ger ...
bank	banken	ban·ken
post office	posten	pos·ten
tourist office	turistinformationen	too·rist·in·for·ma·fhoh·nen

Where's the local internet cafe?
Var finns det lokala internet kaféet? — var fins de loh·kaa·la in·ter·net ka·fey·et

Where's the nearest public phone?
Var ligger närmaste telefonautomat? — var li·ger nair·ma·ste te·le·fohn ow·toh·maat

I'm looking for ...
Jag letar efter ... — yaa ley·tar ef·ter ...

Can I look at it?
Får jag se den? — fawr yaa se deyn

Do you have any others?
Har ni några andra? — har nee naw·ra an·dra

How much is it?
Hur mycket kostar det? — hoor mew·ke kos·tar de

That's too expensive.
Det är för dyrt. — de air feur dewrt

What's your lowest price?
Vad är ditt lägsta pris? — vaad air dit leyg·sta prees

There's a mistake in the bill.
Det är ett fel på räkningen. — de air et fel paw reyk·ning·en

TIME & DATES

What time is it?
Hur mycket är klockan? — hur mew·ke air klo·kan

It's (two) o'clock.
Klockan är (två). — klo·kan air (tvaw)

Half past (one).
Halv (två). (lit: half two) — halv (tvaw)

At what time ...?
Hur dags ...? — hur daks ...

At (10) o'clock.
Klockan (tio). — klo·kan (tee·oh)

in the morning	på förmiddagen	paw feur·mi·daa·gen
in the afternoon	på eftermiddagen	paw ef·ter·mi·daa·gen
yesterday	igår	ee·gawr
tomorrow	imorgon	ee·mor·ron
Monday	måndag	mawn·daa
Tuesday	tisdag	tees·taa

Wednesday	onsdag	ohns·daa
Thursday	torsdag	torsh·daa
Friday	fredag	frey·daa
Saturday	lördag	leur·daa
Sunday	söndag	seun·daa

January	januari	ya·nu·aa·ree
February	februari	fe·bru·aa·ree
March	mars	mars
April	april	a·preel
May	maj	mai
June	juni	yoo·nee
July	juli	yoo·lee
August	augusti	aw·gus·tee
September	september	sep·tem·ber
October	oktober	ok·toh·ber
November	november	noh·vem·ber
December	december	dey·sem·ber

TRANSPORT

Public Transport

Is this the ... to (Stockholm)?	Är den här ... till (Stockholm)?	air den hair ... til (stok·holm)
boat	båten	baw·ten
bus	bussen	bu·sen

Is this the ... to (Stockholm)?	Är det här ... till (Stockholm)?	air de hair ... til (stok·holm)
plane	planet	plaa·net
train	tåget	taw·get

What time's the ... bus?	När går ...?	nair gawr ...
first	första bussen	feursh·ta bu·sen
last	sista bussen	sis·ta bu·sen
next	nästa buss	nes·ta bus

QUESTION WORDS

How?	Hur?	hoor
What?	Vad?	vaad
When?	När?	nair
Where?	Var?	var
Who?	Vem?	vem
Why?	Varför?	var·feur

One ... ticket (to Stockholm), please.	Jag skulle vilja ha en ... (till Stockholm).	yaa sku·le vil·ya haa eyn ... (til stok·holm)
one-way	enkelbiljett	en·kel·bil·yet
return	returbiljett	re·toor·bil·yet

At what time does it arrive/leave?
Hur dags anländer/ avgår den? — hoor daks an·len·der/ aav·gawr deyn

How long will it be delayed?
Hur mycket är det försenat? — hoor mew·ket air dey feur·shey·nat

What's the next station/stop?
Vilken är nästa station/hållplats? — vil·ken air nes·ta sta·fhohn/hawl·plats

Does it stop at (Lund)?
Stannar den i (Lund)? — sta·nar den ee (lund)

Please tell me when we get to (Linköping).
Kan du säga till när vi kommer till (Linköping)? — kan doo say·ya til nair vee ko·mer til (lin·sheu·ping)

Please take me to (this address).
Kan du köra mig till (denna address)? — kan doo sheu·ra mey til (dey·na a·dres)

Please stop here.
Kan du stanna här? — kan doo sta·na hair

Driving & Cycling

I'd like to hire a ...	Jag vill hyra en ...	yaa vil hew·ra eyn ...
bicycle	cykel	sew·kel
car	bil	beel
motorbike	motor- cykel	moh·tor· sew·kel

air	luft	luft
oil	olja	ol·ya
park (car)	parkera	par·key·ra
petrol/gas	bensin	ben·seen
service station	bensin- station	ben·seen· sta·fhohn
tyres	däck	dek

Is this the road to (Göteborg)?
Går den här vägen till (Göteborg)? — gawr den hair vey·gen til (yeu·te·bory)

I need a mechanic.
Jag behöver en mekaniker. — yaa be·heu·ver eyn me·kaa·ni·ker

I've run out of petrol/gas.
Jag har ingen bensin kvar. — yaa har ing·en ben·seen kvar

I have a flat tyre.
Jag har fått punktering. — yaa har fawt punk·tey·ring

GLOSSARY

Note that the letters **å, ä** and **ö** fall at the end of the Swedish alphabet, and the letters **v** and **w** are often used interchangeably (you will see the small town of Vaxholm also referred to as Waxholm, and an inn can be known as a *värdshus* or *wärdshus*). In directories like telephone books they usually fall under one category (eg *wa* is listed before *vu*).

(m) indicates masculine gender, (f) feminine gender and (pl) plural

allemansrätt – literally 'every person's right'; a tradition allowing universal access to private property (with some restrictions), public land and wilderness areas

älv – river

apotek – pharmacy

bad – swimming pool, bathing place or bathroom

bakfickan – literally 'back pocket'; a low-profile eatery usually associated with a gourmet restaurant

bankautomat – cash machine, ATM

bensin – petrol, gas

berg – mountain

bergslags paj – quiche made with venison

bibliotek – library

biljet – ticket

biljetautomat – ticket machines (eg for street parking)

biluthyrning – car hire

bio, biograf – cinema

brännvin – aquavit

bro – bridge

bruk – factory, mill, works

bryggeri – brewery

bulle – bun

butik – shop

centrum – town centre

cykel – bicycle

dag – day

dagens – daily

dagens rätt – fixed–price lunch special

dal – valley

domkyrka – cathedral

drottning – queen

duodji – Sami handicraft

dygnskort – a daily transport pass, valid for 24 hours

ej – not, no

ej motorfordon – no motor vehicles

ekologisk – organic

fabrik – factory

färja – ferry

fästning – fort, fortress

fest – party, festival

fika – coffee and cake

fiskekort – local permits

fisksoppa – fish stew

fjäll – mountain

fjällstation – mountain lodge

fjällstugor – mountain huts

flyg – flight, flying

flygbuss – airport bus

flygplats – airport

folkhemmet – welfare state

folköl – standard–stength beer

förbund – union, association

förening – organisation, association

förlag – company

friluft – open-air

frukost – breakfast

fyr – lighthouse

galleri, galleria – shopping mall

gamla staden, gamla stan – 'old town', the historical part of a city or town

gammal, gamla – old

gatan – street (often abbreviated to 'g')

gatukök – literally 'street kitchen'; kiosk, stall or grill selling fast food

gatukontoret – municipal parking spaces

gåhties – cottages

gákti – traditional Sami clothing

gård – yard, farm, estate

glögg – mulled wine

gräns – border

grillad korv med bröd – hot dog

gruva – mine

hällristningar – rock carvings

hamn – harbour

hembygdsgård – open-air museum, usually old farmhouse buildings

hembygdsområde – old homestead

hemslöjd – handicraft

hjörtron – cloudberry

hotell – hotel

hus – house

husmanskost – homely Swedish fare; what you would expect cooked at home when you were a (Swedish) child

hyrbilar – car hire

i – in

idrottsplats – sports venue, stadium

inlagd sill – pickled herring

järnvägsstation – train station

Janssons frestelse – hearty casserole

joik – see *yoik*

Jugendstil – Swedish Romanticist movement, similar to art nouveau

julbord – buffet

Julmust – sweet dark–brown soft drink

kaj – quay

källare – cellar, vault

kanelbulle – cinnamon bun

kanot – canoe

kardemummabullar – cardamom rolls

karta – map

Kartförlaget – State Mapping Agency (sales division)

kåta – Sami hut

kloster – monastery

knäckebröd – crispbread

kök – kitchen

kombibiljett – combined ticket

konditori – baker and confectioner (often with an attached cafe)

konst – art
kort – card
korv – sausage
kräftor – crayfish
kräftskivor – crayfish parties
krav – organic
krog – pub, restaurant (or both)
krona (kronor) – Swedish currency unit
kung – king
kust – coast
kyrka – church
kyrkogård – graveyard
kyrkstad – church town

lagom – concept of not too much and not too little
lakrits – licorice
län – county
länskort – county pass
länsmuseum – regional museum
länståg – regional train
länstrafiken – public transport network of a *län*
lättöl – light beer
lavin – avalanche
lávvu – tent
lilla – lesser, little
linbana – chairlift, cable car
lingonsylt – lingonberry jam
lussekatt – saffron bun
lufsa – baked pork and potato

magasin – store (usually a department store), warehouse
magasinet – depot
mellanöl – medium–strength beer
Midsommardag – Midsummer's Day; first Saturday after 21 June (the main celebrations take place on Midsummer's Eve)
motti och fläsk – porridge with pork
museet – museum
munk – doughnut meets apple strudel
mynt – coins

nässelsoppa – nettle soup
natt – night
nattklubb – nightclub
naturreservat – nature reserve

naturum – visitor centre at national park or nature reserve
Naturvårdsverket – Swedish Environmental Protection Agency (National Parks Authority)
nedre – lower
norr – north
norrsken – northern lights (aurora borealis)
nubbe – small shot of aquavit
nyheter – news

ö – island
och – and
ordning och reda – concept of tidiness and order
öst – east (abbreviated to 'ö')
östra – eastern
övre – upper

på – on, in
pålägg – toppings for toast etc
palats – palace
palt – meat–filled dumpling
pendeltåg – commuter train
pensionat – pension, guest-house
pepparkaka – gingerbread biscuit
P-hus – multistorey car park
polis – police
polkagris – rock candy
punsch – strong alcoholic punch
pytt i panna – potato hash with sliced beets and a fried egg

rådhus – town hall
rälsbuss – railcar
raukar – limestone formations
RFSL – Riksförbundet för Sexuellt Likaberättigande (national gay organisation)
riksdag – parliament
riksdaler – old Swedish currency
ripa – ptarmigan, a game bird
röding – Arctic char
rum – room

saft – cordial
schlager – Catchy, camp, highly melodic pop tunes that are big on sentimentality, and commonly featured at the Eurovision Song Contest

siida – Sami village units or communities
sjukhus – hospital
sjö – lake, sea
skål – cheers
skärgård – archipelago
skog – forest
slöjd – handicraft
slott – castle, manor house
smörgåsbord – Swedish buffet
snaps – distilled alcoholic beverage
söder – south
sommarkort – summer travel pass
sommarstuga – summer cottage
starköl – strong beer
STF – Svenska Turistföreningen (Swedish Touring Association)
stor, stora – big or large
stortorget – main square
strand – beach, shore
stuga (stugor/na) – cabin (cabins)
stugby – chalet park; small village of cabins
svensk – Swedish
Sverige – Sweden
SVIF – Sveriges Vandrarhem i Förening; hostelling association

teater – theatre
telefonkort – telephone card
torg, torget – town square
torn – tower
trädgård – garden open to the public
tull – customs, toll
tumulus – burial ground
tunnelbana, T-bana – underground railway, metro
turistbyrå – tourist office

väg – road
vandrarhem – hostel
värdshus/wärdshus – inn, restaurant
väst – west (abbreviated to 'v')
västra – western
vecka – week
vik – bay, inlet

yoik – a type of traditional Sami singing (also referred to as *joik*)

Behind the Scenes

SEND US YOUR FEEDBACK

We love to hear from travellers – your comments keep us on our toes and help make our books better. Our well-travelled team reads every word on what you loved or loathed about this book. Although we cannot reply individually to your submissions, we always guarantee that your feedback goes straight to the appropriate authors, in time for the next edition. Each person who sends us information is thanked in the next edition – the most useful submissions are rewarded with a selection of digital PDF chapters.

Visit **lonelyplanet.com/contact** to submit your updates and suggestions or to ask for help. Our award-winning website also features inspirational travel stories, news and discussions.

Note: We may edit, reproduce and incorporate your comments in Lonely Planet products such as guidebooks, websites and digital products, so let us know if you don't want your comments reproduced or your name acknowledged. For a copy of our privacy policy visit lonelyplanet.com/privacy.

OUR READERS

Many thanks to the travellers who used the last edition and wrote to us with helpful hints, useful advice and interesting anecdotes:

Claus Christensen, Dominik Ebneter, Frank Bult, George & Linda Moss, Katy Ionis, Melissa Kang, Morten Fristrup

WRITER THANKS
Benedict Walker

My thanks to Gemma Graham for taking me on for this project, to Michal Greenberg for helping me find a home in Germany, to Ida Sara Lina Burguete Kirkman and MacGyver for being the best Swedish guides anyone could ever ask for, the Lindqvists in Älmhult for bringing a little bit of Japan to Sweden and to Mum, Trish Walker, who never gives up on me, even when I come close. Special thanks to my Forster Mum, Vicki Kirkman, for not giving up either and to Lauren Kirkman, my travel agent for making her mentor proud. Love all round.

Craig McLachlan

Hej hej! A hearty thanks to everyone who helped out during my research trip around Sweden, but especially to my exceptionally beautiful wife, Yuriko, who kept me on track, focused and constantly smiling. Jämtland and the Bothnian Coast and Swedish Lappland were a joy to explore, and a big part of that joy comes from meeting and talking to happy Swedes! – thanks to you all.

Becky Ohlsen

Thanks to my mom, Christina, for rounding up a bunch of extra info from her friends; Paul Smith for inspiring the pinball quest; James Borup for the brewery intel; the Auld Dub in general; and all the various editors in-house at Lonely Planet for helping whip the resulting content into shape.

ACKNOWLEDGEMENTS

Climate map data adapted from Peel MC, Finlayson BL & McMahon TA (2007) 'Updated World Map of the Köppen-Geiger Climate Classification', Hydrology and Earth System Sciences, 11, 163344.

Cover photograph: Icehotel, Jukkasjärvi, E.D. Torial/Alamy©

THIS BOOK

This 7th edition of Lonely Planet's *Sweden* guidebook was researched and written by Benedict Walker, Craig McLachlan and Becky Ohlsen. The previous edition was written by Becky Ohlsen, Anna Kaminski and Josephine Quintero. This guidebook was produced by the following:

Destination Editor Gemma Graham

Product Editor Sandie Kestell

Senior Cartographer Valentina Kremenchutskaya

Book Designer Ania Bartoszek

Assisting Editors Bridget Blair, Carly Hall, Paul Harding, Helen Koehne, Chris Pitts, Sarah Stewart, Saralinda Turner, Fionnuala Twomey, Sam Wheeler

Assisting Cartographer Julie Dodkins

Cover Researcher Naomi Parker

Thanks to Ronan Abayawickrema, Gwen Cotter, Lauren O'Connell, Genna Patterson, Alison Ridgway, Angela Tinson, Tony Wheeler

Index

Map Legend

Sights
- Beach
- Bird Sanctuary
- Buddhist
- Castle/Palace
- Christian
- Confucian
- Hindu
- Islamic
- Jain
- Jewish
- Monument
- Museum/Gallery/Historic Building
- Ruin
- Shinto
- Sikh
- Taoist
- Winery/Vineyard
- Zoo/Wildlife Sanctuary
- Other Sight

Activities, Courses & Tours
- Bodysurfing
- Diving
- Canoeing/Kayaking
- Course/Tour
- Sento Hot Baths/Onsen
- Skiing
- Snorkelling
- Surfing
- Swimming/Pool
- Walking
- Windsurfing
- Other Activity

Sleeping
- Sleeping
- Camping
- Hut/Shelter

Eating
- Eating

Drinking & Nightlife
- Drinking & Nightlife
- Cafe

Entertainment
- Entertainment

Shopping
- Shopping

Information
- Bank
- Embassy/Consulate
- Hospital/Medical
- Internet
- Police
- Post Office
- Telephone
- Toilet
- Tourist Information
- Other Information

Geographic
- Beach
- Gate
- Hut/Shelter
- Lighthouse
- Lookout
- Mountain/Volcano
- Oasis
- Park
- Pass
- Picnic Area
- Waterfall

Population
- Capital (National)
- Capital (State/Province)
- City/Large Town
- Town/Village

Transport
- Airport
- Border crossing
- Bus
- Cable car/Funicular
- Cycling
- Ferry
- Metro station
- Monorail
- Parking
- Petrol station
- S-Bahn/Subway station
- Taxi
- T-bane/Tunnelbana station
- Train station/Railway
- Tram
- Tube station
- U-Bahn/Underground station
- Other Transport

Routes
- Tollway
- Freeway
- Primary
- Secondary
- Tertiary
- Lane
- Unsealed road
- Road under construction
- Plaza/Mall
- Steps
- Tunnel
- Pedestrian overpass
- Walking Tour
- Walking Tour detour
- Path/Walking Trail

Boundaries
- International
- State/Province
- Disputed
- Regional/Suburb
- Marine Park
- Cliff
- Wall

Hydrography
- River, Creek
- Intermittent River
- Canal
- Water
- Dry/Salt/Intermittent Lake
- Reef

Areas
- Airport/Runway
- Beach/Desert
- Cemetery (Christian)
- Cemetery (Other)
- Glacier
- Mudflat
- Park/Forest
- Sight (Building)
- Sportsground
- Swamp/Mangrove

Note: Not all symbols displayed above appear on the maps in this book

OUR STORY

A beat-up old car, a few dollars in the pocket and a sense of adventure. In 1972 that's all Tony and Maureen Wheeler needed for the trip of a lifetime – across Europe and Asia overland to Australia. It took several months, and at the end – broke but inspired – they sat at their kitchen table writing and stapling together their first travel guide, *Across Asia on the Cheap*. Within a week they'd sold 1500 copies. Lonely Planet was born.

Today, Lonely Planet has offices in Franklin, London, Melbourne, Oakland, Dublin, Beijing and Delhi, with more than 600 staff and writers. We share Tony's belief that 'a great guidebook should do three things: inform, educate and amuse'.

OUR WRITERS

Benedict Walker

Uppsala & Central Sweden, The Southeast & Gotland, Malmö & the South Ben had a suburban upbringing in Newcastle, Australia, and spent his weekends and long summers by the beach, whenever possible. Although he's drawn magnetically to the kinds of mountains he encountered in the Rockies and the Japan and Swiss Alps, beach life is in his blood. He loves the thrill of unearthing the best of big cities, but he's always most at home in nature. Writing for Lonely Planet is Ben's dream come true – to date he has contributed to Lonely Planet's *Australia, Canada, Germany, Japan, Switzerland, USA* and *Vietnam* guidebooks.

Craig McLachlan

Jämtland & the Bothnian Coast, Lappland & the Far North Craig has covered destinations all over the globe for Lonely Planet for two decades. Based in Queenstown, New Zealand, for half the year, he runs an outdoor activities company and a sake brewery, then moonlights overseas for the other half, leading tours and writing for Lonely Planet. Craig has completed a number of adventures in Japan and his books are available on Amazon. Describing himself as a 'freelance anything', Craig has an MBA from the University of Hawai'i and is also a Japanese interpreter, pilot, photographer, hiking guide, tour leader, karate instructor and budding novelist. Check out www.craigmclachlan.com.

Becky Ohlsen

Stockholm & Around, Gothenburg & the Southwest Becky is a freelance writer, editor and critic based in Portland, Oregon. She writes guidebooks and travel stories about Scandinavia, Portland and elsewhere for Lonely Planet. Becky grew up with a thick book of Swedish fairytales illustrated by John Bauer, so the deep black forests of Norrland hold particular fascination for her. Hiking through them, she's alert for trolls and tomtes (which, to the untrained eye, look just like big rocks). Though raised in the mountains of Colorado, Becky has been exploring Sweden since childhood, while visiting her grandparents and other relatives in Stockholm and parts north. She's thoroughly hooked on pickled herring and saffron ice cream but has nothing good to say about Swedish beer. Becky also wrote the Plan Your Trip, Understand and Survival Guide sections of this book.

Published by Lonely Planet Global Limited
CRN 554153
7th edition – May 2018
ISBN 978 1 78657 468 8
© Lonely Planet 2018   Photographs © as indicated 2018
10 9 8 7 6 5 4 3 2 1
Printed in China